Management and Behavioural Process

Management and Behavioural Process

K. Aswathappa, Ph. D.
Former Director,
Canara Bank School of Management Studies
Bangalore University,
Bangalore

G. Sudarsana Reddy
M.Com, MBA, MFM, Ph.D
Professor of Management
Bangalore

Himalaya Publishing House

MUMBAI • NEW DELHI • NAGPUR • BANGALORE • HYDERABAD • CHENNAI • PUNE • LUCKNOW • AHMEDABAD • ERNAKULAM • BHUBANESWAR • INDORE

First Edition : 2009

Published by : Mrs. Meena Pandey
for **HIMALAYA PUBLISHING HOUSE PVT. LTD.,**
"Ramdoot", Dr. Bhalerao Marg, Girgaon, **Mumbai - 400 004.**
Phones: 2386 01 70/2386 38 63, Fax: 022-2387 71 78
Email: himpub@vsnl.com
Website: www.himpub.com

Branch Offices:

New Delhi : "Pooja Apartments", 4-B, Murari Lal Street, Ansari Road, Darya Ganj, **New Delhi - 110 002.** Phone: 23270392, 23278631
Fax: 011-23256286

Nagpur : Kundanlal Chandak Industrial Estate, Ghat Road, **Nagpur - 440 018.**
Phone: 2738731, 3296733 Telefax : 0712-2721215

Bangalore : No. 16/1 (Old 12/1), 1st Floor, Next to Hotel Highlands, Madhava Nagar, Race Course Road, **Bangalore - 560 001.**
Phone : 22281541, 22385461, Telefax: 080-22286611

Hyderabad : No. 3-4-184, Lingampally, Besides Raghavendra Swamy Matham, Kachiguda, **Hydrabad - 500 027.** Mobile : 09848130433

Chennai : No. 85/50, Bazullah Road, T. Nagar, **Chennai - 600 017.**
Phone: 044-28144004/28144005

Pune : First Floor, "Laksha" Apartment, No. 527, Mehunpura, Shaniwarpeth, (Near Prabhat Theatre), **Pune - 411 030.**
Phone: 020 - 24496323/24496333

Lucknow : C-43, Sector - C, Ali Gunj, **Lucknow - 226 024.** Phone: 0522-2339329

Ahmedabad : 114, "SHAIL", 1st Floor, Opp. Madhu Sudan House, C.G.Road, Navrang Pura, **Ahmedabad – 380 009.**
Phone: 079-26560126, Mobiles: 09327324149,09314679413

Ernakulam : 39/104 A, Lakshmi Apartment, Karikkamuri Cross Rd., Ernakulam, **Cochin – 622011**, Kerala.
Phone: 0484-2378012, 2378016, Mob- 09344199799

Bhubaneswar : 5 Station Square, **Bhubaneswar (Orissa) - 751 001.** Mobile - 9861046007,
E-mail:- orissa@himpub.com

Indore : Kesardeep Avenue Extension, 73, Narayan Bagh.Flat No. 302, IIIrd Floor, Near Humpty Dumpty School, Narayan Bagh, **Indore (M.P.)** Mob-09301386468

DTP by : **Sri Siddhi Softtek**
Bangalore

Printed by : Heramb Graphics, Bhandup,
Mumbai – 78.

Preface

For a typical businessperson, life is hard. Competition is mounting and though volumes are increasing, margins are becoming thin. Executives are under tremendous pressure. They should perform, show results, declare dividends regularly and ensure that the scripts do not crash in bourses. Today's managers should be competent and competency alone helps them sail through.

Competency comes from knowledge. ***Management and Behavioural Process*** precisely seeks to provide such comprehension to the present and future managers. The book does not provide knowledge about science, technology, politics or economics. It provides the essential learning about how to manage people in organizations.

A typical manager in an organization performs four functions: planning, organizing, leading, and controlling. Each of these activities needs to be handled with circumspection. The manager needs certain principles and norms, particularly people centric, that help him or her manage the functions better. Organastional behaviour contains well-tested principles of managing people in organizations.

There are good books available on management principles and we have standard volumes on organisational behaviour too. Rarely we find a comprehensive book that contains both the management principles and the contents of organisational behaviour. At the same time more and more universities are including a paper on management and organisational behaviour as one of the papers in their respective syllabi.

Management and Behavioural Process seeks to fill the need. The book is divided into two parts: Part 1 contains 10 chapters that describe functions and principles of management. Part 2 with 13 chapters carries a detailed explanation about organisational behaviour. More space is devoted to the second part as human behaviour and behaviour of organizations is too complex and too multidimensional and obviously requires more attention and space.

We have made the book highly student centric. The language used is direct and conversational. Instructors too can expect the book to be handy and useful in as much as it is rich with pedagogic aids and India centric cases.

We thank Anuj Pandey, Neeraj Pandey, and Vijay Pandey for having encouraged us to author this book.

K. Aswathappa

G. Sudarsana Reddy

Brief Contents

Contents

Part - 1
Management

CHAPTER

One

Introduction to Management

LEARNING OBJECTIVES

After reading this chapter you should understand –

1. The nature of management
2. The four functions of management, managerial skills and roles
3. The different types of managers
4. The traits of sucessful executives
5. Evolution of management theories
6. Contemporary trends in management

Nature of Management

Organisations are made (or unmade) by managers who practise the art and science of management. This chapter provides detailed explanation of the nature of management, functions of management, skills required in an efficient manager and typical functions of a manager.

Management is the attainment of organisational goals in an effective and efficient manner through planning, organising, leading and controlling organisational resources.[1] Organisational resources include human beings, money, machines and materials.

Three features emerge from the above description of the nature of management. First, management involves four functions-planning, organising, leading and controlling. Second, these functions are organised to achieve organisational goals. Third, management involves effective and efficient use of resources. To be **effective** is to achieve organisational goals. To be **efficient** is to achieve goals with least wastage of resources. Some managers do either or fail on both. The best managers focus on both effectiveness and efficiency. This focus results in high performance and organisational goals are easily attained as Fig.1.1 shows.

FIGURE 1-1

EFFICIENCY AND EFFECTIVENESS MATRIX

EFFECTIVENESS \ EFFICIENCY	LOW	HIGH
HIGH	Low efficiency/ High effectivenss Manager chooses the right goals to pursue, but does a poor job of using resources to achieve these goals. Result: A product that customers want, but that is too expensive for them to buy	High efficiency/ High effectivenss Manager chooses the right goals to pursue and makes good use of resources to achieve these goals. Result: A prodect that customers want at a quality and price that they can afford
LOW	Low efficiency/ Low effectivenss Manager chooses wrong goals to pursue and makes poor use of resources. Result: A low quality product that customers do not want	High efficiency/ Low effectivenss Manager chooses inappropriate goals, but makes good use of resources to pursue these goals. Result: A high quality product customers do not want

High performing organisations are efficient and effective

(Source: Gareth R. Jones, *et.al., Management*, p.6).

What is to be underlined is that management is not confined to business establishments only. Management is relevant for an individual, a family, an NGO, a government department, and ofcourse in business organisations. An individual becomes successful when he or she plans, organises, and controls several activities, and uses his or her time and other resources efficiently and effectively. Same logic applies to other institutions also.

Functions of Management

As explained above, management involves four important functions: planning, organising, leading and controlling (see Fig.1.2). Each of these will be explained in greater detail in subsequent chapters. Here, a brief description of the four functions follows.

FIGURE 1-2
FUNCTIONS OF MANAGEMENT

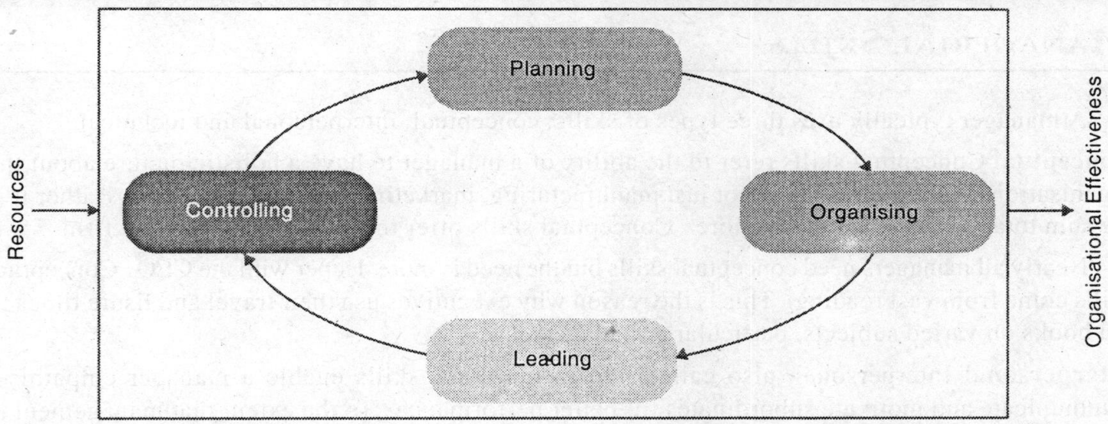

Planning Planning specifies where the organisation should be in the future and establishes appropriate strategies to reach the destination. The other functions — organising, leading and controlling are derivatives of the planning function.

All managers at every level of organisation engage in planning. Plans give them the goal and the actions needed to reach the objective.

Poor or lack of planning may ruin the organisation. It was precisely the lack of planning that resulted in the closure of once famous Binny Mills.

Organising After plans and objectives have been developed, managers must design and develop an organisation that helps them accomplish the objectives. The organising function creates a structure of task and authority relationships that give a practical shape to all the functions of management. Infosys, WIPRO, TCS, L&T, Reliance and ICICI Bank have all organisational structures and reorganised them from time to time to accommodate changing needs. These firms use their respective structures to carry out their stated activities.

Leading Leading is motivating people to achieve organisational objectives. It involves creating a shared culture and values, communicating goals to employees, and infusing them with the desire to perform at higher levels. Leading involves motivating entire departments, and divisions as well as those individuals working closely with the manager. The ability to lead is called 'leadership' which is a great trait. In any successful organisation, it is one person — called the leader, who makes difference to it. Such people who really made the difference are legion. Ratan Tata, Narayana Murthy, Azim Premji, Steve Jobs, Bill Gates, Ramalinga Raju and the likes are the names that shall find a place in the history of business management.

The quality of leadership or the leader need not be the top executive of the organisation. The person is there at every level and the quality is found in all human beings. A janitor making his juniors do a better job of sweeping is as much a leader as the CEO who inspires his or her followers for better performance.

Controlling The last function of management is controlling. This seeks to ensure that the actual performance of the organisation conforms with what was planned for the firm. Controlling typically involves monitoring employees' activities, determining whether the organisation is on target towards its goals, and making corrections as necessary. Managers must ensure that the organisation is moving towards its goals.

MANAGERIAL SKILLS

A manager typically uses three types of skills: conceptual, interpersonal and technical.

Conceptual Conceptual skills refer to the ability of a manager to have a holistic picture about the organisation. An organisation is not just manufacturing, marketing or financing entity. Rather it is the sum total of these and many more. Conceptual skills offer this perspective about a firm.

Nearly all managers need conceptual skills but the need is more deeper with the CEO. Conceptual skills come from vast reading. This is the reason why executives use their travel and lisure times to red books on varied subjects, particularly management.

Interpersonal Interpersonal, also called human relations, skills enable a manager empathise, communicate and motivate subordinates for better performance. To the extent that management is understood as getting things done through people, people management (interpersonal skills) is highly significant.

Technical Technical skills enable people to perform specific tasks proficiently. They include mastery of the methods, techniques and equipment involved in specific functions such as engineering, manufacturing or finance. Technical skills also include specialised knowledge, analytical ability, and the competent use of tools and techniques to solve problems in that specific discipline.

Who needs which type of skills more than the others? The answer is simple — executives need more conceptual skills, employees down the line need more of technical skills and employees at all levels need conceptual skills.

MANAGER'S ROLES

Armed with conceptual, interpersonal and technical skills, manager spends his or her time every day on different roles. A role is a set of specific tasks that a person is expected to perform because of the position he or she holds in an organisation.

Mintzberg's roles of managers are the one's generally explained while detailing tasks of executives. Henry Mintzberg had identified 10 roles of a typical manager as early as 1970s itself.

The passage of time has not diminished his pioneering work. According to him, a manager has 10 roles, broadly categorised under three heads as shown in Table 1.1.

TABLE 1-1

MANAGERIAL ROLES IDENTIFIED BY MINTZBERG

Type of Role	Specific Role	Examples of Role Activities
Interpersonal	Figurehead	Outline future organisational goals to employees at company meetings; open a new corporate headquarters building; state the organisation's ethical guidelines and the principles of behaviour employees are to follow in their dealings with customers and suppliers.
	Leader	Provide an example for employees to follow; give direct commands and orders to subordinates; make decisions concerning the use of human and technical resources; mobiles employee support for specific organisational goals.
	Liaison	Coordinate the work of managers in different departments; establish alliances between different organisations to share resources to produce new goods and services.
Informational	Monitor	Evaluate the performance of managers in different functions, and take corrective action to improve their performance; watch for changes occurring in the external and internal environment that may affect the organisation in the future.
	Disseminator	Inform employees about changes taking place in the external and internal environment that will affect them and the organisation; communicate to employees the organisation's vision and purpose.
	Spokesperson	Launch a national advertising campaign to promote new goods and services; give a speech to inform the local community about the organisation's future intentions.
Decisional	Entrepreneur	Commit organisation resources to develop innovative goods and services; decide to expand internationally to obtain new customers for the organisation's products.
	Disturbance Handler	Move quickly to take corrective action to deal with unexpected problems facing the organisation from the external environment, such as a crisis like an oil spill, or from the internal environment, such as producing faulty goods or services.
	Resource Allocator	Allocate organisational resources among different functions and departments of the organisation; set budgets and salaries of middle and first-level managers.
	Negotiator	Work with suppliers, distributors, and labor unions to reach agreements about the quality and price of input, technical and human resources; work with other organisations to establish agreements to pool resources to work on joint project.

Interpersonal Role Managers assume interpersonal roles in order to coordinate and interact with employees, provide them direction, and offer instructions. In itself, manager plays the role of a *figurehead, leader,* and *liaisoning*. As a figurehead, the manager performs ceremonial and symbolic activities for the department or the organisation. Being a figurehead, the manager needs to visioneer and strategise the activities of the department or the firm.

As a leader, the manager's role is to motivate subordinates for better performance. Relationships with subordinates, communication, and influence are a part of the role of the leader. The liaison role pertains to the development of information sources both inside and outside the organisaiton.

Informational Roles Information roles relate to the tasks necessary to obtain and transmit information. Nearly 75 per cent of the time of the managers is spent on this role. Informational role itself involves three sub-roles. First, a manager acts as a *monitor* and analyses information from inside and outside the organistion. With the information thus collected, the manager can effectively organise and control people and other resources. Acting as a *disseminator*, the manager transmits information to other members of the organisation to influence their attitudes and behaviour. As a *spokesperson*, the manager uses information to promote the organisation so that all the stakeholders respond positively towards it.

Decisional Roles These relate to the methods managers use to plan strategies and utilise resources. As an *entrepreneur*, the manager must decide which programmes and projects to initiate and how to invest resources on them. As a *disturbance handler*, the manager assumes responsibility for handling an unexpected event or crisis that threatens the firm's access to resources.

Under typical conditions, the manager needs to be a *resource allocator*, deciding how best to use people and other resources to increase organisational effectiveness. Being engaged in that role, the manager must also be a *negotiator*, reaching agreements with others. For example, the manager meets and formally negotiates with others — a supplier about a late delivery, the finance officer about the need for additional budget allocations, or the union about a worker grievance.

TYPES OF MANAGERS

Organisations typically use three types of managers to perform efficiently and effectively: First-line managers, middle managers and top managers (also called executives)-arranged in hierarchy. First-line managers report to middle managers and they inturn are subordinated to top managers. These three types of managers are grouped into departments according to their job specific duties and responsibilities. A department like manufacturing, R&D or accounting comprises a group of people who work together and possess similar skills or use the same kind of knowledge, tools, or techniques to perform their jobs. Each department has all the three levels of managers as Fig.1.3 shows.

First-Line Managers First-line managers (often called supervisors) stand at the base of the managerial hierarchy. They are responsible for the daily supervision of the non-managerial employees who actually perform activities necessary to convert inputs into outputs. In otherwords, these are the people who produce goods and services. First-line managers are found in all departments. Primary concern of the first-line managers is the application of rules and procedures to motivate subordinates, give instructions and achieve results. Besides supervisors, the first-line managers are variously called as line managers, section chiefs and office managers.

Middle Managers These managers work at middle levels of the organisation and are responsible to find the best way to organise human and other resources to achieve organisational goals. Typically, middle level managers head various departments in the organisation. In order to increase efficiency, middle managers seek to find ways to help first-line managers and non-managerial employees better utilise resources to reduce manufacturing costs or improve the services provided to the customers. To increase effectiveness, middle level managers are responsible for evaluating whether the goals the organisation is pursuing are appropriate and for suggesting to executives ways in which goals should be changed.

FIGURE 1-3
TYPES OF MANAGERS

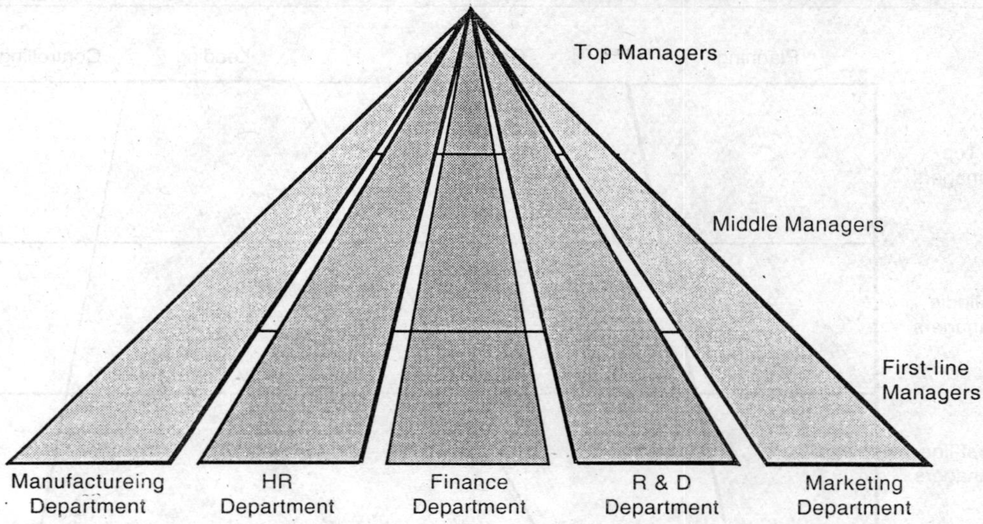

Middle managers ubiquitous. Every company has them. They are the 'glue' that holds companies together, bridging the gap between the top management and lower level workers. They implement strategy and organisational changes, keeping workers engaged during both good and bad economic cycles.

The middle managers translate strategy which can be understood by workers down the line. At the same time, middle managers take note of workers' needs making their own observations of client interfaces and shop floor activity, and relaying that information upto the senior managers. They are a buffer between the top managers and lower level employees.

Since 1980s and early 1990s, the middle managers' job has changed dramatically. Organisations became lean and flat by laying off middle managers and slashing middle management levels. But with the emergence of teams and projects, the role of middle managers has been revived. As leaders of teams and projects, middle managers are in great demand. Today's middle managers work with a variety of projects and teams, some of which might cross geographical and cultural as well as functional boundaries.

Top Managers As Fig.1.3 shows, top managers sit at the top of the hierarchy and are responsible for the entire organisation. They set organisational goals, define strategies to achieve them, monitor and interpret the environment, and make decisions that impact the entire organisation. Communicating shared vision with the employees down the line, shaping and sustaining corporate culture, and nurturing an entrepreneurial spirit that can help the company keep pace with the change are the other important functions of top managers. These managers are ultimately responsible for the success (see Closing Case) or failure of an organisation and their performance is continuously scrutinised by all the stakeholders. Top managers are known by different designations as Chief Executive Officers (CEOs), Presidents, Chairpersons, Managing Directors and Executive Vice Presidents.

FIGURE 1-4
AMOUNT OF TIME MANAGERS SPEND ON THE FOUR FUNCTIONS OF MANAGEMENT

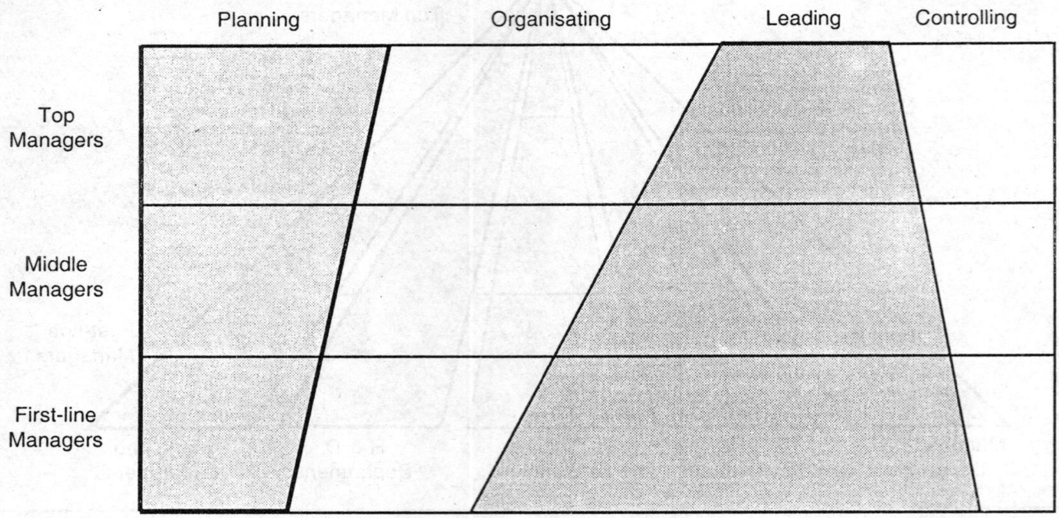

Now we have three level or types of managers and four functions of management. Similarly, we have three types of skills and three types of managers. Two questions pose themselves before us. First, which type of managers are more busy with what function of management? Second, which type of skills are more appropriate for what type of managers? Figures 1.4 and 1.5 seek to answer these questions.

As shown in Fig.1.4, the amount of time that managers spend (read importance) on planning and organising resources to maintain and improve organisational performance increases the higher up they are in the hierarchy. Top managers devote most of their time on planning and organising, the functions that are critical to determining an organisation's long-term performance. The lower a manager's position is in the hierarchy, the more time he or she spends leading and controlling first-line managers or nonmanagerial employees.[2]

Thus, as stated earlier, executives (top managers) need more conceptual skills, first-line managers need more of technical skills and managers at all levels need human skills in equal proportions. (See Fig. 1.5).

Changing Hierarchies of Managers

The tasks and responsibilities of managers at different levels have been changing dramatically in recent years. Flattening of hierarchies, restructuring and empowered teams are the main reasons for changes in hierarchies. As stated earlier, with projects and teams becoming too common in organisations, role of middle managers has shifted towards heading the projects and teams. In addition, middle managers who used to be responsible for coordinating and overseeing the work of first-line managers-but not doing it themselves-now need to perform specific job-related tasks while

FIGURE 1-5
SKILLS REQUIREMENT OF THE THREE LEVELS OF MANAGERS

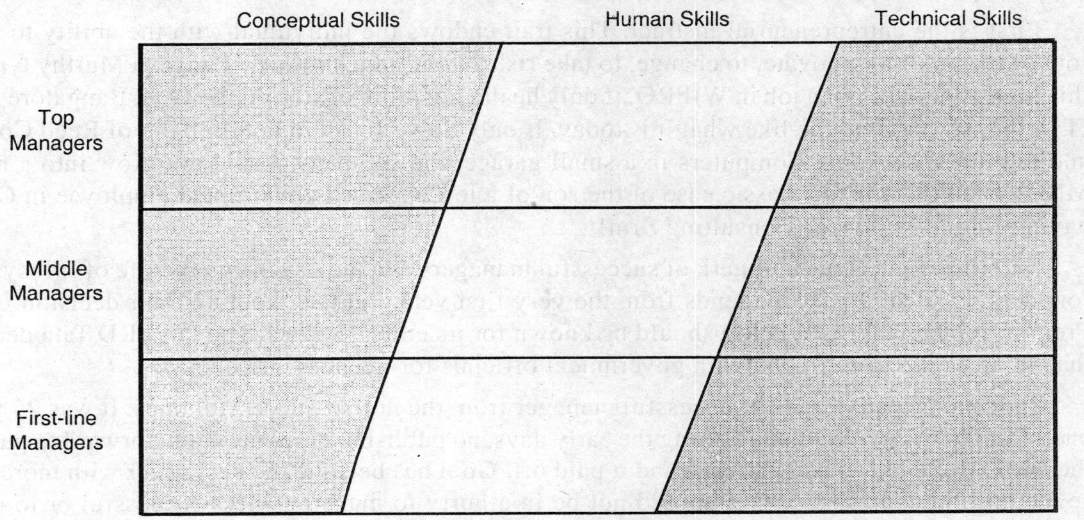

coordinating and monitoring the work of subordinates. Increasingly, top managers are encouraging lower-level managers to look beyond the goals of their respective departments and take a cross departmental view to find new opportunities to improve organisational performance. Stiff competition for resources among firms has put increased pressure on all managers to improve efficiency, effectiveness, and organisational performance. This calls for changing organisational hierarchies.

Empowered teams, also called self-managed teams, cause hierarchical changes in organisations. Empowered teams do not need supervision. They supervise their own work, and monitor the quality of goods and services they produce.

Members of the empowered teams assume many of the responsibilities and duties hitherto performed by first-line managers. What then will happen to first-line managers? They act as coaches or mentors whose job is not to tell employees what to do but to provide advice and guidance and help teams find new ways to perform their tasks more efficiently.

WHAT MAKES MANAGERS SUCCESSFUL?

Managers of all types, particularly the top managers, need to possess certain unique traits which make them successful. One simple answer to the question-what makes a manager tick-he or she is a borne manager. The traits are inherited — the managership is in the blood. Look at the youth of Gujarat. Sons of business fathers automatically become businessmen themselves. Probably Gujarat is the only state in India where fathers having marriageable daughters prefer business boys as husbands. Ambanese stepped into the shoes of the late Ambani, young Bajajs have taken over the reins of Bajaj group of companies, and so are the young Birla's and Junior Premji is succeeding Azim Premji.

Does it mean that successful managers are always borne? The answers 'no'. There are any number of first generation successful entrepreneurs/managers. Narayana Murthy, Anji Reddy, Subrato Bagchi, Steve Jobs and Bill Gates are only a few names that come to one's mind. These icons are made-they have acquired managerial traits. What are the attributes?

First is the entrepreneurial instinct. This trait endows the individual with the ability to think 'out of the box,' to innovate, to change, to take risk and be adventurous. Narayana Murthy typifies this trait. If only he got a job in WIPRO, if only he did not think of starting Infosys, Bangalore (read IT in India) would not be like what it is today. If only Steve Jobs did not drop out of Reed College and did not start Apple Computers in a small garage, the company would not grow into a major MNC! Then there is the classic case of the son of a lowly placed government employee in Orissa having started MindTree Consulting firm!

Determination is the hallmark of successful managers. On the day one in the life of Infosys, the founders decided to pay dividends from the very first year and they kept up their decision. Azim Premji decided that his WIPRO should be known for its ethical values. The late JRD Tata decided that Tatas would never lobby with government officials for licences and quotas.

Patience is what makes a successful manager from the not-so-successful ones. It was 25 years back that Goldrat wrote **Goal**. During the early days, no publisher of repute came forward to publish the book. But Goldrat had patience and it paid off. **Goal** has become the best seller with more than seven million copies sold. One should not be in a hurry to make business successful or to make money. The manager needs to work hard and wait for the traits. Results are sure to come.

Successful manager is able to see opportunities where others fail to identify. Newton was the only man who questioned why apple was falling, though millions earlier to him just saw apples falling. Steve Jobs could use all that calligraphy he learnt in Reed College to design Macintosh Computer.

A successful manager works hard-day in day out-typically 24/7. He or she travels a lot, often globe-trotting. The daily engagements, meetings, schedules, orders, cash flows, rivals, turnovers and many more take a heavy toll on the manager's health. It is work, work all the time.

Reading and acquiring knowledge make the manager keep track of the happenings in the market. An executive is a voracious reader. Azim Premji, Narayana Murthy, or Ratan Tata - you can see them carrying latest books on business management and reading while travelling.

The manager of today is inspired by achievement need. He or she measures success by numbers. The turnover this year is Rs.100 cr. It should go up to Rs.500 cr. next year and to Rs.1000 cr. the following year. Successful managers are ambitious, but not greedy.

It is stating what is too obvious. The successful manager possesses all the tree skills we stated earlier. He or she is endowed with conceptual, interpersonal and technical skills in abundance.

Successful managers are ethically conscious people. They know pretty well that unethical practices get them quick results but quick results are not lasting results. Tatas are known for ethical conduct and corporate governance. Narayana Murthy made Panesh Murthy quit the company as the latter indulged in sexual harassment. Gopalakrishna, the present CEO of Infosys, was made to pay a fine of Rs.5 lakh as he was charged with insider trading offense.

The successful manager is not always focused on turnover and profits. He or she is staying connected to customers and employees. The Internet has given increased knowledge and power to customers, so organisations have to remain flexible and adaptable to respond quickly to changing demands or competition.

Team-building skills make a manager highly successful. Teams of front-line employees who work directly with customers are the basic building blocks of organisations. Instead of managing a department of employees, many managers act as team leaders of changing and temporary projects.

A successful manager believes on the strength and quality of collaborative relationships. Partnerships, both within the organisation and with outside customers, suppliers and even rival firms are regarded as the key to winning organisations. E-business models that digitally link customers, suppliers, partners and other stakeholders require managers to assess and manage relationships far beyond the confines of the traditional organisation.

Building a learning organisation is yet another trait of a successful manager. A learning organisation is built on a climate that values experimentation and risk taking, applies current technology, tolerates mistakes and failures, and rewards out-of-box thinking and sharing of knowledge. Everyone in the organisation participates in identifying and solving problems, enabling the organisation to continuously experiment, improve and increase its capability.[3]

A successful manager is expected to possess self-worth or self competency. Self-worth is the first step in the process of learning to manage others. Effective managers must be abreast of important global trends that have significant impact on their organisations and understand how well their organisations are performing in global markets. Of particular importance is the understanding multicultural differences prevailing across the globe.

Evolution of Management Theory

What do the management theories convey? The five management theories (see Fig.1.6) convey the search for newer concepts, principles and practices of management as discovered by management thinkers over time. Advances in management theory typically occur as managers and researchers find better ways to perform the major management functions: planning, organising, leading and controlling.

The five theories identified in the journey of management thought are: Scientific Management Theory, Administrative Management Theory, Behavioural Management Theory, Management Science Theory and Organisation-Environment Theory.

Scientific Management Theory Dating back to the late 18th century and the early 20th century, scientific theory advocates the application of scientific methods to analyse work and to determine how to complete production tasks efficiently.

Credit for Scientific Management goes to Frederick Taylor who was hired by Midvale Steel Company in the US in 1878. Taylor discovered that production and pay were poor, inefficiency and waste were prevalent, and most companies had unused potential. He concluded that management decisions were unsystematic and no efforts were made to determine the best means of production.

In response, Taylor introduced **Scientific Management** (hence he is called the Father of Scientific Management) which recommended the application of scientific methods to analyse work and to determine the methods to complete the tasks efficiently.

In essence, Taylor advocated the following four principles as part of his Scientific Management:

1. Management should develop a precise, and scientific approach for each element of one's work to replace general guidelines.
2. Management should scientifically select, train, teach and develop each worker so that the right person has the right job.

FIGURE 1-6
THE EVOLUTION OF MANAGEMENT THEORY

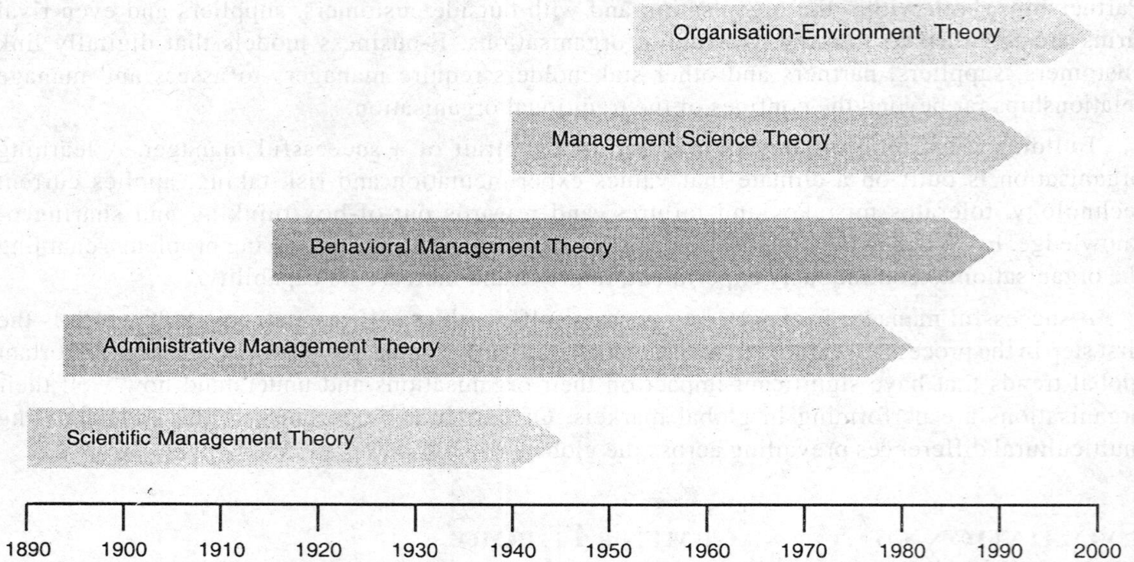

(Source: Gareth R. Jones, *et.al., op.cit.,* p.35).

3. Management should co-operate with the workers to ensure that the job matches plans and principles.
4. Management should ensure an equal division of work and responsibility between managers and workers.[4]

To implement this approach, Taylor introduced time-and-motion studies, and differential piece rate system. The former helped identify one best way of doing a job and the latter benefited workers with additional pay when they exceeded standard levels of output. In addition, Taylor advocated the importance of hiring and training the workers to perform better.

Two more prominent individuals who contributed to Scientific Management were - Frank Gilbreth and his wife Lillian Galbreth. These two refined Taylor's analysis of work measurements and made many contributions to time and motion study.

Taylone popularised the concept of Scientific Management through his two books: **Shop Management (1903),** and **Principles of Scientific Management (1911).** The ideas of Scientific Management dramatically increased productivity across all industries, and they are still important today. Indeed, the concept of arranging work based on careful analysis of tasks for maximum productivity is deeply embedded in today's organisations. Managers in every organisation now carefully analyse the basic tasks that must be performed and try to devise the work systems that will allow their organisations to operate most efficiently.

However, since Scientific Management ignored the human element, it led to increased conflict and often violent clashes on the shop floors. Workers often felt exploited. This was in sharp contrast to the harmony and cooperation that Taylor and his associates had forethought. Table 1.2 presents merits and demerits of Scientific Management.

TABLE 1-2
BALANCED VIEW OF SCIENTIFIC MANAGEMENT

Merits	Demerits
• Improved productivity and performance	• Simplistic motivational assumptions
• Scientific analysis of the work place	• Workers are treated as wheels in a machine
• Linking wages to performance and enhanced earnings for workers	• Potential for exploitation of labour
• Cooperation between management and workers got to be established	• Inter-personal relationships and linkages between environment and organisation ignored
• Demonstrated the importance of personnel selection and training	• Did not acknowledge variance among individuals

Administrative Theory Side by side the proponents of Scientific Management, there were two eminent personalities who were contemplating on a new approach to management. The new approach focused on creating an organisation structure that would facilitate greater efficiency and effectiveness. Organisation structure facilitates allocation of tasks and determines authority relationships that control how employees use resources to achieve organisational goals. The two eminent contributors to the management thought were Max Weber, a German Professor of Sociology and Henry Fayol, the French Manager.

Max Weber developed the famous theory of bureaucracy and Henry Fayol came out with the famous *14 Principles of Management.*

Theory of Bureaucracy Weber's beauracratic theory is based on five principles: (i) labour is divided with clear definitions of authority and responsibility that are legitimised as official duties; (ii) positions are organised in a hierarchy of authority, with each position under the authority of a higher one; (iii) rules and regulations determine and standardise behaviour; (iv) administrative acts and decisions are recorded in writing; (v) management is separate from ownership in any organisation.

Weber believed that organisations that implement all the five principles will establish bureaucratic system that will improve organisational performance.

Though 100 years old and though the term bureaucracy is despised by today's managers, Weber's idea is relevant and is in place in organisations of today. Take away the basic elements of bureaucracy, organisations would collapse like a pack of cards.

Table 1.3 brings out the merits and demerits of bureaucracy.

Fayol's Principles A broad framework for administrative management emerged in 1916 when Henry Fayol, a French mining engineer and executive, published a book summarising his experiences as a manager. Fayol advocated five functions of management, viz., Planning, Organising, Commanding, Coordinating and Controlling (almost identical to the four functions of management explained earlier) and 14 principles (see Table 1.4).

As with bureaucracy, Fayol's principles have stood the test of time and certain principles like line of authority, equity, initiative, esprit de corps and unity of direction were, are and will continue to be relevant in the years to come.

Behavioural Management Theory Three approaches which make up the behaviour theory are the human relations management, human resource perspective and behavioural science approach.

TABLE 1-3

MERITS AND DEMERITS OF BUREAUCRACY

Merits	Demerits
• Efficient performance of routinised activities is ensured	• Inflexible and delayed decisions
• Lends stability to organisations and institutions	• People's element ignored
• Subjective judgements by employees and management avoided	• Rules tend to become ends in themselves
• Respects positions rather than persons	• Difficult to dismantle once established
• Fair and equitable selection and promotion systems tend to improve managers' feeling of security, reduce stress and become ethically conscious	• Difficulty to use bureaucratic principles for the benefit of organisation rather than harming it

TABLE 1-4

FAYOL'S 14 PRINCIPLES OF MANAGEMENT

- *Division of Work* – divide work into specialised tasks and assign reponsibilities to apecific individuals.
- *Authority* – delegate authority along with responsibility.
- *Discipline* – make expectations clear and punish violations.
- *Unity of Command* – each employee should be assigned to only one supervisor.
- *Unity of Direction* – employee's efforts should be focused on achieving organisational objectives.
- *Subordination of individual interest to the general interest* – the general interest must predominate.
- *Remuneration* – systematically reward efforts that support the organisation's direction.
- *Centralisation* – determine the relative importance of superiror and subordinate roles.
- *Scalar chain* – keep communications within the chain of command.
- *Order* – order jobs and material so they support the organisation's direction.
- *Equity* – fair discipline and order enhance employee commitment.
- *Stability and tenure of personnel* – promote employee loyalty and longevity.
- *Initiative* – encourage employees to act on their own in support of the organisation's direction.
- *Esprit de corps* – promote a unity of interest between employees and management.

Human Relations Management Genesis for human relations management was the Hawthorne Studies conducted at the Western Electric Company in the US between 1924 and 1932.

As Professor of Industrial Research at the Harvard School of Business Administration, Mayo was the person, most responsible for conducting the studies and publicising their significance. Naturally, he is called the 'father of human relations movement.'

The Hawthorne project involved three sets of studeies: Illumination Studies, The Relay Assembly Room Study and The Bank Wiring Room Study.

Illumination Studies Illumination studies constituted the first set of experiments and took place between 1924 and 1927. In one of these studies, lighting was decreased over successive periods for the experimental group (the group for whom lighting was altered), while it was kept at a constant level for the control group (a comparison group working in another area). The researchers were surprised to discover that productivity increased roughly at the same rate in both the groups. It was only in the final experiment, where they decreased light to 0.06 foot candle (roughly moonlight intensity), that performance in the experimental group declined as the workers in the group complained that they could hardly see anything. The researchers concluded that factors other than lighting were at work (since output rose in both the groups), and the project was discontinued.

It is from this first round of experiments that the term *Hawthorne Effect* was coined, referring originally to the fact that people's knowledge that they are being studied leads them to modify their behaviour.

The Relay Assembly Room Study Intrigued with the positive changes in productivity, the researchers decided to attempt to determine the causes through further studies. Hence the second set of tests.

The second set of experiments took place between 1927 and 1933. The most famous study involved five women who assembled electrical relays in the Royal Assembly Test Room, where they were away from other workers and the researchers could alter work conditions and evaluate the results. Before the study began, the researchers were concerned about the possible negative reactions from the workers who would be included in the test. To reduce potential resistance, the researchers changed the usual supervisor arrangement so that there would be no official supervisor. Instead, the workers would operate under the general direction of the researchers. The workers were also given special privileges, such as being able to leave their work station without permission, free mid-morning lunch, a workday that was a half-hour shorter, a five-day workweek (a novel idea at that time), and variations in the methods of payment. Generally, productivity increased over the period of study, regardless of how the factors were manipulated.

A Harvard University research group (involved in assessing the results) finally concluded that the change in the supervisory arrangement was the major reason for the increase in the productivity in the Relay Assembly Test Room study and in two related studies involving different work groups. The researchers felt that the physical changes such as rest pauses, free lunches, and incentive payments were of lesser importance.

The Bank Wiring Room Study This study was conducted between 1931 and 1932 and constituted the third set of experiments. The motivation for this study was built on the findings of the second set. For this study, a group of 14 men who wired telephone banks was observed in a standard shop condition. An observer was stationed in the room with instructions to take continuous notes on the workers' actions. The observer was not allowed to give orders or get involved in conversations with the workers. Although, the workers were initially apprehensive about the observer, they settled into more natural and relaxed behaviour after about three weeks. Because the foreman for the work group also supervised other workers in another room, and because the observer was deliberately unobtrusive, the workers were relatively free from constant supervision.

Though the workers were paid according to their output, the observer soon noted that the workers had established an informal daily norm of 6600 units per person. Typically, the men would pace their work so that they reached the norm by the end of the day. Of course, some of the men could do more than 6600 units. But if they indicated that they would prefer to be more productive, they risked becoming victims of harassment.

The researchers concluded that the behavioural norms set by the work group had a powerful influence over the productivity of the group. The higher the norms, the greater the productivity. The lower the norms, the lower the productivity. The power of the peer group and the importance of group influence on individual behaviour and productivity were confirmed in the bank wiring room.

Thus, Hawthorne Studies laid a foundation for understanding people's social and psychological behaviour in the workplace.

The main implication of the Hawthorne Studies, popularly called the Human Relations Management is that the behaviour of managers and workers in the work setting is critical in determining the performance of an organisation.

The Human Resource Approach The human relations approach highlighted the impact of behaviour on performance. Interpersonal behaviour has its impact on satisfaction which in turn may lead to improved performance. This is the typical of the dairy farm model-well fed cows give more milk and satisfied workers tend to perform better. But, as will be stated latter in this book, a satisfied worker is not necessarily a productive worker.

Something else was needed to make the worker a productive employee. Two individuals came out with their own findings in this context. They are: Abraham Maslow, and Douglas McGregor. Their contributions form the human resource approach.

Abraham Maslow came out with a thesis that unmet needs are the causes for problems that people face. From this assumption, Maslow built a hierarchy of needs, starting from physiological and progressing through safety, belonging esteem and self actualisation needs. More details on Maslow's need hierarchy are provided in the chapter on motivation.

Douglas McGregor was not content with the simplistic human relations notions. He challenged the notions. Based on his experiences as a manager and a consultant, McGregor formulated his Theory X and Theory Y which will be explained latter in the chapter on motivation.

The essence of Maslow's and McGergor's prescriptions is the emphasis on daily tasks that people perform. In otherwords, the theme of the human resource approach is the need for designing jobs so that tasks are not perceived as dehumanising or demeaning but instead allow workers to use their full potential. Though there is a shift towards job, concern for employee behaviour is not to be undermined.

Behavioural Science Approach As days went by other thinkers, particularly psychologists, sociologists and anthropologists, began studying people at work. These individuals are known as behavioural scientists, and their approach to management is known as behavioural science approach.

The emphasis of the behavioural science approach lies more on the nature of work, and the degree to which it can fulfill the human need to express skills and abilities. The advocates of this approach believe that an individual is motivated to work for many reasons in addition to making money and forming interpersonal relationships.

The principles of behavioural science approach are being practised in every organisation, behavioural science as a course, more popularly known as **Organisational Behaviour**, is highly popular among the students of commerce and management. The latter part of this book brings out the various principles of behavioural science more clearly.

The behavioural science approach owes its origin to Mary Parker Follet, one of the earliest management thinkers. Being a social philosopher, she pioneered many of the principles and practices of organisational behaviour.

Management Science Theory What makes management science theory different from other approaches is the application of mathematics, statistics, and other quantitative techniques to management decision making and problem solving. Management science in essence is scientific management revisited. TQM, OR, IT, MIS, Lean manufacturing and the like are the buzzwords of management science theory. Originated in 1940, management science approach is highly popular in organisations.

Organisational-Environment Theory Some thinkers on management went beyond the confines of an organisation and tried to understand the impact of external environment on its functioning. The experts concluded that the environment exerts considerable influence on the performance of the organisation. This view is popularly called as the organisational — environment theory. Essentially, this theory examines the interface between organisation and its external environment.

Systems view and contingency approach form part of the organisational-environment theory.

The Systems View The systems view takes a look at how organisations import resources from the external environment, convert them into more useful goods and services, and export them to the market (See Fig.1.7).

FIGURE 1-7
SYSTEMS VIEW OF AN ORGANISATION

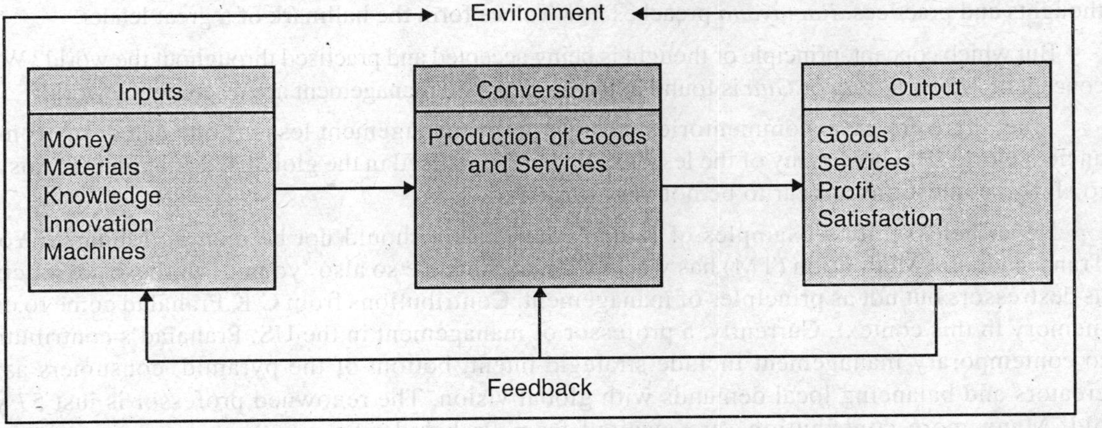

The inputs include several resources such as money, materials, people and machines. The outcome includes products, profit, satisfaction and improved quality of life. Organisations play critical role in this process. It is they that receive the inputs, convert them into more useful products and supply them to consumes to satisfy their needs.

What does the systems approach teach the managers? The main lesson that can be drawn is that the management should focus on efficiency and effectiveness in each part of the organisation, with the understanding that actions taken in one part of the organisation affect its other parts. Each part is interdependent on another and no part can function in isolation.

The Contingency Approach This approach also operates in identical way to that of the systems view. The contingency view posits that organisational structures and control systems that management uses depend on or are contingent upon the characteristics of the external environment within which the firm operates. According to the contingency theory, the characteristics of the environment affect an organisation's ability to obtain resources. Obviously, each department should organise its activities in such a way they are able to access resources from the external environment to the maximum extent. In otherwords, how managers design the organisational hierarchy, choose a control system, and lead and motivate their employees is contingent upon the characteristics of the environment.

The main lesson that can be drawn from the contingency view is that there is no one best way of managing. Each decision and each step that a manager takes are contingent upon the external environment. The environmental forces that impact an organisation's activities include political-legal, technological, economic and social-cultural.

Indian Contributions to Management Practices

India's civilisation is one of the oldest in the world. Management is concomitant of civilisation. In otherwords, management as a discipline has been in practice in India for thousands of years. The way the joint families were managed and the way guilds were organised, led and controlled reveal the prevailing management principles and practices in ancient India.

India has greatest epics which expound the principles of management no end. *Mahabharata* inspires men of action and *Bhagavat Gita* guides men of thought. *Upanishads* are a great source of management thoughts and practices. *Ramayana* preaches how values form the hallmark of a great leader.

But which concept, principle or thought is being accepted and practised throughout the world? Which concept of *Mahabharata* or *Gita* is found in the literature on management anywhere in the world?

True, there are great commentories written on the management lessons one can draw from the ancient works. But how many of the lessons are being practised in the globalised economies? Answers to all these questions appear to be not very positive.

Nevertheless, a few examples of Indian contribution should not be missed. Maharshi Yogi's Transcendental Meditation (TM) has world wide acceptance so also 'yoga'. But these are practised as destressors but not as principles of management. Contributions from C.K.Prahalad come to one's memory in this context. Currently, a professor of management in the US, Prahalad's contributions to contemporary management include strategic intent, bottom of the pyramid, consumers as co-creators and balancing local demands with global vision. The renowned professor is just 57 year old. Many more contributions are awaited from Prahalad who was borne and brought up at Coimbatore in Tamil Nadu.

Contemporary Trends in Management Thinking

Management is a dynamic subject. It is flexible, open, growing, and evergreen discipline. This is the reason why management has survived centuries and is still growing strong.

What is great about management is that the old order is giving place for the new and the transition is smooth. Beginning with scientific management principles, the discipline of management has travelled through focus on people, emphasis on tasks, underlining quantitative techniques and recognising the relevance of external environment.

As on today the following practices are prominent in the management thought.

Inventing and Reinventing Organisations Dynamic managers continually search for ways to unleash the creative potential of their employees and themselves. They are destroying traditional organisation structures, flattening hierarchies and dismantling artificial barriers. Thereon the boss and the subordinates-all to bolster efficiency and effectiveness of organisations.

Globalisation Globalisation throws open new challenges and opportunities. With the world's financial markets running 24 hours a day, and even the remotest corners of the planet only a phone call away, managers of today are expected to think as global citizens. World is their market and their employees do not come from one country or one region. They are a mix of multicultures and multireligious citizens.

Multiculturalism Organisations of today comprise employees with different regions and cultural backgrounds. In otherwords, they have diversity. Diversity needs to be managed effectively as it contributes to innovation and vibrancy. Poorly managed diversity results in flighting away of people.

Quality Managers must become quality conscious. The concept Total Quality Management (TQM) must become a buzzword with every manager. All managers should be thinking about how every organisational process can be conducted to provide goods and services of world class standards. Strong and lasting relationships can be built with customers and suppliers through quality products.

Case: WHERE MANAGEMENT MATTERED

It was 1988, exactly two decades back, that Satyam Computer Services was borne with just 20 people. As years went by, Satyam (this is how the Hyderabad based software company is affectionately called), grew in strengths and as of now it is a $ 2 billion revenue and 53,000 employee company - a remarkable feat by any standard. What is the secret behind this phenomenal success? It is the management provided by Ramalinga Raju, the CEO of Satyam. Truly, management mattered in Satyam as is the case with any successful venture.

It is not just in sales revenue and head count that Satyam is known for. The software giant is known for excellent corporate governance. It has won, among others, the prestigious Golden Peacock Award for corporate governance.

What is unique about Ramalinga Raju? What are his best management practices which made Satyam a darling for job aspirants and a preferred destination for investors?

First about the man. Ramalinga Raju is a highly accredited person graduating as he is, from Ohio University and is an alumnus of Harvard Business School. His outstanding success lies in his simple and passion-driven style of functioning. He has open mind to accept new things and is ever willing to learn from rivals. From Infosys, Raju has learnt the strategies to establish connectivity with investors and to take advantage of capital markets, both within and outside the country. TCS has taught him how to train employees and make them become customer centric in outlook. From WIPRO, Raju has learnt how to focus on improving operational efficiency and how to make sure that every rupee or dollar that gets spent gives maximum mileage.

Raju has open mind to learn from past mistakes. First, he confesses to the mistakes, if ever committed. In an exclusive interview to Dalal Street - Investment Journal (April 2008), Raju made confessions which ran thus: "We assumed that knowledge industry is not capital intensive. We thought we will assemble a team and that our intellectual power will make a difference. But very soon we found that the expenses can be high and no tangible assets were created. We also assumed that it would be an easy take-off, but it was much harder work. Also it took much longer for us to establish ourselves. It was hard on our part to prove customers that we had the competency and the wherewithal to serve them well. Those were the times when we went to meet a customer with a world map in our pocket, so that we could open it and show them where India was."

Raju has the grace to convert wrong assumptions into opportunities.

What are the best management practices of Raju? There are atleast five of them.

Raju has infused entrepreneurial and customer centric spirit in his employees. He has also created a conducive business environment that enables leaders fit to lead and operate in today's environment.

Second, Raju has made Satyam a metrics-driven organisation. Metrics gives an opportunity to employees to objectively express themselves and assess about where they are and where they want to go.

Third, Raju believes in value-adding for Satyam's customers at their business levels. This means understanding their competitive environment, their pain points and addressing those issues effectively. Satyam believes in benchmarking not against past happenings but against pull points from the future.

Fourth, Raju emphasises on the stakeholders' delight. Satyam has an emblem that reads, "Every Satyamite is a leader Delighting the Stakeholders." The spirit of this punch line is in the psyche of every Satyamite. When translated into specifics, what this implies can be better understood by listening to what Raju himself says. In the interview to the Journal, Raju said "If we are servicing a telecom customer and if we do not understand the convergent technologies becoming critical to the success, we are unlikely to service the customer. If we cannot take a bank to the finger tips of every citizen, then it is a failure on our part."

Fifth, Satyam has come to stay a storehoure, a department store of services for the world at large. Satyam provides hundreds of services. From the point of view of large customers who are looking for end-to-end solutions, Satyam becomes one stop shop.

No surprise-Satyam is one of the four in the top league of IT providers. The other three are TCS, WIPRO and Infosys!

Questions

1. What traits does Ramalinga Raju possess as to become successful executive?
2. Which of the functions and principles of management that Ramalinga Raju uses in his daily functioning as the CEO?
3. What lessons can young entrepreneurs of today learn from the experience of the CEO of Satyam?

QUESTIONS

1. What is management? Bring out the four functions of management, each in brief.
2. What roles does a typical manager play every day?
3. Which traits make a manager sucessful?
4. Explain the different types of managers. Whom do you think are the most essential for the sucess of an organisation.
5. Explain –
   (1) Scientic Management
   (2) Hawthorne Studies
6. Describe —
   (1) Administrative Management Theory
   (2) Management Science Theory
7. Why do you think that Indian contribution to management is not much?

REFERENCES

1. Richard L.Daft, *Management*, Sixth Edition, Thompson Learning, 2003, p.5.
2. Gareth R.Jones, et al, *Contemporary Management*, McGraw-Hill, 1998, p.13.
3. Richard L.Daft, op.cit, p.26.
4. Thomas S.Bateman and Scott A.Snell, *Management*, McGraw-Hill, 1999, p.39.

CHAPTER

Two

Ethics and Social Responsibility of Managers

Learning Objectives

After reading this chapter you should understand —

1. The nature of CSR and business ethics
2. The arguments for and against CSR
3. The prominence of CSR
4. The evolving idea of CSR
5. The forces pressuring CSR
6. The sources of business ethics
7. How managers manage ethics
8. The difficulties in decision making
9. The tips for better decision making

SOCIAL RESPONSIBILITY

Social responsibility, also known as Corporate Social Responsibility (CSR), is understood as the obligation of managers to take actions that protect and improve the welfare of society as a whole along with their own interests.

Every decision the businessman takes and every action he contemplates have social implications. Be it deciding on diversification, expansion, opening of a new branch, closure of an existing branch or replacement of men by machines, the society is affected in one way or the other. Even routine matters like overtime and night shifts, outsourcing, and laying off employees due to load-shedding have a social impact. Whether the issue is significant or not, the businessman should keep his social obligation in mind before contemplating any action.

What is significant is that CSR makes a corporation accountable for any of its actions that affect people, their communities, and their environment.

What is equally significant is the fact that CSR extends beyond its regular activities that are carried out in a lawful manner. The social actions which a firm undertakes in the name of its CSR occur "beyond the factory gate" and will benefit the society in general. Successful companies need a healthy society. Education, healthcare, and equal opportunity are essential to a productive workforce. Safe products and working conditions attract customers and minimise the costs of accidents. Efficient utilisation of land, water, energy and other natural resources make businesses more productive. Ultimately, a healthy society creates additional demand for business, as more human needs are met and aspirations grow. Any business that pursues its ends at the expense of the society in which it operates will find its success to be illusory and short-lived.

A healthy society needs successful corporations. No social programme can rival the business when it comes to creating jobs, wealth, and innovation that improve standards of living and social conditions.

How does CSR differ from charity is a question that is relevant here. Charity or philanthropy refers to an idea that a wealthy individual should be bountiful to the weak and poor in the society. Poor feeding and donations to temple construction constitute charity. Charity is undertaken to redeem **karma** a wealthy person has inherited because of misdeeds in his or her previous birth, or to accumulate **punya** for the next birth. Charities are generally occasional and their end use is not monitored.

Unlike philanthropy, CSR is inspired not by self interest but the motive is the interest of the organisation. Maintaining schools, donating computers to village schools, adopting villages, promoting greenery and contributing to ecology and the like benefit society and in turn help contribute to the growth of healthy businesses. Social actions of businesses are being systematised, are periodic and the end uses are subject to social audit.

The CSR Debate There are arguments for and against business's social responsibility. While there are Friedman, Peter Drucker and Dhirubhai Ambani who do not subscribe to CSR, there are more number of people - business, government and academic - who advocate social actions. Knowledge on the debate is useful for any individual to make better judgement of social actions.

Arguments for CSR

There are many arguments in support of socially responsive actions. The more important of them are explained below (See Fig.2.1).

FIGURE 2-1
ARGUMENTS FOR AND AGAINST CSR

Arguments for CSR	*Arguments against CSR*
* Changed public expectations	* Profit maximisation
* Better environment for business	* Society has to pay the cost
* Balance power with responsibility	* Lack of social skills
* Business has resources	* Business has power
* Prevention is better	* Social overhead cost
* Moral responsibility	* Lack of accountability
* Globalisation	* Lack of broad support
* Better employees	* Experts' views

1. Changed Public Expectations of Business One of the most potent arguments for social responsibility is that public expectations from business have changed. It is reasoned that the institution of business exists only because it satisfies the valuable needs of society. Society gave business its charter to exist, and the charter can be amended or revoked at any time that the business fails to live up to society's expectations. Therefore, if business wishes to remain viable in the long run, it must respond to society's needs and give the society what it wants.

2. Better Environment for Business Another argument favouring social responsibility is that it creates a better environment for business. This concept rationalises that a better society produces environmental conditions more favourable for business operations. The firm which is most responsive to the improvement of community quality of life will as a result have a better community in which to conduct its business. Labour recruiting will be easier, and labour will be of a higher quality. Turnover and absenteeism will be reduced.

As a result of social improvements, crime will decrease with the consequence that less money will be spent to protect property, and less taxes have to be paid to support police forces. The arguments can be extended in all directions to show that a better society produces a better environment for business.

3. Balance of Responsibility with Power Another argument for social responsibility is that business's responsibility should be more related to its power. It is reasoned that businessmen have vast amounts of social power. They do affect the economy, minorities, and other social problems. In turn, an equal amount of social responsibility is required to match their social power. If each institution is to perform its social role in an orderly relationship with other institutions, then responsibility must be accepted whenever there is power. Any other arrangement invites irresponsible behaviour.

4. Business has the Resources Another argument for social responsibility is that business has a vast pool of resources in terms of men, talents, functional expertise and money. Probably, business is without peers in respect of the resources it possesses. With these resources at its command, business is in a better position to work for social goals.

5. Prevention is Better Than Cure The last point is that prevention is better than cure. If business delays dealing with social problems now, it may find itself constantly occupied with putting out social fires so that is has no time to accomplish its goal of producing goods and services. Since these social problems must be dealt with at some time, it is actually more economical to deal with them before they develop into serious social breakdowns that consume most of the management's time.

Ford Motor demonstrated its moral responsibility when it recalled 359000 of its Focus cars because of a potential problem with their rear door latches. The problem involving these cars stemmed from a build-up of corrosion around the rear door latches which can eventually prevent them from ensuring security.

Recall of 359000 cars follows as even bigger recall. In Jan. 27, 2005, it was announced that Ford was recalling about 792000 top selling pickup tracks, sport utility vehicles and mini-vans because of possible fire risk from the overheating of their cruise control switches.

6. Moral Responsibility It is said that the acceptance of corporate social responsibility is the morally correct position. This notion suggests that our modern industrial society faces many serious social problems brought on, to a large extent, by large corporations. The corporations therefore have a moral responsibility to help solve or ameliorate these problems. It is this moral obligation that made Toyota recall 9.3 million vehicles since 2004 from the US and Japan. In July 2007, the CEO of Toyota Kolshaki Watanable even deeply bowed before public in apology. A corollary to this notion is that because business firms control so many of the resources in our economy, they should devote some of these resources to the overall betterment of society.

7. Globalisation The recent globalisation of large corporations has led to firms increasingly operating in countries with very different and generally much lower standards of living than found in their respective home countries. More extensive media reach coupled with advances in information technology (e.g. NGO use of websites) has allowed rapid and widespread exposure of alleged corporate abuses even in the remote parts of the globe, as both Shell (oil spills in Nigeria exposed on television documentaries) and Nike (exposure of sweatshop labour conditions in its subcontractor operation in developing countries) have learnt to their cost. Recently, Primark — the discount house of London — cancelled outsouring contracts with three Tamil Nadu based stiching firms on the ground that they were employing child labour. This action was triggered because of BBC's coverage and reporting of the child abuse. Such revelations compel global firms undertake social actions.

Failure to undertake social actions may dent the reputation and brand image of the firms. Infact, firms are likely to be penalised by consumers and other stakeholders, for actions that are not considered socially responsible.

8. Better Employees As stated earlier, labour hiring becomes easier for a socially responsible firm. Employees prefer to work for more socially responsible firms. It is well-known that tobacco companies find it difficult hiring the best talent. This has become more widespread, particularly in tight labour markets as potential and current employees value the corporate social performance of their employers.

Arguments Against CSR

There are arguments against CSR and they are as follows:

1. Profit Maximisation The first and the most forceful argument disfavouring social responsibility is that business has profit maximisation as its main objective. Infact, the business is most socially responsible when it attends to its interests and leaves other activities to other institutions. Since business operates in a world of poverty and hunger, the economic efficiency of business is a matter of top priority and should be the sole mission of business. Business's function is economic, not social and economic values should be the only criteria used to measure success. In this kind of system, managers are the agents of the shareholders, and all their decisions are controlled by their desire to maximise profits for the shareholders while reasonably complying with law and social custom.

2. Society has to Pay the Cost Another argument is that the costs of social responsibility will be passed on to the society and it is the society which must bear them. Can the society afford these additional costs?

3. Lack of Social Skills Business managers are best at managing matters relating to business. They are not equally good at solving social problems. Their outlook is primarily economic and that their skills are the same. They really do not feel at home in social matters. If society is going to depend on someone to work with social problems, why choose a group which is so poorly qualified? Does society really want economic and technical people meddling in social affairs? Will they broaden their outlook and will their skills transfer? Can business really do the job? Is it better equipped than the government and other institutions?

4. Social Overhead Cost Cost on social responsibility is considered to be a social cost which will not immediately benefit the business. Why spend money on an object, the benefits of which will be realised only in the future? It is the heavy social overhead cost which is one of the reasons for the dismal performance of some of our government undertakings.

5. Lack of Accountability Another point of view is that the businessmen have no direct accountability to the people, therefore, it is unwise to give them responsibility for areas where they are not accountable. Accountability should always go with responsibility, and it is poor social control to allow any other kind of arrangement. Until the society can develop mechanisms which establish direct lines of social accountability from business to the public, business must stand clear of social activities and pursue only its goal of profit where it is directly accountable through the market system.

6. Lack of Broad Support Another point is that business involvement in social goals lack support from all groups in society. If business does become socially involved, it will create so much friction among dissident parties that business cannot perform its social assignment. Although many persons desire business to become more socially involved, others oppose the idea. There is lack of agreement among the general public, among intellectuals, in the government and even among businessmen themselves.

7. Friedman and Levitt's Views The most cogent criticism has been voiced by the economist Milton Friedman. Friedman, the apostle of free markets, based his arguments on two principal contentions, one economic and one legal. From the economic perspective, he asserted that if managers spend corporate funds on projects not intended to maximise profits, the efficiency of the market mechanism will be undermined and resources will be misallocated within the economy. On the legal side, Friedman contended that because managers are legal agents of the shareholders, their sole duty is to maximise the financial return to the shareholders. Hence, if they spend corporate funds for social purposes, they are essentially stealing from the stockholders. Moreover, Friedman suggested that if the shareholders want money spent on social causes, they are free to do so individually with their dividends.

The late Dhirubai Ambani believed in running his business effectively and efficiently instead of being concerned about social responsibility.

Theodore Levitt argued against corporate social responsibility fearing that business values might come to dominate society. He posited that business, as an institution, would become the twentieth-century equivalent of the medieval church-the all-embracing institution in society. He suggested that this would not be healthy for society.

Prominence of Social Responsibility

Counter arguments notwithstanding, social responsibility has come to stay. In its **1981 Statement of Corporate Responsibility**, the Business Round Table, a group of 200 leaders of large corporations, said that the pursuit of profit and assumption of social responsibility were not incompatible. Social responsibility has been one of the leading topics at 2003 World Economic Forum (WEF) meetings. A report from the WEF observes that the three pressures of corporate competitiveness, corporate governance, and corporate citizenship, and the linkage among them, will play crucial role in shaping the agenda for business leaders in the coming decade. Similarly, the World Business Council for Sustainable Development (WBCSD), a coalition of 120 international businesses, refers to the increasing calls for firms to assume wider responsibilities in the social arena and claims that social responsibility is firmly on the global policy agenda. Among the many other organisations that are advocating greater attention to social responsibility are the Business for Social Responsibility (BSR), and Business in the Community (BIC).

The government of UK has appointed a minister for social responsibility. The European Commission adopted a new strategy on social responsibility in July 2002. The strategy reads thus: "Many businesses have already recognised that social responsibility can be profitable and social actions have mushroomed. However, the EU can add value in atleast two key ways: by helping stakeholders to make social responsibility more transparent and more credible, and by showing that social responsibility is not just for multinations - it can benefit smaller businesses too.

Indian managers are not lagging behind in undertaking social actions. There are 72 companies that spend one crore and above per annum on social responsibility and 554 firms allocate atleast one lakh rupees every year. Table 2.1 gives more details.

TABLE 2-1

(Rs.cr)

	2004	2005	2006	2007
Reliance Industries	36	38	26	27
Jaiprakash Associates	16	9	17	26
Infosys	14	21	15	21
Ambuja Cements	8	5	15	16
HPCL	7	21	11	15
Total	206	385	314	411

Source: The *Economic Times*, Nov.3, 2007.

The Evolving Idea of Social Responsibility

The social responsibility idea evolved over a period of time. Some major stages in the long history are outlined here.

Business Social Responsibilities in Classical Economic Theory[5] Throughout history, classical economic theory has been the fundamental inspiration of people in business. In the classical economic view, a business is acting in a socially responsible fashion if it utilizes resources as efficiently as possible to produce goods and services that society wants at prices consumers are willing to pay. The sole objective of business is to maximize profits while operating, of course, within the law. If this is done, say classical theorists, firms carry out their major responsibility.

This easily understood goal, derived from Adam Smith's *Wealth of Nations,* was never sought in business practice without reservations. Even Adam Smith voiced a surprising number of exceptions to his principles for social reasons. Throughout our history, business and business people have modified the strict profit maximization principle to address social concerns-not much at first, but more and more over time. Nevertheless, today, this fundamental classical ideology remains entrenched.

The Eighteenth and Nineteenth Centuries In the colonial era, businesses were very small. Merchants practised thrift and frugality, which were dominant virtues then. But charity was a co-existing virtue and the owners of these small enterprises made contributions to schools, churches and the poor.

In the early nineteenth century, companies were not effusive in their social concerns. Charitable contributions continued and grew over time as great fortunes in business were made. In most cases, wealthy entrepreneurs who gave their fortunes to benefit society did so without any reference to the interests of the companies that were the fountainheads of their wealth.

For instance, John D. Rockefeller, who accumulated a fortune in the second half of the nineteenth century, gave in his lifetime, more than $550 million and endowed the Rockefeller Foundation, "*to promote the well-being of mankind throughout the world.*" Andrew Carnegie gave away $350 million during his lifetime to social causes, built 2,811 public libraries and gave 7,689 organs to American churches.

Changing Views of Social Responsibility in the Late Nineteenth and Early Twentieth Centuries During the latter part of the nineteenth century and into the twentieth, a number of forces converged to lead business leaders, especially of the larger corporations, to address social problems out of self-interest. Vigorous industrial growth had many negative social impacts. Business feared new government regulations and sought to blunt their urgency. Business leaders, many of whom by this time were not the original entrepreneurs, but owned only a small part of the stock of the companies they managed, felt freer to use corporate assets for social action. Business sought and found arguments to circumvent the *ultra vires* doctrine.

By the 1920s, three inter-related themes had emerged to justify broader business social responsibility. *First*, managers were *trustees,* that is, agents whose corporate roles put them in positions of power where they could enhance the welfare of not only stockholders, but others such as customers, employees and communities. *Secondly*, managers believed they had an obligation to *balance* the interests of these groups. They were, in effect, coordinators who reconciled the competing claims of multiple stakeholders on their enterprises. And *thirdly*, many managers subscribed to the *service principle,* a principle with two distinct definitions. One definition was a near-spiritual belief that business, simply by operating for profit, had the power to redeem society by creating a broad general welfare. If individual managers served society by making a business economically successful; the aggregate business system would then work to eradicate social injustice, poverty and other ills. A second understanding of the service principle, however, was that although the capitalist system elevated humanity, individual companies and managers were still obligated to undertake social programmes to benefit or serve the public.

These three inter-related ideas-trusteeship, balancing of interests and service-were accepted by more and more business and opinion leaders. Although uplifting, they did not foster lavish contributions for social programmes; nor did they divert most individual managers from their *laissez-faire* attitudes and dominant emphasis on profits.

The Contemporary View of Social Responsibility In the last forty years, the concept of business social responsibility has continued to evolve and expand. Today, the efficient use of resources to make a profit is still seen as the primary social responsibility of business. But added to economic performance are the ideas of previous eras about the meaning of social responsibility. The view that total social responsibilities are broader than simple economic responsibilities, has become more compelling, more accepted by managers and more widely put into practice than ever before.

The range of social programs assumed by managers has continuously expanded since the early years of the century. Today, corporations carry out a wide array of social actions. The span includes programmes for education, public health, employee welfare, housing, urban renewal, environmental protection, resource conservation, day-care centres for working parents and many others. In each of these areas, the programmes that different corporations have implemented run into thousands.[17]

The fundamental reason why the concept and range of social responsibilities have expanded is that accelerating industrial activity continuously changes society. In this situation, social responsibilities arise from the impacts of corporate actions on society. And we know more today about adverse consequences of some business activities. For example, early in this century, carcinogens in industrial effluents were unknown.

Corporate social programmes also arise from a second source-intractable social problems in the corporation's environment. "*A healthy business and a sick society are hardly compatible*," notes Peter Drucker. Racism, wars, violent crime, epidemics such as AIDS and failing schools are societal pathologies a corporation has not caused but may benefit from mitigating.

Forces Pressuring Social Responsiveness

Not all firms are vulnerable to social group pressures and social regulations. Only some firms are pressured to undertake social responsibility actions. The forces that make firms become socially responsive are: government, community interests and demands, environmental concerns, competitive pressures, shareholder/investor pressures, philanthropic requests and initiatives and crises (See Fig.2.2).

FIGURE 2-2
PRESSURES LEADING TO SOCIAL RESPONSIBILITY

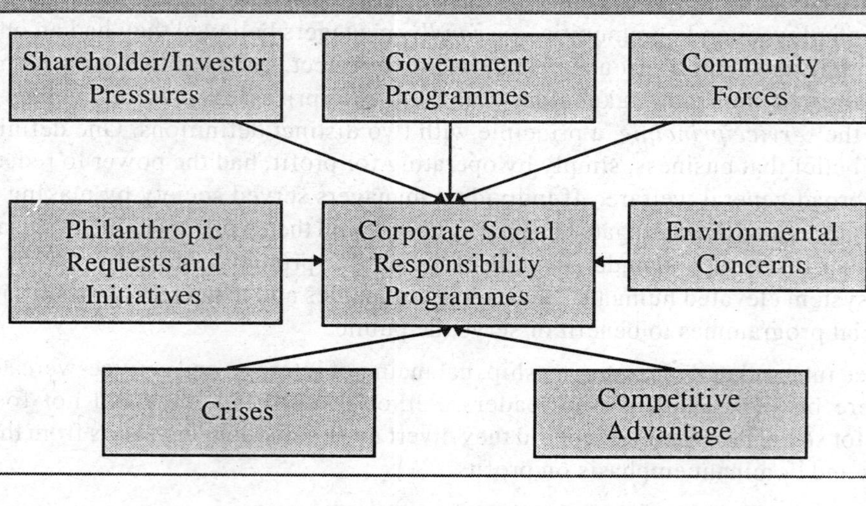

Government Programmes: Government (foreign and domestic) are the most significant forces pressuring firms for social actions. Most government pressures concern compliance with existing regulations. But governments are also major sources of potential rules, a fact which businesses need to take note of. Governments ask businesses to volunteer to help them solve their problems.

Governments mandating social actions are not new. In the 1300s, for example, Londoners who violated the city's smoke pollution ordinances were beheaded. In the US, laws that regulated the purity or quality of certain goods date from colonial times and state and federal efforts to control water pollution began in the late 1800s.

Foreign governments exert pressures on international businesses to abide by codes of conduct that they and international organisations have drafted. These codes expect businesses to respect human rights and social justice, pay fair wages, protect the environment, ensure safety and health of workers, improve worker living conditions, and behave ethically.

Community Interest and Demands Firms undertake many programmes that benefit society in general, not necessarily favouring stakeholders. Programmes can range widely, from helping rebuild disadvantaged sections to providing executive talents to run government undertakings.

MNCs from the US undertake a wide range of programmes in foreign countries, for example, creating scholarships for poor but deserving students from Korea, Malaysia, and Mexico, to pursue higher studies.

Environmental Concerns Environmental programmes of firms mainly result from standards established by government agencies. The Government of India, for example, enacted the Environment Protection Act 1986. The main objective of the Act is to protect and improve the environment and the prevention of hazards to human beings, other living creatures, plant and property. Pollution Control Boards set up under the provisions of the Act. have laid down norms that firms are expected to comply with.

Competitive Advantage Firms believe that by undertaking social actions they would gain competitive edge. Realising this, corporations spend huge sums on social responsibility. U.S. corporate spending on social responsibility shot up from $125 million in 1990 to an estimated $828 million in 2002. Additionally, spending on arts sponsorship amounted to $589 million in 2001.

Competitive advantage comprises four interdependent factors: factor conditions, demand conditions, related and support industries, and context for strategy and rivalry (See Fig.2.3).

Factor Conditions These include the availability of trained workers, high quality scientific and technological institutions, adequate physical infrastructure, transparent and efficient administrative processes and natural resources. All these are the areas that social responsibility actions can influence.

Demand Conditions Demand conditions in a country or a region include the size of the local market, the appropriateness of product standards, and the sophistication of local markets. Sophisticated local customers enhance competitiveness by providing firms with insight into emerging customer needs and applying pressure for innovation.

Social actions can influence both the size and quality of the local market. Apple Computer has donated computers to schools as a means of introducing its products to young people. This provides a clear social benefit to the schools while expanding Apple's potential market and turning students and teachers into more sophisticated purchasers.

Related and Supporting Industries Productivity of a firm can be greatly enhanced by having high quality industries and services close by. While outsourcing from distant suppliers is possible, it is not as efficient as using capable local suppliers of services, components, and machinery. Proximity enhances responsiveness, exchange of information and innovation, in addition to lowering cost on transportation and inventory.

FIGURE 2-3
FOUR ELEMENTS OF COMPETITIVE STRENGTH

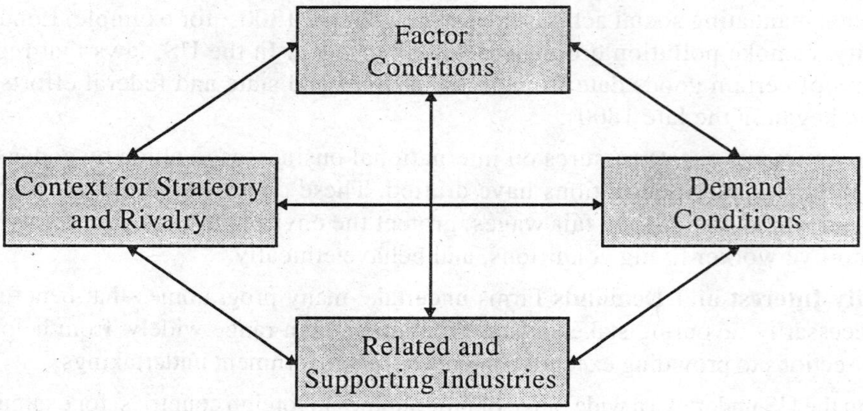

(**Source:** Adapted from Michael E.Porter and Mark R. Kramer, *op. cit., p.60*)

Social responsibility can foster the development of clusters and strengthen supporting industries. American Express, for example, depends on travel related expenditure for a large share of its credit card and travel agency revenues. Hence, it is part of the travel cluster in each of the countries in which it operates, and it depends on the success of these clusters in improving the quality of tourism and attracting travellers.

Context for Strategy and Rivalry The rules, incentives, and norms governing competition in a nation or region have a fundamental influence on productivity. Policies that encourage investment, protect intellectual property, open local markets to trade, break up or prevent the formation of cartels and monopolies, and reduce corruption make a location a more attractive place to do business. Social responsibility can have a strong influence on creating a more productive and transparent environment for competition. For example, 26 US corporations and 38 corporations from other countries have joined to support Transparency International in its work to disclose and deter corruption around the world. By measuring and focussing public attention on corruption, the organisation helps create an environment that rewards fair competition and enhances productivity. This benefits local citizens while providing sponsoring companies improved access to markets.

Shareholders/Investors Pressures Large shareholders such as pension funds have long-range interests in the financial success of their investments. Some of them, obviously, exert pressure on firms to respond appropriately to community social interests. For example, shareholders of Pepsi Co. launched a campaign to force the company to pull out of Myanmar because of the human rights violation of the military regime in that country. Pepsi Co. did oblige the shareholders.

Philanthropic Requests and Initiatives As government funding for charitable causes has been declining there is presurre on the corporate sector to fill the gap, to which the firms have been responding positively.

Crises Firms that do not plan to deal with crises may suffer seriously. So crisis management is an area where proactive prepartion may prevent a crisis or deal with it effectively if it comes.

Basic Elements of Social Responsibility

There are three elements of social responsibility: (i) actions in response to market forces, (ii) mandated social programmes, and (iii) voluntary social programmes.

Actions in Response to Market Market forces have always been dominating corporate activities and the trend will continue in future too. When a business responds to the market place, it is being socially responsible. General Motors is probably the best example to prove that the business of a business is business, and in doing so, the firm can be socially responsive. In 1997, GM employed 6,08,000 people in 56 countries and had a worldwide payroll of $30.4 billion. It made 8.6 million vehicles that were sold through 14,900 dealers. The dealers, in turn, employed another 5,42,000 people. GM paid $1.1 billion in taxes of all kinds to governments. GM's customers paid another $6.8 billion in taxes worldwide while purchasing GM products. In the US, GM withheld an additional $4.9 billion from employees' paycheques, which it remitted to the federal government for income and social security taxes. It also paid $3.7 billion as benefits to its US workers. These statistics illuminate the huge aggregate impact of GM's routine, everyday business operations—operations that broadly support the general welfare and are, in a sense, GM's biggest social programme.

Mandated Social Programmes The second element includes *mandated social programmes*. These programmes are required by government regulations, such as equal opportunity in hiring, or are required by agreements negotiated with stakeholders, such as benefit programmes in wage agreements.

GM is exposed to multiple regulations in many nations, dictating a range of decisions. Continuing with the above example, GM vehicles must comply with tailpipe emission standards; and its fleet must achieve a federally mandated average fuel economy of 27.5 miles per gallon. It must meet state and local noise standards for light vehicles of 80 decibels at 50 feet and another standard for heavy trucks. Its workforce must meet equal opportunity standards. So regulatory guidelines codify for GM societal expectations for responsible operations.

Voluntary Social Programmes These are the third element in social responsibility of businesses. These programmes include promoting ecology, health care, sanitation, rural development fighting AIDS, abolition of child labour, and the like.

Limits of Social Responsibility

The social responsibility actions of managers are limited by cost, efficiency, relevance and scope (See Fig. 2.4). As a result of these constraints, actions fall short of public expectations.

Cost Social responsibility costs money. Whether a company desires to adopt a village, donate to a college or school, build a hospital, maintain parks or undertake relief operations in times of calamity, it costs money and the money could be used for welfare of employees for improving business. As worthy as some social actions may be, they do impose costs either on the business or on some groups in society, or both.

Efficiency The cost of social responsibility can reduce a firm's efficiency and affect to compete in the market place. For example, if a firm is pressured by a local community to keep an outmodel, inefficient plant in operation because closing it would mean loss to local people, while its competitors close their old plants and move operations to other countries to take advantage of lower wages there, the business would not survive at all. The managers who place interests of local employees before the firm's survival, cannot face more efficient competitors.

FIGURE 2-4
LIMITS OF SOCIAL RESPONSIBILITY

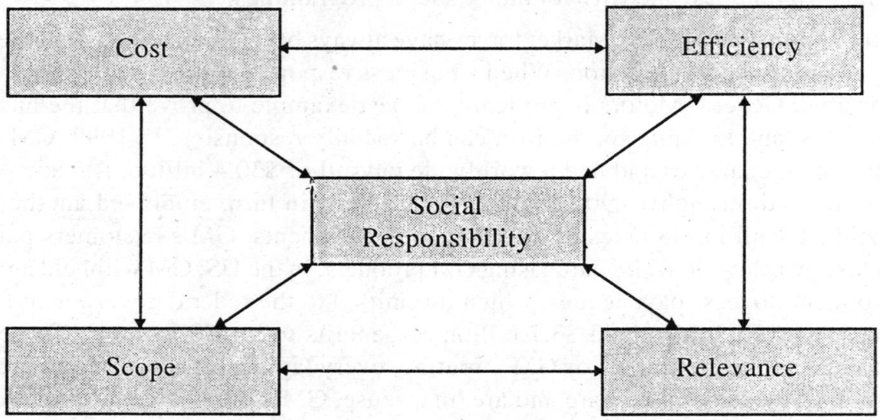

Relevance According to several critics, business has no obligation to society. The only obligation is to run the business successfully. Social responsibility is irrelevant. According to Friedman, for example, "*There is one and only one social responsibility of business: to use its resources and energy in activities designed to increase its profits so long as it stays within the rules of the game...*(and) *engages in open and free competition, without deception and trend...*". Friedman contends that corporate officials are in no position to determine the relative urgency of social problems or the amount of organisational resources that should be committed to a given problem. He also insists that managers who devote corporate resources to pursue personal, and perhaps misguided notions of the social good, unfairly tax their own shareholders, employees and customers. In short, business should produce goods and services efficiently and leave the solution of social problems to the concerned individuals and government agencies.

Often, social responsibility action is undertaken for wrong reasons rendering the exercise to irrelevance and ineffectiveness. Consider what has happened to Brij Mohan Khaitan, the tea giant. In the beginning of 1990s, Khaitan was under tremendous pressure from the Bodo Security Force (BSF). One of his executives was kidnapped and another was gunned down by the militants. BSF demanded hefty sums as a pre-condition for peace. It was at this time that Khaitan reflected and set up a school at a cost of Rs.22 crore. The school could not help Khaitan buy peace from the BSF.

Scope and Complexity Society's problems are too massive, too complex, and too deep seated to be solved by even the most socially conscientious company or even by all companies acting together.

The problems such as environmental pollution-acid rain, ozone depletion, destruction of rain forests; health problems-AIDS, drug and tobacco use; racial discrimination; sex discrimination; ethnic and religious animosities and the like defy solutions however conscientious one might be.

BUSINESS ETHICS

Ethics refers to a system of moral principles-a sense of right and wrong and goodness and badness of actions and their motives and consequences. *Business ethics* refers to the application of ethics to business. To be more specific, business ethics is the study of good and evil, right and wrong and just and unjust actions of businessmen.

Business ethics does not differ from generally accepted norms of good or bad. If dishonesty is considered to be unethical and immoral in society, then any businessman who is dishonest with employees, customers, shareholders or competitors is acting unethically and immorally. If protecting others from any harm is considered to be ethical, then a company that recalls a defective and harmful product from the market is acting ethically. To be considered ethical, businessmen must draw their ideas about what is desirable behaviour from the same sources as anybody else. Businessmen should not try to evolve their own principles to justify what is right and wrong. Employees and employers may be tempted to apply special or weaker ethical rules to business situations. But society does not condone or permit such an exception. People who are in business are bound by the same ethical principles that apply to others.

Two theories are pertinent when one talks about the nature of ethics.

The *theory of moral unity* essentially advocates the principle that business actions should be judged by the general ethical standards of society. There exists only one ethical standard which applies to business and to non-business situations.

Opposed to the theory of moral unity is the *theory of amorality,* which argues that business can be amoral, and the actions of businessmen need not be guided by general ethical standards. Managers may act selfishly because the market mechanism distills their actions into benefits to shareholders and society at large. Adam Smith argued that the 'invisible hand' of the market assures that by "pursuing his own interest (a merchant) frequently promotes that of the society more effectively than when he really intends to promote it."

In this way, capitalism provides moral justification for the pursuit of profit through behaviour which is not purposefully ethical.

However, the theory of amorality is not acceptable to anybody. Everyone agrees that business actions should be subject to the same ethical standards as the one applicable to the society in general.

Sources of Business Ethics

Managers in every society are influenced by three repositories of ethical values: religion, culture and law (see Fig. 2.5). These repositories contain unique systems of values that exert varying degrees of control over managers. A common thread, the idea of *reciprocity* or *mutual help,* runs through all the value systems. This idea reflects the central purpose of all ethics which is to bind the vast

FIGURE 2-5
SOURCES OF ETHICS

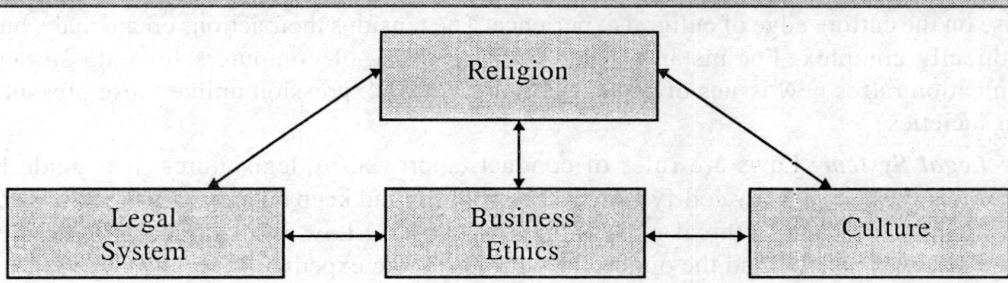

majority of individuals in society into a co-operative whole. Ethical values are a mechanism that controls behaviour in business and in the other walks of life. Ethical restraints are more effective than are cruder controls such as police, law suits or economic incentives. Ethical values channel individual energy into pursuits that are benign to others and beneficial to the society.

Religion One of the oldest sources of ethical inspiration is religion. More than 100,000 different religions exist across the globe. But despite doctrinal differences, the major religions converge on the belief that ethics is an expression of divine will that reveals the nature of right and wrong in business and other areas of life. The world's great religions are also in agreement on fundamental principles which are similar to the building blocks of secular ethical doctrine. The principle of reciprocity towards one's fellow human beings is found in all major religions such as Hinduism, Buddhism, Christianity, Islam, Judaism and Confucianism. The great religions preach the necessity for an orderly social system and emphasise social responsibility in such a way so as to contribute to the general welfare. Built upon such verities are many other rules of conduct.[12]

Cultural Experience Culture, refers to a set of values, rules and standards transmitted among generations and acted upon to produce behaviours that fall within acceptable limits. These rules and standards always play an important part in determining values, because individuals anchor their conduct in the culture of the group. Civilisation itself is a cumulative cultural experience in which people have passed through three distinct phases of moral codification. These stages correspond to the changing economic and social arrangements in human history.

For millions of generations in the *hunting and gathering stage* of human development, ethics was adapted to conditions in which our ancestors had to be ready to fight, face brutal foes and suffer the hostile forces of nature. Under such circumstances, a premium was placed on pugnacity, appetite, greed and sexual readiness, since it was often the strongest who survived. Trade activities in the early civilisations were frequently conducted by brute force and violence.

Civilisation passed into an *agricultural stage* approximately 10,000 years ago, beginning a time when industriousness was more important than ferocity, thrift paid greater dividends than violence, monogamy became the prevailing sexual custom because of the relatively equal numbers of the sexes and peace came to be valued over wars, which destroyed crops and animals. These new values were codified into ethical systems which even guide the managers today.

Two centuries ago, society entered an *industrial stage* of cultural experience, and ethical systems once more began evolving to reflect the changing physical, cultural, institutional and intellectual environment. Large factories and corporations, population growth, capitalist and socialist economic doctrines and technologies have all assaulted the ethical standards of the agrarian stage. Industrialism has not created a distinct ethics, but it has created tensions with old ethical systems based on the values of agricultural societies. It does this by changing values related to what is good and bad. For example, the copious outpouring of material goods from factories has encouraged materialism and consumption at the expense of older virtues such as moderation and thrift. Managers run an industrial enterprise on the cutting edge of cultural experience. The tensions their actions create make business more ethically complex. For instance, the widespread use of computers for data storage and communication raises new issues of privacy and individual expression unlike those present in the agrarian societies.

The Legal System Laws are rules of conduct, approved by legislatures, that guide human behaviour in any society. They codify ethical expectations and keep changing as new evils emerge. But laws cannot cover all ethical expectations of society. Law is reactive; new statutes and enforcement always lag behind the opportunity for corporate expediency.

Whatever ethics that law codifies, it is binding on business. Society expects business to abide by law and obeying law is presumed to be ethical behaviour.

Although society expects business to be law abiding, seldom does the business adhere to the rules. Law breaking in business is common. Taxes are evaded, hundreds of employees die because of occupational diseases, many die because of industrial accidents and million others receive disabling injuries on the job. The blame for these deaths and injuries can be shared by careless employees and by employers who fail to adhere to occupational health and safety laws.

Consumers suffer because of poor quality and high priced products supplied by businessmen. And business causes misery to the society by damaging the environment, disregarding environment protection laws.

Managing Ethics

In the past, it was assumed in most companies that ethics was a matter of individual conscience. But the scenario has changed. Today, many companies are using managerial techniques that are designed to encourage ethical behaviours. Some of the managerial interventions to ensure ethical conduct are explained below. (see also Fig. 2.6).

FIGURE 2-6
MANAGING ETHICS

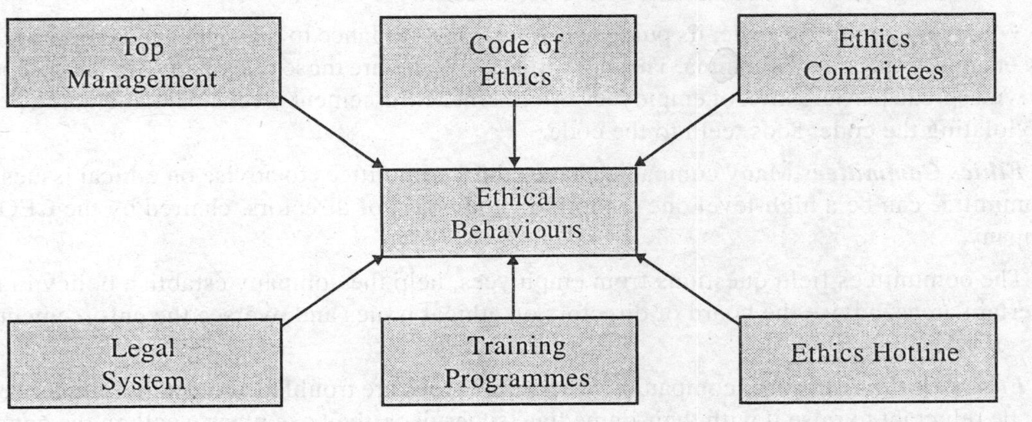

Top Management Top management commitment is necessary to ensure ethical standards in a firm. The chief executive should consciously avoid strategies and actions harmful to employees and society.

Code of Ethics Code of ethics have become popular. Codes vary from book-length formulations to succinct statements which in one or two pages, express a general philosophy for managing conflicts. Nearly 95 per cent of Fortune 500 companies have codes and the trend is visible in our corporate sector also.

Industry associations too have evolved codes of conduct of their own. For example, the Council for Fair Business Practices (CFBP) established in 1966, by leading private sector industrialists in Western India, adopted the following code of fair business practices:

- To charge only fair and reasonable prices and take every possible step to ensure that the prices to be charged to the consumer are brought to his notice.
- To take every possible step to ensure that the agents or dealers... do not charge prices higher than fixed.
- In times of scarcity, not to withhold or suppress stocks of goods with a view to hoarding or profiteering.
- Not to produce or trade in spurious goods of standards lower than specified.
- Not to adulterate goods supplied.
- Not to publish misleading advertisements.
- To invoice goods exported or imported at their correct prices.
- To maintain accuracy in weights and measures of goods offered for sale.
- Not to deal knowingly in smuggled goods.
- Providing after-sales service where necessary or possible.
- Honouring the fundamental rights of the consumers-Right of Safety, Right to Choose, Right to Information and Right to be Heard.
- Discharging social responsibilities and the responsibility to protect the environment and nature's infrastructure.
- Ensuring that the product-warranty is offered in simple, unambiguous and concise language, highlighting the rights of the consumer under it.

Whoever evolves the code, its purpose is to provide guidance to managers and employees when they encounter an ethical dilemma. The most effective codes are those drawn up with the co-operation and widespread participation of employees. An internal enforcement mechanism, including penalties for violating the code, adds teeth to the code.

Ethics Committees Many companies have ethics committees to advise on ethical issues. Such a committee can be a high-level one comprising the board of directors, chaired by the CEO of the company.

The committees field questions from employees, help the company establish policy in new or uncertain areas, advise the board of directors on ethical issues and oversee the enforcement of the code of ethics.

Ethics Hotlines In some companies, when employees are troubled about some ethical issue but may be reluctant to raise it with their immediate supervisor, they can place a call on the company's 'ethics hot line.' A member of the ethics committee receives the confidential call and then quickly investigates the situation. Elaborate steps are taken to protect the identity of the caller, so as to encourage more employees to report any deviant behaviour. This technique is advantageous in as much as ethics hotlines encourage internal whistle-blowing, which is better for a company than to have disgruntled employees take their ethical complaints to the media.

Whistle-blowing is in the news these days. Like the blowing of whistle by a referee to indicate violations of rules in the playfield, whistle-blowing in an organisation refers to disclosure by former or current employees of any illegal, immoral or illegitimate practices involving its employees. Table 2.2 contains some well-known cases of whistle-blowing.

Measures can be taken to protect the interest of whistle-blowing as the Chennai based Murugappa group has done. Since March 2006, the group has implemented a whistle-blower policy. As per the

TABLE 2-2

WHISTLE BLOWING IN ACTION

Sl No.	*Organisation*	*Whistleblower*	*Consequences*
1	Enron	Sherron Watkins	Liquidation of the company
2	Kellog India	Senior Executive (Name not known)	Sacking of two senior executives who were promoted for excellent performance a few months before
3	Director, FBI, US	Coleen Rowly	Attack on the World Trade Centre, US
4	Worldcom	Cynthia Cooper	Company gone bust
5	Xerox	Name not known	CFO made to pay $5.5 million in fines and banned by the SEC from practising accounting
6	Heinz India Jhonson and Johnson Bayer India	Installed Whistle-blowing system	No incident reported
7	LG India	Names not known but 10-12 cases have been reported to head office, South Korea	Not known
8	National Highway	S.K.Dubey Authority of India	S.K.Bubey murdered. Nothing happened to the organisation.
9	Hong Kong City	Lo Pui-Laru Civil Service	Guilty disciplined but Lo has been ostracised by fellow workers

policy, an aggrieved worker can approach the ombudsman through letter, e-mail or call. Ombudsman shall report the matter to the Board. Three such cases have been resolved at the board level since March 2006.

Such protection is necessary as whistle-blowers are praised for some time, they are, in the long-run, isolated, discriminated against and are even subect to physical hazards.

Ethics Training Programmes Nearly all companies which take ethics seriously provide training in ethics for their managers and employees. Such training programmes acquaint company personnel with the official company policy on ethical issues, and they show how those policies can be translated into the specifics of every day decision making. Often, simulated cases based on actual events in the company are used to illustrate how to apply ethical principles to on-the-job problems.

Generally speaking, ethics training is most effective when it is conducted by company managers, and is steered away from abstract philosophical discussions to focus on specifics from the work environment of those attending.

Ethics and Law Law and ethics aim at one thing-defining proper and improper behaviour. But the two are not quite the same. Laws are a society's attempt to formalise-that is, to reduce to written rules-ideas about what is right and what is wrong in various walks of life. However, it is rarely possible for written rules to capture all the subtle shadings that people give to ethics. Ethical concepts are more complex than written rules. Ethics deals with human dilemmas that frequently go beyond the formal language of law and the meanings given to legal rules.

Some of the Acts which seek to ensure fair business practices in our country are the following:

The Foreign Exchange Regulation Act, 1973 now replaced by FEMA

The Companies Act, 1956

The Monopolies and Restrictive Trade Practices Act, 1969, now replaced by the Competition Act, 2002.

The Consumer Protection Act, 1986

The Environment Protection Act, 1986

The Essential Commodities Act, 1955

Table 2.3 shows some of the means of promoting ethics in organisations in different courntries and their popularity

TABLE 2-3
MEANS TO PROMOTE ETHICAL CONDUCT

Means	*India*	*Asia Pacific*	*Global*
Ethics/Code of Conduct	72	73	64
Pre-employement screening	54	37	50
Public source Information	32	25	33
Whistle-blowing system	28	18	28
Fraud training	24	25	29
Others	23	20	27

Note: Figures indicate percentage responses from sample firms who have implemented the system

(**Source:** Survey by Price Waterhouse Coopers, 2003)

As seen from the table, ethics/code is most popular across firms in different regions. Nevertheless, whistle-blowing as a means of promoting ethical conduct is gaining in popularity.

Corporate Culture and Ethical Climate

Corporate culture is a blend of ideas, customs, traditional practices, company values and shared meanings that help define normal behaviour for everyone who works in a company. Every organisation has a culture and it exercises considerable influence on employee behaviour.

Hewlett-Packard is well known for a culture that stresses values and ethics. Called the 'HP Way' by employees, the most important values of the culture are confidence in and respect for people, open communication, sharing of benefits and responsibilities, concern for the individual employees and honesty and integrity.

In some companies, one can feel the blowing of ethical winds. People pick up subtle hints and clues that tell them what behaviour is approved and what is forbidden. This unarticulated understanding among employees is called an *ethical climate*. It is that part of corporate culture that sets the ethical tone in a company.

One way to view ethical climate is diagrammed in Fig.2.7. Three different types of ethical yardsticks are egoism (self-centredness), benevolence (concern for others), and principle (respect for one's own integrity, for group norms, and for society's laws). These ethical yardsticks can be applied to dilemmas concerning individuals, one's company or society at large. For example, if a manager approaches ethics issues with benevolence in mind, he would stress friendly relations with employees, emphasise the importance of team play and co-operation for the company's benefit and recommends socially responsible courses of action. However, if the manager used egoism to

FIGURE 2-7
ETHICAL YARDSTICKS

Ethical Criteria	Focus of Ethical Concern		
	Individual Person	*Company*	*Society*
Egoism	Self-interest	Company interest	Economic efficiency
Benevolence	Friendship	Team interest	Social responsibility
Principle	Personal morality	Company rules and procedures	Laws and professional codes

think about ethical problems, he would be more likely to think first of self-interest, promoting the company's profit and striving for efficient operations at all costs. A company's ethical climate depends on which combination it has of these nine possibilities.

Corporate culture and ethical climate can put much pressure on people to channel their actions in certain directions desired by the company.

Improving Ethical Decision Making

Ethical decisions are difficult to make. They cannot be programmed like production and inventory decisions. But decisions need to be made in business. This section contains practical difficulties in decision making and guidelines which help a manager in making a choice.

Difficulties in Decision Making

There are atleast nine reasons why decision making becomes difficult.

First, managers face dilemmas in deciding on a course of action.

Second, managers confront a distinction between facts and values when making ethical decisions. Facts are statements about *what is* and values are statements about what *ought* to be. *What is* can never define what *ought* to be. For example, the cost of researching, developing and producing a life saving drug may necessitate fixing a high price, as far as the company is concerned. But the price may be perceived by users as exploitative.

Third, good and evil exist simultaneously, in tandem and interlocked. Nestle's sales of infant formula in Kenya and Zambia have led to infant deaths as mothers mixed the powdered food with contaminated local water and their babies died of dysentery. But evidence also shows that the same formula has saved lives of several other infants. Evil should be minimised, but it cannot be eliminated.

Fourth, knowledge about the consequences of an action is limited. One of the principles of decision making is utilitarian. This implies that if an act results in the greatest good of greatest numbers, it is taken as morally acceptable. This principle assumes that the consequences of the act are knowable. But in an uncertain business environment, consequences cannot be easily predicted.

Fifth, antagonistic interests frequently use incompatible ethical arguments to justify their intentions. Thus, the ethical stand of a corporation is often based on entirely different premises from the ethical stand of critics. Animal lovers may argue against slaughter on the ground that beasts are entitled to rights similar to those enjoyed by humans, including the right to life. Poultry growers, on the other hand, contend that raising food animals inure benefits to society.

Sixth, some ethical standards vary with the passage of time. Donations to political parties were forbidden earlier but it is allowed now as Table 2.4 shows. In addition, certain bribes and payments are accepted practices in Asian, African and Latin American countries but are not regarded as ethical in the US. Doing business with close friends and family is a standard practice in the Arab world but is treated as nepotism in Western Europe.

TABLE 2-4

MONEY COMPANIES PAY TO POLITICAL PARTIES

Donations to the Congress and BJP between fiscal 2004 and 2007

Congress		BJP	(Rs. Crore)
2003-04	**52.35**	**2003-04**	**11.69**
Chur Trading Co.	1.00	Public and Political Awareness Trust*	5.50
Jindal Steel and Power	0.50	Bajaj Auto	1.00
General Electoral Trust		Smdutt Builders	0.35
(Aditya Birla Group)	0.50	Jindal Steel and Power	0.25
Brahm Swaroop Brahmchari		Videocon International	0.25
(Jairam Ashram)	0.25	Others	4.34
National Growth	0.05		
Others	0.05		
2004-05	**32**	**2004-05**	**34**
General Electrola Trust	11.21	Public and Political Awareness Trust*	4.00
(Aditya Birla Group)		General Electrola Trust	
Electoral Trust (Tata group)	4.33	(Aditya Birla Group)	2.81
ITC	1.45	Electoral Trust (Tata group)	2.67
Sterlite Industries (India)	1.00	Larsen and Toubro	1.60
Baja Auto	1.00	Adani Wilmar	1.00
Others	13.01	Others	21.92
2005-06	**6**	**2005-06**	**3**
Videcon International Ltd	3.00	Akik Education Centre	0.75
Today House and Infrastructure	0.55	Janakalyan Sahakari Bank	0.50
VM Salgaonkar and Brothers	0.14	General Electrola Trust	
South Indian Research	0.10	(Aditya Birla Group)	0.35
VS Dempo and Co.	0.09	Win Medicare (Modi Group)	0.25
Others	2.12	VS Dempo and Co.	0.06
		Others	1.09
2006-07	**12**	**2006-07**	**4**
General Electrola Trust		Jubilant Enpro	0.05
(Aditya Birla Group)	10.00	Kamaljeet Singh Ahluwalia	0.50
Ranbaxy Laboratories	0.40	Ashapura Minechem	0.10
Modi Group of Industries	0.25	United Phosphorus	0.10
Peninsula Land	0.21	Prime Builders and Developers	0.10
Orbit Construction	0.11	Others	2.70
Others	1.03		

* Managed by the Vedanta group through its Indian subsidiary Sterlite Industries (India)

(***Source:*** Election Commission of India)

Seventh, the ethical behaviour is moulded from the clay of human imperfection. Unethical practices abound everywhere (See Fig.2.8 for different crimes). An honest manager finds himself like a babe in the woods, not able to do anything, surrounded as he is, by dishonesty everywhere.

FIGURE 2-8
THE CORPORATE CRIMES

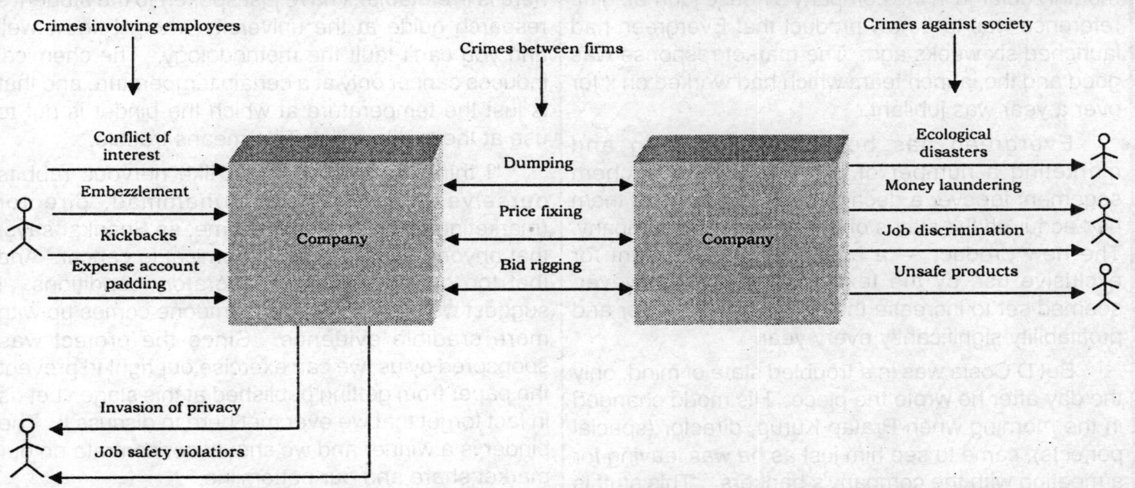

(**Source**: Adapted from *Business and Society* by Frederic, Post and Davis, *op.cit.*, p. 70)

Eighth, the early 21st century presents managers with new and emerging ethical problems that are not solved easily with traditional ethical guidelines. For example, modern ethical theory has not yet developed an adequate principle for weighing human life against economic factors in a decision. Cancer studies may predict that workers exposed to chemicals will become ill in small numbers far in the future. How should this information be balanced against costs of regulation, capital investment or job loss?

Finally, the growth of large scale organisations in the 21st century gives new significance to ethical problems such as committee decision making that masks individual responsibility, organisational loyalty versus loyalty to the public interest and preferential hiring of disadvantaged sections of society. These are ethical problems peculiar to large organisations.

Case

On Hitting a Speed-Breaker

"Looks like we've hit the jackpot, folks." Thus it was that Robert D'Costa, chairman and managing director, Evergreen Chemical Works Ltd., has signed off his monthly column in the company's house journal. The reference was to a new product that Evergreen had launched six weeks ago. The market response was good and the launch team which had worked on it for over a year was jubilant.

Evergreen has been manufacturing and marketing a number of products in the hi-chem segement for over a decade but so far none of them had acquired the status of a winner for the company. The new product — a chemical binder meant for exclusive use by the textile industry — however, seemed set to increase the company's turnover and profitability significantly every year.

But D'Costa was in a troubled state of mind, only the day after he wrote the piece. His modd changed in the morning when Pratap Kurup, director (special porjects), came to see him just as he was leaving for a meeting with the company's bankers. "This stuff is dynamite and I think you should take a look at it," Kurup has said, showing a neatly bound volume. "It is a thesis prepared by a student as part of the research projects we have been sponsoring at the local university. One of its findings is that a chemical we have used in the new binder may be carcinogenic."

D'Costa was surprised and, at the same time, annoyed. "Carcinogenic? What proof does he have, this research students?" he asked. "He was working on rabbits and they have shown signs of skin cancer. It is all documented here," remarked Kurup.

"Rabbits?" said D'Costa. "Give me a break, will you? This binder will put us into the big league and some jerk had to come up with this now. Rabbits, huh? Jesus!"

Sensing that Kurup was somewhat shocked and realising that he himself was perhaps overreacting, D'Costa composed himself quickly and said, "Of course, it certainly needs to be looked into. By the way, have you shown this to Shankar?"

Shankar Rana was director (research) at Evergreen. "He is out of town and is expected only in the afternoon. That's why I thought of giving it to you," said Kurup.

Later in the evening, D'Costa was closetted with all the functional directors. "We have a crisis on our hands," said Rana, who had gone through the thesis in the meantime. "I am familiar with all available material on the chemical so far and there is no mention anywhere of its carcinogenic property. It is not listed anywhere as a hazardous product. But the evidence here is irrefutable. I have just spoken to the student's research guide at the university whom I know well and you can't fault the methodology. The chemical induces cancer only at a certain temperature and that is just the temperature at which the binder is put to use at the textile mills. This means trouble."

"I think we are all acting like nervous rabbits ourselves," said Anwar Mohammad, director (marketing). "This is the first time, as Shankar says, that anyone has linked the chemical to cancer. And that too on rabbits under laboratory conditions. I suggest we play it cool until someone comes up with more credible evidence. Since the project was sponsored by us, we can exercise our right to prevent the paper from getting published at this stage. Let us in fact forget that we ever met here to discuss it. The binder is a winner and we should concentrate on our market share and our bottomline."

"Of course, the product is important for us for the profits it brings in," said D'Costa and added, as an afterthought, "but the crucial issue is whether we can ignore our wider responsibility to society."

"There is also, in the immediate context, the responsibility to out own employees," said Praful Shah, director (manufacturing). "The product is being tested before despatch under a similar temperature at our quality control lab and people there also face the risk. I suggest we discontinue manufacturing the product forthwith."

The discussion continued. Rana said that further research could be conducted at Evergreen's own research centre to ascertain the validity of the student's conclusions. "But I am sure it will only be a repetition of what has been done already," he said, "and perhaps the best option is to refer this to one of our national research laboratories for a more elaborate analysis and particularly regarding its impact on human beings."

Mohammad said this would mean making the matter public, and there would be pressure from all those sel-styled environmentalists and soical engineers who are making a nuisance of themselves' to stop production of the binder at Evergreen.

Even at the end of an hour, there was no consensus at the meeting. The buck of course stopped at D'Costa. What should he do?

QUESTIONS

1. Define the terms CSR and business ethics.
2. Bring out the CSR debate and offer your own opinion on the subject.
3. What are the constraints of CSR?
4. Explain the forces pressuring CSR.
5. State and explain the sources of business ethics.
6. How do managers manage ethics?
7. What are ethical dilemmas? How to manage them?

REFERENCES

1. Laura P. Hartman, *Perspectives in Business Ethics,* McGraw-Hill.
2. Craig N.Smith, "Corporate Social Responsibility: Whether or How", *California Management Review*, 2003.
3. George A. Steiner and John F. Steiner, *Business, Government and Society*, McGraw-Hill.
4. Michael E. Porter and Mark R.Kramer, "The Competitive Advantage of Corporate Philanthrophy". *Harvard Business Review,* Dec. 2002.
5. James E. Post, *et. al., Business and Society,* McGraw-Hill.
6. Gita Piramal, *Business Maharajas,* Penguin.
7. Anne T. Lawrence and James Weber, *Business and Society,* McGraw-Hill.

CHAPTER

Three

Planning and Strategic Management

LEARNING OBJECTIVES

After reading this chapter you should understand —

1. The nature of plans and goals
2. The four levels of planning
3. The six types of planning
4. The planning process that comprises six phases
5. The nature of strategic management and the strategic management process
6. The models of strategic management

As individuals we often talk about goals and plans. So do managers in organisations. What are these goals? Why are they? What are plans? Who plans and who implements? These and other related topics are discussed in this chapter.

Nature of Goals and Plans

A goal is a desired future state that an organisation attempts to realise. Goals are important for atleast four reasons:[1]

(i) Goals provide a sense of direction Without goals, individuals and their organisations tend to grope in the dark. Goals provide them a sense of direction and motivation and inspiration to tread along.

(ii) Goals help focus on efforts Every person and every organisation has limited resources and a wide range of possible ways to use them. In selecting a single goal or a set of related goals, individuals establish priorities and make a commitment about the way they use scarce resources. This is particularly important to an organisation, where managers need to coordinate the actions of many individuals.

(iii) Goals guide plans and decisions Managers need to make long-term and short-term plans. They also need to make decisions to realise the plans. Both in formulating plans and making decisions, goals play critical role.

(iv) Goals help evaluate progress A goal which is specific, measurable and attainable acts as a benchmark to evaluate actual outcome. Goals are an essential part of **controlling**-the process of making sure that actions are in keeping with goals and the plans created to achieve them.

A **plan** is a blue-print for goal achievement and specifies the necessary resource allocations, schedules, tasks, and other actions. Goals specify future ends, plans specify today's means.[2] The word **planning** includes both goal and plan. In otherwords, planning determines organisation's goals and defines the means for achieving them.

Planning is essential for any organisation. An organisation cannot determine its goals and identify resources without planning.

Levels of Planning

In chapter 1, we had described the levels of managers. An organisation shall have three levels of managers: top-level (strategic managers); mid-level (tactical managers); and front-line (operational managers). All the three level managers are actively engaged in planning as explained below:

Strategic Planning Strategic planning involves defining organisation's long-term goals and strategies. Strategic planning has a strong external orientation and covers major activities of the organisation. Senior executives (top-managers) are responsible for the development and execution of strategic plans.

A **strategy** is a pattern of actions accompanied by resource allocations to achieve organisational goals. A firm will have several strategies, as for example, alliance strategy, exporting strategy, licensing strategy, multi-domestic strategy and global strategy.

Tactical Planning Tactical planning is done by mid-managers. Once the strategic plans are in place, mid-managers step in and come out with tactical planning. Tactical planning translates broad strategic goals and plans into specific goals and plans for each activity of the organisation. Tactical plans focus on the major actions that a unit must take to fulfill its part of the strategic plan.

Operational Planning This identifies the specific procedures and processes required at lower levels of the organisation. Front line managers usually develop plans for short periods and focus on routine tasks such as production runs, delivery schedules and human resource requirements.[3]

Types of Planning

Managers typically use a number of planning approaches to achieve better performance. Among the most popular are management by objectives, single-use plans, standing plans, contingency plans, crisis planning and strategic management.

Management by Objectives (MBO) MBO refers to a set of procedures that begins with goal setting and continues through performance review. The MBO process begins with a discussion between the manager and the employees. During the discussion, past performance is reviewed and objectives (goals) for the future are identified. Both the manager and the employees agree upon objectives that are acceptable. Performance appraisals are conducted jointly on a continuous basis, with provisions for regular periodic reviews. At the heart of MBO are the following six elements:

1. Commitment to the programme Commitment from managers and employees is essential for an effective MBO programme. Managers must meet with the employees, set goals together and review performance towards these goals.[4]

2. Set goals This is the most difficult task in MBO. Setting goals involves employees at all levels in the organisation. Goals must be specific, attainable and realistic. They may be qualitative or quantitative, depending on whether or not outcomes are measurable. Whatever the type, the goals must be jointly derived.

3. Deveiop action plans An action plan defines the course of action needed to achieve the stated goals. Action plans are made both for individuals and departments.

4. Review progress A periodic review of progress is important to ensure that the action plans are working. These reviews can occur informally between managers and subordinates. During the reviews, they need to decide what problems exist, and what each can do to resolve them. If necessary objectives may be modified for the next review period.

5. Appraisal of the overall performance Another element in MBO is to carefully evaluate whether annual goals have been achieved for both individuals and departments. Success or failure to achieve goals can become part of the performance appraisal system and dispensation of salary increases and other rewards.

6. Participation As a general rule, the greater the participation of both managers and employees in goal setting, the more likely the goals will be achieved.

A typical MBO programme operates in the way as shown in Fig.3.1.

Single Use and Standing Plans As the term implies, single-use plans are developed to achieve a set of goals that are not likely to be repeated in the future. Standing plans are ongoing and are used to provide guidance for tasks performed repeatedly within the organisation. Single-use plans typically include programmes and projects. Standing plans are organisational policies, rules, and procedures. They pertain to employee illness, absences, smoking, discipline, hiring and dismissals.

Contingency Plans Contingency plans become relevant when environment is changing and is highly volatile. Where socio-cultural, economic, technological and political-legal or any one of

FIGURE 3-1
MODEL OF THE MBO PROCESS

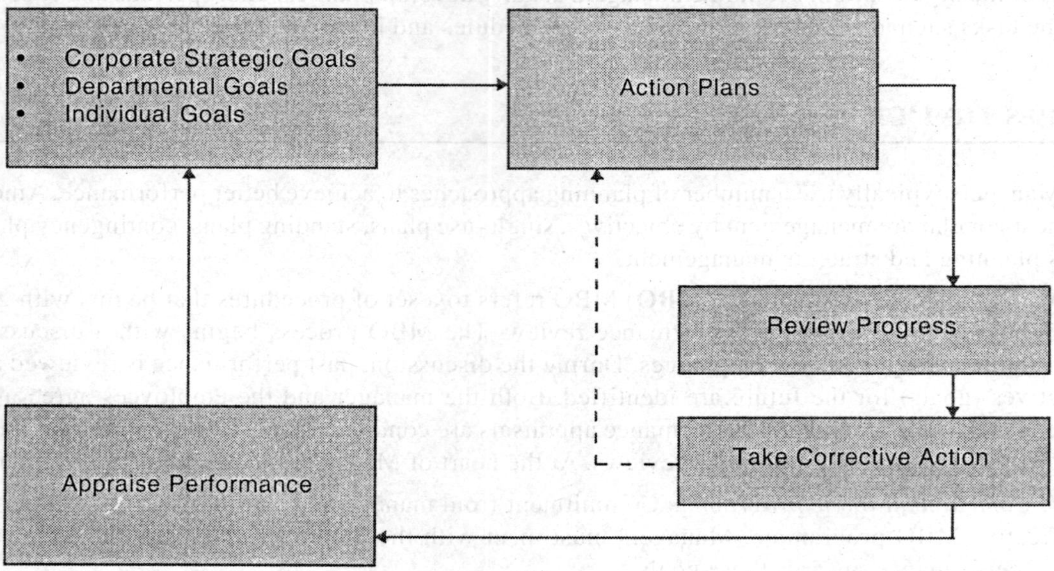

(**Source:** Richard D.Laft, op.cit., p.219)

these changes, plans also need to be changed accordingly. The contingency plans are also called the **scenarios**. Scenarios define company responses to changes in the environment.

Crisis Management Planning Where company response to changes in the environment is sudden, such a plan becomes contingency plan. Sometimes, events are so sudden and devastating they require immediate response. Take the case of the Government of India. The government has a five-year plan and an annual budget. Amidst all these, the government is coming out with short-term urgent action plans to combat raising inflation.

Strategic Management Strategic management is one specific type of planning. The latter part of this chapter contains more details on strategic management.

PROCESS OF PLANNING

Typical planning process involves six steps as shown in Fig.3.2 and explained in this section.

Situational Analysis Planning begins with a situational analysis. Within their time and resource constraints, planners should gather, interpret and summarise all information relevant to the planning issue. A thorough situational analysis studies past events, examines current conditions, and attempts to forecase future trends. It focuses on the internal forces at work in the company or work unit and simultaneously examines the impact of external environment. The outcome of this step is the identification and diagnosis of planning assumptions, issues and problems.

Alternative Goals and Plans Based on the situational analysis, the planners should generate alternative goals that may be pursued in the future and the alternative plans that may be used to

FIGURE 3·2
PROCESS OF PLANNING

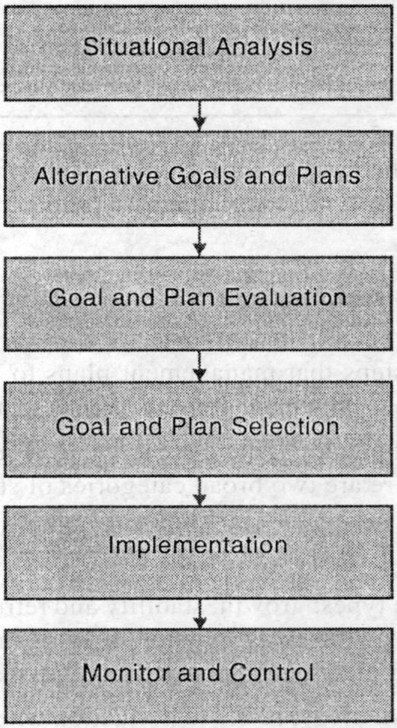

(***Source:*** Thomas S.Bateman and Scott A.Snell, *Management*, p.125)

achieve those goals. This step calls for creativity on the part of managers and employees to think 'beyond box' and come out with alternative goals and plans.

Goal and Plan Evaluation Alternative goals and plans have been identified, the planners must evaluate the merits, demerits, and potential effects of each alternative goal and plan.

Goal and Plan Selection Having shortlisted potential goals and plans, the planner is now in a position to select the most appropriate and feasible goals and plans. Experience, judgement and often intuition play decisive role in the final selection.

Implementation Once managers have selected the goals and plans, they must be implemented appropriately. The best plans and goals go a waste if they are not implemented properly. Managers and employees must understand the plans and goals, marshall resources required to implement them, take part in their implementation and monitor their progress too.

Successful implementation necessitates that the plan be linked to other systems in the organisation, particularly the budget and reward systems. Linking with the budget is necessary as it is the latter that allocates resources for execution of the plan. Similarly, goal achievement should be linked to the organisation's reward system. Many organisations use incentive programmes to encourage employees to achieve goals and to implement plans successfully. Salaries, commissions, promotions, bonuses and other rewards are based on enhanced performance.[5]

Monitor and Control As stated above, managers and employees must not only participate in goal realisation and plan implementation, they should also monitor the performance and control deviations, as and when they occur. Planning is an ongoing and repetitive process. Managers must continuously monitor their performance. They must develop control systems that allow the organisation to take corrective action when plan implementation is not proceeding in the right direction.

STRATEGIC MANAGEMENT

Till now we have explained the nature of goals, plans, planning, types and steps in planning. Strategic management is one specific type of planning. We propose to explain strategic management in detail.

NATURE OF STRATEGY AND STRATEGIC MANAGEMENT

Strategy refers to the basic steps that management plans to initiate to reach organisational goals. Simply told, strategy outlines how management intends to achieve its objectives.

Just as there are three levels of planning, there are three levels of strategies as will be explained later in this chapter. Similarly, there are two broad categories of strategies: grand and global.

A **grand** strategy is the general plan of major action by which a firm intends to achieve its long-term objectives.

Grand strategies fall into three types: growth, stability and retrenched. A **growth** strategy helps achieve growth of a company. Growth can be organic or inorganic. Organic growth is achieved through investment an greenfield projects. Mergers and acquisitions help achieve inorganic growth.

Stability, also called a **pause strategy**, refers to a situation where the company remains content with its current status. It has no ambitious plans to grow. **Retrenchment** means that the organisation goes through a lean phase. Its bottomline is weak. It plans to hive off businesses or even liquidate some or all of them. This results in downsizing, another term for retrenchment.

Simultaneously, a firm may pursue **global strategy**. As the term itself implies, global strategy seeks to foray into international arena. Global strategy itself comprises three types: globalisation, multidomestic and transnational.

Globalisation strategy views world as a single market and expects the firm to offer a standardised product for all countries. In **multidomestic strategy**, each country is treated as an independent market. Products, advertising and sales promotions are highly customised to meet local tasks and needs. A **transnational strategy** seeks to achieve both global integration and local responsiveness. In otherwords, transnational strategy represents a synthesis of both globalisation and multidomestic strategies. A true transnational strategy is difficult to achieve, as one goal requires close global coordination while the other goal requires local flexibility.

Strategic management is the set of decisions and actions used to formulate and implement strategies to achieve organisational goals. Typical questions that present themselves in strategic management are: "What changes and patterns are emerging in the competitive environment? Who are our customers? What products should we offer? How can we offer these products more efficiently?" Answers to these questions help managers make choices about how to position their firms vis-v-vis the rivals. Success does not entirely come from luck. It smiles when right choices and sound decisions are made and are implemented effectively.

What is the difference between planning and strategic management? Strategic management centres around the ways and means of managing competition successfully. The focus is on the extent of competition, its potential to cut into company's market share and how best to outbeat it. Planning, on the otherhand, is an ongoing activity, competition or no competition.

Steps in Strategic Management

Strategic management essentially involves four steps: environmental scanning, strategy formulation, strategy implementation and evaluation and control (See Fig.3.3).

FIGURE 3-3
STRATEGIC MANAGEMENT PROCESS

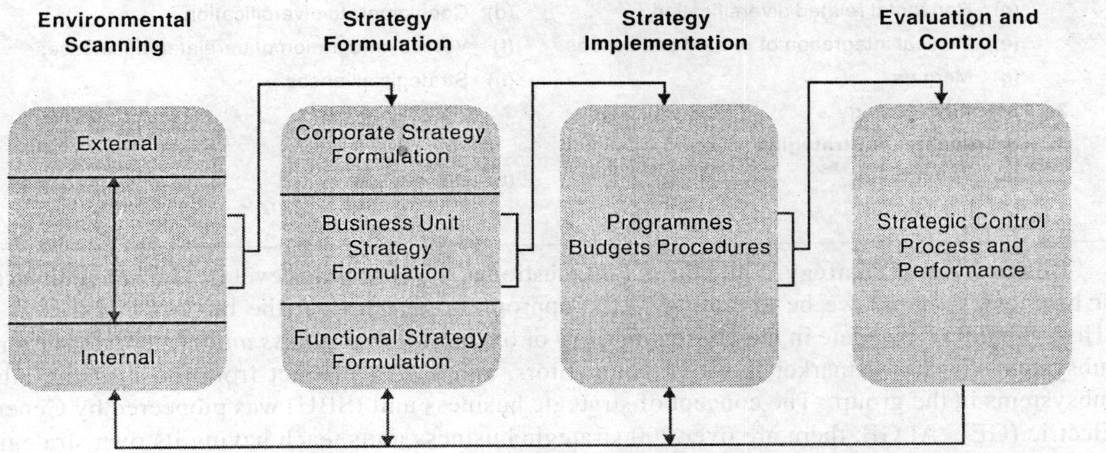

Environmental Scanning As was explained in the previous chapter, environment of an organisation comprises external and internal factors. Environment needs to be scanned in order to determine trends and projections of factors that will affect fortunes of the organisation. Scanning must focus on task environment. Not that elements outside the task environment are ignored, but they receive less attention. Scanning helps identify threats and opportunities prevailing in the environment. In formulating a strategy, a company seeks to take advantage of the opportunities while minimising the threats. What might be a threat to one company may be an opportunity for another. The oil crisis of 1970s threatened oil-fired electrical utilities, but provided a great opportunity for coal producers and shippers.

Strategy Formulation Strategies are formulated at three levels:

1. Corporate level,
2. Business unit level, and
3. Functional level.

Corporate-level Strategy This is formulated by the top management of an organisaiton made up of more then one line of business. The corporate-level strategy of the family-controlled Siyaram Poddar Companies is to continuously innovate in all its businesses with right technology, relentlessly cut costs and focus on the overseas markets. The major questions that need to be answered at this stage are — What kinds of business should the company be engaged in? What are the goals and expectations for each business? How should resources be allocated to reach these goals?

In formulating corporate-level strategies, the company should decide where it wants to be — in 10 or 15 years hence, in at least eight areas — market standing, innovation, productivity, physical and financial resources, profitability, managerial performance and development, worker performance and attitudes, and social responsibility.

Typical corporate level strategies are shows in Table 3.1.

TABLE 3-1
CORPORATE-LEVEL STRATEGIES

1. **Growth Strategies**
   - (a) Internal growth
   - (b) Horizontal integration
   - (c) Horizontal related diversification
   - (d) Conglomerate diversification
   - (e) Vertical integration of related businesses
   - (f) Vertical integration of unrelated businesses
   - (g) Mergers
   - (h) Strategic alliances
2. **Stability Strategy**
3. **Retrenchment Strategies**
   - (a) Turnaround
   - (b) Divestment
   - (c) Liquidation

Business-level Strategy While the major question at the corporate-level is, "In what industries or businesses should we be operating?," the appropriate question at the business unit level is. "How should we compete in the chosen industry or business?" A *business unit* is an organisational subsystem that has a market, a set of competitors, and a goal distinct from those of the other subsystems in the group. The concept of strategic business unit (SBU) was pioneered by General Electric (GE). At GE, there are over 200 strategic business units, each having its own strategies consistent with the organisation's corporate-level strategy.

Table 3.2 shows the business-level strategies of the Siyaram Poddar Companies

TABLE 3-2
BUSINESS-LEVEL STRATEGIES OF THE SIYARAM PODDAR COMPANIES

Siyaram Silk Mills	*Govind Rubber*	*Balakrishna Industries*
• Increase market share from 4 to 5 per cent over the next next two years	• Focus on export to OEMs in Europe, US, Middle East and Africa	• Launching new coated-board products to improve market presence
• Launching new products with the look and feel of polyester wool	• Improving product mix to include more specially products	• Auto parts to be export-led, will account for 60 per cent of tyre production
• Focus shifting to exports	—	• Onus on two/three wheelers as well as replacement market

Functional-level Strategy Each business unit will consist of several departments, such as manufacturing, sales, finance and HRM. Funcational-level strategies identify the basic courses of action that each of the departments must pursue in order to help the business unit to attain its goals. In formulating functional level strategies, managers must be aware that the different functions are interrelated. Each fucntional area, in pursuing its purpose, must mesh its activities with the activities of other departments as shown in Fig. 3.4. A change in one department will invariably affect the way other departments operate. Hence, the strategy of one functional area cannot be viewed in isolation. Rather, the extent to which all functional strategies are integrated determines the effectivesness of the unit's business strategy.

Functional-level strategies of the Siyaram Poddar Group are shown in Table 3.3.

FIGURE 3-4
INTEGRATION AMONG FUNCTIONS

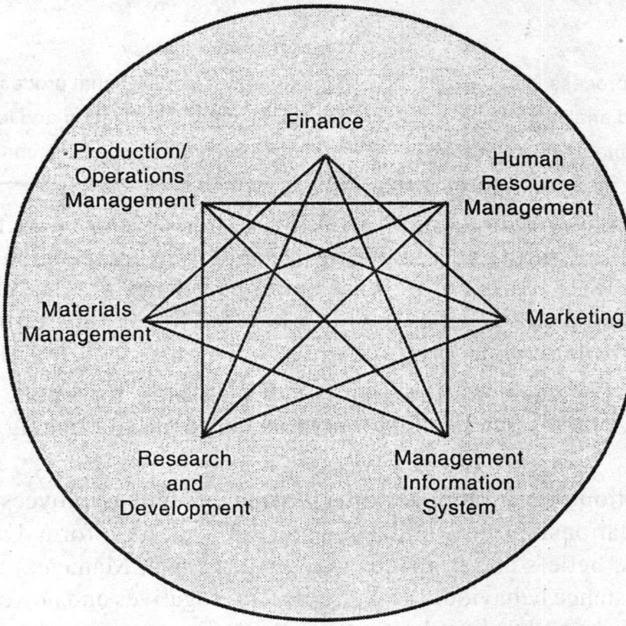

TABLE 3-3
FUNCTIONAL STRATEGIES OF THE SIYARAM PODDAR COMPANIES

Business Unit	*Functional-level Strategies*
Siyaram Silk Mills	• Developing RF 2000, a poly-viscose fabric with the look and feel of poly-wool • Commissioning a new plant at Silvassa to weave 7 lakh metre fabric per month, cost Rs. 30 crore • Relaunching Safari range of fabrics which was discontinued some time back • Installing new machinery to jazz up the Oxemberg line. • Increasing advertisement budget to build brand equity.
Govind Rubber	• Speciality tyres plant in Rajasthan, churning out multicoloured nylon tyres for bicycles • Exports to Europe, US, Middle East and Africa • Tie up with Bajaj Auto, Kinetic Honda and Mahindra & Mahindra • Tapping replacement markets for truck tyres.
Balakrishna Industries	• Big push for exports. Exports to account for 80 per cent of the production • Tie up with Bajaj Auto, Kinetic Honda and Mahindra & Mahindra • Tapping replacement market for truck types.

Strategy Implementation Strategies formulated need to be implemented. Implementation of strategies is, often more difficult than their formulation. Although implementation is the logical step to formulation, the two differ in several ways (See Table 3.4).

TABLE 3-4
DIFFERENCE BETWEEN STRATEGY FORMULATION AND IMPLEMENTATION

Strategy Formulation	*Strategy Implementation*
Strategy formulation is positioning forces before the action	Strategy implementation is managing forces during the action
It focuses on effectiveness	It focuses on efficiency
It is primarily an intellectual process	It is primarily an operational process
It requires good initiative and analytical skills	It requires special motivation and leadership skills
It requires co-ordination among a few individuals	It requires co-ordination among many persons

Implementing strategies requires such actions as altering sales territories, adding new departments, closing facilities, hiring new employees, changing an organisation's pricing strategies, developing financial budgets, formulating new employee benefits, establishing cost-control procedures, changing advertising strategies, building new facilities, transferring managers among divisions, and building a better computer information system.

Strategy-formulation concepts and tools do not differ vastly for small, large or non-profit organisations. However, strategy implementation varies substantially among different types and sizes of organisations.

Strategy implementation poses a threat to many managers and employees in an organisation. New power and status relationships are anticipated and realised. New formal and informal groups are formed whose values, beliefs and priorities may be unknown. Managers and employees may engage themselves in resistance behaviours as their roles, prerogatives and power in the organisation change. Disruption of social and political structures that accompany strategy execution must be anticipated and considered during strategy formulation and managed during strategy implementation.

Guidelines which help ensure that human relationships facilitate but not disrupt strategy implementation include open communication, co-opting as many managers and employees in the strategic management process and matching managers with strategies through transfers, promotions, job enlargement and job enrichment.

Strategy Control Now that the strategies have been implemented, the next logical step is to evolvate the results and initiate corrective actions where necessary. Corrective actions become necessary when results deviate from standards. If expected results have note been achieved, managers may need to change mission and goals, revise the strategies or change the controls themselves. Controls help reduce deviations from targets and provide useful information to the ongoing strategic management process. Chapter 10 gives more details about controls

STRATEGIC MANAGEMENT MODELS

Towards the end of the chapter, it is useful to describe models of strategic management. There are two major models: industrial organisation model and resource based model.

The **industrial organisation** model argues that the primary determinant of a firm's strategy is its external environment. How strategies are formulated and implemented are dictated by the environmental forces surrounding the organisation. This model assumes that the environment presents threats and opportunities to organisations, that firms within an industry control or have equal access to resources, and that these resources are highly mobile between companies. The model argues that organisations should choose to locate themselves in industries that present the greatest opportunities and learn to utilise their resources to suit the needs of the environment.

The industrial organisation model formed the basis for strategic management during the 1980s and hence is called the traditional model.

The second model is the **resource based approach** to strategic management. This model argues that the organisation's resources and capabilities, rather than environmental conditions, should be the basis for organisational decisions and actions. A firm rich in resources and capabilities gains competitive edge and is in a sound position to curve its own strategies, irrespective of the environmental constraints.

In contrasting the two approaches, the industrial organisation model suggests that an organisation's strategy is driven by external considerations; the resource-based model argues that strategy should be driven by internal considerations. The first model argues that strategy drives resource acquisition; the second argues that strategy is determined by resources. Interestingly, both the models carry relevance and application in organisations.

Case

Back from the Brink

The story of HCL Technologies is the typical of how strategic planning can turnaround a company. Once considered a pioneer 10 years ahead of the time, an overconfident software company squanderd the edge and began drifting. In the early 2000s, a mix of arrogance and extreme reliance on its core strength-engineering services-led to hard times at HCL. The company was by far the market leader in that space, which contributed 78% of revenue. A global slowdown hit the company harder than any other. While the whole Indian IT industry was born out of the Y2K and the cost arbitrage phenomenon, HCL looked down upon that business. Then came Vincent Nayar as the CEO in 2005. It is this young man (46 years) who changed the fortunes of HCL Technologies. Secret is strategic planning.

When Nayar took charge as the CEO, the future looked bleak, as traditional outsourcers extended their focus from cost to innovation, while bigger Indian competitors such as TCS, Infosys and Wipro were better placed to play the high volume, low-cost services game.

Today after more than three years of a massive clean up and painful transformation process, the company has turned the corner. Although HCL is still only the fifth largest Indian IT services firm, it looks set to cross the $2 billion revenue mark by 2009 and more importantly, it has emerged as one of the more respected and value centric players in the market.

Nayar put in place a three phase change strategy to get HCL out of the morass and move up the value ladder. The first was a two year process where he introduced more than 75 new initiatives to clean the company's gut. The second was to build strategic tie-ups with companies to jointly offer end-to-end transformation services. The third, which by Nayar's roadmap would be done by 2010, is to bring about a radical shift in HCL business model that would redefine the market place.

One of the first initiatives Nayar undertook was called 'Mirror, Mirror', where he held up a metaphorical mirror during his townhall meetings with employees, to show them the reality that after years of comfortable market leadership, things were not looking too good for the company.

In a desperate attempt to fill in the domain expertise gaps and shore up revenues, HCL went on a string of acquisitions, buying companies such as Gulf Computers and Deutsche Software, Deutsche Bank's India software operation, as well as a part of BT's call centre business. Although the move brought size, analysts questioned the disjointed nature of its operations as a result of serial buys, and the company's weak systems and processes. HCL was also seen as a late entrant into some key verticals, thereby lacking depth in service lines.

While looking at the organisation's structure, Nayar felt that HCL was actually running like a manufacturing operation rather than a knowledge-based business. That's what led to a rather provocatively named initiative called 'Employee First, Customer Second', (EFCS), which played the most crucial role in the turnaround.

Another early initiative-a Comnet clone-was to make the performance review of all senior managers, including Nayar's, accessible to all employees through the intranet. "When thousands of employees all over the world had a chance to view the top management's performance, they truly understood our commitment to transparency," says Nayar. Though the disclosure of performance evaluation was not mandatory for all employees, Nayar claims that in a matter of months, nearly all of them voluntarily started sharing it publicly.

Once the employees' faith was won, Nayar wanted to define what the company's goal was and answer the "who we are" question. The company decided it didn't want to fight the battle on its competitors' turf and hence eschewed the volume game.

After more than two years of the transformation process, the results for HCL have been more than encouraging. Last quarter, the company posted a 9.2% growth compared to an average of 7.6% for its peers. In 2006-07 it bagged 19% of deals worth more than $25 million that came the way of Indian IT companies.

Company Profile

HCL Technologies is the slagship company under the umbrella of HCL Enterprises. HCL Enterprises was founded by Shiv Nadar in 1976 as one of the first Indian "IT Garage Startups". HCL Enterprises has two outfits: HCL Infosystems and the other is the HCL Technologies.

HCL is one of India's global IT services and product engineering companies, providing value-added, software-led IT solutions and services to large and medium scale organisations. HCL is a $2 billion plus having more than 30,000 employees and operating in 25 countries. HCL has the distinction of shipping the first indigenous micro-computer in 1978 at the same time as Apple. In 1983, HCL created a relational database at the same time as Oracle.[6]

Questions

1. What is unique about Nayar's strategies? How did his strategies help HCL's turnaround?

2. What lessons you and the company's rivals can learn from Nayar's strategies?

QUESTIONS

1. What are plans? Goals? Levels of Planning?
2. Bring out the types of planning.
3. Describe the planning process.
4. What is strategic managmenet? Describe the strategic management process.
5. State and explain the models of strategic management.

REFERENCES

1. James,A.F. Stoner, et al., *Management*, PHI, 2007.
2. Richard L.Daft, *Management*, Thomson, 2003.
3. Thomas S.Bateman and Scott A.Snell, *Management*, McGraw-Hill, 1999.
4. Peter Wright, et al., *Strategic Management - Concepts and Cases*, Prentice Hall, 1996.
5. Jeffrey A.Mello, *Strategic Human Resource Management*, Thomson, 2002.
6. The Economic Times, dated May 30, 2008 and company web site.

CHAPTER

Four

Decision Making

LEARNING OBJECTIVES

After reading this chapter you should understand –

1. The nature of decisions and decision making
2. The different types of decisions
3. The conditions under which decisions are made
4. The models of decision making
5. The decision making process
6. The barriers effective decision making
7. The decision making styles
8· The group decision making

In the previous chapter we described plans, planning, strategies and strategic management. Underlying all these are decisions. Plans and strategies are the result of decisions. Better the decision making, better are the plans and strategies.

Corporate world is full of good decisions and bad decisions. When, Ratan Tata and Kumara Mangalam Birla hived off unprofitable businesses, they made sound decisions. The decision of Anand Mahindra, the Vice Chairman of M&M to have a centralised 'office of strategy' other than a federal organisation structure that empowered his group CEOs may be a right decision.

The now liquidated ITT once acquired 20 unrelated companies in one month and managed them all in the belief that sound management principles could be applied to any type of business to make it more profitable, even if the company executives had no expertise in the field. This was a classic case of bad decision. Same is the case when ICI(UK) pulled out of India.

Managers are essentially decision makers. Decision making ability is one of the parametres used to determine the capability of a manager in the present management system. It goes then, without telling, that decision making is highly difficult.

This chapter is devoted to a detailed description of the nature, types, approaches, techniques and other related matters related to decision making in organisations.

Nature of Decision and Decision-making

Decision is understood as making up of one's mind. More specifically, decision refers to making a choice among available alternatives.

Decision making is the process of identifying problems and opportunities and then resolving them. Decision making involves efforts both before and after the actual choice.[1] At the core of decision making are problems and opportunities. A **problem** arises when an actual state of affairs differs from a desired state of affairs. Often, a problem may be an opportunity in disguise. For example, the problem of customer complaints about slow delivery of orders could also be seen as an opportunity to redesign production processes and customer service.[2] Decision making is complete when problems and opportunities are identified and resolved.

Types of Decisions

Decisions are of four types: programmed and non-programmed, innovative and adaptive.

Programmed and non-programmed decisions Programmed decisions, also called routine decisions, represent the choices made in response to relatively well defined and common problems and alternative solutions. Established rules and standard procedures help make routine decisions fairly easily. Placing orders online, processing payroll vouchers, packing and shipping customers' orders, making travel arrangements and the reorder point for manufacturing inventory are the typical programmed decisions. Managers and employees need to guard against the tendency to make routine decisions when a problem actually calls for a non-programmed or innovative decision. Doing so results in **active inertia**, - the rigid devotion to the status quo by attempting to do more of the same old thing but better.[3]

Non-programmed decisions are made in response to situations that are unique, are poorly defined and largely unstructured, and have significant consequences for the organisation. Many non-programmed decisions involve strategic thinking, because uncertainty is great, and decisions are complex. Non-programmed decisions involve such difficult choices as constructing a new facility, launching a new product, acquiring a company, relocate headquarters and the like. The decision of M&M to have a centralised 'office of strategy' is a non-programmed one.

Adaptive Decisions These refer to choices made in response to a combination of moderately unusual problems and alternative solutions. Adaptive decisions typically involve modifying and improving on past routine decisions and practices. These decisions often reflect the concept of **convergence**-a business shift in which two connections with the customer that were previously viewed as competing (e.g. old book stores and Internet book stores) come to be seen as complementary. Those customer connections can include previously competing sales channels, product categories, or distribution channels.[4]

Adaptive decisions also reflect the concept of **continuous improvement**-which refers to a management philosophy that approaches the challenge of product and process improvements as an ongoing effort to increase the levels of quality and excellence. It involves streams of adaptive organisational decisions made overtime that result in a large number of small, incremental improvements year after year. Continuous improvement requires a commitment to constant diagnosis of technical, organisational and managerial processes in search of improvements.[5]

In an environment of continuous improvement, everyone engages in exploration, discovery, and action, continually learns what is effective and what is not, and adjusts and improves accordingly. Fig.4.1 details the concept more clearly. With the continuous improvement philosophy, the organisation can have several benefits: low cost, high quality, flexibility, responsiveness, innovation and speed.

The concept of continuous improvement was first propounded by Toyota Motor Company and has now become a household term in the corporate world.

Innovative Decisions These are decisions based on discovery, identification, and diagnosis of unusual and ambiguous problems and/or the development of unique or creative alternative solutions. Again, the solutions frequently involve a series of small, interrelated decisions made over a period of months or even years. Innovative decisions usually represent a break from the past and hence do not happen in a logical orderly sequence.[6]

Innovative decisions are often preceded by failures and failures should be celebrated as they are the genesis for innovative decision making. Consider the 3M legend from the early 1920s of inventor Francis G.Okie. Okie dreamed up the idea of using sandpaper instead of razor blade for shaving. The aim was to reduce the risk of nicks and avoid sharp instruments. The idea failed, but instead of punishing for the failure, Okie was encouraged to champion other ideas, which included 3M's first blockbuster success: waterproof sandpaper. A culture that permits failure is crucial for innovations.

DECISION-MAKING CONDITIONS

Decision-makers essentially work under five conditions: certainty, risk, uncertainty, ambiguity, and corporate culture.

Certainty This is the condition under which decision makers are fully informed about a problem, alternative solutions are known, and the results of each solution are predictable. Decision making is relatively easy.

FIGURE 4-1
LEARNING CYCLE: EXPLORE, DISCOVER, ACT

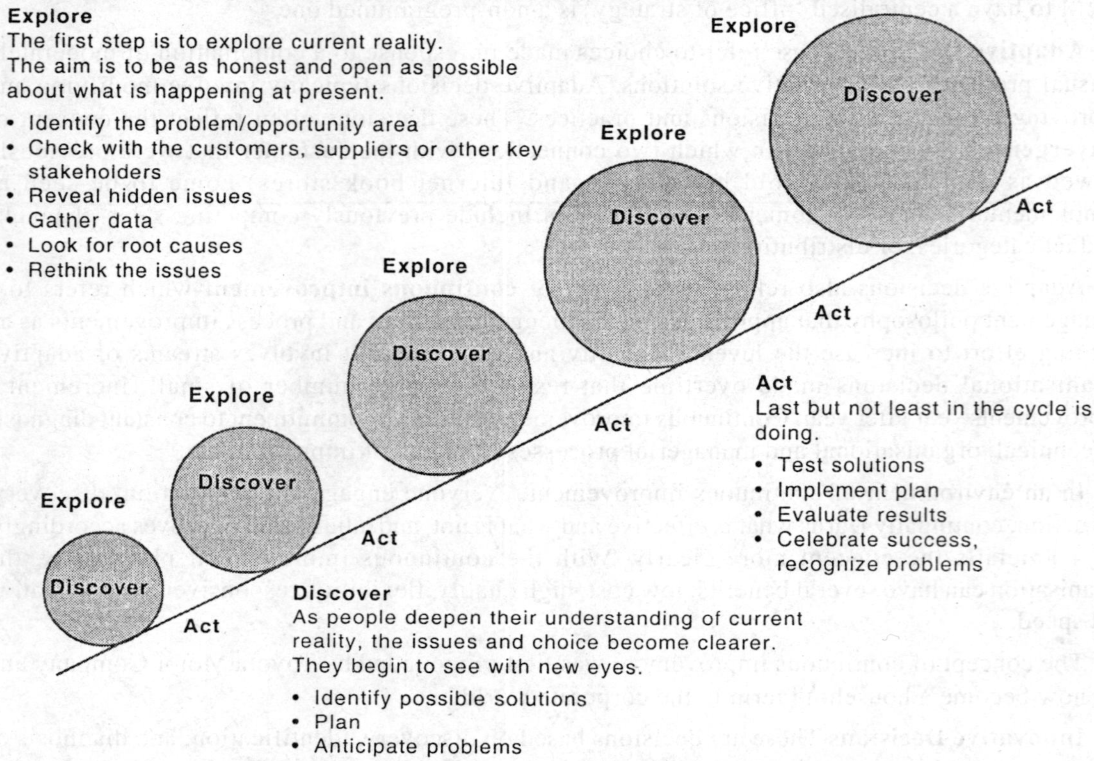

(**Source:** Thomas S. Bateman and Scott A. Snell, *Management*. p.620)

Condition of certainty for decision making is an exception for most managers, thought first-line managers have the privilege of making day-to-day decisions under certainty.

Risk Risk means that a decision has definite goals, information is available, but the future outcomes of the actions are subject to chance. When managers know the possible outcomes of a particular course of action and can assign probabilities to them, there is risk. For example, managers in the biotechnology industry know that there is a 10 per cent probability that a drug will successfully pass advanced clinical trials and a 90 per cent probability that it will fail. These probabilities are known from the experiences of thousands of drugs that have gone through advanced clinical trials. Thus, when managers in the biotechnology industry decide whether to submit a drug for testing, they knew that there is only 10 per cent chance that the drug will succeed. This decision is based on information that is gleaned from past experience.

Uncertainty Under conditions of uncertainty, little is known about the alternative solutions available or their outcomes. Uncertainty arises from two sources. First, managers face situations beyond their control, such as the death of an executive or adverse weather. Second, the managers may not have access to key information. Managers may have to make assumptions from which to forge decisions even though they will be wrong if the assumptions are incorrect. They may have to come out with creative approaches to alternatives and use personal judgement to determine which alternative is the best.

Ambiguity This is by far the most difficult condition to make any decision. Goals are not defined, problems to be solved are not clear, alternatives are difficult to identify and information about outcome is not available. Students face ambiguity when their instructor assigns dissertation task to a group of students but has not given topic, not explained methodology and not guided them in any way. Ambiguity is rightly called a 'wicked' decision problem.

Corporate Culture Corporate culture is a powerful ingredient in decision making. If the corporate culture is authoritarian and conformist, the decision makes tends to be caught by bureaurcy and his/her ability to make dynamic decisions is restricted. In contrast, an innovative and progressive company will permit the decision makers to be more adventerous. Decision maker should understood how the organisation is alternating between risk aversive and ambitious and act accordingly.

MODELS OF DECISION MAKING

The approach managers use to make decisions usually falls into one of the three types - classical, administrative and political. The choice of model depends on the manager's personal preference, whether the decision is programmed or non-programmed, and the extent to which the decision is constrained by uncertainty, risk and ambiguity.

Classical Model This model is based on economic assumptions. Managers are expected to make decisions that are economically sensible and serve the organisation's interests. The assumptions underlying this model are-

1. The manager operates to accomplish goals that are known and agreed upon. Problems are stated specifically and are well defined.
2. The manager strikes for conditions of certainty, gathering all relevant information. All alternatives and the potential results of each are calculated.
3. Criteria for evaluating alternatives are known. The manager selects the alternative that will maximise the ROI to the organisation.
4. The manager is rational and uses logic to assign values, orders preferences, evaluates alternatives and makes the decision that will maximise goal attainments.

The classical model helps the manager understand how to make decisions. It does not describe how managers actually make decisions but provides guidelines for decision making. The classical model is relevant in programmed decisions and when they operate under conditions of certainty or risk, because relevant information is available and probabilities can be calculated.

Administrative Model The administrative model of decision making describes how managers actually make decisions in difficult situations such as uncertainty and ambiguity. The administrative model questions the very assumptions of the classical model. To start with, many of the assumptions are idealistic and are not available. Even if available, managers are not psychologically and mentally prepared to understand, evaluate and make correct decisions. Decision making obviously is an obivously uncertain and risky process.

The administrative model is based on four important concepts: bounded rationality, incomplete information, satisfying and intuition.

Bounded rationality states that managers are bounded by certain cognitive limitations-that is, limitations in their ability to interpret, process and act on information. These limitations constrain managers to determine the optimum decision.

Bounded rationality also suggests that people frequently have inadequate information about (1) the precise nature of the problem facing them, (2) range of feasible solutions, and (3) consequences of each alternative. These conditions create a condition of ***lack of information or ignorance***. Obviously, decisions cannot be optimal.

Satisfying means that decision makers choose the first alternative solution that satisfies minimal decision criteria. The first solution may not be the best but managers are content with it. Rather than pursuing all alternatives to identify the single solution that will maximise economic returns, managers will opt for the first that appears to solve the problem, even if better solutions do exist. The principle of satisfying stems from the bounded rationality concept.

Intuition represents a quick apprehension of a decision situation based on past experience but without conscious thought. Intuitive decision making is not arbitrary or irrational, but is based on years of hands-on experience which helps managers gain quick understanding of the problem and easy identification of a solution without pain taking computations.

Political Model The political model represents the decision-making process in terms of self-interests and goals of powerful external and internal stakeholders. Organisations contain groups with diverse interests each pulling and pushing its own goals and decisions. Decisions are the result of bargaining and discussion among managers. The decision that survives is the decision of the group which is more powerful than others.

The political model reflects reality in the organisations. Decisions are complex and involve many people, information is often ambiguous, resources are limited, and disagreements and conflicts over problems and solutions are normal. In such a scenario whichever group wields more clout carries its decision through. Fig.4.2 illustrates the political decision-making. Table 4.1 carries the different dimensions of the three models of decision-making.

FIGURE 4-2
POLITICAL MODEL OF DECISION MAKING

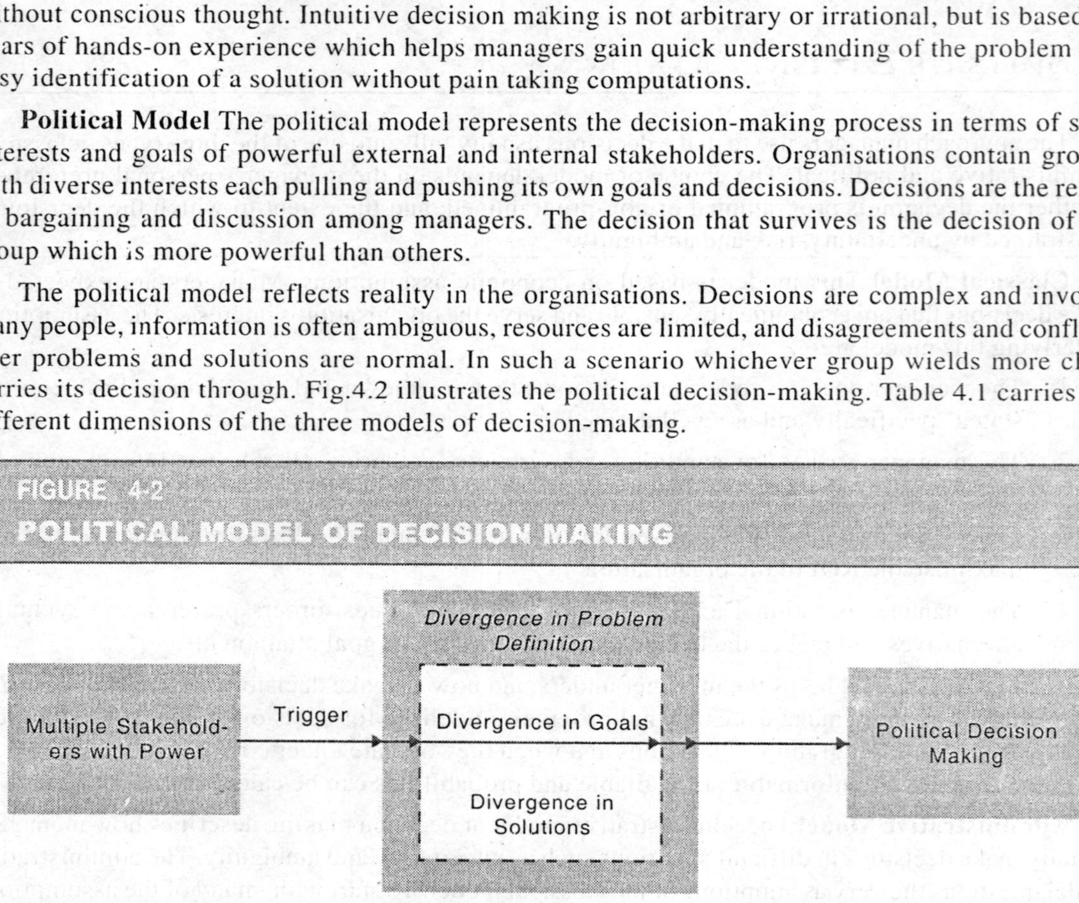

(**Source:** Don Helriegel, *et al., op.cit.,* p.235)

Decision Making Process

When we discuss the steps in the decision making process, we keep classical (also called rational) model of decision making in the background.

TABLE 4-1

CHARACTERISTIC FEATURES OF DECISION MAKING MODELS

Classical Model	*Administrative Model*	*Political Model*
• Clear-cut problems and goals	• Vague problems and goals	• Conflicting goals
• Conditions of certainty	• Condition of uncertainty	• Conditions of uncertainty and ambiguity
• Full information about alternatives and their outcomes	• Limited information about alternatives and outcomes	• Inconsistent view points
• Rational choice by individuals for maximising outcomes	• Satisfying choice for resolving problem using intuition	• Bargaining and discussion among managers

(***Source:*** Richard D. Laft, *op.cit.*, p. 281)

Fig.4.3 shows the typical decision making process. There are six phases in the process: defining and diagnosing the problem progressing through and ending with follow up and control.

FIGURE 4-3

DECISION MAKING PROCESS

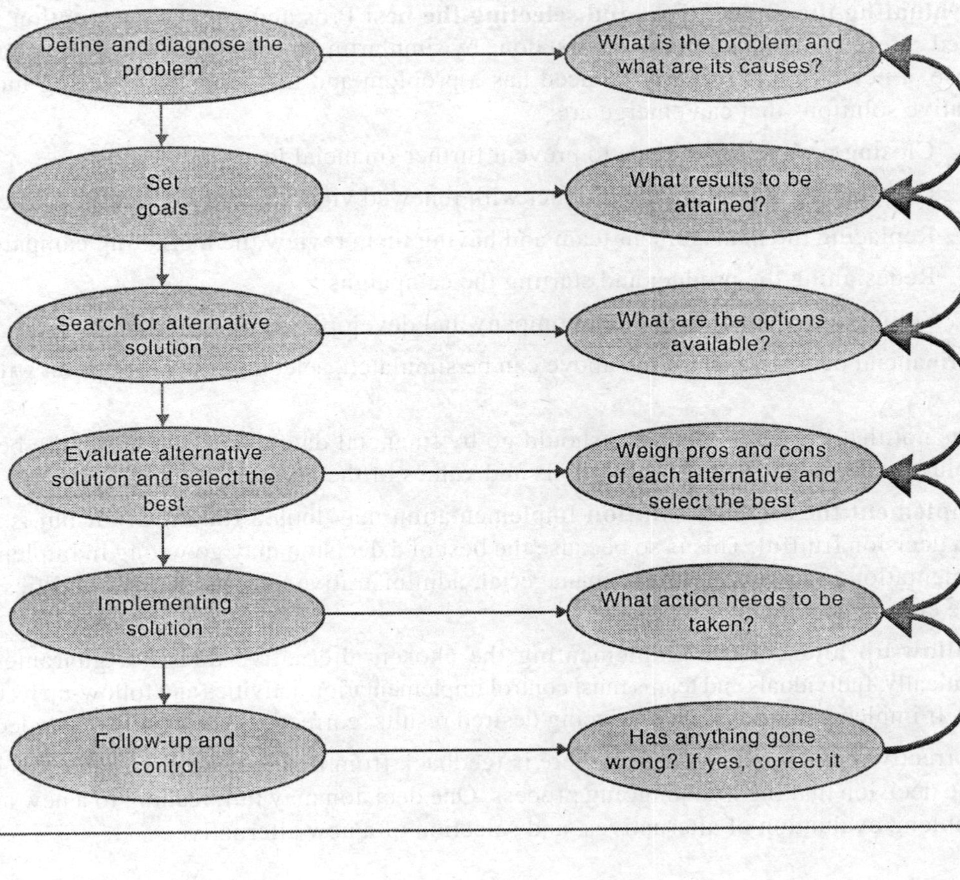

Define and Diagnose the Problem The first step in decision making process is to define the poroblem and identify its probable causes. Problem definition and diagnosis requires three skills from managers: noticing, interpreting and incorporating. **Noticing** involves identifying signals from environment that contribute to the problem. **Interpreting** requires assessing the signals and determining pattern, if any. **Incoporating** calls for integrating the patterns into business goals. Selection of a choice is positive when noticing, interpreting and integrating are properly done.

Set goals Once the problem has been defined and the causes diagnosed, the next step is to set goals. Goals represent the results to be attained and indicate the direction towards which decisions and actions should be aimed at. Goals may be general or operational. **General goals** provide broad direction for decision making in qualitative terms. **Operational goals** state what is to be achieved in quantitative terms, for whom, and within what time period.

Search for alternative solutions Problem having been defined and goals being set, the next stage for decision makers is to generate possible alternative solutions that will help realise the goals. This step might involve seeking additional information, thinking creatively, consulting experts, undertaking research and taking similar actions.

Finding alternative solutions is easy for a programmed decision. Infact, they are available internally in the form of company rules and procedures. Non-programmed decisions, however, require developing new courses of action that will meet the company's needs. For decisions made under conditions of uncertainty and risk not many solutions are available. Only one or two highly customised solutions may be developed by managers.

Evaluating the alternatives and selecting the best Pros and cons of each option need to be weighed carefully. Evaluation can be best done by simularting the financial outcome of each option. Suppose, a new product recently launced has a problem and the company is losing money. The alternative solutions that can emerge are:[7]

- Closing production at once to prevent further financial loss;
- Carrying on marketing the product with renewed vigour but along the same lines;
- Replacing the management team and having them review the marketing campaigns;
- Redesigning the product and starting the campaigns;
- Selling the product to another company and developing a new product.

If financial deta for each of the above can be simulated, selecting the best option will be fairly easy.

It is not that the decision maker should go by financial data only for seleting the best option. The solution should meet the overall goals and values of the organisation.

Implement the selected solution Implementation may look a routine affair but is critical to make a decision fruitful. This is so because the best of a decision may go wrong in implementation. Implementation involves the use of managerial, administrative, and pursuasive abilities to ensure that the chosen decision is carried out.

Follow-up and control Implementing the chosen alternative does not guarantee success automatically. Individuals and teams must control implementation activities and follow-up by evaluating results. If implementation is not producing desired results, corrective action will be needed.

Corrective action can be taken if there is feedback from implementors. Feedback is necessary because decision making is an ongoing process. One decision may fail, leading to a new analysis of the problem, evaluation of alternatives, and selection of a new alternative.

BARRIERS TO EFFECTIVE DECISION MAKING

Decision makers need to guard themselves against certain barriers which impede the effectiveness of decision making. The barriers include ethical issues, escalation of commitment, technology and psychological biases.

Ethical issues Ethics are involved in decision making. They relate to dilammas. Ethical dilemma is a situation in which a person needs to decide whether to do something that is beneficial to self as well as to the organisation, but may be considered unethical and even illegal. Most typically, ethical dilemmas involve risk and uncertainty and non-routine problem situations.

Take a typical situation. You are accompanying a truck loaded with products of your company. The products need to be delivered at the Bangalore market where stock has run out a week back. The truck is caught at the checkpost. The official at the check point is demanding one thousand rupees as bribe notwithstanding the fact that all the documents in support of the truck and the goods there in are in place. If you refuse to pay, the truck will not be released. Contacting head office at Mumbai and getting their help only adds to the delay. In addition, your own inability to handle a simple problem is likely to be revealed. What will you do?

Ethical dilemmas of the type described above do occur affecting the effectiveness of decision making adversely.

Escalation of Commitment Good decision-making demands overriding of previous commitments and discountinuation of old practices that have lost relevance. This means being bold and decisive. However, many managers fall into the trap of **escalating commitment**. Recognised by social psychologists as a common and potentially dysfunctional tendency, it is the tendency to continue with a previously chosen course of action even though it is not working. Managers are typically entrapped to do the old things again and again.

One example for this tendency is the plight of investers who have sunk in their funds on projects with little return until the end. These projects require continous funding and those who pump in the cash, must stay the course in order to receive any return on their investment. On other occassions, investors or project managers frequently become so egoistically involved with the project that their identities are immersed in it. They support the project as potentially viable despite evidence to the contrary, because failure signals a threat to their self-esteem. In addition, organisational inertia or weak culture is responsible for less than satisfactory project to continue.

Technology Organisations are increasingly using computer technologies to facilitate decision making. Artificial intelligence is replacing human brain. We have **expert systems** that reason like a human expert and follow 'either/or' rules or heuristics to make deductions, **fuzzy logic** that reasons beyond either/or choices in more imprecise territory, and **neutral networks** that reason inductively by simulating the brains parallel processing capabilities. Uses for such systems may be found everywhere from banks, where they may help screen loan applications, to hospitals, where they check laboratory results and possible drug interactions, to the factory floor, where they schedule machines and people for maximum production efficiencies.

So far so good. But the decisions made with the help of computer technologies carry the risk of being impersonal and perhaps less compelling in terms of commitment to implementation and follow-through.

Psychological biases Psychological biases often come in the way of making optimum decisions. Such biases include illusion of control, discounting the future, and prior hypothesing bias.

The **illusion of control** is a belief that one can influence events even when one has no control over what will happen. Such overconfidence can lead to failures because decision makers ignore risks and fail to objectively evaluate the odds of success. Relatedly, they may have an unrealistically positive view of themselves or their companies, believe they can do no wrong, or hold a general optimism about the future that can lead them to believe they are immune from risk and failure.

Often decision makers **discount the future**. In the evaluation of alternatives, they weigh short-term costs and benefits more heavily than longer-term costs and benefits.

Managers who have strong prior beliefs about the relationship between two variables tend to make decisions based on those beliefs even when presented with evidence that their beliefs are wrong. In doing so they are falling victims of **prior hypothesis bias**. Moreover, decision makers tend to seek and use information that is consistent with their prior beliefs and to ignore information that contradicts those beliefs.

Decision Making Styles

Decision makers are human beings and human beings have their own styles. Styles influence the decisions. Whatever the styles, good decision makers should not allow emotions and sentiments to cloud objectivity and rationality.

There are two styles of decision making: intutive and rational.

These styles are determined depending on which side of the brain is more dominant. One side of the human brian (left) is believed to the location of emotion, imagination, intution and creativity. The other side (right) is the side of logic, language, maths and analysis.

Decisions tend to be based on hunch and intution if the left side of the decision maker is more dominant. Where the right side is more dominant, decisions tend to be rational and fact-based. Though decision makers tend to have a dominant side, they should aim at achieving a balance between the two sides (see Fig. 4.4).

How do Groups Make Decisions?

The discussion till now centred around individual decision making. Organisaitons today are characterised by teams and groups. Individuals working in teams and groups are also required to make decisions. This section covers discussion on group decision making.

Though decision making is supposed to pass through definite stages, in practice small groups make decisions differently. The popular methods of decision making are:

1. Decision by Lack of Response Ideas after ideas are suggested without any discussion taking place. When the group finally accepts an idea, all others have been bypassed and discarded by simple lack of response rather than by critical evaluation.

2. Decision by Authority Rule In this method, the chairperson, manager, or some other authority makes a decision for the group. This can be done with or without discussion and is highly time efficient. Whether the decision is good, depends on whether or not the authority figure had the necessary information and how well this approach is accepted by other group members.

3. Decision by Minority Two or three group members dominate and force the group to make a decision they agree with. This is often done by providing a suggestion and then forcing a quick

FIGURE 4-4
DECISION MAKING STYLES

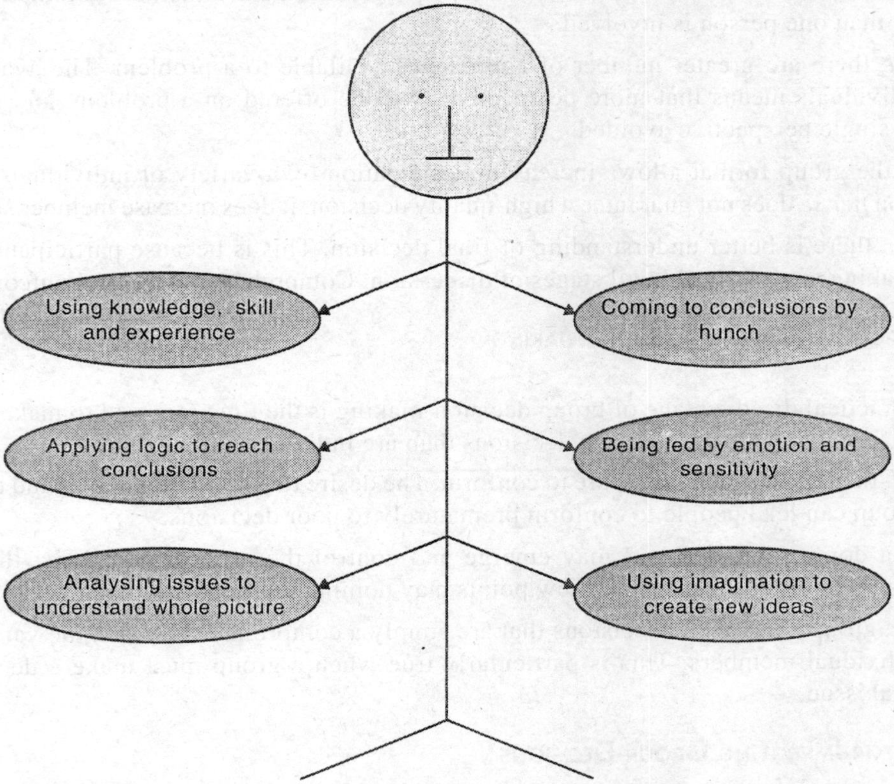

(Adapted from *Manager's Manual,* p. 158)

agreement on it. Questions that emanate from the dominant minority are "Does anyone object?... Let us go ahead then."

4. Decision by Majority Rule Groups can make decisions by majority rule, that is, by voting or polling members to find the majority viewpoint. This method parallels the democratic political system and is often used without awareness of its potential problems. Voting tends to create coalitions of "winners" and "losers." Those in the minority (i.e. the losers) can easily feel left out or discarded without having a fair say. This can detract from the implementation of a decision since support is fragmented in the final result.

5. Decision by Consensus Consensus is a state of affairs where a clear alternative appears with the support of most members, and even those who oppose it feel that they have been heard and had a fair chance to influence the decision outcome. Consensus, therefore, does not require unanimity but requires no outright dissent either.

6. Decision by Unanimity Under this method all group members agree on the course of action to be taken. This is logically a perfect method that is extremely difficult to obtain in actual practice.

Advantages of Group Decision Making

There are several advantages inherent in group decision-making. *First*, groups usually have a greater knowledge base that can be brought to bear on the problem. This is an almost automatic outcome, since more than one person is involved.

Second, there are greater number of approaches available to a problem. The availability of several individuals means that more perspectives will be offered on a problem, and the narrow vision of a single perspective avoided.

Third, the group format allows increased participation by a variety of individuals. Although participation *per se* does not guarantee a high-quality decision, it does increase member satisfaction.

Finally, there is better understanding of final decision. This is because participants in group decision making are involved in all stages of discussion. Comprehension of final outcome is high.

Disadvantages of Group Decision-Making

The most practical disadvantage of group decision-making is the time required to make decisions. Groups are frequently slower to reach decisions than are individuals acting alone.

Second, there is the social pressure to conform. The desire to be a good member and to go along with the group can lead people to conform prematurely to poor decisions.

Third, a dominant individual may emerge and control the group's decisions; this may be particularly true of the leader whose view points may dominate group discussion.

Finally, groups may make decisions that are simply a compromise between the various views held by individual members. This is particularly true when a group must make a decision on a controversial issue.

Strategies for Improving Group Decisions

The effort in group decision making is to take advantage of the group as a decision making resource and to minimise its potential disadvantages. Over the years social scientists have studied ways in which group decision making may be made really effective. Three such ways are: brainstorming, the nominal group technique and the Delphi technique.

Brainstorming Brainstorming technique was developed by Alex Osborn, a partner in an agency. The technique was used originally to develop an ad programme, but it can be used any time an organisation wants to develop creative or free-wheeling ideas. These ideas may depart drastically from generally accepted practice. Procedurally, the technique involves getting six to ten people together to come up with a creative solution to a problem. The idea in brainstorming is to create an atmosphere of enthusiasm and non-judgement in terms of the usefulness of an idea.

Four rules typically govern the brainstorming process:

1. *All criticism is ruled out* Judgement or evaluation of ideas must be withheld until the idea-generation process has been completed.
2. *Freewheeling is welcome* The wilder or more radical the idea, the better.
3. *Quantity is wanted* The greater the number of ideas, the greater the likelihood of obtaining a superior idea.

4. *Combination and improvement are sought* Participants should suggest how ideas of others can be turned into better ones, or how two or more ideas can be combined into still another idea.

Brainstorming is rooted in the notion that harsh and critical judgement discourages people from expressing unorthodox ideas, and that one or more of these otherwise unspoken ideas may be the key to solving the problems at hand. No attempt is made to evaluate responses during the session; it is done later. Brainstorming sessions that last 40 minutes to one hour have been found to be most effective.

Nominal Group Technique (NGT) The major features of the NGT are that it controls the amount of personal interaction and adds structure to the group process. As mentioned earlier, two disadvantages of the group process are that it can be time consuming and that one or two dominant or high-status members may control the group. NGT minimises this problem by suggesting four steps, viz.,

1. Each person writes down ideas, options, or solutions privately without discussing them with others. To save time, this can be done before the meeting.
2. The results of the first step are presented to the group by each person in a round-robin procedure. Each person presents his or her ideas in sequence. There is no discussion, the ideas are written down on a chalk board or large flip chart, so that everyone can see them.
3. After all the ideas have been suggested, the participants may ask questions to clarify an idea or proposal. However, at this point, there is no evaluation, no discussion, and no debate.
4. Each person ranks various proposals privately. The results are tallied to determine the relative support for each idea. The proposal with most tallies is then discussed for possible adoption.

When these steps are followed, NGT has been found to be effective. It integrates the advantages of both group creativity and individual creativity. In many situations it also saves a great deal of time. NGT, therefore, can improve group decision making under otherwise difficult circumstances.

Delphi Technique A third approach, called the Delphi technique, was developed by the Rand Corporation to allow for the benefits of group decision making without members having to meet face to face. In fact, it allows group decision making to be accomplished over large distances and widely scattered members.

The Delphi procedure involves a series of questionnaires distributed over time to a decision making panel. A typical approach works as follows: The first questionnaire states the problem and requests potential solutions. These solutions are summarised by the decision coordinator. The summary is returned to the panel in a second questionnaire. Panel members respond again, and the process is repeated until a consensus is reached and a clear decision emerges.

One of the problems with the Delphi technique relates to the complexity and cost of administering the series of questionnaires. However, it does offer the advantages of group decision making in circumstances when it is physically impossible to convene a group meeting.

Evaluating effectiveness As was mentioned above each technique has its strengths and weaknesses. It is useful to compare one with others on the respective plus and minus points. Table 4.2 does exactly that.

TABLE 4-2
EVALUATING DECISION MAKING TECHNIQUES

Effectiveness Criteria	*Brainstorming*	*NGT*	*Delphi*
Number of ideas	Moderate	High	High
Quality of ideas	Moderate	High	High
Social pressure	Low	Moderate	Low
Time/money costs	Low	Low	High
Potential for inter-personal conflict	Low	Moderate	Low
Feeling of accomplishment	High	High	Moderate
Commitment to solution	Not applicable	Moderate	Low
Builds group cohesiveness	High	Moderate	Low

Case: WRONG DECISION

No one in the world alive today would have missed the name Encyclopedia Britannica. For most of its 230-year history, the **magnum opus** has been viewed as illustrious repository of cultural and historical knowledge. Generations of students and librarians relied on the **Britannica** to research everything from the Aleutian Islands to the history of Zydcco-but that was before CD-ROMs and the Internet became the study tools of choice. Suddenly, the 32-volume collection of encyclopedias seemed destined to fade into history. Britannica was slow to move into electronic media and practically ceded the market to startups such as Microsoft's **Encarta**. Managers made a serious blunder when they sold the company's Cormpton Unit, a CD_ROM pioneer now being used by millians of users. Even when Britannica finally produced a CD_ROM, it was priced at a whopping $1200, which the rival Microsoft was offering cut-rate deals or giving **Encarta** away free with personal computers. When Jacob Safra and a Swiss investment group bought Britannica, new top executives immediately began installing managers who could lead the company into the digital age. Safra believed Britannica could once again be the quality leader. However, decisions had to be made about how to compete with rivals such as Compton's and Microsoft's **Encarta**, as well as the numerous free options available on the Internet.

Questions

1. Assume you are a member of the management team at Britannica, what decisions would you make to successfully compete in today's environment?
2. What alternatives would you consider, and what courses of action would you choose?[8]

QUESTIONS

1. Define the terms 'decision' and 'decision making'. Explain the process of decision making.
2. Bring out the constraining conditions under which decisions are made. How to minimise risk associated with any decision?
3. State and explain the types of decisions.
4. How are group decisions made?
5. Explain the group decision making strategies.

References

1. Richard D.Daft, op.cit., p.273.
2, Don Hellriegel et al., *Management*, Thompson, 2002, p.266.
3. Ibid., p.227.
4. Ibid.
5. Ibid,
6. Richard D.Laft, op.cit., p.277.
7. Robert Heller and Tim Hindle, *Essential Manager's Manual,* Dorling Kindersley, 1998, p.157.
8. Ibid, p.268.

CHAPTER

Five

Organisations

LEARNING OBJECTIVES

After reading this chapter you should understand —

1. The nature of organisation.
2. The different functions of organisation.
3. The factors that influance organisation design.
4. The different types of organisational design.
5. Explian the future design of organisaiton.
6. The certain decisions relevant to organisation design.
7. Know the difference between formal and informal organisations.

Till now we have discussed individual and group behaviors. Intra-personal and interpersonal behaviours, as was pointed out in the first chapter, occur in formal organizations. Strange but true that the structure of an organization will exercise considerable influence on individual and group behaviours. This chapter is devoted to a brief explanation of the nature of organization, structures of organizations, and their impact on the behaviour of individuals and groups.

What is an Organisation? Before quoting a definition on organization straight away, it is advisable to explain its fundamental elements. The elements are: coordination, common goals, division of labour, and integration.

Co-ordination First of all, it is important to recognise that the very idea of organizing stems from the fact that an individual alone is unable to fulfill all of his needs and wishes. Individuals, particularly in modern society, find that they are lacking either in ability, strength, time or endurance to fulfill their basic needs for food, shelter, and safety. As several people coordinate their efforts, however, they find that together they can do more than any of them could have singly. The largest organization – society, makes it possible, through the coordination of the activities of many individuals for all of its members to fulfill their needs. One basic idea underlying the concept of organization, therefore, is the idea of coordination of efforts in the service of mutual help.[(1)]

Common Goals In order for coordination to be helpful, there must exist some goals to be achieved, and some agreement concerning these goals. The goals keep organizational members together and make them work as a team. A second important element underlying the concept of organization then is the idea of achieving a common goal through coordination of activities.

Division of Labour Division of labour refers to dividing work into operations that are narrow in scope in order to increase efficiency with which each operation can be performed. Having divided the work into operations, each operation is assigned to one individual or group of individuals who are more fit in terms of education, skills and experience to do the job. This is the third idea of forming the organization.

A close look at any industrial enterprise will reveal that it comprises several departments – marketing, production, finance and accounting, personnel, research and development, maintenance, management information system and the like – the principle of division of labour being practised.

The division of labour enables the enterprise to function more efficiently. However, departmentalization (another name for division of labour) results in organizational sub-systems that tend to develop unique behavioral attributes. Differences thus emerge between organizational units about their (1) reliance on formality, (2) concerns for work versus people, (3) short-term versus long – term perspectives, and (4) member's orientation towards goals.[2] These attributes give room for organizational conflict.

Integration The fourth and final concept needed to understand organizations is closely related to the idea of integration. If different people are discharging different functions, some integrative function is needed to ensure that all are working towards the commonly agreed upon goals. Integration is mainly achieved through hierarchy of authority-some system for super-ordinate subgroups or individuals to ensure that there is coordination among all through guiding, limiting, controlling, informing and in other ways managing the activities of people.[3]

Coming to the definition of organization – combine the above four elements and we have a definition. However, to quote a formal definition – an organization is defined as "the planned coordination of the activities of a number of people for the achievement of some common, explicit purpose or goal, through division of labour and function, and through a hierarchy of authority and responsibility."[4] What needs emphasis is that organizations are people – individuals working interdependently to achieve shared goals.

Organizations are not just means used by groups of people to achieve some goals. They present different images.

Organization Structure

Once a group of people has established an organization to accomplish shared goals, organizational structure evolves to increase the effectiveness of the organization's control of the activities necessary to achieve its goals. *Organizational structure* is the formal system of task and authority relationships that control how people coordinate their actions and use resources to achieve organization's goals. The principal purpose of organizational structure is one of *control:* to control the means used to motivate people to achieve these goals.[5]

For any organization, an appropriate structure facilitates effective responses to problems of coordination and motivation – problems that can arise for any number of environmental, technological, or human resources. As organizations grow and differentiate, the structure likewise evolves. Organizational structure can be managed and changed through the process of organization design.

Organization design is the process by which managers select and manage elements of structure so that an organization can control the activities necessary to achieve its goals. Organizational structure is the means the organization uses to achieve its goals.

Organization design is about how and why various means are chosen. It is a task that requires managers to strike a balance between external pressures from the organization's environment and internal pressures from, for example, its choice of technology. Achieving the proper balance helps a firm ensure that the organization will survive in the long run.

Importance of Organization Design

There are several reasons why designing an organization's structure is such an important task. Organization design has important implications for a company's ability to deal with contingencies, achieve a competitive advantage, effectively mange diversity, and increase its efficiency and ability to innovate new goods and services. Collectively, these reasons explain why organization design is a vital task in today's competitive global environment.

Dealing with Contingencies. A **contingency** is an event that might occur and must be planned for, such as a changing environment. The design of an organization determines how effectively an organization controls various factors in its environment and obtains scarce resources. For example, an organization's ability to attract skilled employees, loyal customers, or government contracts is a function of the degree to which it can control those three environmental factors.

An organization can design its structure in many ways to increase control over its environment. An organization might change employee task relationships so that employees are more aware of the environment, or it might change the way the organization relates to other organizations by establishing new contracts or joint ventures.

Gaining Competitive Advantage. Increasingly, organizations are discovering that organization design is a source of sustained competitive advantage. **Competitive advantage** is the ability of a company to outperform others because its managers are able to create more value from the resources at their disposal. Competitive advantage springs from a firm's **competences,** manager's skills and abilities in value-creation activities such as manufacturing, research and development, or organization design. Core competences allow a company to develop a strategy to outperform competitors to produce better products or produce the same products but at a lower cost.

The *way* the organization designs its structure is an important determinant how much value the organization creates because organizational design is the means of implementing an organization's *strategy.* Many sources of competitive advantage, such as skills in research and development that result in novel product features or state-of-the-art technology, quickly disappear because they are relatively easy for competitors to imitate. It is much more difficult to imitate good organizational design that brings into being a successful organizational structure. Such imitation is difficult because structure is embedded in the way people in an organization interact and coordinate their actions to get a job done. Moreover, because successful structures take a long time to establish and develop, companies that possess it can have a long-term competitive advantage.

Managing Diversity Differences in the race, gender, and national origin of organizational members have important implications for the values of an organization's effectiveness. The quality of organizational decision making, for example, is a function of the diversity of the viewpoints that are considered and of the kind of analysis that takes place. Similarly, in many organizations, particularly service organizations, a large part of the workforce is socially and economically disadvantaged employees, whose needs and preferences must be taken into consideration. Besides, changes in the characteristics of the workforce, such as an influx of immigrant workers or the aging of the current workforce, require attention and advance planning. An organization needs to design a structure to make optimal use of the talents of a diverse workforce and to develop cultural values that encourage people to work together. An organization's structure determines how effectively mangers are able to coordinate and motivate workers.

Efficiency and Innovation Organizations exist to produce goods and services that people value. The better organizations function, the more value, in the form of more or better goods and services, they create. Historically, the capacity of organizations to create value has increased enormously as organizations have introduced better ways of producing and distributing goods and services. The design and use of new and more efficient organizational structures is equally important. In today's global environment, for example, competition from countries with low labor costs is pressuring companies all over the world to become more efficient in order to reduce costs or increase quality.

Similarly, the ability of companies to compete successfully in today's competitive environment is increasingly a function of how well they innovate and how quickly they can introduce new products and processes. Organizational design plays an important role in innovation. For example, the way an organization's structure links people in different specializations, such as research and marketing, determines how fast the organization can introduce new products.

The Consequences of Poor Organizational Design

Many managements fail to understand the effect of organizational design on their company's performance and effectiveness. Although behaviour is controlled by organizational structure, managers are often unaware of this relationship and pay scant attention to the way employees behave and their role in the organization until something happens.

General Motors, IBM, Sears , Eastman Kodak, and AT&T have all experienced enormous problems in the last decade adjusting to the reality of modern global competition and have seen their sales and profit fall dramatically. In response, they have dramatically reduced their workforces, reduced the number of products they make and even reduced their investment in research and development. Why did the performance of these blue-chip companies deteriorate to such a degree? One reason is that they lost control of their organizational structures. They became so big and bureaucratic that their managers and employees were unable to change and adapt to changing conditions.

The consequence of poor organizational design or lack of attention to organizational design is the decline of the organization. Talented employees leave to take position in strong and growing companies. Resource become harder and harder to acquire and the whole process of value creation slows down. Neglecting design until crisis threatens forces managers to make changes in organizational structure that derail the company's strategy.[6]

KEY FACTORS IN ORGANIZATION DESIGN

Four sets of factors viz, (i) environment, (ii) business strategy, (iii) technology, and (iv) internal contingency factors affect organizational designs, (see Fig 5.1)

FIGURE 5-1
KEY FACTORS IN DESIGN DECISIONS

FACTORS		INDICATORS
Environment	→	Degree of complexity Degree of dynamism Richness
Business Strategy	→	Low cost Differentiation Focused
Technology	→	Technologi cal complexity
Internal Contingency Factors	→	Goals Size Employees

Environmental Factors The environment includes those external stakeholders and forces that directly affect the organization's survival. Major shareholders include customers, suppliers, regulatory agencies, shareholders and creditors. After identifying the relevant stakeholders and forces in the environment, management should assess their characteristics and relative importance to the organization. Environmental characteristics basically vary in terms of complexity and dynamism.

Complexity refers to whether characteristics are few and similar (uniform) or many and different (varied)[7]. Nestle presents a complex environment. The food major has 500 factories in 76 countries and sells its products in a staggering 193 nations almost every country in the world. The company has employees strength of more than 2,10,000. It is the world's biggest maker of infant formula, powdered milk, chocolates, instant coffee, soups, and mineral waters. It is number two in ice cream breakfast cereals and pet food. Roughly, 38 percent of its food sales occurs in Europe, 32 percent in the Americans and 20 percent in Africa and Asia. The company owns 8,500 brands, 750 of these registered in more than one country and 80 are registered in more than 10 countries. In 1998, Nestle grossed sales worth $ 51 billion.

Not a big player like Nestle but a name to be reckoned in India in the food industry is Gujarat Co-operative Milk Marketing Federation, popularity known by its larger than life brand Amul. Amul's environment presents a picture of less complexity. The Rs. 2258 cr. (2000), Amul has just 40 product categories, 300 stock keeping units, 100,000 retailers with refrigerators, 18000 cold chain and 500,000 non-refrigerated retail outlets. Amul's operations are confined mainly to India.

Managing the characteristics of Nestle's is more difficult and challenging than that of Amul.

Dynamism relates to whether environmental characteristics remain basically the same (are stable) or change (are unstable). Unstable characteristics demand revision in organization designs. Dynamism also relates to the need for speed in responding to customers and stakeholders' demands. Organizations increasingly must be able to respond quickly and flexibly.

Environmental richness is a function of the amount of resources available to support an organization. In rich environments, resources are plentiful and uncertainty is low because organizations need not compete for resources. In poor environments, resources are scarce and uncertainty is high because organizations have to compete for the scarce resources.

Environment may be poor for two reasons: (1) The organization is located in a poor country or in a poor region of a country, (2) There is a high level of competition, and organizations are fighting over available resources.[8] In poor environments, organizations need to battle out to attract customers or to obtain the best inputs or the latest technology. The end result of these battles is greater uncertainty for the organization.

Take IT industry for instance. People talk so much about China and even replicating Silicon Valley in that country. But the reality is different. China's firms can boast of little useful intellectual property and no paradigm - bending industrial innovations. China's equity markets are largely closed to private startups, starving entrepreneurs of capital. Its software industry pales besides India's and its stunted pharmaceutical sector has not come up with a single new drug. The country has yet to curb wide spread piracy, suppresses free speech and censors the Internet. China does not have enough number of graduates in science and engineering .[(9)] Obivously, an IT firm desiring to establish operations in China needs to struggle to obtain required quality inputs.

Contrast is India. India is the only country that figures in the high-quality-low -cost segments of the quality cost-matrix. The cost of doing off-shore software development in India is 30 to 80 per cent lower as compared to development in Europe or the U.S. India also has a talent base with enormous potential. It has the world's second largest pool of English speaking scientific manpower. It churns out a huge number of engineers every year and there are plans to triple that number by 2008. More important, the large number of Indian entrepreneurs who have made it big at Silicon Valley has brought a high reputation to the Indian IT industry. No wonder, more than 260 of Fortune 1000 companies outsourced their critical software development from India in the year 2000. The Forrester study conducted in Nov.2001, identified several strengths of India's IT industry. More striking of them are: the country's decade –old experience in the IT area and supportive government policies.[10] IT industry in China generated just $ 850 million revenue in 2001 but in India the revenue in the same year was $ 6 billion. No wonder, Tatas, Wipro, Infosys and Satyam made such great strides in India.

Strategy Choices Many of the top management's choices affect organization design decisions. Strategic choice enable an organization to capitalize on its unique capabilities. Companies need to distinguish and position themselves differently from their competitions in order to build and sustain competitive advantage. Companies have three strategies to build competitive advantage: low cost, differentiation and focused. (See Fig 5.2). Each of these choices affects organization design.

FIGURE 5-2
STRATEGY MODEL

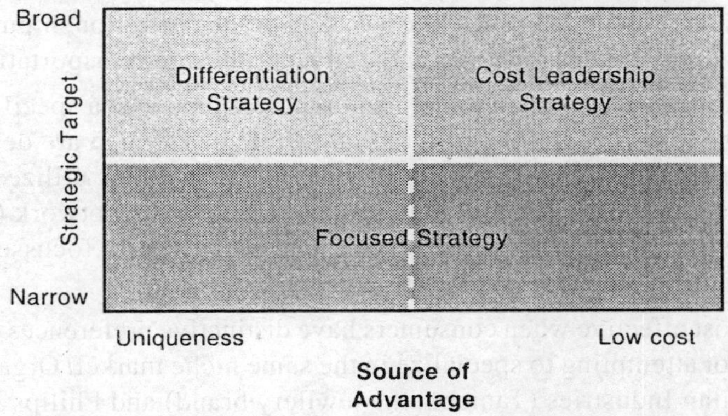

(*Source:* Don Hellriegel, *et. al., op. cit.*, p. 478)

Low cost An organization adopting low cast strategy to gain competitive advantage seeks to offer goods and services to customers at costs lower than its rivals. Such a strategy aims at selling a standardized product that appeals to an average customer in a broad market. The organization must attain significant economies of scale in its operations. Because the environment is stable and uniform, few product modifications are needed to satisfy customers. The organization's design is functional (explained later), with accountability and responsibility clearly assigned to various departments.

Nirma in India has followed low cost strategy and has succeeded in garnering significant market shares in detergents. Similarly Amul follows cost leadership strategy for its ice cream. There are risks associated with low cost strategy. They are: (i) getting "locked in" to a technology and organization design that is expensive to change, (2) the ability of competitors to copy the strategy, and (3) the management not paying attention to changes in the environment.[11]

Differentiation A differentiation strategy is based on providing customers with something that is unique and makes the organization's product or service distinctive from its competitors. An organization that chooses a differentiation strategy typically uses a product design (explained later in this Chapter) where by each product has its own manufacturing and R & D facilities. The key assumption behind this strategy is that customers are waiting to pay a higher price for a product that is distinctive in some way.

A differentiation strategy should be pursued only after careful study of buyer's needs and preferences, to determine the feasibility of incorporating one or more differentiating features into a unique product. A successful differentiation strategy allows a firm to charge a higher price for its product and to gain customer loyalty since customers may become strongly attached to the differentiation features. Special features to differentiate one's product can include superior service, spare parts availability, engineering design, product performance, long life, or ease of use.

A risk of pursing a differentiation strategy is that the unique product may not be valued highly by the customers to justify the higher price. When this happens, a cost leadership strategy will easily defeat a differentiation strategy. Another risk of pursuing a differentiation strategy is that competitors may develop ways to quickly copy the differentiating features. Organizations thus must find durable sources of uniqueness that cannot be quickly or cheaply imitated by rival firms.

A few organizations that have followed differentiation strategy include manufactures of Orient Fans and Captain Cook. Gati, a multimodal transport company, differentiated its services in a highly competitive and uniform market with tangibles like a risk insurance offer for shipments, refund on failure to deliver on time, door- to -door pick up and delivery and safe transportation.

Focused A focused strategy is designed to help an organization target a specific niche with in an industry, unlike both the low-cost and the differentiate strategies, which are designed to target industry wide markets. An organization that chooses a focused strategy may utilize any of a variety of organization designs, ranging from functional to product to matrix to network (explained later in this chapter), to satisfy their customers' preferences. The basic idea in focussed strategy is to specialize in ways that rival firms cannot match effectively.

Focus strategies are most effective when consumers have distinctive preferences or requirements and when rival firms are not attempting to specialize in the same niche market. Organizations using focus strategies include Titan Industries (Tanishq, the jewllery brand) and Philips India (flat TV).

The risks of pursuing a focused strategy include the possibility that numerous competitors recognise the successful focus strategy and copy it; or the market niche may gradually shift towards a broader market. Distinctive customer tastes may blur over time, thus reducing the defensibility of the niche.

Technological Factors Technology has significant impact on organization design in terms of the creation of teams and departments, the delegation of authority and responsibility, sequence of operations and tasks and deciding who is standing where and who is reporting to whom.

The most critical aspects of technology is complexity.

Technological Complexity Viewed from complexity, three types of technology may be distinguished-small batch production technology, mass production technology and continuous process technology (See Fig.5.3). Each of these types has influence on design decisions because each technology presents different control and coordination problems.

Small – Batch Production Here products are custom –produced to meet customer specifications or they are made in small quantities primarily by craft specialists. The main coordination problem associated with this technology is the impossibility of programming activities because production depends on the skills and experience of people working together. An organization that uses small – batch technology needs to give people the freedom to make their own decisions so that they can respond quickly and flexibly to the customer's requests and produce the exact product that the customer wants. For this reason, such an organization has a relatively flat structure (three levels in the hierarchy), and decision making is decentralized to small teams where first-line supervisors have a relatively small span of control (23 employees). With small batch technology, each supervisor and work group decides how to mange each decision as it occurs at each step of the production process. This type of decision making requires mutual adjustment – face – to – face communication with coworkers and often with customers. The most appropriate structure for small-batch technology is an organic structure in which managers and employees work closely to coordinate their activities to meet changing work demands. Hence the relatively flat structure shown in Fig 5.3.[12]

In *mass production technology*, products are manufactured in large quantities, frequently on an assembly line. In organizations using this type of technology, the ability to programme tasks in advance allows them to standardize the manufacturing process and make it predictable. The first-

FIGURE 5-3

TECHNICAL COMPLEXITY AND ORGANISATION DESIGN

Low → Technical Complexity → High

Structural Characteristics	**Small – Batch Technology**	**Mass Production Technology**	**Continuous Process Technology**
Levels in the hierarchy	3	4	6
Span of control of CEO	4	7	10
Span of control of first line supervisor	23	48	15
Ratio of managers to nonmanagers	1 to 23	1 to 16	1 to 8
Approximate shape of organization	 *Relatively flat, with narrow span of control*	 *Relatively tall, with wide span of control*	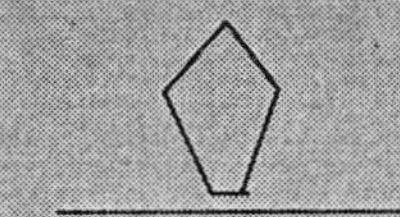 *Very tall, with very narrow span of control*
Type of structure	Organic	Mechanistic	Organic
Cost of operation	High	Medium	Low

(***Source:*** Gareth R. Jones, *Organisational Theory,* p. 366)

line supervisor's span of control increases to 48, because formalization through rules and procedures becomes the principal method of coordination. Decision making becomes centralized and the hierarchy becomes taller (four levels) as managers rely on vertical communication to control the work process. A mechanistic design becomes relevant in order to control work activities in mass production setting and the organizational structure becomes taller and wider, as shown in Fig 5.3.

In *continuous production technology,* products are liquids, solids, or gases that are made through a continuous process. Examples are petroleum products. In this technology, tasks can be programmed in advance, and the work process is predictable and controllable in a technical sense, but there is still the potential for a major systems breakdown. The major problem facing the organization is monitoring the production process to control and correct unforeseen events before they lead to disaster. The consequences of a faulty pipeline in an oil refinery or a chemical plant, for example, are potentially disastrous. Accidents at a nuclear power plant, another user of continuous process technology, can also have catastrophic effects, as accidents at Chernobyl and Three Mile Island showed.[13]

The need to constantly monitor the operating system, and to make sure that each employee conforms to accepted operating procedures, is the reason why continuous process technology is associated with the tallest hierarchy (six levels). Managers at all levels closely monitor their subordinate actions. The diamond shaped hierarchy shown in Fig 5.3 reflects the fact that first-line supervisors have a narrow span of control. Many supervisors are needed to supervise lower-level employees and to monitor and control sophisticated equipment. Because employees also work together as a team and jointly work out procedures for managing and reacting to unexpected situations, mutual adjustment becomes the primary means of co ordination. Thus, an organic design is appropriate for managing continuous process technology, because the potential for unpredictable events requires the capability to provide quick and flexible responses.

Internal Contingency Factors There are many internal forces which have their impact on organizational design. Three most important of them are: (a) organizational goals, (b) size of the organization, and (c) employee characteristics.

Goals The process of organizational design begins with a strategic decision concerning an organization's goals. Over the long run, organizations must provide returns to society and satisfy investors, suppliers, distributors and customers, while operating within governmental, labour and other constraints. Over time, organizations develop a set of goals capable of satisfying these competing groups. Some organizations operate as if flexibility and adaptability were essential to survive. Some emphasise technical superiority. Thus, the relative emphasis of an organization's goals on flexibility, technical superiority, or efficiency is critically important when its managers select an overall structural configuration for the organization.

Organization Size Size of the organization is an important variable which has considerable influence on structure. A small size means more informal structure. Personal relationship but not policies, procedures and rules that matter in task performance.

As the organization grows in size, things tend to become formalized. Manuals, policies, procedures and rules take precedence. Organization becomes bureaucratic. (See Table 5.1)

TABLE 5-1

RELATIONSHIP BETWEEN SIZE AND DESIGN DIMENSIONS

Basic Design Dimensions	*Small Organizations*	*Large Organizations*
Formalization	Less	More
Centralization	High	Low
Specialization	Low	High
Standardization	Low	High
Complexity	Low	High
Hierarchy of authority	Flat	Tall

Organizations attempt to deal with the drift towards bureaucracy by geographically spreading operations and people, empowering employees and downsizing staff strength. There is also a tendency to assign more and more people to specialized roles.

Employee Characteristics Some employees prefer highly structured organizations while others rebel against them. This behaviour may be attributed to age, education, intelligence, and experience of employees.

Old people feel secured in bureaucratic structure but younger ones expect voice in decision - making process. Many young employees are also reluctant to accept the rigid rules and regulations employed by formal organizations.

Better *educated* employees expect participation in decision-making and control processes. Among highly educated personnel, a more flexible organizational structure is likely, with less attention paid to the enforcement of rules and regulations and more to reliance on adhoc groups and informal cooperation to get the work done.

The third employee characteristic is *intelligence*. The higher the individual's intellect, the less likely he or she will accept bureaucratic rules. One obvious reason is that such people often formulate shortcuts which circumvent the rules but get the work done more efficiently. As a result, they are continuously at loggerheads with the bureaucrats, who want things done by the book.[14]

Employee *experience* also influences organizational design. A newly hired employee seeks guidance. Close control may also be needed. Once the employee learns the job, less control is enough. Better experienced the employees are, more flexible organization do they prefer.

TYPES OF ORGANIZATION DESIGN

Having considered the various factors that affect an organization design, let us consider some of the popular designs practised by companies. As we discuss them, we refer to the factors that influence each design.

FUNCTIONAL DESIGN

The oldest and most commonly used design is the functional type. When it is used, the organization is departmentalized on the basis of functions it needs to perform to reach its objectives. Thus, one can see marketing, materials management, production, finance and accounting, personnel and maintenance departments in the functional design of a company engaged in manufacturing (see Fig 5.4). The activities or functions of all these departments are coordinated by the chief executive of the organization. A common theme of functional design proponents is the desirability of standardizing repetitive tasks and making them routine wherever possible. This approach helps reduce errors and lowers costs. Managers can concentrate on exceptions to eliminate any gaps or overlaps.

FIGURE 5-4
FUNCTIONAL DESIGN

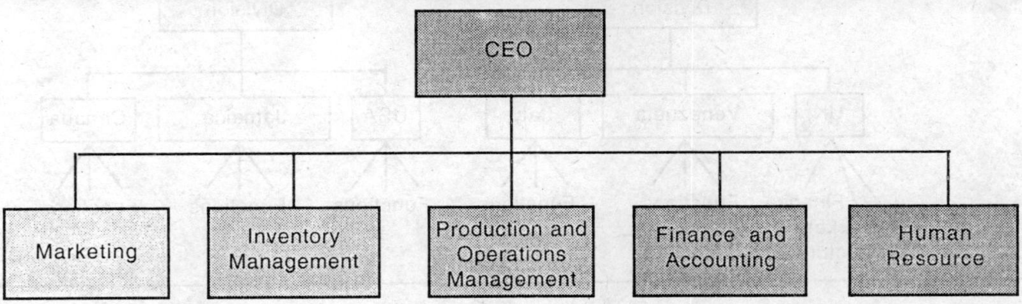

A functional design has both advantages and disadvantages. On the positive side it may be stated that the design permits division of labour and encourages specialization. Secondly, it is easily understood by the employees. It needs no specialized knowledge for them to understand that there are several departments, each performing a separate function, and all departments must work in unison to achieve an organization's goals. Third, functional design eliminates duplication. There is only one marketing department for the entire enterprise, only one production department and so on.

A disadvantage is that the functional design fosters a limited point of view that focuses on a narrow set of tasks. Employees may lose sight of the organization as a whole. Second, horizontal integration across functional departments often becomes difficult as the organization increases the number of geographic areas served and the range of goods and services provided. Third, there is no accountability of each function for total results. Each department functions as a stand-alone unit.

A functional design may be effective when an organization has a narrow product line, competes in a uniform environment, pursues a low-cost or focused business strategy, and does not have to respond to the pressures of serving difficult types of customers. The addition of specialized staff departments to a functional design may enable an organization to lead effectively with same degree of environment uncertainty and dynamism. Staff experts many provide line officers with expert advice, such as dealing with certain technologies.[15] Functional design no doubt is the oldest and simplest form, but it is the most elementary type of design and often represents a base from which other types of design evolve.

PLACE DESIGN

Place design involves establishing an organization's primary units geographically while retaining significant elements of functional design. Popularity called the geographic area design, place design permits locating many tasks required to serve a geographic territory under one manager, rather than grouping functions under different managers or all tasks in one cultural office. (see Fig 5.5).

FIGURE 5-5
PLACE DESIGN

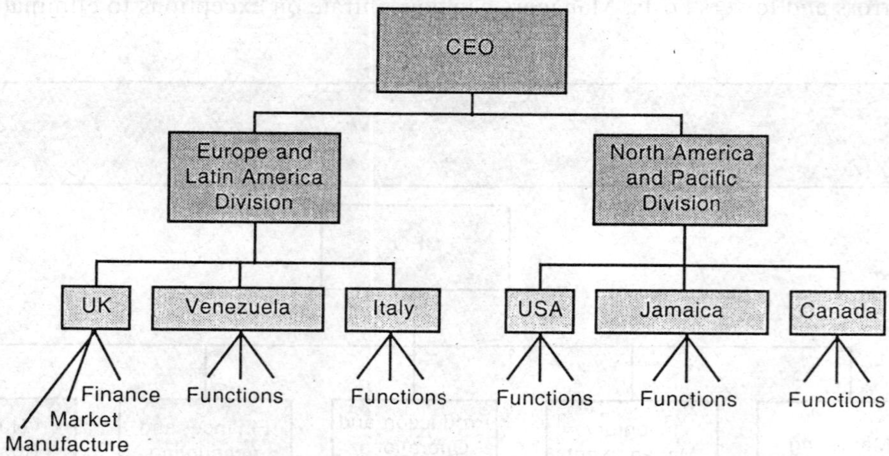

Place design is popularity used by multinational corporations which need to be responsive to local needs. In the U.S. soft drinks have less sugar than in S. America, so the manufacturing process must be slightly different in these two locals. Similarly, in England people prefer bland soups, but Indians enjoy spicy soups. In Turkey, Italy, Spain, and Portugal people prefer a milder and sweeter blend. Geographic design can respond to these performances in tastes easily.

One disadvantage of the geographic area design stems form the duplication of functions. As Fig 5.5 shows, functions are duplicated in all locations. Second, there is the problem of lack of communication among divisions. Third, diffusion of technology is slow as innovations generated in one division (area) may not be adopted quickly by others. Obivously, this arrangement may be suitable for products undergoing rapid technological changes. Finally, employees may begin to emphasise their own geographically based division's goals and needs more than those of the organization as a whole.

A geographic area design is most likely to be used in an organization whose products are not easily transferable across regions and which pursues polycentric corporate philosophy. Nestle and Cadbury are well known organizations using area design. Ranbaxy, an Indian firm has an area design. The company has divided the world in to four regions-India and the Middle East, Europe, CIS and Africa, the Asia Pacific and America.[16]

PRODUCT DESIGN

The product design assigns worldwide responsibility for specific products or product groups to separate operating divisions within a firm. As Fig 5.6 shows, the manager who is incharge of product division has authority for the product line on a global basis.

FIGURE 5-6
GLOBAL PRODUCT DESIGN

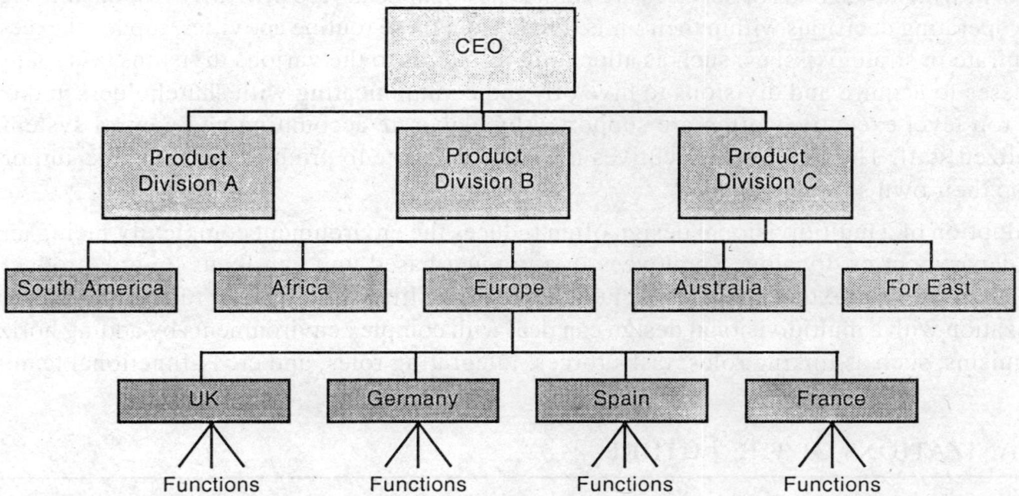

The product designs operate as profit centers. Managers of product division run the operations with considerable autonomy, they have the authority to make important decisions. But, corporate headquarters usually maintain control in terms of budgetary constraints and home office approval for key decisions.

Product design too is mostly followed in global enterprises, though its application in domestic business is not uncommon. When used in a multinational corporation, product design takes the shape as shown in Fig 5.6

A number of benefits are associated with product design. If an organization produces a large number of diverse produces, as in HLL or Motorola, the design allow each major product line to focus on the specific needs of its customers. This would be difficult to achieve if the organization were selling all its product out of one centralized marketing department. Second, under the product design, the company is able to match its marketing strategy to the specific needs of the customers. Third, because managers possess extensive knowledge, they are more able to incorporate new technologies into their products and respond quickly and easily to technological changes that affect their market. Fourth, the product design is an attractive alternative to a functional design when environment and technological factors for each product line are different. Organizations with a product design usually begin with a functional design and then add some place design features as they begin to serve new geographic markets. Eventually, serving multiple customers creates management problems that cannot be effectively dealt with by a functional or a place design alone.

The addition of new product lines, diverse customers, and technological advances also increases the complexity and uncertainity of the company's business environment. When changing to a product design, companies usually do not completely discard functional or place designs. Instead, the product design may incorporate features of functional and place designs into the organization of each product division.

Multidivisional Design

A variation of the product design is the multidivisional design, often referred to as the M-form. In *multidivisional* design, tasks are organized by divisions on the basis of the product or geographic markets in which the goods or services are sold. Divisional heads are primarily responsible for day-to-day operating decisions within their units. Freed from these routine activities, top level executives concentrate in strategy issues, such as allocating resources to the various divisions, assessing new businesses to acquire and divisions to hive off, and communicating with shareholders and others. These top level executives often are supported by elaborate accounting and control systems and specialized staff. The top-level executives may also delegate to product divisions the authority to develop their own strategic plans.[17]

Adoption of a multidivisional design often reduces the environment complexity facing any one team, department or division. Employees in a product based unit can focus on one product line, rather than be overextended across multiple product lines. As with a functional design, an organization with a multidivisional design can deal with complex environments by adding horizontal mechanisms, such as linking roles, tasks forces, integrating roles, and cross-functional teams.[18]

Organizations of the Future

Four types of organization design–matrix, network, virtual, and learning – have emerged in response to certain deficiencies in conventional designs and to rapid advances in technology.

Matrix Design

The most complex form of organization design is the matrix one. The matrix design emerges when one design is superimposed on top of an existing, but different form. The resulting design is quite fluid, with new matrix dimensions being created, escalated, reduced or eliminated as needed. Three features make matrix design distinct from the traditional ones. First, there are managers who report to two different matrix bosses; second, there are the matrix managers who share the subordinates;

and third, there is the top manager who is expected to head the dual structure and balance and adjudicate disputes.[19] (See Fig 5.7).

FIGURE 5-7
MATRIX DESIGN

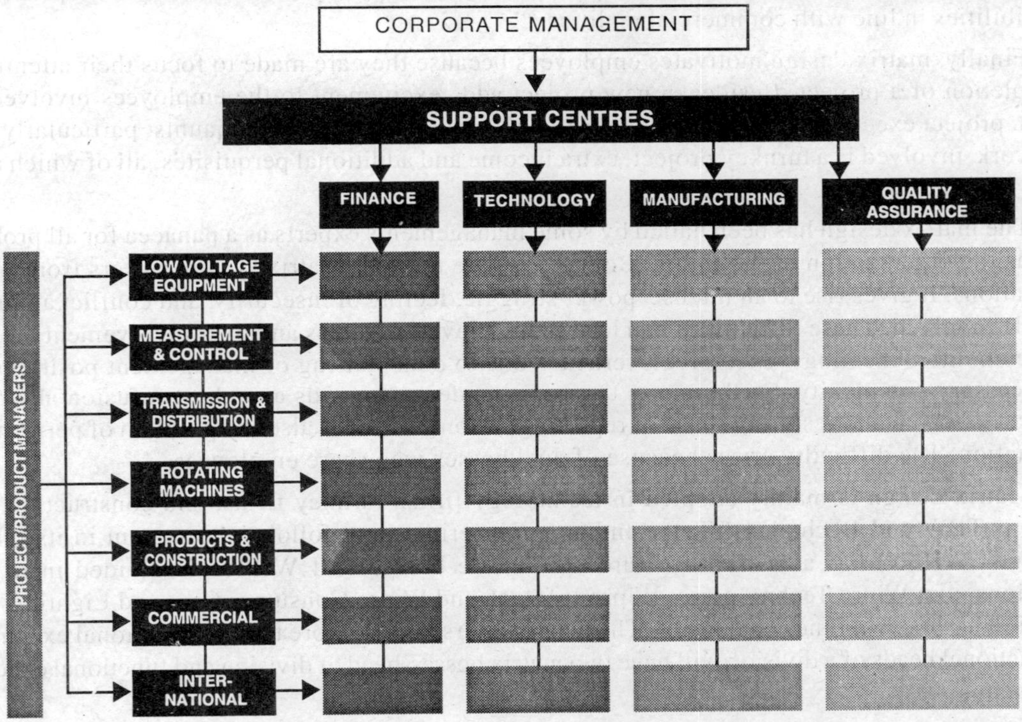

As shown in Fig 5.7 functional design is overlaid on product design. One chain of command in the matrix design is exercised by the functional managers. This authority flows vertically. The second line of command is exercised by the project managers. This line of command flows horizontally. Because the lines of command flow vertically and horizontally, the matrix design is also called the "multiple command" system.

A matrix design has several advantages over more traditional designs. First, the use of cross-functional teams is designed to reduce functional barriers and overcome the problem of subunit orientation. With differences between functions kept to a minimum, integration becomes easier to achieve. The matrix design is basically flexible and is capable of quickly responding to changing product and customer needs.

A second advantage of the matrix design is that it opens up communication between functional specialists and provide an opportunity for team members from different functions to learn from one another and develop their skills. Thus, matrix design facilitates technological progress because the interactions of different specialists produce the innovations that give an organization its core competences.

Third, the matrix enables an organization to maximize its use of skilled professionals, who move from product to product as needed. At the beginning of a project, for example, basic skills of engineers are needed to design and make the product. People move around the matrix to whenever they are most needed; team membership is constantly changing to suit the needs of the product.

Fourth, the dual focus promotes concern for both cost and quality. The primary goal of functional specialists is likely to be technical-producing the highest quality and most innovative product possible. In contrast, the primary goals of product managers are likely to concern cost and speed of development. This built in focus on both quality and cost keeps the team on track and keeps technical possibilities in line with commercial realities.[20]

Finally, matrix design motivates employees because they are made to focus their attention on completion of a project. Besides, a new project adds excitement to the employees involved. For them, project execution may involve visits to new places or even foreign jaunts; particularly when the work involved is a turnkey project; extra income and additional perquisites; all of which add to their motivation.

The matrix design has been hailed by some managements experts as a panacea for all problems and as the organization of the future. Both claims are too tall. Matrix system suffers from serious limitations. It gives rise to an intense power struggle, feeling of insecurity, and conflict among the people involved. These difficulties can lead to high levels of stress and over involvement on group and committee meetings, excessive overheads due to dual staffing of management positions, and unnecessary complexity. Furthermore, there is a tendency towards anarchy-confusion about who reports to whom and resulting sense of reporting to none. There is also the problem of performance evaluation. The difficulty arises because of dual bosses who share employees.

Matrix design is mainly adopted in technology firms, turnkey firms, and construction firms such as TRW and Bechtel. L&T, the Indian engineering giant follows the system in its turnkey projects. WIPRO has a matrix structure. The entire business of WIPRO is divided in to three divisions, viz; Wipro Technologies, Wipro Infotech and Wipro Consumer Care and Lighting. Each division has its own functional heads. The headquarters at Bangalore too has functional executives. A functional heads of a division will have two matrix bosses-head of division and functional executive at headquarters.

Many organizations have started rethinking about the usefulness of the matrix design. Siemens, for example, found the design less suitable for its global operations and has developed a hybrid system, which the company believes will make it more competitive in the international market. Dow Chemicals, instead of abandoning the matrix design, is trying to build 'flexibility' into the system.

Networked Design

A networked design is a cluster of different organizations whose actions are coordinated by contracts and agreements rather than through a formal hierarchy of authority. [21] More often one organization takes the lead in creating the network as it searches for a way to increase effectiveness. As shown in Fig 5.8 the network design typically consists of several satellite organizations beehived around a core firm. The core firm coordinates the network process and provides one or two other cone competencies, such as marketing or product development. Networked design offers flexibility, innovation, quick responses to threats and opportunities and reduced costs and risks. Networked designs accommodate strategic alliances among competing firms.

FIGURE 5-8
NETWORKED DESIGN

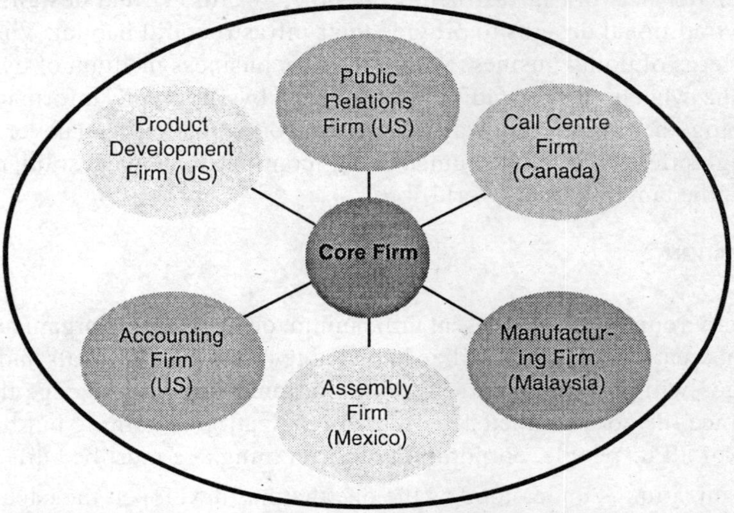

(***Source:*** Steven L. McShane and Mary Ann Von Glinow, *Organisational Behaviour,* Tata McGraw-Hill, 2000, p.581)

VIRTUAL ORGANIZATION

Closely related to networked design is the virtual organization. The term virtual organization represents the new Information Age. The design represents any productive system that enables individuals separated by distance and/or time to work together towards a common goal. Almost inevitably, virtual organizations rely upon computer-mediated communications technologies to bridge the previously insurmountable barriers between their members.[22] Stated more simply, in virtual organizations people use a computer network to work cooperatively and share knowledge quickly and easily regardless of time, distance and organizational boundaries. A virtual organization typically exhibits the following characteristics:

- A reliance for their functioning and survival upon the medium of cyberspace.
- No readily identifiable physical form.
- Boundaries defined and limited solely by the available information technology.[23]

Virtual organization is the latest type of design that managers use to satisfy customer demands. A virtual design permits manager to change an organization's structure quickly to meet changing conditions and situations. Internal departments, job responsibilities, and lines of authority are shifted as needed. Boundaries between an organization and its customers and suppliers are blurred; infact, some customers and suppliers begin to spend more time in the organization than some of its own employees.

- Employees of virtual organization respond quickly to changing customer demands with customized products and services available at any time and place.
- Employees are reciprocally interdependent. The entire workforce must be capable of mastering all the competencies needed to service customers effectively, and

- Managers delegate authority and responsibility to employees while providing them with a clear vision of the organization's goals.

Having said this, it may be stated that any virtual organization can only exist across physical hardware of a computer network infrastructure. In other words, virtual designs though flexible, depend upon more traditional designs to provide their infrastructural habitat. Virtual organization represents new patterns of doing business within the new business medium of cyberspace. Virtual organizations oil the wheels of the traditional economy by supplying information services and linking employees together in different ways. Yet virtual organizations can never replace their real counterparts as long as flesh- and-blood human beings continue to demand solid, physical products and services within the tangible 'real' world.[24]

Learning Organization

In the competitive environment of the present millennium, only a learning organization will survive. Its abilities to learn, create, codify, and utilize knowledge faster than its rivals and quicker than the environment changes-will provide tomorrow's corporation a competitive edge that is sustainable for ever. Indeed, since the core competence of any organization is nothing but the individual and collective learning of all its people, corporation of the coming age must be built around people.

A learning organization is understood as the one that has developed the capacity to adopt and change. Learning organizations, like individuals, constantly learn. In a learning organization, old shibboleth are demolished and a new order is created - a new order that not only encourages managers to look at their people differently, but actually teaches them to look at the world afresh.

Characteristics of the Learning Organization One of the leaders in the field of the learning organization is Senge. His book, *The Fifth Discipline,* puts forward a view that the old methods and procedures of quality improvement, learning from mistakes, and the like are insufficient to enable organizations to survive in the future. Senge puts forward five 'compact technologies' as prerequisites if an organization wishes to become learning focused.

(i) *System thinking:* Managers need to be aware of the open linkages between their own actions and the actions of those around them, within and outside the organization. Senge's view is that managers do not fully grasp a systems perspective because they only perceive and act upon one aspect of a problem rather than understand the broader perspective.

(ii) *Personal mastery:* Organizations need to encourage their employees to continually learn and improve their own skills and abilities. Traditionally organizations have sought to train and develop a select few with the rest placed on a career 'scenic routine'. Senge argues that organizations have wasted a valuable resource by not encouraging all individuals to become constant learning organisms.

(iii) *Mental models:* Mental models are deeply embedded assumptions and generalizations we all carry regarding how the world works and our own actions. It is often subconscious, yet can influence our behaviour in organizations substantially. Senge's view is that these mental models can serve as powerful constraints in an organization's ability to gain new insight and innovations.

(iv) *Building shared vision:* Senge has observed that, throughout history, a shared vision has been a critical component to organizational success. There is an important difference between a vision built around a charismatic leader-which is often transitory - and that built around shared goals. For the development of a learning organization, the building and maintenance of a shared vision offers individuals the support to excel and learn. To develop a shared vision involves communicating descriptions of what the future might hold rather than seeking compliance to a prescribed view.

(v) *Team learning:* Working and sharing information among team members is a vital element of the learning organization. Senge recognizes that many teams exhibit signs of negative synergy of groupthink. Senge stresses the need to overcome such difficulties by encouraging meaningful dialogue. This is accomplished by seeking to suspend assumptions and judgement and to engage in 'free-thinking' with other group members. Table 5.2 contrasts learning organization from its traditional counterpart.

TABLE 5-2
TRADITIONAL VERSUS LEARNING ORGANISATION

Function	*Traditional Organization*	*Learning Organization*
Determination of overall Direction	Vision is provided by top management	There is shared vision that can emerge from many places, but top management is responsible for ensuring that this vision exists and is nurtured.
Formulation and implementation of ideas	Top management decides what is to be done, and the rest of the organization acts on these ideas.	Formulation and implementation of ideas take place at all level of the organization.
Nature of organizational thinking	Each person is responsible for his or her own job responsibilities, and the focus is on developing individual competence.	Personnel understanding their own jobs as well as the way in which their own work interrelates with and influences that of other personnel.
Conflict resolution	Conflicts are resolved through the use of power and hierarchical influence	Conflicts are resolved through the use of collaborative learning and the integration of diverse viewpoints of personnel through out the organization.
Leadership and motivation	The role of the leader is to establish the organization's vision, provide rewards and punishment as appropriate, and maintain overall control of employee activities	The role of the leader is to build a shared vision, empower the personnel, inspire commitment, and encourage effective decisions making through out the enterprise through the use of empowerment and charismatic leadership.

(***Source:*** Fred Luthans, *Organizational Behaviour*, McGraw-Hill, 2000, p.115.)

Creating the Learning Organization At least four sets of capabilities are needed to create a learning organization. They are:

(i) Capabilities of scanning necessary for exposing the organizations to new information, crated internally or acquired externally.

(ii) Capabilities for self-reflection and problem- solving to enable the firm to interpret new information and redefine business knowledge.

(iii) Capabilities to disseminate the new knowledge throughout the organization so that it becomes collective learning.

(iv) Capabilities to act and experiment to enable the organization to practise the new responses it has learnt.

In order to acquire and inculcate these traits in people, there is the need for a shift in the mindset. In the meantime, managers may initiate action on the following lines to create a learning organization:

- Managers must be receptive to the new ideas and overcome the desire to closely monitor and control operations.
- Systems thinking among mangers in the organization needs to be cultivated.
- It is necessary to keep the organization in a state of constant change.
- Diversities need to be cultivated in the functioning of the organizations.
- Create mechanism to unlearn old and obsolete knowledge.
- Disseminate learning throughout the organization systematically.
- Develop a sense of personal efficacy among organizational members.

Need for Learning Organization As the opening paragraph in this section shows, only a learning organization shall survive the emerging competitive global economy. A fundamental revolution (in the form of learning organization) in the theory and practice of management may be vital for India's competitiveness. But even more important, it may prove vital for harnessing the capacities of the Indians to grow and develop their country and address its many critical social and business needs. Table 5.3 brings the need for learning organizations into sharp focus.

TABLE 5-3

NEED FOR LEARNING ORGANISATION

Learning organization is essential because-

- Only it can survive tomorrow's knowledge-based economy.
- Only it can manage tomorrow's intense global competition.
- Only it can cope with tomorrow's rapid fire technological changes
- Only it can handle tomorrow's demanding and fragmented market
- Only it can build a people based work system in a company.

(***Source:*** *Business Today*, Jan. 7-21, 1996).

Lean Production Systems (LPS)

Japan is home of the genisis of lean production systems. Thanks to LPS, Toyota's development time and defects were cut by 50 per cent. Five principles make LPS unique. They are: team work, quality control, customer focus, minimal inventory buffers, and continuous improvement. These principles are not new, but what is new is that all these were integrated and applied in Japanese firms effectively.

Away from Japan, British manufacturing practices, particularly in certain companies (Nissan UK, Ford), were altered over the 1980s and 1990s as a result of the influence of the philosophy of LPS. Output per person has risen considerably; outdated work practices and management have been discorded; there has been a commitment to exacting quality standards and continuous improvement; cooperative working relationships between key constituencies (e.g., workers, managers, suppliers) have been developed; there is a strong emphasis on measurement (e.g., detecting faults and taking remedial action); and a healthier relationship with trade unions.[25]

High Performance Systems (HPS)

HPS borrows concepts from lean production systems but they are distinctive in their own right, and appear to work well in countries where individualism is strong, lifetime employment is weak, and shareholders are powerful-all these point out to the USA. In fact, HPS found takers in AT&T, DuPont, Ford, HP, IBM, Kodak and Xerox. HPS are governed by the following principles:[26]

- customer-focused operating units
- devolved decision making
- streamlined management control, including tighter financial control
- re-engineering of business processes

Customer-focused operating units Organisations obtain reactions from customers, using techniques such as market survey and focus groups, and feed this information directly to managers of operating units. These data would be considered as input in key decision-making processes, including employee selection and performance management.

The rationale for customer focus is that the organizations are more likely to be responsive to changing market trends if managements have routine contact with customers. In such a process, interests and concerns of customers are given serious consideration in important decision-making processes like employee selection, reward systems for creative and effective employees, and the like. In the annual performance appraisal of AT&T executives, for example, one of the criteria used is customer-value added. South West Airlines sought the help of a particular category of customers (frequent fliers) in some of its hiring events.

Devolved decision making In many organizations authority is pushed down the hierarchy giving operating units greater power. This is done by replacing functional groups in organizations (e.g., marketing, finance) with Strategic Business Units (SBUs). SBUs are broad product categories within which are housed functional specializations. An SBU could be subdivided into small operating units. These units are customer oriented, with authority for formulating strategies, and are held responsible for results. The number of SBUs within an organization varies widely.

An SBU acts as a stand-alone unit and the managements controlling it feel that they are running a quasi-independent business, and this has obvious motivational implications.

Streamlined management control/tighter financial control At headquarters there are usually lesser layers of management, leading to wider spaces of control and flatter structures. The operating units receive fewer policy directives from headquarters but tougher financial directives.

Re-engineering of business processes Popularly called BPR, re-engineering involves fundamental rethinking and radical redesigning of business processes in order to achieve dramatic improvements in performance. BPR has resulted in rapid increases in productivity wherever it has been applied.

Design Decisions

Whatever design an organization has, it must make four important structure decisions. These decisions are:(1) Whether or not to use staff experts, (2) what shall be the shape of the organization, (3) whether the organization will be structured in a flexible or rigid way, and (4) how the authority will be distributed.[27] Each of these will have considerable influence on organizational behaviour. A brief discussion of the four decisions, therefore, is in order.

Use of Staff Officers A new organization which has grown successfully over a period exhibits a design as shown in Fig 5.9. This is a "line" organization, wherein all the positions in the organization are in the direct line of authority from the top of the company down to the bottom. Each level in the organization is subordinated to the one above it and there are no advisory specialists. This might work well as long as the company does not grow too large. However, with increased growth the need for specialized experts will emerge. If these specialists are added to the organization, the structure will be called "line and staff" structure. The experts generally include researchers, economists, legal advisers, industrial engineers, and cost accountants (see Fig 5.10).

FIGURE 5-9
LINE ORGANISATION

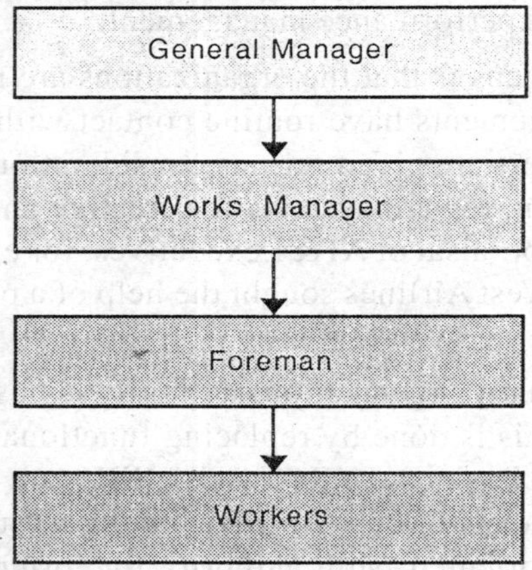

The line-staff emerged as a response to the increasing environmental and functional complexity facing organizations. As firms became larger and more functions were added, it became impossible for managers to keep up with the latest technical developments in their functional area and perform their day to day duties. Also, it was recognized that certain functions were more directly related to the organization's goals than were others. In the military, for example, the "line" engaged in battles, the "staff" provided support functions for those in battle. It is common today in most organizations to find staff units composed of individuals with a great deal of expertise in narrow areas.

The line-staff structure is a method of preserving the authority relationships in organizations in the face of primary and secondary goals. In the line-staff organization, certain functions are considered secondary (staff functions). The principle of line-staff relationship states that line personnel have command authority in their functional areas, staff personnel, on the other hand, are said to have the right to provide advice to line personnel in their(staff) field and expertise. Strictly speaking, it is incorrect to say that line functions are the "most important", since there are instances in which staff functions, secondary in relation to goals, are nevertheless quite important. In these situations, staff people usually possess "functional authority" which can make them equivalent to the line, although such situations are generally temporary.

FIGURE 5-10
LINE AND STAFF STRUCTURE

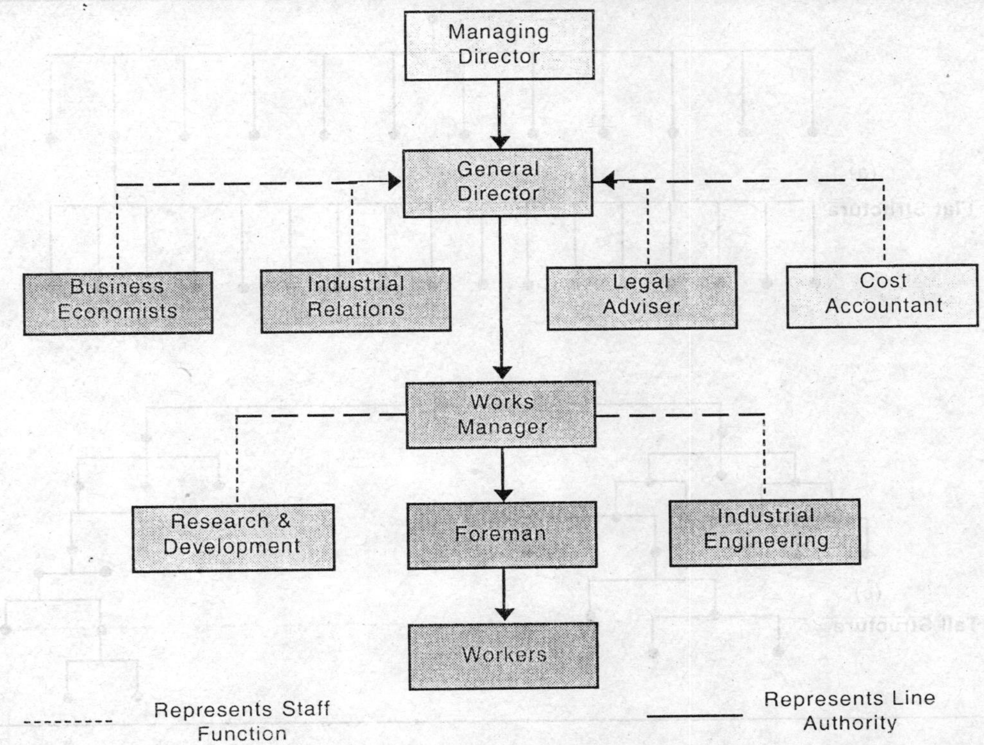

Effect on Behaviour One behavioural implication of line and staff structure is its potential for conflict. Conflict arises between line officers and staff experts and if the conflict is not resolved there will be a flight of people from the organization.

Other behavioral problems that occur in the line-staff structure can be traced to the unity of command principle. Theoretically the line-staff structure is designed to preserve this principle in the light of the existence of primary and secondary organizational objectives. However, because people do not act as mechanically as the organization chart assumes, the system becomes laden with power struggles, influence system, politics and confrontations over authority relationship.

Shape of Organization The shape of an organization refers to the span of control. An organization may have a "tall" structure, wherein the span of control is small, or narrow. A tall design has many hierarchical levels and few workers reporting to each manager. In the alternative, the design may be "flat". The flat design is characterized by large design or wide spans. It has few hierarchical levels and many workers reporting to each manager. As shown in Fig 5.11, two companies with an equal number of employees may have differently shaped designs. Holding the number of employees constant, an increase in the number of levels decreases the span of control, while decreasing the number of levels increases the span of control.

Effect on Behaviour In a tall structure there is scope for increased personal contacts between supervisors and subordinates. The supervisor may create a positive raport with his or she subordinates. The same may not be possible in a flat structure.

FIGURE 5-11
TALL AND FLAT STRUCTURES

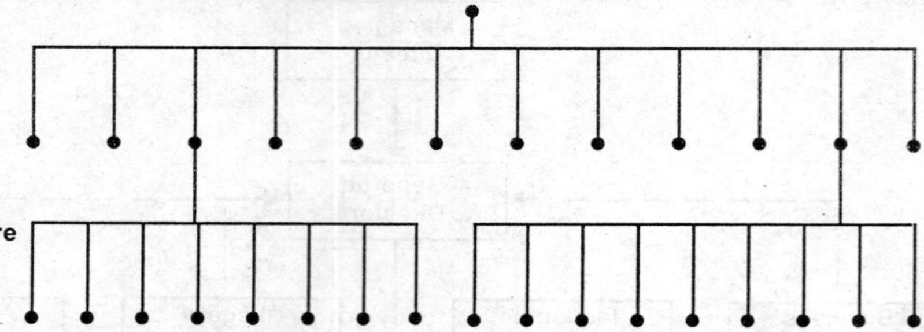

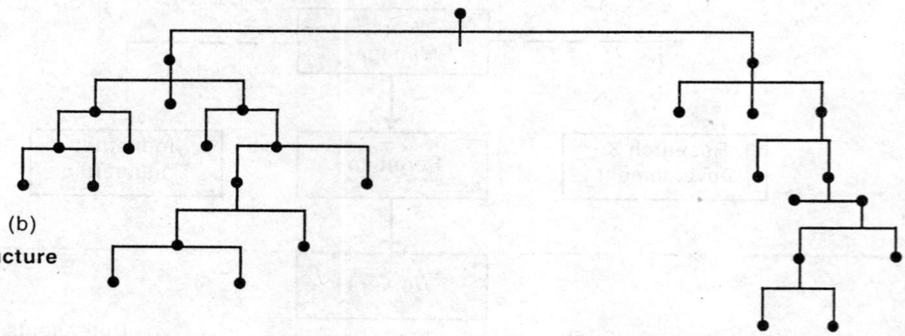

Another behavioural implication is the level of communication. In the flat structure, there are few levels of communication, which means that both downward and upward communications are simplified. There should be less distortion and inaccuracy. The red tape endless communication channels associated with the tall structure are not present in the flat structure.

Overall, from a behavioural point of view, the flat structure is preferable to the tall structure. Employees tend to prefer the structure because it is more free of frequent supervision. They like the autonomy they have, and experience less stress from their job environment. However, manager in the flat structure will have so many people to supervise that they cannot spend much time with any one employee. This can be frustrating for employees who value direct contact with their supervisor. It can also lead to errors by new employees who require training and closer supervision. Table 5.4 compares tall the structure with the flat structure.

Trend towards flat structures It was years ago that the management guru Peter Drucker prophesied in his book. *The New Realities* that only flat structures would survive the 1990's. His prediction has come true, at least in our country. The driving force is competition within and without. A *Business Today* (Dec. 7-21,1993) survey revealed that more than two dozen of the biggest companies were busy reducing the number of management grades, eliminating layers, and redrawing reporting lines within their organizations. ITC, HLL, Godrej & Boyce, RPG Enterprises, Raymond Wollen Mills, Shaw Wallace, and Ballarpur Industries are only some companies which had embarked on the flattening exercise. The survey claimed the following benefits and pitfalls of flat structures:

TABLE 5-4
COMPARISON OF TALL AND FLAT STRUCTURES

Tall Structures	*Flat Structure*
Needed when:	
• Closer control and monitoring is required	• More autonomy and self-control is required
• Mistakes are likely to be costly	• Flexibility and innovation are required
• Tasks/roles are clear: require specialization	• Ambiguous tasks and roles, specialization
• Routine technology	• Non-routine technology
• Inexperienced subordinates	• Experienced subordinates
• Placid, stable environment	• Unstable, turbulent environment

(***Source:*** Madhukar Shukla, *Understanding Organizations*, p.34)

Benefits

(i) Increased growth opportunities for performers.
(ii) Faster decision-making and market response.
(iii) Up-gradation of skills within ranks.
(iv) Better internal communication and interaction
(v) Perceptible decline in overall manpower costs.

Pitfalls

(i) Reduced promotion options for employees.
(ii) Increased work load as layers get trimmed.
(iii) Increased training and development needs.
(iv) Low staff morale during the transition phase.
(v) Rigours of manpower attrition.

Structure Flexibility

Structure flexibility refers to the operating freedom available to an organizational member to perform the tasks assigned to him or her.

With reference to flexibility, there are two distinct structures: "mechanistic" and "organic". The former is characterized by high rigidity, while flexibility is the hallmark of the later. Table 5.5 brings out the contrasting features between the two extremes.

The mechanistic and organic extremes are represented by bureaucracy and matrix structures respectively.

Bureaucracy The term *bureaucracy* often conjures up a host of attributes implying inefficiency, red tapism, paper shuffling, rigid application of rules, and redundance of efforts. This negative connotation is unfortunate since the term, conceived by Max Weber, was originally used to denote an efficient organizational form. Bureaucracy, as conceived by Weber, has the following characteristics:

TABLE 5-5

CHARACTERISTICS OF MECHANISTIC AND ORGANIC STRUCTURES[28]

Organizational Characteristics	*Type of Organization Structure*	
	Organic	*Mechanistic*
Span of control	wide	narrow
Number of levels of authority	few	many
Ratio of administration to production personnel	high	low
Range of time span over which an employee can commit resources	long	short
Degree of centralization in decision making	low	high
Proportion of persons in one unit having opportunity to interact with persons in other units	high	low
Quantity of formal rules	low	high
Specificity of job goals	low	high
Specificity of required activities	low	high
Content of communications	advice and information	instructions and decisions
Range of compensation	narrow	wide
Range of skill levels	narrow	wide
Knowledge-based authority	high	low
Position-based authority	low	high

(*i*) Division of labour.

(*ii*) Well defined hierarchy of authority.

(*iii*) Clearly defined responsibilities and authority.

(*iv*) Heavy dependence on formal rules and procedures.

(*v*) Employment decisions based on merit.

(*vi*) Impersonality of relations.

(*vii*) Promotions based on technical qualifications.

(*viii*) Centralization of authority.

It is indeed paradoxical that though the term bureaucracy is not liked by contemporary management thinkers and practitioners, many of the characteristics of bureaucracy are found in most modern organizations. Study the structure of any large organization, and you find such features as perfect departmentalization, centralized authority, high formalization, and the like. This is indeed a tribute to Max Weber, the German sociologist and political scientist, who conceived the structure long back.

Effect on Behaviour Bureaucratic organization influences organizational behaviour positively as well as negatively. Hierarchy and specialization, for example, help orderly work and clarify human relationships and rules and ensure that people are treated in the same manner. Furthermore, bureaucracy lends stability to organization structures. The background against which Weber propounded bureaucracy bears testimony to the stability part of the structure. It may be recalled that during the early 1900s, when Weber conceived the idea, organizations were in a state of transition due to the influence of the Industrial Revolution and changes in the social structure and process of society. It was during this period that bureaucratic structure was conceived and over a period of time it flourished.

The negative behavioural implications of bureaucracy are: undesirable treatment of all employees alike, absence of adequate means for resolving differences and conflict between ranks and groups, distorted communication because of hierarchical habits, and the tendency to reduce an organization member to become dull, grey, conditioned, "organization man".

Authority Distributions An important structural feature of organizations that influence people's behaviour is the distribution of authority down the line in the hierarchy. At one end there is centralization where authority and decision are concentrated at top management. At the other end is decentralization where both authority and decisions are dispersed throughout lower levels. Fig 5.12 diagrams centralization and decentralization.

FIGURE 5-12
CENTRALISING AND DECENTRALISING AUTHORITY IN THE HIERARCHY

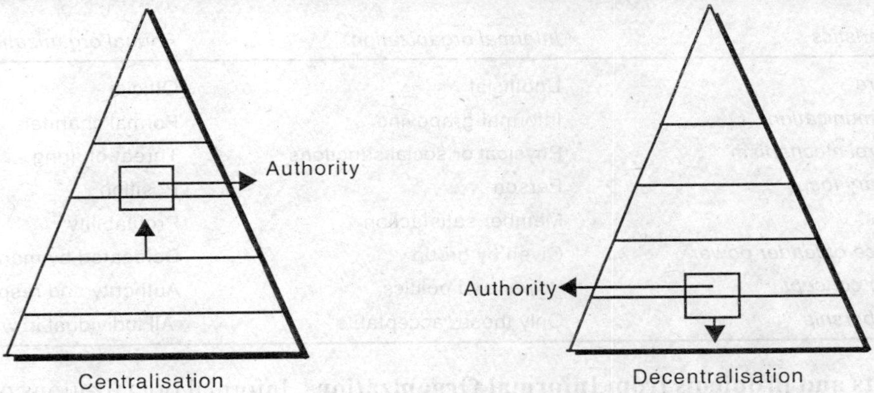

Effect on Behaviour From purely behaviour point of view decentralization is preferable because it recognises and even capitalizes on the importance of the human element. Furthermore decentralization provides an opportunity for individual responsibility and initiative at the lower levels.

Decentralization is also viewed as an effective training device for employees since, theoretically, workers learn to accept greater amount of responsibility earlier than they would under more mechanistic (centralized) systems. As is well known most effective learning occurs by experience. Decentralization allows for the opportunity to experience responsibility which presumably assists in developing innate individual decision-making abilities.

INFORMAL ORGANIZATIONS

Till now we have discussed the formal organization structures. A discussion on formal organization is not complete with out a reference to informal organizations. Hence this section.

An informal organization refers to the patterns of behaviour and influence that arise out of the human interaction occurring within the formal structure. The emphasis in informal organization is on informal relationship.

The concept of informal relationship can be viewed from two perspectives: a macro one that describes the broader, informal, relationships that pervade the entire structure, and a micro one that examines individual behaviour within the confines of smaller, well defined groups. The former perspective is called "informal organization", whereas the latter is called "group dynamics" or " small group behaviour." Group dynamics was discussed in an earlier chapter. The focus here is on informal organizations.

Informal Organization Compared with Formal Organization Table 5.6 summaries the comparison between formal and informal organizations. As seen in Table 5.6, informal organizations come in to existence through emotion but not of logical thought process; primary focus in them is on person but not on position. Communication in them is mainly through informal means but not through formal channels, norms but not rules govern members behaviour, and their goals is member satisfactions and not profitability.

TABLE 5-6

DIFFERENCES BETWEEN FORMAL AND INFORMAL ORGANISATIONS

Characteristics	*Informal organization*	*Formal organization*
1. Nature	Unofficial	Official
2. Communication	Informal-grapevine	Formal channels
3. Control mechanism	Physical or social sanctions	Threat of firing
4. Primary focus	Person	Position
5. Goals	Member satisfaction	Profitability
6. Source of leader power	Given by group	Delegated by management
7. Major concept	Power and politics	Authority and responsibility
8. Membership	Only those "acceptable"	All individual in work groups

Benefits and problems from Informal Organizations Informal organizations offer benefits to members and at the same time pose numerous problems. Among the benefits are: contribution to an effective total system, reduced management work load, greater co-operation, satisfaction and stability to work force, better communication and the like. The potential problem are: development of rumour, encouragement of negative attitudes, resistance to change, development of role conflict, and the like (see Table 5.7)

TABLE 5-7

POTENTIAL PROBLEMS AND BENEFITS ASSOCIATED WITH AN INFORMAL ORGANISATION

Benefits	*Problems*
• Makes an effective total system	• Develops undesirable rumour
• Lightens work load on management	• Encourages negative attitudes
• Helps get the work done	• Resists change
• Tends to encourage co-operation	• Leads to inter-personnel and inter-group conflicts
• Fills in gaps in a manager's abilities	• Develop role conflicts
• Gives satisfaction and stability to workforce	• Rejects and harasses some employees
• Improves communication	• Weakens motivation and satisfaction
• Provides a safety valve for employees emotions	• Operates outside of management control
• Encourages managers to plan and act carefully.	• Supports conformity

Managerial Implications

Formal an informal organizations have specific managerial implications. They are:

1. Manager should not be under an illusion that they alone are responsible for employee behaviour. The organization structure has its own influence. It is the organization or institution which is more important than individuals. People may come and go, but the organization continues.
2. Often, the organization structures is taken for granted, worst still, in many an enterprise a formal chart showing the structure is not in existence. The attendance register is the only proof of X being senior to Y or A reporting to B. This should invite due attention from managers.
3. In an attempt to secure greater economies through division of labour, managers often contribute to conflict. This conflict occurs when individual members or departments form different perceptions about people and work, the importance of following rules, and even how they view the organization's purpose. Thus, re-integrating these specialized groups becomes an important managerial activity.
4. Yet another managerial activity is re-centralization. Authority is often decentralized to lower levels of managements in order to incorporate behavioural ideas into organizational structure. Decentralization, of carried to logical ends, will result in anarchic conditions. Realization of this has led to re-centralization in several undertakings.
5. It is not advisable to over rely on bureaucracy. Though bureaucracy lends stability to the organization, it has the potential of making an organization become sluggish. A sluggish organization fails to capitalize on the talents of its human resources.
6. An organization is a combination of both formal and informal elements. Though informal elements are beneficial, they have dysfunctional consequences too. In order to combat dysfunctional elements, organizational structure must be varied. Managements may, for instance, set time limits for the work of a department, control funds available for the department, or get the activities of the department audited. Sometimes it may be necessary to reorganize the departmental structure of a plant. In order to control informal elements and practices several things may be done; an attempt may be made to integrate informal groups within the structure of the plants , the authority system may be strengthened, the system of specialization may be changed, and the body of rules may be rewritten.[29]

Case

Solectron Corp. – Providers of Supply-Chain Management for Network Organisations

Solectron Corp., founded in 1977, is the world's largest contract electronics manufacturers (CEM). Solectron offers "a full range in integrated supply-chain solution for the world's leading electronics original equipment manufacturers" (OMEs). Headquartered in Milpitas, California, Solectron provides OEM customers with new product design and introduction services, materials management services, high-tech product manufacturing, product warranty services, and end-of-point life support services.

A very successful company, Solectron's fiscal year 2001 revenue was US$8.7 billion. Over the four-year period ending with fiscal 2001, Solectron achieved a compound annual sales growth rate of 43 percent. Solectron has over 40 locations in the Americas, Europe, Asia, and the Pacific Rim.

Solectron has major customer bases in the computer, computer peripherals, telecommunications, and networking industries as well as smaller customer bases in semiconductors, test and industrial controls, medical electronics, avionics, consumer electronics, and global positioning systems. As a contract electronics manufacturer with a wide range of customers, Solectron needs to be flexible. Because of its careful attention to detail in designing its production lines at every facility throughout the world, Solectron can shift jobs or add capacity quickly and seamlessly.

In addition to providing outsourced, design and manufacturing services, Solectron is a global supply-chain facilitator that "helps customers drive speed, efficiency, and cost containment throughout the entire supply chain." Solectron aims "to minimize boundaries in the supply chain... in an effort to help its customers attain the fastest time-to-market with the lowest total costs, while helping them ensure the most efficient allocation of their scarce resources." Essentially, Solectron establishes partnerships with its OEM customers. In doing, so Solectron takes " responsibility for the complete supply chain and for all activities required to support a product from the time of manufacture until its removal from the market." This allows the OEM customers to focus their resources on core competencies such as research and development or sales and marketing.

Contract electronics manufactures, like Solectron, are facilitating the development of "network organizations" and "virtual companies" that often do little beside designing and/or marketing a product. If a client both designs and markets a product, Solectron can handle the manufacturing and/or distribution of the product. If a client's core competency is product design, Solectron can manufacture, market, and distribute it. If a client's strength is marketing products, Solectron can perform all the other supply-chain activities.

Quality is essential in all aspects of Solectron's operations. Quality is essential for securing, developing, and maintaining effective "partnering relationships" with Solectron's customers. Also, Solectron operates on thinner profit margins than its customers do. Consequently, the margin for error is small; anything less than superior quality can have a disastrous impact on the company's bottom line.

Every week the company asks its customers to grade it on quality, responsiveness, communication, service, and technical support. A grade of "B-" or lower initiates a quality-improvement process; a grade of "C" or lower triggers a formal customer complaints resolution process.

Solectron's concern with quality has generated very positive reactions among its customers. Solectron has received more then 250 quality and service awards from its customers. In addition, Solectron is an *Industry week* Best Managed Company Award winner and the first two-time winner of the Malcolm Baldrige National Quality Award for manufacturing.

In order to decrease costs, companies like IBM Corp., Nortel Networks Corp., and Cisco Systems Inc, are increasingly outsourcing work to Solectron and other CEMs. However, when declining sales hit the OEMs, the CEMs are affected negatively - at least in the short term. Over the long term, however, this can mean more business for CEMs like Solectron. Clients may outsource more work in order to shave costs even more and to focus more intensely on their core competencies.

Questions

1. What is a network (or virtual) organization, and how does it differ from more traditional organization structures?

2. Why have network (or virtual) organizations come in to existence? How has Solectron contributed to the rise of these types of organizations?

3. What are the key factors in Solectron's success in facilitating the rise of network (or virtual) organizations?

4. What advantages and disadvantages do you think arise from a network (or virtual) organization relationship?[30]

Questions

1. Define the term organization. Discuss four types of design from the chapter.
2. Discuss the effects of key factors on the design dimensions.
3. Discuss the nature of emerging organizational structures.
4. How would you describe the organization you work for (or your college) on each of the design types. For example, is it very formal or informal organization ?
5. Does your organization show any structural deficiencies discussed in this chapter?
6. What were the original purposes of a bureaucratic approach to organization? Why does bureaucracy receive bad press? What makes an organization organic? Which gets better results, a bureaucracy or an organic structure ? Why ?

References

1. Edgar H. Schein, *Organizational Psychology,* Prentice Hall of India, 1983, p.12.
2. Donald D. White and David A. Bednar, *Organizational Behaviour,* Allyn and Bacon, 1986, p. 73.
3. Edgar H. Schein, *Op.cit,* p. 15.
4. *Ibid.*
5. Gareth R. Jones, *Organizational Theory,* Addison Wesley, 1993, p.11.
6. Ibid, p.16.
7. Don Hellriegel, *et.al, Organizational Behaviour,* Thomson, 2001, p. 475.
8. Gareth R. Jones, *Op.cit,* p. 227.
9. The *Economic Times,* October 27,2002.
10. Aswathappa K. *International Business,* Tata McGraw-Hill publishing Ltd, 2003, p.105.
11. Don Hollriegel, *et.al, Op. cit,* p. 479.
12. Gareth R. Jones, *Op.cit,* p.365.
13. Ibid, p.367.
14. Richard M.Hodgetts, *Organizational Behaviour,* Macmillan, 1991, p.290.
15. Don Hellriegel, *et.al., Op.cit,* p.489.
16. Aswathappa K, *Op.cit,* P.132.
17. Don Hellriegal, *et.al, Op.cit,* p.491.
18. Ibid, p.493.
19. Aswathappa K, *Op.cit,* p.136.
20. Gareth R.Jones, *Op.cit,* p.159.
21. R.E.Miles and EC. Snow, *Causes of Failure in Network Organizations,* California Management Review, July 1992, Pp 53-72.

22. Christopher Bartlett, "Embracing the Virtual Organization", cited in *Managing Organisations*, by Robert H. Rosenfeld and David C. Wilson, McGraw–Hill, Second Edn, p.549.
23. Ibid, p.553.
24. Gray and Starke, *Organizational Behaviour,* Columbus, Merrill Pub Co., 1988, p.344
25. Eugene McKenna, *Business Pyscology and Organisational Behaviour,* Psychology Press Ltd., 2000, p. 462.
26. Ibid, p.463.
27. Hower and Losch, "Organisational Inputs", in *Analysis in Organisational Behaviour*, Richard D. Irwin, 1967, R.168
28. W.Bennis, "*Beyond Bureancracy*", Transaction, July-August, 1965, p.33.
29. Eugene V. Schneder, *Industrial Sociology*, McGraw-Hill, 1971, Pp.119-120.
30. Debra L. Nelson, *et.al., Organisational Behaviour,* Thomson, 2003, Pp. 534-535.

CHAPTER Six

Leadership

LEARNING OBJECTIVES

After reading this chapter you should understand –

1. The nature of Leadership and the importance of Leadership in organisational effectiveness.
2. The difference between Leadership and management.
3. The different leadership styles.
4. The 20th century models on leadership.
5. The emerging issues in Leadership

Success of organisations depends on leaders. Obviously, businesses constantly look for effective leaders and they are not easy to come by. This shortage of effective leadership is not confined to business, but is evident in the lack of able administrators in government, education, hospitals, foundations and every other form of organisation.

In this chapter we focus on the nature, theories and other related topics on leadership.

Nature Of Leadership

The word *leadership* has been widely used by political orators, business executives, social workers, philosophers and scholars both in speech and writing, yet the real meaning has eluded almost everybody.[1] This is clear from the fact that a comprehensive volume summarising research on leadership includes 150 pages of bibliography and cites more than 2500 studies. Yet the last chapter in the book, "Directions for Future Research", concludes that, as far as understanding leadership goes, only a beginning has been made.[2]

We quote a few important definitions on leadership from the existing literature. These definitions reveal the essence of leadership.

1. Leadership is *"the process of encouraging and helping others to work enthusiastically towards objectives."*[3]
2. Leadership is *"the behaviour of an individual when he is directing the activities of a group towards a shared goal"*.
3. Leadership is *"interpersonal influence, exercised in a situation and directed, through the communication process, towards the attainment of a specified goal or goals"*.
4. Leadership is *"an interaction between persons in which one presents information of a sort and in such a manner that the other becomes convinced that his outcomes (benefits/costs ratios) will improve if he behaves in the manner suggested or desired"*.[4]
5. Leadership is *"both a process and property. The process of leadership is the use of non-coercive influence to direct and coordinate the activities of the members of an organised group towards the accomplishment of group objectives. As a property, leadership is the set of qualities or characteristics attributed to those who are perceived to successfully employ such influence.*[5]
6. Leadership is *"the relationship in which one person (the leader) influences others to work together willingly on related tasks to attain goals desired by the leader and / or group.*[6]

The core points that run through all these definitions and which constitute the essence of leadership are the following :

(a) Leadership refers to the ability of one individual to influence others.

(b) The influence is exercised to change the behaviour of others.

(c) Behaviour is changed through non-coercive means.

(d) Change of behaviour is caused with an objective of achieving a shared goal.

(e) The person influencing others (leader) possesses a set of qualities or characteristics which he or she uses to influence others, as the opening case indicates.

(f) Leadership is a group phenomenon. It involves interaction between two or more people.

LEADERSHIP AND MANAGEMENT

Management, managership and leadership are terms which are so closely related that the distinctions among them have become blurred. It is useful to place each of them in its right perspective.

Management is a process of planning, organising, coordinating, directing and controlling the activities of others.

Managership is the authority to carry out these functions.

Leadership, as mentioned above, is the process of influencing for the purpose of achieving shared goals.

Both managership and leadership are management tools with which managers can influence the behaviour of employees to achieve organisational goals. The distinction between them can be made on the basis of the qualifications that managers have. Managers, by virtue of being in a managerial position, have managership, but they may not possess leadership or the ability to influence other people.[7]

John Kotter draws the distinction between leadership and management more clearly. For him, management involves coping with complexity; while leadership is about coping with change. He states that "each system of action involves deciding what needs to be done, creating networks of people and relationships that can accomplish an agenda and then trying to ensure that those people actually do the job."[8] Fig. 6.1 provides Kotter's basic distinction between how managers and leaders accomplish these three tasks.

FIGURE 6-1
KOTTER'S DISTINCTION BETWEEN MANAGERS AND LEADERS

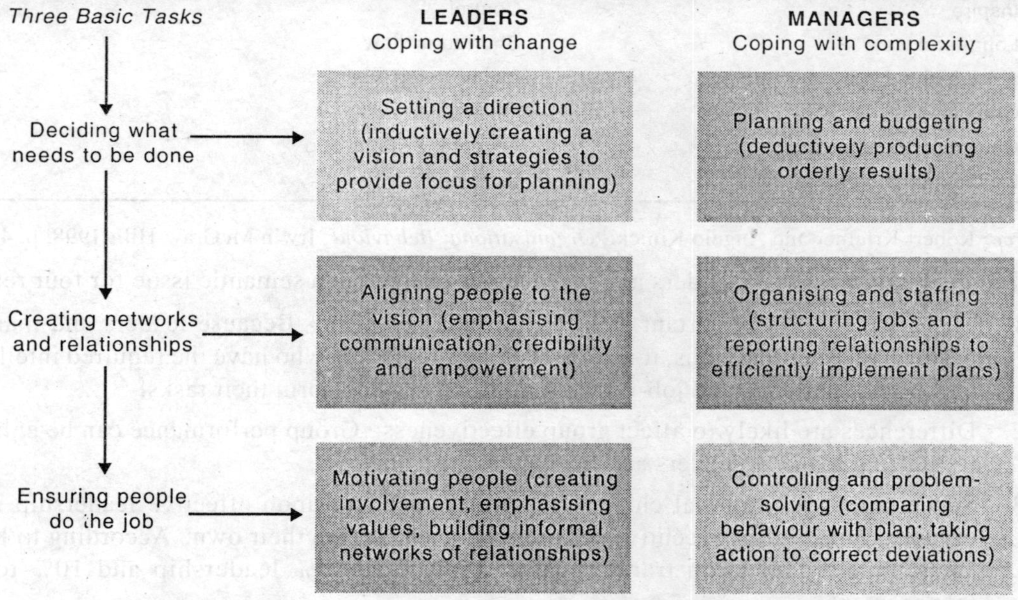

(***Source:*** Curtis W. Cook and Philip L. Hunsaker, *Management and Organisational Behaviour*, p. 492)

There are certain other differences between leaders and managers.

1. Leaders *have followers*, but managers do not have. Subordinates may obey managers out of fear but such compliance is not a response to leadership. Similarly, all leaders are not managers. Leaders have followers but do not possess authority to manage, informal leaders for example. Managership is a fundamental characteristic of a manager.
2. Leaders *have emotional appeal*. They are expected to be charismatic people with great visions who can alter the mood of their followers and raise their hopes and expectations. On the other hand, managers are expected to be rational decision-makers and problem solvers. They are expected to use their analytical minds in the process of establishing and achieving organisational goals.
3. Leaders *fulfill follower's needs*. Managers and leaders try to meet organisational and employees' personal needs. But the emphasis differs. The main aim of a manager is to meet organisational goals. Similarly, the main job of a leader is to satisfy his followers' needs.[9]
4. Peter Drucker and Warren Bennis have rightly pointed thus : "Management is doing things right, leadership is doing right thing. Management lies in climbing the ladder of success; leadership determines whether the ladder is leaning against the right wall." Table 6.1 brings distinction between management and leadership to sharp focus.

TABLE 6-1

DIFFERENCES BETWEEN LEADERS AND MANAGERS

Leaders	*Managers*
Innovate	Administer
Develop	Maintain
Inspire	Control
Long-term view	Short-term view
Ask what and why	Ask how and when
Originate	Initiate
Challenge the status quo	Accept the status quo
Do the right things	Do things right

(***Source:*** Robert Krietner and Angelo Kinicki, *Organisational Behaviour*, Irwin McGraw-Hill, 1998, p. 497)

The distinction between leaders and managers is more than a semantic issue for four reasons:

1. The distinction is important from hiring point of view. Because leaders and managers perform distinct functions, it is important to hire people who have the required intellectual abilities, experience and job-relevant knowledge to perform their tasks.
2. Differences are likely to affect group effectiveness. Group performance can be enhanced by staffing a mix of leaders and managers.
3. Successful organisational change is highly dependent upon effective leadership in any organisation. Senior executives cannot create change on their own. According to Kotter, successful organisation transformation is 70% to 90% leadership and 10% to 30% management.

4. Distinction between leading and managing highlights the point that leadership is not confined to people in particular positions or roles. Anyone from the bottom to the top of an organisation can be a leader. Many an informal leaders have contributed to organisational effectiveness.

In a typical organisation, both leadership and management roles are combined in every individual. Whether one is a leader or manager depends on what role he or she performs at any given time. In fact, backed by leadership traits, an executive is in a stronger position to perform managerial functions that result in desired outcomes. Of course, several situational factors influence how effectively the end results have been obtained. Fig. 6.2 summarises the above process.

FIGURE 6-2
A CONCEPTUAL FRAMEWORK FOR UNDERSTANDING LEADERSHIP

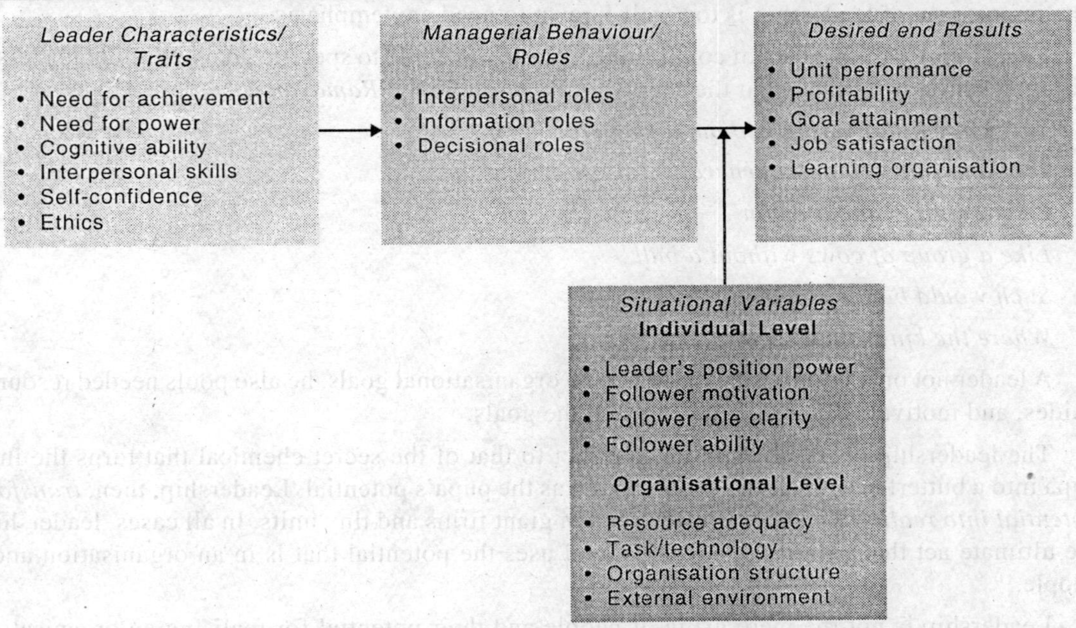

(*Source:* Robert Kreitner and Angelo Kinicki, *Organisational Behaviour*, p. 496)

Leadership is a Mutual Influence Process The discussion on the nature of leadership till now makes a reader believe that leadership is unidirectional i.e., the leader influencing his followers. It is true that leadership refers to the influence of the leader on followers. At the same time, the characteristics of employees and their tasks do yield influence on the leader. Leadership is, therefore, a mutual influence process.

Leader's Influence on Followers Why is leader able to influence his followers ? What makes followers simply obey whatever their leader says ? A leader is able to change the behaviour of his followers because he enjoys power which comes to him from at least five sources. They are [10] : (1) *reward power* which refers to the leader's capacity to reward followers, (2) *coercive power* which is the flip side of reward power and refers to the leader's capacity to coerce or punish followers, (3) *legitimate power* which refers to the power a leader possesses as a result of occupying a particular position or role in the organisation, (4) *expert power* that refers to power that a leader possesses as a result of his knowledge and expertise regarding the tasks to be performed by subordinates ; and (5) *referent power* which is dependent upon the extent to which subordinates identify with, look up to and wish to emulate the leader.

Followers' influence on Leader The fact that the followers and situations will influence their leader is a recent discovery. Several sources of influence on the leader's behaviour are identified. The more important of them are : (1) responses or performance of subordinates; (2) characteristics of subordinates, namely, male or female, young or old, personal background and the like; (3) the nature of the task; (4) organisational policy and climate; (5) peers and their influence on the leader; and (6) influence of superiors on the leader.

Importance of Leadership

The importance of leadership is too well-known to need any emphasis.

Leadership is the process of committing a group of people to specific goals. Without leadership, an organisation would be what the sage Valmiki wrote in the *Ramayana*:

"Like a heard of cattle without a keeper

Like an army without a general

Like a night without moon

Like a group of cows without a bull

Such would be the country

Where the king is not seen".

A leader not only commits his followers to organisational goals, he also pools needed resources, guides, and motivates subordinates to reach the goals.

The leadership process is similar in effect to that of the secret chemical that turns the insect pupa into a butterfly with all the beauty that was the pupa's potential. Leadership, then, *transforms potential into reality*. This role is often seen in giant firms and tiny units. In all cases, leadership is the ultimate act that identifies, develops, and uses the potential that is in an organisation and its people.[11]

Leadership is not the mere using of people and their potential for realising an organisation's goals. It has the ultimate aim of raising the level of human conduct and ethical aspiration of both the leader and the led. This aspect of leadership is what Burns calls the *transforming leadership*. The leader should elevate, inspire, and evangelise his followers to higher things in life.

High sounding words indeed! In reality, effect of leadership on organisational effectiveness seems to be relative because of the following possibilities:

- Poorly performing organisations find it difficult to attract best leaders.
- Not all leaders have the same abilities and experience.
- Environmental and organisational factors can override any effects the leader may have.
- Organisations continue to flourish even after the change of leadership.

Formal and Informal Leadership

Formal leadership occurs when a manager leads by exercising formal authority. The exercise of formal authority through such acts as assigning duties derives, from the manager's official position within the organisation's hierarchy of authority. Any employee who is assigned a managerial position has the opportunity and responsibility to exercise formal leadership in relation to subordinates. Some managers have a better understanding of the authority and formal relationship with subordinates provided by a managerial position; thus, they are more influential in ensuring that subordinates' work effort are productive. These managers are better leaders.

Informal leadership arises when a person without formal authority is influential in directing the behaviour of others. Although not formally appointed or elected, he becomes a leader through his actions or personal attractions.

Formal and informal leadership coexist in almost every work situation. Manager must often work with subordinates who defer to a strong informal leader within their peer group. Managers themselves may act as formal leaders in some situations and as informal leaders in others. When acting as a formal leader, the manager follows the chain of command and exerts influence downward in the hierarchy of authority from manager to subordinates. By contrast, when acting as an informal leader, the manager influences employees outside the formal organisational chain of command. Interpersonnal charisma or persuasiveness is required for informal leadership because the informal leader lacks formal authority.

Leadership Styles and Their Implications

Leadership style is the typical approach a particular person uses to lead people. Stated differently, the behaviour the leader exhibits during supervision of subordinates is known as *leadership style*. Style is said to comprise two distinct elements – the leader's *assumptions* about-subordinates and the leader's actual *behaviour* while interacting with subordinates. Although this distinction is not made in academic circles (where emphasis is more on leader behaviour), it is important to keep in mind, particularly when changes in leader behaviour are desired. A change in leader behaviour can be achieved by either changing the leader's assumptions about people or by first forcing behavioural change of the leader and then hoping for attitudinal change later.

In the meanwhile, the study of leadership styles is useful because it focuses on what the leader actually does in getting work accomplished through people.

Our discussion of leadership style is divided into four types : (i) Styles based on the amount of authority retained by the leader ; (ii) Styles based on the relative emphasis placed on the task to be performed versus that placed on people; (iii) Styles based on the assumptions about people made by the leader; (iv) Likert's four styles; and (v) Enterpreneurial leadership styles.

Styles Based on Authority Retained

This is the classical approach to classifying the leadership styles and is useful even today. Styles in this approach are classified depending on how much authority is retained by the leader versus how much is delegated to the subordinate employees. We have the familiar three-way classification of authoritarian, participative and free-rein leadership.

Authoritarian Style Known in its acronym as autocratic style, authoritarian style involves retention of full authority by the leader. Leader decides, decision is passed on to subordinates, instructions about the implementation of decision are given and the subordinates are expected to do what the leader has told them to do. Assuring that the leader is competent, the advantage of this leadership style is that tasks are efficiently completed, since there is no opportunity for the time consuming two-way communications associated with democratic styles.

The primary problem with authoritarian leadership style is that workers are made aware of what to do, but not why. This may lead to (1) low employee morale, and (2) workers following leader directions lose initiative and avoid responsibility for any errors.

But there are some workers who prefer autocratic leader. They feel secure under his or her leadership. In such cases, productivity and morale of the workers tend to be high.

Participative Style: There are three related types of participative leaders : consultative, consensual and democratic.

Consultative leaders solicit opinions from group before making a decision, yet they do not feel obliged to accept the group's thinking; these leaders make it clear that they alone have final authority to make final decisions.

Consensual leaders encourage group discussion on an issue and then make a decision that reflects the general agreement (consensus) of group members. Consensual leaders delegate more authority to the group than do the consultative leaders. This style leads to considerable delay in decision-making because every member has to give his/or her consent.

Democratic leaders confer final authority on the group. They function as collectors of opinion and take a vote before making a decision. Democratic leaders delegate full authority to subordinates. This style is more relevant for community activities than for work settings.

The participative style has merits. Firstly, it is highly effective where group comprises competent and motivated members who want to get involved in making decisions and giving feedback to the leader. Secondly, employees' feelings of self-worth and satisfaction are increased because the leader conveys a sense of confidence in employee judgement. Thirdly, participation allows employees to satisfy high-level needs such as esteem and self-actualisation by allowing them to take part in decision-making. Fourthly, employee participation in decision-making improves the quality of decisions, because when more people think about problem it is likely that a better solution will be found. Finally, there will be less resistance to change because those who have developed the solution will usually support its implementation.

This particular style seems to have only academic interest. In practice the style may not work. Neither the leader has large heart to share authority with others. Nor the subordinates have physical and mental preparedness to take part in decision-making. Where both these are possible, decision-making is likely to get delayed.

Free-rein style Also called laissez-faire, free-rein leader chooses not to adopt a leadership role and actually abdicates leadership position, generally relinquishing it to someone else in the work group. While technically not a leadership style (it is more the absence of one), it does warrant brief mention since the absence of leadership may have a positive or negative effect.

On the positive side, free-rein leadership works when the group is composed of highly committed members. On the negative side it may be stated that the leader abdicates leadership role because of his or her own incompetency, the fear of failure, or the perceived social cost of ostracisation by the workgroup.

STYLES BASED ON TASK VERSUS PEOPLE EMPHASIS

Another standard way of classifying leadership styles is based on the relative concern the leader places on the task to be performed vis-à-vis the people performing the task.

A leader who places greater emphasis on task performance tends to exhibit the following behaviours :

(i) Organising and defining the roles of the group members.

(ii) Explaining what activities each has to do and when, where and how tasks are to be accomplished.

(iii) Establishing well-defined patterns of organisation, channels of communication and ways of task accomplishment.

A leader who places greater emphasis on people tries to gain their relationships by exhibiting such behaviours as :

(i) Establishing channels of communication.

(ii) Extending psychological support to them.

(iii) Developing mutual trust.

(iv) Developing empathy for them.

Depending on task emphasis or people emphasis, four combinations are possible as shown in Fig. 6.3.

FIGURE 6-3
FOUR KEY LEADER BEHAVIOURS

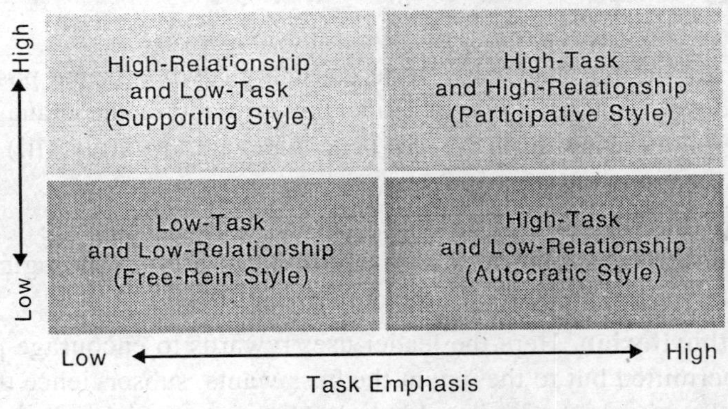

A brief description of each style follows :

High-Task and Low-Relationship A high-task and low-relationship leader emphasises showing employees how to get the tasks accomplished and spends minimum time giving psychological support. This style may be effective where the employees are inexperienced with the work to be performed. The high-task and low-relationship style may also be well suited to situations where seasonal help is involved. Seasonal employees may be unfamiliar with the task and these require direct guidance on performing the work properly. A high-task and low-relationship leader is not necessarily rude or discourteous. The leader simply takes the expedient route of focusing on work rather than people.

High-Task and High Relationship This leader spends considerable time showing people how to get the work accomplished and providing them psychological support. The high-task and high-relationship style is considered generally useful because it results in high productivity and personal satisfaction. A more critical look at this style would suggest that it works best in situations where people need an active and involved leader. When employees are lacking in self-confidence and technical skill, the high-task and high-relationship style is particularly effective.

High-Relationship and Low-Task A leader using the high-relationship and low-task style gives employees much encouragement and support but a minimum of guidance about the task accomplishment. In some situations employees need more psychological support rather than technical instructions. The high-relationship and low-task style is suitable for such situations.

Low-Relationship and Low-Task A leader using this style is neither here nor there. It is essentially a free-rein style. Subordinates are given considerable latitude in performing their work. They are also given very little psychological support, encouragement and praise. They are, therefore, free to run their own show. When subordinates are highly skilled and psychologically mature, this style can be effective.

Styles Based on Assumptions about People

Depending on what assumptions a leader makes about his or her followers, two styles may be distinguished. This two-way classification is based on McGregor's famous Theory X and Theory Y assumptions about people. These assumptions are pointed out later in this chapter. In the meantime it may be stated that *Theory X* leaders are autocratic. They distrust people and believe in close supervision and tight-control over the subordinates. *Theory Y* leaders are participative, they trust subordinates and allow them to participate in decision-making.

Likert's Four Styles

Developing on the notion that leadership style consists of two extreme positions-autocratic and democratic-Likert develops four styles of leadership to capture the management culture of an organization: (i) exploitative authoritative, (ii) benevolent authoritative, (iii) consultative, and (iv) participative.

Exploitative authoritative As an exploitative authoritarian, the leader uses sanctions, communication is downward, superiors and subordinates are psychologically distant, and the decisions are generally made at the top of the organization.

Benevolent authoritarian Here the leader uses rewards to encourage performance, upward communication is permitted but to the extent the boss wants, subservience to boss is widespread, and there is some delegation in decision making, though major decisions are made by the people at the top of the hierarchy.

Consultative Here the leader uses rewards, communication is two-way although upward, communication is cautious and limited, some involvement is sought from employees, and as in the benevolent authoritarian style, subordinates are involved in decision-making in a limited way.

Participative The leader disperses economic rewards and makes full use of group participation and involvement in setting performance standards and improving methods and procedures. Subordinates and superiors are psychologically close, and group decision-making is widespread in the organization. There is a tendency among a number of individuals to belong to more than workgroup in order to promote intergroup links and understanding.

ENTREPRENEURSHIP LEADERSHIP STYLE

An entrepreneur is a person who coverts an innovative idea into business. The word entrepreneur is generally associated with small-scale industry. What is an entrepreneurship leadership style? Based on both their personality characteristics, and the circumstances of operating a business, many entrepreneurs use a similar leadership style. The most notable features of this style are :

(i) Impatience and brusquences towards employees because the entrepreneur is always busy.

(ii) A heavy task orientation combined with a very direct-approach to giving instructions to employees.

(iii) A charismatic personality that inspires others to want to do business with him or her despite the impatience.

(iv) A much stronger interest in dealing with customers than employees.

(v) A strong dislike for bureaucratic rules and regulations.

(vi) Anxiety to consolidate business gains as quickly as possible.

Some of the styles described above will be referred to again later in different contexts.

THEORIES OF LEADERSHIP

From the beginning of the 20th century, many distinguished authors and researchers have contributed to the rich knowledge on leadership. Without the forward-looking visions of past generations (some of whom are listed in Table 6.2), we would not have the insights that we have today. While, examining all the earlier contributions is rather unnecessary, we focus on certain works, which are relevant even today.

Historically, focus on leadership in theories shifted from one dimension of leadership to another. Early leadership research focused on the leader himself or herself to the virtual exclusion of other variables. It was assumed that leadership effectiveness could be explained isolating psychological, physical characteristics, or traits, which were presumed to differentiate the leader from the other members of the group.[12]

As the years went by the focus shifted from the personality of the leader to his or her behaviour while delegating tasks to subordinates and communicating with them. It was believed by the behaviourists that a leader's effectiveness depended upon behaviours and not on traits alone.

More recently the situation in which the leader operates has been given much importance. It is believed that the leadership effectiveness depends on the situation in which the leader operates.

We shall discuss a few important theories on leadership with an assertion that any theory will be complete only when it covers three important dimensions of leadership, namely:

1. The leader and his or her psychological attributes;
2. The follower with his or her problems, attitudes, and needs; and
3. The group situation in which followers and leaders relate with one another.[13]

To concentrate on any one of these three factors represents over-simplification of an intricate phenomenon.

TABLE 6-2

SIGNIFICANT LEADERSHIP THEORIES AND MODELS

Contributor	*Theory or Model*	*Year of Publication of Significant Research*
Taylor	Scientific Management	1911
Mayo	Hawthorne Studies	1933
Barnard	Executive Function	1938
Coch-French	Michigan Studies	1948
Stogdill	Ohio State Studies	1948
Homans	Human Group	1950
Maslow	Hierarchy of Needs	1954
McGregor	Theory X – Theory Y	1957
Tannenbaum-Schmidt	Continuum of Leader Behaviour	1957
Blake-Mouton	Managerial Grid	1964
Argyris	Maturity-Immaturity	1964
McClelland	Achievement Theory	1965
Odiorne	Management by Objectives	1965
Herzberg	Motivation – Hygiene	1966
Likert	Systems 1-4	1967
Fiedler	Contingency Model	1967
Reddin	3-D Management Style	1967
Olsson	Management by Objectives	1968
Hersey-Blanchard	Situational Leadership	1969
Vroom-Yetten	Contingency Model	1973
House-Mitchell	Path – Goal	1974
Vroom	Expectancy Theory	1976
House	Charismatic Leadership	1977
Burns	Transformational Leadership	1978
Kerr-Jermier	Substitutes for Leadership	1978
McCall-Lombardo	Fatal Leadership Flaws	1983
Greenleaf	Servant Leadership	1983
Bennis-Nanus	Leadership Competencies	1985
Tichy-Devanna	Transformational Leadership	1986
Manz	Super Leadership	1989
Yuki	Integrating Leadership Model	1989
Covey	Principle-Centered Leadership	1991
Fisher	Principle Self-Directed Work Teams	1993
Johnson	SOAR Model	1994
Pansegrouw	Transformational Model	1995
Gyllenpalm	Organisational Cone	1995
Whetter-Cameron	Empowerment	1995
Tichy	Leadership Engine	1997
Ball	DNA Leadership	1997
Byham-Cox	Empowerment	1998
Fairholm	Values-Base Leadership	1998
Cohen	8 Universal Laws of Leadership	1998
Ulrich, Zenger, Smallwood	Results-Based Leadership	1999
Wheatley	Leadership and the New Science	1999

(***Source:*** Paul Hersey, *et al*, *Management of Organisational Behaviour*, Pearson, 2001, p. 87)

The theories of leadership considered in the following pages are :

(a) Trait theory
(b) Leader behaviour theory
(c) The Managerial Grid
(d) Contingency theories

Besides, the famous Theory X and Theory Y of McGregor has also been considered.

TRAIT APPROACH

The trait theories of leadership focus on the individual characteristics of successful leaders. According to the theories, leaders possess a set of traits which make them distinct from followers. An attempt must, therefore, be made to identify and measure these traits.

Attempts were indeed made in the past to identify such qualities. Ralph Stogdill, for instance, surveyed more than 5000 leadership studies and concluded that successful leaders tend to have the following qualities.[14]

(i) A strong desire for accomplishment
(ii) Persistent pursuit of goals
(iii) Creativity and intelligence used to solve problems
(iv) Initiative applied to social situations
(v) Self-assumed personality
(vi) Willingness to accept behavioural consequences
(vii) Low susceptibility to interpersonal stress
(viii) High tolerance of ambiguity
(ix) Ability to influence other people
(x) Ability to structure social interactions

Most of the research on leadership conducted till now concentrated mainly on the unique qualities of successful leaders. There has been little systematic study of the personal traits of unsuccessful leaders. Probably ineffective leadership is associated with such qualities as poor temperament, self centeredness, inability to get along with others, lack of vision, lack of character and mental health problems such as aggression, depression, disorganization, paranoia, neurosis and procrastination. In addition, some attitudinal factors seem to be associated with ineffective leaders. These include : (1) overconcern with morale, (2) failure to maintain an objective attitude, (3) lack of a sense of proportion, (4) practising "polarization" or seeing others as either good or bad, (5) idealism in decision-making and (6) over eagerness to do the "right" things.

Evaluation of the Trait Theory The trait approach to leadership has been severely criticised by many. Some of the limitations of the theory are the following :

(i) The list of personality traits of successful leaders is too long and there seems to be no finality about it. Although hundreds of traits have been identified, no consistent pattern has emerged.

(ii) How much of which trait a successful leader must have is not clear. Furthermore, certain traits, particularly psychological, cannot be quantified.

(iii) The theory assumes that a leader is born and not trained. This assumption is not acceptable to the contemporary thinkers on the subject.

(iv) Contrary to what the theory assumes, leadership effectiveness does not depend upon the personality of the leader alone. Other variables like the situation, the task, the organisation and the characteristics of followers will equally determine the effectiveness of leaders.

(v) It is well known that people who fail as leaders and people who never achieve positions of leadership often possess some of the same traits as successful leaders. Thus, for example, although taller people may generally be more successful as leaders, many tall people have neither the inclination nor the capabilities to be leaders. At the same time, many short people have risen to positions of leadership.

(vi) There is little consensus on the meaning of words used to label traits. In a study of extensive leadership qualities a researcher demonstrated the magnitude of this problem when he asked 75 top executives to define the term "dependability", a trait associated with effective leadership. The executives defined this trait in 147 different ways. Even after similar definitions had been combined, 25 different definitions remained.[15]

It does not mean to say that the trait theory of leadership is irrelevant. With all its limitations, the theory is still relevant because of certain merits.

One merit relates to the qualities of successful leaders. Focusing on personality traits, a review of studies carried out from 1900 to 1957 showed that leaders tend to be consistently better adjusted, more dominant, more extroverted, more masculine, and more conservative and have greater interpersonal sensitivity than non-leaders.[16]

The *second* merit relates to the influence of personality on one's effectiveness "... person's personality, what he fundamentally is as a person, is an ever present and massive influence on how and with what success, he functions as a manager."

"The personality of man is his inner life, including such inner elements as background, life history, beliefs, life experiences, attitudes, prejudices, self-image, fears, loves, hates, hopes and philosophy of life. In this sense, a man is like an iceberg : only a small fraction of what he appears above the surface (his observable behaviour, what he does); the rest is his inner life, the 7/8th of the iceberg that lie, unobservable, below the surface."

However, the manager's inner personality causes or 'spills over' into his behaviour which, in turn, affects others with whom he works, eliciting from them either cooperative or resistance reactions. And, therein lies the manager's fate : cooperative reactions from his people spell success, resistance reactions, however irrational from the manager's view-point, usually assure his failure."

"...It is clear that there is an influential relationship between a manager's total personality and his success as a manager on the job. I have submitted this precise concept to several thousand practising managers over the years and based on their experience virtually all acknowledge its validity."[17]

Third, the view that leaders are born, not made is in fact, still popular (through not among researchers). After a lifetime of reading popular novels and viewing films and television shows, perhaps most of us believe, to some extent, that there are individuals who have predisposition to leadership, that they are naturally braver, more aggressive, more decisive and more articulate than other people.[18]

Finally, the theory has certain practical implications also. If leadership traits could be identified, then nations and organisations would become far more sophisticated in selecting leaders. Only those people who possess the designated leadership traits would become politicians, officers and managers. Presumably, organisations and societies would then operate more effectively.[19]

BEHAVIOURAL THEORIES

Beginning in the late 1940's and continuing through the early 1960's researchers moved away from an emphasis on traits and towards the study of leader behaviours. This new approach differed from the trait oriented research in at least two ways. First, actual leader behaviours instead of personal traits were the main focus. Second, where as most trait studies sought to separate leaders from non-leaders, leader behaviour studies wanted to determine how various kinds of specific behaviour affect the performance and satisfaction of followers. Thus, the difference between the two approaches is summarized in Table 6.3.

TABLE 6-3
DIFFERENCE BETWEEN TRAIT AND BEHAVIOUR THEORIES

Theories	*Emphasis*	*End result*
Trait theories	Study personal characteristics	Separate leaders from non-leaders
Leader behaviour theories	Study how a leader behaves	Followers' performance and satisfaction.

The Ohio State University studies and the University of Michigan studies are the two important behavioural theories.

Ohio State University Studies These well publicised studies were started shortly after World War II. The main objective of the studies was to identify the major dimensions of leadership and to investigate the effect of leader behaviour on employee performance and satisfaction. From a list of leader behaviours in a wide variety of situations, two leadership dimensions were identified.

(i) The *initiating structure*, which refers to leader behaviour that defines and organises the group tasks, assigns the tasks to employees and supervises their activities.

(ii) *Consideration* refers to leader behaviour that can be characterised by friendliness, respect, supportiveness, openness, trust and concern for the welfare of the employees.

The main point in the study is that both consideration and initiating structure are not seen as being placed on a continuum. That's, rather than a leader necessarily being low on one dimension when high on the other, the leader could be high on both, low on both, or high on one and low on the other as seen in the quadrants shown in Fig. 6.4.

The findings of the Ohio State studies can be summarized as follows :

(i) Consideration was positively related to low absenteeism and grievance, but it was negatively or neutrally related to performance.

(ii) Initiating structure was positively related to employee performance but was also associated with such negative consequences as absenteeism and grievances.

(iii) When both consideration and structure were high, performance and satisfaction tended to be high. But in some cases, high productivity was accompanied by absenteeism and grievances.[20]

The University of Michigan Studies These studies were conducted during the same period as those at Ohio State and resulted in identical conclusions. As in the Ohio State University studies, researchers at the University of Michigan distinguished between two dimensions of leadership : production-centered and employee-centred. *Production-centred* leaders set rigid work standards, organised tasks down to the last detail, prescribed the work methods to be followed and closely

FIGURE 6-4
LEADER BEHAVIOURS AND LEADERSHIP STYLES

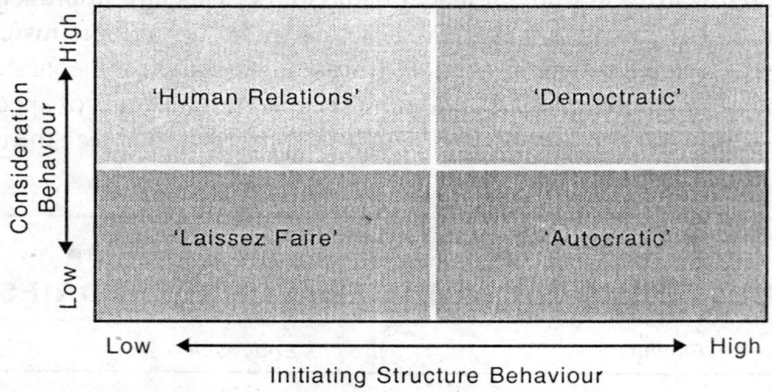

(***Source:*** Schermerhorn *et al, Organisational Behaviour*, p. 587)

supervised subordinates' performance. *Employee-centred* leaders, on the other hand, encouraged employee participation in goal setting and in other work related decisions, and helped ensure high performance by inspiring respect and trust.

At first the findings of Michigan studies seem to refute the Ohio state research because they place leadership on a continuum such as the one shown in Fig. 6.5 and concede that the further to the right the leaders go, the better off they are. But a deeper analysis reveals that employee and work orientation are two separate dimensions and that a leader can be either high or low on one or both. Thus, the two styles discovered by the Michigan researchers were similar to those of the Ohio State people. The production-centred leadership factor and the initiating-leadership structure factor both measured work orientation, while the employee-oriented factor and the consideration factor both measured people orientation.

FIGURE 6-5
A PRODUCTION-CENTRED/EMPLOYEE-CENTRED LEADERSHIP CONTINUUM

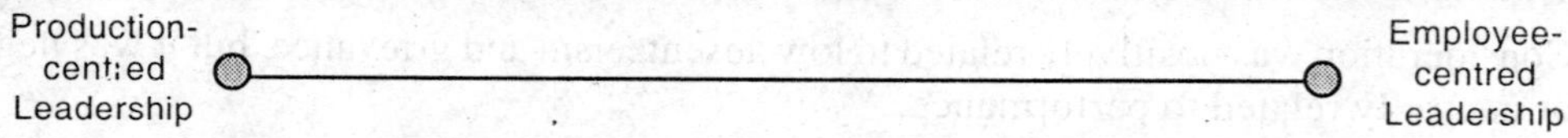

Evaluation of Behavioural Theories In leader behaviour theories, unlike in the trait theories, the focus was on what leaders did – how they delegated the tasks, how they communicated with and tried to motivate their subordinates, how they carried out their tasks and so on. The theories underlined that the behaviours can be learnt and an individual trained in the appropriated leadership behaviours would be able to lead more effectively. This is the main contribution of the leader behaviour theory.

Behavioural theorists, however, could not successfully identify a consistent relationship between leadership behaviour and group performance. General statements could not be made because results would vary over different range of circumstances. What was missing consideration of the situational factors that influence success or failure.[21]

Leader-member Exchange (LMX) Theory Also called the vertical dyad model, this approach too focuses more on leader behaviours. A vertical dyad consists of two persons who are linked hierarchically, such as a supervisor and a subordinate. The leader behaviour depends on who the subordinate is. The theory is advocated by George Graen and his associates.

The basic idea behind the LMX theory is that leaders form two groups, in-groups, and out-groups, of followers. In-group members tend to be similar to the leader, and get greater responsibilities, more attention, and more rewards. They work within the leader's inner circle of communication. As a result, in-group members are more satisfied, have lower turnover, and have high organizational commitment. In contrast, out-group members are outside the circle and receive less attention and fewer rewards. They are managed by formal rules and policies.

An important implication of the LMX model is that leadership can be understood better by examining dyads (pairs of relations) made up of leader and member (a vertical relationship) rather than by concentrating on what one might call the average leadership style. Graen and his associates contend that much of the past studies on leadership presume the existence of an average style that a leader exhibits towards all members of a workgroup. An average style not being practical, a leader divides the subordinates into in-group and out-groups and behaves differently towards each group (see Fig.6.6).

FIGURE 6-6
CONTRASTING VIEWS OF LEADER-SUBORDINATE

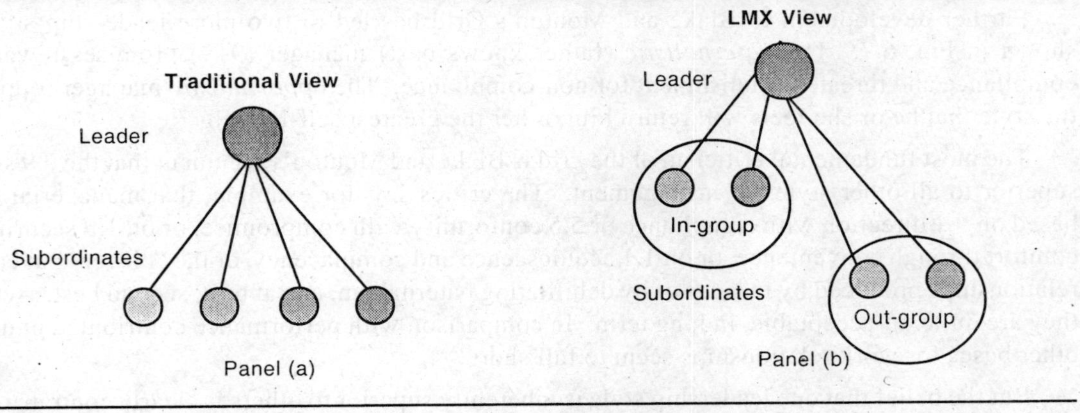

(***Source:*** Robert P. Vecctio, *Organisational Behaviour,* p.375)

Panel (a) in Fig.6.6 portrays the traditional view of how leaders and subordinates are perceived. All subordinates are created equally — they have equal access to the leader, equal influence in decision making, equal sharing of information, and equal social distance from the leader. Panel (b) however, reflects the vertical dyad linkage perspective, wherein the in-group members enjoy a better relationship with the leader than the out-group members. The differing distances of the subordinates from the leader reflect differences in the equality of working relationships, and therefore, differences in influence, authority, and access to information.

Why is the model called the Leader Member Exchange theory? The theory emphasizes the social exchange that takes place between leader and followers. The social exchange view states that group members make contributions at a cost to themselves and receive rewards accordingly. Interaction continues because members find the social exchange mutually rewarding.

The LMX model has its applications in any situation where the leader is required to influence followers; whether it is the Vice-chancellor of a university, director of a B-School, or executive in an organization, there are bound to be in-groups and out-groups. There is no doubt that in-group members are more close to the boss than those belonging to the out-group. But the problem with the model relates to the categorization of subordinates into in-group and out-group. Who is with in-group and who is with out-group? Is group alignment permanent? What are the criteria to categorize an employee into one group or other? These are difficult questions for which no easy answers are available.

The Managerial Grid A graphic depiction of a two dimensional view of leadership style has been developed by Blake and Mouton. They proposed a Managerial Grid based on the styles of 'concern for people' and 'concern for production' which correspond to the Ohio State dimensions of consideration and initiating structure or the Michigan dimensions of employee centred and production centred. Fig. 6.7 shows a diagram of the Managerial Grid.

The grid identifies five basic styles of leadership. The 9,1 (task management) leader is primarily concerned with production and has little concern for people. This person believes in getting work done at all costs. The 1,9 (country club management) leader is primarily concerned with people. The 5,5 (middle of the road management) leader represents a moderate concern for both. The 9,9 (team management) style demonstrates high concern for both production and people and is, therefore, the ideal approach to leadership. The 1,1 (impoverished management) has minimum concern for people and production. The model is useful to managers in as much as it helps them identify their current styles and develop the most desirable style.

Further development to Blake and Mouton's Grid has led to two more leadership styles as shown in Fig. 6.7. The *paternalistic* (father knows best) manager (9+9) promises reward for compliance and threatens punishment for non-compliance. The *opportunistic* manager (opp) uses the style that he or she feels will return him or her the greatest self-benefits.[22]

The most fundamental criticism of the grid is Blake and Mouton's argument that the 9,9 style is superior to all other styles of management. The critics say, for example, that managerial styles based on 9,1 direction with compliance or 5,5 conformity with compromise, or on 1,9 security and comfort through convenience, or on 1,1 acquiescence and complacency, or the "clever" but corrupt relationships produced by facades or by debilitating paternalism, are at best, second best. Actually they are quite un-acceptable, in long term. In comparison with performance contributed under 9,9 other bases for work relationships seem to fall short.

But the belief that one leadership style is inherently superior to others is clearly contratry to the contingency idea of leadership. It seems unlikely that the 9,9 management style is appropriate for organisations experiencing different growth rates, labour relations, competition and a host of other differentiating problems.

CONTINGENCY THEORIES OF LEADERSHIP

It became increasingly clear for people studying the leadership phenomenon that predicting leadership effectiveness was more complex than identifying a few traits or preferable behaviours. The failure to obtain consistent results led to a focus on situational or contingency theories of leadership. As the name itself implies, contingency theories of leadership are derived from the basic proposition that the most effective behaviour for leaders to engage in is contingent upon characteristics of the situation in which the leaders find themselves. Thus, the types of questions we must ask ourselves regarding leadership range from those such as "is an employee oriented

FIGURE 6-7
THE MANAGERIAL GRID

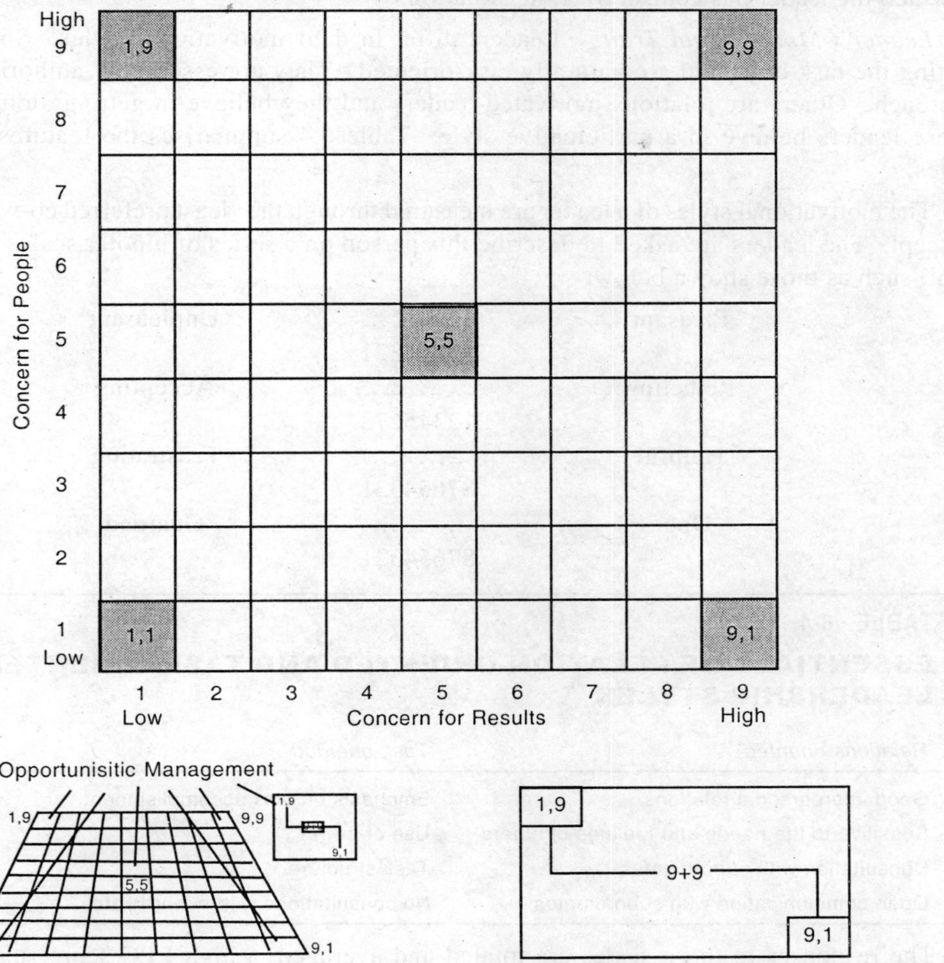

In Opportunisitic Management, people adapt and shift to any grid style needed to gain the maximum advantage. Performance occurs according to a system of selfish gain. Effort is given only for an advantage for personal gain.

9+9 : Paternalism/ Maternalism Management :

Reward and approval are bestowed to people in return for loyalty and obedience; failure to comply leads to punishment.

(***Source:*** Debra L. Nelson, *et al,* p.397)

leadership more effective than a production-oriented one"? to new questions such as, "under what conditions (in what type of situation) will employee oriented leadership be effective, and under what different types of conditions will production-oriented leadership be effective.?"[22]

Fiedler's contingency model, the path-goal theory and the situational leadership theory are the three most popular contingency theories of leadership.

Fiedler's Theory Fiedler's model postulates that effectiveness of a leader depends upon (1) his motivational style, and (2) the favourableness of the situation. Leaders are motivated by either interpersonal relations or task-goal accomplishment. The situational favourableness is the extent to which the leader has control over the situation.[23]

Leader's Motivational Traits Leaders differ in their motivational styles. Some believe in getting the task done and are naturally task-oriented. They are essentially authoritarian in their approach. Others are relations-motivated leaders and they believe in getting along with others. These leaders believe in a participative style. Table 6.4 summarises the features of these two styles.

The motivational styles of a leader are measured through the "least preferred co-workers" (LPC) concept. The leaders are asked to describe this person on a series of bipolar scales (usually 16 in total) such as those shown below:

Pleasant	 87654321	Unpleasant
Rejecting	 12345678	Accepting
Helpful	 87654321	Frustrating
Open	 87654321	Guarded

TABLE 6-4

ESSENTIALS OF RELATION-ORIENTED AND TASK-ORIENTED LEADERSHIP STYLES

Relations-oriented	*Task-oriented*
Good interpersonal relations	Emphasis on task accomplishment
Sensitive to the needs and feelings of others	Use of power
Consultation with subordinates	Task structure
Open communication with subordinates	No consultations with subordinates

The responses to these scales are totaled and averaged, a high LPC score suggests that the leader has relations-orientation, while a low LPC indicates a task-orientation. Fiedler's logic is that individuals who rate their least preferred co-worker in a relatively favourable light on these scales derive satisfaction out of interpersonal relations; those who rate the co-worker in a relatively unfavourable light get satisfaction out of successful task performance.

Situational Factors According to Fiedler the situation is favourable to the leader when he has influence and control over his subordinates' performance. Three factors are hypothesised to determine situational favourability : (1) leader-member relations, (2) task structure, and (3) position power.

Leader-Member Relations When the relationship between the leader and the subordinates is good and the leader can count on the loyalty of his subordinates, the leader's influence and control are high. Poor leader member relations, on the other hand, impair the leader's control and contribute to an unfavourable situation to the leader.

Task-Structure This factor describes the extent to which the task has a well defined goal, has methods of operation that can be easily defined, whose accomplishment can be easily measured, and also leads to a unique solution. A high degree of task structure contributes to a favourable situation for the leader as it enables him to influence and control the behaviour of a subordinate on a structured task. When the task is unstructured, the situation is not favourable to the leader who is less likely to have any influence and control over his subordinate's behaviour.

Position Power Position power comprises formal authority and reward power. Authority exists to command needed resources for task accomplishment and reward power to award a reward for good performance and punishment for laxity on the part of subordinates. The greater the power, the greater the leader's control over subordinates and the more favourable the situation is to the leader.

Over all, situational favourableness is determined by the combination of these three situational factors. A high control situation occurs where the leader has good leader-member relations, highly structured tasks and strong position power. A low control situation exists when the leader has poor relationships with subordinates, unstructured tasks and weak position power. Between these two situations exists a moderate control situation.[24]

Leadership Match According to the contingency theory, a task-oriented leader will perform better than a relations-oriented one in high or low control situations. Whereas a relations-oriented leader will do well in moderate control situations (See Fig. 6.8)

FIGURE 6-8
LEADERSHIP EFFECTIVENSS IN THE CONTINGENCY THEORY

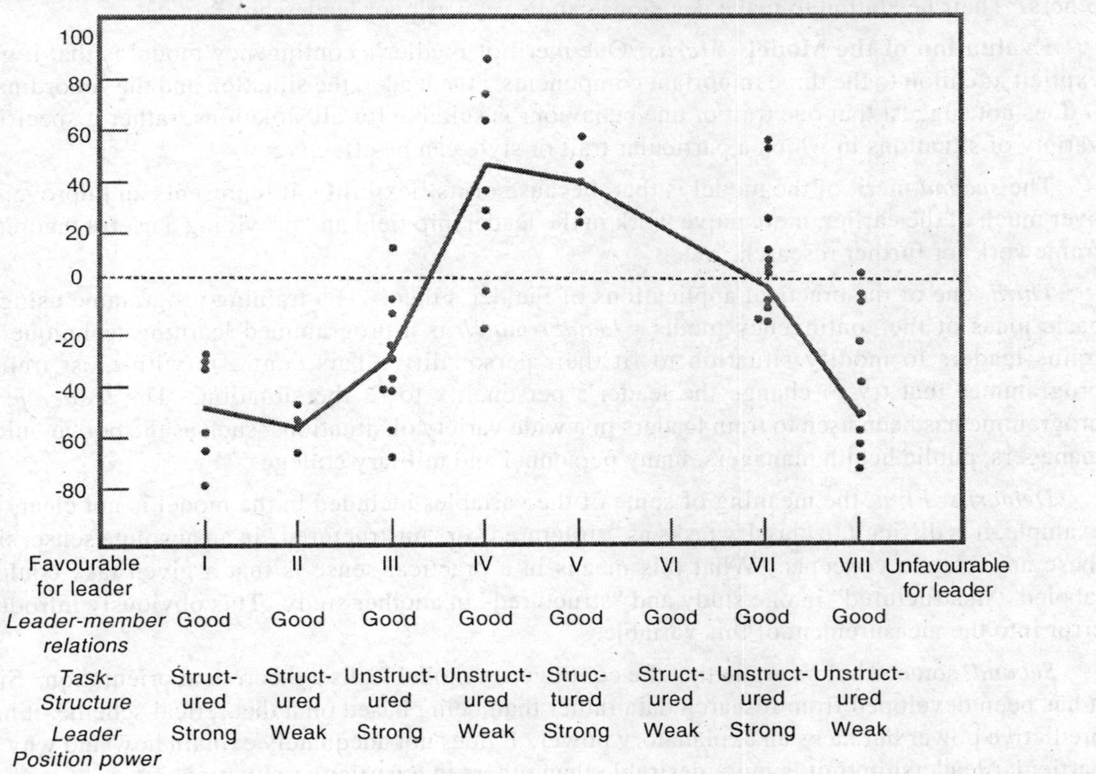

(***Source:*** F.E. Fiedler, *A Theory of Leader Effectiveness*, p. 27)

What are the reasons for such phenomena? Why does a task motivated leader perform well in both high control and low control situations? Similarly, why does relations motivated leader do well in a moderate control situation? Reasons are not difficult to seek.

High-control Situation Since task performance is controlled in high-controlled situations, task-motivated leaders should be able to relax and even become considerate toward their subordinates. By doing so, they can meet the needs of both the organisation and its members. On the other hand, relation-oriented leaders, who pride themselves on being able to solve problems with interpersonal skills, do not find much challenge in this situation. Since their subordinates are willing to comply with their wishes, the managers do not have much opportunity to use their interpersonal abilities.

Moderate-control Situation Relation motivated leaders perform best in this situation because they are able to accomplish task-goals by using their interpersonal skills. They are sensitive to the needs of group members, encourage others to participate in the group process, and incorporate different viewpoint in solving complex problems. On the other hand, task-motivated leaders are so engrossed in accomplishing the task that they are not able to deal patently with interpersonal conflicts and pay little attention to the needs and feelings of their work group members.

Low-control Situation In this situation, task motivated leaders should be able to provide the direction that the employees want. When the situation is chaotic, people will be more concerned with direction and leadership than with interpersonal likes or dislikes. Although leaders may irritate subordinates at times by being directive, they can quickly achieve task-oriented goals by structuring and monitoring the group tasks. On the other hand, relation motivated leaders are so concerned with interpersonal relationships, that they feel uneasy about making decisions without consulting others. Their hesitation to make decisions can be seen as poor leadership.[25]

Evaluation of the Model *Merits:* One merit of Fiedler's contingency model is that it gives explicit attention to the three important components : the leader, the situation and the subordinates. It does not suggest that one trait or one behaviour is suitable for all situations, rather it specifies a variety of situations in which a particular trait or style can be effective.

The *second* merit of the model is that, because of its flexibility, it represents an improvement over much of the earlier, more naïve work in the leadership field and providing a useful theoretical framework for further research.[26]

Third, one of the practical applications of Fielder's theory is a training programme using the basic ideas of the contingency model. *Leader match* is a programmed learning technique that trains leaders to modify situation to fit their personality. This contrasts with most training programmes that try to change the leader's personality to fit the situation. The *leader match* programme has been used to train leaders in a wide variety of situations, such as the police, middle managers, public health managers, many personnel and military colleges.

Demerits First, the meaning of some of the variables included in the model is not clear. For example, it is difficult to classify tasks as "structured" or "unstructured" in an absolute sense, since these are relative concepts. What this means in a practical sense is that a given task could be labeled "unstructured" in one study and "structured" in another study. This obviously introduces error into the measurement of this variable.[27]

Second, some scholars argue that the contingency model lacks a theoretical orientation. Since it has been developed from research data rather than being based on a theoretical scheme, it has a predictive power but lacks an explanatory power. It does not adequately explain how and why one particular leadership trait is more desirable than others in a particular situation.[28]

Third, there is the question of what the LPC scale measures. It does not satisfactorily explain how and why leaders who describe least preferred co-workers in negative terms are considered to be task-motivated and those who describe them in positive terms are considered relation-motivated. Therefore, the theory generally lacks explanatory power.[29]

Fourth, the LPC score instrument is itself criticised. It is said that the score does not reveal the leader behaviour but suggest only his feelings towards his least preferred co-worker.

Fifth, no attention is given to the actual technical competence of the leader or the subordinates. The theory assumes adequate technical competence both in the leader and in the followers.[30]

In conclusion, it may be stated that Fiedler has clearly made an important contribution towards understanding leadership effectiveness. His model has been the object of much controversy and probably will continue to be so. Field studies fall short of providing full support and the model could benefit by including additional moderating variables. But Fiedler's work continues to be a dominant input in the development of a contingency explanation of leadership effectiveness.

Path – Goal Theory of Leadership One of the most respected approaches to the study of leadership currently discussed is the path goal theory developed by Robert House.

The essence of the theory is that the leader's job is to use structure, support and rewards to create a work environment that helps employees reach the organisation's goals.[31] According to the theory the leader must clarify goals for the subordinates and clear the path for realising the goals. The theory is called path goal because its major concern is how the leader influences the subordinates' perceptions of their work goals, personal goals and paths to goal attainment. The theory suggests that a leader's behaviour is motivating or satisfying to the degree that the behaviour increases subordinate goal attainment and clarifies the paths to these goals.[32]

The path goal theory is closely related to the expectancy theory of motivation discussed in Chapter 8. The expectancy theory holds that motivation is the product of a desire for an outcome (valence), the belief that effort will lead to performance (instrumentality) and the hope that performance will result in desired outcome (expectancy). The path goal theory focuses on how leaders might influence motivation by increasing the availability and attractiveness of rewards and by strengthening the expectancies that effort can result in performance and performance in rewards.

As was mentioned earlier, the path goal is one of the contingency models. The leader's effectiveness, according to the path goal theory, in influencing rewards and expectancies depends on the characteristics of the environment and the characteristics of the subordinates. As Fig. 6.9 shows, the ultimate effect of leadership behaviour on motivation and satisfaction is contingent upon the characteristics of environment and of the subordinates and follower perceptions about effort-reward linkages.[33]

The figure shows four different kinds of leader behaviour and two categories of contingency variables. Together, the behaviours and contingencies influence the motivation for task performance and satisfaction of employees.

The four dimensions of leader behaviour are directive, supportive, achievement oriented, and participative. The true meaning of these dimensions as they would be reflected in actual leader behaviours is illustrated in Table 6.5. Path-goal theory suggests that depending on the followers and the situation, these different leader behaviours can increase goal clarity of followers, enhance their level of satisfaction, and raise their expectations that effort will result in effective performance, which in turn, will lead to valued rewards.

Evaluation of the Theory The path-goal theory deserves appreciation in as much as it suggests that leaders should first assess the situation and select a leadership behaviour appropriate to the

FIGURE 6-9
THE PATH-GOAL THEORY OF LEADERSHIP

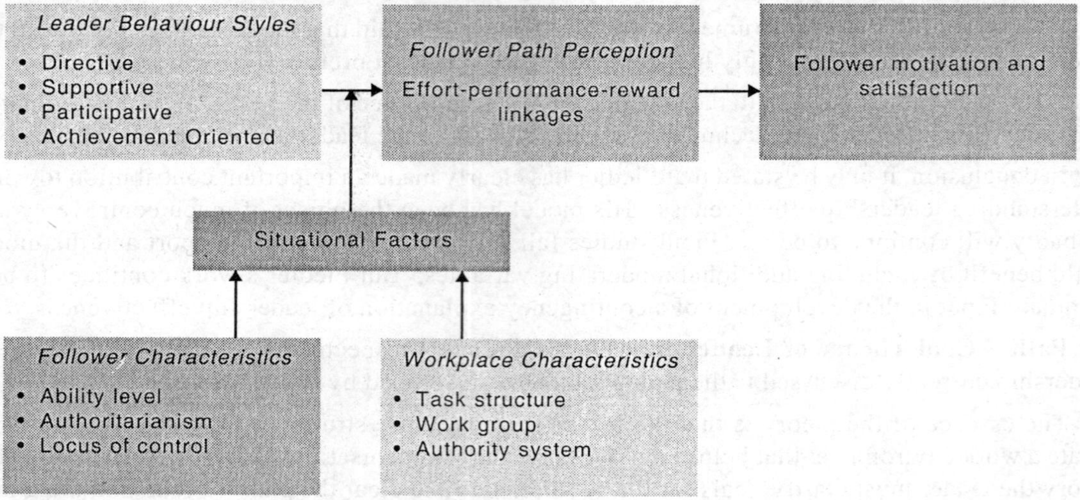

TABLE 6-5
LEADER BEHAVIOUR DIMENSIONS IN PATH-GOAL THEORY

Leader Directiveness

Letting subordinates know what's expected.
Providing specific guidance as to what should be done and how.
Making leader's part in the group understood.
Scheduling work to be done.
Maintaining definite standards of performance.

Leader Supportiveness

Showing concern for status and well-being of subordinates.
Doing little things to make the work more pleasant.
Treating members as equals.
Being friendly and approachable.

Leader Participativeness

Consulting with subordinates.
Soliciting subordinate suggestions.
Taking these suggestions seriously.
Maintaining definite standards of performance.

Leader Achievement-orientedness

Setting challenging goals.
Expecting subordinates to perform at their peak levels.
Showing a high degree of confidence in subordinates.
Constantly emphasising excellence in performance.

situational demands. By exhibiting the appropriate behaviours, leaders can enhance followers' effort-to-performance expectancies, performance-to-reward expectancies, or valences of the outcomes. These increased expectancies and valences will improve subordinates' effort level and the rewards attained, which in turn, will enhance followers' performance and satisfaction.

An example will better explain what has been stated above. Suppose we have a set of followers who are in a newly created work unit and do not have a clear understanding of their roles. If afterwards, there is role ambiguity, the path-goal theory posits that the leader should play a directive role to clear role ambiguity of his or her followers. Because role ambiguity is a source of unpleasantness and conflicts, its removal through leader's directive behaviour tends to increase employee satisfaction. Fig.6.10 illustrates this process. Similarly, leaders may look at the leadership situation and note that follower's performance is not satisfactory. The leader may also conclude that the current situation may not offer attractive incentives for increased performance. In this case, the leader may use directive behaviour to increase the value of the rewards (or valence) which, in turn, will increase employee performance.

FIGURE 6-10
EXAMPLE OF APPLYING PATH-GOAL THEORY

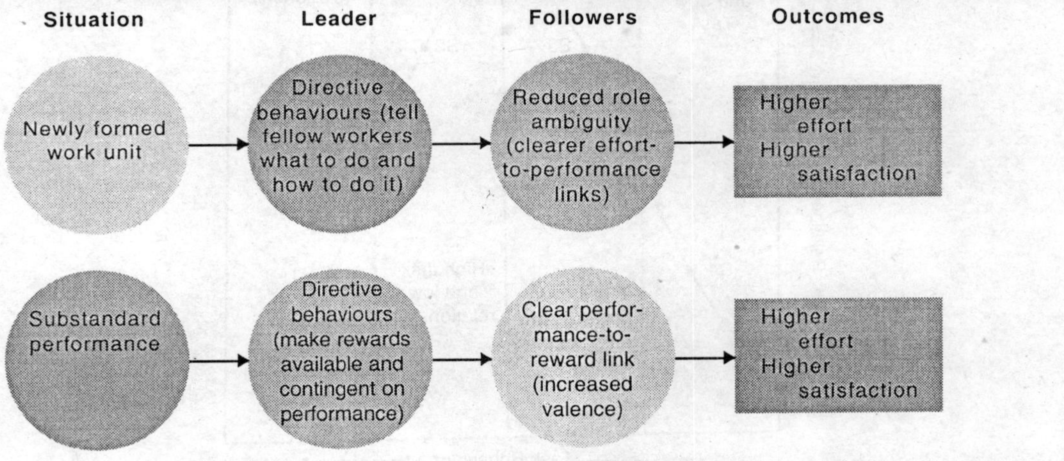

(***Source:*** Richard L. Hughes *et al, Leadership*, p. 4)

Another merit of the path-goal theory is its simplicity. The theory illustrates that as models become more complicated, they may be more useful to researchers and less appealing to practitioners. This does not mean they prefer simplicity to validity-they generally appreciate the complexity of the leadership process. But neither do they want a model that is so complex as to be indecipherable.

On the negative side of the model, two criticisms are identified. First, the simplicity of the theory is itself its drawback. Critics point out that the theory fails to capture all elements of the leadership process. Second, the theory is yet to be extensively tested.

The Situational Leadership Theory Paul Hersey and Kenneth Blanchard have developed a situational model of leadership that adds "maturity" of followers as a contingency variable which deserves due consideration. The two authors feel that situational leadership requires adjusting the leader's emphasis on task behaviours (i.e., giving guidance and direction) and relationship behaviour (i.e., offering socio-emotional support) according to the maturity of follower in performing their tasks. *Maturity* in this context is understood not as age or emotional stability but as desire for achievement, willingness to accept responsibility and task-related ability and experience. The goals and knowledge of the followers are important variables in determining effective leadership style.

Hersey and Blanchard believe that the relationship between the leader and subordinates moves through four phases-a kind of life cycle-as subordinates develop and mature and that managers need to vary their leadership styles with each phase (See Fig. 6.11). In the initial phase – when subordinates first enter the organisation – a high task orientation by the manager is most appropriate. Subordinates must be instructed in their tasks and familiarized with the organisation's rules and procedures.

FIGURE 6-11
THE SITUATIONAL THEORY OF LEADERSHIP

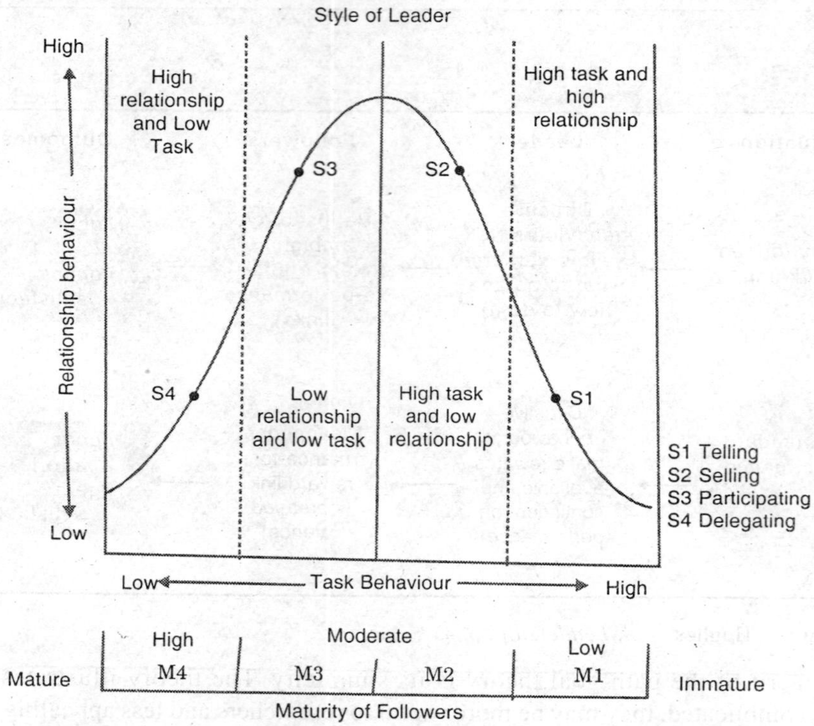

(*Source:* Hersey and Blanchard, *Management of Organisational Behaviour*, p. 152)

At this stage a non-directive manager causes anxiety and confusion among new employees, however, a participatory employee relationship approach would also be inappropriate at this stage because subordinates cannot yet be regarded as colleagues. This style is called the "directing" or "telling" approach of leadership.

As subordinates begin to learn their tasks, task-oriented management remains essential, as subordinates are not yet willing or able to accept full responsibility. However, the manager's trust in and support of subordinates can increase as the manager becomes familiar with subordinates and desires to encourage further efforts on their part. Thus, the manager may choose to initiate employee-oriented behaviours. This style is called "selling" or "coaching" approach to leadership.

In the third phase (here it is the "participating" or "supporting" style), the subordinates' ability and achievement motivation are increased and subordinates actively begin to seek greater responsibility. The manager will no longer need to be directive (indeed, close direction might be resented). However, the manager will continue to be supportive and considerate in order to strengthen the subordinates' resolve for greater responsibility.

"Delegating" is the style which the manager follows in the final stage. Here, the manager can reduce the amount of support and encouragement as subordinates gradually become more confident, self-directing and experienced. Subordinates are "on their own" and no longer need or expect a directive relationship with their manager.

Evaluation The situational leadership theory has generated considerable interest because it recommends a leadership type that is dynamic and flexible rather than static. The motivation, ability and experience of subordinates must be constantly assessed in order to determine which style combination would be most appropriate under flexible and changing conditions. If the style is appropriate, according to Hersey and Blanchard, it will not only motivate employees but will also help them move towards maturity. Further, the theory gives specific attention to followers and their feelings about a task or jot to be done. Finally, the theory is one of the more popular leadership training module available today. Partly enhanced by the success of Blanchard's book *The One Minute Manager*, many organisations make use of the model and its associated instruments.

The theory is however, weak on three counts. *First*, the theory requires that a leader be perceptive enough to determine a subordinate's maturity development level on a task. How to assess the maturity level is a difficult task.

Secondly, situational leadership, like most contingency theories, is heavily based on the need for style flexibility. Is it possible to change style as subordinates mature? Although, it is desirable that the leaders are adaptable, there is a strong belief that this is not possible.

Finally, the theory assumes that the nature of the task being supervised is such that the leader can treat each employee in a slightly different way. There is no doubt that this is a reasonable assumption in many cases. But in practice can a leader exhibit different leadership styles when all members of the group perform the task together ? This question remains unanswered.

Thus, viewed from conceptual and methodological perspective, the theory remains an intuitively appealing model that needs empirical validation.

Vroom-Yetton Model One of the tasks of a leader is to make decisions. Because the decisions reached by leaders often have far-reaching effects on their subordinates, one major determinant of leader effectiveness clearly is the adequacy with which they perform this key task. Leaders who make good decisions will be more effective in the long run than leaders who make bad ones. How do leaders make good decisions? Stated differently, how much participation should leaders invite from subordinate?

Participation in decision making is an important variable in determining job satisfaction, productivity, stress, and turnover. Thus, the manner in which leaders handle their issue can be crucial in determining their effectiveness.

Reverting to be question-how much participation in decisions by subordinates should leaders allow-an easy answer to this is provided by the normative decision theory of Vroom and Yetton. The model suggests that there are five decision-making styles, ranging from highly autocratic to highly participative. In the order of importance, the five styles are:

- **Autocratic I (AI)**-A leader solves a problem using information that is readily available.
- **Autocratic II (AII)**-A leader obtains additional information from subordinates and then solves the problem.

- **Consultative I (CI)**-A leader shares the problem with subordinates on an individual basis and obtains their ideas and suggestions. Further, the leader chooses a solution to the problem at hand.
- **Consultative II (CII)**-A leader shares the problem with subordinates as a group. The final decision may or may not reflect subordinate input.
- **Group (G)**-A leader meets with subordinates as a group. However, he or she acts as a chairperson who focuses and directs discussion, but does not impose his or her will on the group. Subordinate's participation is sought.

Which of these styles is most appropriate for a given situation depends on a number of factors. Vroom and Yetton identify seven questions that need to be answered to determine the appropriate style. These underlying contingencies (or decision rules) focus on such issues as whether subordinates can be trusted to approach the problem from a perspective that is congruent with organizational goals. The seven questions can be arranged in a sequential fashion that permits matching leadership style to a given situation.

Fig.6.12 shows the decision tree that Vroom and Yetton devised for selecting the best or most appropriate style. The seven decision rules are listed across the top of the model. For each question, a leader is to provide a yes or no answer. At the end of each branch in the tree is a designated style, denoted by AI, AII, CI, CII, or G.

The theory can be better explained by studying an example. Consider a manager who is required to deal with a purchase department typist who is not typing enough purchase orders each day (the answer to Q.A is yes). If the manager has a clear understanding of why the typist is a poor performer (B=yes), if the subordinate must accept the manager's decision in order for the solution to work (D=yes), and if the manager is also certain that his or her decision will be accepted by the subordinate (E=yes), then the manager should take a non-participative approach to dealing with the problem (AI).[34]

The Vroom-Yetton model provides a useful devise for diagnosing a situation. It prescribes a specific type of behaviour (hence the theory is called normative model) for a leader who is confrônted with a particular problem.

This theory makes an important contribution to the understanding of leadership. In so far as there is widespread current interest in allowing subordinates to participate in decision making, the normative decision theory is useful in giving leaders clear guidance as to when such a move may be expected to improve task performance.

Although the model offers specific guidelines to leaders, its utility is limited to the leader decision-making tasks.

Recently, proponents of the theory have sought to modify the model to answer its critics. For example, it can be very difficult to always answer the seven decision rules with a simple yes or no answer. Often, a manager has only a sense of what is likely to occur. In such cases, he or she may be able to give probability estimates but not simple and firm answers. To address this and other related issues, Vroom and his associates have made a number of modifications, such as allowing probabilistic responses. As a result, the model is evolving into a very complex and unwieldy set of mathematical equations. Nonetheless, managers who are not particularly interested in precise mathematical advice, may be because of lack interest or time, will continue to use the decision tree presented in Fig.6.12 as a quick guide to selecting a leadership style.[35]

McGregor's Theory X and Theory Y McGregor's Theory X and Theory Y are probably the most widely known of all the theories, having been discussed much in textbooks, journals and

FIGURE 6-12
VROOM-YETTON MODEL

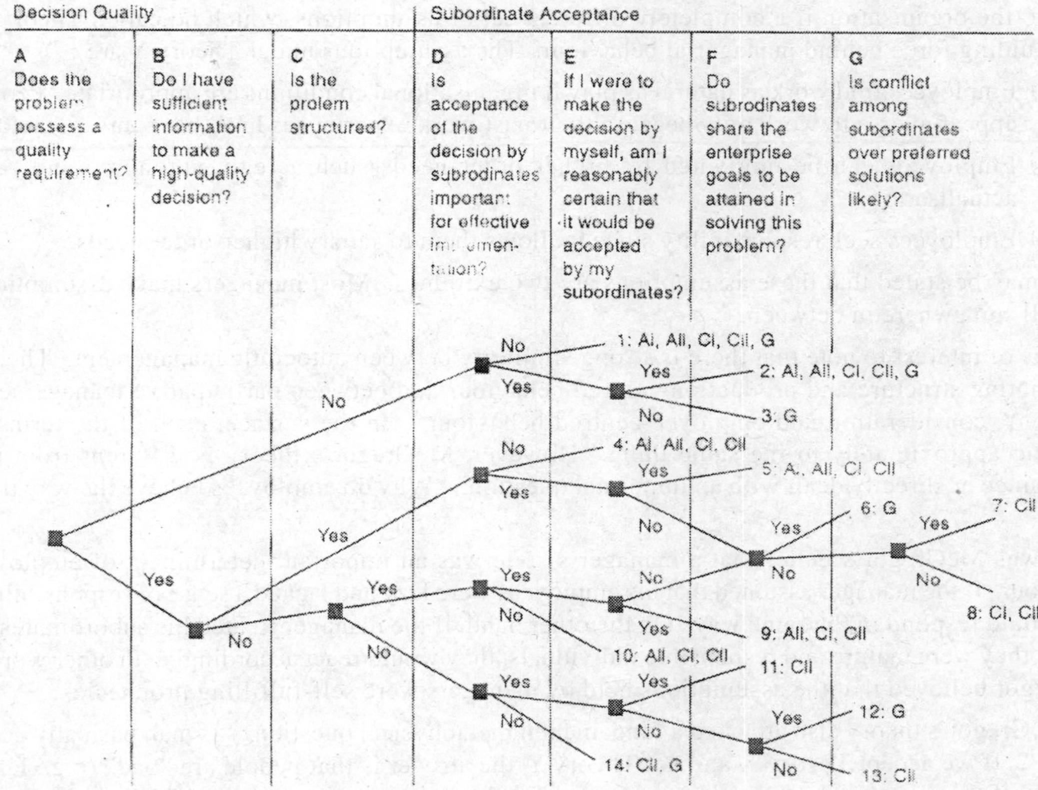

Decision-Making Methods

AI = Autocratic decision without subordinates' input

AII = Autocratic decision using ingormation gathered from suboridinates

CI = Consultative decision with problem discussed individually with each subordinate

CII = Consultative decision with problem discussed with subordinates as a group

G = Group decision

Note: The numbers 1–14 denote Problem Types.

---

management training programmes. It is difficult to determine whether Theory X and Theory Y are leadership theories or theories of motivation. We include the theories in a discussion on leadership because of the assumptions a leader makes about his subordinates. It should not, however, be forgotten that the theories have implications for employee motivation.

McGregor argued that traditional managerial behaviour was inappropriate since it was based on some questionable assumption about employees. Appropriately labeled Theory X by McGregor, these assumptions were :

(i) Employees are inherently lazy and will avoid work unless forced to do it.

(ii) Employees have no ambition or desire for responsibility; instead they prefer to be directed and controlled.

(iii) Employees have no motivation to achieve organisational objectives.

(iv) Employees are only motivated by physiological and safety needs.

McGregor contended that many managerial practices were based on Theory X assumptions and pointed to such examples as hierarchical models of organisation where one person controls another, or on a small scale, a quality control inspector who checks on the behaviour of others. He further believed that Theory X assumptions were outdated and that employees would contribute far more to the organisation if a completely different set of assumptions, which he called Theory Y, were guiding force behind managerial behaviour. The assumptions under Theory Y are :

(*i*) Employees find work as natural as play if organisational conditions are appropriate. People appear averse to work only because their past work experiences have been unsatisfactory.

(*ii*) Employees can be motivated by higher order needs such as ego, autonomy and self-actualisation.

(*iii*) Employees seek responsibility since it allows them to satisfy higher-order needs.

It may be stated that these assumptions are two extremes. Most managers make assumptions that fall somewhere in between.

It is of interest to note that there is strong similarity between autocratic management, Theory X, initiating structure and production-centred behaviour and between participative management, Theory Y, consideration and employee-centred behaviour. On the surface, each of the terms is referring approximately to the same thing. However, McGregor's theory is different from the other, since he directly dealt with an important question: "Why do employees behave the way they do?"

It was McGregor's belief that a manager's style was an important determinant of employee behaviour. If the manager assumed that his employees were lazy and lacked a sense of responsibility, they would respond in the same way. On the other hand, if the manager treated his subordinates as though they were mature and responsible individuals, they would react accordingly. In other words, McGregor believed that the assumptions held by managers were self-fulfilling prophecies.

McGregor's theory also attacked a fundamental metaphysical question : "Is man basically good or bad"? If we accept Theory X and not Theory Y, the answer is that people are "bad" (e.g., lazy) because of the way they have been treated.[36]

Till now we have examined the various theories on leadership. Before closing this chapter, it is useful to take another look at the theories. Fig. 6.13 provides a review of the theories covered in this chapter.

What Does it Mean?

Till now we have discussed the nature and theories of leadership. The relevant questions now are what does this discussion mean? In what way will the discussion help a practising manager discharge his or her functions more effectively? The following paragraphs will answer these questions.

1. The manager must understand that leadership is a two-way influencing process. Just as the leader influences his followers, the actions and performance of subordinates will influence the behaviour of their leader. The leader must realise this and accept the influence of followers on him.

2. Whatever may be the criticism against the trait theory of leadership, there is no gainsaying the fact that effective leadership demands certain unique qualities. One such quality is *competence*. The leader must be competent enough to perform a task better than what his or her followers are capable of. This earns him or her enormous respect from his or her followers. Competence

FIGURE 6-13
ESSENCE OF LEADERSHIP THEORIES

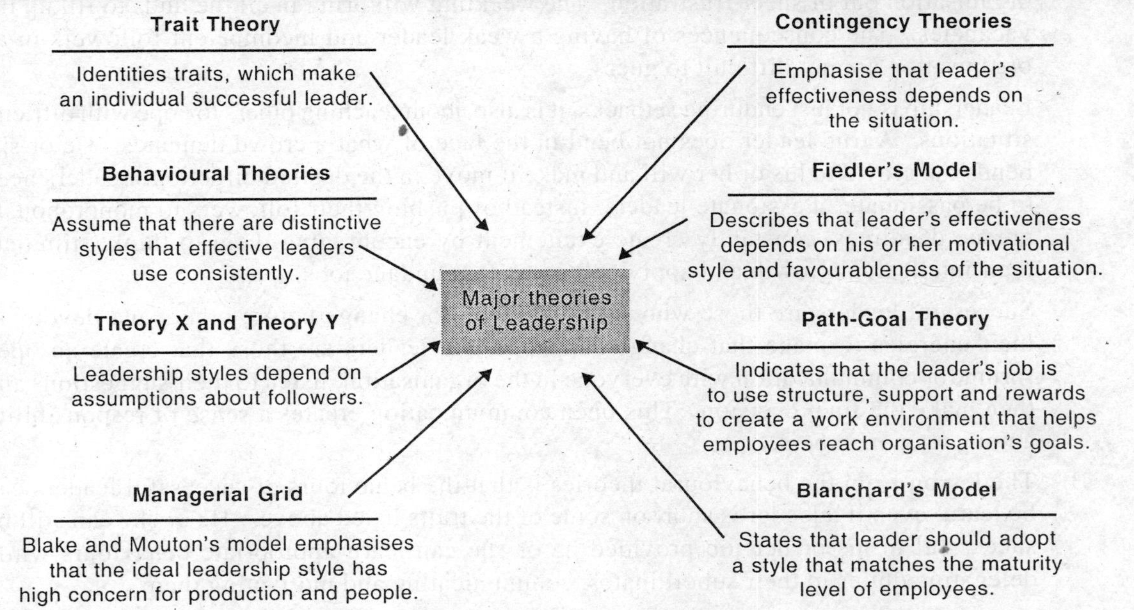

gives robust *confidence* to the leader about himself or herself and about his or her team. It is the confidence which equips him or her to face any adverse situation with courage. It also enables the leader to kindle hope in his or her followers when their spirits are down, which is usually the case when the organisation is passing through a lean period. A leader needs to be an *intellectual*. He or she needs to understand not only the intricacies of the immediate task before him or her, but must also have knowledge about the political, economic, social and cultural milieu operating beyond his or her company's gate. The leader should also be *visionary* to visualize and map out the future for his or her organisation 15 to 20 years ahead and even beyond. *Communication skill* is yet another quality which a leader needs to be endowed with. He or she need not be a great orator but must be able to express his or her ideas fluently and with clarity. What makes a successful leader distinct from unsuccessful ones is the *courage* to make quick decisions. A leader who oscillates in making decisions will miss opportunities to rivals. Success in business lies in seizing an opportunity before others do and exploiting it to one's advantage. A leader needs to be even tempered however trying the situation may be. Losing his or her temper will make him or her lose his or her balance. Besides, anger betrays the weakness of an individual. *Selflessness* pays rich dividends to the leader. True, success has come to the organisation thorough his or her dynamic leadership, but the active involvement of the followers should not be forgotten. Wisdom lies in making others feel winners and not in arrogating all credit to one self. The leader must have sincerity of purpose. He or she must complete the task that he or she initiates. Above all the leader must be a man of character. The leader's job is not mere realisation of goals. He or she has the bigger responsibility of ennobling and elevating his or her subordinates to higher things in life.

It is essential that an individual who is richly endowed with all these qualities and more should alone be appointed as the leader. Any laxity on this condition will result in bringing a weakling and crowning him or her with the position of leadership. Such a leader will experience insecurity in the company of subordinates who may be smarter. He or she will treat them as his or her rivals instead of as followers and will ensure that they quit the organisation out of sheer frustration. The weakling will bring in all the duds to fill up the vacancies. The consequences of having a weak leader and incompetent followers in an organisation are not difficult to guess.

Leadership is not just enduring setbacks, it is also about teaching others to cope with difficult situations. A true leader does not bend in the face of what a crowd demands. He or she bends the crowd to his or her will and make it move in the desired direction. Leaders need to be passionate. Passionate leaders, instead of pushing their followers to monotonously pursue deadlines, constantly create excitement by encouraging them to think, stimulate their intellectual growth and apply new ideas to mundane jobs.

Successful leaders are those who sense the need for change before others and devote all their energies to make that change happen. Good leaders are those that create an open forum for communication with everyone in the organisation, listen to their suggestions and then make the final decision. This open communication creates a sense of responsibility among team members.

3. The lesson from the behavioural theories is that the behaviours of successful leaders can be learnt even if a leader is short on some of the traits listed above. He or she can still be successful in his or her job provided he or she can learn appropriate behaviours while delegating duties to their subordinates, communicating and motivating them.
4. A leader can learn a valuable lesson from contingency theories; the effectiveness of leadership depends on situations – the tasks to be accomplished, the skills and expectations of subordinates, the organisational environment, the past experiences of the leader and his or her followers and the like. An individual who is successful as a leader in one situation may do poorly in another. Specifically contingency theories encourage managers to :
   - Examine their situation – the people, task and organisation.
   - Be flexible in the use of various skills within an overall style.
   - Consider modifying elements of their jobs to obtain a better match with their preferred style.

Thus, a successful leader does not have one best way of doing things. He or she needs to follow different styles suiting different situations. Matching a particular style to a specific situation is the essence of effective leadership.

Given below is a list of 12 different work situations (see Table 6.6). Against each situation the most appropriate leadership style is recommended. The situation-style match given in the table is not comprehensive and is not the ideal one but it does help a leader understand the uniqueness of the situation and adopt an appropriate style.[37]

5. Finally, McGregor's Theory X and Theory Y can be an eye opener to any leader. Most leaders assume that their follower are under Theory X though they are, in effect, under Theory Y. The leader needs to learn a new theory of working with people – Theory Z.
6. Good leaders are likely to be good followers. Although there are distinctions between their social roles, the attributes and behaviours of leaders and followers may not be distinct.

TABLE 6-6
SITUATION – STYLE MATCH

Situation	Recommended Leadership Style
1. People in a state of confusion or panic because of crisis such as materials shortage, equipment failure, or natural disaster.	High task and low relationship or authoritarian.
2. Complex technology, inexperienced employees.	High task and low relationship at the outset.
3. Undesirable, repetitive jobs, average employees.	High relationship and low task.
4. Self-sufficient, capable workers performing job.	Low task and low relationship
5. Employees dislike working, job is undesirable.	High relationship and high task.
6. Start-up of new operation, job descriptions are vague.	High relationship and high task.
7. Group of people "doing time" until retirement.	High relationship and low task.
8. Inexperienced but well meaning employees.	High relationship and high task.
9. Repetitive work; employees with average motivation.	High relationship and low task.
10. Employees are performing independent tasks requiring coordination by leader.	High task; emphasis on relationship depends on emotional maturity of employees.
11. Emotionally immature employees; average skill level.	High task and low relationship.
12. Employees are child like or "prima donnas" but talented.	High relationship and low task.

Contemporary Issues on Leadership

Topics of contemporary interest relating to leadership are transformational leadership, women as leaders and charismatic leadership.

Transformational Leadership: In explaining the concept of transformational leadership, two styles of leadership are talked of. They are : transactional and transformational. Transactional leaders determine what subordinates need to do to achieve their own and organisational objectives, classify those requirements and help subordinates become confident that they can reach their objective by expanding the necessary efforts.[38] The styles of leadership we discussed till now belong to the transactional leadership. Transformational leadership implies a process whereby an individual attempts to elevate his or her consciousness (*chetana*) so that various common place conflicts and dualities begin at higher levels of synthesis.[39] Stated differently, transformational leadership attempts to change the whole organisation from one "style" or "culture" to another. As was pointed in the beginning of this chapter, transformational leadership has the ultimate aim of raising the level of human conduct and ethical aspiration of both the leader and the led. The leader's main thrust is to elevate, inspire and evangelise his or her followers (and himself or herself) to higher things in life.

The late J.R.D. Tata comes to one's memory in the context. His qualities of head and heart moved everybody who ever came into contact with him. If Tata group of companies stand distinct in our corporate world – in terms of profitability, professional management and social responsiveness – credit goes to the transformational leadership of J.R.D. Transformational leaders are characterised by distinct skills. They are : (1) *anticipatory skills* – foresight into a constantly changing environment; (2) *visionary skills* – a process of persuasion and example by which a person or leadership team induces a group to take action in accord with the leader's purposes or, more likely, the shared purposes of a larger groups; (3) *value* – congruence skills – the need of corporate leader to be in touch with employees' economic, safety, psychological, spiritual, sexual, aesthetic and physical needs in order to engage people on the basis of shared motives, values and goals; (4) *empowerment skills* – the willingness to share power and to do so effectively; and (5) *self-understanding* – introspective or self-understanding skills as well as frameworks within which leaders understand both their own needs and goals of those of their employees.[40]

We need more of transformational leaders for our economy. Our economy is now thrown open for global competition. Foreign companies are entering our country in a large number. In order to maintain our own identity and to sustain our ethos and at the same time to accept what is good for our business we need more transformational leaders. Specifically, we need more of J.R.D. Tatas.

Women As Leaders

Historically, women have been discriminated against in our male dominated society. Most girls were married when they were in their teens; widow remarriages were considered to be a social taboo; education beyond the primary or at the most school level was rare; girls, especially in rural and small towns, were deliberately undernourished and denied access to outside world; and women were considered to be fit to cook food but not to work in business establishments. Even the Constitution has not been free from bias against the fair sex. Throughout the Constitution, women are referred to only six times, and in five of them, they are clubbed together with men and children. Equality of gender has not been explicitly expounded as a specific Constitutional value, though Articles 14 and 15 guarantee equality of status, opportunity, social, political and economic justice.

The picture is not totally different today. The report of the National Committee on the Status of Women has made startling revelations. Major findings in the report are: a decline in the sex ratio due to excessive mortality among women and female children; disparity in access to health care and widening gap between women and men in literacy; education and training for employment. Daily newspapers publish reports about rape, bride burnings, dowry deaths and wives beaten to death. Women are afraid of going out alone after dark and cannot go for shopping without male escorts.

As we go into the future, discrimination against women will certainly go and they will sure occupy equal status along with male counterparts. Seeds for better tomorrow have already been sown. Today's girls are better educated, more assertive and more bold. Added to this is the women's liberation movement, to protect and improve the lot of women. Business and other professional activities are multiplying, demanding the services of talented people, including women. The Government is also keen on uplifting the status of women.

Women in Business Participation of women in business as owners, managers and employees is less encouraging, considering the size of the population and the vast opportunities available. While women account for 48 per cent of the population, the recent Census put the female work-force at 20.85 per cent. Those that take up jobs are content with lower paid jobs. Women occupying top positions are few and far between. Reasons are not difficult to seek. The main reasons are:

1. Women are known to have lower attachment to work and are, therefore, content with lower positions;
2. They do not consider themselves as primary earners and withdraw from the labour force once family income reaches adequacy;
3. They lack education and training commensurate with men as marriage and home-making take precedence; and
4. They are less preferred to men in recruitment and selection because of legal and other problems mentioned below.

Problems of Female Employment: Facts apart, people belonging to fair sex are generally employed, partly because for certain jobs they are best fit, and partly because suitable male candidates are not available. On being employed, women pose additional problems to employers. Provisions of the Factories Act and the Maternity Benefit Act should be complied with. Then there is the defiant attitude of a male worker to work under a woman manager or unwanted chivalrous attitude if the former is a boss. Further, women should be paid equal wages as male counterparts, though the former are less prepared to take up duties involving more physical strain. Payment of equal pay has been made mandatory.[41]

Two questions regarding women in leadership positions need to be addressed. The first concerns the skills and abilities necessary to lead: Are women more, or less, people-oriented than male leaders? Are women more, or less, job-oriented than men? The second question is related to subordinates' responses to male and female leader: Will female leaders not be permitted to lead because of the stereotypes and biases of their employees?

With regard to the first question no differences are observed in the skills and abilities of male and female leaders. In other words, there are no differences in the orientation of the two groups. Regarding the second question what we stated above holds good. There is the defiant attitude of a male worker to work under a woman manager or unwanted chivalrous attitude if the former is a boss.

Yet another issue relevant in this context is the effect of *glass ceiling.* Glass ceiling refers to the barrier that keeps women away from reaching the highest levels in organisations. Glass ceiling takes several forms. The well known barrier is the way women have been streotyped. They should cook and not work. The other barriers are highly subtle — fewer opportunities to learn, fewer opportunities for advancement, fewer chances of expatriation, fewer opportunities to work in projects that would enhance their visibility exclusion from networks and dyads and the like. Ideally, the glass ceiling should crack into pieces and the signs towards that are visible through the way women are getting educated empowerd and top positions, here and there, being occupied by them.

Charismatic Leadership Charisma is a leadership trait that can help influence employees to take early and sustained action. Charismatic leaders are dynamic risk-takers who show their expertise and self-confidence, express high performance expectations, and use symbols and language to inspire others. They can also be mentors who treat employees individually and guide them to take action.[42]

Table 6.7 contains 10 features of charismatic and non-charismatic leaders.

What is the effect of charismatic leadership on followers' performance and satisfaction ? There is a positive correlation between charismatic leadership and high performance and satisfaction among the followers. People working for charismatic leaders are motivated to work extra, because they like their leaders and express greater satisfaction in working with them.

However, charismatic leadership may not always be needed to achieve high levels of employee performance. It may be most appropriate when the follower's task has an ideological component. This may explain why, when charismatic leaders surface, it is more likely to be in politics, religion, wartime, or when a business firm is introducing a radically new product or facing a life – threaturning crisis. Such conditions tend to involve ideological concerns.

Charismatic leaders may become a liability to an organisation once the crisis and need for dramatic change subside. This is so because, in times of peace, charismatic leader's overwhelming self-confidence often becomes a liability. He or she is unable to listen to others, becomes uncomfortable when challenged by aggressive subordinates, and begins to hold an unjustifiable belief in his or her "rightness" on issues.

TABLE 6-7

BEHAVIOURAL COMPONENTS OF CHARISMATIC AND NON-CHARISMATIC LEADERS

	Non-charismatic Leader	*Charismatic Leader*
Relation to Status Quo	Essentially agrees with status quo and strives to maintain it	Essentially opposed to status quo and strives to change it
Future Goal	Goal not too discrepant from status quo	Idealised vision which is highly discrepant from status quo
Likableness	Shared perspective makes him/her likable	Shared perspective and idealized vision makes him/her a likable and honourable hero worthy of identification and imitation
Trustworthiness	Disinterested advocacy in persuasion attempts	Disinterested advocacy by incurring great personal risk and cost
Expertise	Expert in using available means to achieve goals within the framework of the existing order	Expert in using unconventional means to transcend the existing order
Behaviour	Conventional, conforming to existing norms	Unconventional or counter normative
Environmental Sensitivity	Low need for environmental sensitivity to maintain status quo	High need for environmental sensitivity for changing the status quo
Articulation	Weak articulation of goals and motivation to lead	Strong articulation of future vision and motivation to lead
Power Base	Position power and personal power (based on reward, expertise and liking for a friend who is a similar other)	Personal power (based on expertise, respect and admiration for a unique hero)
Leader-Follower	Egalitarian, consensus seeking, or directive. Nudges or orders people to share his/her views	Elitist, entrepreneur and exemplary. Transforms people to the radical changes advocated

(*Source:* Richard M. Hodgetts, *Organisational Behaviour*, p. 234)

Peter F. Drucker observes that charisma makes a leader inflexible convinced of his or her own infallibility, with inability to change. "History Knows" writes he, "no more charismatic leaders than this century's triad of Stalin. Hitler, and Mao – the misleaders who inflicted as much evil and suffering on humanity as have ever been recorded. This is what happened to Stalin, Hitler and Mao and it is a common place in the study of ancient history, that only Alexander the Great's early death saved him from becoming an ineffectual failure."

Emotional Intelligence Emotional intelligence refers to one's ability to monitor own and others' emotions, discriminate among them, and use the information to guide his or her thoughts and actions. Specifically, emotional intelligence consists of the following four dimensions.[44]

(i) *Emotional atonement or self awareness and people skills.* The person is good at reading his or her own feelings, can empathize with others, and accept other people's feelings.

(ii) *Emotional management.* The person's emotions do not overwhelm him or her, and they are appropriate to the situation.

(iii) *Self-driven.* Self-motivation is connected with denial of gratification. People who deny immediate gratification and exhibit patience for rewards are more socially competent and self-reliant than those who crave for immediate gains.

(iv) *Self-management skills.* This refers to handling situations without being subsumed or overwhelmed by them.

Effective leaders possess emotional intelligence. The hallmarks of emotional intelligence, namely, self-awareness, empathy, adaptability, and self-confidence, are learned capabilities, and they can be developed.

Case

GE's Controversial Leader

In 1981, John W. Welch, Jr., became CEO of General Electric. His appointment ushered in an era of disdain for the elaborate planning and centralised control that had been the hallmark of his predecessor, Reginald Jones. "Jones felt the others would be caretakers," says one former GE vice president, "Welch was the one who would take the company in radical directions if necessary."

Indeed, Welch has proved to be anything but a caretaker. He quickly articulated a plan to change GE from a manufacturing company deriving more than half its revenues from heavy industry to one reaping a larger share of its earnings from technology and services. He also stated that GE would sell those of its businesses that weren't either first or second in their markets.

Since becoming CEO, Welch has sold more than 250 businesses and used $ 20 billion to purchase more than 300 new ones. Among the acquisition are the RCA Corporation, the Employers Reinsurance Company, 80 percent of Kidder, Peabody & Company, the medical equipment business of Thomson SA, the appliance-making Roper Corporation and the chemical business of the Borg-Warner Corporation. In the process, he has eliminated more than 200,000 jobs through forced retirements, layoffs, resignations and outright divestitures.

His moves have caused revenues to increase by 50 percent – up to about $ 70 billion. Admirers say that Welch has vision and is transforming GE from a stodgy bureaucracy to a nimble company much more fit for the challenges ahead. He was named "CEO of the Year" by the American Management Association in 1991. Detractors have dubbed Welch "Neutron Jack," after the bomb that destroys people but leaves buildings intact.

A notorious disliker of bureaucracy and red tape, Welch has cut layers of management, eliminating the group and sector levels that once fell between the heads of the various businesses and the CEO. Having fewer hierarchical levels fit in with his basic philosophy that managers should have the freedom to run their businesses as they see fit and to react to the fast-changing environment.

"The early '80s were a hardware decade, getting the right stuff in the right place," Welch says. "The '90s and late '80s are what we call software. We're working desperately to get everyone participating in the process. To be a winner in the '90s, you've got to have the creativity of everybody in the organisation."

To that end, Welch has recently identified four types of leaders. Type One leaders deliver on commitments and share in the values of the company. Such leaders have a promising future at GE, says Welch. Type Two leaders do not deliver on commitments and do not share company values. These leaders will not survive at GE. Type Three leaders miss commitments but share company values, so they will usually be given a second chance. Type Four leaders deliver on commitments, make all the numbers, but do not "share in the values we must have," says Welch. The Type Four leader "is the individual who typically forces performance out of people rather than inspires it : the autocrat, the big shot, the tyrant. Too often all of us have looked the other way," according to Welch. The tendency is to allow Type Four managers to continue to function "because 'they always deliver' – at least in the short run." Now, says Welch, "in an environment where we must have every good idea from every man and woman in the organisation, we cannot afford management styles that suppress and intimidate."

In order to further promote creativity and innovation, Welch has been advocating the development of a "boundaryless" company, in which workers at all levels are encouraged to communicate and share ideas with one another. He has also instituted the Best Practices Program, in which GE employees study the attitudes and management practices of other admirable companies and adapt the best for use at GE. Another means of fostering change is GE's Work-Out Program, in which managers and their subordinates meet in a forum similar to a New England town meeting and seek ways to eliminate unnecessary work and solve problems together.

According to Welch, "Leadership starts with absolute integrity. Leaders need to define and communicate their vision. They must have enormous energy and the ability to energise and excite others. Leaders embrace change – they know it creates opportunities. Leaders are accountable and decisive. They set and meet aggressive targets. They act sooner rather than later on issues." He noted recently, "I don't know what the world's going to be; all I know is it's going to be nothing like it is today. It's going to be faster; information is going to be everywhere." As a result, he says, everyone at GE needs to come to work each day "on the razor's edge of a competitive battle."

Questions

1. Analyse the sources of power that are likely to be used by the four types of leaders identified by Welch. Note particularly the contrast between Type one and Type Four managers.

2. Use path-goal theory to analyse Welch's leadership approach.

3. Is Welch a transformational leader? Why, or why not? What should Welch do next?[45]

QUESTIONS

1. What aspects of a leadership situation might be important that have not been identified by the situational leadership approaches already discussed in this chapter?
2. Organisations annually spend a great deal of money on leadership training. Is this a wise investment? Are their less costly ways of improving leadership effectiveness?
3. Is there a cause-and-effect relationship between leader behaviour and follower performance? What is the nature or direction of the relationship? How strong is the relationship?
4. Is everyone cut out to be a leader? Explain.
5. Has your MBA programme helped you develop any of the traits that characterise leaders?
6. Does it make more sense to change a person's leadership style or the situation? How would Fiedler and House answer this question?
7. In your view, which leadership theory has the greatest practical application? Why?
8. Identify three charismatic leaders and describe their leadership traits and behavioural style.
9. Critically examine the trait theory of leadership.
10. Does leadership make any difference to the effectiveness of an organisation? Defend your position.

REFERENCES

1. Ralph M. Stoglill, *Handbook of Leadership*, New York, The Free Press, 1974.
2. *Ibid*.
3. Keith Davis and J.W. Newstrom, *Human Behaviour At Work*, New York, McGraw-Hill. 1989, p. 204.
4. G.A. Yukl, *Leadership in Organisations*, New Jersey, Prentice Hall, 1981.

5. J.L. Gray and F.A. Starke, *Organisational Behaviour – Concepts and Applications*, Columbus, Merrill Publishing Co., 1988, p. 219.
6. George R. Terry and S.G. Franklin, *Principles of Management*, Illinois, Richard D. Irwin, 1987, p. 327.
7. Chung and L.C. Megginson, *Organisational Behaviour – Developing Managerial Skills*, New York, Harper and row, 1981, p. 280.
8. John Kotter, *"What Leaders Do"*, Harvard Business Review, May-June 1990, p. 104.
9. D.C. Feldman and H.J. Arnold, *Managing Individual and Group Behaviour in Organisations*, New York, McGraw-Hill, 1983, p. 291.
10. Keith Davis and Newstrom, *Op.cit.*, p. 204.
11. Andrew J.H. Durbin, *The Practice of Supervision*, p. 317.
12. Robert Tannebaum and Fred Massarik, *"Leadership : A Frame of Reference", in Leadership and Organisation – A Behavioural Science Approach*, New York, McGraw-Hill, 1961, p. 22.
13. Ibid, p. 24.
14. Cited in *Organisational Behaviour – Developing Managerial Skill*, by Chung and Megginson, *Op.cit.*, pp. 283-284.
15. R.D. Mann, *"A Review of the Relationships between Personality and Performance in Small Group", Psychological Bulletin*, 56 (1959) pp. 241-70.
16. J.L. Gray and F.A. Starke, *Op.cit.*, p. 233.
17. James Ownes, *"The Use of Leadership Theory", Organisational Behaviour – A Managerial Approach*, eds. by H.R. Kundson and C.P. Fleenor, Cambridge, Winthrop Publishers, 1978, p. 244.
18. James A.F. Stoner, *Management*, New Delhi, Prentice Hall of India, 1984.
19. Ibid, p. 470.
20. John R. Schermerhorn, Jr., *et.al.*, *Managing Organisational Behaviour,* New York, John Wiley and Sons, 1985, p. 586.
21. Chung and L.C. Megginson, *Op.cit.*, p. 285.
22. Debra L. Nelson and James C. Quick, *Organisational Behaviour,* Thomsen-Western, 2003, p. 398.
23. D.C. Feldman and H.J. Arnold, *Op.cit.*, p. 307.
24. Chung and L.C. Megginson, *Op.cit.*, p. 288.
25. Ibid., p. 291.
26. Ibid., p. 292
27. Joe Kelly, *Organisational Behaviour – Its Data, First Principles, and Applications*, New Delhi, Surjeet Publications, 1987, p. 366.
28. Chung and L.C. Megginson, *Op.cit.*, p. 293.
29. Ibid., p. 293
30. E.H. Schein, *Organisational Psychology*, New Delhi, Prentice Hall of India, 1983, p. 117.
31. Keith Davis and Newstrom, *Op.cit.*, p. 207.
32. Robert J. House and Terence R. Mitchall, "Path Goal Theory of Leadership", *Organisational Behaviour - A Management Approach* by H.R. Knudsen and C.P. Fleenor, *Op.cit.*, p. 252.
33. Ibid., p. 253.
34. Rober P. Vecchio, *Organisational Behaviour,* The Dryden Press, 1995, p. 372.
35. Ibid., p. 241.

36. J.L.Gray and F.A. Starke, *Op.cit.,* p. 241.
37. Andrew J.H. Dubrin, *The Practice of Supervision*, New Delhi, Universal Book Stall, 1988, p. 231.
38. Stoner, *Op.cit*., p. 480.
39. S.K. Chakraborthy, *Management Transformation by Values*, p. 13
40. Stoner, *Op.cit*., p. 481.
41. K. Aswathappa, *Essentials of Business Environment*, Mumbai, Himalaya Publishing House, 1991, p. 424.
42. John W. Newstrom and Keith Davis, *Op.cit.*, 9th Edition, p. 280.
43. Stephen P. Robbins, *Op.cit.*, 6th Edn., p. 391.
44. Eugene McKenna, *Business Psychology and Organisational Behaviour,* Psychology Press Ltd., 2000, p.80.
45. Kathryn M. Barton and David C. Martin, *Management*, McGraw-Hill, 1998, p. 441.

CHAPTER Seven

Communication

LEARNING OBJECTIVES

After reading this chapter you should understand –

1. The nature of Communication.
2. The Communication can destroy or create interpersonal relations.
3. The process of Interpersonal communication.
4. The three types interpersonal communication.
5. The strategies available to overcome the barriers.
6. The flow of Organizational communication.
7. There exist informal communication and formal.

Organizations comprise people who interact with each other to achieve shared goals. Employees are the organization's brain cells, and communication represents the nervous systems that carries this information and shared meaning to vital parts of the organizational body.[1] Large organizations require innovative strategies to keep these communication pathways open. Smaller business may have fewer structural bottlenecks, but they too can suffer from subtle communication barriers.[2]

Communication is one of the most widely discussed topics of OB. The attention is justified because of the role of communication in influencing interpersonal behaviour in organizations. This chapter is devoted to a brief discussion of the nature of communication, its significance, interpersonal and organizational communication, barriers to communication and the ways to overcome the barriers.

Meaning and Definition

Like any other topic on OB, communication too has been defined by several authors. One researcher uncovered as many as 95 definitions, none of them being widely accepted.[3] For our purpose communication may be understood as the process of exchanging information and understanding between people.

This simple definition of communication directs our attention to the three important issues:

1. Communication involves transmission and reception of messages. As communicators, people use symbols to create messages. They cannot literally communicate to other individuals a meaning, attitude, perception, belief, or feeling. Rather, they use a message or messages to represent what they see, feel, or experience. Just as an artist uses a brush and paint to depict a beautiful sunset or landscape, so too, do communicators use messages to represent their perceptions, thoughts and feelings.[4]

2. Communication involves people, at least two - one to transmit the message (sender) and another to receive the message (receiver). Traditionally, the focus was on the sender and his communication skills for effective communication. Of late, the role of the receiver, and the art of listening are being underlined as requisites for making communication effective.

3. The definition refers to the process of communication. Communication is best described as a process because it is active, continuous, reciprocal, and dynamic. For convenience, we can discuss separate elements of the communication process such as senders, receivers, or messages as if they were static and discrete. However, any model that portrays communication as beginning what a sender and proceeds until it reaches a receiver inadequately represents the dynamics of communication.[5]

Significance

Effective communication is important for managers in organizations to perform their basic functions of planning, organizing, leading, and controlling. The process of communication makes it possible for managers to carry out their tasks and responsibilities. Information must be communicated to managers so that they will have basis for planning; the plans must be communicated to others in order to be carried out. Organizing requires communicating with others about their job assignments. Leading requires managers to communicate with subordinates so that group goals can be achieved. Written and oral communications are an essential part of controlling. Managers can carry out their management functions only by interacting and communicating with others. The communication process is thus the foundation upon which the management functions depend.[6]

Managers, in general, spend as much as 37.5 hours per week in communicating.[7] Thus, a large share of managerial time is devoted to the activity of communication. Rarely are managers alone at their desks thinking, planning or contemplating alternatives. In fact, managerial time is spent largely on face-to-face or telephone communication with subordinates, peers, supervisors, suppliers, or customers. When not conferring with others in person or on the telephone, managers may be writing or dictating memos, letters or reports sent to them. Even in those few periods when managers are alone, they are frequently interrupted by communications.[8] The time spent by managers on communication and the attention it receives from them speak about the importance of communication.

For organizations to function successfully, effective communication is a basic requisite. Inter-personal, inter-group and intragroup communications are essential for information to flow, ideas to generate, and feelings to be exchanged. What communication does for an organization resembles what the bloodstream does for an organism. The bloodstream supplies all the cells of the organism with oxygen; the communication system supplies all the units-departments, people of the organization with information. Deprived of oxygen, the cells malfunction and die; deprived of necessary information, individuals and departments within the organization malfunction, which can certainly lead to a sort of terminal ineffectiveness for them and for the organization as a whole.[9]

Communication is significant as it serves four major functions within a group or organization: control, motivation, emotional expression and information.[10]

Communication helps *control* member behaviour in more than one way. Organizations have authority, hierarchies and formal guidelines that employees are required to follow, when employees, for instance, are required first to communicate any job-related grievance to their boss; to follow their job description; or to comply with company policies, communication is performing a control function.

Communication fosters *motivation* by clarifying to employees what is to be done, how well they are doing, and what can be done to improve performance if it is below standard.

For many employees, their work group is a primary source for social interaction. The communication that takes place within the group is a fundamental mechanism by which members show their frustrations and feelings of satisfaction. Communication, therefore, provides a release for the emotional expression of feelings and for fulfillment of social needs.

Communication provides *information* to individuals and members for taking a decision by identifying and evaluating alternative choices.

Communication can play a major role in changing people's *attitudes*. It is said that a common approach in moulding or changing an employee's attitudes is to supply information on the objects or issues towards which attitudes are directed. Company magazines, bulletin boards, pamphlets, meetings, educational programmes, newspaper advertising, and many other forms of written and verbal communications, formal and informal in character, are used for this purpose. Underlying their use is the belief that communication is a powerful factor in molding attitudes - that well informed individuals will have "sounder" attitudes than will ill-informed individuals.[(11)]

Communication is the essence of *social behaiour*. In everyday living, the mere presence of another person encourages communication. It is a universal human propensity and, as some state, "You cannot not communicate".[12]

Most importantly, communication plays an important role in *knowledge management*, particularly in minimizing the "silos of knowledge" problem that undermines an organization's potential. This relates to the increasing importance of communication in decision making. As organizational environments become more complex, decision makers need information from many people to perceive problems, recognize new product ideas, and identify emerging customer needs. Cannon, the Japanese optics and electronics firm, recognized this through its emphasis on "heart-to-heart and mind-to-mind communication". This corporate philosophy encourages employees worldwide to share information on customers and products so that they can make more informed choices about corporate actions. British Telecom does the same thing. By encouraging on going communication, employees create "knowledge moments" – instances where shared knowledge results in better decisions.

As a part of knowledge management, APTECH, the Indian computer educator has been developing and implementing a company wide Enterprise Information System(EIS). EIS extends across the entire network of over 1200 centres in 30 countries and covers every element of its training operations, from centre automation to academics to quality administration to online delivery of education to complete integration into the SAP ERP systems that are used for accounting, logistics and distribution. The ardous but exciting systems journey has demanded a revisiting of many processes, budgetary controls and the entire materials management processes of requisitioning, ordering, printing and supply from central stores to regional and country offices to each education centre and finally into the hands of the quarter million students in APTECH. [13]

The discussion on communication in this chapter is divided in to two parts: inter-personal communication and organizational communication. Inter-personal communication is discussed here. Organizational communication will be considered later in this chapter.

Inter-personal Communication

The process of inter-personal communication is illustrated in Fig 7.1

The model comprises several parts: (1) the sender, (2) encoding (3) the message, (4) the channel, (5) decoding (6) the receiver, and (7) feedback.

Each of these components needs elaboration.

The communication process begins with the **sender** of the source. The sender has an intended message to communicate. The characteristics of the sender influence the communication process. The sender's attitudes, credibility and other attributes influence the way he or she perceives and interprets the objects or events to be communicated. His or her personality also influences the manner in which the message is transmitted. A sensitive person, for instance, will look at the communication process from the receiver's perspective, an insensitive person will be primarily concerned with his or her own needs.[14]

The sender **encodes** the information to be transmitted by translating it into a series of symbols or gestures. Encoding is necessary because information can only be transferred from one person to another through representations or symbols. Encoding can be fairly simple, such as seeing a picture of what one wants and then ordering a sandwich and milk shake. It can also be extremely difficult, such as finding the right words to explain why an employee's performance leaves much to be desired.

FIGURE 7-1
A MODEL OF THE INTERPERSONAL COMMUNICATION PROCESS

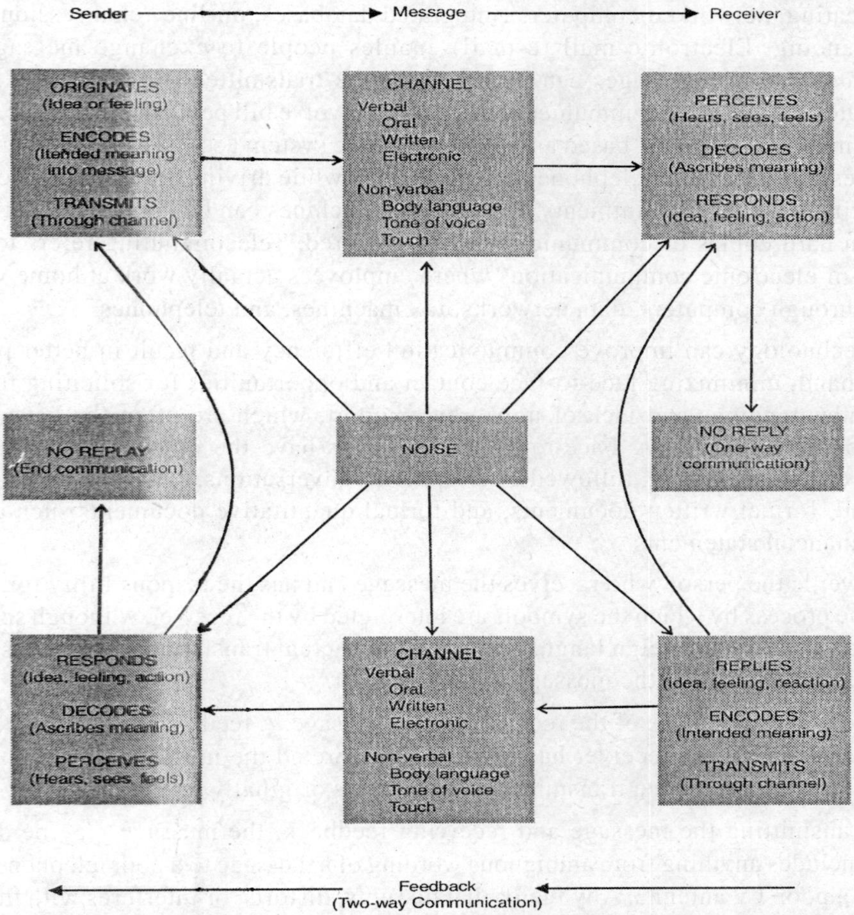

(*Source:* Adapted from ***Management** and Organisational Behaviour*, by Curtis W. Cook and Philip L. Hunsaker, p. 275)

The **message is the physical** form in to which the sender encodes the information. "When we speak, the speech is **the message**. When we write, the writing is the message. When we gesture, the movements of our **arms, the exp**ressions on our face are the messages."[15]

The **channel is the medium th**rough which the message is transmitted. Oral communication via sound waves is **the verbal ch**annel utilized in speeches, meetings, phone calls, or informal discussions**.** Face-to-face **oral com**munication accounts for 81 percent of a manager's communication each week, of which **45 percent** is with subordinates, 15 percent with superiors, 18 percent with peers, and 24 percent **with people** external to the organization.

Nonverbal channels such as touch, facial expression, and tone of voice can convey nuances of meaning mere words **are not cap**able of communicating. Although aware of nonverbal signals, many of us fail **to recognize t**heir importance in amplifying, changing, or negating verbal communication.

Written communication channels include letters, memorandums, reports, manuals and forms. Written materials provide hard copies for storage and retrieval in case documented evidence is needed later.

Electronic channels include e-mail, voice mail, portable telephones, facsimile (fax) machines, telecommunicating, networked computers (integrated databases, on-line "chat session," etc.), and video conferencing. Electronic mail (e-mail) enables people to exchange messages through computers. Interpersonal messages can just as easily be transmitted overseas as to an adjacent office. Computer-to-computer communications can also involve bill payments, invoices, or purchase orders. Voice mail is a computer-based answering machine system accessed by telephone to receive or transmit messages. Cellular telephones can be utilized while driving, during luncheon meetings, or while walking between appointments. Portable fax machines can be hooked up in a car or other location when hard copies of communications are required. Telecommuting refers to one of the ultimate uses of electronic communications where employees actually work at home while linked to the office through computers, data networks, fax machines, and telephones.

On-line technology can improve communication efficiency and result in better productivity. On the other hand, minimizing face-to-face contact and opportunities for soliciting feedback can lead to misunderstandings and lack of nonverbal support, which are often the keys to effective communication and motivation. Face-to-face discussions have the potential for being the most complete and effective channel, followed by telephone conversations, informal letters and memos, electronic mail, formal written documents, and formal quantitative documents such as computer printouts of financial statements.

The receiver is the person who receives the message and has the responsibility for *decoding* it. Decoding is the process by which the symbols are interpreted by the receiver. Although some complex messages (such as those in foreign languages) require an actual translation, in most cases decoding is simply the interpretation of the message by the receiver.

A **feedback** is the response of the receiver to the message. A feedback is desirable because the sender can discover that the receiver has correctly interpreted the message. It is a check on how successfully the sender has been transmitting messages as originally intended.

In both transmitting the message and receiving feedback, the message may be disrupted by *noise*, which includes anything from ambiguous wording of a message to a poor telephone connection or static from a poor TV antenna. Any factor that disrupts, distorts, or interferes with the receiver's ability to receive the message is called noise.

Noise, it may be stated, is not a part of communication process. It is, infact, a barrier.

Types of Interpersonal Communication

There are several forms of interpersonal communication in organizations. By far, the most common form is the **spoken word**, since it is the quickest. Further, oral communication is likely to be quite accurate because messages can be clarified through ongoing dialogues.

In addition to oral communication, there is **written communication** which supplements the former. Employees devote large portion of their workdays to send messages in written form. Memos, letters, reports, orders, e-mail, and the like can serve as the permanent records, in addition to conveying messages.

A third form of communication is **non-verbal** which consists of unspoken cues that a communicator sends in conjunction with a spoken or written messages.[15] For example, a person's tone of voice, facial characteristics, eye behaviour, head-nodding, nose-thumbing, thumb movement are all non-verbal cues. One's posture and manner of walking also may have communication significance. A person may walk as though he or she is "master of all he or she surveys", or he or she may walk in a manner which indicates utter despair. Popularly called 'body language', human physical movements indicate varied meanings. Frown on the face, for instance, means expression of unhappiness and raised eyebrows indicate disbelief or amazement. Even the physical distance between two individuals engaged in private conversation reflects the nature of their relationship. Strangers converse at greater distances than acquaintances, or close friends or lovers show the greatest physical proximity. Less talked about but equally significant are such non-verbal symbols as the sort of clothes a person wears, the kind of car he or she drives, his or her hair style, and his beard. Also, a barrier across the road tells us we should go no further, and junk lying on the roadside tells us someone has been careless, if not malicious.[(16)] And not be ignored are the style of print (handwritten, typed, or printed) and kind of paper used in a written message which are important non-verbal characteristics.

Though verbal and non-verbal communications are separated, both operate at the same time. The verbal part of a message conveys content or information. The non-verbal component indicates how the verbal message should be interpreted and thus is a metacommunication.

Whenever verbal and non-verbal messages contradict each other, we are more likely to believe the non-verbal. In fact, it has been suggested that the total impact of a message is a function of the following:[17]

$$\text{Total impact} = .07 \text{ verbal} + .38 \text{ vocal} + .55 \text{ facial}$$

BARRIERS TO EFFECTIVE COMMUNICATION

Because of the complexity of the communication process, problems arise at every stage resulting in distortion of communication. Noise, as a barrier, was identified in the communication model. Some more barriers to effective communication are explained below. For convenience of study, the barriers have been classified into three categories - sender related barriers, situation related barriers and receiver related barriers (See Fig 7.2)

Sender Related Barriers The sender is responsible for defining the communication, encoding ideas, thoughts, and feelings to messages that can be understood by the receiver, and creating a favourable communication climate. When this responsibility is not appropriately discharged, communication is bound to be ineffective.[18]

The following communication barriers are caused by or related to the sender.

Communication Goals There must be some goal or objective in communication. This goal provides the sender with the basis for formulating the message. Lack of such a goal can lead to formulation of incoherent messages.

Communication Skills Communication skills refer to clarity of thought, correct word usage, grammatical accuracy, proper delivery of messages, correct spelling or pronunciation, and proper organization of sentences or speeches. Absence of these make it difficult for the receiver to understand the message clearly.

Interpersonal Sensitivity Lack of interpersonal sensitivity is another reason why communication may fail to achieve its goal. The sender may convey the message clearly and correctly to the receiver but fails to get intended results because the message does not motivate the receiver to respond positively. Insensitive individuals often use a language which is offensive to the receivers. They are also indifferent to the needs and feelings of others.

FIGURE 7-2
COMMUNICATION BARRIERS

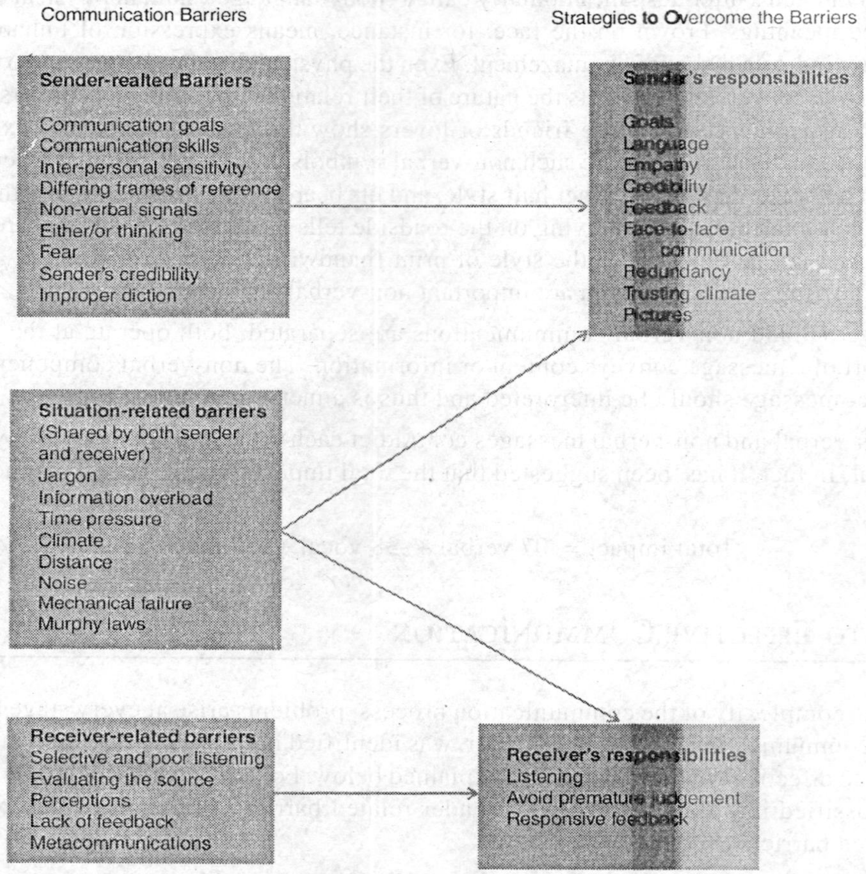

Differing Frames of Reference Effective communication requires that the encoding and decoding process be based upon a common field of experience. Lack of shared experience may result in miscommunication.[19]

Improper Diction The way the sender utters a word or a phrase is, often, not clear to the receiver. English is spoken differently in different states. There are Telugu, Tamil, Hindi, Bengali and Malayalam accents to the language depending in which state the language is being spoken. For many people 'school' becomes 'ischool', 'statistics' is 'istatistics', 'which' is 'wuch', 'Mahatma' is 'Magatma' and 'Canara Bank' is 'Kanara Bank'. Some senders speak in a low pitch-infact they do not seem to be talking they are whispering. Communication obviously fails in such circumstances.

Inconsistent Non-verbal Signals The tone of voice, facial expressions and bodily postures can help or hinder communication. For example, a quarrel at home may make the boss shout unnecessarily or speak in an angry voice to his or her subordinates at work.

Either or Thinking An individual's behaviour is often based on "either or" thinking. Early in one's life a person learns to use such so-called polar terms as near/far, objective/ subjective, black/ white, that/this, and he or she thinks and speaks in this way. But most of the things do not conform to these convenient extremes. By taking the position of either-or, a person is committed to a position where compromising or viewing a situation correctly is not possible. This places rigidity in communication.[20]

Fear Fear is another barrier to effective communication. A person under the influence of fear is likely to lose balance and his or her communication skills will be affected adversely. On the other hand, fear is likely to promote effective communication by making the sender more alert while transmitting a message.

Sender Credibility A sender's credibility refers to the attitudes the receiver has towards the reliability or trustworthiness of the sender's message. Expertise, reliability, intentions, warmth, dynamism, and reputation are the characteristics which contribute to credibility. The amount of faith the receiver places on the message depends on his or her evaluation of the sender. The more receiver trusts the sender, the greater will be the receiver's willingness to listen to the sender's messages. No receiver will take a sender seriously if there is a wide chasm between what he or she preaches and he or she practises.[21]

Receiver Related Barriers The receiver is responsible for effective communication as much as the sender is. Communication will be effective when the receiver evinces keen interest in the message transmitted and provides a feedback to the sender. If the receiver fails to do this, poor and ineffective communication results. Barriers related to the receiver are as follows:

Selective and Poor Listening Selective listening refers to the people's tendency to hear only what they want. We are likely to listen to what we like to listen to and disregard information that creates cognitive dissonance or is threatening to our self-esteem. We try to ignore information that conflicts with established beliefs or values.

Poor listening also distorts communication. There are six bad habits that prevent effective listening: (1) faking attention, (2) listening too hard for the small details that major points are missed, (3) refusing to listen when the subject-matter is difficult, (4) dismissing a subject prematurely as uninteresting, (5) criticizing the delivery or physical appearance of the sender, and (6) yielding to distractions.

Evaluating the Source The receiver has a tendency to evaluate the sender and not the message. If the receiver says, " I don't like the person" or "I don't like what the person is saying". The messages hardly reaches the receiver.

Perceptions The receiver's perceptions - stereotyping, projection and halo effect - make communication ineffective. *Stereotyping*, as was explained in Chapter 6, refers to the tendency to categorise people into a single class on the basis of some trait. Typing the sender with others on a common trait, the receiver loses objectivity and openness which are essential for effective communication. *Projection* is a perceptual process by which we try to attribute our own thoughts and feelings to others. Projection interferes with accurate comprehension of communication because people only perceive mirror images of their own thoughts, not the actual images trying to be conveyed by others.[(22)] The *halo effect* refers to the process of forming opinion based on one element from a group of elements and generalising that perception to all other elements. The good attendance record of an employee, for instance, may cause positive judgement of his or her productivity, attitudes, or quality of work. The halo effect is likely to distort communication by colouring the receiver's perceptions.

Lack of Responsive Feedback Non-response, or inappropriate response discourages the sender of the message. A non-response means that the receiver is not interested in the message, and it is difficult to communicate with such a person. An appropriate response hurts the sender's ego or feelings.

Metacommunication Metacommunication means an additional idea accompanying every idea that is expressed. The following incident involves a typical metacommunication: A superintendent and his foreman were standing at the latter's office. Upon hearing the girls in the office burst into loud laughter, the superintendent said, "The girls seem happy this morning - the way they are talking and laughing". That was his communication. From this sentence, the foreman got one or more of the following messages, "Your secretaries are loafing on the job", "Your secretaries do not take their work seriously", "You are not exercising proper control." Later, the foreman reprimanded the girls and changed their working stations (at the expense of good morale).[23]

The receiver is more likely to concentrate on the metacommunication than on communication itself. This results in miscommunication.

Situation Related Barriers Several communication barriers are attributed to factors other than the sender and the receiver. These barriers are explained below:

Jargon Jargon means unintelligible or meaningless talk or writing, familiar only to a group or profession. It is full of special words known only to the members of a group. Each profession has its own jargon or special vocabulary. When it is used outside the group, it becomes unintelligible.

The following story clearly brings out how jargon acts as a barrier to effective communication.

An American plumber wrote to the Bureau of Standards in America saying that he found hydrochloric acid good for cleaning clogged drains. He wanted to know whether he was doing the rights thing. The Bureau replied: "The efficacy of hydrochloric acid is indisputable, but the corrosive residue is incompatible with metallic permanence." The plumber wrote back and said he was happy that they agreed. The Bureau wrote again: "We cannot assume responsibility for the production of toxic and noxious residues with hydrochloric acid and suggest that you use an alternative procedure." The plumber wrote again saying how happy he was that they agreed with him. Finally, the Bureau wrote thus: "Don't use hydrochloric acid. It eats the hell out of pipes."

Well, the plumber didn't use it. The plumber understood when it was written in plain English. He had not understood earlier as it was all written in jargon.

Information Overload When receivers are bombarded with more messages than they can possibly handle, they experience communication overload. Because of this information overload, the receiver cannot accommodate a heavy load of message from the sender. Poor or miscommunication will be the result.

Time Pressure Time pressure can cause poor communication by preventing the sender from providing adequate information to the receiver. As a result, communication may become relatively superficial, and this superficiality can adversely affect effective communication.

Communication Climate The climate in which communication takes place influences its effectiveness. If communication takes place in an atmosphere of trust and confidence, it is likely to produce a positive response. If a message is incomplete, the receiver is likely to fill in the missing part with favourable interpretations. Conversely, if communication takes place in a climate where distrust prevails, even a well intended message can be negatively distorted.[24]

Noise Noise, as was shown in Fig 7.1 affects communication adversely. Noise will disrupt, distort, or interfere with the receiver's ability to receive the messages accurately.

Distance There will be delay in communication if the distance between the sender and the receiver is long. This is particularly true if the mode of communication is letter writing. Communication delayed is communication denied.

Mechanical Failure The failure of mechanical equipment in disruption of communication is too clear for needing any elaboration.

Murphy's Laws on Communication It is useful to quote the laws codified by the Murphy Centre for the Codification of Human and organizational Laws. After extensive research, the Centre has codified certain laws relating to the communication. Two of them are:

1. Communication usually fails-except by chance.
2. If a message can be understood in different ways, it will be understood in just the way that does the most harm.

Overcoming the Barriers

Barriers can be overcome if conscious efforts are made by both the sender and the receiver. The efforts shall be on the following lines:

Sender's Responsibility Being the initiator of the communication process, the sender has the following responsibilities:

Setting Communication Goals The sender must set clear goals for communication. Depending on the purpose, modes of communication should vary. If the purpose is to disseminate information, a well organized talk or written communication shall serve the purpose. On the other hand, if the purpose is to change the attitude or opinion of the of the receiver, a more skillful and emphatic communication is needed.[25]

Using Appropriate Language Since language can be a barrier, the sender should structure messages in ways that will make them clear and understandable to the receiver. The sender must use appropriate and simple words so that the receiver can understand them correctly. He or she must avoid the use of jargon, particularly when the receiver is not familiar with it. The receiver should realize that language is meant for conveying a message and not to exhibit one's richness of vocabulary.

Practising Empathic Communication The sender must understand the receiver frame of reference (assumptions, attitudes, and beliefs) to understand how the message will be received and interpereted. This form of communication is known as empathic communication. It requires the communicators to place themselves in each other's frame of reference. Empathic communication will slove many problems associated with communication.[26]

Improving Communicator's Credibility Expertise and trustworthiness are the determinants of one's credibility. Expertise refers to one's mastery over the topic under discussion. Trustworthiness refers to the quality of showing by action what one preaches. The sender's credibility can be increased by mastering the subject of communication and building up trustworthiness.

Encouraging Feedback Effective communication can be achieved by obtaining feedback from the receiver. Feedback enables the sender to know whether the receiver has understood the message or not. Two-way communication promotes effective communication.

Using Face-To-Face Communication Effective communication can be achieved through face-to-face communication rather than through memos or letters. Furthermore, people are accustomed to expressing themselves more freely and with fewer reservations when talking rather than writing.

Using a Correct Amount of Redundancy If a message is important or complicated, it is often necessary to repeat it in several different ways so that the receiver will understand it. Unnecessary redundancy or the overuse of clinches, however, will make the message dull to the receiver. Redundancy is less necessary in written than in oral communication.

Developing Trusting Climate Effective communication cannot take place if a climate of trust does not exist between the sender and the receiver. It is imperative that an environment of trust is created before any genuine communication is attempted.

Using Picture It is said that "one picture is worth a thousand words." The sender must, therefore, make use of illustrations and charts to put across the message clearly. But care should be taken to ensure that the picture fits with the message.

Receiver's Responsibility The receiver has greater responsibility to make communication effective. If the receiver plays his or her part well, communication can be effective, irrespective of the barriers. The role of the receiver will be on the lines stated below.

Effective Listening Listening is an essential requirement of effective communication but its importance is not, unfortunately, recognized by many. Reading, writing and public speaking are taught to students in schools and colleges , but students are left to falter along on their own when it comes to listening.

Most listeners believe that listening is just a matter of sitting back and absorbing information like a sponge. Effective listening does not just happen. It requires much hard work and effort on the lines suggested in Table 7.1. The table contains 10 principles of good listening. These principles identify the major differences between good and bad listeners. Note what the good listener will do against each principle of listening.

Listening can achieve much more than effective communication. Active listening is an important way to bring about changes in people. Clinical and research evidence clearly shows that sensitive listening is the most effective agent for individual personality change and group development. Listening brings about changes in people's attitude towards themselves and others, and also brings about changes in their basic values and personal philosophy. People who have been listened to in this new and special way become more emotionally mature, more open to their experiences, less defensive, more democratic, and less authoritarian.

When people are listened to sensitively, they tend to listen to themselves with more care and make clear exactly what they are feeling and thinking. Group members tend to listen more to each other, become less argumentative, more ready to incorporate other points of view. Because listening reduces the threat of having one's ideas criticised, the person is better able to see them for what they are, and is more likely to feel that these contributions are worth while.

Not the least important result of listening is the change that takes place with in the listener himself or herself. Besides the fact that listening provides more information than any other activity, it builds deep positive relationships and tends to alter constructively the attitudes of the listener. Listening is a growth experience.[27]

Barriers to Effective Listening Despite its importance in promoting effective communication, active listening is often neglected. Many factors contribute to difficulties in listening.

Physiological limitations Poor listening can be partly blamed on our physiological process. Most individuals have the ability to speak at about 120 words per minute, while our brains have the ability to recognize words at the rate of 600 or more words per minute. This gap creates a great deal of idle time for our brains to be wandering or processing other fragments of information from various sources.

TABLE 7-1

PRINCIPLES OF EFFECTIVE LISTENING

Principles	Good listener	Bad listener
1. Look for areas of interests	Seeks personal enlightenment and/or information, entertains new topics as potentially interesting.	Turns out dry subjects, narrowly defines what is interesting.
2. Overlook errors of delivery	Attends to meaning and content, ignores delivery errors while being sensitive to any message in them.	Ignores if delivery is poor, misses messages because of personal attributes of the communicator.
3. Postpone judgement	Avoids quick judgements, waits until comprehension of the core message is complete.	Quickly evaluates and passes judgements, inflexible regarding contrary messages.
4. Listen for ideas	Listens for ideas and themes. Identifies the main points.	Listens for facts and details
5. Take notes	Takes careful notes and uses a variety of methods for doing so.	Takes incomplete note using only one system.
6. Be actively responsive	Responds frequently with nods, and other responses, shows active body state, works at listening.	Passive demeanour, few or no responses, little energy output.
7. Resist directions	Resists being distracted, longer concentration, span, places loaded words in perspective.	Easily distracted, focuses on loaded or emotional words, short concentration span.
8. Challenge your mind	Uses difficult material to stimulate the mind, seeks to enlarge understanding.	Avoids difficult material, does not seek to broaden knowledge base.
9. Capitalize on mind speed	Uses listening time to summarise and anticipate the message, attends to implicit as well as explicit messages.	Daydreams with slow speakers, becomes preoccupied with other thoughts.
10. Assist and encourage the speaker	Asks for clarifying information or example, uses reflecting phrases, helps to rephrase the idea.	Interrupts, asks trivial questions, makes distracting comments.

Inadequate background information Most listeners do not have full information to engage in meaningful conversation.

Selective memory Some employees treasure every accolade and never hear a single criticism. Others hear only the complaints and never the praise. We have a tendency to hear – and remember- what we want.

Selective expectation Many employees expect to be withdrawn and not to be heard. This suits managers because they are always busy with immediate tasks and no time to listen to each employee.

Fear of being influenced or persuaded Some managers hold certain beliefs so dear to their hearts that they are biased – unable to entertain. Another's point of view about a matter. Typically mangers who feel this strongly about an issue have a tendency to turn off speakers, disputing their cherished beliefs even before they are fully explained.

Bias and being judgment When you don't like a person, it's hard to hear what he or she says. Sometimes this bias is based on wrong or incomplete information.

Partial listening and distractions Managers may hear the literal words, but miss the connotation, facial expressions, or tone of voice. In essence, he or she gets only part of the message.

Selective perception Selective perception is a process where we select or pay attention to only that information that adheres to or reinforces our own beliefs, views, or needs, causing severe distortion of messages.

Interference from emotions Communication is susceptible to interference by emotions. Though we use communication to express our emotions, not everyone is able to understand, control, or explain their feelings adequately or fully. Emotions are neither right or wrong but rather an expression of human reactions. By observing nonverbal cues, we are better able to interpret the true level and type of other's emotional states. We can then utilize empathy to neutralize emotional responses, paying the way to begin work on understanding the content of the communication. The emotional state of both the sender and the receiver must be considered in eliminating problems in the communication process.

Avoiding Evaluative Judgement The receiver must avoid making premature judgements about the sender and his or her message. Such judgement, positive or negative, will distort communication. It is the responsibility of the receiver to create a climate that fosters acceptance, trust and understanding.

Providing Responsive Feedback Responsive feedback refers to the understanding of the message by the receiver, and what he or she feels about the problem. The purpose of sending responsive feedback is to engage in constructive dialogue and to achieve a common ground in communication.

Organizational Communication

All the factors discussed in connection with interpersonal communication apply to communication in organizations also. But there are certain unique features about the latter which need special treatment. They are: factors of communication, communication flows, communication networks, and informal communication.

Factors Influencing Organizational Communication

Four factors influence the effectiveness of organizational communication. They are: formal channels of communication, authority structure, job specification and information ownership.

Formal Channel of Communication A formal channel of communication is a means of communication that is endorsed and probably controlled by managers. Examples include newsletters, memos and reports and staff meetings.

Formal channels influence effectiveness of communication in two ways. *First*, the formal channels cover an everwidening distance as organizations develop and grow. For example, effective communication is usually far more difficult to achieve in a large multiplant conglomerate than in an organization with a single plant. *Second,* the formal channels of communication can inhibit the free flow of information among organizational levels. An assembly line worker, for example, will often communicate problems to a supervisor rather than to the plant manager.

Authority Structure The organization's structure has a similar impact on communication effectiveness. Status and power differences in the organization help determine who will comfortably communicate with whom. The content and accuracy of the communication will also be affected by authority differences. For example, conversation between a Vice Chancellor and an assistant clerk may well be characterized by somewhat strained politeness and formality.

Job Specialization Specialization tends to separate people in organizations, because jobs are, by nature, separate identifiable collections of activities. Once people are separated, they tend to develop their own interpersonal styles and acquire their own perspectives about organization's goals and means to realize them.

Job specialization facilitates communication within differentiated groups. Members of the same work group are likely to share the same jargon, time horizons, goals, tasks, and personal styles. However, communication between groups is likely to be inhibited.

Information Ownership The term information ownership means that individuals possess unique information and knowledge about their jobs. For example, a darkroom employee may have found a particularly efficient way to develop photoprints. A department head may have a particularly effective way of handling conflict among employees. And a sales person may know who the key decision makers are in his or her major accounts. Such information is a form of power for the individuals who possess it. With such information they are able to function better than their peers. Many individuals with skills and knowledge are unwilling to share this information with others. As a result, completely open communication within the organization does not take place.

COMMUNICATION FLOWS

Within organizations there are five directions in which communications flow: downward, upward, lateral, diagonal, and external (See Fig 7.3).

FIGURE 7-3
COMMUNICATION FLOWS IN ORGANISATIONS

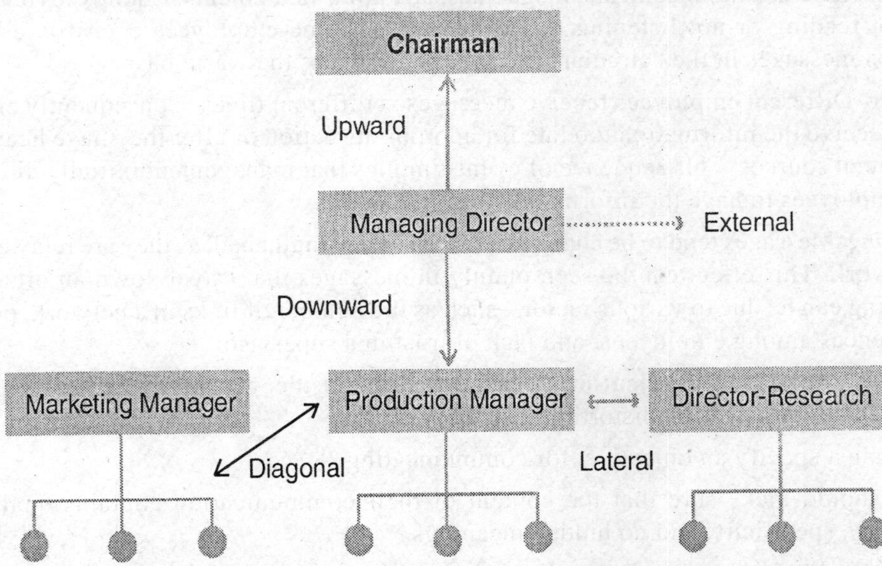

Downward Flow Downward flow refers to the communication from superiors to subordinates an corresponds to the chain of command or line of authority. The primary purpose of this type of flow is to convey job related information to employees at lower levels. Employees need these information inputs to carry out their jobs and to meet the expectations of their superiors. Absence of downward flow results in role ambiguity, stress and anxiety among employees. Typical downward communication includes group meetings, budgets, operational procedures, circulars, company publications, and the like.

There are five specific reasons for downward communication. They are:

(a) **Specific task directives** Instructions about the job are specifically worked out and are communicated to the employees through direct orders, training sessions, training manuals and written directives.

(b) **Job rationale** This information is designed to provide employees with a full understanding of the job and how it relates to other jobs.

(c) **Procedures and practices** In addition to instructions about the job, employees are also informed about other obligations and privileges in the system, for example, they are told about vacations, sick leave, rewards and sanctions.

(d) **Feedback** This is an appraisal about how a person performs assigned tasks.

(e) **Indoctrination of goals** This includes communication of the organization's ideology presented in the corporate mission.

Distortion of Downward Communication Distortions occur rendering downward communication generally ineffective. There are four reasons for this distortion. They are:

(a) *Reliance upon written diffusion methods* Many organizations rely too heavily on written and mechanical manuals, films, news letters, public address systems, and booklets. These are used instead of contact and face-to-face communication.

(b) *Message overload* In some organizations employees are over-burdened with bulletins, memos, letters, announcements, magazines, and policy statements. Employees tend to react by not reading or not listening to the messages. Some employees even file all or most written messages in the "circular file", better known as the waste basket.

(c) *Timing* Different employees receive messages at different times. Consequently employees may receive the information too late for appropriate action or after they have heard it from unofficial sources. This sequence of events implies that management initially did not want the employees to have the information.

(d) *Filtering* Messages tend to be changed, shortened, or lengthened, as they are relayed through a network. This effect can be seen plainly in messages that travel down an organization. Filtering can be due to various factors, such as the number of links in a network, perceptual differences among employees, and lack of trust in a supervisor.

Improving Downward Communication Managers must consider the following three elements to make downward communication distortion free:

(a) They must specify an objective for communicating.

(b) They should make sure that the content of their communication contains qualities like accuracy, specificity, and no hidden meanings.

(c) They should employ the best communication technique to get the message across to the receiver.

Additionally, placing too much faith in the downward flow is not desirable. Managers who assume that their supervisory hierarchy is an adequate channel for transmitting messages that will readily be received by employees may be subject to rude shocks.

Upward Flow Upward or bottom-up flow is designed to provide feedback on how well the organization is functioning. Lower level employees are expected to provide upward communication about their performance and problems.

Upward communication encourages employees to participate in the decision making process and to submit valuable ideas. It also provides feedback on how well subordinates have understood downward communication.

Furthermore, upward communication serves as a way for supervisors to get to know the subordinates, as a way of diagnosing misinterpretations, as a way of disclosing first symptoms of tension and difficulties, and as a way of making subordinates views more visible to superiors. In addition, when organizations give employees the opportunity to voice dissatisfaction to higher levels, employees tend to be more committed to the organization.

The most common forms of upward communication include suggestion boxes, open door policies, group meetings, grievances, questions, and feedback.

Distorting Upward Communication The basic problem in upward communication stems from the nature of the hierarchical organization. The traditional role of managers is to direct, coordinate, and control the people below them. These managers are less in the habit of listening to their subordinates than in telling them how to perform. Subordinates, too, fall into a traditional mind set, they expect to listen to their bosses rather than to be listened to.

Filtering of information may also take place. Employees will not send messages upward that supervisors do not want to hear. This is especially true if the information affects the subordinates adversely. Subordinates will not only tell the supervisors what he or she wants to hear, but will also tell the supervisor only what they want the supervisor to know. Moreover, many subordinates perceive that full and objective reporting may be personalized by the supervisor or may be regarded as espionage by peers.

In general, employees tend to fear that expressing their true feelings about the company to their boss could be a dangerous act. The boss is often seen as untrustworthy, a person to whom it is dangerous to talk with full candour.

Additionally, employees have little opportunity to send communication upward. Their managers are not available many times. The nature of hierarchy also impedes upward communication as numerous employees attempt to communicate to one or a few managers high in the organization. It is, therefore, difficult for a manager to communicate with many subordinates on individual basis.

Another problem with upward communication is that organizations typically rely on lower level members to initiate it. Instead of actively soliciting information and providing channels for receiving it, managers frequently adopt an open-door policy and assume that individuals who have something to communicate will do so voluntarily.[28]

Improving Upward Communication Management can develop upward communication by encouraging better listening, by building trust and by responding to messages that are received. Various practices may also be used to improve upward communication: counselling, grievance systems, consultive supervision, meetings, suggestion systems, and job satisfaction surveys.

Four prevalent strategies for encouraging upward communication are the open door policy, suggestion systems, participation in social group and the encouraging of letters from employees.

The *open-door policy* states that employees are welcome to come to their manager's offices, or perhaps to those of other managers, to discuss any matter that concerns them. The policy is attractive in theory because it indicates a willingness to communicate, but it has limitations in practice.

Psychological and social barriers frequently make employees reluctant to approach a manager. A climate of openness and trust must be present to assure the success of this tactic. For instance, an employee must not be afraid of revealing ignorance about a topic when discussing it with a higher level manager. Employees cannot be afraid of saying something that will incur their manager disfavour. An interesting variation of the open-door policy is the system of Management by Wandering Around (MBWA). Here, managers are encouraged to develop more open communications by strolling around the office or production plant and talking to subordinates.

Suggestion systems are formal programmes that encourage individual employees to recommend work improvements. If managed correctly, these programmes can be tremendously successful. At times, suggestion systems are less successful because they rely primarily on written communication; hence, the motivation that comes from face-to-face communication is lacking. Another problem is that often no incentive is offered for the employees to make recommendations.

Participation in informal, casual recreational events furnish good opportunities for upward communication. This type of communication is generally spontaneous. The upward communication is not the primary purpose of event but a natural by product. Japanese companies have systemized this strategy by providing managers with an expense account regularly entertaining their subordinates.

Employee letters supply the final upward communication technique to be mentioned here. Many companies have a periodic newsletter in which they print letters from their employees as well as responses from various managers. Some large companies have newsletters at lower organizational levels - such as at production facilities - to encourage more letters and responses.

In summary, upward communication requires special attention because the very nature of the hierarchical organization works against it. This valuable channel of information will not be maximized unless specific procedures are implemented and managers are continually sensitive to the psychological and sociological problems inherent in the proceeds.

Lateral Communication Also called horizontal communication lateral flow takes place between peers. It is needed to achieve co-operation among group members and between work groups. Furthermore, lateral flow provides emotional and social support to individuals. It contributes to the development of friendship and informal work groups.

There are several purposes why horizontal communication takes place. First is *task coordination*. Heads of sections or departments may meet monthly to discuss how each section or department contributes to the company's goals. Another purpose is *problem solving*. The members of a section or a department may assemble to discuss how to handle a threatened budget and may employ some of the techniques such as Delphi Technique and Nominal Group Technique to solve the problem. Another reason for horizontal communication is *information sharing*. Here, members of different departments may meet to share information. A final reason is *conflict resolution*. Members of one department may meet to discuss a conflict within the department or with another department.

Problems in Horizontal Communication Horizontal communication is often discouraged at least four reasons. *First*, too much horizontal communication may weaken the organization structure. Too many messages flowing in all directions would lead to anarchy.

Second, departments do not generally like to share information with other departments because of rivalry.

Third, too much of job specialization results in each department becoming an island by itself having little in common to share with other departments.

Finally, management may not have encouraged frequent horizontal communication.

Improving Horizontal Communication As was mentioned above, excessive reliance on horizontal communication may undermine the authority structure of an organization, but too little lateral communication can result in a rigid and inefficient organization. Consequently, the correct balance between vertical and horizontal communication must be found. This can be accomplished through flexible procedures that provide guidelines about when and how employees should use horizontal communication.

How can the problem of rivalry and competition be overcome? Task forces and committees composed of employees from different departments working on common problems are often a viable solution. When employees are working toward common goals, they are more likely to be co-operative rather than competitive. Another strategy is to conduct training sessions on teamwork in which employees gain an appreciation of horizontal communication.

Diagonal communication Diagonal communication takes place between a manager and members of other work groups. A manager needs this kind of communication to interact with employees in other managers' jurisdictions regarding his or her particular function - that is functional authority. For example, a cost accountant interacts with plant personnel who deal with cost data. The diagonal communication network usually does not appear on the organizational chart, but a number of such networks are found in large organizations.[(29)]

External Communication External communication takes place between a manager and outside groups like suppliers, government, creditors, banks, financial agencies, environmentalists, consultants, and the like. A business enterprise cannot operate in a vaccum. It must maintain contacts with outside agencies and external communication is needed for the purpose.

COMMUNICTION NETWORKS

While the downward, upward, lateral, diagonal and external flows are general, there are specific flows which exist within these broad categories. In upward communication, for example, an employee who wishes to communicate with the production manager may be required to do so through the foreman who is the immediate superior. These specific flows within the broad categories are called communication networks. A communication network may be understood, therefore, as the pattern of communication flows among various positions in an organization. Networks may also emerge spontaneously in the course of interpersonal interaction. Whatever their use is, communication networks are a fact of organizational life. Particularly, networks created by organizations are useful in as mush as they protect higher level managers from being swamped with unwanted information.[30] They enhance coordination, and reinforce authority structure. Furthermore, communication networks in groups can be important in determining who gets what information and how satisfied the members are with their functions or places in the groups.[(31)]

Most studies of communication networks have taken place in groups created in a laboratory setting. As a result, the research conclusions have limited application because of their artificial settings and small groups involved.

Though based on studies conducted in laboratories, communication networks can be extended to organizations. For simplicity's sake, let us assume that there are only five persons in an organization, viz., A, B, C, D, & E. The *wheel net* in Fig 7.4 represents four workers, and a supervisor who is placed in the midst of the workers. Workers have no interaction among themselves. All communication must pass among themselves and pass through the supervisor. Wheel is, therefore, a highly centralized network. The same is true of *'Y'*. In a *chain*, communication can move up or

FIGURE 7-4
COMMUNICATION NETWORKS

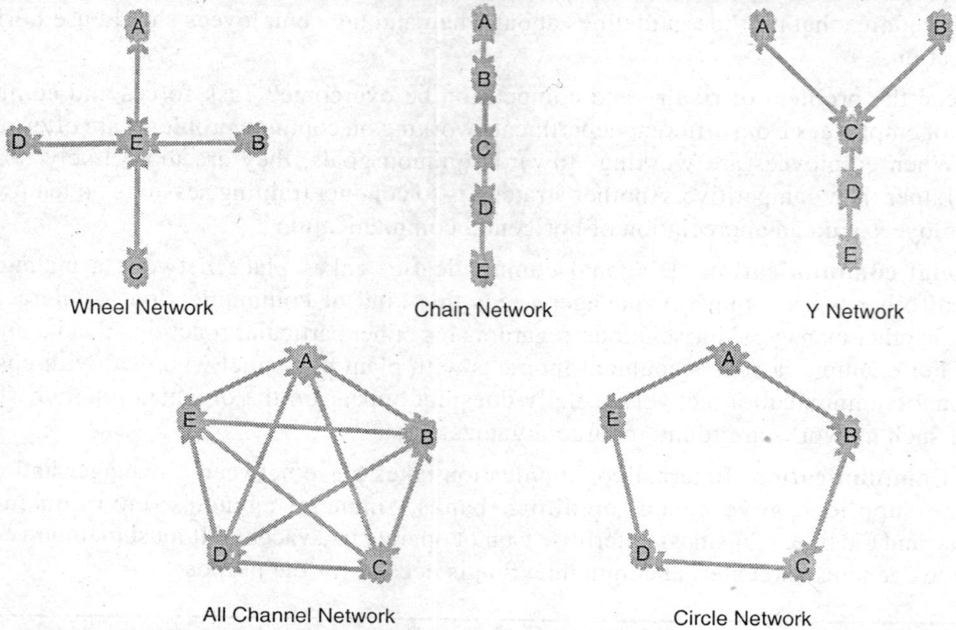

down, but not laterally. The chain has all the appearances of an organizational chain of command - first reporting to the second, second to the third and so on. The *circle network* allows each member to converse with the person on his or her left or right and no farther. In *all channel net*, every member has easy access to every other members in the group.

The relevant question now is which network is better than the other? The answer is difficult because each network has its own advantages and limitations, as shown in Table 7.2. Thus, among all the nets, chain scores high on all the factors. Then comes 'Y', followed by all channel and others.

TABLE 7-2
PERFORMANCE OF NETWORKS

Factors	*Wheel*	*'Y'*	*Chain*	*Circle*	*All channel*
Speed	Fast	Moderate	Fast	Slow	Fast
Accuracy	Good	High	Good	Poor	Moderate
Emergence of leadership	Very pronounced	Moderate	Marked	None	None
Satisfaction	Low	Moderate	Moderate	High	High

(***Source:*** Adapted from Bavelas and Barrett, "An Experienced Approach to Organizational Communication", Personnel, March 1951.)

Communication Roles

The specific functions an individual serves in an organization's communication network shall constitute his or her *communication role*. Four such roles have been identified :[32] gatekeeper, liaison, isolate, and cosmopolite.

Gatekeepers A gatekeeper is an individual who passes information to others or controls messages. Common examples of gatekeepers are secretaries and assistants to executives. A gatekeeper who has the ability to control the information or time its release actually controls the final decision. Generally executives depend on gatekeepers who wield influence at higher levels in organizations.

Liaisons An individual who serves as a communication link between groups, but is not a member of either group, is a liaison. This person serves as a bridge between groups that need to exchange messages. Organizations that use liaisons to link departments are relatively more effective than firms that do not.

Isolates An isolate is someone who has very little or no conflict with other members of the organization. Certain jobs, such as night guard and messenger, are characterized by the absence of contacts with other organizational members. Yet some people whose jobs offer more opportunities for contact may still remain uninformed. They may consciously choose not to socialize with coworkers or participate in grapevines. Feelings of isolation tend to be associated with such social isolation.

Cosmopolites A cosmopolite is a person whose communication network frequently extends into the organization's external environment. Cosmopolites are more interested in national rather than local affairs and tend to have stronger professional affiliations. They are also likely to change jobs more frequently than other employees. Like liaisons, cosmopolites can serve a gate keeping function in that the firm's contact with and information from the outside world needs to be passed through them.

Communication Policies and the Communiction Audit

An organization's *communication policy* states (i) a set of objective the organization wishes to achieve through communication, (ii) guidelines or directives to be applied to decision-making about communication related issues, or (iii) a combination of both. The communication policy is either formally expressed or informally understood - mostly the latter. Consequently, implementation of the policy is not always feasible.

The *communication audit* is a tool for auditing communication policies networks and activities. When an audit is used, organizational communication is viewed as a group of communication factors related to organizational goals.

Communication activities are not ends in themselves, but are means of achieving organizational goals. Sometimes communication specialists will minimize the importance of organizational goals and put too much emphasis on the communication process. A communication audit should focus on communication as a means to meet the overall goals.

The four major communication networks that need to be audited are the following:

(i) The regulative or task-related networks pertaining to policies, procedures, rules, and superior-subordinate relationships;

(ii) The innovative network, which includes problem solving, meetings, and suggestions for change;

(iii) The integrative network, which consists of praise, rewards, promotions and those items that link enterprise goals with personal needs;

(iv) The information-instructive network, which includes company publications bulletin boards, and the grapevines.

The communication audit then, is a tool for analyzing the relationship of communication to the managerial functions. The audit should be used not only when problems occur, but also to prevent communication-related problems from arising. The audit can take many forms and may include observations, questionnaires, interviews, and analysis of written documents. Each audit should be followed by a formal report defining the current condition of communications, explaining whether organizational goals are being achieved.[33]

INFORMAL COMMUNICTION

The discussion till now has been on formal communication. There is informal communication, popularly, known as grapevine. Grapevine exists outside formal communication channels in organizations and is carried out either in face-to-face interaction or over the phone. The informal communication may be task-related (e.g., shortcutting long chains of command) or social-related (e.g., exchanging personal information, gossip, and rumours).[34]

The word *grapevine* originated during the Civil War in America, during which period telegraph lines were strung loosely from tree to tree in vine-like fashion. Messages sent over this haphazard system often became garbled, and any.false information or rumour that came along was therefore ironically said to come from the grapevine.

The following characteristics of the grapevine are worth noting:

1. Grapevines are found in every organization and they are virtually impossible to eliminate. It is only natural for employees to discuss matters of mutual concern, and even the closet monitoring of their conversations will not prevent them from occurring.
2. Information usually travels more rapidly through the grapevine than through official communication channels.
3. The grapevine is a more spontaneous form of expression and hence intrinsically more gratifying and credible than formal communication.
4. In situations, where official censorship and filtering occur, grapevine information is more informative.
5. On non-controversial topics related to the organization, most of the information communicated through the grapevine (about 75 percent) is accurate. Emotionally charged information however, is more likely to be distorted.
6. The number of people who serve as actual links in the grapevine is generally small (estimated to be less than 10 percent of the group).[35]

Three types of grapevine have been identified: chain system, cluster system, and gossip systems: [36] (see Fig 7.5). Some grapevines operate as a single-strand, chain system in which one member tells another, who in turn tells another, and so on. But such grapevines are uncommon. Most organizational grapevines operate as a cluster system in which a few individuals inform a cluster, or set of other people. A third type of grapevine, the gossip system, occurs when a single member

FIGURE 7-5
TYPES OF GRAPEVINE SYSTEMS

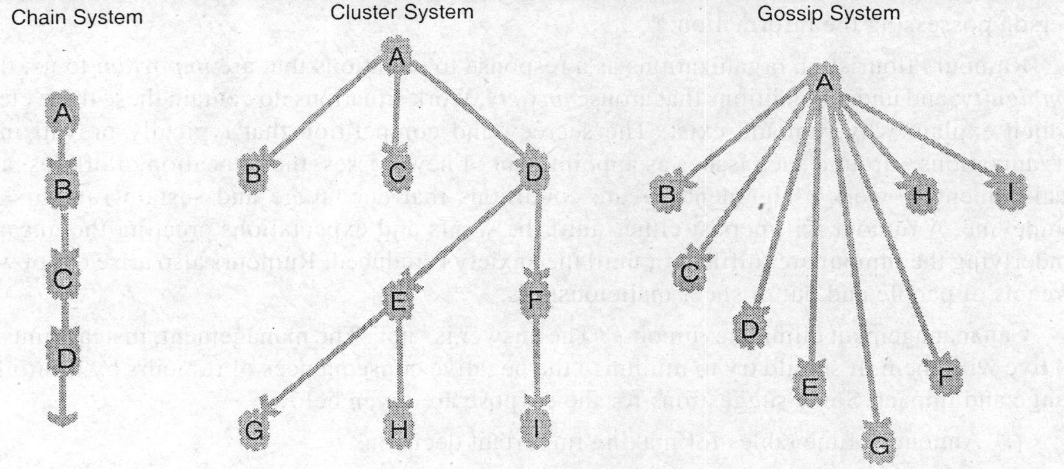

(*Source:* Robert P. Vecchio, *op. Cit,* p. 554)

non-selectively communicates with everyone he or she meets. Most organizational grapevines are cluster systems, with occasional 'gossips' adding to the rate of spread.

Grapevines are inevitable in organizations. They play positive as well as negative roles. On the positive side are listed several benefits that occur to the management because of grapevines. Grapevine is an effective tool for developing corporate identity, building team work, and motivating people. It supplements formal communication channels to make the total communication system more effective.

In a sense, the degree of grapevine activity is a measure of a firm's spirit and vitality. If employees are so disinterested in their work that they do not engage in pep talk, they are obviously maladjusted. If they are so indifferent about their associates that they even eschew chattering about who will get promotion, who brought in the big contract or which young executive is dating whose secretary, they are patently abnormal. A lively grapevine reflects the deep psychological need of people to talk about their jobs and their company as a central life of interest. Without it the company would literally be sick.

What should not be missed is the most positive contribution grapevine makes to the organization's communication system - it is the speed of spreading the message. The speed of grapevines can be attributed to the fact that the messages are oral rather than written. Morever, people enjoy passing on timely information because it makes them appear in touch and well informed and there is social value attached to bringing surprising news to others.

Grapevine has been criticized too. It tends to be accurate when the information is noncontroversial. With controversial information, the grapevine can be erroneous, it is also said that the speed with which the grapevine spreads information makes it difficult to check false rumours.[37]

Rumour: As was pointed out above, 75 per cent of grapevine information is accurate. The remaining 25 percent which is inaccurate, constitutes rumour. Rumour, therefore, is the injudicious and untrue information that is communicated without factual evidence to back it up.

Rumour is generally perceived to be dangerous because of its potential to fish in troubled waters. But not always. Rumours serve at least four purposes: to structure and reduce anxiety; to make sense of limited or fragmented information; to serve as a vehicle to organize group members, and possibly outsiders in to coalitions; and to signal a sender's status or power that he is the only person possessing the information.[38]

Rumours flourish in organizations as a response to situations that are *important* to us; there is *ambiguity*; and under conditions that arouse *anxiety*. Work situations do contain these three elements which explain why rumours exist. The secrecy and competition that typically prevail in large organizations - around such issues as appointment of new bosses, the relocation of offices, and the realignment of work assignments-create conditions that encourage and sustain rumours or the grapevine. A rumour will persist either until the wants and expectations creating the uncertainty underlying the rumour are fulfilled or until the anxiety is reduced. Rumours also arise out of wishful dreams of people and out of sheer maliciousness.

Can management eliminate rumours? The answer is "no". The management, instead, must learn to live with them. It should try to minimize the negative consequences of rumours by limiting their range and impact. Some suggestions for the purpose are given below:

(i) Announce time tables for making important decisions

(ii) Explain decisions and behaviour that may appear inconsistent or secretive.

(iii) Get at the root of the rumour and confront it with facts.

(iv) Identify rumour mongers and discipline them.

(v) Take the assistance of the labour union to fight rumours.

COMMUNICTION MEDIA

Communication in organizations can take a variety forms but the most popular media are (a) written communication, (b) oral communication, and (c) non-verbal communication.

Written communication Written communication is more common in organizations. Reports, notes, letters, memos, and organizational handbooks are the most common forms of written communication. Managers prefer written communication because it provides a record of what has been transmitted and it can be reread if first reading was not clear.

The problems with written communication are : (i) many managers are not good in drafting, they prefer verbal medium; (ii) superior often refuse to read written reports of any substantial length, preferring to be briefed verbally about the contents; and (iii) some written communications, such as job descriptions and policy manuals, are continually in need of updating, a task that is highly time consuming.[39]

Oral Communication Face-to Face verbal orders, telephone discussions, speeches and discussions at meetings are forms of oral communication. Most managers prefer oral communications because it is faster and provides for immediate feedback. Face-to Face communication is more popular form of oral communication.

Face-to-face communication is not always possible. In dealing with large groups the manager is often forced to choose a more appropriate form of communication, such as speech. Even with a small group and informal talk with limited discussion afterwards may be the best the manager can do. Each step away from one-on-one communication reduces the degree of interaction and, therefore, the extent of information exchanged.

Non-verbal Communication Three major forms of nonverbal communication are: kinesics, proxemics, and para language.

Kinesics is another name for body language. Body language includes such forms as gestures, facial configurations, and other movements of the body.

The face and the hands are particularly important sources of body language in work situations. Examples are eye contact, eye movement, smiles and frowns, touching and furrowed brow.

Proxemics deals with the way people use physical space and what it means. A manager's office is larger than those of others; contains better quality furniture and more trappings than any one else; and is often in the corner of the building. Managers use physical space to send right messages to others.

Para language refers to how people verbalise the message. Specifically, para language includes voice tension, quality, volume, a speech rate, and pitch. Variation of any of these can mean different things.

INFORMATION TECHNOLOGIES

Information technologies are mainly used as channels of communication. The Internet, World Wide Web (WWW), Electronic mail (e-mail), voice mail and telecommuting constitute the state of the art information technologies.

The *Internet* is an integral global network of computers that gives users access to information and documents. Anyone with a personal computer, modem, and proper software can access the Internet free and obtain and share information with others via e-mail, which are electronic messages transmitted to and from Internet host computers.

Organizations use the Internet to explain their benefits to newly hired employees.

The World Wide Web (WWW) is the part of the Internet that supports a retrieval system for a vast amount of information and documents on all topics. Web sites, or home pages, are formatted addresses that provide access to that material.

Electronic mail (e-mail), as stated earlier, enables people to exchange information through computers. Until several years ago, if an employee wanted to discuss an idea with his or her boss, the employee had to wait for days to get an appointment with the boss. Today, the same employee can simply send an e-mail to the boss (like the employees at Microsoft do - read opening case of this chapter). Quick and easy access to this medium of communication has the potential to radically change internal coordination and integrating systems and communication with external suppliers and customers.

Voice mail is a computer based message system that people access by telephone. Voice mail is human equivalent of e-mail. Although more expensive than an e-mail system, voice mail is a richer information medium than e-mail. Voice mail is an excellent medium for sending short, simple, and non-controversial messages.

Telecommunicating is the practice of working at home while being electronically linked to the office. Employees who work at a customer's office or communicate with the office or plant via a laptop computers or mobile phone would be classified as telecommuters. Telecommunity often involves the use of computer-based software, e-mail, voice mail, fax machines, and related technologies.

Telecommunicating jobs includes sales person, real estate agent, computer systems analyst, data entry clerk, consultant, attender, security broker, and copy editor. Millions of employees have already formed telecommunicating arrangements with their employers, and their number is growing. Wipro is one example of a company which has been using telecommunicating successfully. However, telecommunicating is not for everyone, some telecommunicators experience a sense of isolation, stagnation, or compulsive overwork.

The potential advantages of telecommuting are fairly obivous. They allow people to communicate with one another more easily, quickly, and with much less expense. However, some problems need to be guarded against. First, these technologies have not been effective for promoting interpersonal relations or complex team problem solving where face-to-face dialogue is needed. Second, information technologies can breakdown the boundaries between work time and non-work time. A medical transcriber who works full-time from her home, for example, finds herself typing a tape but is interrupted by her husband, children, and telephone. Third, the Intranet/internet may erode the delegation of authority by creating too much and too frequent communication between superiors and subordinates. Fourth, e-mail opens the possibility of wasting time on increased volumes of meaningless data with the consequence of unnecessary work overload. Finally, for most individuals, e-mail lacks confidentiality. Most e-mail messages can easily be read by others who have computers and access to the same intranet or to the Internet.

Managerial Implications

Manager must understand that communication is an essential concomitant of an organization. Perhaps no other topic can rival communication in its impact on organizational behaviour. Whether in motivating employees, building high morale among employees, providing satisfaction in work, contributing to employee development and growth or moulding employee attitudes, the role of communication is considerable. Not to be ignored is the role of communication in enabling the management to discharge its basic functions and in facilitating successful functioning of organizations.

In any organization, the manger's foremost responsibilities are the development and maintenance of an effective communication system. Unfortunately, managers perceive their role of communication as one of transmitting messages. An effective communication system requires skills both in sending and receiving messages. In addition, barriers occur at every level of the communication process. A manager must identify the barriers, understand why they have occurred, and take steps to prevent their occurrence. No price should be too high and no effort too heavy for the manager in his or her drive towards improving the communication system.

Case: A Case of Misunderstood Message

Indane Biscuits is located in an industrial area. The biscuits factory employs labour on a daily basis. The management does not follow statutory regulations and are able to get away with violations by keeping the concerned inspectors in good books.

The factory has a designated room to which employees are periodically called either to hire or to fire.

As a part of National Safety Day the Industries Association, of which the Indane Biscuits is a member, decided to celebrate collectively at a central place. Each of the members was given specific tasks.

The Personnel Manager, Indane Biscuits, desired to consult his supervisors and to inform everybody through them about the safety day celebrations. He sent a memo requesting them to be present in the room meant for hiring and firing. As soon as the supervisors read the memo they all got panicky thinking that now it was their turn to get fired. They started having 'hush-hush' consultations. The workers also learnt about it and since they had a lot of score to settle with the management, they extended their sympathy and support to the supervisors. As a consequence everybody struck work and the factory came to a grinding halt.

In the meantime, the Personnel Manager was unaware of the developments and when he came to know of it, he went immediately and tried to convince the supervisors about the purpose of inviting them and the reason why that particular room was chosen. The Personnel Manager, had selected the room because no other room was available. But the supervisors and the workers were in no mood to listen.

The Managing Director, who rushed to the factory on hearing about the strike, also couldn't convince the workers.

The matter was referred to the labour department. The enquiry resulted in all irregularities of the factory getting exposed and imposition of heavy penalties. The Personnel Manager was sacked. The factory re-opened after prolonged negotiations and settlements.

Questions

1. Identify the communication barriers in this case.
2. Identify the flows of communication in Indane Biscuits.
3. What role did grapevine play in Indane Biscuits ?

Questions

1 Describe the communication process, identify its key parts. Give an example of how this process operates with both oral and written messages.

2 "Ineffective communication is the fault of the sender." Do you agree? Discuss yes or no.

3 Describes the advantages and limitations of each of the communication networks: (a) wheel, (b) circle (c) chain, (d) all chain.

4 Observe your own behaviour, and discuss what non-verbal communication habits you typically use. Do you notice some habits that mislead receivers?

5 What are the barriers that check effective communication? How can these barriers be overcome?

6 Discuss why rumours occur in organizations? How do you manage them ?

7 What are some of the potential problems with upward and downward communications? How can managers alleviate these problems?

8 Some claim that e-mail can take so much time reading and replying so that they are actually a drain on productivity? Do you agree? Why?

9 How does communication affect the interpersonal influence topics discussed in Chapters 4-11?

10 If your job transfers you to a foreign culture, what nonverbal communication practices must you be sensitive to?

11 If a person of a different gender supervises you, what non verbal problems might you encounter?

References

1. Steven L. McShane and Mary Ann Glinow, *Organisational Behaviour*, TMH, 2000, p.231.
2. Ibid, p.232.
3. Ibid.
4. F.E.X. Dance, " The Concept of Communication," *Journal of Communication*, June 1970, pp. 201-202.
5. Donald D. White and David A. Bednar, *Organizational Behaviour*, Boston; Allyn and Bacon, Inc., 1986, p.405
6. Ibid., p.406
7. James A.F Stoner, *Management*, New Delhi, Prentice Hall of India, 1984, p. 494.
8. Klemmer and Snyder, "Measurement of Time Spent on Communication", *Journal of Communication,* June 1972, pp. 142-52.
9. James A.F. Stoner, *Op.cit.,* p. 494.
10. David R. Hampton, *Contemporary Management*, New York, McGra-Hill, 1981, p.399
11. Stephen P. Robbins, *Organizational Behaviour - Concepts, Controversies, and Applications*, New Delhi, Prentice Hall of India, pp. 267 – 268.
12. Morris S. Viteles, *Motivation and Morale in Industry*, Bombay, Allied Pacific (P) Ltd., 1962, p. 415.
13. George, R. Terry and Stephen G. Franklin, *Principles of Management*, New Delhi, All India Traveller Bookseller, 1987, p. 354.
14. Ganesh Natarajan, *Knowledge Management,* Tata McGraw-Hill, 2000, p.83.
15. Kae H.Chung and Leon C. Megginson, *Organizational Behaviour*, New York, Harper and Row, 1981 p.193.
16. D.K. Berlo, *The process of Communcation*, New York, Holt, Rinehart, and Winston, 1960, p.54.
17. David J. Cherrington, *Organizational Behaviour*, Boston, Allyn and Bacon, 1989, p.565.
18. Normal L. Munn, et al., *Introduction to Psychology*, New Delhi, Oxford and IBH Publishing Co., 1972, p.584.

19. Robert P. Vecchio, *Organizational Behaviour,* The Dryden Press, 1995, Pp 539-540.
20. David R. Hampton, *Op.cit.,* p.409
21. Kae H. Chung and Leon C. Megginson, *Op.cit.,* p. 199.
22. George R. Terry and Stephen G. Franklin, *Op.cit.,* p. 363.
23. Kae H. Chung and Leon C. Megginson, *Op.cit.*, p.200.
24. D.C. Feldman and H.J. Arnold, *Managing Individual and Group Behaviours in Organizations*, New York, McGraw-Hill, 1983, p.367.
25. Wayne Baty, "Vital Factors in Interpersonal Communication", *Organizational Behaviour*, Ed. By H.R Knudson, Cambridge, Winthrop Publishers, 1978, p.86.
26. Kae H. Chung and Leon C. Megginson, *Op.cit.,* p.202.
27. Ibid., p.203
28. Ibid., p.204
29. C.R. Rogers and R.E. Farson, "Active Listening", *Organisational Behaviours*, Ed. By H.R. Knudson, *Op.cit.,* p.94.
30. David J. Cherrington, *Op.cit.,* p.589
31. Kae H. Chung and Leon C. Megginson, *Op.cit.,* p. 196.
32. Joseph Reitz, *Behaviour in Organizations*, Illinois, Richard D. Irwin, 1977, P. 349.
33. Robert P. Vecchio, *Op.cit.,* p.545
34. Gray and Smeltzer, *Management,* New York, MacMillan, 1990, p.566.
35. D.C. Feldman and H.J. Arnold, *Op.cit.*, p.361.
36. Sutton and Porter, "A Study of the Grapevine in a Governmental Organizations", *Personnel Psychology*, Vo. 21(1968), pp. 223 – 230.
37. Robert P. Vecchio, *Op.cit.*, p.554
38. Fred Luthans, *Organizational Behavior*, New York, McGraw-Hill, 1989, p. 389.
39. Keith Davis, "*The Care and Cultivation of the Corporate Grapevine*", *Op.cit.,* p.386.
40. Hirschhorn, "Managing Rumours", in *Cutting Back*, Ed. By Hirschhorn, San Francisco, Jossey-Bass, 1983, pp. 49-52.

CHAPTER

Eight

Motivation — Theories and Principles

LEARNING OBJECTIVES

After reading this chapter you should understand –

1. The nature of Motivation.
2. The importance of Motivation.
3. The factors that affect Motivation.
4. The Motivation theories are of two broad categories – early and contemporary theories.

NATURE OF MOTIVATION

Motivation makes ordinary people extraordinary, average performers into outstanding achievers and weak organisations into most successful ones.

This chapter focuses on theoretical foundations for motivation. The next chapter describes application of principles of motivation to organisational settings.

Every organisation must –

- Attract competent people and retain them with it.
- Allow people to perform tasks for which they were hired, and
- Stimulate people to go beyond routine performance and overreach themselves in their work.

Thus, if the organisation were to be effective it must address the motivational challenges involved in arousing people's desires to be productive members of the organisation.[2]

A basic principle is that the performance of an individual depends on his or her ability backed by motivation. Stated algebraically, the principle is :

$$\text{Performance} = f\,(\text{ability} \times \text{motivation})$$

Ability refers to skill and competence of the person to complete a given task. However, ability alone is not enough. The person's desire to accomplish the task is also necessary. Organisations become successful when employees have abilities and desire to accomplish given tasks.

Motivation in simple terms may be understood as the set of forces that cause people to behave in certain ways. The framework given in Fig. 8.1 helps us understand the nature of motivation better.

FIGURE 8-1
FRAMEWORK OF MOTIVATION

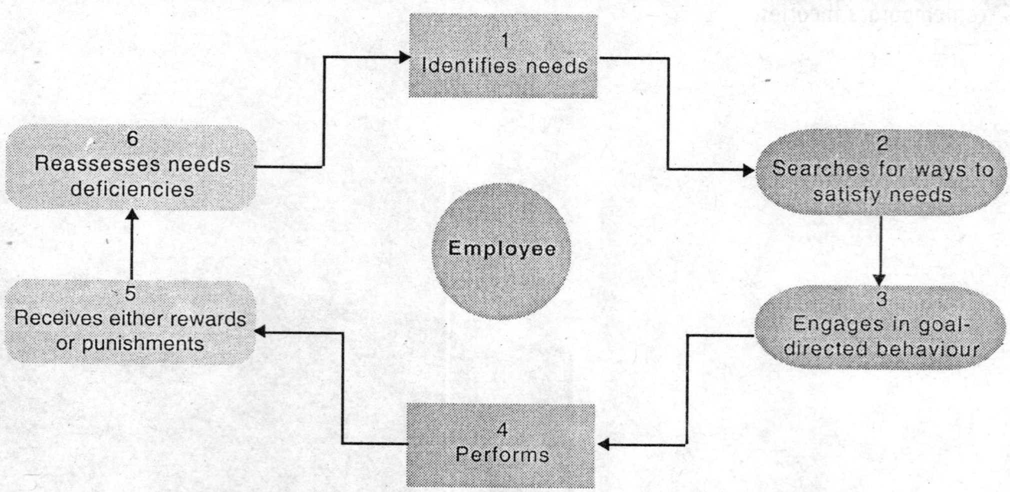

The framework (Fig 8.1) comprises six steps. Motivation process, as shown in the Fig. 8.1, begins with the individual's needs (step 1). Needs are felt deprivations which the individual experiences at a given time and act as energizers. These needs may be psychological (e.g., the need for recognition), physiological (e.g., the need for water, air, or food), or social (e.g., the need for friendship). These deprivations force the individual to search for ways to reduce or eliminate them (step 2).

Motivation is goal directed (step 3). A goal is a specific result that the individual wants to achieve. An employee's goals are often driving forces and accomplishing those goals can significantly reduce needs. For example, some employees have strong drives for advancement and expectations that working long hours on visible projects will lead to promotions, and greater influence. Such needs and expectations often create uncomfortable tension within these individuals. Believing that certain specific behaviours can overcome this tension, these employees act to reduce it. Employees striving to advance may seek to work on major problems facing the organisation in order to gain visibility and influence with senior managers (step 4). Promotions and raises are two of the ways that organisation seek to maintain desirable behaviours.[3] They are signals (feedback) to employees that their needs for advancement and recognition and their behaviours are appropriate (step 5). Once the employees have received either rewards or punishments, they reassess their needs (step 6).

Some definitions on motivation are worth citing in this context.

1. *"Motivation is the result of processes, internal or external to the individual, that arouse enthusiasm and persistence to pursue a certain course of action."*[4]
2. *"... how behaviour gets started, is energised, is sustained, is directed, is stopped and what kind of subjective reaction is present in the organisation while all this is going on"*[5]

IMPORTANCE OF MOTIVATION

As stated in the beginning of this chapter, motivation coupled with ability leads to performance. Not only are employees motivated to perform allotted tasks, they look for better ways to do a job. This statement can apply for corporate strategists, and to production workers who are looking for better ways to do a job. When people actively seek new ways of doing things, they usually find them. It is the responsibility of managers to make employees look for better ways of doing jobs. An understanding of the nature of motivation is helpful in this context.

Second, a motivated employee generally is more quality oriented. This is true whether we are talking about a top manager spending extra time on data gathering and analysis for a report, or a clerk taking extra care when filing important documents. In either case, the organisation benefits, because individuals in and outside the organisation see the enterprise as quality conscious. A clear understanding of the way motivation works helps a manager make his employees quality oriented.

Third, highly motivated workers are more productive than apathetic workers. Much has been written recently about the high productivity of Japanese workers and the fact that fewer workers are needed to produce an automobile in Japan than elsewhere. The high productivity of Japanese workers becomes the question of management's ability to motivate its employees. An appreciation of the nature of motivation is highly useful for managers.

Fourth, every organisation requires human resources, in addition to the need for financial and physical resources for it to function. Three behavioural dimensions of human resources are significant to the organisation : (1) people must be attracted not only to join the organisation but also to remain in it; (2) people must perform tasks for which they are hired, and must do in a dependable manner;

and (3) people must go beyond this dependable role performance and engage in some form of creative, spontaneous, and innovative behaviour at work. In other words, for an organisation to be effective, it must come to grips with the motivational problems of stimulating both the decision to participate and the decision to produce at work.

Fifth, motivation as a concept represents a highly complex phenomenon that affects, and is affected by a multitude of factors in the organisational milieu. A comprehensive understanding of the way in which organisation functions requires that increasing attention be directed towards the question of why people behave as they do on their jobs. An understanding of the topic of motivation is thus essential in order to comprehend more fully the effects of variations in other reactions (such as leadership style, job realisation and salary systems) as they relate to performance, satisfaction and so forth.

Sixth, yet another reason why increasing attention is paid towards motivation can be found in the present and future technology required for production. As technology increase in complexity, machines tend to become necessary yet insufficient vehicles of effective and efficient operations. Modern technology can no longer be considered synonymous with the term "automation". Consider the example of the highly technologically based space programme in the Indian Space Research Organisation (ISRO). The Polar Satellite Launch Vehicle's (PSLV) lift-off has been the result of 12 years of developmental work, transfer of technology to private industry, smoothening the manufacture of components and subsystems, complex project management and dedicated work by literally thousands in the ISRO, industry and other national laboratories and research institutes. With this feet India has joined the exclusive club of half a dozen nations that can build and more importantly, launch its own satellites.

The secret behind the success of ISRO has been its employees who are both capable of using and are *willing to use* the advanced technology to reach the goals.

Seventh, while organisations have for some time viewed their financial and physical resources from a long-term perspective, only recently have they begun seriously to apply this same perspective to their human resources. Many organisations are now beginning to pay increasing attention to developing their employees as future resources (a "talent bank") upon which they can draw as they grow and develop. Evidence for such concern can be seen in the recent growth of management and organisation development programmers, in the increased popularity of "assessment center" appraisals, in recent attention to manpower planning and in the emergence of "human resources accounting" systems. More concern is being directed, in addition, towards stimulating employees to enlarge their job skills (through training, job design, job rotation and so on) at both blue-collar and white-collar levels in an effort to ensure a continual reservoir of well-trained and highly motivated people.

MOTIVATIONAL CHALLENGES

The framework of motivation (Fig. 8.1) shows that the task of motivation is simple. But in reality, the task is more challenging.

One reason why motivation is a difficult job is that the workforce is changing. Employees join the organisations with different needs and expectations. Their values, beliefs, backgrounds, lifestyles, perceptions and attitudes are different. Not many organisations have understood these and not many OB experts are clear about the ways of motivating such diverse workforce.

Motivating employees is also more challenging at a time when firms have dramatically changed the jobs that employees perform, reduced layers of hierarchy, and jettisoned large numbers of employees in the name of right-sizing or down-sizing. These actions have significantly damaged the levels of trust and commitment necessary for employees to put in efforts above minimum requirements. Some organisations have resorted to hire and fire and pay-for-performance strategies almost giving up motivational efforts. Such strategies may have some effect (both positive and negative) but fail to make an individual overreach himself or herself.

Third, motives can be only inferred; they cannot be seen. The director of a B-school finds two girls working in his office showing varying performance, though both of them are of same age, same educational qualification and identical work experience. What motivates one girl but fails with another is difficult to understand.

The dynamic nature of needs often poses challenge to any manager in motivating his or subordinates. An employee, at any given time, has various needs, desires and expectations. Further, these factors change over time and may also conflict with each other. Employees who put in extra hours at work to fulfill their needs for accomplishment may find that these extra hours conflict directly with needs for affiliation and their desire to be with their families.

THEORIES ON MOTIVATION

There is no shortage of models, strategies and tactics for motivating employees. As a result, firms constantly experiment with new motivational programmes and practices. For discussion purposes, it is useful to classify motivational models into two general categories: early and contemporary. (See also Fig. 8.2)

EARLY THEORIES

Scientific Management: Scientific Management is the name given to a philosophy and set of methods and techniques that stressed the scientific study and organisation of work at the operations level for the purpose of increasing efficiency. Several luminaries contributed their ideas to the philosophy of Scientific Management but the movement is more associated with F.W. Taylor who is remembered as the "Father of Scientific Management."

Scientific Management had contributed several techniques which are relevant even today. The techniques are :

(i) Scientific method of doing work.

(ii) Planning the task.

(iii) Scientific selection, training and remuneration of workers.

(iv) Standardization.

(v) Specialization and division of work.

(vi) Time and motion studies.

(vii) Mental revolution.

Coupled with Taylor's logical and rational approach to management was simple theory of human behaviour. People are primarily motivated by economic rewards and will take direction if offered an opportunity to improve their economic positions. Put simply, Taylor's theory stated that:

FIGURE 8-2
MOTIVATIONAL MODELS

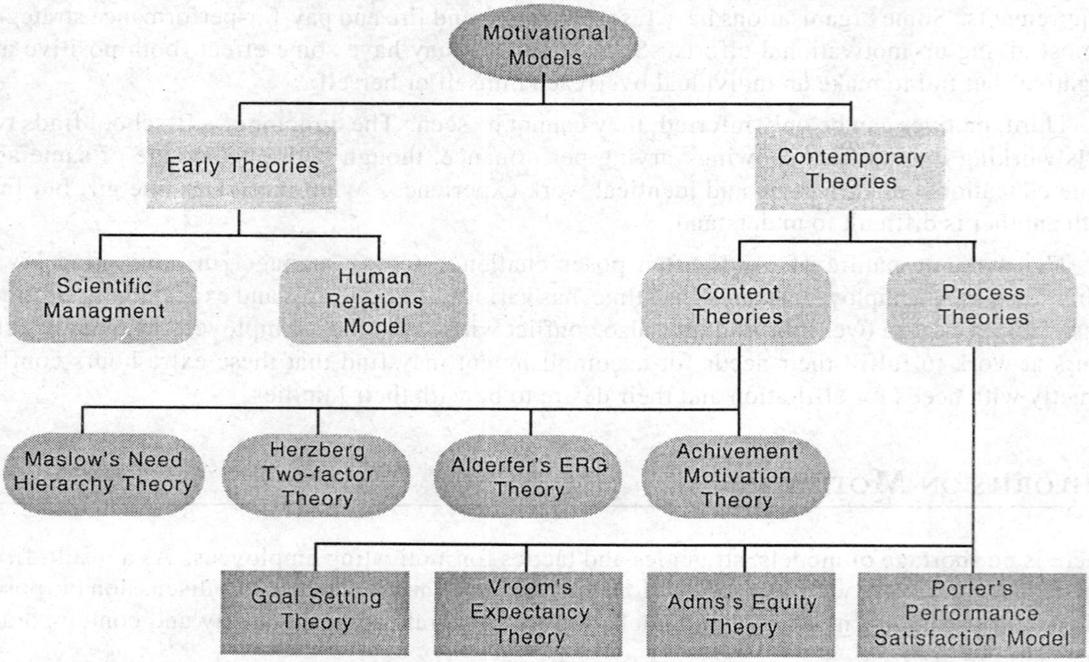

(i) Physical work could be scientifically studied to determine the optimal method of performing a job.

(ii) Workers could thereafter be made more efficient by being given prescriptions for how they were to do their jobs.

(iii) Workers would be willing to adhere to these prescriptions if paid on a differential piece work basis.

Scientific approach to motivation has been criticised severally. In particular, behavioural scientists have argued that Taylor and his colleagues dehumanised workers by treating them as mere factors of production, who could be manipulated completely through economic incentives.

The most fundamental problem with Taylor's approach from a motivational viewpoint is concerned with his rather simplistic assumption about human behaviour. Taylor believed that workers would be motivated more by the need for money (this assumption is called the 'rabble hypothesis'). He thought that the primary interest of the worker is economic gain in the form of higher wages. Contrary to this rabble hypothesis, worker seeks satisfaction of a variety of needs in the work place-need for security, social fulfillment and a challenging jobs, including pay.

Taylor's over simplified and routine jobs, instead of benefiting the workers, created boredom and dissatisfaction in them. The workers lost their abilities to think, willingness to take initiative and preparedness to use skills effectively.

Taylor's contribution is being appreciated now than when he was alive. For example, Peter Drucker believes that Taylor's work has had the same degree of impact upon the world as the work of Karl Marx or Sigmund Freud. The basic tenets of Scientific Management – science, not rule of thumb; harmony, not discord; co-operation, not individualization; maximum output, not restricted output; and the development of each person to his greatest efficiency and prosperity were relevant during Taylor's days, are relevant today and will continue to be so in days to come.

Human Relations Model It became clear that the assumption that workers were primarily motivated by money, proved to be inadequate. Elton Mayo and other human relations researchers found that the social contacts which the workers had at work places were also important and that the boredom and repetitiveness of tasks were themselves factors in reducing motivation. Mayo and others also believed that managers could motivate employees by acknowledging their social needs and by making them feel useful and important.

As a result, employees were given some freedom to make their own decisions on their jobs. Greater attention was paid to the organisation's informal work groups. More information was provided to employees about the manager's intentions and about the operations of the organisation. The Scientific Management model workers had been expected to accept management's authority in return for high wages made possible by the efficient system designed by management and implemented by the workers. In the Human Relations Model, workers were expected to accept management's authority because supervisors treated them with consideration and were attentive to their needs.

The problem with the Human Relations Model is its undue reliance on social contacts at work situation for motivating employees. Social contacts, though desirable by themselves will not always help motivate workers.

Notwithstanding what the early theories contain, there is no gainsaying the fact that for motivating employees it is necessary to ensure the feeling in them that the employees are gaining something from their actions. It is not enough that accomplishment of a task is important for the welfare of the organisation. To energise an employee, managers must make the accomplishment of work tasks contribute to the welfare of the employee as well. This is the realm of content theories of motivation. **Content theories of motivation** outline what workers want and need and therefore what tools managers can use to motivate their subordinates.

Additionally, motivating employees means that their actions must be properly *directed*. This implies that the employees have learnt what needs to be done and how and when to do it. Directing behaviour is the realm of **process theories of motivation**. These theories describe how managers can use knowledge of subordinates' needs and desires to direct subordinate behaviour appropriately.[5]

Content Theories

Maslow's need hierarchy theory, Herzberg's two-factor theory, Alderfer's ERG theory, McClelland's achievement theory and Murray's manifest needs theories are classified as content theories. These theories use individual needs to help in the understanding of job satisfaction and work behaviours. Needs reflect either physiological or psychological deficiencies. Hunger, for example, is a physiological need, desire for emotional support is a psychological need. Needs are an additional aspect of individual attributes which complement his / her demographic, contemporary and psychological characteristics.

Although content theories disagree somewhat concerning the exact nature of the needs, they do agree that

Individual needs → Activate → Tensions → That Influence → Job satisfaction and Work behaviour

Stated more clearly, content theorists suggest that the manager's job is to create work environment that responds positively to individual needs. Such things as poor performance, undesirable behaviours and decreased satisfactions can be partially explained in terms of dissatisfied needs. Also, the motivational value and rewards can be analysed in terms of "activated" needs to which a given reward either does or does not respond.

Maslow's need Hierarchy Theory The need hierarchy model of motivation propounded by Abraham Harold Maslow is undoubtedly the simplest and most widely discussed theory of motivation. The essence of the theory may be summarized thus :

(a) People are wanting beings whose needs can influence their behaviour. Only unsatisfied needs can influence behaviour, satisfied need do not act as motivators.

(b) Since needs are many, they are arranged in an order of importance, or hierarchy (hence the nomenclature need-hierarchy theory of motivation), from the basic to the complex.

(c) The person advances to the next level of hierarchy, or from the basic to the complex, only when the lower level need is at least minimally satisfied.

(d) Further up the hierarchy the person is able to go, the more individuality, humanness and psychological health he will display.

The Needs Maslow' need hierarchy divides human needs into five levels as shown in Fig. 8.3. Each level represents a group of needs – not one need for each level.

The most basic level of needs comprises the primary or physiological ones. So long as they are unsatisfied, they monopolise a person's consciousness and have virtually exclusive power to motivate behaviour. However, when they are satisfied, they cease to be motivators.

FIGURE 8-3
MASLOW'S HIERARCHY OF NEEDS — DOMINANCE OF PHYSIOLOGICAL NEEDS

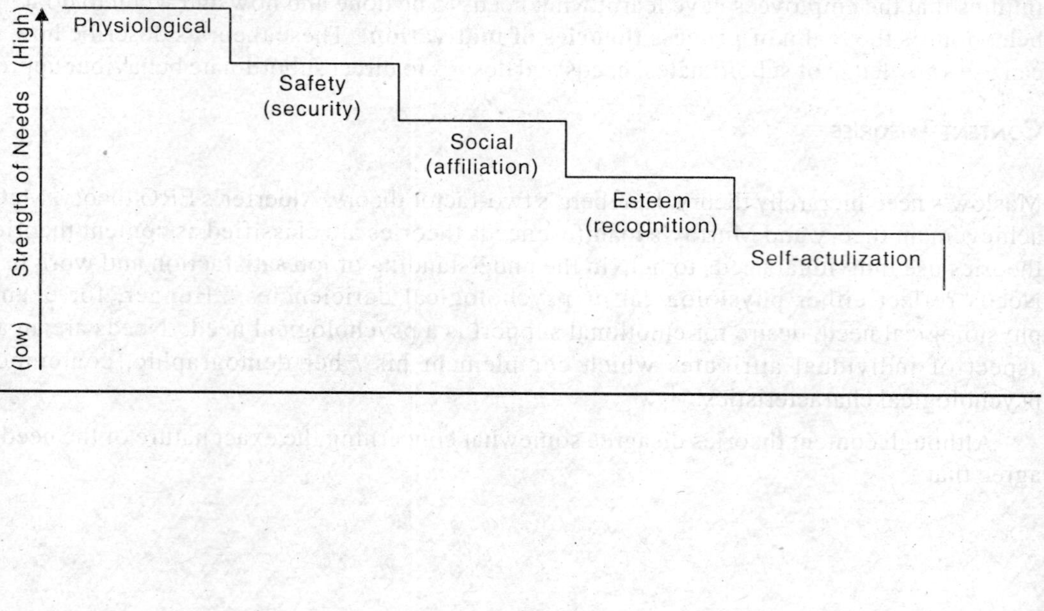

FIGURE 8-4
SAFETY NEEDS DOMINANT IN THE NEED STRUCTURE

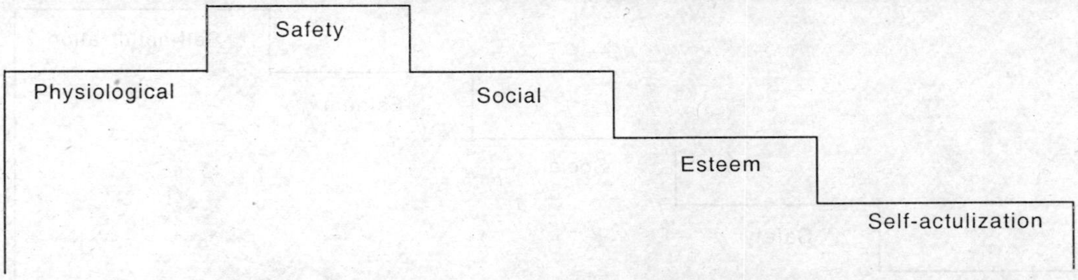

FIGURE 8-5
SOCIAL NEEDS DOMINANT IN THE NEED STRUCTURE

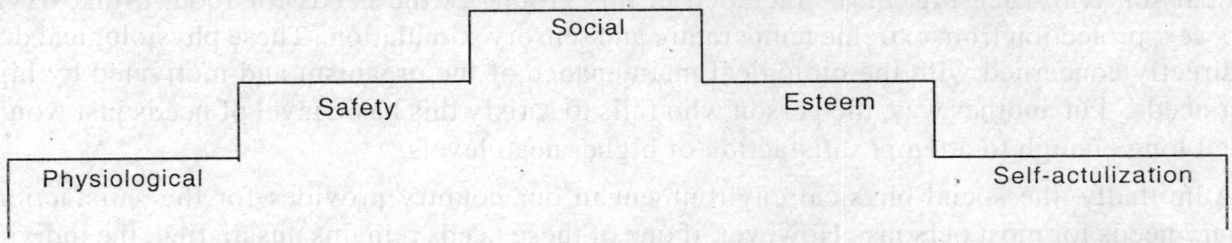

FIGURE 8-6
ESTEEM NEEDS DOMINANT IN THE NEED STRUCTURE

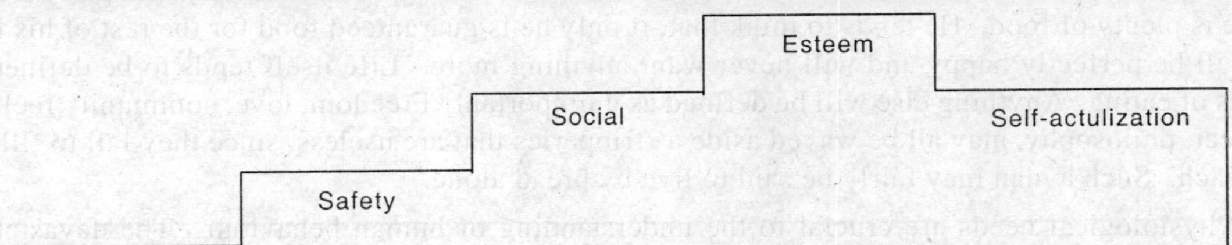

(Figures 8.3 to 8.7 are based on *Management and Organisational Behaviour* by Paul Hersey and others).

The satisfaction of primary needs does not produce contentment, instead, it unleashes a new series of discontents. The secondary needs now begin to acquire the power to motivate. People do not stop wanting; after physiological needs are fulfilled, they begin to want, in succession, safety, love, esteem and self-realisation. Maslow also suggested that people can travel down as well as up the hierarchy. Loss of existing satisfaction of primary needs, for example, can reactivate the level and increase its relative importance. A detailed description of each level needs follows.

FIGURE 8-7
SALF-ACTULIZATION NEEDS DOMINANT IN THE NEED STRUCTURE

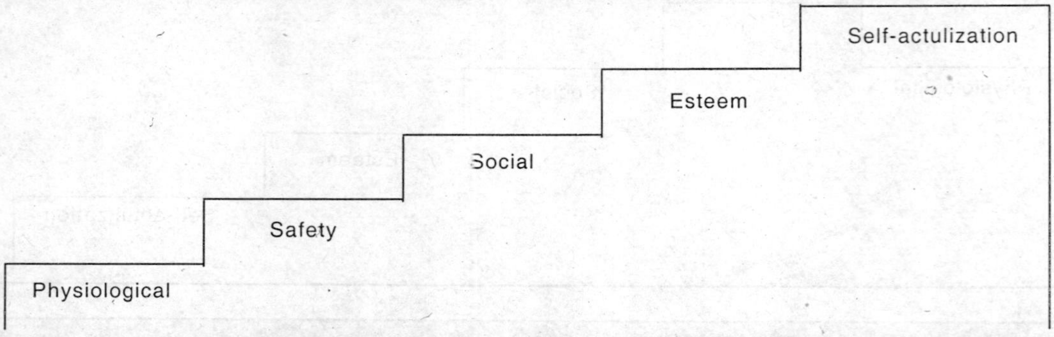

Physiological Needs The most basic, powerful and obvious of all human needs is the need for physical survival. (See Fig. 8.3). Included in this group are the needs for food, drink, oxygen, sleep, sex, protection from extreme temperature and sensory stimulation. These physiological drives are directly concerned with the biological maintenance of the organism and motivated by higher order needs. Put another way, the person who fails to satisfy this basic level of needs just won't be around long enough to attempt satisfaction of higher need levels.

Admittedly, the social-physical environment in our country provides for the satisfaction of primary needs for most persons. However, if one of these needs remains unsatisfied, the individual rapidly becomes dominated by that need, so that all other need quickly become nonexistent or decidedly secondary. The chronically hungry person will never strive to compose music, or build a brave new world. Such a person is much too preoccupied with getting something to eat. Maslow adds :

For our chronically and extremely hungry man, Utopia can be defined simply as a place where there is plenty of food. He tends to think that, if only he is guaranteed food for the rest of his life, he will be perfectly happy and will never want anything more. Life itself tends to be defined in terms of eating. Anything else will be defined as unimportant. Freedom, love, community feeling, respect, philosophy, may all be waved aside as fripperies that are useless, since they fail to fill the stomach. Such a man may fairly be said to live by bread alone.

Physiological needs are crucial to the understanding of human behaviour. The devastating effects on behaviour produced by a lack of food or water have been chronicled in numerous experiments and autobiographies. One terrifying example of the behavioural effects brought about by prolonged food deprivation occurred when a Peruvian airliner crashed deep in the jungles of South America in 1970. Trapped with a dwindling supply of food, the survivors, including a catholic priest, resorted to eating the victims of the crash. This incident illustrates how deeply ingrained social and moral taboos can give way to biological drives under stressful conditions. Without doubt, physiological needs dominate human desires, forcing themselves on one's attention before higher order goals can be pursued.[7]

In the organisational context, physiological needs are represented by employees concern for salary and basic working conditions. It is the duty of managers to ensure that these needs of the employees are met so that they can be motivated to strive for gratification of higher order needs.

Safety Needs Once physiological needs are met, another set of motives, called safety or security needs, become motivators. (See Fig. 8.4) The primary motivating force here is to ensure a reasonable degree of continuity, order structure and predictability in one's environment. Maslow suggested that the safety needs are most readily observed in infants and young children because of their relative helplessness and dependence on adults.

Safety needs exert influence beyond childhood. The preference for secured income, the acquisition of insurance and owning one's own house may be regarded as motivated in part by safety seeking. At least in part, religious and philosophic belief systems may also be interpreted in this fashion. Religions and philosophies help a person organise his world and the people in it into a coherent and meaningful whole, thus making the person feel "safe." Other expressions of the need for safety occur when individuals are confronted with real emergencies, eg., war, crime, waves, floods, earthquakes, riots, social disorganizations and similar other conditions.[8]

Security needs in the organisational context correlate to such factors as job security, salary increases, safe working conditions, unionization and lobbying for protective legislation. Managerial practices to satisfy the safety needs of employees include pension scheme, group insurance, provident fund, gratuity, safe working conditions, grievance procedure, system of seniority to govern lay-off and others. Arbitrary or unpredictable actions, actions which create feeling of uncertainty (particularly regarding continued employment), favouritism, or discrimination on the part of superiors hardly create feeling of security in an employee's mind.

Social Needs Also called belonging and love needs, these constitute the third level in the hierarchy of needs. (See Fig. 8.5). These needs arise when physiological and safety needs are satisfied. An individual motivated on this level longs for affectionate relationship with others, namely, for a place in his or her family and or reference groups. Group membership becomes a dominant goal for the individual. Accordingly, the person will feel keenly the pangs of loneliness, social ostracism, friendliness and rejection, especially when induced by the absence of friends, relatives, a spouse or children.[9]

Unlike Freud who equated love with sex, Maslow believed that love involves a healthy, loving relationship between two people, which includes mutual respect, admiration and trust. Maslow also stressed that love needs involve both giving and receiving love. Being loved and accepted is instrumental to healthy feelings of worth. Not being loved leads to feelings of futility, emptiness and hostility.

In the organisational context, social needs represent the need for a compatible work group, peer acceptance, professional friendship and friendly supervision. Managers do well to encourage informal groups. Besides, supervision needs to be effective and friendly behaviour with subordinates pays.

Unfortunately, many managers view friendly relations of employees with their peers as a threat to the organisation and act accordingly. Managers have often gone to considerable lengths to control and direct employees' relationships in ways that are opposed to the natural groupings of human beings. Therefore, when a manager assumes that informal groups always threaten the organisation, and actively strives to break up existing groups, the individuals affected may become resistant, antagonistic and uncooperative. These resistant actions are often consequences or symptoms, not causes, for the manager may have thwarted the satisfaction of social needs and perhaps even safety needs.

Self Esteem Needs Next in Maslow's hierarchy are esteem or egoistic needs. (See Fig. 8.6). Maslow classified these needs into two subsidiary sets : self-respect and esteem from others. The former includes such things as desire for competence, confidence, personal strength, adequacy, achievement, independence and freedom. An individual needs to know that he is worthwhile and capable of mastering tasks and challenges in life. Esteem from others includes prestige, recognition, acceptance, attention, status, reputation and appreciation. In this case individuals need to be appreciated for what they can do, i.e., the must experience feelings of worth because their competence is recognised and valued by others.

Satisfaction of the self-esteem needs generates feelings and attitudes of self-confidence, worth, strength, capability and of being useful and necessary in the world. In contrast, the thwarting of these needs leads to feelings and attitudes of inferiority, ineptness, weakness and helplessness. These negative self-perceptions, may, in turn give rise to basic discouragement, sense of futility and hopelessness in dealing with life's demands and a low evaluation of self *vis-à-vis* others. Maslow emphasised that the most healthy self-esteem is based on earned respect from others rather than on fame, status, or adulation. Esteem is the result of effort – it is earned. Hence, there is a real psychological danger of basing one's esteem needs on the opinions of others rather than on real ability, achievement and adequacy. Once a person relies exclusively upon the opinions of others for his own self-esteem, he places himself in psychological jeopardy. To be solid, self-esteem must be founded on one's actual worth rather than on external factors beyond one's control.

In the workplace self-esteem needs correspond to job title, merit pay increase, peer/supervisory recognition, challenging work, responsibility, and publicity in company publications. Managerial practices to fulfill these needs include challenging work assignments, performance feedback, performance recognition, personal encouragement and involving employees in goal getting and decision-making.

Self Actualisation Needs Finally, if all the earlier four level needs are satisfied, the need for self-actualisation comes to the fore (see Fig. 8.7). Maslow characterised self-actualisation as the desire to become everything that one is capable of becoming. The person who has achieved this highest-level presses towards the full use and exploitation of his talents, capacities and potentialities. In other words, to self-actualize is to become the total kind of person that one wants to become to reach the peak of one's potential.

The need for self-actualisation is distinctive, in that it is never fully satisfied. It appears to remain important and insatiable. The more apparent satisfaction of it a person obtains, the more important the need for more seems to become.

Though the impulse to realise one's potential is natural and necessary, only a few, usually the gifted, ever do so. Maslow himself estimated that less than one percent of the population fulfills the need for self-actualisation. Maslow advances three reasons for this. *First*, people are invariably blind to their own potentialities. *Second*, the social environment often stifles development towards self-fulfillment. Women, for example, were stereotyped for long, to be housewives. This prevented them from reaching self-fulfillment. A *final* obstacle is the strong negative influence exercised by the safety needs. The growth process demands a constant willingness to take risks, to make mistakes, and to break old habits. This requires courage. It logically follows that anything that increases the individual's fear and anxiety also increases his tendency to regress towards safety and security.

In an organisation, self-actualisation needs correlate to desire for excelling oneself in one's job, advancing an important idea, successfully managing a unit and the like. By being aware of the self-actualisation needs of subordinates, managers can use a variety of approaches to enable subordinates to achieve personal as well as organisational goals.

Maslow's theory represents a significant departure from economic theories of motivation. As a result the theory has an important impact in two ways. First, the theory presents an entire array of non economic worker needs. If an employee does not respond to economic incentives, managers have alternative sources of employee motivation to consider. Second, Maslow's hierarchy provides an important explanation for the changing motivation of workers over time. When a new employee first starts on the job, needs lower on the hierarchy – Physiological or safety needs – are likely to command the most attention. Later, as these needs are fulfilled, the employee's attention will turn to the fulfillment of higher – order needs, such as gaining the acceptance and respect of coworkers.[10]

Fig. 8.8 illustrates one's ascension up the hierarchy of needs. The individual is able to go further up only when his previous needs are satisfied. If unsatisfied, the needs will hold his concentration till they are satisfied. Thus there is satisfaction – progression dimension in Maslow's model.

FIGURE 8-8

FLOW DIAGRAM OF NEEDS SATISFACTION

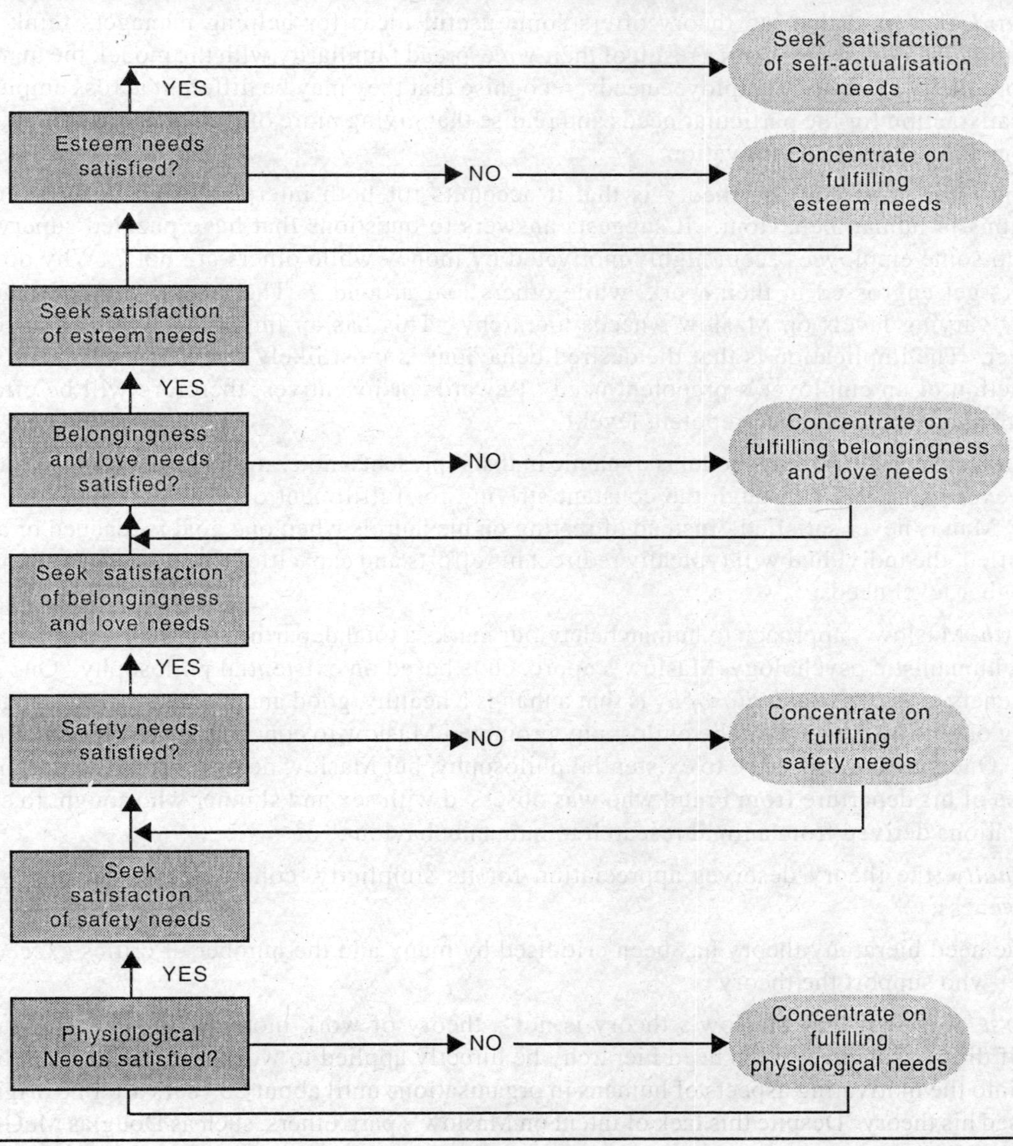

(***Source:*** T. Herbert, *Dimensions of Organizational Behaviour*, p.23)

What is the role of a typical manager ? The task is to lift the employees from lower level needs to the higher level ones. Employees must be motivated to aspire for self-actualisation needs.

Evaluation of the Model Maslow's theory represents a significant departure from economic theories of motivation. As a result the theory has an important impact in two ways. *First*, the theory presents an entire array of non-economic worker needs. If an employee does not respond to economic incentives, managers have alternative sources of employee motivation to consider.

Second, Maslow's hierarchy provides an important explanation for the changing motivations of workers overtime. When a new employee first starts on the job, needs lower on the hierarchy – physiological or safety needs – are likely to command the most attention. Later, as these needs are fulfilled, the employee's attention will turn to the fulfillment of higher – order needs, such as gaining the acceptance and respect of co-workers.

Third, it is said that the theory offers some useful ideas for helping managers think about motivating their employees. As a result of their widespread familiarity with the model, the managers are more likely to identify employee needs, recognise that they may be different across employees, offer satisfaction for the particular needs and realise that giving more of the same reward may have a diminishing impact on motivation.

The *fourth* merit of the theory is that it accounts for both interpersonal and intrapersonal variations in human behaviour. It suggests answers to questions that have puzzled supervisors. Why do some employees seem highly motivated by money while others are not ? Why do some workers get engrossed in their work, while others loaf around ? The answer may be that they occupy varying levels on Maslow's needs hierarchy. This has an important implication for the manager. The implication is that the desired behaviour is most likely to occur if it results in the satisfaction of an employee's prepotent need. Rewards or incentives, therefore will be effective when they are linked to the prepotent level.[11]

Fifth, the need hierarchy model is dynamic in that it presents motivation as a constantly changing force, expressing itself through the constant striving for fulfillment of new and higher levels of needs. Man is never satisfied. Instead of resting on his laurels when one goal is reached or a need is satisfied, the individual will typically redirect his efforts and capacities towards the attainment of still higher level needs.[12]

Sixth, Maslow's approach to human behaviour marks a total departure from earlier approaches. Called humanistic psychology, Maslow's approach is based on existential philosophy. One of the basic tenets of *existential philosophy* is that a man is a healthy, good and creative being, capable of carving out his own destiny. The philosophy prompted Maslow to conceptualise self-actualisation needs. One may not subscribe to existential philosophy, but Maslow deserves to be complimented because of his departure from Freud who was obsessed with sex and skinner who sought to extend observations derived from animal research to human behaviour.

Finally, the theory deserves appreciation for its simplicity, commonness, humanness and intuitiveness.

The need hierarchy theory has been criticised by many and the number of critics exceeds the number who support the theory.

First, it is said that Maslow's theory is not a theory of work motivation. In fact, Maslow, himself did not intend that his need hierarchy be directly applied to work motivation. He did not delve into the motivating aspects of humans in organisations until about 20 years after he originally proposed his theory. Despite this lack of intent on Maslow's part, others, such as Douglas McGregor, in his widely read book "The Human Side of Enterprise", popularized Maslow's theory in management literature.

Second, the hierarchy of needs simply does not exist. At all levels needs are present at given time. An individual motivated by self-actualisation needs, for example, cannot afford to forget his food.

Third, assuming hierarchy does exist among needs, it may not be the same in all countries. Maslow's hierarchy applies to American and British managers. Japanese managers, however, would seem to have hierarchy that places social and security needs higher, because they are less well satisfied than self-actualisation. Northern European managers would seem to have a hierarchy that reverses Maslow's positioning of safety and love. These and other variations imply that Maslow's hierarchy may be better reflection of the culture of its birth than a guide to motivation in other cultures.[13]

Table 8.1 brings out different ordering of needs n six different countries.

TABLE 8-1
ORDERING OF NEEDS ACROSS COUNTRIES

Country	*Need Priority*
United States and Japan	Self-actualisation, esteem, safety, physiological and social
France	Self-actualisation, esteem, physiological, safety and social
Germany	Self-actualisation, physiological, esteem, social and safety
India	Physiological, self-actualisation, esteem, social and safety
Malawi	Physiological, self-actualisation, esteem, safety and social
China	Self-actualisation, safety, physiological and social

(***Source:*** Manao Thakur, *et al, International Managment,* Tata McGraw-Hill, 1997, p.177)

Because of the differing need priorities organisations, particularly MNCs, need to adopt different personnel policies and practices to meet local needs. This was what Honda did in the U.S when it set up its plant.

Fourth, not only are there differences across countries in needs hierarchy, there are variations within countries and among individuals. Within a country, culturally disadvantaged employees may feel stronger deprivation of lower level needs, whereas culturally advantaged employees seek satisfaction of higher level needs.

Maslow himself pointed out that individuals differ in the relative intensity of their various needs. For example, some individuals remain strongly influenced by feeling of insecurity despite objective conditions that satisfy the needs of most similarly situated persons.

Fifth, Maslow's assumption about psychological health is not acceptable to many. His existential philosophy is also questioned by the critics. Contrary to Maslow's belief, many individuals may stay content with lower level needs – physiological or safety needs. They may not move farther in the hierarchy of needs in search of satisfaction.

Sixth, it has also been pointed that managers will not have time to leisurely diagnose of where every employee is on Maslow's hierarchy. Further more, they may not be free to supply rewards tailor-made to each of them. Given these constraints in addition to the presence of cultural and individual differences in patterns of need satisfaction, how can manager make any practical use of Maslow's theory ?

In spite of its serious limitations, the need hierarchy theory is important because of its contribution in terms of making management reward diverse needs of humans at work. Their names of hierarchy are not important. But some of them, particularly higher level needs like esteem and actualisation needs, are important to the content of work motivation.

Motivation –Hygiene Theory Another very popular theory of motivation is that proposed by psychologist Frederick Herzberg. This model, which is variously termed the two-factor theory, the dual factor theory, and the motivation-hygiene theory, has been widely accepted by managers concerned with the problem of human behaviour at work.

There are two distinct aspects of the motivation-hygiene theory. The first and more basic part of model represents a formally stated theory of work behaviour. It is this two-factor model of motivation which is considered in this chapter. The second aspect of Herzberg's work has focused upon the behavioural consequences of job enrichment and job satisfaction programmes. The second aspect will be considered in the next chapter.

Herzberg and his associates Mausner, Peterson and Capwell began their initial work on factors affecting work motivation in the mid-50s. Their first effort entailed a thorough review of existing research to the date on the subject. Based on this review, Herzberg carried out his now famous survey of 200 accountants and engineers. Herzberg used the critical incident method of obtaining data for analysis. The respondents were essentially asked two questions : (1) When did you feel particularly good about your job ; and (2) When did you feel exceptionally bad about your job ?

Responses obtained from this critical incident method were interesting. It was revealed that factors which made respondents feel good were totally different from those which made them feel bad. As seen in Fig. 8.9, certain characteristics tend to be consistently related to job-satisfaction (factors on the right-side of the figure), and others to job-dissatisfaction (factors on the left-side of the figure).

Intrinsic factors, such as achievement, recognition, the work itself, responsibility, advancement and growth seem to be related to job-satisfaction. These factors are variously known as motivators, satisfiers and job content factors. When questioned when they felt good about their work, respondents tended to attribute these characteristics to themselves. On the other hand, when they were dissatisfied, they tended to extrinsic factors, such as company policy and administration, supervision, work conditions, salary, status, security and interpersonal relations. These factors are also known as dissatisfiers, hygiene factors, maintenance factors or job content factors. Herzberg chose the term hygiene and maintenance to describe these factors as they help prevent occurrence of undesirable consequences.

According to Herzberg, satisfaction and dissatisfaction are not opposite poles of one dimension, they are two separate dimensions. Satisfaction is affected by motivators and dissatisfaction by hygiene factors. This is the key idea of Herzberg and it has important implications for managers.

To achieve motivation, managers should cope with both satisfiers and dissatisfiers. Improve hygiene factors – dissatisfaction is removed from the minds of employees. A favourable frame of mind is not created for motivation. Provide satisfiers, motivation will then take place. Managers should be realistic not to expect motivation by only improving the "hygiene" work environment.

This is the crux of the two-factor theory of motivation. Fig. 8.10 diagrams the essence of the Herzberg's model.

FIGURE 8-9
HERZBERG'S HYGIENES AND MOTIVATORS

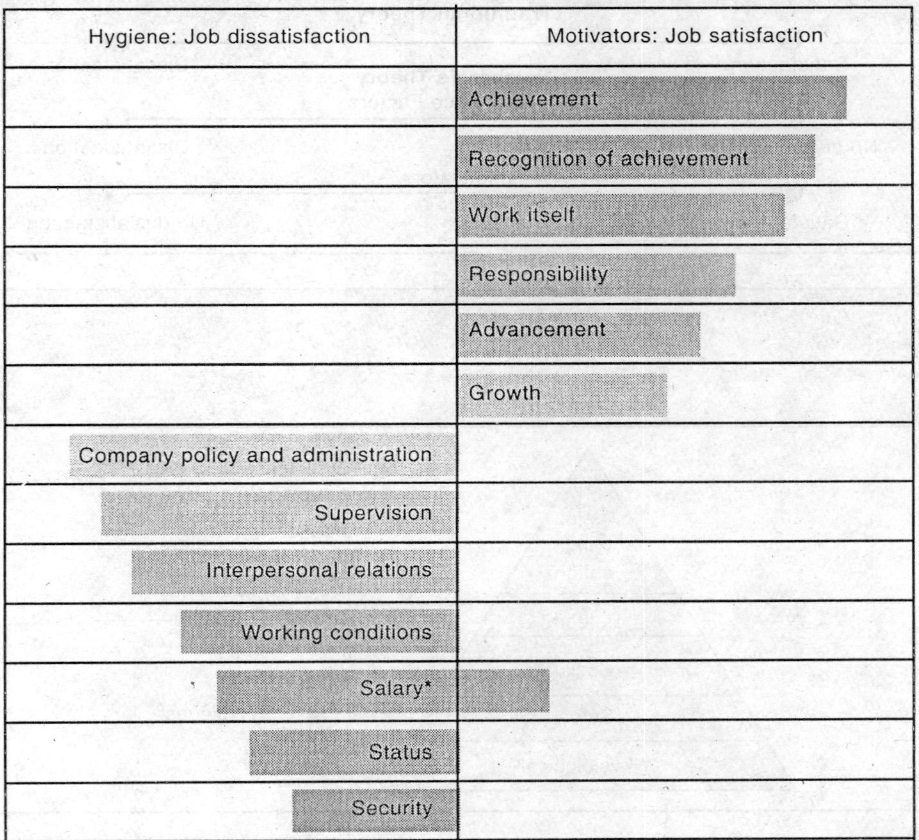

* Because of its ubiquitous nature, salary commonly shows up as a motivator as well as hygiene. Although primarily a hygiene factor, it also often takes on some of the properties of a motivator, with dynamics similar to those of recognition for achievement.

Need Hierarchy and Two-factor Theories Compared and Contrasted There are similarities and dissimilarities between Maslow's need hierarchy and Herzberg's hygiene-motivation theories of motivation. Both of them have become very popular and have been widely accepted by academics and managers. The most striking similarity between the two theories is that they assume that specific needs energise behaviour. Further more, there appears to be a great deal of agreement as to the totality of human needs. Fig. 8.11 shows how the needs in both the models might be related. It is reasonable to argue that Herzberg's motivators satisfy the higher order needs of Maslow's i.e., self-esteem and self-actualisation.

The hygiene factors are the equivalent of the physiological, security and social needs of the need hierarchy model.

The differences between the two models are presented in Table 8.2.

FIGURE 8-10
ESSENCE OF THE TWO-FACTOR THEORY

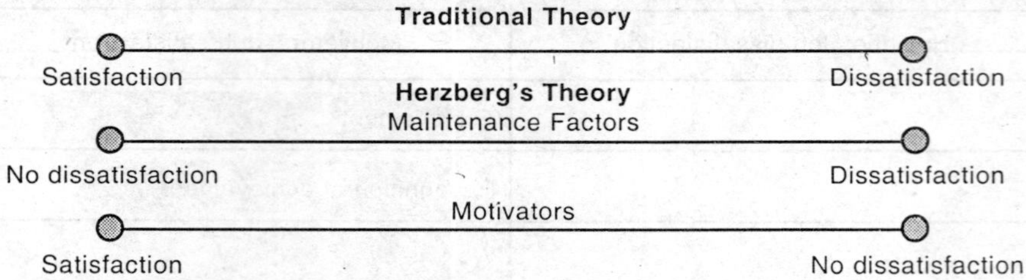

FIGURE 8-11
A COMPARISON OF MASLOW'S NEED HIERARCHY AND HERZBERG'S TWO-FACTOR THEORY

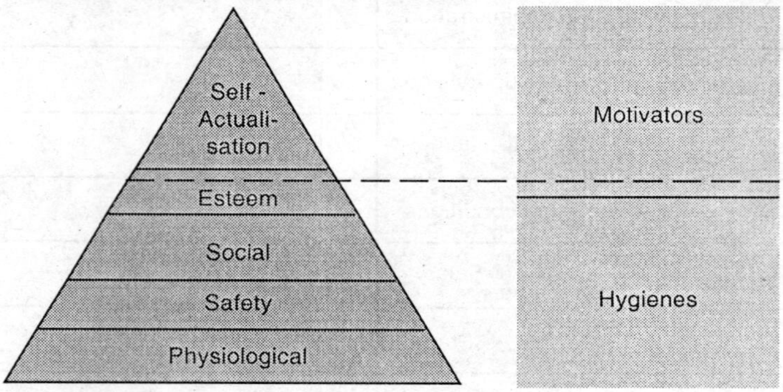

Evaluation of the Two-Factor Theory Like the need hierarchy theory, the hygiene – motivation theory has been the subject of appreciation and criticism. The criticisms of the theory are the following :

(a) The procedure that Herzberg adopted is limited by its methodology. When things are going well people claim credit for themselves. Contrarily, they blame failure on the extrinsic environment.

(b) The reliability of Herzberg's methodology is questioned. Since raters have to make interpretations, it is possible that they may contaminate the findings by interpreting one response in one manner while treating another similar response differently.

(c) The theory, to the degree that it is valid, provides an explanation of job-satisfaction. It is not really a theory of motivation.

(d) No overall measure of satisfaction was utilised. In other words, a person may dislike part of his job, yet think the job is acceptable.

(e) The theory is inconsistent with previous research. The motivation hygiene theory ignores situational variables.

TABLE 8-2

DIFFERENCE BETWEEN MASLOW'S AND HERZBERG'S MOTIVATIONAL THEORIES

Issue	*Maslow*	*Herzberg*
Type of theory	Descriptive	Prescriptive
The satisfaction performance relationship	Unsatisfied needs energise behaviour, this behaviour causes performance	Needs cause performance
Effect of need satisfaction	A satisfied need is not a motivator (except self – actualisation)	A satisfied (hygiene) need is not a motivator, other satisfied needs are motivators
Need order	Hierarchy of needs	No hierarchy
Effect of pay	Pay is a motivator if it satisfies needs	Pay is not a motivator
Effect of needs	All needs are motivators at various times	Only some needs are motivators
View of motivation	Macro view – deals with all aspects of existence	Micro view – deals primarily with work related motivation
Worker level	Relevant for all workers	Probably more relevant to white – collar and professional workers

(f) Herzberg assumes that there is a relationship between satisfaction and productivity. But the research methodology he used looked only at satisfaction, not at productivity. To make such research relevant, one must assume a high relationship between satisfaction and productivity.

(g) The two factors are not actually distinct. Both motivators and hygienes contribute to both satisfaction and dissatisfaction.

(h) Thanks to Herzberg's theory, there has been a tremendous emphasis on motivators. The importance of hygiene factors has been ignored.

A study conducted by Sarveswara Rao G.V. (1972) revealed certain facts which are worth quoting here. The findings are : (1) the two-factor theory is an over generalisation of facts and it is methodologically bound; (2) satisfaction and dissatisfaction are two distinct feelings; (3) both motivators and hygiene factors contribute to both satisfaction and dissatisfaction, although the relative influence of the two factors vary according to occupational levels and (4) motivators have more potential influence on both satisfaction and dissatisfaction.

There are certain merits of the theory. One of the most significant contribution of Herzberg's work was the tremendous impact it had on stimulating thought, research and experimentation on the topic of motivation at work. Before 1959, little research had been carried out in the are of work motivation and the research that did exist was largely fragmentary. Maslow's work on the need hierarchy theory and others were largely concerned with laboratory based findings, or clinical observations and neither had seriously addressed the problems of the work place at that time. Herzberg filled this void by specially calling attention to the need for increased understanding of the role of motivation in organisation.[14]

Second, Herzberg's theory offers specific action recommendation for managers to improve motivational levels. Herzberg cleared many misconceptions concerning motivation. For example, he argued that money should not be viewed as the most potent force on the job. He advanced a strong case for "content" factors which have a considerable bearing on behaviour. According to Herzberg, it is these content factors and not money that are primarily related to work motivation.

Third, the job design technique of job enrichment is the contribution of Herzbeg.

Finally, Herzberg has two-dimensionalised the needs, instead of five as was done by Maslow.

All things considered, it may be stated that Herzberg's theory has been widely read and few managers are unfamiliar with his recommendations. The increased popularity since the mid-1960s of vertically expanding jobs to allow workers greater responsibility in planning and controlling their work can be largely attributed to Herzberg's findings and recommendations.

ERG Theory A modification of Maslow's need hierarchy was proposed by Clay Alderfer. Alderfer's views on motivation arose from the results of questionnaires he gave to over 100 employees at several levels in a bank. Alderfer's work led him to propose that there are **three** (rather than Maslow's five) primary categories of human needs. These categories are :

(a) *Existence:* The basic physiological needs (hunger and thirst) and protection from physical danger.

(b) *Relatedness:* Social and affiliation needs and the need for respect and positive regard from others.

(c) *Growth:* The need to develop and realise one's potential.

By establishing these broader categories of human needs, Alderfer retained the idea of a hierarchy of needs, but offered a less rigid version of Maslow's "satisfaction-progression" hypothesis.[15] For example, since Maslow's social and esteem needs are together in Alderfer's ERG model under the umbrella of "relatedness" needs, neither takes fulfillment precedence over the other.

Where Maslow proposed "satisfaction-progression" model, Alderfer came out with "frustration-regression" hypothesis (see Fig. 8.12). If fulfillment of a higher order need is blocked – if something prevents the higher – order need from being fulfilled – an individual's attention will *regress* back

FIGURE 8-12

TWO KEY COMPONENTS OF ERG THEORY; SATISFACTION — PROGRESSION AND FRUSTRATION-REGRSSION

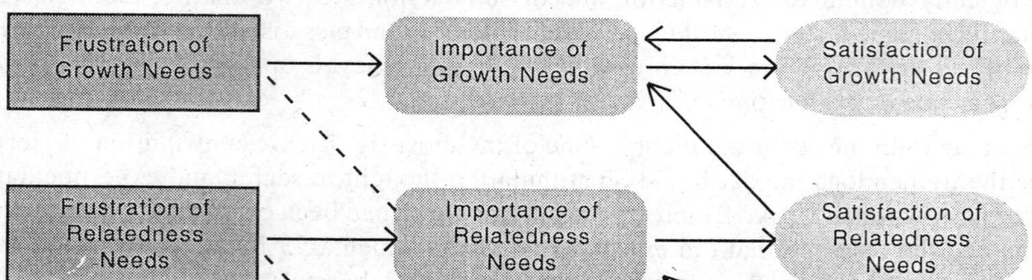

(*Source:* Richard M. Hodgetts, *Organisational Behaviour*, MacMillan, 1991, p.134)

towards fulfillment of needs lower in the hierarchy. For instance, if relatedness needs are relatively fulfilled but growth – need fulfillment is blocked, an individual's attention will return to fulfillment of relatedness needs. Besides, Alderfer's ERG theory assumes that growth needs become *more* rather than less important as they become fulfilled.[16]

Evaluation of the Theory Advantages of the ERG theory are as follows:

- First, The ERG theory is more consistent with our knowledge of individual differences among people. Variables such as education, family background and cultural environment can alter the importance or driving force that a group of needs holds for a particular individual. The evidence demonstrates that people in other cultures rank the need categories differently, for instance, natives of Spain and Japan place social needs before their psychological requirements. This would be consistent with the ERG theory. The ERG theory, therefore, represents a more valid version of the need hierarchy.
- Second, although there is some evidence to counter the theory's predictive value, most contemporary analysis of work motivation tends to support Alderfer's theory over Maslow's and Herzberg's. Overall, the ERG theory seems to take some of the strong points of the earlier content theories, but is less restrictive and limiting.

Disadvantages of the theory are as follows:

The theory does not offer clear cut guidelines. The ERG theory implies that individuals will be motivated to engage in behaviour which will satisfy one of the three sets of needs postulated by the theory. In order to predict what behaviour any given person will be motivated to engage in would require an assessment of that person to determine which of the three needs were most salient and most important to that person. The individuals would then be predicted to engage in behaviour which would lead to the attainment of outcomes, with the capacity of fulfilling these salient needs.[17]

Research on Alderfer's modifications to Maslow's theory has been supportive. Both laboratory and field studies have generated support for Alderfer's three categories and their hierarchical fulfillment relationship. Other studies have supported Alderfer's seemingly paradoxical contention that strength of need will increase when a need is either highly satisfied or highly unsatisfied.[18]

Achievement Motivation Theory The Achievement Motivation theory provides a final content theory of motivation. The theory has been advocated by David C. McClelland and his associates. It was in the late 1940s that David C. McClelland and his friends began to study three needs that motivate human behaviour-power, affiliation and achievement. McClelland believes that each person has a need for all the three (as well as for others) but that people differ in the degree to which the various needs motivate their behaviour.

A brief description of these three needs follows :

Need for Achievement (nAch) Employees with a high need for achievement derive satisfaction from achieving goals. Succeeding a task is important to the high achiever. Although people with a high need for achievement are often wealthy, their wealth comes from their ability to achieve goals. In most societies goal achievement is rewarded financially. High achievers are not motivated by money *per se*; money is their indicator of achievement. High achievers prefer immediate feedback on their performance, and they generally undertake tasks of moderate difficulty rather than those that are either very easy or very difficult. They dislike tasks with high risks because they get not achievement satisfaction from happenstance success. Similarly, they dislike easy tasks because there is no challenge to their skills. High achievers also prefer to work independently, so that successful tasks performance (or failure) can be related to their own efforts rather than to someone else's.

McClelland believes that the need for achievement can be learned and he has cited numerous instances in which people developed the need to achieve. He believes that economically backward cultures can be changed if the need to achieve can be stimulated. If McClelland is right, the achievement motivation theory is particularly attractive, because the motive can be taught to an individual or a group.

That the need for achievement can be learned was demonstrated in the Kakinada project in our country, way back in 1970s. In this ambitious project, researchers attempted to raise the achievement motivation of businessmen in Kakinada. The attempt was a success. The businessmen made plans that would help them realise their goals to become successful entrepreneurs, and told each other about their goals and their methods of reaching them. The businessmen became more productive as entrepreneurs; they started several large industries, enlarged their businesses and hired more than five thousands of their villagers. In a ten year reassessment of the programme, achievement motivational levels and results were still exceptional.

Developing Achievement Motives McClelland and his associates have made specific suggestions for developing a high achievement need. They are :

(a) Give employees periodic feedback on performance. This will provide information that will enable them to modify or correct their performance.

(b) Provide good models of achievement. Employees who are "heroes" should be available for others to emulate.

(c) Arrange tasks so that employees call pursue moderate challenges and responsibilities. Avoid tasks that are either extremely difficult or extremely easy.

(d) As much as possible, employees should be able to control their own destiny and imagination. They should be trained, however, to think realistically and positively about how they will accomplish goals.

Though McClelland placed emphasis on nAch motives, he also studied need for power and affiliation.

Need for Power (nPow) The employees exhibiting the needs for power derive satisfaction from the ability to control others. Actual achievement of goals is less important than the means by which goals are achieved. Satisfaction is derived from being in positions of influence and control. Individuals with a high nPow derive satisfaction from being in positions of influence and control. Organisations that foster the power motive tend to attract individuals with a high need for power (for example, military and political organisations).

Need for Affiliation (nAff) Individuals exhibiting this need as a dominant motive derive satisfaction from social and interpersonal activities. There is a need to form strong interpersonal ties and to 'get close' to people psychologically. If asked to choose between working at a task with those who are technically competent and those who are their friends, high nAff individuals will choose their friends.

Needs of individuals and their work preferences are summarized in Table 8.3.

Evaluation of the Theory Like any other theory on motivation, McClelland's theory too has been criticised, criticisms often being unfair. In the first place, the critics question whether motives can be taught to adults. Considerable psychological literature suggests that the acquisition of motives normally occurs in childhood and is very difficult to change once it has been established. McClelland, however, Counters that there is strong evidence from politics and religion to indicate that adult behaviour can be drastically altered in a relatively short time.

TABLE 8-3

WORK PREFERENCES OF PERSONS HIGH IN NEED FOR ACHIEVEMENT, AFFILIATION AND POWER

Individual Needs	*Work Preferences*	*Example*
High need for achievement	Individual responsibility Challenging but achievable goals Feedback on performances	Field sales person with challenging quota and opportunity to earn individual bonus.
High need for affiliation	Interpersonal relationships Opportunities to communicate	Customer service representative Member of work groups subject to group bonus plan.
High need for power	Control over other persons Attention; Recognition	Formal positions of supervisory responsibility; appointment as head of special task force or committee.

The *second* criticism of this theory questions the contention that the needs are permanently acquired. McClelland is the only theorist who argues that the needs can be socially changed through education and training. Opponents contend that the change may be only temporary similar to the one which occurs at an evangelistic meeting or a political rally.

The *third* criticism relates to the methodology used by McClelland and his associates to advocate the theory. These researchers used the famous Thematic Apperception Test (TAT) of Murray as the main tool to determine basic needs. While projective techniques as TAT have many advantages over structured questionnaires, the interpretation of responses is more subject to research's bias.

On the positive side, it may be stated that the findings of McClelland highlight the importance of matching the individual and the job. Employees with high achievement needs thrive on work that is challenging, satisfying, stimulating and complex; they welcome autonomy, variety and frequent feedback from supervisors. Employees with low achievement needs prefer situations of stability, security and predictability, they respond better to considerate than to impersonal high-pressure supervision and look to the work place and co-workers for social satisfaction. McClelland's research also suggests that managers can, to some extent, raise the achievement need level of subordinates by creating the proper work environment – permitting their subordinates a measure of independence, increasing responsibility and autonomy, gradually making tasks more challenging and praising and rewarding high performance.

Thus, McClelland's work seems to have numerous practical applications at least in the economic realm. It would appear that the current problem is to concentrate on the development of an environment that will support the desired need, be it affiliation, power or achievement, or to change the need to fit the environment. The essence of the theory is that

Individual needs + responsive work environment $\xrightarrow{\text{can create}}$ work motivation and job satisfaction

How true and how relevant the essence is!

Implications of Content Theories For a student it looks as though all the content theories – need hierarchy, two-factor, achievement motivation and ERG – look alike. Infact, it appears basically two theories have become too many.

There are similarities in the types of needs proposed by these theories. As shown in Fig. 8.13, these theories propose similar types of needs, but divide them into slightly different categories.

FIGURE 8-13
MATCHING CONTENT THEORIES

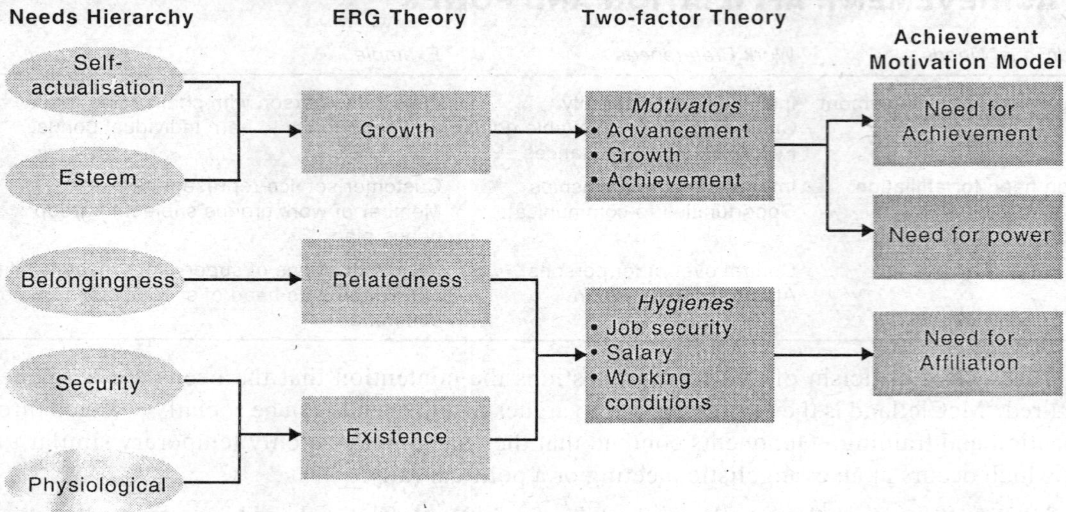

(***Source:*** Don Hellriegel, *et al., Organisational Behaviour,* p.145)

Both Maslow and Alderfer, for example, build a hierarchy of needs, whereas Herzberg proposed two discrete continua for two need categories.

Herzberg's hygiene factors correspond with the lower three levels of Maslow's theory. Similarly, Herzberg's motivation factors parallel the top two levels of Maslow's hierarchy.

There are also similarities between need-hierarchy and ERG theories. The existence needs in the ERG theory correspond to the physiological and safety needs of Maslow's hierarchy. The related needs overlap with the interpersonal needs and the need for respect from others in Maslow's theory. Finally, the growth needs correspond to Maslow's self-esteem and self-actualisation needs.

McClelland's can likewise be dovetailed with other theories. The need for affiliation clearly is analogous to relatedness needs in the ERG theory, belongingness in Maslow's hierarchy and interpersonal relations in Herzberg's theory. The need for power overlaps with Alderfer's relatedness and growth needs; the need for achievement fits well with Alderfer's growth needs and Maslow's self-actualisation needs.

Similarities notwithstanding, each theory, has served an important function in the evolution of management theories of work motivation. Need-hierarchy theories highlighted the importance of non-economic needs such as Maslow's esteem needs or Alderfer's relatedness needs – in motivating employees. Herzberg's two-factor theory raised in manager's minds an important distinction between extrinsic and intrinsic sources of motivation. McClelland's theory drove home the idea that some needs are learned.

Taken together, all the content theories emphasise the variety of possible worker needs. This has two important implications for OB practitioners.[19] First, these theories remind managers that there is no such thing as an ideal job design. While our later discussions of job design will focus on how to make jobs more enlarged, more enriched and more involving, it should always be remembered that more of any of these job features, is only better for a worker who wants or needs more. This conclusion has led some management thinkers to suggest that an important point of selecting a new employee is finding one whose needs fit what the job has to offer.

A second implication of content theories for OB practitioners is the need to tailor compensation schemes to different individual needs. Incentive schemes, for example, allow workers to choose their own rewards, the inspiration behind this practice being content theories of motivation.

Directing Behaviour — Process Theories

Content theories discussed till now, explain the dynamics of employee needs, such as why people have different needs at different times. By understanding an employee's needs, we can discover what motivates that person. Process theories do not explain how needs emerge. Rather, they describe the process through which needs are translated into behaviour. Specially, process theories explain why someone with a particular need engages in a particular direction, intensity and persistence of effort to satisfy the need. The most popular process theories are : expectancy theory, equity theory, goal-setting theory and Porter's performance – satisfaction model.

Expectancy Theory of Motivation Expectancy theory is based on the idea that work effort is directed towards behaviour that people believe will lead to desired outcomes. Through experience, we develop expectations about whether we can achieve various levels of job performance. We also develop expectations about whether performance will lead to desired outcomes. Finally, we direct our efforts towards outcomes that help us fulfill our needs. A basic premise of the expectancy theory is that employees are rational and not impulsive. They think about what they have to do to be rewarded and how much the rewards mean to them before they perform their jobs. (See Fig. 8.14).

FIGURE 8-14
EXPECTANCY THEORY

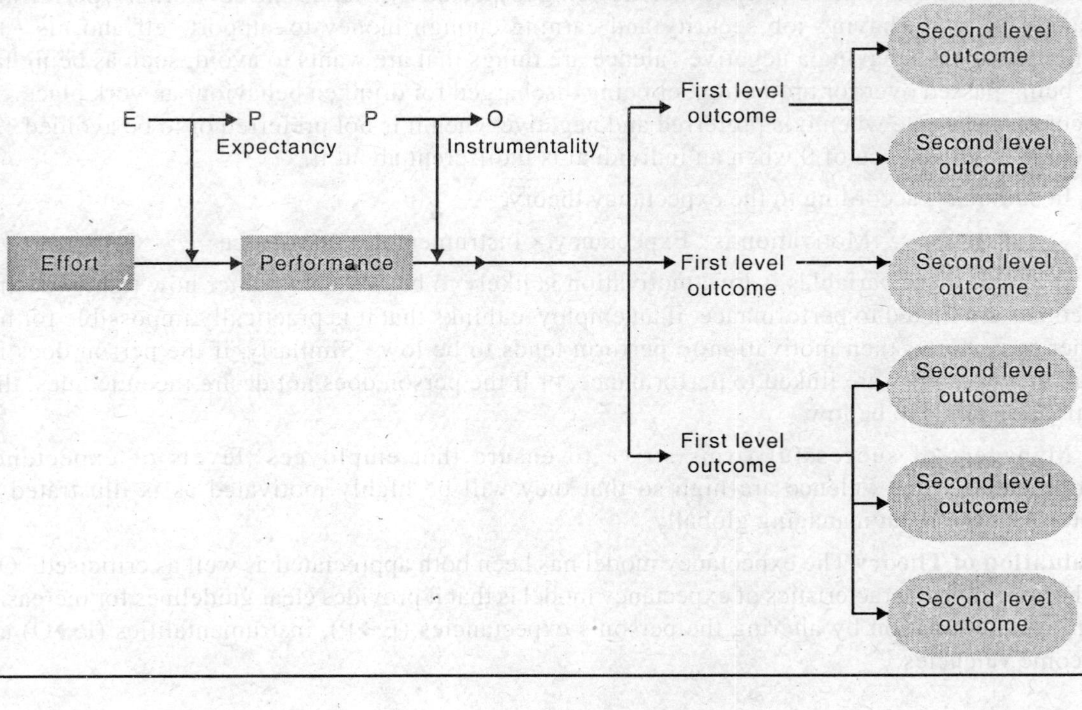

Four important variables need to be explained to understand the expectancy model better. They are : first-level and second-level outcomes, expectancy, valence and instrumentally.

First-level and Second-level outcomes Performance achieved as a result of efforts is the first level outcomes. Performance may be reflected through productivity, absenteeism, quality of work and the like. Second-level outcomes are the rewards (positive or negative) that the first level outcomes are likely to produce. They include a pay raise, promotion, peer acceptance and job security.[20]

Expectancy The belief that a particular level of effort will be followed by a particular level of performance is called expectancy. Expectancy is simple probability and therefore ranges from 0, indicating no chance that a first-level outcome will occur after the behaviour, to +1 (indicating certainty that a particular first-level outcome will follow a behaviour).

Expectancy can be restated as follows :

Effort-to-Performance (E →P)

Instrumentality This is the perception by an individual that first-level outcomes are associated with second-level outcomes. In other words, instrumentality is the relationship between the first-level outcomes and the second-level outcomes. It can have values ranging from –1 to +1. A -1 indicates that the attainment of a second-level outcome is less likely if a first-level outcome has occurred. A +1 suggests that the attainment of a second-level outcome is more likely if the first-level outcome has been attained. If there is no relationship between the first-level outcome and the second-level outcome, instrumentality is said to be 0.

Instrumentality can also be stated as follows :

Performance-to-outcome or (P→O)

Valence The fourth element in the expectancy model is valence. Valence is an individual's preference for a second-level outcome. Valence can have values ranging from negative to positive. Outcomes having a positive valence include being respected by friends and co-workers, performing meaningful work, having job security and earning enough money to support self and his / her family. Outcomes having a negative valence are things that are wants to avoid, such as being laid off, being passed over for promotion, or being discharged for drunken behaviour at work place. An outcome is positive when it is preferred and negative when it is not preferred or to be avoided. An outcome has a valence of 0 when an individual is indifferent about it.

In summary, according to the expectancy theory,

Motivation is : Expectancy × Instrumentality × Valence

If any of these variables is low, motivation is likely to be low. No matter how tightly desired outcomes are linked to performance, if an employee thinks that it is practically impossible for him or her to perform, then motivation to perform tends to be low. Similarly, if the person does not think that outcomes are linked to performance, or if the person does not desire the outcomes, then motivation tends to be low.

Managers of successful firms strive to ensure that employees' levels of expectancy, instrumentality and valence are high so that they will be highly motivated as is illustrated by Motorola's efforts at managing globally.

Evaluation of Theory The expectancy model has been both appreciated as well as criticised. One of the appealing characteristics of expectancy model is that it provides clear guidelines for increasing employee motivation by altering the person's expectancies (E→P), instrumentalities (P→O) and outcome valencies.[21]

Several practical implications of expectancy theory are shown in Table 8.4. The contents of the table are self-explanatory.

TABLE 8-4

APPLICATION OF EXPECTANCY THEORY

Variable	*Objective*	*Applications*
E→P Expectancies	To increase the belief that employees are capable of performing the job successfully	• Select people with required skills and knowledge. • Provide required training and clarify job requirements. • Provide sufficient time and resources. • Assign simpler or fewer tasks until employees can master them. • Provide examples of similar employees who have successfully performed the tasks. • Provide counseling and coaching to employees who lack self-confidence.
P→O instrumentalities	To increase the belief that good performance will result in valued outcomes	• Measure job performance accurately. • Clearly explain the outcomes that will result from successful performance. • Describe how the employee's rewards were based on past performances.
Valences of outcomes	To increase the expected value of outcomes resulting from desired performance	• Distribute rewards that employees value. • Individualise rewards. • Minimise the presence of counter-valent outcomes.

(***Source:*** Steven L. Mc Shane and Mary Ann Von Glinow, *op. cit*, p. 77)

The expectancy model is a cognitive theory. Individuals are viewed as thinking, reasoning beings who have beliefs and anticipations concerning future events in their lives. They do not simply act impulsively. It is a model which values human dignity.

This theory also assumes that individuals do not act on the basis of strong internal drives, unmet needs, or the application of satisfiers or dissatisfiers.

The expectancy theory helps managers see beyond what Maslow and Herzberg showed that motivation to work can only occur when work can satisfy unsatisfied needs. Vroom's theory implies that managers must make it possible for an employee to see that effort can result in appropriate need satisfying rewards. This may require special efforts, for example, affirmative action to correct the damage caused by any discriminative action in the past. In any case, it is necessary to build and maintain a climate of expectancies that will support requisite levels of motivation to work.

Despite its general appeal, the expectancy model has some problems. Like any newer model, it needs to be tested to learn how will research evidence support it. For example, the numerous relationships among the three variables are still open to question. It is also important to discover what kinds of behaviour the model explains and to which situations it does not very well apply.

Contrary to the assumption of the expectancy theory that individuals make decisions consciously, there are numerous instances where decisions are made with no conscious thought. This is particularly true for routine jobs. It is proved that people often make decisions and later try to rationalize them, rather than use the process indicated in the expectancy theory to make the decision in the first place.

Also, although Vroom's model emerges as an important theory of motivation, it has not been fully tested empirically. It is complex and thus its validity is difficult to test in its entirety. Most studies that have attempted to test its validity have been only marginally successful. Some critics even argue that the theory has only limited use because it tends to be valid only in situations where the effort-performance and the performance-reward linkages are clearly perceived by the employees. Since many individuals in organisations are rewarded on the basis of seniority, education, job requirements and positions rather than on their actual performance, the theory tends to be idealistic.

Further the model raised some fundamental questions.[22] Is it so complex that managers will tend to use only its highlights and not explore its details and implications ? Will other managers ignore it altogether? Many managers in operating situations do not have the time or resources to use a complex motivational system on the job. However, as they begin to learn about it, perhaps they can use parts of it.

Limitations apart, the expectancy model is useful in as much as it serves as a heuristic decision tool to guide managers in dealing with the complexity of motivation in organisations. Motivation principles such as encouraging employee performance (valence and expectancy) and matching rewards to performance (instrumentality) can be drawn from the theory. These principles can be used to guide managers in designing organisational rewards, work systems, management by objective and goal setting.

Equity Theory The equity theory is another process theory. The theory owes its origin to several prominent theorists like Festinger, Heider, Romans, Jacques, Patchen, Weick and Adams. However, it is Adam's formulation of the equity theory which is a highly developed and researched statement on the topics. Therefore, Adam's formulation is considered here.

Like any other theory, the equity theory is also alternatively known as the "social comparison" theory and "inequity" theory. True to its name, the equity theory is based on the assumption that individuals are motivated by their desire to be equitably treated in their work relationships. When employees work for an organisation, they basically exchange their services for pay and other benefits. The equity theory proposes that individuals attempt to reduce any inequity they may feel as a result of this exchange relationship. For example, if employees feel that they are either overpaid or underpaid, the equity theory posits that they will be motivated to restore equity.

Four terms are important in the theory :

- *Person*: The individual for whom equity or inequity exists.
- *Comparison other*: Any group or individual used by a person as a referent regarding inputs and outcomes. Comparison other is also called relevant other.
- *Inputs*: Characteristics which individuals bring with them to the job : education, skills, experience and the like. These are subjectively perceived by a person. (See Table 8.5)
- *Outcomes*: Pay, promotion and fringe benefits received from a job. These are also subjectively perceived by a person. (See Table 8.5)

The theory proposes that the motivation to act develops after the person compares inputs / outcomes with the identical ratio of the relevant other. Inequity is defined as the perception that person's job inputs / outcomes ratio is not equal to the inputs / outcomes ratio of the comparison other.

The basic equity proposal assumes that, upon feeling inequity, the person is motivated to reduce it. Further, the greater the felt inequity, the greater the motivation to reduce it. Thus, inequity as motivation force will act as follows:

Individual perceives inequity → Individual experiences tension → Individual wants to reduce tension → Individual takes action

TABLE 8-5
EXAMPLES OF INPUTS AND OUTCOMES IN ORGANISATIONS

Inputs	*Outcomes*
Age	Challenging job assignment
Attendance	Fringe benefits
Interpersonal skills	Job perquisites (parking space or office location)
Communication skills	Job security
Job effort (long hours)	Monotony
Level of education	Promotion
Past experience	Recognition
Performance	Responsibility
Personal appearance	Salary
Seniority	Seniority benefits
Social status	Status symbols
Technical skills	Working conditions
Training	

(***Source:*** Don Hellriegel, *et al, op. cit,* p. 152)

When attempting to reduce inequity, the person may try a number of alternatives, some of which are :

- Altering his or her inputs.
- Altering his or her outcomes.
- Distorting his or her inputs and outcomes cognitively.
- Leaving the field.
- Trying to alter or cognitively distort input and outcomes of the comparison other, or force him or her to leave the field.
- Changing the comparison other.

Fig. 8.15 contains three different equity relationships : equity, negative inequity and positive inequity. Assume the two people of the equity relationships in Fig. 8.15 have equivalent backgrounds and perform identical tasks. Only their hourly pay rates differ. Equity exists for an individual when his or her ratio of perceived outcomes to inputs is equal to that of the comparison other (See part A in Fig. 8.15). If the comparison other enjoys greater outcomes for similar inputs, negative inequity will be perceived (See part B in Fig. 8.15). On the other hand, a person will experience positive inequity when his or her outcome to input ratio is greater than that of the comparison other (See part C in Fig. 8.15).

It is not that the person feeling inequity alone gets motivated to restore equity. The person with a feeling of equity also gets motivated but to maintain the current situation.

Evaluation of the Theory Like any other theory of motivation, the equity theory has advantages and limitations. On the advantages it may be stated that the theory has generated extensive research, with many of the results being supportive.

Second, the theory recognise the influence of social comparison processes on motivation. Individuals are concerned not only with the absolute amounts of rewards they receive for their

FIGURE 8-15

NEGATIVE AND POSITIVE INEQUITY

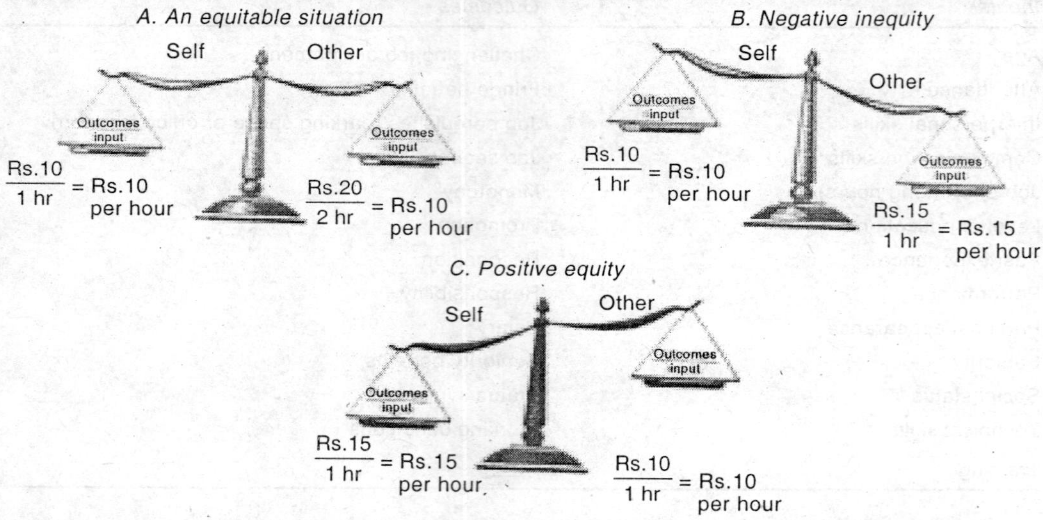

efforts, but also with the relationship between their inputs and outcomes and the inputs and outcomes of others. Any perceived injustice motivates them to restore equity.

Third, compared to the content theories the equity theory adopts a realistic approach to motivation. The equity theory posits that a major share of motivated behaviour is based on the perceived situation rather than on the actual set of circumstances. Where Maslow saw behaviour largely as a result of personality need variables, and where Herzberg saw behaviour as the result of objective job content and job context factors, the equity theory generally argues that it is the perceived equity of the situation that stimulates motivation and satisfaction. In other words, if an employee "thinks" he or she is paid less than his or her co-workers for the same quantity and quality of work, he or she would, according to the equity model, be dissatisfied and would move to reduce the inequity through various means. Such a hypothesis is particularly interesting in view of several findings which indicate that workers generally tend to overestimate the salaries or benefits of others.

The equity theory has its share of criticisms. The central theme of the model is the judgement of fair treatment. The difficulty is that not everyone equally appreciates the concept of fairness. Equity predictions, therefore, are more likely to apply to people who are morally mature that is, individuals guided by a normal system in which the fair distribution of rewards is a fundamental tenet.

The theory is not clear about the areas mentioned below :

(a) Is a given factor an input or an outcome? For example, "responsibility" is viewed by some as input and as output by others.

(b) How does a person choose (or change) the comparison other ?

(c) Under what circumstances will each method of inequity resolution be used? The feeling of inequity may force one to quit the job, but may force a change of comparison other in another. Individual differences obviously influence this activity.

(d) What is the relationship between inputs and outcomes? If (as seems likely) they are perceived by employees to be interrelated (e.g., more outcomes cannot be attained without additional inputs), the prediction of employee behaviour is more difficult.

(e) Will the findings generated in laboratory experiments hold in actual organisations? One analyst of the equity theory has noted that most studies supporting it have been laboratory experiments with student subjects.

Regardless of these problems, the equity theory continues to offer us some important insights into employee motivation.

Managing the Equity Dynamic Fig. 8.16 shows that the equity comparison actually intervenes between a manager's allocation of rewards and his / her impact on the work behaviour of subordinates. Managing the equity dynamic thus becomes quite central to the manager who strives to maintain healthy psychological contracts, that is, fairly balanced inducements and contributions among subordinates. Rewards that are received with feeling of equity can foster job satisfaction and performance and rewards received with feelings of negative inequity can damage these key work results. The burden lies with the manager to take control of the situation and make sure that any negative consequences of the equity comparison are avoided or at least minimised, when rewards are allocated.

FIGURE 8-16
THE EQUITY COMPARISON

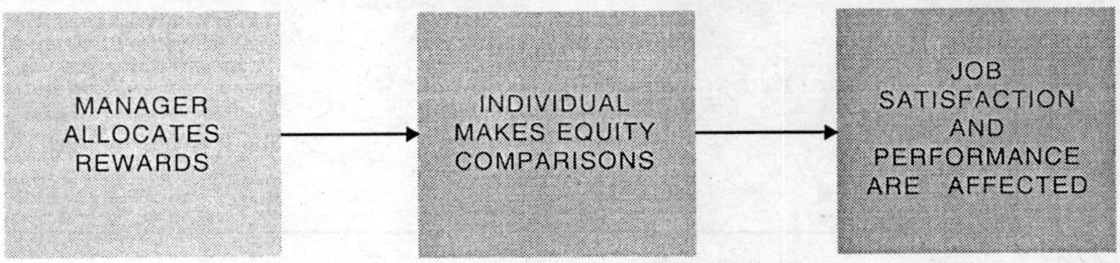

Here are two tips to the practising managers for maintaining equity dynamic at their work :

(a) Recognise that an equity comparison is likely to be made by each subordinate whenever visible rewards such as pay, promotions and the like are allocated.

(b) Anticipate felt negative inequities. Carefully communicate to each individual your evaluation of the reward, an appraisal of the performance upon which it is based and the comparison points you consider to be appropriate.

Also remember, feelings of inequity are determined solely by the individual's interpretation of situation. Thus, the assumption that every employee in a work situation will perceive his / her annual pay raise as fair is incorrect. It is not how a manager feels about the allocation of rewards that matters; rather it is how the individuals receiving the rewards feel or perceive them that will determine the motivational outcomes of the equity dynamic. Indeed, this whole area of perception is so important that we devoted the entire Chapter 17 for its discussion.

Porter and Lawler's Model Lyman Porter and Edward Lawler III, two OB researchers, developed an expectancy model of motivation that stretches beyond Vroom's work. This model attempted to —

(a) Identify the source of people's valences and expectancies, and

(b) Link effort with performance and job satisfaction.[23] Fig. 8.17 illustrates the model.

FIGURE 8-17
PORTER AND LAWLER'S EXPECTANCY MODEL

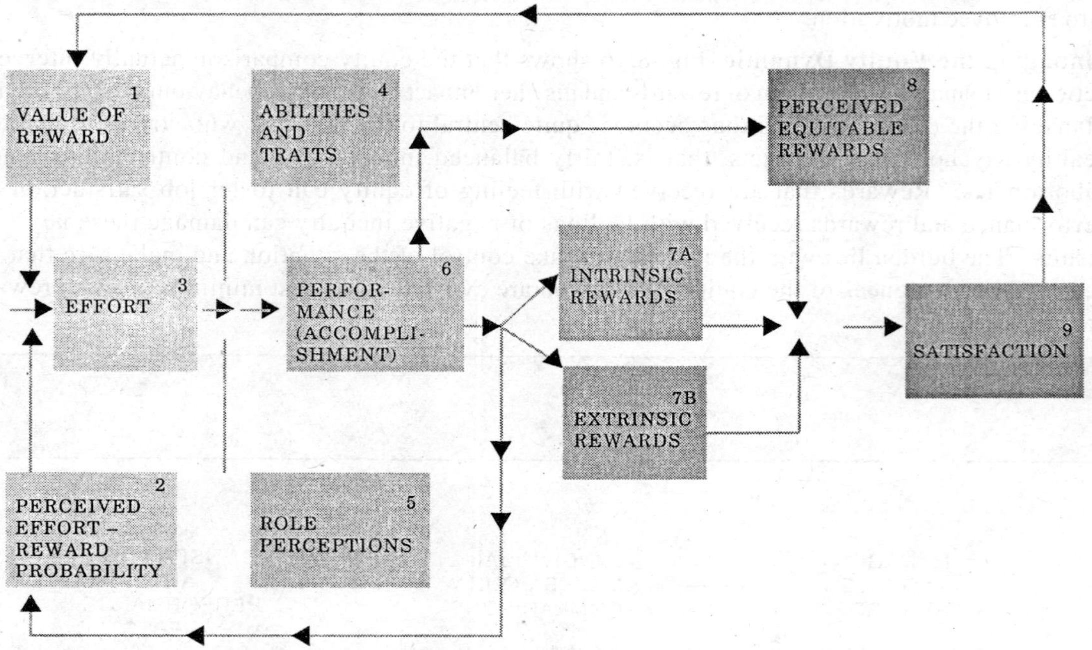

Predictors of Effort Effort is perceived as a function of the perceived value of a reward (the reward's valence) and the perceived effort-reward probability (an expectancy). Employee should exhibit more effort when they believe they will receive valued rewards for task accomplishment.

Predictors of Performance Performance is determined by more than effort. Fig. 8.17 indicates that the relationship between effort and performance is moderated by an employee's abilities and traits and role perceptions. That is, employees with higher abilities attain higher performance for a given level of effort than employees with lesser abilities. Similarly, effort results in higher performance when employees clearly understand and are comfortable with their roles. This occurs because effort is channeled into the most important tasks. For example, stage fright can render an otherwise well prepared actor or speaker ineffective.[24]

Predictors of Satisfaction Performance begets intrinsic and extrinsic rewards to employees. Intrinsic rewards are intangible outcomes such as achievements. Extrinsic rewards are tangible outcomes such as pay and recognition. Now, job satisfaction is determined by employees' perceptions of the equity of the rewards received. Fig. 8.17 further shows that job satisfaction affects employees' subsequent valence of rewards. Finally, employees' future effort → reward probabilities are influenced by past experience with performance and rewards.

Goal-setting Theory A goal is basically a desirable objective, the achievement of which is uppermost in the mind of a person. Goals are used for two purposes in organizations:

(a) As motivational devices in the sense that employees work towards meeting these goals.

(b) As a control device when performance is monitored in relation to the goals set for individuals and departments.

We focus on the first purpose in this context.

The basic idea behind the goal-setting theory is that a goal serves as a motivator because it causes people to focus their inputs and their jobs and organizations. It is the job of managers to ensure that employees divert their resources towards achieving goals. Proponents of the goal-setting theory argue that it works by directing attention and action, mobilizing effort, increasing persistence, and encouraging the development of strategies to achieve the goals (recollect Fig.8.1). Feedback regarding results is also an essential element.

Originally focusing on the second purpose (stated above), goal-setting is developing into a motivational theory as researchers attempt to better understand the cognitive factors that influence its success. Essentially there are three elements in the goal-setting theory (see Fig.8.18).

FIGURE 8-18
GOAL-SETTING PROCESS

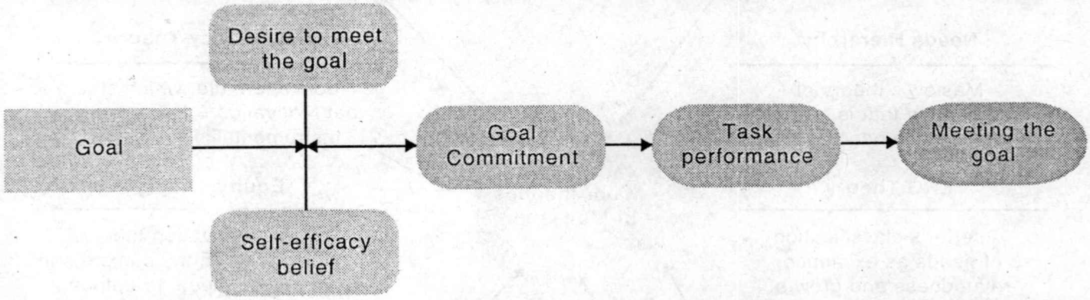

First is the desire in an individual to attain his or her goal. It is the nature of any human being to have goals and entertain the desire to reach them. When individuals succeed in meeting a goal, they feel competent and successful.

The second element is the acceptance by individuals of job and organizational goals as personal goals. This is the idea of *goal commitment*-the extent to which people invest themselves in meeting a goal. Where desire to meet a goal is strong, commitment to the goal tends to be high. Similarly, goal commitment depends on the person's ability to reach the goals. Obviously, the more strongly the individual believes that he or she is capable of meeting a goal, the more strongly he or she will accept it as his or her own.

Finally, goal-setting theory posits that beliefs about self-efficiency and goal commitment influence task performance. This makes sense because only when an individual has the necessary skills and abilities and a strong commitment will he or she perform the task which leads to goal attainment.

The success of goal-setting in motivating employees depends on establishing goals that have the appropriate attributes or characteristics. In particular, goals should be specific, measurable, attainable, realistic, and time-bound–SMART in acronym.

Goal-setting theory is an effective model of motivation in as much as it offers specific guideline for employee motivation-set realistic attainable, and time-bound goals. Under proper conditions, such goals tend to enhance performance.

REVIEW OF THEORIES

Towards the end, it is useful to take another look at all the theories described in this chapter. Fig. 8.19 helps us have a review of all the models.

FIGURE 8-19
ESSENTIALS OF MOTIVATIONAL THEORIES

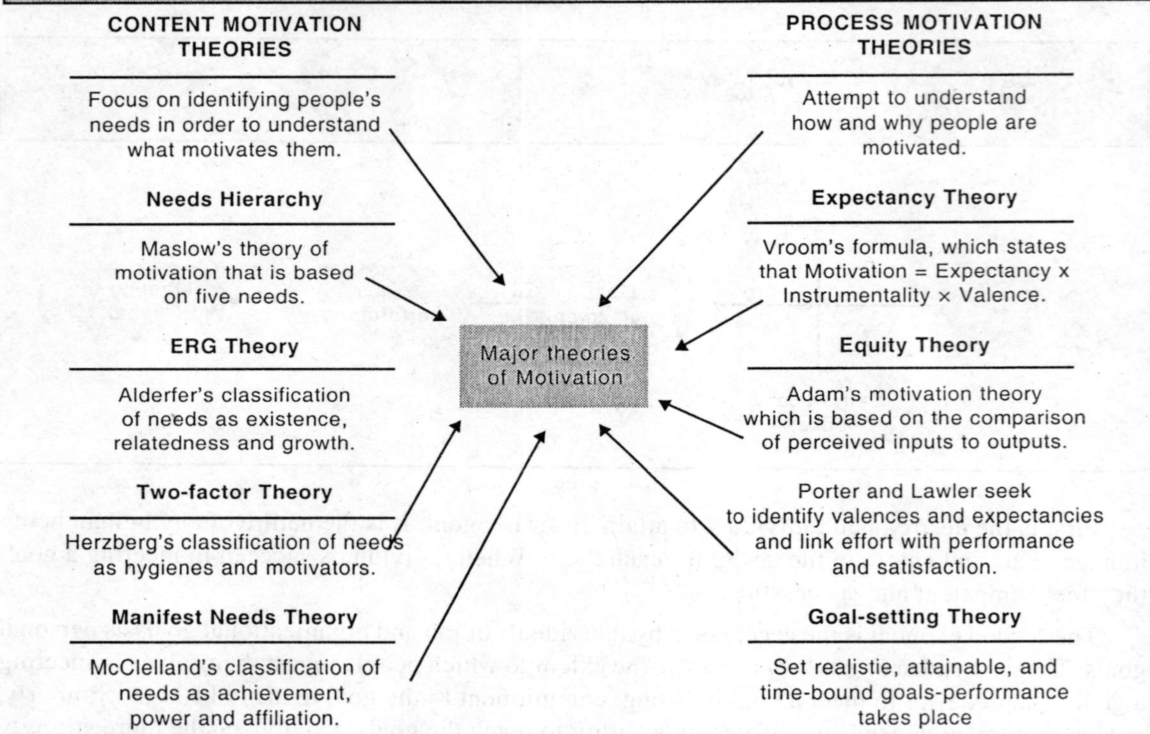

Case

THE MANAGER'S MEMO

From : R. Prince, Manager, Word Processing Center

To : E. Switzer-Greer, Manager, Personnel Department

Re: Department Policies

Unfortunately, some members of my staff are less than conscientious when it comes to arriving on time in the morning and after their lunch break. In addition, some of the word-processing staff are not very motivated to do their best.

I think that the most effective way to reduce this problem would be a clear, simple, understandable policy to motivate the employees. I have developed the following guidelines for punctuality and output :

- All employees are to be punctual. At 8.30, which is starting time, I will patrol the word-processing department and make a note of anyone who is late. Anyone who is late three times will be laid off.
- All employees are to let me know when they go to lunch. They must be back at their desks within one hour. Anyone who is late three times will be laid off.
- Based on five years experience with this department, a reasonable quantity of work is 15 pages a day of original typing or 30 pages of revisions. Employee's annual raises will be based on whether they exceed, meet or fall below this level of output.
- Raises will be computed as follows : An employee who exceeds the standard level will receive a 6 percent raise. An employee who meets the standard level will receive a 3 percent raise. An employee who falls below the standard level will receive no raise for the year.

I believe this four-point policy is easy to remember and understand. Please let me know whether you think the policy will be effective in motivating employees to be on time and to work diligently while they are here. Also, I'm interested in seeing any suggestions you have for improving this policy.

Questions

Assume you are the manager of the personnel department, write a response to this memo. To support your position, refer to the motivation theories described in the chapter. In phrasing your response, keep in mind that you can benefit by reinforcing certain behaviours of the word-processing manager (such as seeking good policies and consulting you).[25]

Questions

1. What is motivation? Why is it a critical issue of interest to managers in organisations?
2. Critically examine the need hierarchy theory of motivation.
3. Compare and contrast Maslow's need hierarchy theory with Herzberg's two factor theory of motivation.
4. What is the ERG theory of motivation? Discuss its merits and limitations.
5. What is the essence of Vroom's expectancy model of motivation? What are its merits and limitations?
6. What do you understand by equity theory of motivation? What are the ways of restoring equity to situation of inequity?
7. Bring out the essence of Porter and Lawler's theory of motivation. Do you think that the model is comprehensive? Yes or no – justify either way.
8. Think of a person who, in the past, did an excellent job of motivating you. Which of the following approaches did he use? Why?

(a) Lower order or higher order needs?

(b) Motivational or maintenance factors?

(c) ERG needs?

(d) Behaviour modification?

9. Critically examine the Achievement Motivation theory.

10. Name two outcomes in your job or classroom that have negative valence for your personality. How does a knowledge of these help someone who is trying to motivate you?

11. Discuss some organisational problems that might be resolved using the motivation models discussed in this chapter. What are the potential problems in using the theories?

12. Discuss the difficulties that are encountered when managers use motivation theories (eg., equity and expectancy) that rely on subjective employee responses.

13. At what level in Maslow's hierarchy of needs are you living? Are you basically satisfied at this level?

14. If you are being inequitably paid in your job, which strategy do you think would be the most helpful to you in resolving the inequity? What tactics would you consider using?

References

1. Don Hellriegel *et al, Organisational Behaviour,* South Western, 2001, p. 132.
2. *Ibid.*
3. Ibid, p. 133.
4. J.L. Gray and F.A. Starke, *Organisational Behaviour – Concepts and Applications,* Merrill Publishing Co., 1988. p. 104.
5. R.M. Steers and L.W. Porter, *Motivation and Work Behaviour,* McGraw-Hill, 1975, p. 5.
6. Gregory B. Northcraft and Margaret A. Neale, *Organisational Behaviour,* The Dryden Press, 1990, p. 135.
7. Larry A. Hjella and Daniel J. Ziegler, *Personality Theories : Basic Assumptions, Research and Application,* McGraw-Hill, 1976, p. 257.
8. Ibid p. 259.
9. Ibid.
10. Gregory B. Northcraft and Margaret A. Neale, *Op cit,* p.137.
11. H.R. Bobbitt, *et al, Organisational Behaviour,* Prentice Hall, 1978, p. 142.
12. Theodone T. Herbert, *Dimensions of Organisational Behaviour,* McMillan, 1976, p. 225.
13. David R. Hampton, *Contemporary Management,* McGraw-Hill, 1983, p. 54.
14. R.M. Steers and L.W. Porter, *Op. cit.,* p. 5.
15. Gregory B. Northcraft and Margaret A. Neale, *Op. cit.,* p. 139.
16. Ibid
17. Feldman and Arnold, *Managing Individual and Group Behaviour in Organisations,* McGraw-Hill, 1983, p. 11.

18. Gregory B. Northcraft and Margaret A. Neale, *Op.cit,* p.139
19. Ibid, p. 145.
20. Don Hellriegel, *et.al., Op. cit,* p.147.
21. Steven L. McShane and Mary Ann Vanglinow, *Organisational Behaviour,* Tata McGraw-Hill, 2000, p. 77.
22. K.H. Chung and L.C. Megginson, *Organisational Behaviour - Developing Managerial Skills,* Harper & Row, 1981, p. 142.
23. Robert Krietner and Angelo Kinicki, *Organisational Behaviour,* Irwin, McGraw-Hill, 1998, p. 231.
24. Ibid.
25. Gregary B. Northeraft and Margaret A. Neale, *Organisational Behaviour,* Pp. 174-175.
26. Speech delivered by Steve Jobbs, CEO of Apple Computers on June 12, 2005, to mark stanford Commencement Day.

CHAPTER

Nine

Applied Motivation Practices

LEARNING OBJECTIVES

After reading this chapter you should understand —

1. The motivational practices available in the hands of managers.
2. The power of Rewards as motivators.
3. The forces of motivation.
4. The OB Mod is another motivational practice.
5. The nature of Goal setting.
6. How to motivate problem employees.
7. The QWL is a powerful motivational practice.
8. How MBO, flexi time, flexi benefits, help motivate employees.

In the previous chapter, the nature of and the theories of motivation were described in detail. A knowledge about the theories, though useful is not enough to motivate employees. A manager must know specific ways which help him or her motivate his or her subordinates. There are several motivational practices and applications for motivating employees. Some of them are: rewards, job design, behaviour modification, empowerment, goal setting, motivating problem people, quality of work life and others (See Fig.9.1).

FIGURE 9-1
MOTIVATIONAL PRACTICES

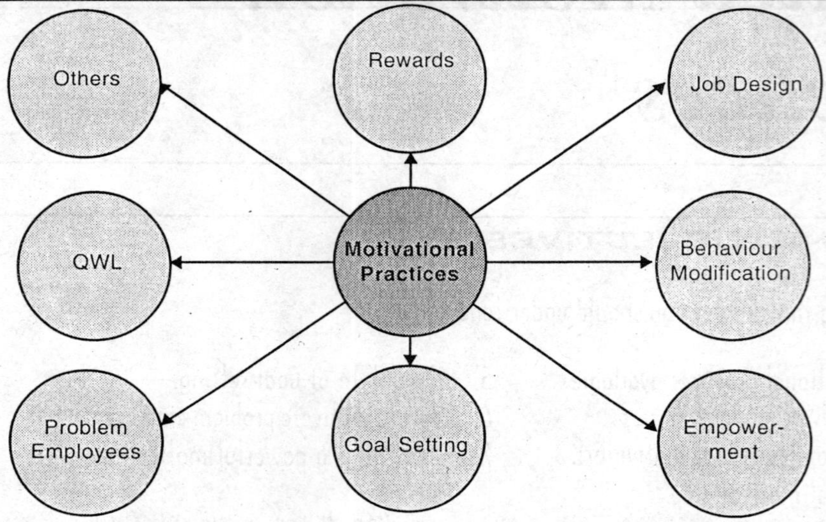

Rewards

People join organizations expecting reward. Firms distribute money and other benefits in exchange for the employees availability, competencies and behaviours.

Fig 9.2 identifies four types of rewards: Membership and seniority, job status, competency and performance.[1]

Membership and Seniority-Based Rewards

Benefits an employee receives depend on the firm on which he or she joins. An MBA taking up a job in Wipro or Infosys gets more benefits than the boy or girl who joins a state government undertaking.

In the same firm, a senior employee receives more benefits than his or her junior employee. Advancement, pay raises, retirement benefits, and perquisites depend on seniority of an employee.

There are advantage and limitations associated with membership and seniority based rewards. Membership-based rewards attract job applicants but the problem is that such rewards may not directly motivate job performance. Seniority-based rewards tend to reduce turnover but may fail to motivate achievers to perform better. Another problem with membership-based rewards is that they discourage poor performers from leaving the firm voluntarily because alternative jobs are simply not available to them.[2]

FIGURE 9-2
TYPES OF ORGANISATIONAL REWARDS

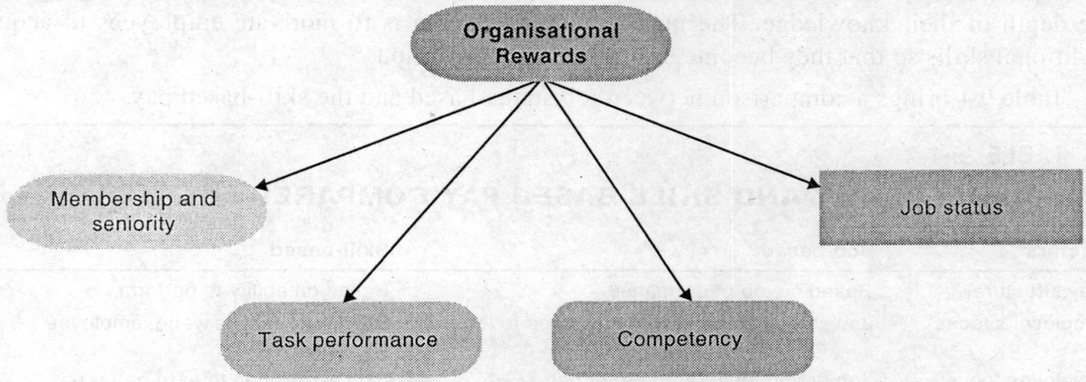

Job status-Based Rewards

Every firm rewards employees for the status of the jobs they are holding. Firms use **job evaluation** system which helps establish differentials in status of jobs. Status differentials are used as the basis for establishing salary/wage differentials.

Jobs that require more skill and effort, have more responsibility, and have difficult working conditions would have more value and consequently would be placed in higher pay grades. Firms that do not use job evaluation systems still reward job status based on pay survey information about the labour market.

A supervisor will receive higher rewards than a purchasing assistant as the job of the former enjoys better status than the latter. It has more value to the organization (calculated by job evaluation systems or pay survey) and therefore employees in that job receive more status-based rewards in the organization. High status job holders are also rewarded with more perquisites.

One advantage of status-based pay is that it helps maintain feelings of equity. Job evaluation systems try to maintain **internal equity;** that is, to ensure that employees feel their pay is fair when compared to how much other jobs in the firm are paid. Pay surveys help maintain **external equity;** that is, to ensure that employees feel their pay is fair when compared to how much people in other firms are paid.[3] Job-based rewards also motivate employees to compete for positions higher up the organizational hierarchy.

Job-based rewards are criticized by many. For one thing, such benefits fail to motivate achievers to perform better. Just because an employee holds a high priced job, he or she is rewarded better, notwithstanding the level of performance attained by the individual. Further, employees tend to exaggerate their job description and job specification to garner higher grading for their jobs through job evaluation systems. Higher grades confer higher rewards on the jobs.

Competency-Based Rewards

Increasingly organizations are linking rewards to competencies of employees. Competencies are reflected through skills, knowledge, and traits that lead to desirable behaviours. Employees are expected to have several competencies, and these competencies are evaluated by observing specific behaviour patterns.

Where rewards are linked to competencies what emerges is the skill-based pay. In the skill based pay, employees are paid on the basis of number of jobs they are capable of discharging, or on the depth of their knowledge. The purpose of this system is to motivate employees to acquire additional skills so that they become useful to the organization.

Table 9.1 brings a comparison between job status-based and the skill-based pay.

TABLE 9-1

JOB-BASED PAY AND SKILL-BASED PAY COMPARED

Factors	Job-based	Skill-based
Pay structure	Based on job performance	Based on ability to perform
Employer's focus	Job carries wage; employee linked to job	Employee carries wage; employee linked to skills
Employee focus	Job promotion to earn better pay.	Skill acquisition to earn better pay.
Procedures required	Assess job content; value jobs	Assess skills; value skills
Advantages	Pay based on value of work performed.	Flexibility; reduced workforce.
Disadvantages	Potential personnel bureaucracy; inflexibility	Potential personnel bureaucracies; cost controls

(***Source:*** Aswathappa K, *Human Resource and Personnel Management*, TMH, 2002, p. 258).

Competency- based rewards have merits. They have been praised for developing a better-skilled and flexible workforce. Customer needs are met more quickly and employees can handle any job with felicity. Product or service quality tends to improve because employees who have work experience in several jobs are more likely to know where problems originate. Moreover, employees find it easier to discover ways to improve the work process as they learn more skills and tasks in that process. Rather than paying to jobs, skill-based pay rewards skills, underlining the principle that employees are hired for their skills and not just to hold on to jobs.

Skill-based rewards, however, result in pay disparities which may demotivate employees. They are also expensive.

PERFORMANCE BASED REWARDS

The trend that is emerging recently is to link pay to performance rather than to seniority or membership. Firms in N. America, Europe, and Asia are paying their employees more for performance than ever before. For instance, in a recent survey of 210 large firms in Tokyo, Japan, 24 percent currently awarded pay increases on the basis of performance than seniority.[4]

Performance-based rewards are many, but the most common among them are:

- Organizational rewards → Stock options, Profit sharing
- Team rewards → Gain sharing, Special bonuses
- Individual rewards → Piece rate, Commission, Merit pay, Bonuses

Profit sharing is an organizational performance-based reward. In profit sharing, designated employees are allowed to share in the profit earned by a company. **Employee stock option schemes (ESOPS)** confer ownership of the firm on employees. ESPOS encourage employees to buy share of the company and reward than through dividend and market appreciation of the shares.

Team rewards are common where firms rely on teams to get the work done. Some teams are rewarded with special bonuses or gifts if they collectively achieve specific goals. A **gain sharing plan** is a type of team reward that motivates team members to reduce costs and increases labour efficiency in their work process. Gain sharing plans use a predetermined formula to calculate cost savings and pay bonus to all teams members. Typically, the company shares the cost savings with employees.

Individual rewards are quite common in organizations. The most common is the *piece rate* which links pay to the units produced by an employee. *Commissions* are paid to salespeople on the actual sales shown by them. *Merit pay* is based on an individual's performance. This is gradually replaced by reasonable *bonuses* for accomplishing specific tasks or for achieving certain goals. Although these bonuses are often determined from team or organizational performance, they may also result from satisfactory completion of individuals goals.

Do rewards, particularly monetary ones, really motivate? Put another way, does money motivate employees? The answer is 'yes' and 'no'.

MONEY Money is understood to be a powerful motivator for more than one reason. In the *first* place, money is fundamental for completion of a task. Work, unless it is voluntary or "play", involves a contract between two parties "guaranteed" by the payment of money. The employee takes pay as the reward for his or her work, and the employer views it as the price for using the services of the employee.

Second, as a medium of exchange, money is the vehicle by which employees can buy numerous need-satisfying goods and services they desire. *Third*, money is one of the hygiene factors, and improving maintenance factors is the first step in efforts directed towards motivation. *Fourth*, money also performs the function of a "score card" by which employees assess the value that the organization places on their services and by which employees can compare their "values" to others. *Fifth*, reinforcement and expectancy theories attest to the value of money as a motivator. In the former, if pay is contingent upon performance, it will encourage workers to high levels of effort (see Fig 9.3). Consistent with the expectancy theory, money will motivate to the extent that it is seen as being able to satisfy an individual's personal goals and is perceived as being dependent upon performance criteria.

Sixth, money acts as punctuation in one's life. It is an attention getting and affect producing mechanism. Money has, therefore, tremendous importance in influencing employee behaviour. *Seventh*, money is easily vulnerable for manipulation. Other factors like satisfaction, responsibility, a challenging job and the like are nebulous. Payments and the plans with which they are linked are manipulatable. *Finally*, money will be a powerful motivator for a person who is tense and anxious about lack of money. Many worries and concerns are financially based. It is relaxing to receive sufficient money to clear the outstanding bills and past debts which have been causing tensions.

But behavioural scientists think otherwise. They downgrade money as a motivator. They prefer, instead, other techniques such as challenging jobs, goals, participation in decision-making and other non-monetary incentives for motivating employees. The opposition of behavioural scientists to money as a motivator is understandable for at least six reasons. *First*, money is not important to all people. High achievers, for example, are intrinsically motivated. Money has little impact on the people. *Second*, people fail to see a direct linkage between monetary rewards and performance. In these days of unionization, protective legislation, seniority based promotions, and the cost of living

FIGURE 9-3
FEEDBACK FROM EMPLOYEE

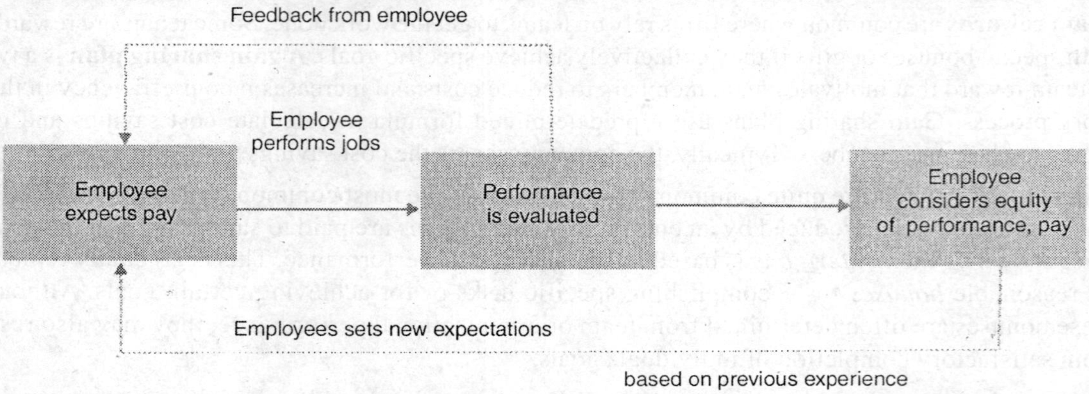

indexation, pay raises do not depend on performance. *Third*, for money to motivate the difference in pay increases between a high performer and an average performer must be significant. In practice it rarely is. *Fourth*, management must have the discretion to reward high performers with more money. This is not possible, thanks to strong unionization. *Fifth*, relationship among employees are often ruptured because of the scramble for monetary rewards. *Finally*, financial incentives discourage risk-taking propensity of people. Whenever people are encouraged to think about what they will get for performing a task, they become less inclined to take risks or explore possibilities.

The conclusion is that money can motivate some people under conditions. Put in another way, money cannot motivate all people under all circumstances. Studies too attest to the same assertion. Saiyadain and Monappa.[(5)] for example, found that only 33 percent of managers chose their jobs for remuneration. In another study conducted by Mirza S Saiyyadain[6] it was concluded that 72 percent of the students who opted for management education gave challenging jobs and freedom to make decisions as predominant reasons, while money was indicated by only 55 percent. In the same study, 23 percent of the engineers with one to seven years experience, in a state electricity board, indicated money to be important, while job content variables and supporting services were perceived as more important.

In yet another study conducted by the leading management consultancy firm. A.F. Ferguson and Co, it was revealed that only 14.8 percent of MBAs and engineering graduates preferred remuneration as the reason for joining particular organizations. The study also revealed that 48 percent wanted growth opportunities, 24 percent desired job contents, 6.6 percent expected company culture to be good and 6.6 percent went by company image. [7]

JOB DESIGN

Besides rewards, OB specialists emphasize job itself as a source of motivation. The process of assigning tasks to a job, including interdependency of those tasks with other jobs, is called *Job Design*.[8] A job is a set of tasks assigned to and performed by one person. Some jobs have very few tasks, each requiring limited skill or effort. Other jobs include a very complex set of tasks and can be accomplished by only a few highly trained professionals.

Job design has a critical impact on organization and employee objectives. From the organization's perspective, the way tasks and responsibilities are grouped can affect productivity and costs. Jobs that are not satisfying or are too demanding are difficult to fill. Boring jobs may experience higher turnover. For an employee, motivation and job satisfaction are affected by the match between job factor (content, qualifications and rewards) and personal needs. A thoughtful job design, therefore, can help both the organization and its employees achieve their objectives.

Poorly designed job, on the other hand, may lead to lower productivity, employee turnover, absenteeism, complaints, sabotage, unionization, resignations and other problems.

It was Herzberg who conceived job design as an important instrument to motivate employees. Since then, job design has been used extensively all over the World.

Factors Affecting Job Design

Job design is affected by organizational, environmental, and behavioural factors. (see Fig 9.4)

FIGURE 9-4
FACTORS AFFECTING JOB DESIGN

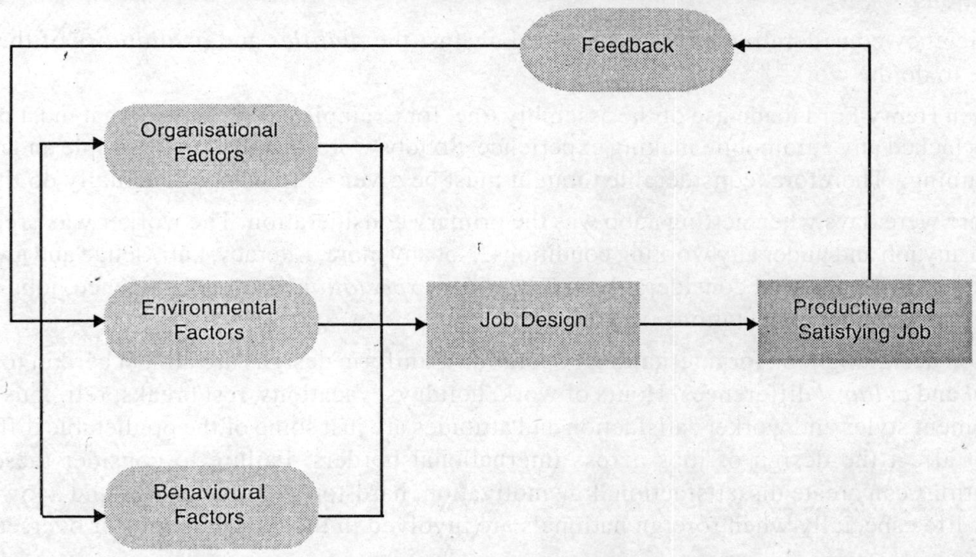

Organizational Factors These include characteristics of task, workflow, ergonomics and work practices. With regard to *task characteristics*, it may be states that job design requires the assembly of a number of tasks in to a job or a group of jobs. An individual may carry out one main task, which consists of a number of interrelated elements or functions.

On the other hand, task functions may be split between a team working closely together or strung along an assembly line. In more complex jobs, individuals may carry out one main task, each with a number of functions or these tasks may be allocated to a group of workers or divided among them. Complexity in a job may be a reflection of the number and variety of tasks to be carried out, or the range and scope of the decisions that have to be made, or the difficulty of predicting outcomes.

The *flow of work* in an organization is strongly influenced by the nature of the product. The product usually suggests the sequence and balance between jobs if the work is to be done effectively. For example, the frame of a car must be built before the fenders and doors can be added later. After the sequence of jobs is determined, the balance between jobs is established.

Ergonomics is concerned with designing and shaping jobs to fit the physical abilities and characteristics of individuals so that they can perform the jobs effectively. Ergonomics helps employers design jobs in such a way that workers' physical abilities and job demands are balanced. It does not alter the nature of job tasks but adopt location of tools, switches and other facilities, keeping in view that the handling of the job is the primary consideration.

Work practices are set ways of performing work. These methods may arise from tradition or collective wishes of employees. Work practices till now, were determined by time and motion study techniques. A new technique has now emerged, which if introduced, could drastically alter the work practices in industrial undertakings. Called MOST (Maynard Operating Sequence Technique) the technique uses a standard formula to list the motion sequence ascribed in index values. There will be resistance from the workers to the introduction of MOST but the benefits from the technique should help cope with opposition.

Environmental Factors These include employee abilities and availability and social and cultural expectations.

Efficiency consideration must be balanced against the *abilities* and *availability* of the people who are to do the work.

When Henry Ford made use of the assembly line, for example, he was aware that most potential workers lacked any automobile making experience. So jobs were designed to be simple and required little training. Therefore, considerable thought must be given as to who will actually do the work.

There were days when getting a job was the primary consideration. The worker was prepared to work on any job and under any working conditions. Not any more. Literacy, knowledge and awareness of workers have improved considerably, so also their *expectations* from jobs. Hence, jobs must be designed to meet the expectations of workers.

When designing jobs for international operations, uniform designs are almost certain to neglect *national* and *cultural* differences. Hours of work, holidays, vacations, rest breaks, religious beliefs, management styles and worker satisfaction and attitudes are just some of the predictable differences that can affect the design of jobs across international borders. Failure to consider these social expectations can create dissatisfaction, low motivation, hard-to-fill job openings and a low quality of work life especially when foreign nationals are involved in the home country or overseas.

Behavioural Elements Behavioural factors have to do with the human needs and the necessity to satisfy them. Behavioural factors include feedback, autonomy, use of abilities and variety.

Job Design Approaches

Five approaches to job design are popular in the literature on O.B. They are: job rotation, job engineering, job enlargement, job enrichment and socio technical systems. All these are explained in the subsequently paragraphs. (see Fig 9.5).

Fig 9.5 contains two dimensions- **Impact and Complexity.** The impact dimension on the vertical axis, is the degree to which a job design approach is linked to factors beyond the immediate job, such as reward systems, performance appraisal methods, leadership, customer needs, organization design, working conditions, and team composition and norms. The complexity dimension, on the

FIGURE 9-5
COMPARISON OF FIVE JOB DESIGN APPROACHES

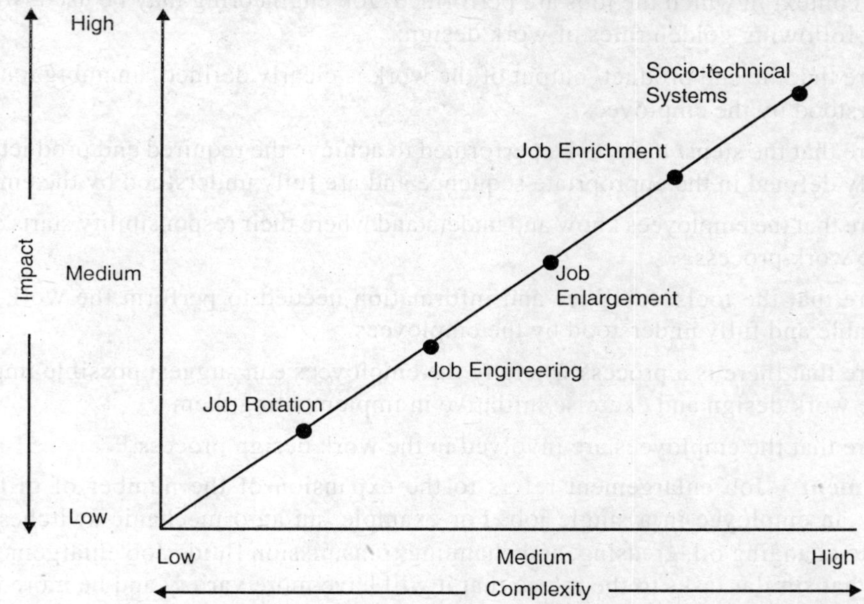

(***Source:*** Don Hellriegel, *et al, op. cit,* p. 447)

horizontal axis, is the degree to which a job design approach requires (1) the involvement of individuals with diverse competencies at various organizational levels; and (2) a high level of decision-making competency for successful implementation.[9]

Job Rotation Job rotation refers to moving employees from job to job to add variety and reduce boredom by allowing them to perform a variety of tasks. When an activity is no longer challenging, the employee would be rotated to another job, at the same level, that has similar skill requirements. It reduces boredom and disinterest through diversifying the employee's activities. Other benefits are also available. Employees with a wider range of skills give management more flexibility in scheduling work, adapting to changes and filling vacancies. Job rotation also has drawbacks. Training costs are increased, work is disrupted as rotated employees take time to adjust to a new set-up. It can demotivate intelligent and ambitious trainees who seek specific responsibilities in their chosen speciality.

Job Engineering Job engineers focuse on the tasks to be performed, methods to be used, workflows among employees, layout of the workplace, performance standards, and interdependencies among people and machines. Experts often examine these job design factors by means of time-and motion studies, determining the time required to do each task and the movements needed to perform it efficiently.

Specialization of labour is the hallmark of job engineering. High levels of specialization are intended to (1) allow employees to learn a task rapidly; (2) permit short work cycles so that performance can be almost automatic and involve little or no mental effort; (3) make hiring easier because low-skilled people can be easily trained and paid relatively low wages; and (4) reduce the need for supervision, leading to simplified jobs and standardization.[10]

Although job engineering also can create boring jobs, it remains an important job design approach because the resulting cost savings can be measured immediately and easily.

The approach continues to be successfully used, particularly when it is combined with a concern for the social context in which the jobs are performed. Job engineering may be used, with success, subject to the following golden rules of work design:

- Ensure that the end product/ output of the work is clearly defined, unambiguous, and fully understood by the employees.
- Ensure that the steps/ tasks to be performed to achieve the required end product/ output are clearly defined in the appropriate sequence and are fully understood by the employees.
- Ensure that the employees know and understand where their responsibility starts and finishes in the work process.
- Ensure that the tools, facilities and information needed to perform the work are readily available and fully understood by the employees.
- Ensure that there is a process whereby the employees can suggest possible improvements in the work design and exercise initiative in implementing them.
- Ensure that the employees are involved in the work design process.[11]

Job Enlargement Job enlargement refers to the expansion of the number of different tasks performed by an employee in a single job. For example, an auto mechanic switches from only changing oil to changing oil, greasing, and changing transmission fluid. Job enlargement attempts to add somewhat similar tasks to the job so that it will have more variety and be more interesting.

Job enlargement approach to job design has been criticized and appreciated too.

An enlarged job can motivate an individual for five reasons:

(a) *Task variety* Highly fragmented jobs requiring a limited number of unchanging responses tend to be extremely monotonous. Increasing the number of tasks to be performed can reduce the level of boredom.

(b) *Meaningful work modules* Frequently, jobs are enlarged so that one worker completes a whole unit of work, or a major portion of it. This tends to increase satisfaction by allowing workers to appreciate their contribution to the entire project or product.

(c) *Ability utilization* Workers derive greater satisfaction from jobs that utilize their physical and mental skills and abilities better. Enlarged jobs tend to fulfill this condition. However, management must be careful not to enlarge jobs too much, because jobs that require more skills and ability than the worker possesses lead to frustration and present obstacles to task accomplishment. Enlarged jobs with optimal levels of complexity, on the other hand, create tasks that are challenging but attainable.

(d) *Worker-paced control* Job enlarged schemes often move a worker from a machine-paced production line to a job in which the worker paces himself or herself. Workers feel less fatigued and likely to enjoy their work more if they can vary the rhythm and work at their own pace.

(e) *Performance feedback* Workers performing narrow jobs with short performance cycles repeat the same set of motion endlessly, without meaningful end point. As a result, it is difficult to count the number of finished performance cycles. Even if they are counted, the feedback tends to be meaningless. Enlarged jobs allow for more meaningful feedback, and can be particularly motivating if it is tied to evaluation and organizational rewards.

FIGURE 9-6
CHARACTERISTICS OF AN ENRICHED JOB

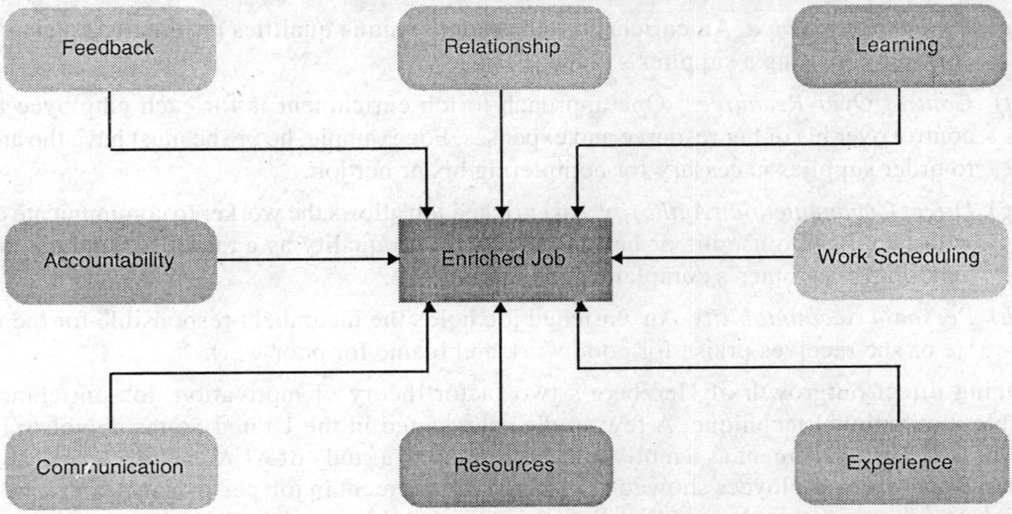

Although the benefits of job enlargement are several, certain disadvantages cannot be lost sight of. First, training costs tend to rise. Workers may require additional training for their new, enlarged tasks. Besides, if the job enlargement programme involves breaking up on existing production line of work systems and redesigning a new system and training employees to adjust to it, the costs can be substantial. Moreover, productivity may fall during the introduction of a new system. Another drawback is that unions often argue for increased pay because of the increased workload. Finally, even after enlargement, many jobs may still be routine and boring.

Job Enrichment First coined by Herzberg in his famous research with motivators and maintenance factors, job enrichment has become a popular concept.

It simply means adding a few more motivators to a job to make it more rewarding. To be specific, a job is enriched when the nature of the job is exciting, challenging, and creative, or gives the jobholder more decision-making, planning and controlling powers.

According to Herzberg an enriched job has eight characteristics. These features are described below and illustrated in Fig 9.6.[12]

(a) *Direct Feedback* Employees should be able to get immediate knowledge of the results they are achieving. The evaluation of performance can be built in to the job (as in an electronic spell-checker indicating the presence of absence of errors) or provided by a supervisor.

(b) *Client Relationship* An employee serves a client or customer directly has an enriched job. The client can be outside the firm (such as mechanic dealing with a car owner) or inside (such as a computer operator running a job for another department).

(c) *New Learning* An enriched job allows its incumbent to feel that he is growing mentally. An assistant who clips relevant newspaper articles for his boss is, therefore, doing an enriched job.

(d) *Scheduling Own Work* Freedom to schedule one's own work contributes to enrichment. Deciding when to tackle which assignment is an example of self-scheduling. Employees who perform creative work have more opportunity to schedule their assignments than do employees performing routine jobs.

(e) *Unique Experience* An enriched job has some unique qualities or features, such a quality controller visiting a supplier's place.

(f) *Control Over Resources* One approach to job enrichment is for each employee to have control over his or her resource and expenses. For example, he or she must have the authority to order supplies necessary for completing his or her job.

(g) *Direct Communication Authority* An enriched job allows the worker to communicate directly with people who use his or her output, such as a quality as a quality assurance manager handiing a customer's complaints about quality.

(h) *Personal Accountability* An enriched job holds the incumbent responsible for the results. He or she receives praise for good work and blame for poor work.

Being direct outgrowth of Herzberg's two factor theory of motivation, job enrichment is a valuable motivational technique. A few studies conducted in the United States demonstrated the usefulness of job enrichment as a motivator. For example, a study of AT & T with clerical and other telephone company employees showed a positive improvement in job performance and satisfaction after job enrichment.[13] Another study with technicians, engineers, and sales representatives showed similar results.[14]

Not that any study is needed to demonstrate the usefulness of job enrichment in helping motivate employees. It can be the knowledge of everyone, specially for people working in government establishments. A lab technician in the health department of a state government experiences frustration after 20 years of working in the same capacity. The incumbent hardly finds the job interesting. The only regular work the employee does, on every working day, is to sign the attendance register at 10 a.m. He naturally plans to take voluntary retirement. The frustration of such employees, whose number unfortunately is considerable, can be remedied by enriching the jobs.

The other benefits of job enrichment are job satisfaction, growth opportunities, scope for self-realization to employees, better employee performance, and less absenteeism, turnover and grievances to organizations, and full use of human resources and more effective organizations to the society.

Some Cautions About Job Enrichment

Since job enrichment has been so well publicized in recent years as a method of increasing worker motivation, one can easily be misled about its possibilities. Although job enrichment can cause increased employee motivation, there are some other factors that should be considered.

(i) **Job enrichment is not a substitute for good management** Regardless of how enriched jobs might be in an organization, if other environmental factors in the organization are not adequate, job enrichment will have little or no effect. Job enrichment is not a substitute for good supervisory practices, wages, and company policies.

(ii) **"Enriched" is a relative term** As a general rule, job enrichment presupposes that jobs with little responsibility should be improved to provide more responsibility for the incumbent. However, we must remember that describing a job as one with "little responsibility" carries an implicit assumption about the person occupying that role. While the job may appear to be boring to the observer, the person actually performing the job may find it quite challenging.

(iii) Enriching jobs may create a "snow ball" effect Given that organizations have a fixed amount of authority to distribute among the members, enriching one person's job means taking authority away from another (most likely the managers). This not only presents systems design problems(for example, rewriting job descriptions), but it can also present a practical barrier, since labour unions may resist a scheme that eliminates jobs.

(iv) Job enrichment assumes that workers want more responsibility Clearly if we take the extreme case of a worker who is motivated by lack of responsibility, then job enrichment for this person would be a disaster. For workers who, for a variety of reasons, are satisfied with their current level of responsibility, job enrichment may cause more problems than it cures.

(v) Job enrichment may have negative short-run effects For a short time after an increase in job responsibility, it is not usual for organizations to experience a drop in productivity, as workers become accustomed to the work systems. After this initial drop; however, there will be increased productivity.

(vi) Job enrichment may become static People become bored in their jobs because their capacity to make decision is not fully utilized. Even through the job is changed to utilize this capacity, there is ample evidence to suggest that personal capacity is a dynamic, developing attribute, it is likely, therefore, that after a period of time (the exact amount varies from person to person) the worker will outgrow the enriched job. If this occurs, additional enrichment will be a required to fully utilize the individual's increased capacity. If jobs cannot be changed over time to use this capacity, the workers could be transferred to another job at a higher level of work (promoted).

(vii) Participation can affect the enrichment process Herzberg originally recommended that workers should not to be involved in the enrichment process. His logic was that workers are often conditioned to see their jobs in terms of "hygiene" factors and are unable to respond to the job content. No doubt this is a factor that management must consider in the participation process, but recent research has indicated that participation can have a positive effect.

(viii) Change is difficult to implement: As is too well-known, any change is resisted and this applies to job enrichment also. In fact, job enrichment theory is a paradox: on the one hand we have a theory telling us that changing jobs through increasing the level of responsibility will result in increased motivation. On the other hand, our knowledge about change processes tells us that this type of change is one of the most difficult things to implement in a work situation. The initiation of a job enrichment programme must take this factor into account. In other words, do not expect employees to jump for joy at the announcement of a job enrichment programme.

Sociotechnical Systems The sociotechnical systems approach focuses on organizations as made up of people with various competencies (the social systems) who use tools, machines and techniques (the technical system) to create goods or services valued by customers and other stakeholders. Thus, the social and technical systems need to be designed with respect to one another and to the demands of customers, suppliers, and other stakeholders in the external environment. Because of their impact, socio technical systems are complex and have an impact on the way work is performed throughout the organization.[15] As shown in Fig 9.5, this model influences how effective an organization will be. All firms are socio technical systems, but they seldom reflect the principles underlying this approach.

The goal of technical model is to find the best possible match between the technology available, the people involved, and the needs of an organization. A crucial feature of this model is the recognition of tasks interdependence, which become basis forming teams. Teams being formed, the specific tasks to be performed by team members are considered, along with relationship among all these tasks. This approach, as with job enrichment, has been widely used in industrial establishments.

Ergonomics Ergonomics is with another approach to job design but not shown in Fig 9.5. Ergonomics focuses on minimizing the physical demands and risks of work. This approach helps ensure that job demands are consistent with people's physical capabilities to perform them with least risk. It involves the design of aids (ranging from hand tools to computer software to instruments) used to perform tasks. Where jobs are well designed (through ergonomics), workers report less physical effort and fatigue, fewer aches and pains, and hence fewer health complaints. The likelihood of accidents is reduced, and employees have more favourable attitudes towards their work and experience job satisfaction. But on cost side, equipment investments are high and training requirements tend to increase.[16]

Ergonomics has become more relevant now because employees stay in the workforce longer and jobs are altered to meet their changing physical needs. Its relevance is also felt more now because of the need to accommodate individuals with physical disabilities (e.g. hearing impaired, loss of mobility in the limbs).

MODEL OF JOB DESIGN

The Job Characteristics Model developed by Richard Hackman and G R Oldham seeks to bring the job close to the person. Figure 9.7 outlines the Job Characteristics Model.[17] This model suggests that five core job characteristics result in the employee experiencing three favourable psychological states, which in turn lead to positive outcomes. (See Fig. 9.7.) The five core job characteristics are explained as follows:

1. **Skill variety:** The degree to which a job includes difficult activities and involves the use of multiple skills and talents of the employee.
2. **Task identity:** The degree to which the job requires completion of a whole and identifiable piece of work that is doing a job from beginning to end with a tangible outcome.
3. **Task significance:** The degree to which the job has a substantial impact on the likes or work of other people.
4. **Autonomy:** The degree to which the job provides the employee with substantial freedom, independence and discretion in scheduling the work and in determining the procedure to be used in carrying it out.
5. **Feedback:** The degree to which the employee possesses information of the actual results of his or her performance.

Hackman and Oldham's model seeks to integrate the five job characteristics to give an overall Motivating Potential Score (MPS) for each job's potential for motivating the incumbents.

FIGURE 9-7
JOB CHARACTERISTICS MODEL

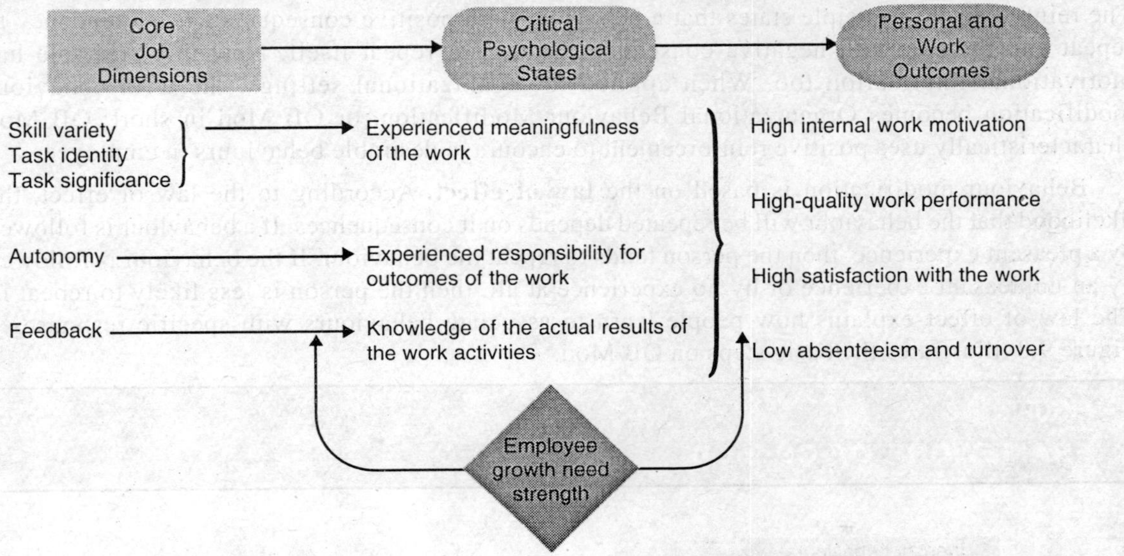

(***Source:*** Debra L Nelson, *et al.*, *Organizational Behaviour*)

An individual's MPS is determined thus —

$$\text{MPS} = \frac{\text{(Skill Variety)} + \text{(Task Identity)} + \text{(Task Significance)}}{3} \times \text{(Autonomy)} \times \text{(Feedback)}$$

The Job Characteristics Model contains a moderator - growth need strength. This moderator explains why jobs theoretically high in MPS will not automatically generate a high level of motivation and satisfaction for all workers. This means that employees with a low growth need are less likely to experience a positive outcome when their job is enriched.

The job characteristics theory further suggests that core job dimensions stimulate three critical psychological states based on the relationship specified in the model.

The three critical psychological factors are:

1. **Meaningfulness of the work:** The extent to which the employee experiences the job as the one which is meaningful, valuable and worthwhile.
2. **Responsibility for work outcomes:** The extent to which the employee feels accountable for the outcome of the work he or she does.
3. **Knowledge of results:** The extent to which the employee has feedback on his or her performance on the job.

Hailed as highly relevant approach to job design, the Job Characteristics Model has been empirically tested with the results being supportive of the theory.

BEHAVIOUR MODIFICATION

We may recall that in Chapter 6, we stated that one of the principle of learning is reinforcement. The reinforcement principle states that a behaviour with positive consequence has a tendency to repeat and the one with negative consequence does not repeat itself. Now this principle has motivational implication too. When applied to organizational settings, the term behaviour modification becomes Organizational Behaviour Modification, or OB Mod in short. OB Mod characteristically uses positive reinforcement to encourage desirable behaviours in employees.

Behaviour modification is based on the **law of effect.** According to the law of effect, the likelihood that the behaviour will be repeated depends on it consequences. If a behaviour is followed by a pleasant experience, then the person tends to repeat the behaviour. If the behaviour is followed by an unpleasant experience or by no experience at all, then the person is less likely to repeat it. The law of effect explains how people learn to associate behaviours with specific responses.[18] Figure 9.8 illustrates the basic steps on OB Mod.

FIGURE 9-8
FRAMEWORK OF OB MOD

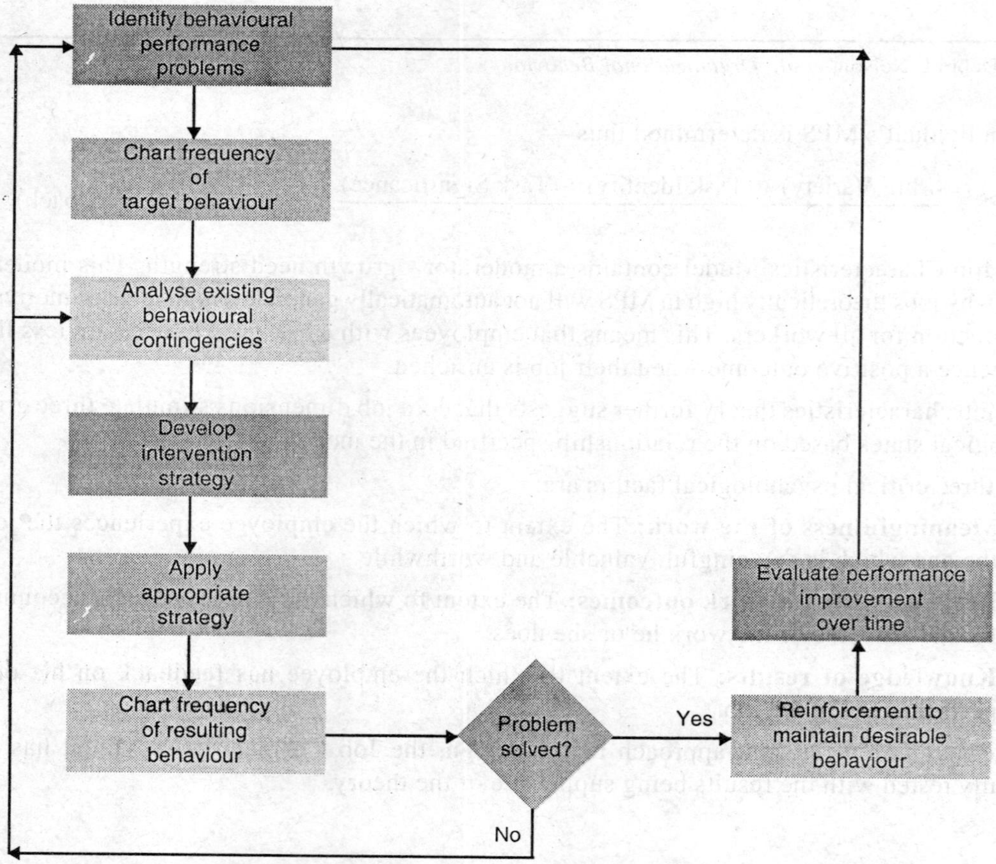

(*Source:* Cook and Hunsaker, *Management and Organizational Behaviour*, p. 241)

Identify Behaviour Problem

The first step is to identify the critical behaviours that make a significant impact on the employee's job performance. For example, the manager of a garments store might decide that most important behaviour for salespeople working in the store is to greet customers warmly and exhibit the clothes they want to see. Three kinds of activities are associated with this behaviour, the behavioural event itself, the performance that results, and the organizational consequences that befall the individual.[19]

In the second step, the manager measures **base line performance**- the existing levels of performance for each individual. This usually is stated in terms of a percentage frequency across different time intervals. For example, the garments store manager may observe that a particular salesperson presently is greeting around 50 percent of the customers each day as desired[20]. Charting baseline performance serves as a point of reference for desirable or undesirable behaviour.

The third step is to identify the existing behavioural contingencies, or consequences of performances; that is what happens now to employees who perform at different levels? If a salesgirl in the garment store works hard, does she get a reward or just get fired? For instance, the manager of the garments store may observe that when customers are greeted warmly and assisted competently, they buy something 50 percent of the time, where as the customers who are not properly greeted and assisted make a purchase only 30 percent of the time. Thus the salesgirl earns both gratification from the sales manager and higher commission .

The popular A-B-C of behaviour modification should be recollected in this context. There are two contingencies to any behaviour: the antecedents that precede behaviour and the consequences that follow the behaviour. Together these variables form the A-B-C model as shown in Fig 9.9.

Antecedents are events preceding the behaviour, informing the employees that certain behaviours will have particular consequences. An antecedent may be a sound from computer signaling that email has arrived or a request from the boss to complete a task with in the stipulated time. These antecedents signal employees to establish certain behaviours in order for certain consequences to occur.[21]

Although antecedents are important, behaviour modification mainly focuses on the consequences, consequences are events following behaviours that influence its future occurrence. If a behaviour is followed by a pleasant experience, then the person is more likely to repeat the behaviour. If the behaviour is followed by an unpleasant experiences or by no response at all, then the person is less likely to repeat it.

The fourth and fifth steps in OB Mod (Fig 9.8) represent designing and applying an appropriate intervention strategy. This may involve establishing linkage between performance and reward. Various kinds of positive reinforces are used to guide employee behaviour in desired directions. The garments stores manage may introduce commission on sales to sales persons, whereby sales people can earn a given percentage of commission on every rupee of sales made. Reinforcement of this type helps shape the behaviour of sales people. In addition, an individual salesperson who does not get reinforced may model the behavior of more successful salespersons.

After the intervention step, the manager again measures performance to determine whether the desired behaviour has been achieved. This is called charting frequency of desirable behaviour (Fig 10.8). If desired behaviour has not been achieved, the manager needs to redesign the intervention strategy or repeat the entire process. For instance, if the salespeople in garment store are still not greeting customers properly, the manager needs to look for other terms of positive reinforcement, perhaps a higher percentage of commission.[22]

FIGURE 9-9
A-B-C OF BEHAVIOUR MODIFICATION

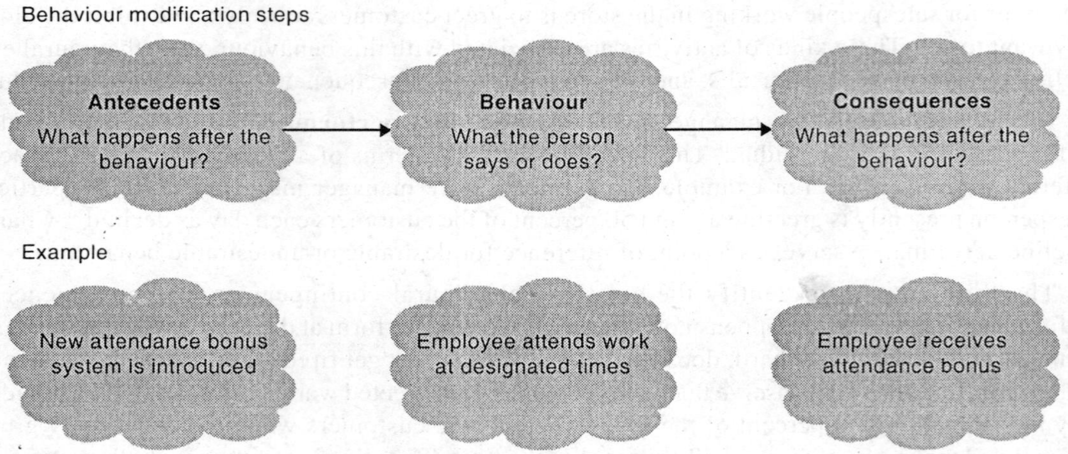

If performance has increased, the manager must try to maintain the desirable behaviour through some schedule of positive reinforcement. For e.g., higher percentage of commission might be granted for every additional sale.

Finally, monitoring the performance overtime is necessary. Motivation exhibited by the sales people needs to be sustained over a period of time. This needs evaluation of performance and reinforcing desirable behaviours.

OB Mod in Practice

OB Mod has been used by a number of organizations to reduce cost, increase attendance, improve productivity, improve safety, increase satisfaction , reduce labour cost, and increase profit. The organizations which benefited include General Electric, Standard Oil, B.F. Goodrich Chemical Co., Emery Air Freight, Michigan Bell etc. all in the United States.

Despite the positive results that OB Mod has demonstrated, it is not without its critics. Is it a technique for manipulating people? Does it decrease an employee's freedom? If so, is such an action on the part of managers unethical? And do non-monetary reinforcers like feedback, praise, and recognition get old after a while? Will employees begin to see these as ways for management to increase productivity without providing commensurate increase in their pay? There are no easy answers to questions such as these.

Empowerment

Empowerment is one of the concepts discussed much in OB. Empowerment is what young job aspirants are looking for in organizations. More than monetary rewards, it is the feeling that employee 'owns' the job that motivates him or her now–a–days. Empowerment may be understood as "a process of enhancing feeling of self-efficacy among organizational members through the identification of conditions that foster powerlessness and through their removal by both formal organizational practices and informal techniques of providing efficiency information."[23] Empowered employees are energetic and passionate. They aspire to do better job because they get personally rewarded for doing so.

Empowerment consists of five stages. (See Fig 9.10) The first stage involves identifying conditions existing in the organizations that lead to feelings of powerlessness on the part of organizational members. These conditions manifest through poor communication, centralized resources, authoritarian styles of leadership, low incentive value rewards, low task variety and unrealistic performance goals.

FIGURE 9-10
EMPOWERMENT STAGES

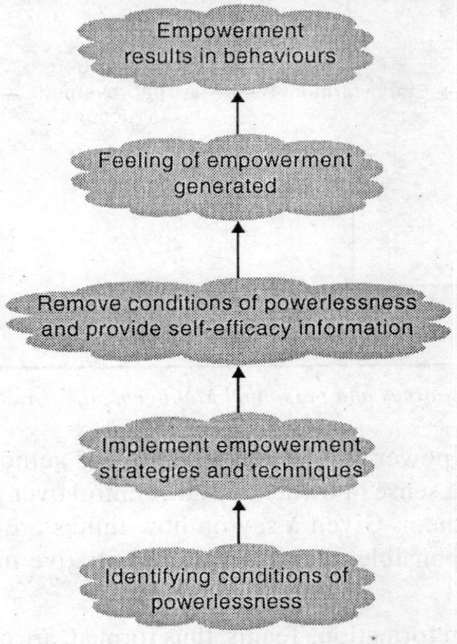

Diagnosis being completed as suggested above, the next stage is to introduce empowerment strategies and techniques. Use of participating management, implementing merit-pay systems, and job enrichment are examples of possible empowerment practices.

The use of the programmes (stated above) is designed to accomplish two objectives in the third stage. One is simply to remove the conditions identified in the first stage as contributing to powerlessness. The second, and more important, is to provide self-efficacy information to subordinates. Self efficacy describes a beliefs in one's effectiveness. Individuals high in self efficacy tend to be confident and self-assured and feel they are likely to be a successful in whatever endeavors they undertake.

Receiving such information results in feeling of empowerment in the fourth stage. This is because increasing self-efficacy strengthens effort-performance expectancies. (see expectancy theory of motivation in the previous chapter). Finally, the enhanced empowerment feelings from stage four are translated into behaviour in the fifth and final stage. These behavioural consequences of empowerment include increased activity directed towards task accomplishment.[24]

Empowerment is facilitated by a combination of factors including values, leadership actions, job structure, and reward systems as illustrated in Fig 9.11.

FIGURE 9-11

FACILIATORS OF EMPOWERED TEAMS

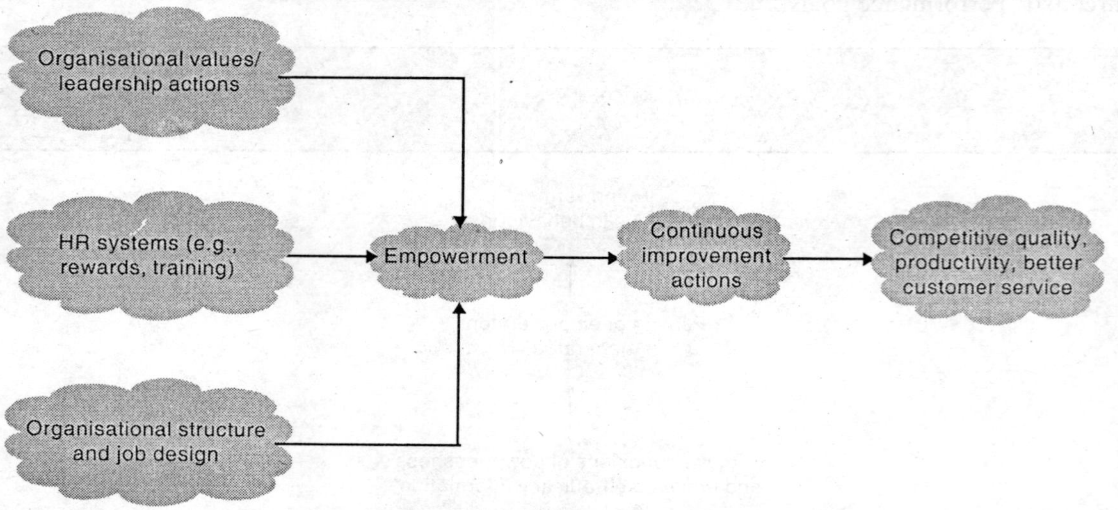

(***Source:*** Aswathappa K., *Human Resources and personnel Management,* 3rd Edn., TMH, 2003, p. 356).

Empowerment occurs when power of decision marking and authority to share resources go to employees who then experience a sense of ownership and control over jobs. Empowered employees knew that their jobs belong to them. Given a say on how things are done, employees feel more responsible. When they feel responsible, they show more initiative in their work, get more done, and enjoy the work more.[25]

Empowerment demands team formation. Teams, thus formed, are called self-directed or simply empowered teams. Wipro Corporation has nearly 30 such teams and Titan, ABB, Tata Information Systems too have their own empowered teams. The 60,000 tonnes per annum polyester filament yarn plant of Reliance at Hazira went on stream within 14 months mainly because its technical teams were empowered to make critical decisions at the worksite. Self directed teams are distinguished by the following characteristics features:

- They are empowered to share various management and leadership functions.
- They plan, control and improve their own work processes.
- They set their own goals and inspect their own work.
- They often create their won schedules and review their performance as a group.
- They may prepare their own budgets and co-ordinate their work with other departments.
- They usually order materials, keep inventories and deal with suppliers.

- They are frequently responsible for acquiring any new training they might need.
- They may hire own replacement or assume responsibility for disciplining their own members.
- They and not others outside the team, take responsibility for the quality of their products or services.[26]

Information sharing is another building block of empowerment. Employees need to be informed about the business and demonstrate how their work fits in. One of the most important measures of job satisfaction is whether employees find meaning in their work - if they know what they are working towards and understand how their work affects other employees and the organization as a whole.

The following tips may be useful in empowering employees:

- Delegate responsibility and along with it authority.
- Replace the managerial 'parent' role with that of 'partner' role.
- Have tolerance for mistakes committed by subordinates. Demonstrate this tolerance through deeds and words.
- Share information with subordinates. Empowered employees need sufficient information to get full perspective.
- Allow teams to form. Teams are the best vehicles to empowerment.
- Performance feedback is always important: it is particularly important for newly empowered employees. Feedback enhances learning and can provide needed assurance that the job is being mastered.

Empowerment needs to be implemented with caution. Where employees suffer from inflated egos and are highly self-centered, empowerment does not work. Many employees entertain the feeling that they are subjugated to be led and not to lead. Empowerment has no appeal to such subordinates. When employees look for secured but not challenging jobs, empowerment sounds hollow.

GOAL SETTING THEORY

Goal setting is one of the most effective and widely practised tools of motivation. Goals are the immediate or ultimate objectives that employees are trying to accomplish from their work efforts in organisations. Goal setting is the process of motivating employees by establishing performance goals. That goal motivates any individual is an established fact. We tend to relax and slacken our efforts if we are not clear about what we want to achieve. A student does not do well in an examination if he or she does not keep a target in mind - target may be a first class or securing distinction. An individual may not rise in personal life if he or she does not have clear career goals. It does not mean that performance of an individual is nil in the absence of a goal. The theory emphasises that with clear goals performance tends to increase.

Why goals motivate employees? There are at least five reasons which explain the correlation between goals and motivation.[27] First, they lead employees to compare their present performance with the goal. To the extent that individuals fall short of the goal, they feel dissatisfied and work harder to attain it - as long as they believe that it is possible for them to do so.

Second, when individuals succeed in reaching a goal, they feel competent and successful; such feelings are desirable and can serve as a strong incentive to extra effort. Third, the existence of a goal clarifies what level of performance is required. Once this level is established, individuals can focus on developing effective strategies for attaining it.

Fourth, the theory calls attention to the important role of self - efficacy - individuals' beliefs about their ability to perform at given levels. If people do not have confidence in themselves, their effort and performance will decrease. In contrast, if they conclude that they can reach the goal, motivation and performance will be enhanced.

Finally, goal setting theory indicates that goals will guide behaviour only when they are accepted by the self and by others. If others concerned do not accept the goals, performance of an employee will not increase. Similarly, if the goal is not acceptable to the self, its effect on the behaviour of the person will be minimal.

Goals need to fulfill certain requisites if they were to impact employee behaviour.

One requirement is that goals must be specific. Specific goals lead to higher output than do vague goals such as "Do your best". Acceptance of the goal and commitment towards its achievement will have effect on employee behaviour and satisfaction. Similarly, organizational support towards goal attainment supported by individual abilities and traits leads to goal realisation. As a result of performance, a person receives various intrinsic and extrinsic rewards, which in turn, influence satisfaction (See Fig.9.12).

FIGURE 9-12
GOAL SETTING REQUISITES

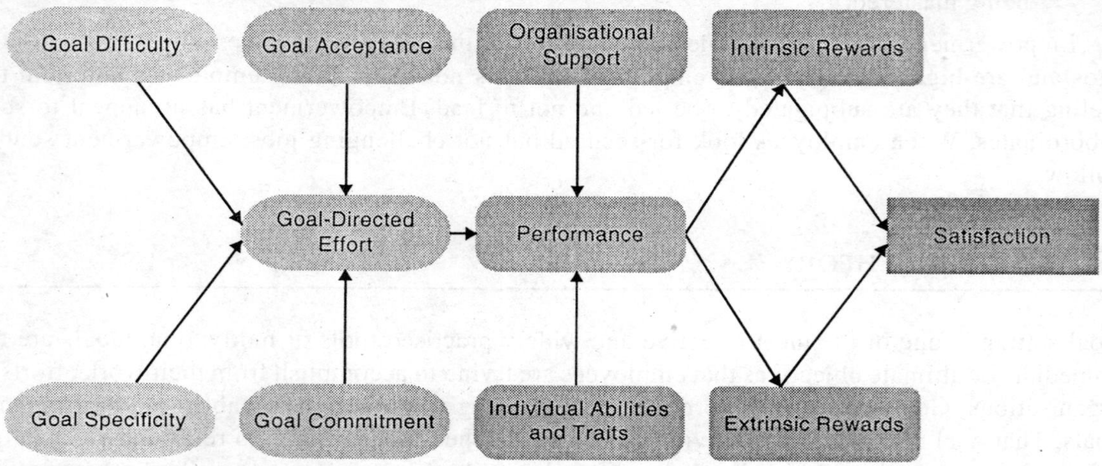

(*Source:* Gregory Moorhead and Rieky W. Griffin, *op.cit.*, p.362)

Goal setting theory is a very powerful technique of motivation. When used correctly, carefully monitored, and actively supported by managers, goal setting can improve performance. However, neither goal setting nor any other technique can be used to correct every problem.

PARTICIPATIVE MANAGEMENT

Participative management is yet another motivational tool used by managers to motivate employees. It refers to the association of workers and their representatives with the decision-making process.

At what level of decision-making can participation be allowed is a relevant question. There are three groups of managerial decisions which have a direct impact on employee behaviour. They are social, economic, and personnel decisions. Economic decisions include financial aspects — the methods of manufacturing, shut-down, lay-offs, mergers, and other similar functions. Personnel decisions refer to employee living, promotions, demotions, transfers, job design, and the like. Social decisions refer to hours of work, welfare measures, safety, health, and the like. The answer to the question raised above is that employees should be allowed to participate in all these decisions.

In practice, participation by employees is effected through several methods like:

- participation at the board level
- participation through share ownership
- participation through joint councils, committees, and works councils
- participation through collective bargaining
- participation through job enlargement and job enrichment
- participation through quality circles
- participation through empowered teams

The greatest fall out of participative management is that the employee identities himself or herself with the job and organization and this leads to improved motivation and enhanced task performance. Stated diffantly, participation leads to reduced conflict and stress, more commitment to goals, better acceptance of change, and improved communication. It is not difficult to explain why participation motivates. It is almost a matter of common sense that humans will take greater pride and pleasure in their work if they are allowed participatory freedom in shaping the policies and decisions which affect their work.

PROBLEM EMPLOYEES

No organisation is free from some sort of problem employees. Motivating problem employees is obviously a challenge to managers like Annette and Paolo. Managers need to understand that it is highly difficult to control actions of problem people. Nor is it possible to change them.

Four principles need to be satisfied. The principle are:

1. Everyone has motivational energy. Although many problem employees display a marked lack of drive and commitment in their jobs, these qualities are usually alive and well in other areas of their lives;
2. The energy which the problem employees possess is often blocked in the workplace. The blockage may occur because of new and sudden stresses at home or may accumulate incrementally over the years, the product of frustrated dreamers or broken promises at work;

3. Removing blockage of energy requires people participation. To motivate an employee to work towards organizational goals, it is necessary to find his or her locus of energy and leverage it. Instead of pushing solution on people with the force of argument, the manager should pull solutions out of them;
4. Beyond a certain point there is no need to show mercy to problem people.

The following are some tips to deal with problem employees.

1. Try to reach out to the employee even if it appears to be capitulation on the part of the boss. This is necessary in the interest of the organization. Failing, think of the next.
2. Change the place of work. Probably new boss, new peers and new environment may change the employee. Failing this, think of the next.
3. Issue verbal threats - threats of severe actions. Severity of actions contemplated to vary from workers to managers. Higher the hierarchy, graver the severity. Failing, think of the next.
4. Translate threats into actions. If problem employees are workers, suspension may work. If the problem employees are managers, sack them.

Just as there are problem employees there are individuals who are committed and motivated but who often go unnoticed, unrecognized, and unrewarded, particularly in large organisations. Files move, work goes on, activities and functions continue to take place in organisations because of such employees.

Who has heard of a widow, a sweeper, in a B-School? The poor lady has health problems. She cannot bend her body to sweep the premises. But she wants the building to be kept clean and tidy. She has struck on a novel idea. She has appointed a boy to do her work and pays him Rs.500 every month from her own salary!

Such unsung and unheard heroes and heroines are found in the corporate sector too. Popularly called B players, they are parallel to the best supporting actors and actresses at the Bollywood. The B players exhibit unique characteristics as described in Table 9.2.

TABLE 9-2

PROFILE OF B PLAYERS

- They are not stars. Neither are they laggards. They do their jobs competently, steer the course, and define the organization's values and culture.
- They receive the least attention from the top management, since they are unambitious and unexiting.
- They make up five per cent of any company's bell curve.
- The B player is the wheel in an organizational machine that never squeaks and hence never gets any lubricant.
- They maintain perfect work-life balance.
- They differ from stars (A players) not in intelligence but in drive and attitude.
- They stick on with an organization, because they value the comaraderie and security of a known team. But they do leave, when things are mismanaged.
- They are the solid citizens, the juggernauts who give stability to organizations.

Like problem employees, B players need to be handled carefully. Organizations are taking notice of B players and have unique policies to manage them. Coca-Cola India, for example, regularly does an duster analysis based on performance feedback, dividing employees into five levels-high potentials, promotables, matches, mismatches, and non-performers. The 'matches' form Coke's majority B group. The company has career paths for all B players.

Hindustan unilever has created a special category for the top employees within the B category. Popularly called the sustained high performers (SHPs), these individuals get the same increments as the top 15 per cent of high potentials.[28]

Quality of Work Life

The term "quality of work life" means different things to different persons, for example, to a worker on an assembly line, it may just mean a fair day's pay, safe working conditions, and a supervisor who treats him with dignity. To a young new entrant, it may mean opportunities for advancement, creative tasks and a successful career.

There are many factors which can contribute to quality of work life. They are:

1. Adequate and fair compensation.
2. A safe and healthy environment.
3. Jobs aimed at developing and using employee's skill and abilities.
4. Growth and security; jobs aimed at expanding employee capabilities, rather than leading to their obsolescence.
5. An environment in which employees develop self-esteem and a sense of identity.
6. Protection and respect for employee's right to privacy, dissent and equity.
7. A sensible integration of job career and family life and leisure time.

It would not be incorrect to say that quality of work life, in fact, covers all aspects of worker's life with special reference to his or her interaction with his or her work and his or her working environment. The following are suggested:

1. **Adequate and fair compensation,** adequacy to the extent to which the income from full time work meets the needs of the socially determined standard of living.
2. **Safety and healthy working conditions,** including reasonable hours of work and rest pauses, physical working conditions that ensure safety, minimize risk of illness and occupational diseases and special measures for protection of women and children.
3. **Security and growth opportunity,** including factors like security of employment and opportunity for advancement and self-improvement.
4. **Opportunity to use and develop creativity,** such as work autonomy, nature of supervision, use of multiple skills, worker's role in total work process and his or her appreciation of the outcome of his or her own effort and self-regulation.
5. **Respect for the individuals' personal rights,** such as the application of the principles of natural justice and equity, aceptance of the right of free speech and the right to personal privacy in respect of the worker's off-the- job behaviour.
6. **Work and family life,** including transfers, schedule of hours of work, travels requirements and overtime requirements.

It is worth noting that often the conditions that contribute to motivation (equitable salaries, financial incentive and effective employee selection) will also contribute to the quality of work life.

Some of these activities (like job enrichment) might contribute indirectly to the quality of work life by tapping the worker's higher order needs, and motivating them. Still other activities may contribute directly to the quality of work life providing for a safer work place, less discrimination on the job, and so forth.

Others

The other motivational techniques used in organizations to influence employee behaviour include management by objective (MBO), flexible working hours, two-tier pay systems, flexible benefits and the like.

MBO refers to a formal set of procedures that begin with goals setting and contributes through performance review. The key of MBO is that it is a participative process, actively involving managers and subordinates at every organizational level. Propounded by Peter F. Drucker in 1954, MBO has motivational potential because the participants become ego involved in decisions thy have made. They tend to accept the decisions as their own and feel personally responsible for implementing them.

A systems of *flexible working hours*, also called flexi time, to suit the convenience of individual employees has often been pointed out as one of the techniques of motivation. Various work weeks are being used, all with the aim of lengthening the leisure between work periods. Most common are the four-day 40 hours week with three days off (4/3), the three day, 36 hours week with four days off (3/4); and the seven-day, 70 hours with seven days off (7/7). Of these the 4/3 arrangement is highly popular.

The benefit claimed for flexitime are numerous. They include reduced absenteeism, increased productivity, reduced overtime expenses, a lessening in hostility towards management, elimination of tardiness, and reduced traffic congestion around work sites.

In terms of motivational theories, flexitime corresponds to the diverse needs of the work-force. It appeals to an individual's growth need (ERG theory) or desire for autonomy (motivation hygiene theory).

Two-tier pay system This provides for offering significantly lower wage rates to newly hired employees than those already employed in the same job. The two-tier pay system is seen everywhere in organizations. A junior lecturer in a university is paid less than a senior grade lecturer. Similarity, a worker in a factory, with 15 to 20 years of experience, is put on a higher scale than a beginner.

The two-tier system is said to place a premium on experience and loyalty. It will induce a new recruit to stick to the same organization.

The two-tier pay system corresponds to the equity theory but in a negative way. Junior lecturer or worker perceives inequity or injustice being done to him or her as he is paid less than his or her senior though both attend to the same work. This, it is claimed results in an increased turnover rate among those newly hires. But what happens in practice does not prove the claim.

Flexible benefits These allow employees to pick and choose from among the menu of benefits package that is individually tailored to his or her own needs and situations. The programme seeks to replace the traditional fringe benefits programmes which apply uniformly to all employees. The idea of flexible benefits operates on the following lines. An organization sets up a flexible spending account for each employee, usually based on some percentage of his or her salary, and then a price tag is put on each benefit. Options might include inexpensive medical plus with high deductibles; expensive medical plus with low or no deductibles; hearing, dental and eye coverage, vacation options; extended disability; a variety of savings and pension plans; life insurance; college tuition reimbursement plans; and extended vacation time. Employees then select benefit options until they have spent the amount in their respective accounts.

Consistent with the expectancy theory thesis that organizational rewards should be linked to each individual employee's goals, flexible benefits individualize rewards by allowing each employee to choose the compensation package that best satisfies his current needs.

Case

MOTIVATING PARTNERS AT STARBUCKS

Starbucks, with more than 3,300 locations worldwide, serves millions of coffee lovers each week. Having a history of excellent growth and profitability, Starbucks continues to expand. It opens "virtually a store a day". In addition to sales of whole bean coffees, fresh brewed espresso beverages, pastries and confections, and coffee-related accessories and equipment in company-operated retail stores, Starbucks sells whole coffee beans through other outlets including supermarkets and online. It also manufactures and sells a line of premium ice creams and the bottled Frappucino coffee drink.

Famed for its coffee products, the company also enjoys a glowing reputation as a progressive employer. Known for its employee policies and motivational programs, Starbucks has been included in *Fortune* magazine's list of "The 100 Best Companies to Work For" in 1998, 1999 and 2000.

The basis of Starbucks reputation as a great place to work is contained in the six guiding principles that form the foundation of the company's mission statement. One of these guiding principles is to "provide a great work environment and treat each other with respect and dignity". Starbucks tries to "create a work environment that is lively, exciting, and full of enthusiasm."

One overt symbol of the guiding principle is the name to all Starbucks' employees. Every one is called a partner. More important than the name, however, is a company culture devoted to developing and motivating the partners. "Starbucks has created a culture dedicated to challenging employees... to be their best," Starbucks is dedicated to investing in, supporting and engaging its partners in the continual reinvention of the company.

The challenge to "be their best" begins with training. All new coffee store employees (referred to as baristas) receive 25 hours of classroom training under the guidance of partners who have been specially trained. The training includes coffee knowledge and customer service skills. Management trainees participate in up to 12 weeks of classes. They also receive coaching on leadership skills, diversity awareness, advanced customer service, succession planning and career development.

Starbucks' motivational programs for its partners consist of "a special blend of employee benefits" and a work life/personal life program that focuses on the physical, emotional, mental, and creative aspects of each individual.

The company offers a comprehensive benefits package to all partners, including part-time employees who work a minimum of 20 hours per week. The benefits package includes full medical and dental insurance coverage, disability and life insurance, vacation days, a retirement savings plan with matching company contributions, discounted stock purchase plans, and stock options as part of Starbuck BEAN STOCK program. Starbucks established the BEAN STOCK program in 1991 as a way of investing in the employee partners and creating ownership throughout the company.

The work/life program includes on site fitness services, flexible work schedules, referral and educational support for child care and elder care issues, and a program that links employees who have shared interests and hobbies. Starbucks continually seeks to develop programs that address the life stages and personal need of its partners. In fact, the company conducts periodic surveys of its partners to assess their needs and it responds accordingly with appropriate work/life solutions. "We will ask our partners constantly what's important to them and consider these things as we plan into the year 2003 and beyond," says a Starbucks manager.

Open communication and innovative thinking both of which positively influence the partners' motivation - are encouraged through various partner relations mechanisms. These mechanisms include *Mission Review*, *Open Forums*, and the *Warm Regards* recognition program. *Mission Rreview*, "encourages partners to tell the company how they're feeling and ask any questions." *Open Forums* are held on a regular basis to review performance, recognize achievements, and consider the future. The *Warm Regards* program recognizes "outstanding achievement that embodies the guiding principles, mission, and goals of Starbucks."

These programs benefit both the partners and the company. One of the benefits for Starbucks is a reduction in operating costs. The company has relatively low health-care costs, reduced absenteeism, and one of the lowest turnover rates in the restaurant industry. The lower turnover rate also reduces training costs. Another benefit for Starbucks is the quality of customer service that grows out of the partners commitment to the company.

"We're profitable because of the value system of our company" observes Howard Schulz, Starbucks' Chairman and Chief Global Strategist. "American companies have failed to realize that there's tremendous value in inspiring people to share a common purpose of self-esteem, self-respect, and appreciation." Starbucks is "about people – a humanistic approach to doing business that produces bottom-line results."[28]

Questions

1. Given Starbucks' benefits package and work/life program, what insights have you gained about its approach to employee motivation? Explain your answer.

2. What needs does Starbucks appeal to through its benefits package, and work/life program?

3. What is important to you in terms of your personal work motivation? How do the things that motivate you fit with Starbucks' approach to motivating partners?[29]

QUESTIONS

1. Can money act as motivator? 'Yes' or 'no', discuss.
2. What is job design? Describe approaches to job design.
3. Describe, in your own words, the motivational practices explained in this chapter.
4. What are the similarities and differences between gain-sharing and profit-sharing plans? Which systems would motivate you to achieve greater performance? Why?

REFERENCES

1. Nigel Nicholson, "How to Motivate Your Problem People", *Harvard Business Review,* January 2003, p. 58.
2. Steven L. McShane and Mary Ann Von Glinow, *Organizational Behaviour,* TMH, 2000, p. 98.
3. Ibid, p. 99
4. "Corporate Restructuring Sweeps Japan", *Focus Japan*, March 23, 1996.
5. Mirza S. Saiyadain and Arun Monappa, *Profile of Indian Managers,* New Delhi, Vidhyavahini, 1977.
6. Mirza S. Saiyadain. "Job Enrichment: Problems and Prospects", *Vikalpa,* IIMA, 1976.
7. *Business India*, Jan 6-19, 1992.

8. Steven L. McShane and Mary An Glinow, *Op. cit.,* p. 107.
9. Don Hellriegel, *et.al.*, *Organizational Behaviour,* South-Western, 2001, p. 446.
10. Ibid , p. 448.
11. Ibid
12. Frederick Herzberg, *et.al.*, "The Wise Old Tusk", *Harvard Business Review,* Sept-October, 1974, p. 70.
13. Robert Ford, "Job Enrichment Lessons for AT&T", *Harvard Business Review,* Jan-Feb, 1973, p. 106.
14. W.J. Paul, *et.al.,* "Job Enrichment Pays Off", *Harvard Business Review,* March- April , 1969, p. 78.
15. Don Hellriegel, *et.al., Op.cit.*, p. 450.
16. D.C Feldman and H.J Arnold, *Managing Individual and Group Behaviour in Organizations,* McGraw-Hill, 1983 p.144.
17. Debra L. Nelson, *et al, Organisational Behaviour,* Thomson, 2003, p. 174.
18. Steven L. McShane and Mary Ann Von Glinow, *Op.cit.*, p. 42.
19. Gregory Moorhead and Ricky W. Griffin, *Organizational Behaviour,* Jaico, 2000, p. 168
20. Ibid.
21. Steven L. McShane and Mary Ann Von Glinow, *Op.cit.,* p. 42.
22. Gregory Moorhead and Ricky W. Griffin, *Op.cit.,* p. 168.
23. John Ivanesvich and Michael T. Matteson, *Organizational Behaviour and Management,* Irwin McGraw-Hill, 1999, P. 378.
24. Ibid.
25. Richard S.Willins, *et.al.*, *Empowered Teams*, Jossey Bass Publishers, 1991, p. 3
26. Ibid p. 4.
27. Robert A. Baron, *Psychology,* PHI, 1996, p. 680.
28. Nigel Nicholson, *Op.cit,* p 59.
29. Debra L. Nelson, *et.al., op.cit.,* Pp. 177-178.

CHAPTER

Ten

Managerial Control

LEARNING OBJECTIVES

After reading this chapter you should understand –

1. The nature and significance of control
2. The control cycle
3. The bureaucratic, marketing and financial controls are the strategies to achieve organisational control
4. The use of quality standards, ABC, EVA, MVA and Clan are the recent trends in organisational control

NATURE OF CONTROL

Organisations use control function to ensure that the goals are reached with least wastage of resources. Obviously, control is an important function, nay, as important as the planning function itself. Infact, planning and control are considered to be Siamese twins of management.[1] Plans, once made, must be properly implemented. If they are not carried out properly, management must take steps to correct the problem. Thus, planning facilitates control, and control facilitates planning. Planning lays down a framework for the future and thus provides a blueprint for control. Control systems, in turn, regulate the allocation and utilisation of resources and in so doing, facilitate the process of planning.

Control is typically understood as any process that directs the activities of individuals towards the achievement of organisational goals. If activities are not proceeding towards goals achievement, corrective steps need to be initiated. An essential part of the control process is taking corrective actions when needed.

Control can occur at three places in organisations: before the event, during the event and after the event. A local automobile dealer, for example, can focus his attention before, during or after the sale of new cars. Careful selection of new cars and cautious selection of sales staff are ways to ensure high quality or profitable sales even before they take place. Monitoring how sales people act with customers would be considered control during the sales task. Counting the number of new cars sold during the month or contacting the buyers about their satisfaction with the transactions would constitute control after sales have occurred.[2] These three types of controls are formally called feed forward, concurrent and feedback and are illustrated in Fig.10.1.

IMPORTANCE OF CONTROL

For many people control conjures up negative images - restraining, forcing, delimiting, watching or manipulating. This perception is far from reality as control plays several positive roles as described here.

How control facilitates planning was explained earlier. The other benefits of control are: better quality, coping with change, faster cycles, facilitate delegation[3] and innovation.

Better quality Control ensures better quality of goods and services. Rigid quality standards are set and made sure that actual quality corresponds with the standards. Where deviations occur, corrective actions are taken. This is the role of control.

Coping with change Change is inevitable in organisations. Government policies change. Competition intensifies. Technology changes. The control function aids managers in responding to the threats and opportunities posed by changing environment by helping the managers detect the changes.

Create faster cycles Organisations gain competitive edge through reduced cycle time. Orders once accepted, need to be executed fast without causing delay. Control function facilitates faster cycles of production by defining schedules and adhering to them strictly.

FIGURE 10-1
CONTROL FOCUS

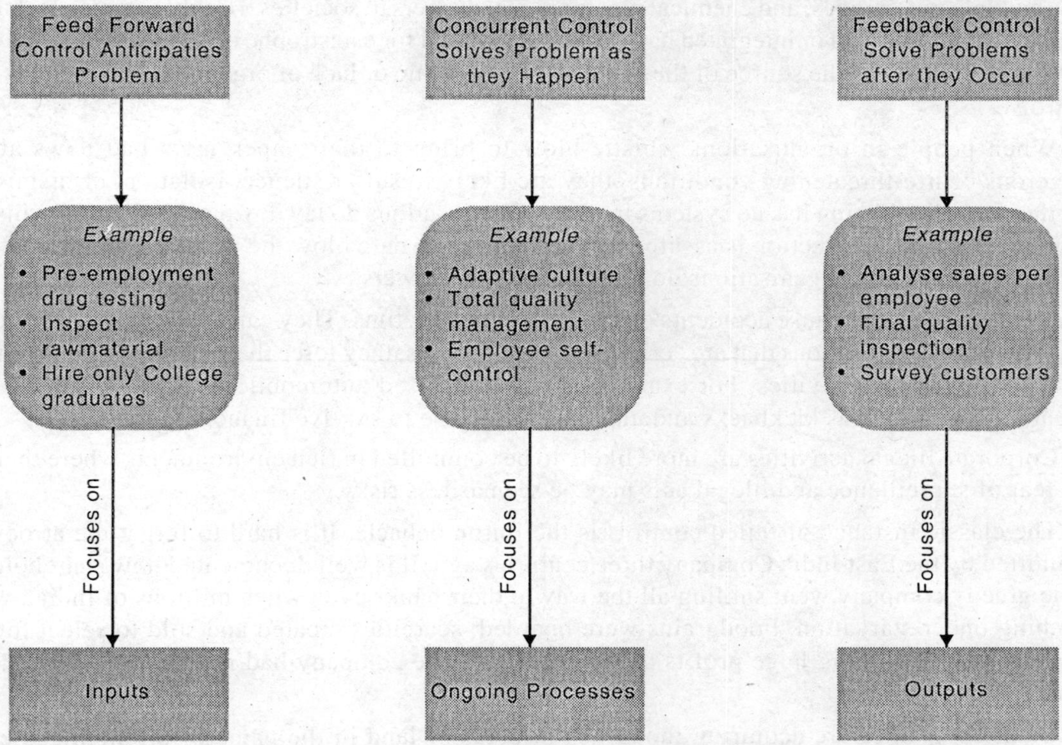

(**Source:** Adapted from *Management* by Hellriegel, et al., p.656)

Delegation Modern management demands delegation and participative management. Delegation does not mean that the managers are absolved of their responsibilities. Rather, delegation changes the nature of control process. Under the traditional autocratic system, the manager would specify both the standards for performance and the methods for achieving them. In the new dispensation, employees are empowered to define goals, set standards and evaluate progress. Manager's job is just to observe but not interfere in the work of employees.

Lack of controls or the wrong kinds of controls can cause irreparable damage to organisations. Ineffective control systems result in problems ranging from employee theft to financial losses from unauthorised foreign exchange speculations.

Innovation Controls may help raise the level of innovation in an organisation. Successful innovation takes place when managers can create an organisational setting in which employees feel empowered to be creative and in which authority is decentralised and employees down the line feel free to experiment and take risks.

Several of the evils associated with organisation stem from lack of or wrong control systems. Organisations misbehave, engage in misconduct, and create disasters.[4] The buck for such evils stops at control — the absence or the presence of it.

Large organisations are known to emit toxins and escape with impunity. Chemical plant disaster in Bhopal, Chernobyl nuclear disaster in Russia and GE's letting of harmful industrial chemicals into the Hudson River are only a few instances. 'Normal accidents' like actual and potential disasters in nuclear plants, nuclear weapon systems, recombinant DNA production, ships carrying highly toxic or explosive cargoes, and chemical plants are real dangers to societies. Highly complex technical systems that are coupled or integrated have a strong potential for catastrophe not because of individual employee error that is the source of the accident but systemic or lack of organisational systems and controls.

When people in organisations whistle-blow to bring to their supervisors bad news about dangerous or life-threatening conditions, they are likely to suffer silence, isolation, or dismissal. Not that whistle-blowing has no systems in place. Organisations do lay down procedure for whistle-blowing and strong protection is assured to the people who dare blow the whistle. Systems are not implemented because organisations do not like whistle-blowers.

Organisations can cause accidents or can be accident victims. They can also engage in criminal acts. There are organisations that are "crime-coercive," that is, they force their members or customers to engage in illegal activities. For example, some franchised automobile dealers are forced into illegal practices such as kickbacks and unrecorded income to survive financially.

Corporate illegal activities are more likely to be committed in rich environments where there is less fear of surveillance and illegal acts may be seen as less risky.

The classic instance of failed controls is the Enron debacle. It is hard to forget the atrocities committed by the East India Company three centuries ago. It is well documented how shareholders of the greedy company went smiling all the way to their banks even when millions of Indian were perishing under starvation. Foodgrains were hoarded, scarcities created and sold to select few at very high prices earning huge profits to the company. The company had monopoly over trade in gains.

Giant companies are acquiring thousands of acres of land in the name of promoting special economic zones (SEZs) thus depriving poor families of their lands and livelihood. The Polepally Pharma Special Economic Zone and other projects in Mahabubnagar district of Andhra Pradesh have resulted in the displacement of 350 poor families. 25 of the land-losers died of trauma and demoralisation. This is the trend and not just an isolated event throughout India and probably beyond.

The Control Cycle

The control cycle typically involves four stages, as shown in Fig.10.2. The steps are: setting performance standards, measuring performance, comparing performance against standards and identifying deviations and taking remedial actions.

Set Performance Standards Every organisation has goals, including profitability, innovation, customer satisfaction and the like. A standard is the level of expected performance for a given goal. Standards are performance targets that establish desired performance levels, motivate performance, and serve as benchmarks to evaluate actual performance. Standards can be set for any activity-financial, manufacturing, human resource, legal compliance and the like.

The number of standards of performance managers set can run into hundreds. Managers at each level are responsible for selecting those standards that will best allow them to evaluate the performance of their unit, division or the organisation.

FIGURE 10-2
THE CONTROL CYCLE

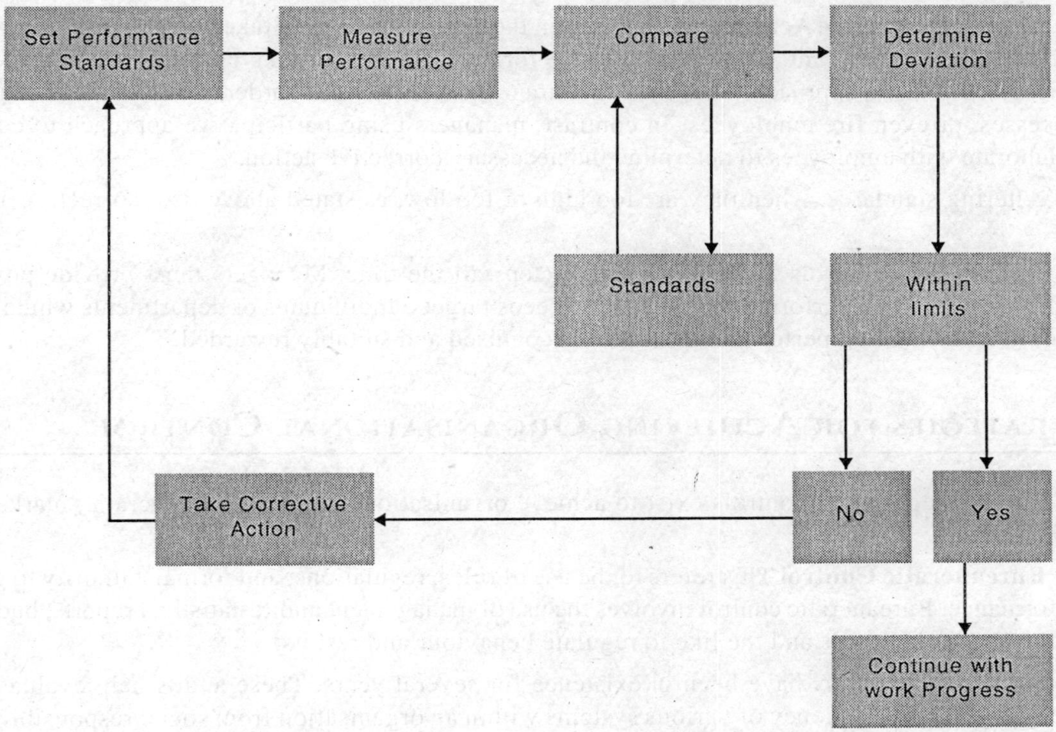

(**Source:** Thomas S.Bateman and Scott A.Snell, *Management*, p.544)

Measure Performance Once managers have decided which standards or targets they will use to evaluate performance, the next step in the control process is to measure actual performance. Managers can count units produced, days absent, papers filed, samples distributed and rupees earned.

Managers do not rely exclusively on quantitative measures. They observe things in organisation-especially employee participation and learning. Managers have to observe for themselves whether employees are participating in decision making and possess opportunities to acquire knowledge.

Compare Performance to Standards The third step in the control process is comparing performance with the standard. In this step, the manager evaluates the performance and identifies deviations, if any. For some activities relatively small deviations from the standards are acceptable, while in others a slight deviation is serious. Managers therefore must carefully analyse and evaluate the results.

Where performance exceeds standards, managers tend to raise standards themselves for the next time period. However, if performance is too low and standards are not reached, or if standards are set too high so that employees cannot achieve them, managers must decide to take corrective action. Taking corrective action is easy when the reasons for poor performance can be identified-high labour cost, for instance. Labour cost can be reduced by installing more machines, constituting cross-functional teams, or down-sizing the headcount. Often, reasons for poor performance are hard to identify. Changes in the environment such as the emergence of a new global competitor, a recession, or an increase in interest rates might be the reason for performance falling short of standards. Notwithstanding the difficulty, managers should identify reasons and proceed to the next step.

Taking Corrective Action The final step in the control cycle is to take corrective action where deviations are significant. Managers exercise formal authority to take corrective action, if they believe in top-down approach. They may encourage workers to work harder, redesign the production processes, or even fire employees. In contrast, managers using participative approach to control collaborate with employees to determine the necessary corrective action.

Altering standards, when they are too high or too low, as stated above, is a corrective action too.

It is not that controls involve corrective steps all the time. Managers must provide positive reinforcement when performance meets or exceeds targets. Individuals or departments which have exhibited outstanding performance must be recognised and suitably rewarded.

STRATEGIES FOR ACHIEVING ORGANISATIONAL CONTROL

Three categories of controls exist to achieve organisational control: bureaucratic, marketing, and financial.

Bureaucratic Control This refers to the use of rules, regulations, and formal authority to guide performance. Bureaucratic control involves the use of management audit, statistical reports, budgets, performance appraisals and the like to regulate behaviour and results.

Management audits have been in existence for several years. These audits help evaluate the effectiveness and efficiency of various systems within an organisation from social responsibility to accounting control. Management audit may be external or internal.

An *external audit* occurs when one organisation (an audit firm) evaluates another one. Even a company can also conduct external audits of rivals and other firms for strategic decision-making purposes. The external audit (i) investigates other firms for possible merger or acquisition; (ii) determines the soundness of a company that will be used as a major supplier; or (iii) discovers the strengths and weaknesses of a competitor to maintain or better exploit the competitive advantage of the investigating organisation.[5] External audit mainly depends on published data.

Internal audits assess (1) what the company has done for itself and (2) what it has done for its customers or other users of its goods and services. Several criteria such as financial stability, production efficiency, sales effectiveness, human resource development and social responsibility are used to assess and evaluate the company. The audit reviews the company's past, present and future.

Budgetary control is one of the most commonly used method of bureaucratic controls. Budgetary control is the process of finding what has been done and comparing the results with the corresponding budgets to identify accomplishments or to remedy differences.

Market Control This involves the collection and evaluation of data related to sales, prices, costs and profits for guiding decisions and evaluating results. *Customer monitoring* is the major control in marketing. Customer monitoring consists of ongoing efforts to obtain feedback from customers concerning the quality of goods and services. Such monitoring is done to prevent problems or identify and solve them.

Financial Controls These include the mechanisms for preventing or correcting the misallocation of resources. External auditing firms and/or internal auditing department monitor the effectiveness of financial controls.

Financial statements and financial analysis are the major mechanisms of financial control.

Financial statements include income statement and balance sheet. Balance sheet represents a statement of assets and liabilities of a firm on a given date. In addition to assets and liabilities, balance sheet provides owners' equity. Assets are what the firm owns; liabilities are what it owes to others and owners' equity is the difference between assets and liabilities and is the company's networth in retained earnings and equity.

Income statement, popularly known as *profit and loss statement*, summarises the firm's financial performance for usually one year. Some firms prepare income statements more frequently. The profit and loss statement shows revenues coming into the firm from all sources and all outflows in the form of expenses. Expenses subtracted from income give profit. Where expenses exceed income, the result is loss suffered by the firm. This is called the bottom line of a company.

Ratio analysis is another mechanism of financial control. Ratios are statistics that express the relationships between performance indicators such as profits and sales, sales and inventory and the like (see Fig.10.3 for typical ratios).

It is not enough if ratios are calculated. Managers should know how to interpret them. For example, a return on investment of 10 per cent does not mean anything unless it is compared with that of the previous year and of other organisations.

FIGURE 10-3
COMMON FINANCIAL RATIOS

(A) Activity Ratios	
Inventory turnover	Total sales/average inventory
Conversion ratio	Purchase orders/customer inquires
(B) Liquidity Ratios	
Current ratio	Current assets/current liabilities
(C) Leaverage Ratios	
Debt ratio	Total debt/Total assets
(D) Profitability Ratios	
Profit on sales	Net income/sales
Gross margin	Gross income/sales
Return on investment	Net income/total assets

Trends in Controls

Companies are responding to changing environment and are devising new control mechanisms to serve organisational objectives. The new control mechanisms are international quality standards, activity based costing, economic value added, market value added and clan.

International Quality Standards Quality control systems have become international. Many countries have endorsed a universal framework for quality assurance called ISO 9000, a set of international standards for quality management systems established by the International Organisation for Standardisation in 1987 and revised in 2000. By the end of 1999, more than 340,000 organisations in 150 countries, including India, had been certified to demonstrate their commitment to quality. ISO 9000 has become the recognised standard for evaluating and comparing companies on a global basis.

Activity Based Costing (ABC) Organisations ascertain costs of producing goods and services. These figures will help fix prices and control costs. Traditional methods of cost finding assign costs to various departments or functions, such as marketing, manufacturing, human resource management and the like. The trend now is to assign costs to activities/processes, hence the title ABC. ABC attempts to identify all the activities needed to produce goods and services and allocate costs accordingly. For example, ABC may assign cost to such activities as recruitment, training, processing purchase orders, shipping goods or internal transport. ABC allocates costs across business processes, it provides more accurate picture of the costs of various goods and services.

ABC seeks to highlight wasted activities or activities that cost too much relative to the benefits they provide to the organisation. By providing this type of information, ABC has emerged as a valuable method of streamlining business processes.

Economic Value Added (EVA) Companies are increasingly using EVA system to gauge financial performance. EVA may be understood as net (after-tax) operating profit minus the cost of capital invested in the company's tangible assets. Assessing performance in terms of EVA is intended to capture all the activities a company can undertake to add value from its functions. Each job, department or process in the firm is measured by the value added.

The Godrej group has been using EVA with results being highly positive. Since EVA has been introduced, all the group companies have cutdown the use capital dramatically. Infact, many of the businesses have been working on negative working capital.

Market Value Added (MVA) Also called market capitalisation (market cap in short), MVA represents the value of all shares multiplied by current market rate. If MVA is greater than all the capital invested in the company in the form of shares, debentures, and retained earnings, the firm has positive MVA. A favourable MVA and EVA go together.

Clan Control Clan control presupposes employee empowerment. Empowered employees decide on their own, monitor progress and correct themselves, should deviations occur. They are expected to work in the interest of the organisation. There is trust between managers and employees. This trust replaces the traditional authoritarian approach to control. This does not mean that the managers do not exercise control. Empowerment implies self imposed control.

QUESTIONS

Case

Salespersons and Their Expense Accounts

Vinay Mishra, sales and marketing manager, Bingo Ltd., was not too keen on having another drink. But the client was in the mood for one and had to be humoured. The order was too important to let anything jeopardise the negotiations.

As they were departing from the hotel an hour later, Sanjay Dixit, his deputy, noted with concern that Mishra was looking washed out. "Are you okay?" he asked. "Why don't you come in my car? I will drop our friend at the company guest house and then leave you at your place."

"I must go home," said Mishra. "My wife and son would be waiting. I will drive on my own. Don't bother," and added with a wink, "We will get this order for sure."

The next day, there was a pall of gloom at the Bingo office. Mishra had hit a vehicle on the road head on and died within minutes of being hospitalised.

The tragedy raised several issues at Bingo. Mishra had died while on duty and his dependents were entitled to more than the usual terminal benefits. The amount had to be substantial. There was also the matter of his having had to imbibe an extra drink, much against his liking, just to get that order. There was a general feeling that Bingo was morally responsible for his death.

On learning from Dixit about the above-normal consumption of liquor on the night of the accident, personnel director Vinod Chalke decided to look at that specific issue in some detail. He began to examine the records, over the last eight years, of sickness and absenteeism among the company's sales staff. There were 65 people in the sales and marketing department who were all entitled to an expense account with varying limits and a company vehicle each-either a car or a two-wheeler. After probing, with the help of an internal auditor, into the expense statements of a number of salesmen and marketing executives, Chalke was able to arrive at certain conclusions.

A week later, he decided to make a presentation of his findings to the executive committee of the company headed by Vinod Datar, the managing director.

Chalke began by saying that two salespersons had died in traffic accidents during the period. The accidents had happened during weekends while they were off duty. But 23 others had been involved in accidents during working hours. They had suffered minor injuries and had been hospitalised for brief periods ranging from two days to a week. All the 23 accidents had happened during the post-lunch period. "I am not suggesting anything at the moment," he said, "but it points to something significant."

What was, however, revealing, according to Chalke, was the trend in leave of absence among the sales staff. All of them had regularly taken sick leaves. A look at the expense statements of individual salesmen had proved that they had invariably entertained a major client over dinner the previous day. "It is easy to surmise that every such absenteeism was because of a hangover," said Chalke.

"That deserves a closer look," said a somewhat shocked Datar. "In our pursuit of sales orders, production and profits, we are losing our humanity and our bearings somewhere. It is bad enough that we had to lose Mishra. We can't have any more fatal accidents on our collective conscience."

"That brings me to the point I was trying to make," said Chalke. "I suggest that alcohol be disallowed as an expense item with immediate effect. This will forestall all potential fatalities. Bingo has always nurtured the image of a company which takes care of its people and such a step would be quite in order."

"We would take care of them less if as a company we ceased to make profits," said Gautam Biswas, the marketing director. "We make profits only when we get sales orders. And we can't get enough sales orders unless we entertain clients. I don't want to sound morbid but if a salesman can't hold a drink, he should look for a job in another department."

Chalke said he had spoken informally to a couple of salespersons and they had mentioned that they would be quite happy not to have a drink with clients or if they were to entertain them less frequently.

Biswas said that it was a momentary reaction induced by the recent tragedy and insisted that entertaining was an essential part of securing more sales.

"Why don't we do it in the office itself?" asked Shankar Shetty, the finance director. "We can convert a part of our executive canteen in the top floor into an entertainment lounge with provision for a liquor cabinet."

Chalke said that workers on the shopfloor downstairs might not like the idea because two of them had only recently been warned for working on the machines under the influence of alcohol. "We can't have double standards in the company," he added.

Datar was in a dilemma. Clearly, he had to have a new control mechanism in place. What should he do?[6]

1. What do you understand by control? Bring out its importance.
2. Bring out the nature of control. Explain the control cycle.
3. State and explain the strategies to achieve control in organisations.
4. State and describe the recent trends in control.

REFERENCES

1. Thomas S.Bateman and Scott A.Snell, *Management*, McGraw-Hill, 1999, p.543.
2. Richard D.Laft, *Management*, Thomson, 2003, p.655.
3. James,A.F.Stoner, et al., *Management*, PHI, 2007, pp.562-563.
4. Richard H.Hall and Pamela,S.T.Olbert, *Organisations*, Pearson, 2005, pp.13-15.
5. Thomas S.Bateman and Scott A.Snell, op.cit., p.548.
6. R. Chandrasekhar, *The Buck Stops Here*, Macmillan, Pp.108-110.

Part - 2
Organisational Behaviour

CHAPTER

Eleven

A Prelude to Organisational Behaviour

LEARNING OBJECTIVES

After reading this chapter you should understand —

1. The nature of organisations, reasons why they exist, and organisational effectiveness
2. The nature of organisational behaviour, its foundations, its importance, and limitations
3. Historical evolution of organisational behaviour
4. Human resource approach, contingency approach, productivity approach, systems approach, and interactionalism approach to the study of organisational behaviour

NATURE OF ORGANISATIONAL BEHAVIOUR

Few things touch our daily life as much as organisations do. We depend on organisations for education, employment, food, clothing, shelter, health, wealth, recreation, travel, and much more. They touch every aspect of human life, as told in the opening case, from birth to death. In fact, life becomes unlivable *sans* organisations.

But most of us have a casual attitude towards organisations. We notice their importance when they fail to deliver their goods and services to us. For example, when trains stop running we take notice of the indifferent services rendered by railways. When electricity fails, we blame the state electricity board for its incompetent and corrupt administration. When doctors in a government hospital strike work, we blame the government, and so on. It is essential for us to understand what these organisations are, how do they function and how to make them more effective in their functioning. These and other related issues are addressed in this book.

WHAT ARE ORGANISATIONS?

Organisations are as old as the human race itself. Archaeologists have discovered massive temples dating back to 3500 **BC** that were constructed through the organised actions of many people. The fact that these impressive monuments were built suggest that not only did complex organisations exist, but that the people in them worked cohesively for common causes.[1]

We have equally impressive examples of contemporary organisations such as Hong Kong's new island airport at Chek Lap Kok, the Hiberria Oil Platform off the East Coast, North America, and the complex network of computer connections - the Internet.

What, then, are these powerful constructs that we call organisations? They are groups of people who work independently towards some purpose. Organisations are not physical structures; rather; they are people who work together to achieve a set of goals. People who work in organisations have structured patterns of interactions, meaning that they expect each other to complete certain tasks in an organised way.

Who creates these organizations ? Often an individual or a group of people, who believe that they possess the necessary skills and knowledge, form an organization to produce goods and services. In this way organizations like rèstaurants, Wipro, and design studios are created. At times, several people form a group to respond to a perceived need by creating an organization. People with a lot of money may invest jointly to build a vacation resort. A group of people with similar beliefs may build a new place of worship or citizens of a state may float a new political party.[(2)]

In general, entrepreneurship is the term used to describe the process by which people recognize opportunities, garner resources and put them to use to produce goods and services. The rewards of entrepreneurship are as varied as the spiritual satisfaction derived by the believers who build a place of worship, or the profit generated for the founders and shareholders of a resort that successfully responded to people's recreational needs.

WHY DO ORGANISATIONS EXIST?

In the beginning of this chapter, we stated that life is unlivable without organizations. This is a broad statement about the usefulness of organisations in any society. Specifically, organisations play five different roles (See Fig 11.1), thus , reiterating their role. As seen from the figure, an

FIGURE 11-1
FIVE REASONS WHY ORGANISATIONS EXIST

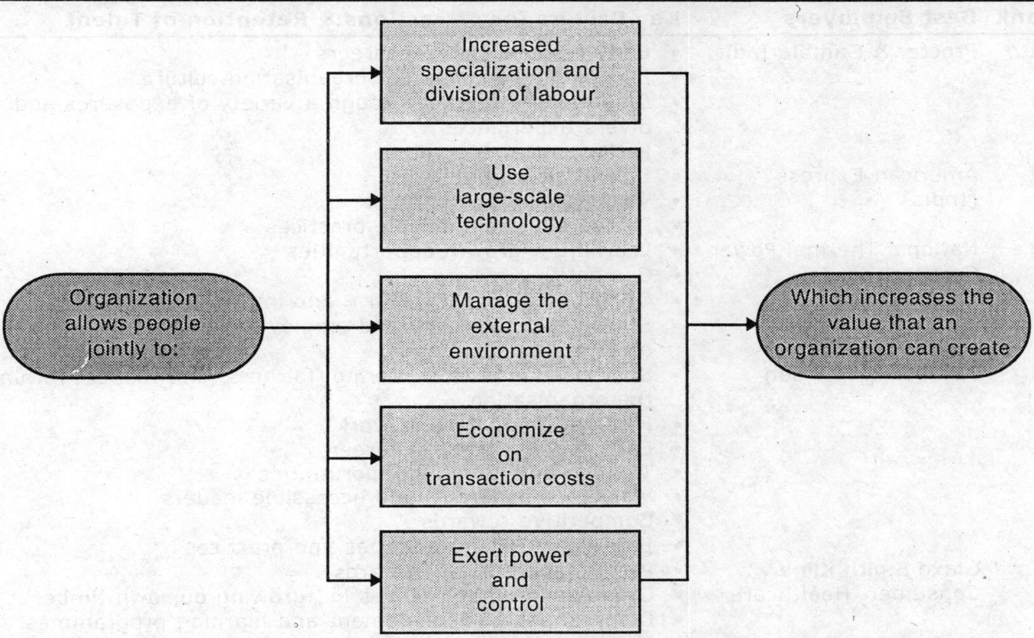

organization allows people to jointly increase specializations and division of labour, use large - scale technology, manage the external environment, economize on transaction costs, and exert power and control - all of which, increase the value the organization can create.[3]

To Increase Specialization and the Division of Labour People who work in organizations may become more productive and efficient at what they do than people who work alone. For many kinds of productive work, the use of an organization allows the development of specialization and division of labour. The collective nature of organization allows individuals to focus on a narrow area of expertise, which allows them to become more skilled or specialised at what they do.

There are several firms, such as Wipro, which have provided enabling environments for individuals to enhance their skills for orgnization and individual growth. The *Business Today* and Hewitt Study[4] has identified the best employers in India and the top 10 of them, together with reasons why they have been ranked thus, are shown in Table 11.1.

To Use Large-scale Technology Organizations are able to take advantage of the economies of scale and scope that result from the use of modern automated computerized technology. **Economies of scale** are the cost savings that result when goods and services are produced in large volumes by automated production. **Economies of scope** are the cost savings that result when an organization is able to use under - utilized resources more effectively because they can be shared across several different products or tasks. Economies of scope (as well as of scale) can be achieved, for example, when it is possible to design an automated production line that can make several different types of products simultaneously.

To Manage the External Environment: Pressures from the environment in which organizations operate necessitate organizing productive resources. An organization's environment includes not

TABLE 11-1
10 Best Employers

Rank	Best Employers	Key Drivers for Attractions & Retention of Talent
1.	Procter & Gamble India	• Early responsibility in careers • Flexible and transparent organisation culture • Global opportunities through a variety of exposures and divers experiences • Performance recognition
2.	American Express (India)	• Strong global brand • Value-based environment • Pioneers in many people practices
3.	National Thermal Power Corporation	• Learning & growth opportunities • Competitive rewards • Opportunity to grow, learn, and implement • Strong social security and employee welfar performance oriented culture
4.	Johnson & Johnson	• Strong value of trust, caring, fairness, and respect within the organisation • Freedom to operate at work • Early responsibility in career • Training and learning opporutnities • Visible, transparent, and accessible leaders • Competitive rewards • Innovative HR programmes and practices
5.	Glaxo Smith Kline Consumer Healthcare	• Performance-driven rewards • Organisation that believes in ' growing our own timber' • Comprehensive development and learning programmes • Flat organisation, where performance could lead to very quick career progression • Challenging work content • Exhaustive induction and orientation programme • Competitive reward
6.	Tata Steel	• Organisation philosophy and culture • Job stability • Freedom to work and innovate
7.	Colgate-Palmolive India	• Company brand • Open, transparent and caring organisation • Management with strong principles and values • Training and development programmes • Structured career planning process • Global career opportunities
8.	Wipro	• Company's brand as an employer • Early opportunities for growth • High degree of autonomy • Value compatibility • Innovative people programmes
9.	Indian Oil Corporation	• Company brand image • Work culture • Learning and growth opporutnities • Challenging work assignments • Growing organization
10.	Tata Consultancy Services	• The group brand equity • Strong corporate governance and citizenship • Commitment to learning and development • Best in people practices • Challenging assignments • Opportunity to work with Fortune 500 clients

(**Source:** *Business Today*, 14 September, 2003)

only economic, social and political factors but also the sources from which it obtains inputs and the market-place into which it releases its outputs. Managing complex environments is a task beyond the abilities of most individuals, but an organization has the resources to develop specialists to anticipate or attempt to influence the many demands from the environment. This specialization allows the organization to create more value for itself, its members, and its customers.

Ranking is done every year. In a study during 2006-07, the best employers identified were: (see Table 11.2).

TABLE 11-2
Best Employers

Rank	Name of the Company/Group	Year of Incorporation	Global Revenue	No. of Employees
1	A.V.Birla Group	1949	$ 12 billion	88,000
2	Satyam Computer Services	1987	Rs. 4,793 crores	40,000
3	J.W.Marriott	1999	$ 100 million (India)	2,100 (India)
4	Eureka Forbes	1982	Rs. 850 crores	8,064
5	Cisco India	1995	$ 30 billion	2,200 (India)
6	Godrej Products	2001	Rs. 657 crores	1,190
7	Agilent Tech	1999	$ 4.97 billion	1,250 (India)
8	Scope International	2000	$ 135 million	4,600 (India)
9	TCS	1968	Rs. 11,214 crores	83,500
10	Kotak Mahindra Bank	2003	Rs. 937 crores	5,293

To Economize on Transaction Costs When people cooperate to produce goods and services, certain problems arise as they learn what to do and how to work with others to perform a task effectively. People have to jointly decide who will do which tasks (the division of labour), who will get paid what amounts, and how to decide if each worker is doing his or her share of the work. The costs associated with negotiating, monitoring, and governing exchanges between people are called **transaction costs.** Organization's ability to control the exchanges between people reduces the transaction costs associated with the exchanges.

To Exert Power and Control Organizations can exert great pressure on individuals to conform to task and production requirements in order to increase production efficiency. To get a job done efficiently, it is important for people to come to work in a predictable fashion, to behave in the interest of the organization, and to accept the authority of the organization and its managers. All these requirements make production less costly and more efficient but put a burden on individuals who must conform to these regulations. When individuals work for themselves, they need to address only their own needs. When they work for an organization, however, they must pay attention to the organization's needs as well as their own. Organizations can discipline or fire workers who fail to conform and can reward good performance with promotion and increased rewards. Because employment, promotion, and increased rewards are important and often scarce, organizations can use them to exert power over individuals.

Taken together, these five factors help explain why more value can often be created when people work together, coordinating their actions in an organized setting, than when they work alone. Over time, the stability created by an organization provides a setting in which the organization and its members can increase their skills and capabilities, and the ability of the organization to create value additions by leaps and bounds. In the last ten years, for example, Infosys has grown to become the most powerful software company in the world because Narayana Murthy, its founder, created an organizational setting in which people are given the freedom to develop their skills and capabilities to create valuable new products.

Organizational Effectiveness

It is essential that organizations should function effectively if they are to be useful. Ineffective organizations are no better than sick people. Organizations are said to be effective when they produce quality goods and services at reasonable cost without compromising on profit-making. The other requirement of effectiveness is that the organizations should seek to satisfy their diverse stakeholders. Stakeholders are all the people and groups affected by, or that can affect, an organization's decisions, policies, and operations.[5] Some of the stakeholders are so primary that an organization's existence and activities depend on them. These stakeholders include customers, suppliers, employees, and investors. But an organization's stake goes beyond these primary interest groups and extends to such groups which are affected by the firm's primary activities and decisions. These groups, called secondary stakeholders, include local communities, government departments, foreign governments, social activist groups, media, and the general public. The connections of these groups with organizations are many and often conflicting. It is the duty of managers to keep all the stakeholders satisfied and the extent of satisfaction derived by stakeholders speaks about the effectiveness of an organization.

The Role of Organizational Behaviour

Organizational Behaviour (OB) helps firms achieve effectiveness in their activities. Organizations, as stated earlier, comprise people and OB helps in utilizing these resources for achieving organizational effectiveness. People generally possess physical strength, skills of some kind, executive skills, and organizing abilities. OB helps harness these qualities and use them for achieving organizational goals.

Definition and Meaning of OB

The definitions on OB are many. However, three features need to be emphasized in any definition:

- OB is the study of human behaviour;
- The study is about behaviour in organizations; and
- Knowledge about human behaviour would be useful in improving an organization's effectiveness.

Combining the above three features, OB may be understood to be the study of human behaviour in organizational settings, of the interface between human behaviour and the organization, and of the organization itself. Knowledge gained from such a study is useful in improving organizational effectiveness. The following definitions are appropriate:

OB refers to the behaviour of individuals and groups within organizations and the interaction between organizational members and their external environments.[6]

OB is a field of study that investigates the impact that individuals, groups and structure have on behaviour within organizations for the purpose of applying such knowledge towards improving an organization's effectiveness.[7]

To sum up, OB obviously comprises individual behaviour, group behaviour and of the organization itself. Understanding of the subject is complete when all the three are studied carefully. The study of individual behaviour alone is incomplete because the actions of the employee influence and are influenced by the organization where he or she works. Again, studying only organizations without learning about the people amounts to looking at only part of the picture.

The influence of environment on the interface between individuals and organizations cannot be overlooked. Fig.11.2 illustrates the integrative study of OB. It shows the linkages among human behaviour in organizational settings, the individual-organizational interface, the organization, as well as the environment surrounding the organization.

FIGURE 11-2
THE NATURE OF ORGANISATIONAL BEHAVIOUR

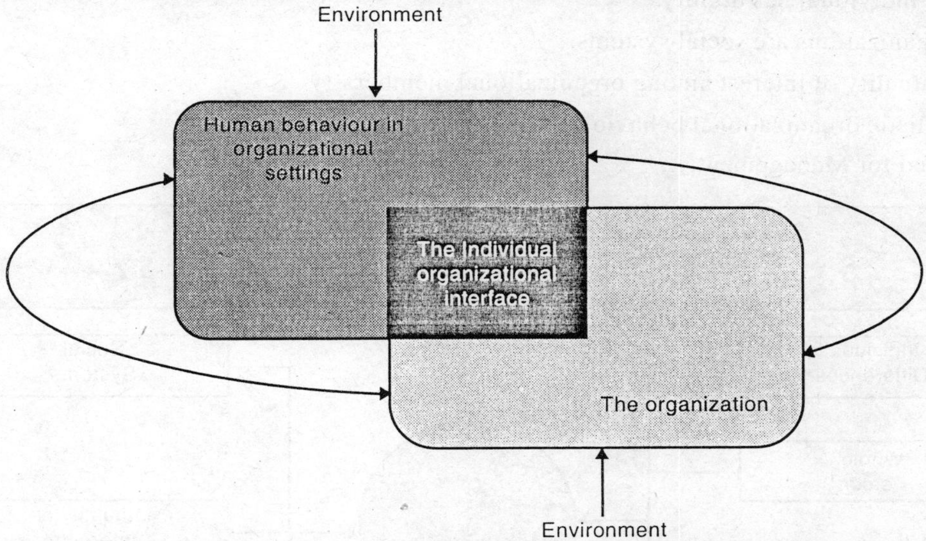

(**Source:** Gregory Moorhead and Ricky W.Griffin, *Organizational Behaviour*, p.5)

The field of OB is both exciting and complex. Many variables and concepts accompany the interaction shown in Fig.11.2 and together these factors greatly complicate the manager's ability to understand, appreciate, and manage people in an organization. They also provide unique opportunities to enhance personnel and organizational effectiveness.

OB has emerged as a distinct field of study. It is an area of expertise with a common body of knowledge. OB is also an applied field. It applies the knowledge gained about individuals and groups and the effect of structure on behaviour in order to make organizations work more effectively.

OB should not be mistaken as representing the whole management. It represents only the behavioural or people approach to management. Other recognized approaches to management include the process, quantitative systems and contingency approaches.

FOUNDATIONS OF OB

The subject OB is based on a few fundamental concepts which revolve around the nature of people and organizations. These concepts are not peculiar to the field of OB. Every discipline, be it a social science or a physical science, will flourish on definite assumptions. For example, the famous principle which runs through financial accounting is that for every debit there shall be a corresponding credit. Similarly, the law of gravity is common whether it is in Mumbai or Bangalore.

Coming to OB, the basic assumptions distinct to the discipline are (see Fig.11.3):

- There are differences between individuals.
- A whole person.
- Behaviour of an individual is caused.
- An individual has dignity.
- Organizations are social systems.
- Mutuality of interest among organizational members.
- Holistic organizational behaviour.
- Need for Management.

FIGURE 11-3
FOUNDATIONS OF OB

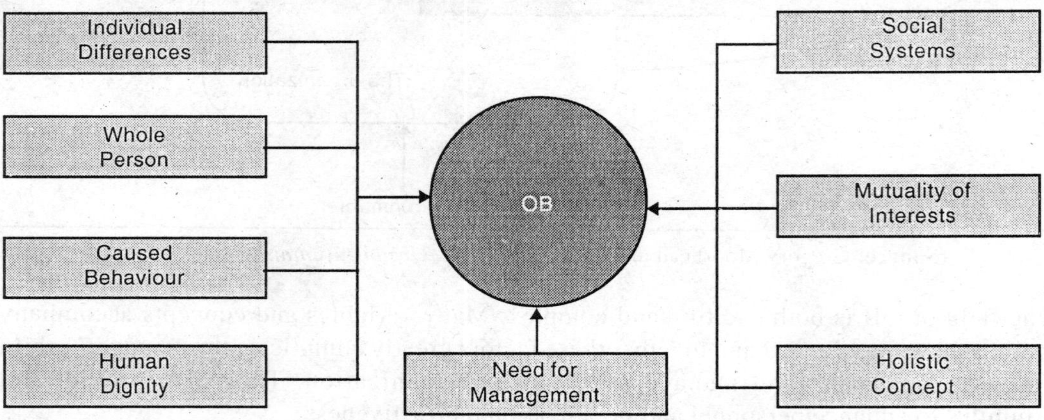

Whilst the first four concepts centre around people, the next two are concerned with organizations. The last one is a combination of the first five assumptions. A brief explanation of each assumption follows.

1. Individual Differences People have much in common (they become excited by the arrival of a new child in the family or they are grieved by the loss of a loved one), but each person in the world is also individually different. Each one is different from the others in several ways. Whether it is intelligence, physique, personality, diction, or any such trait, one can find striking differences. The idea of difference comes originally from psychology. From the day of birth, each person is unique and individual experiences after birth make people even more different. Individual differences mean that management can cause the greatest motivation among employees by treating them differently. If it were not for individual differences, some standard, across-the-board way of dealing with all the employees could be adopted and minimum judgement would be required thereafter.

It is because of individual differences that OB begins with the individual. Only a person can take responsibility and make decisions, a group, by nature, cannot do so. A group is powerless until individuals therein act.

2. A whole Person When an individual is appointed, his/her skill alone is not hired, his/her social background, likes and dislikes, pride and prejudices-are also hired. A person's family life cannot be separated from his or her work life. It is for this reason that managers should endeavour to make the workplace a home away from home. They not only strive hard to develop a better employee out of a worker, but also a better person in terms of growth and fulfillment.

3. Caused Behaviour The behaviour of the employee is caused and not random. This behaviour is directed towards some one that the employee believes, rightly or wrongly, is in his/her interest. Thus, when a worker comes late to his or her work, pelts stones at a running bus, or abuses the supervisor, there is a cause behind it. The manager must realize this basic principle and correct this behaviour and tackle the issue at its root.

4. Human Dignity This concept is of a different order from the other three just discussed because it is more an ethical philosophy than a scientific conclusion. It confirms that people are to be treated differently from other factors of production because they are of a higher order in the universe. It recognizes that people want to be treated with respect and dignity and should be treated. Every job, however simple, entitles the people who do it to proper respect and recognition of their unique aspirations and abilities. The concept of human dignity rejects the old idea of using employees as economic tools.

Ethical philosophy is reflected in the conscience of humankind, confirmed by the experience of people in all ages. It has to do with the consequences of our acts to ourselves and to others. It recognizes that life has an overall purpose and accepts the inner integrity of each individual. Since organizational behaviour always involves people, ethical philosophy is involved in one way or the other in each action. Human decisions cannot and should not be made devoid of values.

5. Organizations are Social Systems From sociology we learn that organizations are social systems; consequently activities therein are governed by social as well as psychological laws. Just as people have psychological needs, they also have social roles and status. Their behaviour is influenced by their group as well as by their individual drives. In fact, two types of social systems exist side by side in organizations. One is the formal system and the other is the informal social system.

The existence of a social system implies that the organizational environment is one of dynamic change, rather than a static set of relations as revealed in an organization chart. All parts of the system are interdependent and are subject to influence by any other part.

6. Mutuality of Interest Mutual interest is represented by the statement that 'organizations need people and people also need organizations'. Organizations have human purpose. They are formed and maintained on the basis of some mutuality of interest among their participants. People see organizations as a means to help them reach their goals, while, at the same time, organizations need people to help attain organizational objectives. If mutuality is lacking, it makes no sense to try to assemble a group and develop cooperation, because there is no common base on which to build. Mutual interest provides a superordinate goal that unites the variety of needs that people bring to organizations. The result is that people are encouraged to attack organizational problems rather than each other.

7. Holistic Concept When the above six fundamental concepts of OB are placed together, a holistic concept emerges. This concept interprets people-organization relationships in terms of the whole person, whole group, whole organization, and the whole social system. It takes an all-encompassing view of people in organizations in an effort to understand as many of the possible factors that influence their behaviour. Issues are analysed in terms of the situation affecting them rather than in terms of an isolated event or problem.

8. Need for Management While describing the nature of OB above, we made an observation that the knowledge about the subject would be useful in improving an organisation's effectiveness. Now, who would use the knowledge about OB for organisational effectiveness? The answer is 'management'.

The nature of management, functions of management and other related topics were explained in Part 1 of this book.

Importance of OB

A study of OB is beneficial in several ways. In the first place, OB provides a road map to our lives in organizations. Every one of us has an inherent need to know about the world in which we live. This is particularly true in organizations, as they have a profound effect on our actions and behaviours.

People bring to their work place their hopes and dreams as well as their fears and frustrations. Much of the time, people in organizations may appear to be acting quite rationally, doing their fair share of work, and going about their tasks in a civil manner. Suddenly, a few people appear distracted, their work slips, and they even get withdrawn. Worse still, one may find someone taking advantage of others to further his or her personal interests.

Occasionally, you are likely to get caught up in anxiety-provoking organizational changes that involve redeployments or even layoffs. Such a range of human behaviours makes life in organizations perplexing. But those who know what to look for and have some advance ideas about how to cope with pressures are more likely to respond in ways that are functional, less stressful, and even career-advancing.[8] We, therefore, need to map out organizational events so that we can function in a more secure and comfortable environment.

Second, the field of OB uses scientific research to help us understand and predict organizational life. This is not to say that this knowledge is absolute. The decisions and actions that people in organizations make are determined by a complex combination of factors. Besides, the field of OB is not a pure science. Nevertheless, it helps us make sense of the workplace and, to some extent, predict what people will do under various conditions.

Third, OB helps us influence organizational events. Though it is good to understand and predict organizational events, most of us want to influence the environment in which we live. Whether one is a marketing specialist or a computer programmer, he or she needs to know how to communicate effectively with others, manage conflict, make better decisions, ensure commitment to ideas, help work teams operate more effectively, and the like. OB theories and concepts will help us influence organisational events.

Fourth, OB helps an individual understand himself/herself and others better. This helps improve interpersonal relations considerably. Of particular significance are topics like attitude, perception, leadership, communication, T.A. and conflict, an understanding of which will change the very style of talking and functioning of an individual. It is no exaggeration that the MBA graduate always remembers, with satisfaction, OB among all the subjects of his/her course, even after graduation.

Fifth, a manager in a business establishment is concerned with getting things done through delegation. He or she will be successful when he or she can motivate subordinates to work for better results. OB will help the manager understand the basis of motivation and what he or she should do to motivate subordinates.

Sixth, the field of OB is useful for maintaining cordial industrial relations. If an employee is slow in his or her work, or if his or her productivity is steadily declining, it is not always because of denial of promotion or a poor work environment. Similarly, if the union of workers gives a strike call, the basic issue may not be a demand for more wages, higher bonus, a better canteen, or for three pairs of uniform in the place of two. Often the indifferent attitude of the boss makes the worker lazy. Similarly, reluctance of the management to talk to union leaders about issues might provoke them to give a strike call. In other words, relations between management and employees are often strained for reasons which are personnel issues, not technical. Human problems need to be tackled humanely. OB is very useful in this context as it helps understand the cause of the problem, predict its course of action, and control its consequences (see Fig.11.4). It is also a human tool for human benefit. The field of OB serves as the basis for human resource management.

FIGURE 11-4
THE BASIC PROCESS OF OB

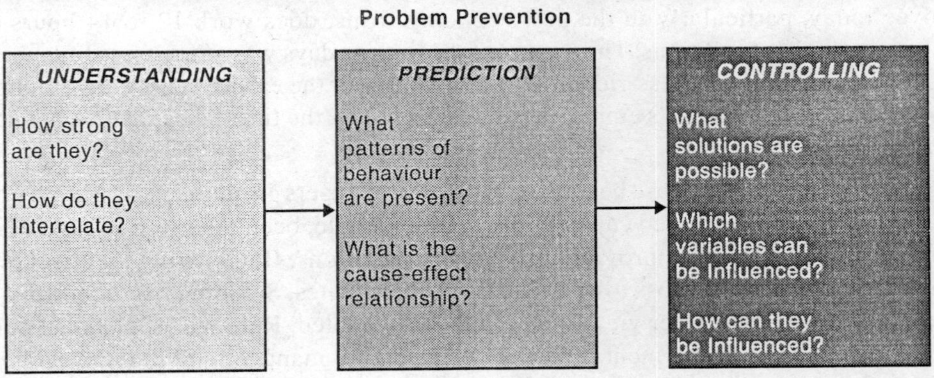

Seventh, the subject of OB is also useful in the field of marketing. In the dynamic mechanism of the flow of goods and services from producer to consumer, awareness of the nature of individual and social processes has an immediate or long-range contribution to the success or failure of the enterprise. Consumer choice behaviour, the nature of influence, and the channels involved, represent leading topics for behaviour research in this area. Innovation and the diffusion of new products, creativity, and the learning of responses are equally important social and individual phenomena that contribute to the total process.

Eighth, the most popular reason for studying OB is that the reader is interested in pursuing a career in management and wants to learn how to predict behaviour and apply it in some meaningful way to make organizations more effective. A successful manager should have good 'people skills' which include the ability to understand one's employees and use this knowledge effectively to make them more efficient.

Finally, in the last couple of years, our economy has been witnessing a upward trend; every sector of the economy doing pretty well, registering an overall growth rate of seven per cent per annum. In order to sustain this trend, effective management of all sectors of the economy, particularly the industrial sector, is of paramount importance. Effective management does not mean competent utilization of technical or financial resources alone. Rather, it implies efficient management of human resources. This is where OB comes into the picture. It is a discipline which enables a manager to motivate his or her subordinates towards higher productivity and better results.

SHORTCOMINGS OF OB

The shortcomings of the subject OB that should not be lost sight of. To start with, though the subject helps an individual understand human behaviour better only in the workplace, he or she may be a failure on the domestic front. People who have a thorough grounding of behavioural disciplines have sometimes proved to be total wrecks in their personal lives.

The subject of OB has not contributed to improved interpersonal relations in organizational settings. Jealousies, back-stabbing, leg-pulling, intrigues, harassment, and inequalities in rewards go side by side with nice lectures, training programmes, discussions, smiles, assurances, niceties and the like (Recollect the opening case). An employee is not sure when a pink slip will be handed out or when a reward will be announced. History seems to be repeating itself. In the earlier days, a worker was exposed to 12 to 14 hours of work and was made to work under inhuman conditions. An employee today, particularly in the new economy firms, does work 12 to 14 hours a day but under for better working conditions. The worker of the bygone days was stress-free. Today's employee is always under pressure and stress-ridden. While a worker of the earlier years died of lung diseases caused by fumes and dust; today's employee gets burnt out by the time he or she reaches 45 years of age (See also closing case).

The subject of OB has almost become a fad with managers in most organizations. Common uniforms, open offices, and shared canteens have, for example, been practised in several industrial establishments in the name of improving interpersonal relations. But wearing identical clothes has not changed the attitude of the boss towards his/her subordinates. Seldom is the subordinate treated as an equal, and rarely are his/her views respected and accepted. Removal of physical palisades in the office has not abolished the mental barriers between the manager and the managed. The boss and the subordinates may eat the same food in the same canteen. Still, the former expects his/her subordinate to serve him/her the food and treat him/her differently. The dual personalities of managers are often bewildering. Outwardly, they talk about participative management, equality of opportunities, empowerment, and open door policies. Behind the veneer of all this pep talk, is the harsh reality that most of these bosses are feudal lords who expect the subordinates to be slaves. Any deviation from this makes the boss feel insecure. The smart subordinate is feared, hounded, and is finally made to quit.

OB is selfish and exploitative. It serves only the interest of the management. It is the product of capitalist societies. With high emphasis on motivation, efficiency, and productivity, the subject breeds a competitive spirit among the employees. They are not allowed to function and live in harmony with one another.

A serious problem that has plagued the subject is the tendency of managers to expect quick-fix solutions from behavioural programmes. This expectation makes the managers address the symptoms while neglecting the underlying problems or to fragment their efforts within the firms.

Critics of OB wonder whether the ideas that have been developed and tested during periods of organizational growth and economic plenty will endure with equal success under different conditions.

Future environment shall be marked buy shrinking demand, scarce resources, and more intense competition. When organizations stagnate, decline, or encounter a threat of closure, there will be conflict and stress. Under these conditions, will the conflict resolution strategies work? Will the motivational models be relevant? Will the leadership styles be practicable? No easy answers are available to these and other related questions.

Finally, OB will not totally abolish conflict and frustration, it can only reduce them. It is a means to improve, not an absolute answer to problems. It is only a part of the whole fabric of an organization. We can discuss OB as a separate subject; but to apply it, we must relate it to reality. However improved, OB will not solve unemployment. It will not make up for our own deficiencies. It cannot substitute for poor planning, inept organizing, or inadequate controls. It is only one of the many systems operating within a larger social system.

The shortcomings of OB, however, should not detract the reader from the greatest contribution of the discipline to human life-understanding human behaviour. Life in and outside organizations would not be what it is if we fail to understand ourselves and our fellow beings better.

CONTEMPORARY OB

Three aspects of the subject deserve mention here:

1. OB is interdisciplinary in focus;
2. A particular set of concepts is accepted as defining the scope of OB; and
3. OB assumes that there is no 'one best' answer to a problem.

An Interdisciplinary Focus OB is an applied behavioural science. It has drawn heavily from a number of applied behavioural sciences such a psychology, sociology, and anthropology. It has also drawn from such subjects as economics, history, political science, engineering and medicine (Also see Fig.11.5).

Psychology It is the science or study of behaviour, and includes animal as well as human behaviour.

Animals like rats and monkeys are used for carrying out psychological experimentation and the conclusions drawn from such experiments are sought to be generalised with reference to human behaviour.

Psychology is concerned with individual behaviour and has contributed greatly to the intra-individual dynamics of human behaviour. In other words, intra-personal aspects of organizational behaviour like motivation, personality, perception, attitude, opinion, and learning owe their study to psychology.

Psychologists themselves are becoming increasingly important these days and the number of professional psychologists has also been growing. They hold important positions in various sectors. Some are academicians with specialization in experimental, social, or clinical psychology. Others can be found in business, industrial, and government organisations. For example, there are educational psychologists and counsellors who work with school children. Some industrial psychologists function mainly in industry, where they are involved in screening and training employees. More recently, their functions have been expanded to include training, developing effective leadership, performance appraisal, job design, and work-stress.

FIGURE 11-5
MAJOR DISCIPLINES AND THEIR CONTRIBUTIONS TO OB

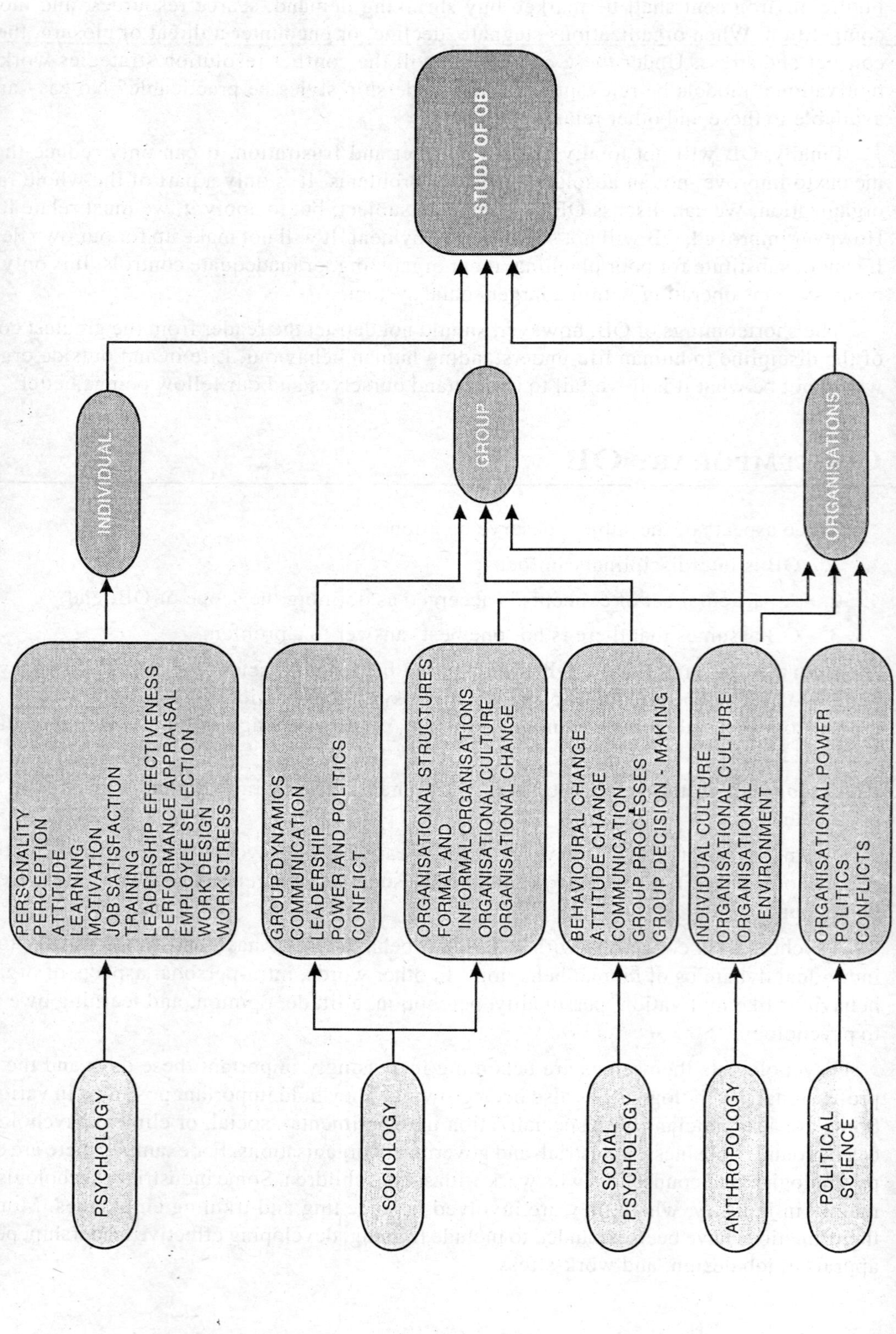

Sociology If psychology is the study of individual behaviour, sociology addresses itself to the study of group behaviour. It studies the behaviour of people in relation to their fellow human beings. Sociologists have enriched organizational behaviour through their contribution to the study of interpersonal dynamics like leadership, group-dynamics, communication, formal and informal organisations, and the like.

Social Psychology This subject borrows concepts from both psychology and sociology. It focuses on the influence of people on one another. One of the areas receiving considerable attention from social psychology is change-how to reduce resistance to it and implement it successfully. Additionally, social psychology is useful in measuring, understanding, and changing attitudes, communication patterns, the ways in which group activities can satisfy individual needs, and in group decision-making process.

Anthropology It is the study of the human race, in particular, its culture. Culture has significant influence on human behaviour. It dictates what people learn and how they behave.

Every organisation will have its own distinct culture. Some organizations particularly, closely held ones, are secretive, publicity-shy, and are less inclined to encourage participative management.

Some organisations, the Tatas for example, take employee welfare and social responsibility as their main goals. The culture of the organisation will have an influence on the employee. His or her attire, perception about things good and bad, and his or her style of functioning are influenced by the culture of his or her organisation.

Political Science Contributions from political scientists for a better understanding of OB are significant. Political scientists study the behaviours of individuals and groups within a political environment. Specific topics of concern to political scientists include conflict resolution, group coalition, allocation of power, and how people manipulate power in their self-interest.

In the past, the term 'politics' was considered to be a dirty word. Not any more. Organisations are becoming political entities and a better understanding of them cannot be had without understanding the political perspective as well.

Engineering: This discipline, too, has influenced OB. Industrial engineering, in particular, has long been concerned with work measurement, productivity measurement, workflow analysis and design, and labour relations. Obviously, all these are important for OB as will be made clear in the subsequent chapters.

Most recently medicine has also come into play in connection with the study of OB, specially in the area of stress. Increasingly, research is showing that controlling the causes and consequences of stress, within and outside of organizational settings, is important for the well-being of both the individual and the organisations.(9) Stress management is covered, in greater detail in Chapter 23.

Scope of Organizational Behaviour Organisational behaviour, as mentioned earlier, is the study of human behaviour within organisations. The subject encompasses the study of individual behaviour, interpersonal behaviour, and of the organisations themselves.

Intrapersonal behaviour covers such aspects as personality, attitude, perception, learning, opinion, motivation, job satisfaction, and stress management.

Interpersonal behaviour includes group dynamic, team dynamics, intergroup conflict, leadership, communication, Transaction Analysis, and the like.

About *organizations*, the study covers such aspects as their formation, structures, effectiveness and, formal and informal organisations.

These three levels of analysis are not necessarily mutually exclusive. The field of organizational behaviour embraces them as being complementary. In the past, these three levels of analysis were pursued with little coordination by behavioural scientists. Now, however, a major contribution of those interested in OB is the attempt to integrate these three levels of analysis, although this will require much effort. The individual focus is no more important or valuable to the manager within an organisation than is the group or formal organisational focus. There is no need to choose one level of analysis and exclude the others. Managers in business, health care, education, government, and religious organisations all have problems in common that require an interdisciplinary approach. This can be provided by OB because it emphasizes on all these levels of analysis-the individual, the group, and the formal organisation.

All the above, and other, topics have been discussed in detail latter in the book. It may be emphasised that the subject of OB applies to all types of organiszations though the focus in this book is towards business establishments only. This is so because the book is primarily addressed to management students preparing themselves for occupying important positions in industrial and business enterprises.

There is No 'One Best' Way What is the most effective way to motivate people? What style of leadership works best? Should groups or individuals make organisational decisions? Although questions such as these appear to be quite reasonable, there is a basic problem with all of them. That is, they suggest that there is one best approach: one best way to motivate, to lead and to make decisions.[10]

Specialists in the field of OB today agree that there is no one best approach when it comes to such complex phenomena. When it comes to studying human behaviour in organizations, there are no simple answers. OB scholars recognize that behaviour in work settings is the complex 'result of many interacting forces.' This fact has been recognised in what is known as the contingency approach (discussed in the next section), an orientation that is the hallmark of contemporary OB. OB literature is obviously replete with phrases such as 'it all depends', 'other things being equal', 'under certain conditions' and the like, implying that a certain behaviour is contingent or a solution is workable only under certain conditions.

Contextual Perspective of OB

Several contextual perspectives have increasingly influenced OB: the human resource approach, the contingency approach, the productivity approach, the systems approach and the interactionalism approach (see Fig.11.6).

Human Resource Approach This approach recognises the fact that people are the central resource in any organisation and that they should be developed towards higher levels of competency, creativity, and fulfillment. People thus developed will contribute to the success of the organisation.

The human resources approach is also called the *supportive approach*, in the sense that the manager's role changes from control of employees to active support to their growth and performance.

The supportive approach contrasts with the traditional management approach. In the traditional approach, managers decide what employees should do and closely monitor their performance to ensure task accomplishment. In the human resources approach, the role of managers changes, as stated above, from structuring and controlling to supporting.

FIGURE 11-6
APPROACHES TO THE STUDY OF OB

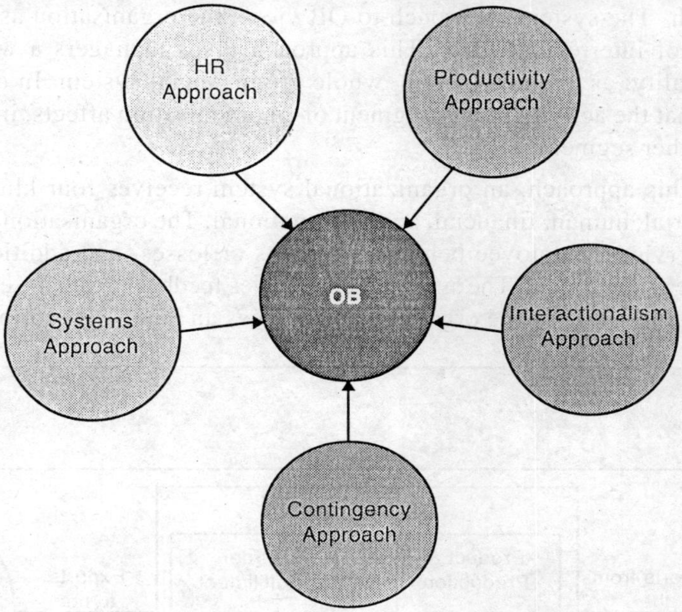

Contingency Approach The contingency approach is another useful way of looking at OB. This approach assumes that there is no 'one best way' available in any organisation. It suggests that in most organisations situations and outcomes are contingent on, or influenced by, other variables (see Fig.11.7).

As seen from Fig.11.8, the contingency approach to OB differs from the universal approach. The universal model, shown at the top of the figure, presumes a direct cause and effect linkage between variables. For instance, it suggests that whenever a manager encounters a certain problem or situation (such as motivating employees for higher efficiency and greater output), a universal approach does exist (such as raising pay), that will lead to the desired outcome. The contingency

FIGURE 11-7
UNIVERSAL APPROACH vs CONTINGENCY APPROACH

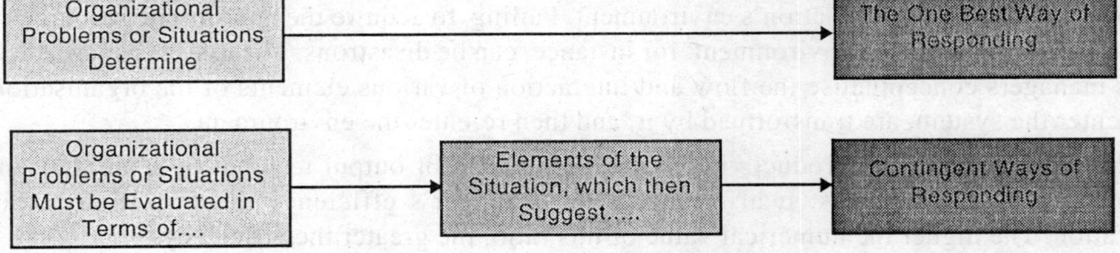

(**Source:** Moorhead and Griffin, *Op.cit.*, p.19)

approach, on the other hand, acknowledges that several other variables affect the relationship. In other words, the appropriate managerial action or behaviour in any given situation depends on the elements of that situation.[11]

Systems Approach The systems approach to OB views the organisation as a united, purposeful system composed of interrelated parts. This approach gives managers a way of looking at the organisation in totality: as a whole person, whole group, social system. In doing so, the systems approach tells us that the activity of any segment of an organisation affects, in varying degrees, the activity of every other segment.

According to this approach, an organizational system receives four kinds of inputs from its environment: material, human, financial, and informational. The organisation converts these inputs into products or services, employee behaviour, profits or losses, and additional information and supplies these to the environment. The system then receives feedback from the environment regarding the outputs (see Fig.11.8). Thus the organisation becomes an input-transformation-output system.

FIGURE 11-8
SYSTEMS APPRAOCH TO OB

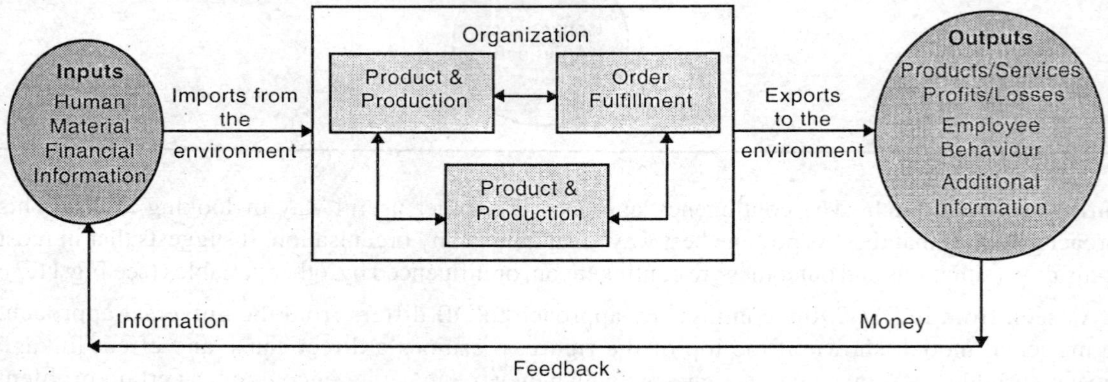

Managers should not become passive spectators of organisational systems. A key function of managing is to adapt to transform system elements to achieve goals within a dynamic environment. Managers need to work with people and allocate resources to carry out tasks within an environment of change. The main purpose of this book is to train managers to manage organisational systems more effectively.

The systems approach has functional consequences for managers. For one thing, it underscores the importance of an organisation's environment. Failing to acquire the appropriate resources and to heed feedback from the environment, for instance, can be disastrous. The systems approach also helps managers conceptualise the flow and interaction of various elements of the organisation as they enter the system, are transformed by it, and then re-enter the environment.

Productivity Approach Productivity, which is the ratio of output to input, is a measure of an organisation's effectiveness. It also reveals the manager's efficiency in optimising resource utilization. The higher the numerical value of this ratio, the greater the efficiency.

Productivity is generally measured in terms of economic inputs and outputs, but human and social inputs and outputs also are important. For example, if better OB can improve job satisfaction, a human output or benefit occurs.

In the same manner, when employee development programmes lead to a by-product of better citizens in a community, a valuable social output occurs. OB decisions typically involve human, social, and/or economic issues, and so productivity, usually a significant part of these decisions, is recognised and discussed extensively in the literature on OB.

Interactionalism: Interactionalism is a relatively new approach to understanding behaviour in organisational settings. First presented in terms of interactional psychology, this view assumes that individual behaivour results from a continuous and multidirectional interaction between characteristics of the person and of the situation. More specifically, interactionalism attempts to explain how people select, interpret, and change various situations. Fig.11.9 illustrates this perspective.[(12)] It should be noted that the individual and the situation are presumed to interact continuously. This interaction is what determines an individual's behaviour.

FIGURE 11-9
INTERACTIONALIST PERSPECTIVE TO OB

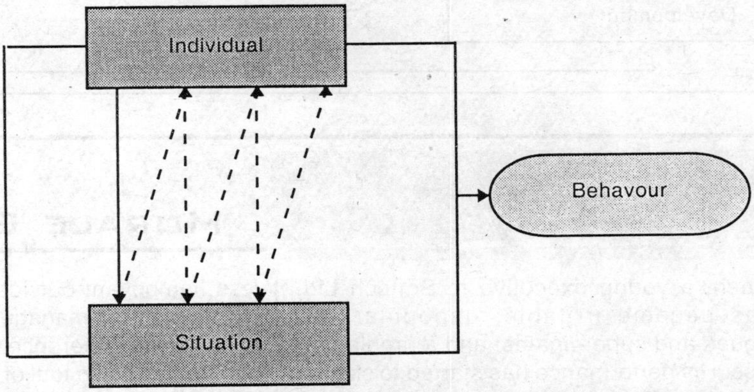

(**Source:** Moorhead and Griffin, *Op.cit.*, p.20)

OB MODEL

We follow a model (see Fig.11.10) for discussion in this book.

As seen from the figure, individual behaviour comprises such aspects as personality, perceptions, attitudes, learning, and motivation. Group behaviour covers such topics as group dynamics, leadership, power and politics, communication and conflict. Study of organisations includes the nature of organisations and organisational change and development. Now, individual behaviour will influence and is influenced by group behaviour, which inturn has impact on behaviour of organisations. The cumulative effect of all these behaviours is felt on organisational effectiveness which in turn has impact on individual, group and organisational behaviours.

FIGURE 11-10
OB MODEL

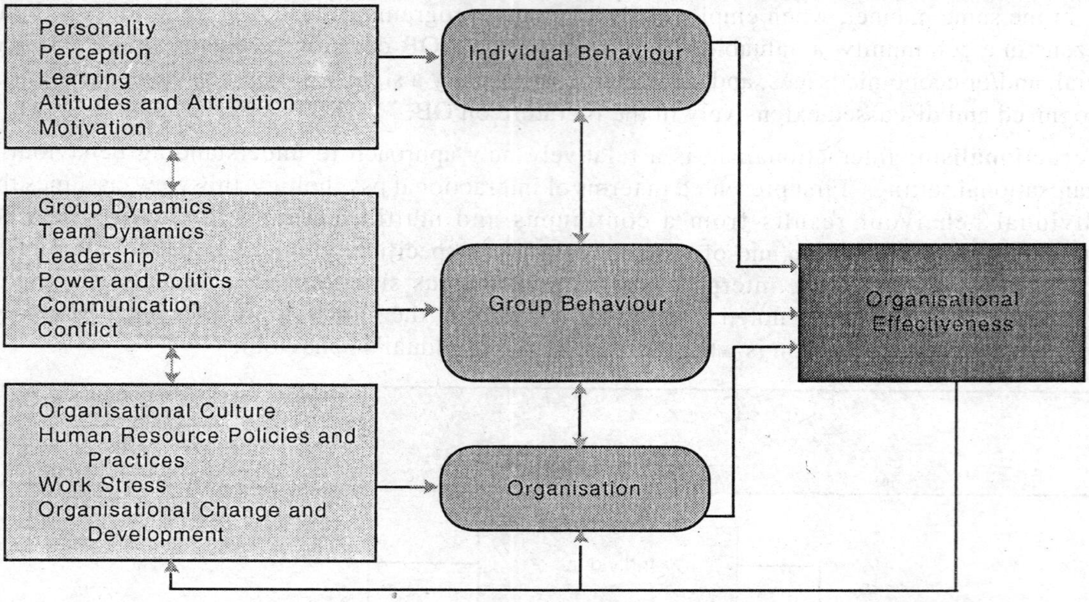

Case

MORALE GONE BUST

Dinesh, a young executive in Softech Ltd., has become irritable, unpopular with colleagues and subordinates; and a problem for the boss. His performance has started to slacken and mistakes plague his every action and recommendation. What is surprising is just three months back Dinesh was quite opposite of all these. He also has a brilliant track record. With a gold medal from a prestigious B-school, Dinesh entered his vocational area of finance and proved an instant success. He has revamped the cost and budgetary control systems, set up a management accounting procedure, and created a reliable and efficient management information system. Dinesh received awards and is slated to climb up the organisational hierarchy further.

Yet, such a man has gone to pieces all of a sudden. Several things transpired against Dinesh. His only son has turned out to be a spastic child, he has been overlooked for a promotion, with a less flamboyant outsider being preferred for the No.1 slot by the management, which has suddenly exhibited its preference to a traditional accountant and he has fallen foul of a powerful line executive.

To compound the problem further, what had been a mild flirtation with an office colleague has assumed the proportion of a major sex scandal.

With his emotional relationships in a mess and worried about his son's health and his own future in Softech, Dinesh's morale has gone bust. His self-confidence has been rudely shaken.

QUESTIONS

1. How would the knowledge of OB help describe these sudden happenings in the life of Dinesh?
2. Compare the character of Dinesh with Vijay (opening case) and draw similarities and dissimilarities.
3. What should Dinesh do now?

QUESTIONS

1 Define Organizational Behaviour. Why do we study the subject?

2 Discuss how OB is an interdisciplinary subject.

3 State the various approaches to the study of OB. Explain each.

4 Explain the different foundations of OB.

5 Besides those cited in the Chapter, what reasons can you think of for the importance of OB?

6 Identify some managerial jobs that are greatly affected by human behaviour and others not so. Which would you prefer? Why?

7 Identify two students in a class who exhibit contrasting behaviours. Using the knowledge you have gained from reading this chapter analyse how and why such behaviours contrast.

8 Explain the following statement: "People influence organizations, and organizations influence people".

9 Do you use the contingency approach in your daily affairs? Explain the circumstances under which it is used.

10 Your friend suggests that OB courses are only useful to people who enter management careers. Do you agree with your friend? Why?

REFERENCES

1. Richard D.Laft, *Management*, Thomson, 2003, p.5..
2. Gareth R.Jones, *Organizational Theory*, Second Edition, Addison-Wesley Pub.Co. 2000, p.4.
3. Ibid, p.7.
4. *Business Today*, September 14, 2003.
5. James E.Post, Anne T.Lawrence and James Weber, *Business and Society*, Ninth Edition, McGraw-Hill, 1999, p.9.
6. Curtis W.Cook and Phillip L.Hunsaker, *Management and Organizational Behaviour*, Third Edition, McGraw-Hill, Irwin, 2001, p.5.
7. Stephen P.Robbins, *Organizational Behaviour-Concepts, Controversies and Applications*, PHI, 1989, p.6.
8. Curtis W.Cook and Phillip L.Hunsaker, *op.cit.* p.5.
9. Moorhead and Griffin, *Organizational Behaviour*, Jaico, 1999, p.15.
10. Jerald Greenberg and Robert A.Baron, *Behaviour in Organizations*, Prentice Hall of India, 1999, p.11.
11. Moorhead and Griffin, *op.cit.*, p.20.
12. Ibid, p.20.

CHAPTER

Twelve

Historical Evolution of Organisational Behaviour

Learning Objectives

After reading this chapter you should understand that —

1. Why one should know the historical roots of organisational behaviour
2. How the subject organisational behaviour has evolved over a period of time

With regard to organisational behaviour, its history will tell us how the subject has evolved, over a period of time, to its present stage. It will help us understand, for instance, how management came to impose rules and regulations on employees, why many employees in organisations do standardised and repetitive tasks on assembly lines and why a number of organisations in recent years have replaced their assembly lines with team-based work units.

Interestingly, many contemporary managers today have come to appreciate the value of history. For example, managers glean insights from *Mahabharata*, *Iliad* and other great works. And some organisations such as Tatas, Godrej and Salgaocars have corporate historians, others such as Coca-Cola, openly proclaim their heritage as part of their employee orientation programmes.

Concern for the welfare of workers in management of business enterprises has been in existence since ages. Kautilya's *Arthasastra* states that there existed a sound base for systematic management of human resources as early as the 4th century B.C. itself. The government then, took an active interest in the operation of public and private sector enterprises and provided systematic procedures for regulating employer-employee relationships.

Elsewhere, human resource in organisations received management's attention much earlier. As early as 1800 B.C. itself, 'minimum wage rate' and 'incentive wage plan' was included in the Babylonian code of Hammurabi.

But experts of human behaviour have tried to chronicle the growth of the subject only from the beginning of the 19th century. The early part of the 19th century is significant because it was during this period that the Industrial Revolution took place that resulted in the total transformation of the then industrial environment.

Platitudes about minimum wage rate, incentive wage plan and sound base for systematic management of human resources apart, there is no gainsaying the fact that life for an average employee, prior to the 19th century, was miserable to say the least. Working conditions in factories were brutal and back breaking. People worked from dawn until dusk under intolerable conditions of disease, filth, danger and scarcity of resources. They had to work this way to survive, so that they had little time to improve job satisfaction[1].

Industrial Revolution

Then came the Industrial Revolution which brought about materialism, discipline, monotony, boredom, job displacement, impersonality, work interdependence, and related behavioural phenomena.[2] Nevertheless, the Industrial Revolution was responsible for planting the seed for potential improvement. Industry created surplus of goods and knowledge that eventually gave workers increased wages, shorter hours, and more work satisfaction. In this new industrial environment Robert Owen, a young Welsh factory owner, about the year 1800, was one of the first to emphasise the human needs of employees. He refused to employ young children. He taught his workers cleanliness and temperance and improved their working conditions. Owen could demonstrate in his own factory that it paid to devote as much attention to 'vital machines' as to 'inanimate machines.' His methods entitled him to be called the 'father of personnel management.' This could hardly be called modern organisational behaviour, but a beginning in that direction was, however made.[3]

In 1835, Andrew Ure published his *The philosophy of Manufactures,* in which, he included the human factor as one of the factors of production, besides the mechanical and commercial parts.

Believing in the importance of the human factor, Ure provided workers with hot tea, medical treatment, and sickness payments.

Nearer home, around this time J.N. Tata took a special interest in the welfare of his workers. He installed the first humidifiers and fire sprinklers in his factories. In 1886, he instituted a pension fund, and in 1895, began to pay accident compensation. He was decades ahead of his time and miles ahead of his competitors. The Empress Mills experiments showed that not only profits but people mattered to him.[4]

The ideas of Owen, Ure and Tata were accepted slowly or not at all, and they often deteriorated into a paternalistic, do-good-approach than a genuine recognition of the importance of people at work.

Scientific Management

The very mention of scientific management brings Taylor to our memory. He is appropriately called the 'father of scientific management' as he converted broad generalisations into practical tools. He was also responsible for awakening interest in workers in the 1900s. Taylor advocated the selection of right people for right jobs, training them adequately, placing them in jobs for which they were best suited, and remunerating them handsomely. To be sure, Taylor's goal was technical efficiency, but at least management was awakened to the importance of human resources, which was hitherto neglected.

Taylor published his major work *Principles of Scientific Management* in 1911. During that decade, interest in human conditions at work was accelerated by World War I.

Taylor's ideas were criticised-particularly, his belief in rationalising everything and holding the assumption that human behaviour is based on 'rabble hypothesis.'

But Taylor's ideas are practised even today. Companies such as UPS still use some of the basic concepts introduced during the scientific management era in their efforts to become even more efficient.

The scientists who were closely influenced by Taylor were the industrial psychologists Frank and Lillian Gilbreth. This husband - and - wife team pioneered time-and-motion study, a type of applied research designed to classify and streamline the individual movements needed to perform jobs with the intent of finding "the one best way" to perform them. Although this approach appears to be highly mechanical and dehumanising, Gilbreths had great concern for human beings.

Scientific management was criticised by employees and theorists for its over emphasis on task accomplishment and monetary incentives at the cost of respect for human beings. A new approach that treated workers as human beings was desired.

The Human Relations Movement

Failure of Scientific Management gave birth to the human relations movement which is characterised by heavy emphasis on employee cooperation and morale. Under this, people were to be treated as human beings and not as machines, listening to their needs and problems and involving them in decision-making in matters relating to working conditions. There are varied and complex reasons for this human relations position. Historically, three of the most important contributing factors would be the Great Depression, the labour movement, the results of the now famous Hawthorne Studies.[5]

The stock exchange crash of 1929 in America marked the beginning of the Great Depression. The consequences of the **Depression** were wide spread unemployment, decline of purchasing power, collapse of markets, and lowering of the standard of living of people. This phenomenon was world wide and not confined to America alone.

One positive outcome of the **Depression** was that management began to realise that production alone could not be its major function. Marketing, finance, and personnel were also required in order for a business to survive and grow. The Depression's aftermath of unemployment and insecurity bought to the surface, human problems that managers were now forced to recognise and cope with. Personnel departments were either created or given more emphasis, and most managers now began to develop a new, awakened view of the human aspects of work. Human relations took an increased significance as an indirect, and in some cases, direct result of the Depression.[6]

Mere creation or strengthening of personnel departments did not improve the plight of workers. Production still preceded people in order of importance in organisations. Decent hours of work, fair wages, and adequate working conditions were sacrificed for more production. There were people like Taylor, Ford, and Sloan who sincerely believed in giving labour due share. Such noble hearted souls were few and far between. In general, exploitation of labour continued.

Labour Movement: Continued exploitation made workers realise that their protection lay in their own hands. They formed strong unions and this had the desired effect on management. Management began to place primary emphasis on employee relations, and secondary attention was given to wages, hours of work, and conditions of employment.

Unfortunately, the human relations role also often came about for wrong reasons. In too many cases, it was forced on managers by labour, threatening them with consequences of non-compliance. Ideally, it would have been better, had, human relations developed because of intrinsic motivation of practising managers, to better understand and provide for the welfare of their employees.[7]

HAWTHORNE STUDIES

Although the Depression and the labour movement were at least, important indirect causes of the practice of human relations, the Hawthorne studies dominate the academic discussion on historical development. The studies gave academic status to the study of organisational behaviour.

The studies were carried out at the Western Electric Company's Hawthorne works in Cicero, a suburb of Chicago, and are closely linked with the name of Elton Mayo. As Professor of Industrial Research at the Harward School of Business Administration, Mayo was the person, most responsible for conducting the studies and publicising their significance. Naturally, he is called the 'father of human relations movement.'

When they started, the Hawthorne studies reflected the scientific management tradition of seeking greater efficiency by improving the tools and methods of work-in this case lighting. GE wanted to sell more tubelights, so, along with other electric companies, it supported studies on the relationship between lighting and productivity that were to be conducted by the National Research Council. The research involved three sets of studies.

Illumination Studies Illumination studies constituted the first set of experiments and took place between 1924 and 1927. In one of these studies, lighting was decreased over successive periods for the experimental group (the group for whom lighting was altered), while it was kept at a constant level for the control group (a comparison group working in another area). The researchers were surprised to discover that productivity increased roughly at the same rate in both the groups. It was only in the final experiment, where they decreased light to 0.06 foot candle (roughly moonlight intensity), that performance in the experimental group declined as the workers in the group complained that they could hardly see anything. The researchers concluded that factors other than lighting were at work (since output rose in both the groups), and the project was discontinued.

It is from this first round of experiments that the term *Hawthorne Effect* was coined, referring originally to the fact that people's knowledge that they are being studied leads them to modify their behaviour.

The Relay Assembly Room Study Intrigued with the positive changes in productivity, the researchers decided to attempt to determine the causes through further studies. Hence the second set of tests.

The second set of experiments took place between 1927 and 1933. The most famous study involved five women who assembled electrical relays in the Royal Assembly Test Room, where they were away from other workers and the researchers could alter work conditions and evaluate the results. Before the study began, the researchers were concerned about the possible negative reactions from the workers who would be included in the test. To reduce potential resistance, the researchers changed the usual supervisor arrangement so that there would be no official supervisor. Instead, the workers would operate under the general direction of the researchers. The workers were also given special privileges, such as being able to leave their work station without permission, free mid-morning lunch, a workday that was a half-hour shorter, a five-day workweek (a novel idea at that time), and variations in the methods of payment. Generally, productivity increased over the period of study, regardless of how the factors were manipulated.

A Harvard University research group (involved in assessing the results) finally concluded that the change in the supervisory arrangement was the major reason for the increase in the productivity in the Relay Assembly Test Room study and in two related studies involving different work groups. The researchers felt that the physical changes such as rest pauses, free lunches, and incentive payments were of lesser importance.

The Bank Wiring Room Study This study was conducted between 1931 and 1932 and constituted the third set of experiments. The motivation for this study was built on the findings of the second set. For this study, a group of 14 men who wired telephone banks was observed in a standard shop condition. An observer was stationed in the room with instructions to take continuous notes on the workers' actions. The observer was not allowed to give orders or get involved in conversations with the workers. Although, the workers were initially apprehensive about the observer, they settled into more natural and relaxed behaviour after about three weeks. Because the foreman for the work group also supervised other workers in another room, and because the observer was deliberately unobtrusive, the workers were relatively free from constant supervision.

Though the workers were paid according to their output, the observer soon noted that the workers had established an informal daily norm of 6600 units per person. Typically, the men would pace their work so that they reached the norm by the end of the day. Of course, some of the men could do more than 6600 units. But if they indicated that they would prefer to be more productive, they risked becoming victims of harassment.

The researchers concluded that the behavioural norms set by the work group had a powerful influence over the productivity of the group. The higher the norms, the greater the productivity. The lower the norms, the lower the productivity. The power of the peer group and the importance of group influence on individual behaviour and productivity were confirmed in the bank wiring room.

Thus, Hawthorne Studies laid a foundation for understanding people's social and psychological behaviour in the workplace.

Organisational Behaviour

The human relations movement thus started, continued and flourished for a long time. Unfortunately, the movement grew so fast that much fadism and shallowness developed. Some practitioners began to emphasise the big smile, 'being nice to people', and 'keep them happy', while subtly trying to manipulate employees. Naturally, the human relations movement received serious criticism.

In course of time, the term 'human relations' lost its flavour, although it continues to be used, especially at the operating level-because of its appropriateness. As the field became more mature and research based, the new term that arose to describe it was 'organisational behaviour.'[11] Experts trace this development to the late 1950s and early 1960s.

Organisational behaviour has made considerable strides since 1960s, although there have been occasional steps backward as well. Managers increasingly recognise the value of human resources and strive to better understand people and their role in complex organisation and competitive business situations. This realisation has come from the subject, organisational behaviour.

- Fig 12.1 brings out milestones in the history of organisational behaviour.

FIGURE 12-1
MILESTONES IN THE HISTORY OF ORGANISATION BEHAVIOUR

Industrial Revolution	Robert Owen, Andrew Ure and J.N. Tata provided certain welfare facilities. The ideas degenerated into paternalistic approach.
Scientific Management–Early 20th Century	Taylor believed in rationalising production. He believed that human behaviour was based on 'rabble hypothesis.'
Human Relations Movement during 1920s to 1940s	Great Depression, labour movement and Hawthorne studies led to the movement. The movement subsequently became a fad
	Organisational behaviour – 1950's

Question

1 Sketch the historical growth of the subject organisational behaviour.

References

1. Keith Davis and Newstrom, *Human Behaviour at Work: Organisational Behaviour*, New York : McGraw Hill, 1989, p. 7.
2. Perline, M.M. and Kurtis, L.T., *Automation – Its Impact on Organised Labour*, Personnel Journal, Vol. 48, No. 5, 1969, p. 340.
3. Keith Davis and Newstrom, *Op.cit.*, p. 7.

4. R.M. Lala, *The Creation of Wealth,* Mumbai: IBH Publishing Company, 1981, p. 13.
5. Fred Luthans, *Organisational Behaviour*, New York: McGraw-Hill, 1989, p.13.
6. *Ibid.*, p.14.
7. *Ibid.*, p.14.
8. Stephen, P.Robbins, *Organisational Behaviour-Concepts, Controversies and Applications*, New Delhi: Prentice Hall of India, 1989, p. 212.
9. Fred Luthans, *Op. cit.*, p. 19.
10. Keith Davis and Newstrom, *Op.cit.*, p. 8.
11. *Ibid.*, p. 9.

CHAPTER

Thirteen

Organisational Culture, Creativity and Innovation

LEARNING OBJECTIVES

After reading this chapter you should understand that —

1. The nature of Culture.
2. The types of cultures.
3. The sources of Culture.
4. How to sustain Culture.
5. The effects of Culture – functional and dysfunctional.
6. The difficulties of Changing organisational culture.
7. The nature of Creativity.
8. The different ways and methods of enhancing creativity.
9. The natuer of Innovation.

Organizational culture has assumed considerable importance nowadays because of its impact on employee performance and satisfaction. A discussion on organizational culture is, therefore, highly appropriate in a book on OB. Hence this chapter. We propose to discuss in this chapter the nature, functional and dysfunctional consequences, creation and sustenance, ways of changing, and other related aspects of organizational culture.

MEANING AND DEFINITION

By culture we mean that complex whole which includes knowledge, belief, art, morals, law, custom, and other capabilities and habits acquired by man in a society. Two terms are key to the concept culture: history and shared phenomenon. With regard to the first, it may be stated that cultural mores of a society are passed on from generation to generation. The second key term which is basic to culture implies that the cultural ethos are shared among the members of a society.[1]

Having known the meaning of culture, we may attempt to define organizational culture. Organizational culture (or its sister term corporate culture) has been defined as the philosophies, ideologies, values, assumptions, beliefs, expectations, attitudes and norms that knit an organization together and are shared by its employees.[2]

The following ten characteristics help us understand the nature of culture better.[3] When these characteristics are mixed and meshed, we get the essence of culture.

1. **Individual Initiative** The degree of responsibility, freedom, and independence that individuals have.
2. **Risk Tolerance** The degree to which employees are encouraged to be aggressive, innovative, and risk-seeking.
3. **Direction** The degree to which the organization creates clear objectives and performance expectations.
4. **Integration** The degree to which units within the organization are encouraged to operate in a coordinated manner.
5. **Management Support** The degree to which mangers provide clear communication, assistance and support to their subordinates.
6. **Control** The number of rules and regulations, and the amount of direct supervision that is used to oversee and control employee behaviour.
7. **Identity** The degree to which members' identify with the organization as a whole rather than with their particular work group or field of professional expertise.
8. **Reward System** The degree to which reward allocations are based on employee, performance criteria in contrast to seniority, favouritism, and so on.
9. **Conflict Tolerance** The degree to which employees are encouraged to air conflicts and criticisms openly.
10. **Communication Patterns** The degree to which organizational communications are restricted to the formal hierarchy of authority.

Organizational members tend to internalize cultural practices and like to indoctrinate newcomers into such mores. Some of these practices are so thoroughly internalized that no one questions them – they are taken for granted that is, they get institutionalized.

Besides institutionalization, deification or glorification is another process that tends to occur in strongly developed organizational cultures. Heroes emerge, especially among the founding fathers of the organization, whose sacrifices, valorous deeds, and ingenuity in the difficult initial years of the organization or during later crises periods are embellished into stories and sagas. The organization itself may come to be regarded as precious in itself, as a source of pride, and in some sense unique. Organizational members begin to feel a strong bond with it that transcends material returns given by the organization, and they begin to identify with it. The organization turns into a sort of clan.[4]

CULTURAL DIMENSIONS

Over the years a number of organizational cultures have been identified. The more interesting of these are as follows:

Levels of Culture Three levels of culture may be distinguished. These include national culture, business culture, and the occupational and organizational cultures. (See Fig 13.1). All these levels influence the effectiveness of management.

FIGURE 13-1
LEVELS OF CULTURE

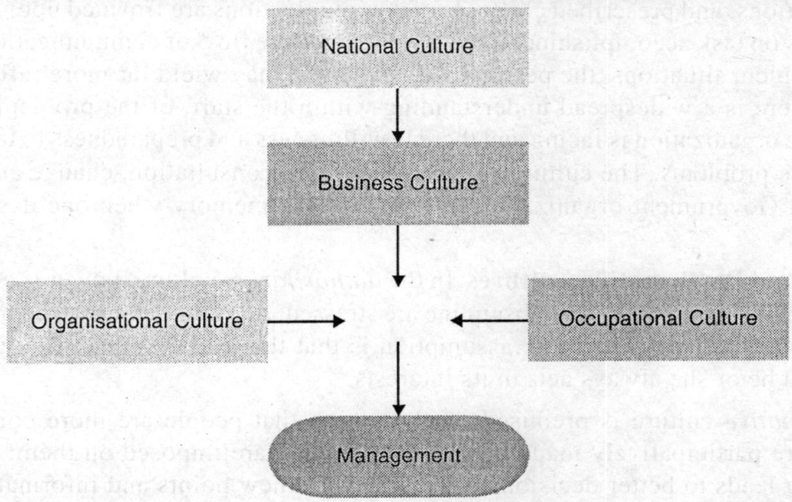

National culture is the dominant culture with in the political boundaries of the nation-state. The dominant national culture usually represents culture of the people with the greatest population or the greatest political or economic power. Formal education is usually taught, and business is usually conducted in the language of the dominant culture. National culture has considerable significance for international managers who need to manage cultural diversities.

Business culture represents norms, values, and beliefs that pertain to all aspects of doing business in a culture. Business culture tells people the correct, acceptable ways to conduct business in a society.

National culture impacts business culture considerably. In any society, business closely interweaves with the broader culture's values norms and beliefs. Examples include the priorities given to age and security, the role expectations for women within a family, and expectations concerning how those managing should behave towards subordinates.

Business culture influences all aspects of work and organizational life. This includes how managers select and promote employees, lead and motivate their subordinates, structure their organizations, select and formulate their strategies, and negotiate with other business people.

Different occupational groups, such as physicians, lawyers, accountants and craftspeople, have distinct cultures, called *occupational cultures.* Occupational cultures are the norms, values, beliefs, and expected ways of behaving of people in the same occupational group, regardless of which organization they work for. The occupational culture cannot be ignored by the manager just because of the dominant importance of national and business cultures.

Organization culture, as stated earlier, represents beliefs, attitudes and norms that knit an organization together and are shared by its employees, as the opening case reveals.

Mechanistic and Organic Cultures The *mechanistic* organizational culture exhibits the values of bureaucracy and feudalism. Organizational work is conceived as a system of narrow specialism and people think of their careers mainly within these specialisms. Authority is thought of as flowing down from the top of the organization down to the lower levels and communication flows through prescribed channels. There is a great deal of departmental loyalty and inter-departmental animosity, a strong "we" versus "they" perception. This sort of culture resists change and innovation.

Contrast is the *organic culture*. Formal hierarchies of authority, departmental boundaries, formal rules and regulations, and prescribed channels of communications are frowned upon. There is great deal of emphasis on task accomplishment, team work, and free flow of communication - formal and informal. In problem situations, the persons with expertise may wield far more influence than the formal boss. There is a widespread understanding within the staff, of the problems, threats, and opportunities the organization is facing and there is willingness and preparedness to take appropriate roles to solve the problems. The culture stresses flexibility, consultation, change and innovation.[5] CMC, a Central Government organization, comes to one's memory when one describes organic culture.

Authoritarian and Participative Cultures In the *authoritarian* culture, power is concentrated on the leader and obedience to orders and discipline are stressed. Any disobedience is punished severely to set an example to others. The basic assumption is that the leader knows what is good for the organization and he or she always acts in its interests.

The *participative* culture is premised on the notion that people are more committed to the decisions that are participatively made than to those which are imposed on them. Further, group problem-solving leads to better decisions because several new points and information are shared during discussions.[6] Participative cultures tend to emerge where most organizational members are professionals or see themselves as equals.

Dominant and Sub-cultures Many big companies have a dominant culture and several cells of sub-cultures, which are attached to different roles, functions, and levels. If the sub-cultures are accepted, a natural conclusion is that very few beliefs, attitudes, or values are shared by all organisational members. A dominant culture, normally referred to as the organisational culture, reflects core values that are shared by the majority of the employees. In effect, this is the distinctive personality of the organisation.

By contrast, sub-cultures are found in departments, divisions, and geographical areas, and reflect the common problems or experiences of employees who reside in these areas. A sub-culture could consist of the core values of the dominant culture as well as the values unique to the department or area to which it relates.[7] There could be differences and clashes between sub-culture and another and between subcultures and the dominant culture.

Strong, Weak, and Unhealthy Cultures Distinction is also made between strong and weak cultures. In a strong culture, the core values of the organisation are widely shared and eagerly embraced by a large number of employees who are deeply committed to them.

A strong culture will have a significant influence on employee behaviour manifesting in reduced turnover, lower absenteeism, increased cohesiveness, and postitive attitudes. This is so because there is a high agreement among members about what the organisation stands for. The result is the creation of an internal atmosphere of high behavioural control. Behavioural control brought in by strong culture is much more powerful than the one that results from formal rules and regulations. In addition, organisations sharing strong culture tend to perform better than those without such a culture. In recent years, as organisations have created flatter structures, introduced team systems of working, reduced bureaucratic control, and empowered employees, some would argue that the shared meaning generated by a strong culture ensures that everyone is moving in the same direction.

Strong culture has dysfunctional consequences. It tends to lead to groupthink, collective blind spots, and resistances to change and innovation. It tends to discourage diversity as strong culture would not accommodate the diverse behaviours and strengths that people of different backgrounds can bring to the organization.

Weak Cultures A weak culture is characterized by the presence of several sub-cultures, sharing of few values and behavioural norms by employees, and existence of few sacred traditions. In weak-cultured organizations, there is little cohesion across the organization-top executives do not repeatedly expose any business philosophy or exhibit commitment to particular values or extoll the use of particular operating practices. Because of the lack of shared values, organizational members have no deeply felt sense of identity. The lack of corporate identity tends to result in few employees viewing the company as a place to work and their work as a way to make a living.

Unhealthy Cultures There are organizations which have unhealthy cultures. One unhealthy trait is a politicized internal environment that allows influential managers to operate autonomous 'fiefdoms' and resist needed change. In politically dominated cultures, many issues get resolved on the basis of turf, vocal support or opposition by powerful executives, personal lobbying by a key executive, and coalitions among individuals or departments with vested interests in a particular outcome. What is best for the organization plays second fiddle to personal aggrandizement.

Another feature of unhealthy cultures is that of promoting managers who are good at staying within their budgets, exerting close supervisory control over their units, and handling administrative detail as opposed to managers who understand vision, strategies, and culture-building and who are good leaders, motivators, and decision makers. While the former are adept at internal organizational manoeuvring, they may lack the entrepreneurial skills an organization needs among its senior executives to introduce new ideas, reallocate resources, build new competitive abilities, and fashion new culture.

Finally, unhealthy culture is also characterized by an aversion to looking outside the organization for superior practices and approaches. Sometimes, an organization enjoys undisputed leadership in the industry and its managers become inbred and arrogant. It believes it has all the answers or can develop them on its own. Insular thinking and inward-looking solutions often precede a decline in performance. Several well-knowns organizations such as Bank of America, Citicorp, Ford, and Xerox had unhealthy cultures during the late 1970s and early 1980s. GM, Kmart and Sears, and L&T in India do exhibit unhealthy cultural traits now.

How is Culture Created?

Culture is essentially learnt. What applies to the learning process applies to culture too. Basically, an organizational culture forms in response to two major challenges that confront every organization: (1) external adaptation and survival, and (2) internal integration.

External adaptation and survival have to do with how the organization will find a niche in and cope with its constantly changing external environment. External adaptation and survival involve addressing the following issues:-[8]

- *Mission and strategy:* Identifying the primary purpose of the organization; selecting strategies to pursue this mission.
- *Goals:* Setting specific targets to achieve.
- *Means:* Determining how to pursue the goals, including selecting an organization structure, and reward system.
- *Measurement* Establishing criteria to determine how well individuals and teams are accomplishing their goals.

Internal integration has to do with the establishment and maintenance of effective working relationships among the members of an organization. Internal integration involves addressing the following issues:

- *Language and concepts* Identifying methods of communication and developing a shared meaning for important concepts.
- *Group and team boundaries* Establishing criteria for membership in groups and teams.
- *Power and statuses* Determining rules for acquiring, maintaining, and losing power and status.
- *Reward and punishment* Developing systems for encouraging desirable behaviours and discouraging undesirable behaviours.

An organizational culture emerges when members share knowledge and assumptions as they discover or develop ways of coping with issues of external adaptation and international integration.

Having understand the challenges that evoke organizational culture, it is necessary to state the sources from where corporate cultures emerge. Organizational culture generally comes from critical incidents, leaders, property rights, organizational structure, organizational ethics and characteristics of employees (see Fig 13.2).

Culture Formation Around Critical Incidents Norms and beliefs arise around the way members respond to critical incidents. Something emotionally charged or anxiety producing may happen, such as an attack by a member on the leader. Because everyone witnesses it and because tension is high when the attack occurs, the immediate next set of behaviours tends to create a norm.

Suppose, for example, that the leader counter-attacks, that the group members "concur" with silence or approval and that the offending member indicates with an apology that he or she accepts his or her "mistake". In those few moments a bit of culture has begun to be created-the norms that "we do not attack the leader in this group; authority is sacred." The norm may eventually become a belief and then an assumption if the same pattern occurs. If the leader and the group consistently respond differently to attacks, a different norm will arise. By reconstruction the history of critical incidents in the group and how members deal with them, one gets a good indication of the important cultural elements in that group.

FIGURE 13-2
WHERE DOES AN ORGANISATIONAL CULTURE COME FROM?

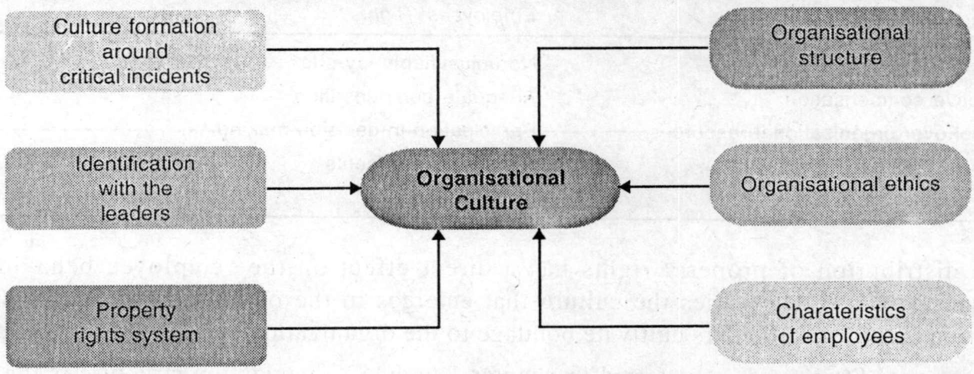

Identification with Leaders A second mechanism of culture creation is the modeling by leader figures that permits group members to identify with them and internalize their values and assumptions. When groups or organizations first form, there are usually dominant figures or "founders" who help establish the early culture. They have a vision or mission of what the organization should be. They are unconstrained by previous customs or ideologies. The small size that typically characterizes any new organization further facilitates the founders imposing their vision on all organizational members. Because the founders have the original idea, they also typically have biases on how to get the idea fulfilled. The organization's culture results from the interaction between (1) the founder's biases and assumptions, and (2) what the original members who the founders initially employ learn subsequently from their own experiences.

The late J.R.D. typifies this type of culture creation. His supportive-consultive role, his belief on professionalism, and assumption that only honesty and fair dealing will pay have made the vast Tata empire what it is today.

Property Rights Corporate culture, particularly its values, stems from how the organization distributes its property rights - the right the organization gives to its members to receive and use organizational resources. Property rights define the rights and responsibilities of each stakeholder group and cause the development of different norms, values and attitudes towards the organization.[9] Table 13.1 identifies some of the property rights commonly given to the managers and to the workforce.

Shareholders have the strongest property rights of all stakeholder groups because they own the resources of the organization and share in its profits. Next come the managers who are entitled for attractive stock options and compensation. The wholetime directors of Reliance Industries, for example, drew compensation of Rs 35.58 cr. during 2001-2002. They command resources of the organization and are responsible for decision making. Managers are vested with strong property rights because it is they who make or mar organizations.

Employees too have property rights in the form of secured jobs, adequate compensation, pension and benefits and in some cases stock options (For example, a former canteen boy at Infosys who used to serve tea, now runs the cafeteria and holds enough company stock to be counted as a millionaire).

TABLE 13-1
COMMON PROPERTY RIGHTS GIVEN TO MANAGERS AND EMPLOYEES

Managers' rights	*Employees' Rights*
Stock options	No unjustifiable lay-offs
Attractive compensation	Adequate compensation
Control over organizational resources	Participation in decision making
Decision making	Pension and benefits
	Stock options

The distribution of property rights has a direct effect on the employee behaviour and performance. It also determines the culture that emerges in the organizations. Where property distribution is fair, stakeholders cultivate bondage to the organization and develop strong culture.

Organizational Structure As started in chapter 1 and 18, organization structure is the formal system of tasks and authority relationships that an organization establishes to control its activities. The structure goes beyond this. It influences organizational culture.

Recall from the previous chapter that mechanistic structures have many levels of authority. Highly centralized and standardized and organic structures have few levels of authority and decentralized structures rely on mutual adjustment. In mechanistic structures, people have relatively little personal autonomy and desirable behaviour includes being cautious, "boss is always right" attitude, and respecting traditions. Obivously, a mechanistic structure is likely to give rise to a culture in which predictability and stability are desired end results. In organic structures, people have more freedom to choose and control their own activities, and desirable behaviours include being creative or courageous and risk taking. Thus an organic structures is likely to give rise to a culture in which innovation and flexibility are desired end states.[10]

Organizational Ethics Organizational ethics (part of organizational cultures) are the moral values, beliefs rules that establish the appropriate way for organizational stakeholders to deal with one another within the organization's environment. Organizational ethics outline the right and wrong ways to behave in a situation.

Bribery and corruption are the major issues when one is talking about ethics. Bribery is a deliberate attempt to pursue someone (usually in position of power and authority) to act improperly in favour of the briber by offering money or gifts or any other material gain. Bribery has been at the root of corruption. Corruption then is the abuse of public office for private gain. Bribery and corruption are discouraged by an ethically strong organization, such as Tatas.

Characteristics of People within the Organization The ultimate source of organizational culture is the people who make up the organization. Organizations are composed of people and it is they who contribute to cultures. People differ in their personalities, values, and ethics. Naturally, organizations which hire and retain people tend to develop distinctly different cultures. People may be attracted to an organization whose values match theirs; similarly, an organization selects people who share its values. Overtime, people who do not fit in quit. The consequence is that people inside the organization become more and more similar, the values of the organization become more and more parochial, and the culture becomes more and more distinct from that of similar organizations. This "People make the place" view of organizational culture has dysfunctional consequences which will be explained later in this Chapter.

CULTURE ARTIFACTS

Organizational culture having emerged, manifests itself through stories, rituals, ceremonies, language, symbols and statements of principles. All these exhibits together constitute the culture artifacts.

Stories Stories about past corporate incidents serve as powerful social prescriptions of the way things should (or should not) be done. As they are told and retold, stories give meaning and identity to organization members and are specially helpful in orienting new employees. The strength of stories lies in the fact that the listeners are left to draw their own conclusions.

The following themes generally appear in stories across different types of organization: [11]

Stories about the CEO These stories may reflect whether the CEO is 'human' or how he or she reacts to mistakes.

Stories about getting fired. Events leading to employee firings are recounted.

Stories about how the company deals with employees who have to relocate. These stories relate to the company's action towards employees who have to move- whether the company is sympathetic or not.

Stories about how the company deals with crisis situations, as revealed by the experience of Brij Mohan Khaitan, the tea baron. Crisis is no news to him. He survived a bomb attack in London, riots of pre-Independence Calcutta and the Naxalite movement. But the crisis from ULFA and Bodo militants in Assam was too much for Khaitan. On march 18, 1992 one of his executives Subhir Roy and his driver were abducted by BSF-another militant organization in Assam. Roy and his driver were released after 20 days of captivity. Khaitan apparently bought peace from the militants. Today, the gardens are guarded night and day by Khaitan's private army. Two thousand armed guards, forty per garden, patrol its perimeters constantly. No manager is allowed to go outside the garden without some protection. He built a school in Assam investing Rs.22 cr to provide good education to children. His protective attitudes towards his executives has earned him their unflinching loyalty.[12]

Stories whether lower level employees can rise to the top. Often, these stories describe a person who started out at the bottom and eventually became the CEO.

To be effective as cultural tools, stories must be credible. One cannot tell stories about flat structures and then have parking space reserved for managers. Stories not backed by the reality, can lead to cynism and mistrust. Credible stories prescribe norms for employee behaviour.

Rituals Rituals are everyday organizational practices that are repeated routinely. They help dramatize the organization's culture. They also help achieve desired behaviour from employees and build commonality of culture. Examples include dress of organizational members, how visitors are greeted, how fellow employees are greeted, how often senior executives visit subordinates, how much time employees take for lunch and the like.

Ceremonies Ceremonies are more formal artifacts than rituals Elaborate sets of activities that are enacted time and again on important occasions are known as organizational ceremonies. These occasions provide opportunities to reward and recognise employees whose behaviour is congruent with the values of the company. Ceremonies send a message that individuals who both espouse and exhibit corporate values are heroes to be admired. Examples of ceremonies include cleberating launch of a new contract or newly won contract, publicly rewarding employees and the like.

Language The language of the workplace speaks highly about the organization's culture. Many organizations and units within organizations use language as a way to identify members of a culture or subculture. By learning this language, members attest to their acceptance of the culture and in so doing, help preserve it.

Organizations, overtime, often develop unique terms to describe equipment, offices, key personnel, suppliers, customers, or products that relate to its business. New employees are frequently overwhelmed with acronyms and jargon that, after six months on the job, have become fully part of their language. Once assimilated, this terminology acts as a common denominator that unites members of a given culture or subculture.

It is not that each organization and its subunits have their own language, often each profession develops its own language.

Structures And Symbols The size, shape, location and age of buildings might reveal organization's culture. British Airways has changed its corporate culture by changing its headquarters building. The old multistory headquarters near London's Heathrow Airport reinforced hierarchial and bureaucratic values that the airline wanted to cast off. The new headquarters is designed with a central village square and work units spreading out of it. Executives are located with their units, not cloistered on a separate executive floor.

Inside a building there is a treasure trove of physical artifacts. Desks, chairs, cafeteria food and wall hangings, dress atire are just a few of the things that might convey cultural meaning.

Statement of Principles Yet another artifact of corporate culture is the direct statement of principles. Some organizations have explicitly written principles for all to see. Some other companies make explicit the moral aspects of their culture by *publishing codes of ethics* - specific statements of a company's ethical values. Statement of the type enables the newly hired employees to understand the culture of their organization.

SUSTAINING THE CULTURE

Having created culture, it needs to be kept alive in the organization. There are strategies which organizations employ to sustain their cultures. Such approaches include selecting and socializing employees, actions of founders and leaders, culturally consistent rewards, managing the cultural network and maintaining stable workforce. (see Fig 13.3).

FIGURE 13-3
STRATEGIES FOR SUSTAINING CULTURE

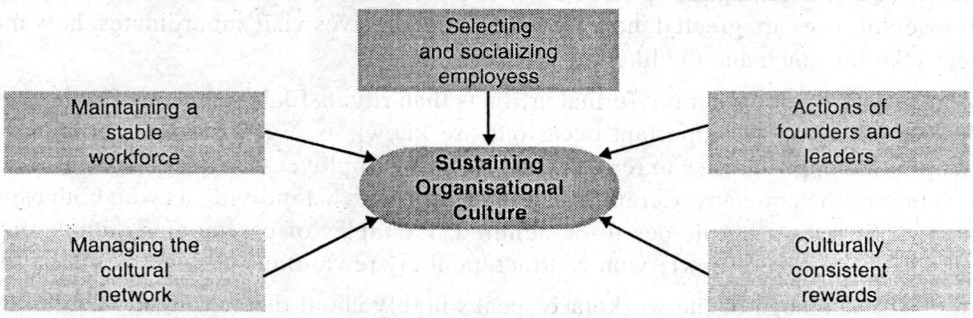

Selecting and Socializing Employees The main purpose of *hiring process* is to hire right people for right jobs. When, for a given job, two or more candidates, with identical skills and abilities are available, final selection is influenced by how well a candidate fits into the organization. By identifying candidates who can jell with the organizational culture, selection helps sustain culture considerably.

Job applicants too look at an organization from its culture perspective before seeking entry in to it. In fact, more than pay and perquisites an organization offers, its cultural artifacts which often attract or detract job seekers.

Along with selecting people with compatible values, companies maintain strong culture through the effective *socialization* of new employees. Organizational socialization refers to the process by which individuals learn the values, expected behaviours, and social knowledge necessary to assume their roles in the organization.

Socialization can be conceptualized as a process made up of three stages: *Pre-arrival*, *encounter* and *metamorphosis*. The first stage encompasses all the learning that occurs before a new member joins the organization. In the second stage, the new employee sees what the organization is really like and confronts the likelihood that expectation and reality diverge. In the third stage, the relatively long lasting changes take place. The new employee masters the skills required for his or her new roles, and makes the adjustment to his or her work group's values and norms.

Actions of Leaders and Founders We have already stated the role of leaders in creating organizational culture. We emphasize that the founders and leaders play a significant role in sustaining organizational culture. Founders are visionaries whose energetic style provides a powerful role model for others to follow. The founder's cultural imprint often remains with the organization for decades. For example, the culture at Microsoft calls for working exceptionally long hours, because that is what the co-founder Bill Gates has always done.

Inspite of the founder's effect, subsequent leaders can break the organization away from the founder's values if they apply the transformational leadership concept described in Chapter 16. Transformation leaders strengthen organizational culture by communicating and enacting their vision of the future. Cultural values are pertinently reinforced when leaders behave in ways that are consistent with the vision.

Culturally Consistent Rewards Reward systems strengthen corporate culture when they are consistent with cultural values. Aggressive cultures might offer more performance-based individual incentives, whereas paternalistic cultures would more likely offer employee assistance programs, medical insurance, and other benefits that support employee well-being.

Managing the Cultural Network Organizational culture is learned, so an effective network of cultural transmission is necessary to strengthen the firm in underlying values and beliefs. The cultural network exists through the organizational grapevine. It is also supported through frequent opportunities for interaction so that employees can share stories and re-enact rituals. Senior executives must tap into the cultural network, sharing their own stories and creating new ceremonies and other opportunities to demonstrate shared meaning. Company magazines and other media can also strengthen organizational culture by communicating cultural values and beliefs more effectively.

Maintaining a Stable Workforce An organization's culture is embedded in the minds of its employees. The director of a B-school in Bangalore was aghast when a retired employee appeared one morning at his (Director's) office and told him that he came to the school because he dreamt about it the previous night. Organizational stories are rarely written down; rituals and celebrations do not usually exist in manuals; organizational metaphors are not found in corporate directories.

Thus, organizations depend on a stable workforce to communicate and reinforce the dominant beliefs and values. The organization's culture can literally disintegrate during periods of high turnover and downsizing because the corporate memory leaves with these employees. Organizational culture also weakens during periods of rapid expansion or mergers because it takes time for incoming employees to learn about and accept the dominant corporate values and beliefs. For this reason, some orghanizations keep their culture intact by moderating employment growth and checking turnover problems.

Effects of Culture

Cultural effects may be both functional, as well as dysfunctional. Talking about the latter, it may be stated that culture leads to groupthink, collective blindspots, and resistance to change and innovation.

As was mentioned earlier, culture makes an organization a clan. The clan form in an industry possesses a few potentially disabling weaknesses. A clan always tends to develop xenophobia, a fear of outsiders. In the words of the President of one major Type Z Company: 'We simply can't bring in an outsider at top levels. We have tried it, but the others won't accept him. We consider that to be one of our biggest problems.' In other ways too, the Type Z resists deviance in all forms. Because the glue that holds it together is consistency of beliefs rather than application of hierarchy, it tends indiscriminately to reject all inconsistency. The trouble is that it is difficult, perhaps impossible, to discriminate in advance between a deviant idea that is useful and adaptive and one that is simply stupid and immoral. Companies such as IBM, General Motors, and Xerox, in which motivation is critical, typically segregate their researchers and those who come up with new product ideas, sometimes locating them on the opposite end of the continent from headquarters in order to shield from the oppressive corporate culture. What happens, of course, is that those scientists indeed become deviant from the mainline culture, develop lots of different ideas, and then discover that the headquarters decision makers reject their ideas as being too deviant.[13]

Another problem from well-knit culture relates to the management of diversity. Strong cultures put considerable pressure on employees to conform. But modern organizations are known for diversity of workforce. Workforce diversity is being accepted and even encouraged. Obviously, there develops conflict between the need for conformity and the advantage of having employees with diverse behaviours and strengths.

Culture acts as a barrier to mergers and acquisitions. Historically, financial matters were alone considered to decide which company should acquire which company or which unit would merge with which firm. In recent years, cultural compatibility has become the primary concern. While a favourable financial statement or product line may be the initial attraction of an acquisition company, whether the acquisition actually works seems to have more to do with how well the cultures of the two organizations match with each other. Where there is a mismatch, acquisitions are likely to fail, as happened to the takeover of Poysha Industries Ltd. by Tinplate Co.of India Ltd. The latter acquired the former in 1991, but the big-brother attitude of the acquirer was too much for the acquired and the marriage broke down in 1994.

On the positive side, culture in an organization serves the following purposes:

- effective control
- promotion of innovation
- strategy formulation and innovation

- strong commitment from employees[14]
- performance and satisfaction.

Effective Control Culture serves as a control mechanism that shapes behaviours of employees. As strong culture seeps through the organization, people register do's (e.g. perform effectively and keep a firm grip on quality) and don'ts (e.g, engage in poor team work or be disrespected to employees). When employees do not act in accordance with the beliefs and values of the culture, managers and colleagues are likely to intervene and initiate corrective actions.

Promotion of Innovation Innovation and creativity are emerging issues in the domain of organizational culture. Both creativity and innovation will be explained in detail in the latter part of this chapter. Suffice it to state now that organizational culture contributes to creativity and innovation by the development of norms that support such a process.

Strategy Formulation and Implementation Organizational culture has considerable influence on strategy formulation and implementation, particularly on the latter. Culture provides inputs to the company to adopt a particular strategy. Motorola's culture, for example, is built around high investment in R&D, quality, and customer care. This culture has bolstered the strategy of the company, providing the impetus for the development of new products-e.g. lightweight cellular telephones and wristwatch pagers-which were hailed as major technological breakthroughs.

Culture energizes people in the company to do their jobs in a strategy-supportive manner and help execute strategies. A culture, where frugality and thrift are values strongly shared by organization members, is conducive to successful execution of a low-cost leadership strategy. Similarly, a culture where creativity, embracing change, and challenging the status quo are pervasive themes, is very conducive to successful implementation of a product innovation and technological leadership strategy. A culture built around such principles as listening to customers, encouraging employees to take pride in their work, and giving employees a high degree of decision-making responsibility, is very conducive to successful execution of a strategy of delivering superior customer service.

What happens when there is a conflict between culture and strategy? Conflict between culture and strategy sends mixed signals to organizational members and forces a choice which is not desirable. Should employees be loyal to the culture and resist actions to pursue the strategy? Or should they go along with the strategy and engage in behaviours that will erode certain valued aspects of the culture? Such conflict weakens commitment of both. To avoid such a possibility, it is advisable to change the culture to fit the strategy. IBM did this when its bureaucratic and mainframe culture clashed with the shift to a PC-dominated world and the emergence of the Internet economy.

Strong Commitment from Employees Culture provides a sense of identity to members and increases their commitment to the organization as told in the opening case. When employees internalize the values of the company, they find their work intrinsically rewarding and identity with their fellow workers. Motivation is enhanced, and morale boosts.

Commitment is said to go through three phases—*compliance, identification*, and *internalization*. With regard to compliance, people conform in order to obtain same material benefit. When they reach the identification stage, the demands of culture are accepted in order to maintain good relationships with colleagues. In the final phase-internalization-people find that the adoption of the cultural values of the organization produces intrinsic satisfaction because these values are in line with their personal values. In many ways, this is an ideal state as far as the acceptance of organizational values is concerned, and, if widespread, is indicative of a strong culture.

Performance and Satisfaction Culture has significant impact on performance. Comparative studies of Japanese and American management methods suggest that the relative success of Japanese companies in the 1980s could be partly explained by their strong organizational cultures emphasizing employee participation, open communication, security, and equality.

Culture has a performance-enhancement quality for at least four reasons. First, as stated above, strategy implementation is made easy through culture. Second, strong culture is characterized by goal alignment; that is all employees share common goal. Third, strong culture creates a high level of motivation because of the values shared by the members. Finally, strong culture provides control mechanism without the oppressive effect of bureaucracy.

That culture contributes to performances needs a rider. Under stable conditions, culture can contribute to enhanced organization performance. However, if the environment is changing, culture can become a liability.

There is correlation between organizational culture and employee satisfaction. But individual needs of employees may moderate the relationship between culture and satisfaction. In general, satisfaction will be the highest when there is a congruence between individual needs and culture. For instance, an organization whose culture would be characterized as low in structure, having loose supervision, and rewarding employees for higher achievement is more likely to have more satisfied employees if those employees have a high achievement need and prefer autonomy. Thus, job satisfaction often varies according to the employees' perception of the culture.

CHANGING ORGANIZATIONAL CULTURE

Culture of an organization needs to be changed, particularly when the company's culture is weak, unhealthy, or when it acts as an obstacle in implementing a new strategy. Culture change should be preceded by diagnosing the existing values and beliefs of the organization. OB experts have developed a number of useful approaches for diagnosing organizational culture. These fall into there different, yet complementary approaches: the behavioural approach, the competing values approach, and the deep assumptions approach.

The behavioural approach This approach emphasizes the surface level of culture-the pattern of behaviours that employees exhibit. This approach provides specific descriptions about how tasks are performed and how interpersonal relations are managed in organizations.

The competing values approach This approach seeks to assess an organization's culture in terms of how it resolves a set of value dilemmas. The approach suggests that an organization's culture can be understood in terms of two important 'Value Pairs', each pair consisting of contradictory values placed at opposite ends of a continuum, as shown Fig.13.4. The two value pairs are (i) internal focus and integration versus external focus and differentiation, and (ii) flexibility and discretion versus stability and control. Organizations continually struggle to satisfy the conflicting demands placed on them by these competing values. For example, when faced with the competing values of internal versus external focus, companies must choose between attending to the integration problems of internal operations and the competitive issues in the external environment. Too much emphasis on the environment can result in neglect of internal efficiencies. Conversely, too much attention to the internal aspects of organization can result in missing important changes in the competitive environment.

The competing values approach provides indications of where an organization's existing values fall along each of the dimensions and quadrants shown in Fig.13.4: clan culture, ad-hocracy culture, hirarchial culture, and market culture. For example, if an organization's values are focused on

FIGURE 13-4
THE COMPETING VALUES APPROACH TO CULTURE

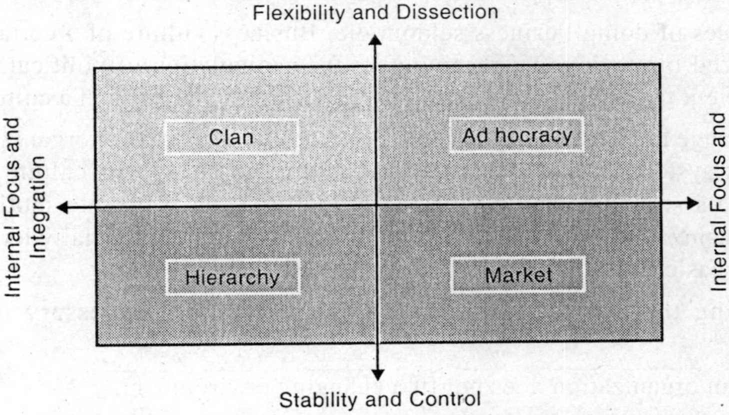

(***Source:*** Thomas G. Cummings, *et. al., Organisational Development and Change,* p. 507)

internal integration issues and emphasize innovation and flexibility, it exhibits a clan culture. On the other hand, a market culture characterizes values that are externally focused and emphasize stability and control.

The Deep Assumptions Approach This approach focuses on the deepest levels of organizational culture-the generally unexamined, but tacit and shared assumptions that guide members' behaviour and which have a powerful impact on employee performance. Diagnosing culture from this perspective typically begins with the most tangible level of awareness and then works down to the deep assumption.

The method operates on the following lines:

An OB expert brings a group of people for a culture workshop, for example, a senior management team or a cross section of managers, old and new members, labour leaders, and staff. The group first brainstorms a range of artifacts, such as behaviours, symbols, language, and physical space arrangements. From this list, the values and norms that would produce such artifacts are deduced. In addition, the values espoused in formal planning documents are listed. Finally, the group attempts to identify the assumptions that would explain the constellation of values, norms, and artifacts.[15]

Difficulties in Changing Having understood the existing culture, the OB expert needs to take steps to change the norms, values, and beliefs. Before doing so, it is advisable to be aware of the difficulties in changing the organizational culture.

It may be stated that those advocating culture change generally focus on more superficial elements, such as norms and artifacts. These elements are easier to change than the deeper elements of values and basic assumptions. We focus on the difficulties faced in changing the deeper elements of culture.

Deeper elements of organizational culture represent assumptions about organizational life which members do not question and have difficulty in envisioning anything else. Besides, members do not want to change their cultural assumptions. The culture provides a strong defence against external uncertainties and threats. It represents past solutions to difficult problems. Members also have vested interests in maintaining the status quo. They may have developed personal stakes, pride, and power in the culture and may strongly resist attempts to change. Further, cultures that provide firms with a competitive advantage may be difficult to replicate, thus making it difficult for less successful firms to change their cultures to approximate the more successful ones.

Age old practices of doing business seldom die. Business culture of a certain community in India is characterized by paying and receiving graft, manipulation of political and bureaucratic authority, and efficient tax dodges. It is extremely difficult to change such a culture.[16]

Finally, any change in culture demands change in the configuration of organizational members, the property rights system, and organizational structure. To change its culture, an organization needs to redesign its structure, and revive the property rights it uses to motivate and reward employees. The organization might also need to change its people, especially its top management team. All these are easier said than done.

Notwithstanding the difficulties, culture change becomes necessary in the following circumstances:

- culture of an organization does not fit a changing environment,
- if the industry is extremely competitive and changes rapidly,
- if the company is mediocre or worse,
- if the organization is about to become a very large one, or
- if the company is smaller and growing rapidly.

Organizations facing these conditions need to change their cultures to adapt to the situations or to operate at higher levels of effectiveness. They may have to attempt or supplement attempts at cultural change with other approaches, such as managing around the existing culture and modifying strategy.

Guidelines for Changing The following practical advice can serve as guidelines for culture change:[17]

(i) *Formulate a clear strategic vision.* Effective culture change should start with a clear vision of the organization's new strategy and of the shared values and behaviours required to make it work. This vision provides the purpose and direction for change in culture. It serves as an yardstick for defining the organization existing culture and for deciding whether proposed changes are consistent with the core values of the organization.

(ii) *Display top management commitment.* Culture change must be managed from the top of the organization. Chief executives and other responsible people should be strongly committed to the new values and need to create constant pressures for change. They must have the staying power to see the changes through.

(iii) *Model culture change at the highest levels.* Senior executives should communicate the new culture through their own actions. Their behaviours need to reflect the kinds of values and actions being sought.

(iv) *Restructure the organization to support the new culture.* Culture change needs supporting modifications in organizational structure, human resource systems, control mechanisms, and leadership styles. These changes can help orient people's behaviours to the new culture.

(iv) *Select and socialize new comers and terminate deviants.* Changing organizational membership is necessary to change corporate culture. People need to be selected and terminated in terms of their consequence with the new culture. This is especially important in key leadership positions, where people's actions can significantly promote or hinder new values, beliefs, and actions.

(vi) *Develop ethical and legal sensitivity* Culture change can ignite tensions between organizational and individual interests, resulting in ethical and legal problems for individual members. Promoting performers, demoting laggards, and terminating deviants lead to ethical and legal problems. Guidelines for minimizing such tensions would be: setting realistic values for culture change and not promising what the organization cannot deliver; providing mechanisms for member dissent and diversity, such as internal review procedures; and educating managers about the legal and ethical pitfalls inherent in culture change and helping them develop guidelines for resolving such issues.

CREATIVITY IN ORGANIZATIONS

As stated earlier, organizational culture promotes creativity and innovation. We propose to examine the two in that order.

Nature of Creativity Creativity refers to the process by which novel but situationally appropriate outcomes are brought about.[18] The essence of creativity is the element of freshness, originality, and novelty that is also appropriate to the context. If a manager gives dictation standing on his head, there is novelty but the act is hardly appropriate. In other words to call anything creative, the act must be unique and appropriate to the context. The social and technological changes that organizations face require creative decisions. Managers of the future need to develop special competencies to deal with the turbulence of change, and one of these important competencies is the ability to promote creativity in organizations.

It is not that creativity is needed now more than ever before. In fact most of the inventions we are enjoying today were discovered hundreds or even thousands of years ago. But business being so complex and competitive now, a firm gains competitive edge if it is creative.

Creativity Process Although it is difficult to describe how people come out with creative ideas, researchers have developed a model that outlines the various stages of the creative process. Specifically, the model, shown in Fig.13.5, specifies that the process of creativity occurs in the following four stages:

Preparation Creative ideas do not come out of thin air. Preparation is an important condition for creativity. Preparation involves developing a clear understanding of what one wants to achieve through a novel solution.

Incubation Incubation is a process of reflective thought and is often conducted subconsciously. During incubation, the individual engages in other pursuits while the mind considers the problem and works on it. Incubation plays a powerful role in dissolving previously held notions about a problem. It does not involve forgetting about the problem or issue; rather it involves putting the problem on the back burner. The problem is still simmering in one's mind, but it is not at the forefront of his or her attention.

Along with dissolving fixed notions of the problem, incubation assists in divergent thinking. Divergent thinking involves reframing the problem in a unique way and generating different approaches to the issue.[19]

Insight Individuals experience insight at some point during the incubation stage. Insight refers to the experience of suddenly becoming aware of a unique idea. These flashes of inspiration do not

FIGURE 13-5
STEPS IN THE CREATIVE PROCESS

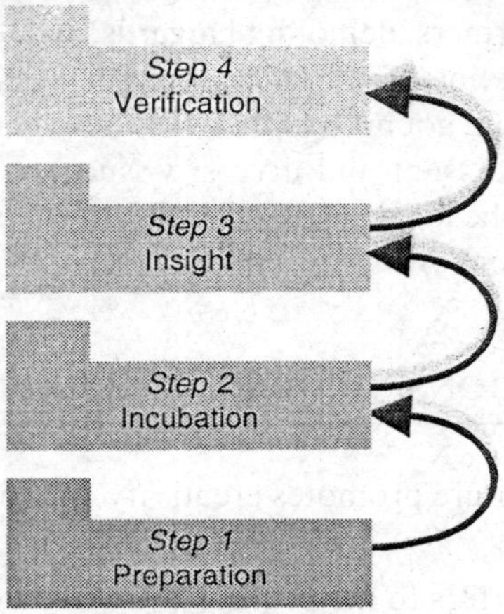

follow any particular schedule; they might come at any time of the day or night. They are also fleeting and can be lost quickly if not documented. With this in mind, many people carry small voice recorders that allow them to capture their ideas before they are lost. Similarly, writers keep diaries, artists keep sketch pads, and lyricists keep tape recorders handy to capture ideas whenever inspiration strikes.

Verification Ideas are generated at the insight-stage. But coming up with ideas is one thing, and verifying whether they are of any value is quite another. Assessing the usefulness of an idea requires consciously thinking about it and subjecting it to evaluation and experimentation. At the verification stage, tenacity may be critical, because other people often resist creative ideas or quickly reject them as impractical.

Although the steps explained above suggest that creative process follows an order, creative insight does not happen in such an orderly or neat fashion. For example, incubation may occur during verification. Besides, the process is often repetitive because initial ideas may be unsatisfactory and require further vision. Also, incubation might very well occur during the verification stage.

Characteristics of Creative Individuals

It is said that creative people possess intellectual and personality characteristics different from their less creative counterparts. Some of the traits of creative people include:

1. A willingness to give up immediate gain to reach long-range goals
2. A great amount of energy
3. An irritation with the status quo
4. Perseverance
5. A pursuit of hobbies and specialized interests
6. A belief that fantasy and daydreaming are not a waste of time[20]
7. Inventive thinking style
8. High intellectual abilities

METHODS OF ENHANCING CREATIVITY

Creative ideas are known to emerge by some kind of mysterious bolt from the blue. Not only Moran, but many people who are considered highly creative have similar experiences.

Nevertheless, OB experts have identified several techniques which help improve creative ability among individuals. One such technique is *brainstorming*. This technique is used to train individuals to be more creative. In a brainstorming session, a group of people are encouraged to exchange ideas freely in an atmosphere characterized by little censorship or criticism when presented with a problem group members try to generate as many *alternative solutions* as they can. At this point, the quality of the ideas is not important, rather sheer number is emphasized. Outlandish ideas are especially encouraged-they may turn out to be creative. Later, the recorded proposals are refined and evaluated.

Another technique which helps promote creativity is *grid analysis.* In this technique, ideas or materials of possible relevance to a problem are listed on two sides of a two-dimensional grid. Then each possible combination of ideas is created and examined for its usefulness as a solution. For example, a marketing firm may be interested in promoting alternative uses for its current products. To uncover such novel uses, they may list their products on the horizontal axis, and target customers or products that they do not manufacture, on the vertical axis. The resulting combinations may suggest new markets for their products, or the possible conversion of their equipment of goods for the manufacture of other products. [21]

Yet another technique of promoting creativity is *lateral thinking,* first developed by De Bono. This technique is designed to help people escape from habitual mind patterns called vertical thinking.

With vertical thinking, each step in the cognitive process follows the previous step in an unbroken sequence; it could be considered rational because only relevant information is considered at each stage. For example, within an organization there are many habitual ways of processing and analysing information based on vertical thinking.

But lateral thinking poses a deliberate and provocative challenge to one's preconceptions. It emphasizes thinking in sideways mode and invites restructuring conventional ways of looking at a problem. For example, a problem could be looked at from the angle of solution, and then go backwards to the beginning of the process and look at it afresh. It is not necessary to be correct at each step of tackling a problem; in fact, one could go down the wrong alleyway, but there could be weird logic in such a deviation because from this vantage point a better pathway may be visible. One could also use what was once considered irrelevant information as a means to arrive at a new way of examining a problem.[22]

CREATIVITY-INDUCING FACTORS

Having techniques to promote creativity is not enough. There needs to be supporting environment and facilities to encourage people search for novel ideas. Following are some of the factors which help induce creativity: (1) creative people, (2) organizational support, (3) organizational culture, (4) diversity, (5) exposure, and (6) sufficient time and resources. (See Fig. 13.6).

Creative people We have stated earlier the characteristics of creative people. Selecting creative people is the starting point in enhancing creativity in organizations.

Organizational support Organizational support to creativity may come in several ways. First, set goals for creativity. For instance, 3M Company has set a goal that 35 per cent of its total revenue

FIGURE 13-6
CONDITIONS FOR CREATIVITY

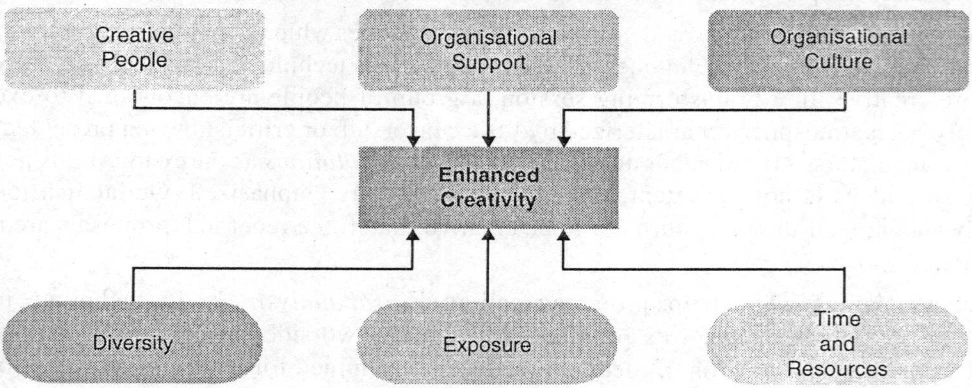

should come from new products developed in the past four years. Second, firms encourage employees to take risks and are prepared to accept the inevitable failures that result from those risks. Corporate leaders allow employees not only to make mistakes, but also encourage them to try out ideas where failure is more than a remote possibility. Third, some companies help employees break out of their shells and become risk-takers. Finally, organizations make jobs intrinsically motivating. Employees tend to be more creative when they believe their work has a significant impact on the organization and/or the larger society.

Organizational culture Openness to new ideas, friendly supervision, team building, participative decision making, flexible organization structures, and the like help promote creative thinking.

Diversity When companies are staffed by people from diverse ethnic and cultural groups, they are bound to think differently about the situations they face. Divergent thinking is a key element in creativity. It is well understood that highly creative ideas emanate from California's Silicon Valley because over one-third of its resident engineers and scientists come from countries outside the US. Many MNCs have realized the benefits of diversity and hence follow a geocentric polity while hiring people.

Exposure Exposing employees to varying kinds of experience, such as foreign assignments, seminars, or extended leaves help enhance creative thinking.

Time and Resources It is no secret that people tend to be more creative when they have adequate funds, material, facilities, information, and time. This requirement does not mean that creativity flourishes in the most lavish work settings. Rather, people simply need enough resources to be able to explore alternatives and test their ideas.

It is not enough to take positive steps to promote creativity. It is also essential to guard against ways which hinder creativity. Table 13.3 contains certain hindrances to creative thinking.

INNOVATION IN ORGANIZATIONS

A creative idea needs to be converted into a product so that it fulfills needs and wants of users. The process of converting a creative idea into a useful product is called innovation. Specifically,

TABLE 13-3
SIXTY-ONE WAYS TO BLOCK CREATIVITY

A good idea but.
Against company policy.
Ahead of the times.
All right in theory.
Be practical.
Can you put it into practice?
Costs too much.
Don't start anything yet.
Have you considered.
I know it won't work.
It can't work.
Too many projects now.
It doesn't fit human nature.
It has been done before.
It needs more study.
It's not budgeted.
It's not good enough.
It's not part of your job.
Let me add to that.
Let's discuss it.
Let's form a committee.
Let's make a survey first.
Let's not step on toes.
Let's put it off for a while.
Let's sit on it for a while.
Let's think it over for a while.
Not ready for it yet.
Of course, it won't work.
Our plan is different.
Some other time.
Surely you know better.
That's not our problem.
The boss won't go for it.
The new people won't understand.
The old timers won't use it.
The timing is off.
The union won't go for it.
There are better ways.
They won't go for it.
Too academic.
Too hard to administer.
Too hard to implement.
Too late.
Too much paperwork.
Too old fashioned.
Too soon.
We have been doing it this way for a long time and it works.
We haven't the manpower.
We haven't the time.
We're too big.
We're too small.
We've never done it that way.
We've tried it before.
What bubble head thought that up?
What will the customers think?
What will the union think?
What you're really saying is.
Who do you think you are?
Who else has tried it?
Why hasn't someone suggested it before if it's a good idea?
You are off base.

(***Source:*** A Dale Timpe, *op.cit*, p.178)

innovation may be defined as the successful implementation of creative ideas within an organization.[23] As may be seen from Table 13.4, some companies are more innovative than others.

Innovative Process

Innovation, like creativity, does not occur in a jiffy. The process is spread over several stages and consumes several months and/or years. There are four stages in the process of innovation (See Fig.13.7). A brief explanation of each stage follows.[24]

Stage one involves setting the agenda for innovation. This involves creating a mission statement- a document describing an organization's overall direction and general goals. Top management should be committed to innovation and motivated to implement the idea.

Stage two sets the stages. At this stage, broad goals are narrowed down into more specific tasks and needed resources are gathered to meet them.

TABLE 13-4

THE MOST INNOVATIVE COMPANIES OF THE TWENTIETH CENTURY

An effective measure of an organization's innovativeness is the number of U.S. patents it holds. Based on this, the following companies may be considered the most innovative companies of the twentieth century.

Rank	Company	Number of Patents
1	General Electric Co.	50,837
2	IBM Corp.	32,498
3	Westinghouse Electric Corp.	28,005
4	AT&T Corp.	24,578
5	General Motors	23,948
6	E.I.Du Pont de Nemours & Co.	23,559
7	Hitachi Ltd.	19,645
8	Eastman Kodak Co.	19,576
9	Canon Kubushiki Kaisha	18,876
10	United States Navy	17,805

(***Source:*** Greenberg and Baron, *Behaviour in Organization,* p.537)

FIGURE 13-7

INNOVATION PROCESS

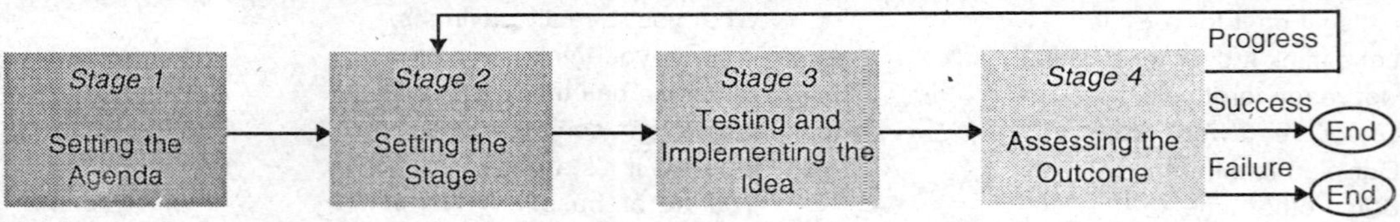

At ***stage three***, the ideas are actually implemented. In other words, life is given to innovation. At ***stage four***, an assessment of the idea is made. What happens to the idea depends on the results of the assessment. Three outcomes are possible. If the resulting idea has been a total success, it will be accepted and carried out in the future. This ends the process. Likewise, the process ends when the idea proves to be a total failure. However, if the new idea shows promise and makes some progress towards the organization's objectives but still has problems, the process is likely to start all over again at stage two.

Case

Changing the Culture of UTC

United Technologies Corporation (UTC) is a $ 21 billion conglomerate composed of six different businesses: Pratt & Whitney (aircraft engines), Otis (elevators), Carrier (air conditioners), Hamilton Standard (aviation systems), Sikorsky (helicopters), and UT (automotive systems). When George David took over as CEO, he found himself in charge of a collection of companies, some of which, like Otis, were performing well, some of which, like Pratt & Whitney, were performing poorly. Indeed, in the early 1990s, Pratt &Whitney was losing over $ 500 million a year. As David started to analyze why some units were performing well and some poorly, he began to realize that at least part of the answer lay in the way the different divisions operated.

Pratt & Whitney was the company's oldest business and had the most prestige in the organization. In the jet aircraft business, it takes many years to develop a new engine, and research and development costs are enormous, often running into the billions. Possessing this long-term research orientation, Pratt & Whitney had gradually developed into a very tall, inflexible organizational structure that was coordinated from the top. The master plan for new engine development was decided by the top-management teams, which then allocated to various teams of design engineers the responsibility for developing specific parts for the new engine. Top managers coordinated the whole project, and over the years this top down, centralized approach had slowed project development. Moreover, middle managers had become internally focused in their part of the project and not externally on the needs of the company's customers - the airlines that provided passenger service. The result was that the company had missed opportunities to develop aircraft engines that suited the needs of airlines in the new deregulated airline industry, which valued fuel efficiency and engines that were easy and cheap to maintain.

David compared this stodgy, conservative operating culture with the way Otis, the division that he had previously been in charge of, operated. At Otis managers' mindset was very different and they had entrepreneurial, quick-moving and customer-driven values. At Otis, managers had to work closely with their customers to understand their specific needs. Every elevator project is different and each elevator must be custom-built for the building in which it is to be placed. Consequently, top managers had decentralized decision making to lower-level managers, empowering the people on the spot to find the best way to despond to each customer's unique needs. This decentralized approach also speeded up decision making and project completion. The division's entrepreneurial values also encouraged managers to experiment with new elevator designs and to search for new kinds of customers, particularly international customers, with the result that Otis had become the largest and most profitable elevator company in the world.

David decided that to increase the profitability of the whole UTC empire he needed to transfer Otis's culture to the other divisions-in particular, to Pratt & Whitney, the loss-making division. In a series of radical moves, David replaced many of Pratt & Whitney top managers with Otis executives, including Karl J. Krapek, who became president. He then slashed Pratt & Whitney's workforce by 40 percent, laying off many middle managers. David then began to empower middle managers and created product development process. These teams were also given the responsibility to liaise with important customers to ensure that the new engines that Pratt & Whitney developed suited the needs of airlines in the 1990s and beyond. David and Krapek's goal is to replace the long-term engineering mindset of Pratt & Whitney's managers with a new customer-driven focus.

Questions

1. Why were the cultures of Pratt & Whitney and the Otis divisions different?
2. How has David tried to change Pratt & Whitney's culture, and what more can he and Krapek do?[25]

QUESTIONS

1 Define organizational culture. Trace and explain the various cultural dimensions.
2 How is organizational culture created and sustained?
3 Bring out the positives and negatives of organizational culture.
4 What are the obstacles to change organizational culture? How can change be brought about?
5 What is creativity? Explain the process of creativity.
6 How can creativity be enhanced in organizations?
7 What is innovation? Explain the process of innovation.
8 Do academic institutions have different organizational cultures? In what ways might these cultures be said to differ?
9 Have you ever worked for an organization whose culture is in need of a change? If so, what were the problems? What could have been done to change the culture?
10 Name a company with a distinct culture. What do you think are the company's values? Has the culture contributed to organization's performance? Explain.

REFERENCE

1. Gary Dessler, *Managing Organizations,* The Dryden Press, 1995, Pp. 394-395.
2. Ralph H. Kilman, *et.al., Issues in Understanding and Changing Culture,* California Management Review, 1986, p.89.
3. Stephen P. Robbins, *Organizational Behaviour,* Prentice Hall of India, 1991 p. 579
4. Pradip N. Khandwalla, *Organizational Design for Excellence,* Tata McGraw Hill, 1992, p. 9.
5. Ibid, p. 11.
6. Ibid, p.12.
7. Eugene McKenna, *Business Psychology and Organisational Behaviour,* Psychology Press Co. 2000, p. 472.
8. Ibid, p.473.
9. Gareth R. Jones, *Organizational Theory,* Pearson Education, 1993, p. 192.
10. Ibid, p. 197.
11. Debra L. Nelson and James Campbell Quick, *Organizational Behaviour-Foundations, Realities and Challenges,* 4th Edn, Thomson, 2003, p. 541.
12. Gita Piramal, *Business Maharajas,* Viking, 1996, p. 232.
13. William Ouchi, *Theory Z,* Addision Weseley Pub. Co., 1981, p.88.
14. Eugene McKenna, *Op. cit.*, p. 484.
15. Thomas G. Cummings, *et.al., Organisation Development and Change,* Thomson, 2002, p.505.
16. Pradip Chanda, *The Second Coming,* Tata McGraw-Hill, 2000, p. 150.
17. J.Burrey, *Organisational Culutre: Can it be a Source of Sustained Competitive Advantage*, Academy of Management Review, 1986, p.70.
18. Pradip N. Khandwalla, *Corporate Creativity,* Tata McGraw-Hill Pub. Co., 2003, p.4.

19. Steven L. Mcshane and Mary Ann Von Glinow, *Organizational Behaviour,* Tata McGraw-Hill, 2003, p.296.
20. Robert P. Vecchio, *Organisational Behaviour,* The Dryden Press, 1995, p.418.
21. Ibid, p. 421.
22. Eugene McKenna, *Op.cit.*, p. 241
23. Jerald Greenberg and Robert A. Baron, *Behaviour in Organisations,* Prentice Hall of India, 2003, p. 536.
24. Ibid, p. 538.
25. Gareth R. Jones, *Op.cit.,* p. 160.

CHAPTER

Fourteen

International Organisational Behaviour

LEARNING OBJECTIVES

After reading this chapter you should understand that —

1. The trends in IB.
2. How Culture influences employee behaviour and impact of norms, values, and beliefs varies across countries.
3. The need for customizing OB practices.
4. The Individual behaviour across cultures.
5. The important areas of interpersonal behaviours.
6. How technological advancement makes organization designs across cultures similar.

Trends in International Business

The world has entered an era of unprecedented global economic activity, including world -wide production, distribution, and increasingly large number of international joint ventures, multinational mergers and acquisitions, and global strategic alliances. Examples of new global operations and alliances abound, with most major firms earning more from their international operations than from domestic markets. MNCs such as ABB, Honda, British Petroleum, Siemens, Motorola, and Eastman Kodak each do business in more than 50 countries. The assets of most MNCs are owned by different nationalities and their employees hail from different countries (see Table 14.1). The post-World War II years saw a major expansion of world trade. From 1948 through 1972, world exports grew from $ 51 billion to $ 415 billion, representing a sevenfold increase in monetary terms and a fourfold increase in volumes. By 1980, international imports exceeded $ 1 trillion as compared with $ 800 billion in 1975. In the 1990s world exports grew from $4.3 trillion in 1990 to $7.1 trillion in 1999, an increase of 66 per cent.

Thus, the modern business enterprise has no place to hide. It has no place to go but everywhere.[1]

Cultural Differences and Similarities

The discussion in this chapter centres around the behaviour of people in organizational settings against an international perspective. We, therefore, focus on cross-cultural impact on employee behaviour. Four generalizations can be made in this context: (1) behaviour across cultures, (2) culture determines behaviour, (3) cultural clusters, and (4) cultural diversity.

Behaviour Across Countries

Behaviour in organizational settings varies across cultures. Human resource practices, too, vary across cultures. Here are some representatives examples.[2]

(a) The concept of an hourly wage plays a minor role in Mexico. Labour law requires that employees receive full pay for 365 days a year.

(b) In Australia and Brazil, employees with one year of service are automatically given 30 days of paid vacation.

(c) In Japan, remuneration levels are determined using the objective factors of age, length of service, and educational background rather than skill, ability, and performance. Performance does not count until after an employee reaches 45 years of age.

(d) In the UK, employees are allowed up to 40 weeks of maternity leave, and employers must provide a government mandated amount of pay for 18 of those weeks. In India, a woman employee is entitled for full wages during the previous six weeks and the subsequent six week period of pregnancy, and the employer is bound to pay the amount.

(e) In 87 per cent of large Swedish companies, the heads of human resources are on the board of directors.

The differences are glaring in performance appraisal-a sensitive area in OB. The experience of Shell Oil is worth recollecting in this context.[3] The head office of the MNC had established the

TABLE 14-1

WHO OWNS THE MOST IN FOREIGN COUNTRIES?

Rank	Company	Country	Industry	Assets ($ billion)		Total	Foreign
				Total	Foreign	Employees	Employees(%)
1	Royal Dutch Shell	United Kingdom Netherlands	Petroleum	102.0	63.7	106,000	75
2	Ford	United States	Motor vehicles	219.4	60.6	337,778	29
3	Exxon	United States	Petroleum	87.9	56.2	86,000	64
4	General Motors	United States	Motor vehicles	198.6	51.6	692,800	26
5	IBM	United States	Computers	81.1	43.9	219,839	53
6	Volkswagen	Germany	Motor vehicles	52.4	NA	242,318	40
7	General Electric	United States	Electronics	251.5	33.9	216,000	17
8	Toyota	Japan	Motor vehicles	116.8	32.8	172,675	16
9	Daimler-Benz	Germany	Transport Communication	66.5	27.9	330,551	24
10	Elf Aquitaine	France	Petroleum	48.9	27.7	89,500	49
11	Mobil	United States	Petroleum	41.5	26.2	58,500	47
12	Mitsubishi	Japan	Diversified	109.3	NA	36,000	31
13	Nestle	Switzerland	Food	38.7	25.4	212,687	97
14	Nissan Motor	Japan	Motor vehicles	80.8	NA	143,310	24
15	ABB	Switzerland	Electronic equipments	29.1	24.8	207,557	94
16	Matsushita Electric	Japan	Electronics	92.2	NA	265,397	42
17	Roche Holdings	Switzerland	Pharmaceuticals	25.9	23.4	61,381	83
18	Alcatel Alsthom	France	Electronics	51.2	23.1	197,000	59
19	Sony	Japan	Electronics	47.6	NA	156,000	58
20	Fiat	Italy	Motor vehicles	59.1	22.5	251,333	38
21	Bayer	Germany	Chemicals	27.4	22.4	146,700	53
22	Hitachi	Japan	Electronics	92.5	22.2	331,852	24
23	Unilever	United Kingdoms/ Netherlands	Food	28.4	22.0	307,000	90
24	Philips	Netherlands	Electronics	27.8	NA	253,000	83
25	Siemens	Germany	Electronics	50.6	21.2	376,000	42

(***Source:*** Adapted from data in UNCTAD 1996)

criteria to be used for appraisal in its subsidiaries. But the prioritization of the criteria was left to the subsidiaries. As a result, the outcome of the evaluations could be quite different from country to country, because what was regarded as the most important criterion in one subsidiary might be ranked much lower on the evaluation list of another. The MNC actually used the HAIRL system of appraisal. The five criteria in this acronym stood for: (a) Helicopter- the capacity to take a broad view from above; (b) Analysis - the ability to evaluate situations logically and completely; (c) Imagination- the ability to be creative and think outside the box; (d) Reality- the ability to use information realistically; and (e) Leadership - the ability to effectively galvanize and inspire personnel. When Shell's subsidiaries were asked to prioritize these five criteria from top to bottom, the results were as follows:

Netherlands	*France* .	*Germany*	*Britain*
Reality	Imagination	Leadership	Helicopter
Analysis	Analysis	Analysis	Imagination
Helicopter	Leadership	Reality	Reality
Leadership	Helicopter	Imagination	Analysis
Imagination	Reality	Helicopter	Leadership.

Obivously, employees in different subsidiaries were being evaluated differently.

Culture Determines Behaviour

Culture is an important factor for variations in behaviour. True, there are other factors like differing standards of living and varied geographical conditions which can cause variations in behaviour, but culture is the determining factor. To elaborate on this statement, let us begin with the nature of culture. Culture may be understood as the pervasive and shared beliefs, norms, and values that guide the everyday life of individuals. These beliefs, norms, and values are passed on to future generations through cultural rituals, stories, and symbols.

Cultural norms prescribe behaviours and practices. That is, they tell us what we can do and what we cannot. For example, norms prescribe when and whom we can marry, and what clothes we can or cannot wear to a function or to the office.[4]

Cultural values tell us what is most dear to our hearts. Fig. 14.1 shows the cultural values of three representative countries.

FIGURE 14-1
CULTURAL CONTRASTS IN VALUE

Americans	Japanese	Arabs
1. Freedom	1. Belonging	1. Family security
2. Independence	2. Group harmony	2. Family harmony
3. Self-reliance	3. Collectiveness	3. Parental guidance
4. Equality	4. Age/Seniority	4. Age
5. Individualism	5. Group consensus	5. Authority
6. Competition	6. Cooperation	6. Compromise
7. Efficiency	7. Quality	7. Devotion
8. Time	8. Patience	8. Very patient
9. Directness	9. Indirectness	9. Indirectness
10. Openness	10. Go between	10. Hospitality
11. Aggressiveness	11. Interpersonal	11. Friendship
12. Informality	12. Hierarchy	12. Formal/Admiration
13. Future-orientation	13. Continuation	13. Past and present
14. Risk-taking	14. Conservative	14. Religious belief
15. Creativity	15. Information	15. Tradition
16. Self-accomplishment	16. Group achievement	16. Social recognition
17. Winning	17. Success	17. Reputation
18. Money	18. Relationship	18. Friendship
19. Material possessions	19. Harmony with nature	19. Belonging
20. Privacy	20. Networking	20. Family network

(*Source:* Farid Elashmawi, et al, *Multi-cultural Management,* p.63)

Americans, for example, value freedom most - freedom to choose one's own destiny- whether it leads to success or failure . Japanese culture, on the other hand, finds a higher value; in belonging; one must belong to and support a group in order to survive. Belonging to a group is more important than individualism. Arab culture on the other hand is less concerned with individualism or group-belonging, concentrating instead on their own family security and relying on god for destiny. Individual identity is usually based on the background and position of each person's family.[5]

Cultural symbols, stories, and rituals It is important to communicate the norms, values, and beliefs of a society or a group to its members. Culture is passed from one generation to another through its symbols, stories, and rituals. Culture is continuously reinforced when people see symbols, hear stories, and engage in rituals.

Another key feature of culture is that cultural values, norms, and beliefs are shared by a group of people. The group must accept that these norms, values, and beliefs are by and large correct and compelling. This means that although people in any culture do not have the same way all the time, culture makes behaviour predictable most of the time. Marriage in India, for example, makes a woman wear certain things like *mangala sutra* which a married female in Western or American culture is not expected to do so.

Cultural values also have a major influence on the way people relate to each other and also to what they aspire for in a job. In many hierarchical cultures (e.g., India, Japan, etc), the meaning and value of a job lies more in the status than in the pay packet. In these cultures, people also expect recognition for their seniority and age. On the other hand, in more egalitarian cultures (e.g., US, Germany, etc.), people expect reward and compensation for their performance rather than for their seniority.

That culture influences behaviour and human resource practices is stating only part of the story. Its impact stretches beyond and determines the type of business a society engages in. For example, French culture is known for its emphasis on elegance, elitism, and concern for form. Not only does this get reflected in its 1200 museums, its 5000 varieties of wine (which are classified, like the French society, from superior to ordinary table wine), more than 50,000 drama performances per year, but also in the fact that France has always been the capital of fashion industry.

On the other hand, Mexican culture is known fort its 'pro-death' values. Mexicans celebrate the *Day of the Dead*, have folk art forms which feature skeletons, adorn the graves as a work of art, and even have a popular magazine called La Calavera (meaning The Skeleton)! Not surprisingly, life insurance is not a flourishing business in Mexico. In the mid-1990s, less than 20 per cent of the employed population had life insurance cover, and the insurance premium formed just about 1.5 per cent of the GDP (as compared to 5.5 per cent in Brazil, and close to 9 per cent in the U.S).

Besides, the cultural values of the society define the meaning and reason of business and how it is organized. In many cultures, high profits and market capitalization are not criteria for doing business. In many Arab and Latin countries (e.g., Italy, Spain, Latin American countries, Saudi Arabia, etc.) the business firm is seen as an extension of the family and family honour comes before profits. Similarly, in France, business firms are culturally seen as social institutions which uphold national pride.

Such cultural differences have a direct impact on the strategic orientation of companies across cultures. For instance, one study of comparison between the financial and strategic focus of US and Japanese companies found that while US companies emphasized more on profits, dividends, and stock prices, the Japanese companies focused more on new product development and market share.

The cultural values also influence how the business is organized and conducted in a society. In collective societies (e.g., China, Saudi Arabia, Spain, etc.), for instance, personal contacts play an important role in conducting business. The guanxi (meaning interpersonal relationships) system in China encourages people to conduct business based on personal relationships. This is in sharp contrast to more individualistic societies where personal relationships are deliberately kept away from professional relationships.

Similarly, consider the *keiretsu* of Japan. A keiretsu (e.g., Sanwa group, Mitsubishi group, Mitsui group, etc.) normally consists of a network of trading companies, manufacturing companies, banks, insurance companies, and many satellite manufacturing units. What binds them together are a number of business linkages, such as interlocking shareholding, intra-group loans, and intra-group trade. The close- knit nature of the keiretsu helps the group to avoid hostile takeover, share knowledge, avoid redundancies by reallocating people within the group, keep prices in control through preferential buying, and so on. The structure and working of keiretsu clearly reflect the Japanese values of collectivism and interdependence.

Cultural Clusters

Though cultures across countries vary, there are similarities nevertheless. To the extent that there are similarities, the need to customize products to meet local demands is minimized. Countries that share cultural similarities form *cultural clusters.* Not that a cultural cluster does not have differences, but the similarities are predominant. Fig.14.2 shows certain cultural clusters, which is on the basis of language similarities.

FIGURE 14-2
CULTURAL CLUSTERS

Anglo	Nordic	Germanic	Latin American	Latin European
Australia	Denmark	Austria	Argentina	Belgium
Canada	Finland	Germany	Chile	France
Ireland	Norway	Switzerland	Colombia	Italy
New Zealand	Sweden		Mexico	Portugal
South Africa			Peru	Spain
UK			Venezuela	
USA				
Near Eastern	**Arab**	**Far Eastern**	**Independent**	
Greece	Abu Dhabi	Hong Kong	Brazil	
Iran	Bahrain	Indonesia	India	
Turkey	Kuwait	Malaysia	Israel	
Portugal	Oman	Philippines	Japan	
Spain	Saudi Arabia	Singapore		
	UAE	Taiwan		
		Thailand		
		Vietnam		

(***Source:*** Adapted from *International Business* by Darrell Mahoney, *et al*, p.384)

International businesses utilize the culture-clustering approach in formulating their global strategies. Many firms from New Zealand focus their first exporting efforts on Australia. Hong Kong firms have been very successful in exploiting China's markets. Canadian firms are more comfortable working with British partners than are Japanese firms.[6]

Improvements in communication and transportation have made clustering possible. Thanks to cable and satellite TV, people in different parts of the world watch and enjoy the same entertainment programmes and serials. Lower airfares generated by increased airline competition mean that more tourists can learn firsthand about other cultures. MNCs facilitate this process of *cultural convergence*, for better or for worse, through their advertisements that define appropriate lifestyles, attitudes, and goals and by bringing new management techniques, technologies, and cultural values to the countries in which they operate.

HOFSTEDE'S CULTURAL DIMENSIONS

In a discussion on cultural clusters, reference should be made to the pioneering work done by Dutch scientist Geert Hofstede. He identified four cultural dimensions around which countries have been clustered with people in each group exhibiting identical behaviours. The four dimensions are: power distance, uncertainty avoidance, individualism, and masculinity.

Power Distance Power distance is the extent to which less powerful members of institutions and organizations accept that power is distributed unequally.[7] Countries in which people blindly obey the orders of superiors have high power distance.

High power distance countries have norms, values and beliefs such as-

- inequality is fundamentally good,
- every one has a place; some are high, some are low,
- most people should be dependent on a leader,
- the powerful are entitled to privileges, and
- the powerful should not hide their power.

The dimension of power distance can be measured in a number of ways. For example, the basic motivational assumption in high power distance countries is that people dislike work and try to avoid it. Consequently, managers believe that they must adopt Theory X leadership style, that is, they must be authoritarian, must force workers to perform, and must supervise their subordinates closely.

Organizational structures and systems tend to match the assumption regarding leadership and motivation. In high power distance countries, decision making is centralized. Those at the top make most of the decisions. Organizations tend to have tall structures. They will have a large proportion of supervisory personnel, and the people at the lower levels often will have low job qualifications. Such structures encourage and promote inequality between people at different levels. On the other hand, organizations in low power distance countries tend to be decentralized and have flatter structures. They will have a smaller proportion of supervision personnel and the lower state of workforce will consist of highly qualified people.

The US, Austria, Ireland, Norway, and New Zealand represent cultures with low power distance. France, India, Singapore, Brazil, Mexico, and Indonesia are examples of societies with a high power distance.

Uncertainty Avoidance Uncertainty avoidance is the extent to which people feel threatened by ambiguous situations, and have created beliefs and institutions that try to avoid these. There are countries with high uncertainty avoidance and there are those characterized by low uncertainty avoidance. Denmark and Great Britain are examples for a low uncertainty avoidance culture. Germany, Japan, and Spain typify high uncertainty avoidance societies.

Countries with citizens who do not like uncertainty tend to have a high need for security and a strong belief in experts and their knowledge. Countries with low uncertainty avoidance have people who are more willing to accept that risks are associated with the unknown, and that life must go on in spite of this.[8]

Specifically, high uncertainty avoidance countries are characterized by norms, values, and beliefs which accept that:

- Conflict should be avoided,
- Deviant people and ideas should not be tolerated,
- Laws are very important and should be followed,
- Experts and authorities are usually correct, and
- Consensus is important.

Obviously, low uncertainty avoidance societies tend to represent the antonym of the above characteristics.

The effect of uncertainty avoidance has several manifestations. Countries with high uncertainty avoidance cultures have a great deal of structuring of organizational activities, more written rules, less risk-taking by managers, low labour turnover, and less ambitious employees.

Low uncertainty avoidance societies have organization settings with less structuring of activities, fewer written rules, more risk-taking by managers, higher labour turnover, and more ambitious employees. The organization encourages employees to use their initiative and assume responsibility for their actions.

Individualism Individualism is the tendency of people to look after themselves and their family only. Opposite of this is collectivism which refers to the tendency of people to belong to groups and to look after each other in exchange for loyalty. Individualism is common in the US, Canada, Australia, Denmark, and Sweden. The people of Indonesia, Pakistan, and a number of South American countries exhibit collectivism.

Specifically, countries high on individualism have norms, values, and beliefs which accept that:

- People are responsible for themselves,
- Individual achievement is ideal, and
- People need not be emotionally dependent on organizations or groups.

In contrast, collectivist countries believe that:

- One's identity is based on one's group membership,
- Group decision making is best, and
- Groups protect individuals in exchange for their loyalty to the group.

The effects of individualism/collectivism can be seen in organizations also. Organizations in collectivist societies tend to promote nepotism in selecting managers. In contrast, in individualistic societies, favouritism shown to friends and relatives is considered to be unfair and even illegal. Further, organizations in collectivist cultures base promotions mostly on seniority and age, whereas in individualist societies they are based on one's performance. Finally, in collectivist cultures, important decisions are made by older senior managers as opposed to individualist cultures, where decision making is an individual responsibility.

Masculinity Masculinity refers to a situation in which the dominant values in a society are success, money, and other material things. Hofstede measured this dimension on a continuum ranging from masculinity to femininity.

High masculine cultures have norms, values, and beliefs that:[9]

- Gender roles should be clearly distinguished,
- Men are assertive and dominant,
- Machismo or exaggerated maleness is good,
- People—especially men-should be decisive,
- Work takes priority over other duties, such as family, and
- Advancement, success, and money are important.

In highly masculine societies, jobs are clearly defined by gender. There are men's jobs and women's jobs. Men usually choose jobs that are associated with long-term careers. Women usually choose jobs that are associated with short-term employment, before marriage.

Cultural Diversity-Source of Energy Cultural diversity can be an important source of energy in enhancing organizational effectiveness. More and more organizations are realizing the virtues of cultural diversity, but surprisingly little do they know how to manage it. Organizations that adopt a multinational strategy can become more than a sum of their parts. Operations in each culture can benefit from operations in other cultures through an enhanced understanding of how the world looks and works.

We divide the remaining part of this chapter into three sections: individual behaviour in the global context, group or interpersonal behaviour in an international environment, and organization structure in a cross-country perspective.

Individual Behaviour in the Global Perspective

As stated above, individual behaviour varies across cultures. These variations can be studied in terms of motivation, rewards, cultural adjustment, and managerial responses.

Motivation Across Cultures

We studied the nature, importance, and theories of motivation in Chapter 9. Here, we focus on motivation of employees in international settings.

In a multicultural work environment, not everyone is motivated by the same factors. Motivational procsses, approaches, and applications reflect the culture of the country directly or indirectly. Motivational appeals, rewards for performance, and punishment for the absence of it need to be culture-specific.

Table 14.2 shows the motivational approaches and cultural factors for three distinct cultures: American, Japanese, and Arab.[10]

Management Styles Management styles are important and effective motivators in each culture. American styles are characterized by professionalism and friendliness. Japanese managers motive employees through continuous counsel and persuasion. The Arab manager will be most effective in a parenting-type role that includes coaching and personal attention.

TABLE 14-2
CULTURAL CONTRASTS IN MOTIVATION

	American	*Japanese*	*Arab*
Management Styles	Leadership; Friendliness	Persuasion; Functional group activities	Coaching; Personal attention; Parenthood
Control	Independence; Decision-making; Space, Time, Money	Group harmony	Of others/parenthood
Emotional Appeal	Opportunity	Group participation; Company success	Religion; Nationalistic; Admiration
Recognition	Individual contribution	Group identity; Belonging to group	Individual status; Class/society; Promotion
Material Awards	Salary; Commission; Profitsharing	Annual bonus; Social services; Fringe benefits	Gift for self/family; Family affair; Salary increase
Threats	Loss of job	Out of group	Demotion
Cultural Values	Competition; Risk-taking; Material possession; Freedom	Group harmony; Achievement; Belonging	Reputation; Family security; Religion; Social status

(***Source:*** Farid Elashmawi, *et al, op.cit,* p.144)

In India:-

- Employees of MNCs are paid much more than their counterparts in host countries for identical work.
- Different industries have different wage and salary structures resulting in disparities in remuneration for identical work.
- Wide gaps exist between wages and salaries of employees in the organized sector and of those in the unorganized sector, the latter earning much less than the former.
- Differences exist between earnings of employees in the government sector and those in the private sector.
- Within the government sector, salary differences exist among employees of different departments.

The area of international compensation is complex primarily because MNCs must cater for three categories of employees: parent country nationals (PCNs), third country nationals (TCNs), and host country nationals (HCNs). The key components of multinational compensation include base salary, foreign service inducement/ hardship programmes, allowances, and benefits.

Base salary is the foundation block for international compensation. Other compensation components are linked to the base salary. Foreign service inducement generally forms a percentage of base pay. Such payment varies, depending upon the assignment, actual hardship, tax consequences, and length of assignment.

Allowances include cost of living allowance, housing allowance, home leave allowance, education allowance, relocation allowance, and spouse assistance. Benefits cover such schemes as pension plans, medical coverage, social security benefits, vacations and special leave, airfares, rest and rehabilitation leave, emergency provisions in case of death or illness, and the like.

Control All people are motivated by the power of being in control of their own lives or work space. Americans feel good about being independent and in control of their own destinies. Japanese motivation comes through group harmony and consensus. Whereas the Arab manager strives for control of others through a parenting relationship.

Emotional Appeal Americans respond to available opportunity. Sentiments may not evoke response. The Japanese are motivated by reputation and company success, which are allied with their cultural values of belonging and group achievement. Arab motivation comes from an appeal to the sense of self within the authority structure.

Recognition Americans want to be directly recognized for their individual contributions and achievements. Japanese recognition comes through identification with the group. Recognition in Arab cultures generally results from the individual's status in the hierarchy. When a department reaches its goal, the recognition will first go to the head and then percolate down to the lowest level employees.

Material Reward The American rewards that are culturally appropriate reflect the values of the macro culture. Americans measure individual success more in terms of material possessions. Monetary rewards motivate Americans. The Japanese are motivated by rewards shared among the group, such as bonuses, social services, and fringe benefits available to group members. Arabs are motivated by gifts for the individual and family, which reflect admiration or appreciation for the individual's achievement.

Threats Threats motivate people for the wrong reasons. Since the Americans' identities are often directly linked to their jobs, the threat of being fired is significant to them. For the Japanese, the greatest threat is the fear of exclusion from the group. To the Arab, a demotion is a threat to one's reputation and status.

Cultural Values As stated earlier, motivational tools and processes reflect each unique culture. In the American culture, competition, risk-taking, material possessions, self-reliance, and freedom are all motivational values. In contrast, group harmony, belonging, and achievement are important and valued tools in motivation of Japanese employees. The Arab workers value reputation, authority, and social status and respond to these values in their motivation process.

Compensation Across Cultures

Compensation includes wages and salaries, incentives such as bonuses, and pension benefits. There are wide variations both among countries and among organizations within countries, concerning how to compensate employees. A country's economic development, cultural traditions, legal institutions, government policies, and the role of labour unions all affect compensation. Consider the following examples:[11]

- Japanese workers earn over three times the wages of the workers in the other East Asian countries such as Taiwan, Singapore, and Korea.
- Although not required by law, Korean and Japanese workers expect significant bonuses at least twice a year.
- In Denmark, over 80 per cent of employees belong to unions, and agreements between unions and employees' associations determine minimal and normal pay.
- In Germany, there is a statutory minimum of eighteen paid holidays a year. Also consider the following:[12]

The model shown in Fig.14.3 helps the multinational manager in solving the issue relating to international compensation.

FIGURE 14-3
THREE SETS OF COMPENSATION

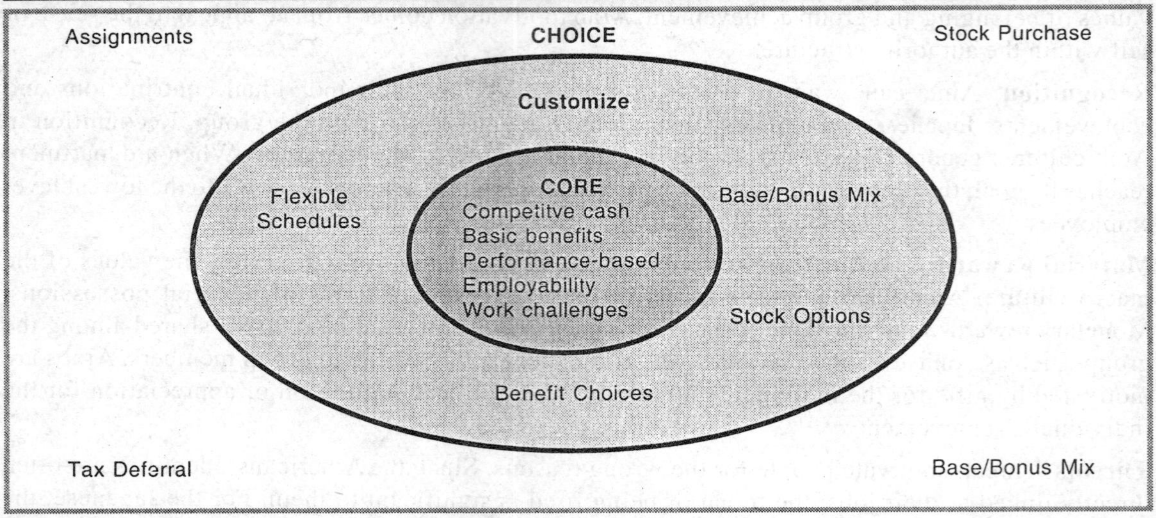

(***Source:*** Peter J.Dowling et al, *International Human Resources Management*, p.199)

The model (Fig.14.3) clubs forms of total compensation into three sets: core, crafted, and choice. Specific practices in the *core* section may vary according to market and local conditions. The *crafted set* of compensation elements assume that regional managers have discretion to choose from a menu of compensation forms, while alternatives in the *choice* set offer flexibility for employees to select among various forms of compensation.[13]

Cultural Adjustment

The process of cultural adjustment is a critical determinant of expatriate (an individual who lives and works away from his/her home country) performance. Adjustment to a foreign culture is multifaceted, and individuals vary in terms of their reactions and coping behaviours.

The concept of an adjustment cycle or curve (popularly called the U curve), depicted in Fig. 14.4 is helpful in demonstrating the typical phases that may be encountered during cultural adjustment. The curve is based on psychological reactions to the overseas assignments and comprises four phases.

Phase 1 begins with reactions prior to the assignment-the expatriate may experience a range of positive and negative emotions such as excitement, anxiety, fear of the unknown, sense of adventure, and so on. There can be an upswing of mood upon arrival in the assignment country that produces what has been referred to as the 'honeymoon' or 'tourist' phase. Then, as the novelty wears off, realities of every day life in the alien land begin to unfurl, homesickness sets in, and a downswing may commence-a feeling that 'the party is over', which can create negative appraisals of the situation and location leading to a period of crisis **(phase 2)**. This can be a critical time, and how the expatriate copes with the psychological adjustment at this phase has an important outcome in terms of success

FIGURE 14-4
THE PHASES OF CULTURAL ADJUSTMENT

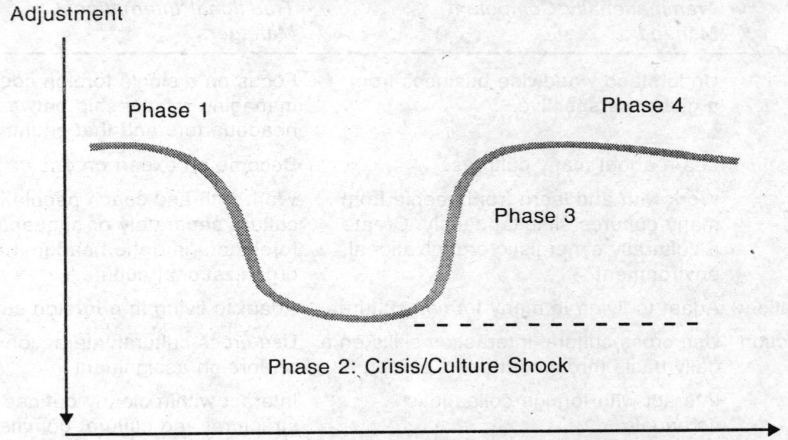

(*Source:* Peter J.Dowling, *op.cit*, p.133)

or failure. There is a suggestion that 'failure as an early recall' may be triggered at this point (indicated by the dotted line in Fig.14.4). Once the individual passes this crisis point, as he or she comes to terms with the demands of the new environment, there is an upswing **(phase 3)** as the person begins to adjust to the new environment. This levels off over time to what has been described as healthy recovery **(phase 4)**[14]

The bottom of the U-shaped curve (Fig.14.4) is marked by *culture shock* which is the expatriate's reaction to a new, unpredictable, and therefore, uncertain environment. Culture shock is not a disease, but rather a natural response to the stress of immersing oneself in the new environment. Severe culture shock is often a positive sign indicating that the expatriate is becoming deeply involved in the new culture instead of remaining isolated in an expatriate ghetto.[15]

Managerial Responses

Managerial responses vary across cultures. Specific behaviours depend upon the attitudes managers hold about employees. Three primary attitudes can be distinguished in this context: ethnocentric, polycentric, and geocentric. *Ethnocentric managers* perceive foreign countries and their people as inferior to those of the home country. These managers believe that the practices of the home country are the best. A *polycentric manager* sees all countries as different and hard to understand. Such managers tend to leave their foreign offices alone, believing that local managers are most likely to understand their own needs. *Geocentric managers* recognize similarities as well as differences among countries. Such managers attempt to draw on the most effective techniques and practices, wherever they originate.

Managerial responses are also shaped by the culture of the land. Managers in Japan, for instance, strongly believe that a manager should be able to answer any question he or she is asked. Thus, they place a premium on expertise and experience. In contrast, Swedish managers have the least concern for knowing all the answers. They view themselves as problem solvers and facilitators who make no claim to omnipotence.

TABLE 14-3
TRANSNATIONLLY COMPETENT MANAGERS

Transnational Skills	*Transnationally Competent Managers*	*Traditional International Managers*
Global perspective	Understand worldwide business from a global perspective.	Focus on a single foreign country and on managing relationship between headquarters and that country.
Local responsiveness	Learn about many cultures.	Become an expert on one.
Synergistic learning	Work with and learn from people from many cultures simultaneously. Create a culturally synergistic organizational environment.	Work with and coach people in each foreign culture separately or sequentially. Integrate foreigners into the headquarter's national organizational culture.
Transition and adaptation	Adapt to living in many foreign cultures.	Adapt to living in a foreign culture.
Cross-cultural interaction	Use cross-cultural interaction skills on a daily basis throughout one's career.	Use cross-cultural interaction skills primarily on foreign assignment.
Collaboration	Interact with foreign colleagues as equals.	Interact within clearly defined hierarchies of structural and cultural dominance.
Foreign experience	Transpatriation for career and organization development.	Expartriation or inpatriation primarily to get the job done.

(Source: Nancy J.Adler and Susan Bartholomew. 'Managing Globally Competent People', *Academy of Management Executive,* August 1992).

Managerial behaviour is rapidly changing, particularly among European managers. In general, these managers are becoming career-oriented, better educated, more willing to work co-operatively with labour, more willing to delegate, and also more cosmopolitan.

Finally managers in the international environment need different competencies and skills, as shown in Table 14.3. Alder and her colleagues have identified some of the transnational skills that are needed for the newly emerging global economy.[16]

INTERPERSONAL BEHAVIOUR ACROSS CULTURES

Just as individual behaviour varies across cultures, so do group behaviour. Important areas of interpersonal behaviour include leadership, multicultural teams, negotiations, and communication.

LEADERSHIP ACROSS CULTURES

In the chapter on leadership, we examined the nature, theories, and styles of leadership. We propose to examine the effectiveness of leadership in international settings in this section.

A multinational leader needs to possess certain unique qualities (apart from those listed in the trait theory) to become successful in global settings. What an international manager needs is **emotional intelligence**. Emotional intelligence refers to a set of five individual and social competencies, including self-awareness, self-regulation, motivation, empathy, and social skills.[17] *Self-awareness* is the ability to recognize and understand one's moods, emotions, and drives, as well as their effects on other people. Leaders with a high level of self-awareness exhibit self-confidence, a realistic self-assessment, and a self-deprecating humour. *Self-regulation,* the second quality, is the ability to control or redirect disruptive impulses and moods-the ability to think before doing. Leaders with a high level of self-regulation exhibit trustworthiness, integrity, comfort with ambiguity, and openness to change.

Motivation, the third component in emotional intelligence, is reflected in a passion to work for reasons that go beyond money or status. Leaders high on motivation exhibit remarkable organizational commitment, drive to achieve, and optimism (even in the circumstances of failure).

The fourth emotional intelligence quality is *empathy.* Empathy refers to understanding the emotional make up of other people and skill in treating people according to their emotional reactions. Leaders with a high level of empathy demonstrate an ability to build and retain talent in their organization, show cross-cultural sensitivity, and become known for offering great service to clients and customers.

Social skill is the fifth competency in emotional intelligence. Social skill refers to the proficiency in managing relationships and building networks, along with an ability to find common ground and to build rapport. Leaders with a high level of social skill are effective at leading change, show a superior ability to build and lead teams, and become known for their persuasiveness.[18]

Leadership in the International Context In international settings, leadership needs to be situational, that is, successful leadership in multinational companies requires that managers adjust their leadership styles to fit the different situations. This adjustment must occur not only in response to traditional contingency factors such as subordinates characteristics but also in response to the cultural and institutional context of the multinational's country locations.[19] (see Fig.14.5).

As seen from Fig. 14.5, in an international setting, the leader's behaviour and traits are influenced by subordinate's characteristics and work settings are influenced by the national context. The national context includes the national culture, business culture, and social institutions.

It is advisable to elaborate on the Fig.14.5.

Leader Behaviour and Traits National culture, business culture, and social institutions define the array of preferred and acceptable leader behaviour and traits for managers. Recollecting Hofstede's cultural dimensions, in high power distance countries, subordinates expect the leader to act with authority. Educational systems train managers to act as an elite social class.

Subordinate's Characteristics National and business cultures influence workers' needs and levels of achievement motivation. Additionally, a country's socioeconomic development and institutional support for education affect the quality and availability of education and training for workers. Consequently, a leader must modify his or her style to fit the types of workers available in a particular nation.

Work Setting Culture and social institutions affect the choices managers make in designing organizations and subunits. These organizational characteristics, in turn, affect the leader's options in the work setting: that is, task characteristics such as routine work, and organizational characteristics such as formalized jobs. In fact, the organizational context can be so powerful that, in some situations, leader behaviour may not even be necessary. For example, a highly formalized organization may not require much leader supervision.[20]

Universalism in Leadership In recent years, a new issue has cropped up in the literature on leadership. The issue relates to the universalism of leadership. That is, whether or not effective leaders act similarly regardless of their respective cultures. Transformational leadership is projected as an approach which can cut across all cultural barriers and be effective in any organization anywhere in the world and represents a higher level of leadership. Transformational leaders are visionary agents with a sense of mission who are capable of motivating their followers to accept new goals and new ways of doing things. Specifically, the transformational leader:[21]

FIGURE 14-5
NATIONAL CONTEXT CONTINGENCY MODEL OF LEADERSHIP

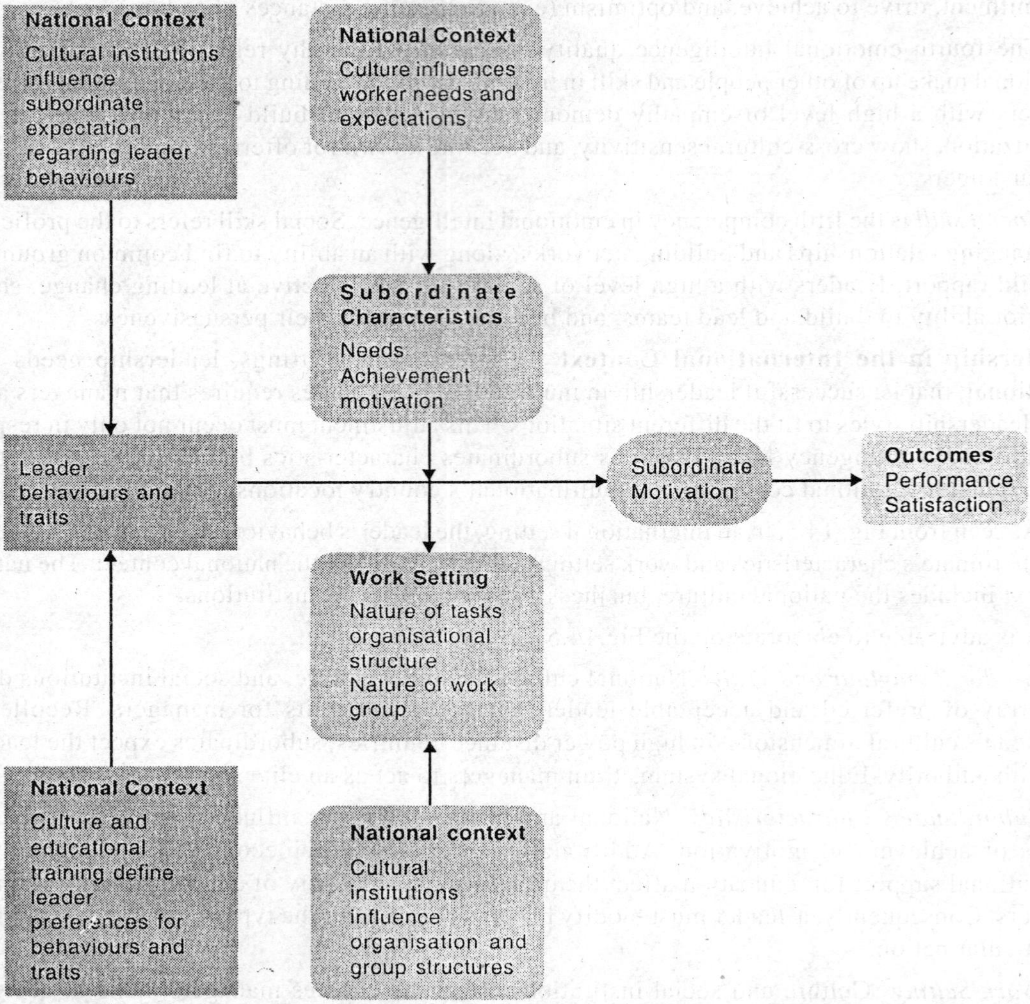

(*Source:* Adapted from John B.Cullen, *op. cit*, p.543)

- *Articulates a vision* Presents in vivid and emotional terms an idealized vision of future for the organization-what it can and should become-and makes this vision clear to followers.
- *Breaks from the status quo* Has a strong desire to break from tradition and do things differently; is an expert in finding ways to do things differently; challenges subordinates to find new solutions to old problems.
- *Provides goals and a plan* Has a vision that is future oriented, and provides clear steps for followers to transform the company.

- *Gives meaning or a purpose to goals* Places the goals in emotion-laden stories or a cultural context so that subordinates see the need to follow the leader's ideals and to share a commitment to radical change; helps subordinates envision a future state of a better organization.
- *Takes risks* Is willing to take more risks with the organization than the average leader.
- *Is motivated to lead* Seeks leadership positions and displays strong enthusiasm for the leadership role; acts as a role model.
- *Builds a power base* Uses personal power based on expertise, respect, and the admiration of followers.
- *Demonstrates high ethical and moral standards* Behaves consistently and fairly with a known ethical standard.

Contrary to popular belief, transformation leaders are not new to the present century. The German sociologist Max Weber recognized the existence of transformational leadership throughout history. This type of transformational leadership he called 'charisma' and he noted that it had existed in all cultures. According to Weber, Jesus Christ and Muhammad were among the first transformational leaders. Most people also consider Mahatma Gandhi and Martin Luther King as representatives of transformational leadership.

Transformational leaders succeed because subordinates respond to them with high levels of performance, personal devotion, reverence, excitement regarding the leader's ideas, and a willingness to sacrifice for the good of the company. However, true transformational leaders are rare. They seem to arise when an organization needs a change or faces a crisis.[22]

Does transformational leadership really work equally effectively in all cultures? The answer does not seem to be a definite 'yes'. Leader behaviours need to vary from country to country. For example, transformational leaders need to be more directive in less developed countries than in developed ones. Moreover, cultures can create some problems in using universal leadership concepts in countries such as Japan, where the use of contingent reward systems is not as widely used as in the West. These reward systems can also become meaningless in Arab and Turkish cultures where there is a great belief that things will happen 'if God wills' and not because a leader has decided to carry them out. Obviously, though transformational leadership has universal appreciation, it needs to be fine-tuned when applying in any particular country.

MULTICULTURAL TEAMS

Although diversity refers to many characteristics, including gender, race, profession, nationality, age, and ethnicity, this section focuses on cultural differences. Homogeneous teams are those with all members coming from the same cultural group; multicultural teams are those with members coming from more than one culture. Multicultural teams can be divided into three types:

- *Token teams,* in which only one member is from another culture. An example would be a group of Japanese retailers and a British attorney who are looking into the benefits and shortcomings of setting up operations in Bermuda.
- *Bicultural teams* have members from two cultures. An example would be a team of four Mexicans and four Canadians who have formed a team to investigate the possibility of investing in Russia.

- *Multicultural teams* have members from three or more cultures. An example is a group of three Americans, three German, three Uruguyans, and three Chinese managers who are looking after mining operations in Chile.

Managing Culturally Diverse Teams As will be stated in Chapter 21, properly managed diverse groups can result in several benefits such as better hiring efforts, increased sales and market share, increased innovation and creation, and higher productivity. Some of the ways to better manage multicultural teams are task-related selection, establishing a vision, equalizing power, and creating mutual respect.[23]

Task-related selection: Leaders should select team members based on their task-related abilities rather than on ethnicity. Team members should be homogenous in ability levels but heterogenous in attitudes. Such members help maximize team effectiveness.

Establishing a vision: Members of diverse teams have more difficulty agreeing on their purpose and task than do members of homogenous groups. Global alliances often become troubled because partners from different cultures do not clearly understand each other's intent-their purpose, goals, and strategy- because they are initially unable to communicate with each other. The main task of leaders is to help teams agree on his or her vision or super-ordinate goal that cuts across individual differences. Super-ordinate goals give general direction and focus to the team's activities. Such goals requiring collaboration and cooperation generally decrease prejudice and increase mutual respect.

Equalizing power: Teams generally produce more and better ideas if all members participate. Cultural dominance (disproportionate power vested in members of one culture over those from other cultures) is therefore, counterproductive because it stifles non-dominant team members' contributions. In multicultural teams, leaders must guard against vesting disproportionate power in host-country members, members of the home country, members from the most technologically advanced or economically developed countries, or members with ideologies most consonant with their own. Team leaders should manage the distribution of power according to each member's ability to contribute to the task, not according to some preconceived gradient of relative cultural superiority.

Creating mutual respect For most teams to work effectively, members must respect each other. Prejudice is the antonym of mutual respect. Equal status, close contact, and cooperative efforts towards a common goal decrease prejudice. Team leaders can enhance mutual respect by selecting members of equal ability, making prior accomplishments and skills known to all team members, and minimizing early judgement based on ethnic stereotypes.

Negotiating Globally

Negotiation is the process of bargaining with one or more parties to arrive at a solution that is acceptable to all. Business negotiations often involve one party attempting to influence another to make a particular decision or sign a contract. A negotiation becomes cross-cultural when the parties involved belong to different cultures and, therefore, do not share the same ways of thinking, feeling, and behaving. All global negotiations are cross-cultural.

Negotiation, as an approach to conflict resolution was discussed in Chapter 14. Conflict presupposes the existence of disagreement between two parties and negotiation seeks to remove such differences. The discussion on negotiation here focuses on management of business negotiations and not on conflict resolution.

Negotiating cross-culturally is one of the single most important global business skills. Global negotiations contain all of the complexity of domestic negotiations, with the added dimension of cultural diversity.

Negotiation is not always the best approach to doing business. Many times such strategies as 'take-it-or-leave-it' or bargaining become more effective. Negotiating, compared to bargaining or the take-it-or-leave-it approach, is time-consuming and patience-testing. As a rule, managers should negotiate when any one of the following conditions exists:[24]

- Their power position is low relative to their counterpart.
- The trust level is high.
- Sufficient time is available to explore each party's multiple needs, resources, and options.
- Commitment, not mere compliance, is important to ensure that all parties carry out the agreement.

Fig.14.6 summarizes the above conditions. Negotiating is generally the preferred strategy for creating win-win solutions in global business.

FIGURE 14-6

WHEN TO NEGOTIATE?

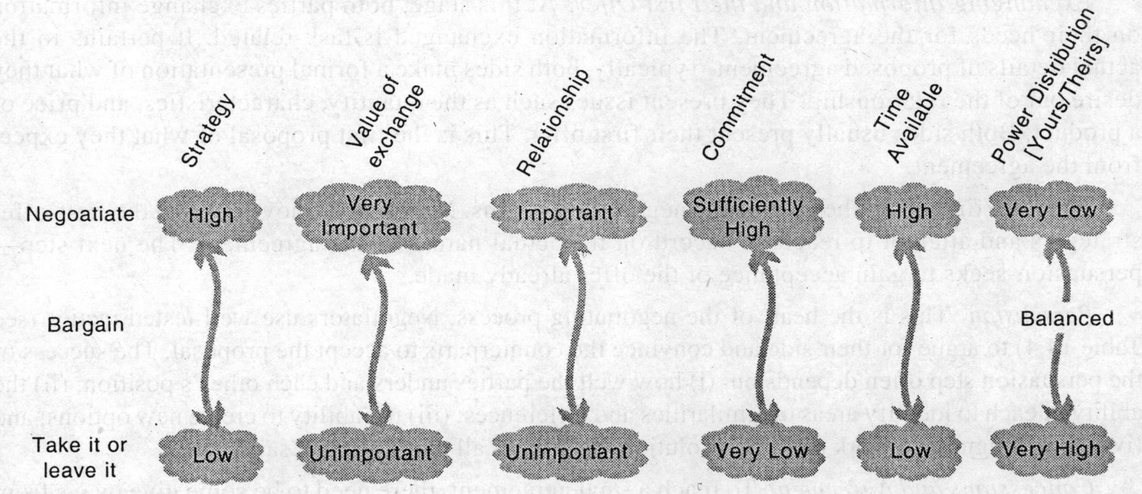

(***Source:*** Nancy J.Adler, *op.cit*, p.212)

Steps in Negotiation: The process in global negotiation comprises several steps. Although each multicultural negotiation is unique and may combine two or more steps or repeat some, the negotiation process involves five steps leading to the final step, an agreement. The negotiation steps include preparation, building the relationship, exchanging information, and the first offer, persuasion, concessions, and agreement (see Fig.14.7).

Preparation: Effective international negotiation strategy needs preparation. Preparation involves that the negotiator gathers extensive information on the issue to be negotiated, on the setting in which the negotiation will take place, and on the firm and people involved. The negotiator needs to do extensive research on nature and negotiation styles of the foreign culture.

FIGURE 14-7
STEPS IN INTERNATIONAL NEGOTIATIONS

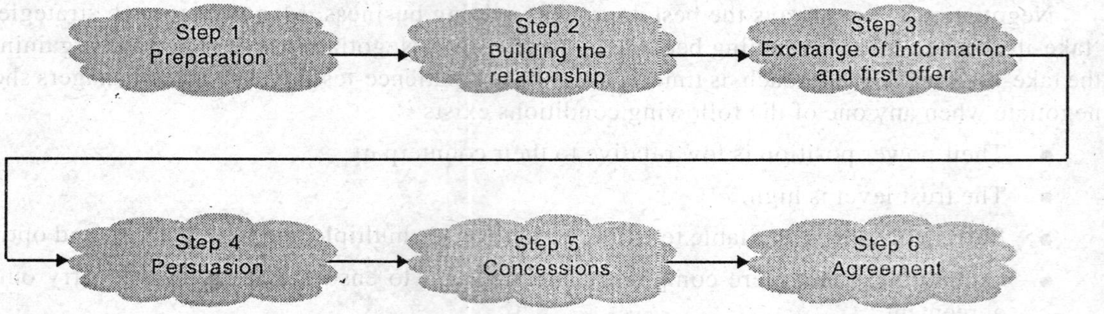

Building the Relationship: Having planned well, the negotiator is ready to begin direct communication with his or her negotiating partners. At this stage, the negotiators do not focus on the business issues. Rather, they focus on social and interpersonal relations. Negotiators get to know each other personally. The relationship building phase generally takes place at a location different from the formal negotiation place.

Exchanging Information and the First Offer: At this stage, both parties exchange information on their needs for the agreement. The information exchanged is task-related. It pertains to the actual details of proposed agreement. Typically, both sides make a formal presentation of what they desire out of the relationship. They present issues such as the quantity, characteristics, and price of a product. Both sides usually present their first offer. This is the first proposal of what they expect from the agreement.

After the first offer, the core of the negotiation begins. Negotiators move beyond the first-offer strategies and attempt to reach an accord on the actual nature of the agreement. The next step—persuasion-seeks to gain acceptance of the offer already made.

Persuasion This is the heart of the negotiating process. Negotiators use well-tested tactics (see Table 14.4) to argue for their side and convince the counterparts to accept the proposal. The success of the persuasion step often depends on: (i) how well the parties understand each other's position; (ii) the ability of each to identify areas of similarities and differences; (iii) the ability to create new options; and (iv) the willingness to work towards a solution that allows all parties to feel satisfied.[25]

Concessions and Agreement To reach a final agreement, there need to be some giveaways from both sides. Making concessions requires that each side relaxes some of its demands to meet the other party's needs. Concessions having been made, final agreement emerges. The final agreement is the signed contract, agreeable to all sides. The agreement must be understood in principle by all people from different national and business cultures.

Communicating Across Cultures

Successful international negotiation requires effective cross-cultural communication. Additionally, in global businesses, activities such as leading, motivating, decision making, problem solving, and exchanging information and ideas depend on the ability of managers and employees from one culture to communicate successfully with colleagues, clients, and suppliers from other cultures.

TABLE 14-4

NEGOTIATING TACTICS

Tactic	Description	Example
Promise	I will do something you want me to do, if you do something I want you to do (conditional, positive).	I will lower the price by $5 if you increase the order by 100 units.
Threat	I will do something you don't want me to do, if you do something I don't want you to do (conditional, negative).	I'll walk out of the negotiation if you leak this story to the press.
Recommendation	If you do something I want you to do, a third party will do something you want (third party positive).	If you lower your price, more teenagers will be able to buy your product.
Warning	If you do something I don't want you to do, a third party will do something you don't want (third party negative).	If you don't settle, the press will spill this whole sordid story on the front page of every newspaper in the country.
Reward	I will give you something positive (something) you want now, on the spot (unconditional, positive).	Let's make it easier on you tomorrow and meet closer to your office. I have really appreciated your willingness to meet at my building.
Punishment	I will give you something negative (something you don't want) now, on the spot (unconditional, negative).	I refuse to listen to your screaming. I am leaving.
Normative Appeal	I appeal to a societal norm.	Everybody else buys our product for $5 per unit.
Commitment	I will do something you want (unconditional, positive).	I will deliver 100 units by June 15.
Self-disclosure	I will tell you something about myself.	We have had to lay off 100 employees this month. We really need to sign a major contract by the end of the year.
Question	I want to ask you something about yourself.	Can you tell me more about your Brazilian operation?
Command	I order you to do something.	Lower your price.

(*Source*: Nancy J. Adler, *op.cit.*, p.235)

Communication is the process of transferring meanings from sender to receiver. On the surface, this appears to be a fairly straight-forward process. But there are great many problems in the international scenario that can result in the failure to transfer meanings correctly.

Mistakes in cross-cultural communication often go unnoticed by the communicators, but these mistakes have the potential to cause damage to international relationships and negotiations. Mistakes or misinterpretations of the subtle gestures of the hands and face, the use of silence, what is said or not said, and the intricacies of dealing with age and status often provide pitfalls for international managers.

Crucial issues in intercultural communication are: language and culture, differences between high and low context cultures, use of interpreters, non-verbal communication, and attribution errors.[26] If these are taken care of, inter-cultural communication will be effective.

Language and Culture Language is the foundation of every culture. It is an abstract system of word meanings and symbols related to all aspects of culture. Language includes speech, written characters, numerals, symbols, and gestures of non-verbal communication.

The interrelationship between language and culture is very strong and often the former determines the latter. Words provide the concepts for understanding the world. All languages (there are approximately three thousand of them) have limited sets of words. These restricted word sets, in turn, constrain the ability of the users to understand or conceptualize the world. Since language structures the way we think about what we see and behave - it determines control patterns.

The above hypothesis that language determines cultural patterns is, however, not acceptable to several experts. Many social scientists argue that language does not determine human thought and behaviour patterns. For example, humans possess the physical ability to make millions of colour distinctions, yet languages are recognised in the number of colours they can express. The English language distinguishes between yellow and orange, but some other languages do not.[27] The word *punya* is popular in Indian languages but there is no equivalent of it in the English language.

Obviously, it is not that languages determine culture. It is culture that comes first and requires the development of certain concepts and thus certain words. Notwithstanding the arguments, there is close interrelationship between language and culture.

High- and Low-Context Languages The world's languages can be classified, based on whether the message conveyed is explicit or implicit, into two groups. Languages in which people state things directly and explicitly are called *low context.* The words provide the meaning and there is no need to interpret the situation to understand the import of the words. Languages in which people state things indirectly and implicitly are called *high context.* In the *high - context* language, communications have multiple meanings that can be interpreted only by reading the situation in which they occur. So important are the ideas of high and low context that many people refer to the whole culture as being high or low context.[28]

Most northern European languages, including German, English, and the Scandinavian languages, are low context. People use explicit words to communicate direct meanings. In contrast, Asian and Arabic languages are high context. In Asian languages, often what is left unsaid is just as important as what is said. Silent periods and the use of incomplete sentences require a person to interpret what the communicator does not say by reading the situation. Arabic introduces interpretation into the languages with an opposite tack. Extensive imprecise verbal and non-verbal communication produces an interaction where reading the situation is essential for comprehension.

Communication between high context and low context people is a challenge for international managers. Translated words for a low context speaker have explicit meanings but the same may have a multitude of meanings for a high context speaker. In international negotiations, the negotiators should realize that communication will have errors. Moreover, even good translations may require contextual interpretations for effective communication.

Use of Interpreters In cross-cultural communication, use of a language foreign to both the parties, is common. The international manager is at an advantage if he or she speaks more than one language fluently. US Americans speak only English but their European counterparts are generally bilingual or even multilingual.

Increasingly, companies are making use of the services of interpreters in international negotiations. The interpreter's role is to provide a simultaneous translation of a foreign language while a person speaks. This requires greater linguistic skills than speaking a language or translating written documents. Good interpreters are not only bilingual but also have the technical knowledge and vocabulary to deal with technical details common in business transactions.[29]

To simplify the increasing diversity of languages in businesses, some MNCs use one language as the corporate language. Increasingly, this language is English, as it is being used in a majority of countries. Using English allows companies a more consistent culture while dealing with the linguistic diversity of their employees and customers. However, even companies which have a corporate language, have permanent translators on their rolls to manage such issues as interaction with the international press, translation of local product information, and negotiations with other companies.[30]

Non-verbal Communication Non-verbal communication includes facial gestures, voice intonation, physical distance, smile, battling of eyelid, kiss, handshake, and even silence. Non-verbal communication supplements or enhances spoken communication.

It is easy to misinterpret the meanings of non-verbal communication of another culture. Take for example body language. In the US, when a manager keeps his or her feet on the desk, it means the boss is relaxing and the others can also do the same. But such gestures are frowned upon in India.

Take another non-verbal communication medium-touching. In greeting one another, people may shake hands, embrace, or kiss. In routine interaction, people may touch or pat each other in a variety of ways. The type of touching deemed appropriate is deeply rooted in society's cultural values. Russian men, for example, often kiss other men outside their family as a form of greeting; Brazilian men hug in greeting.

A multinational manager meets with all forms of non-verbal communication styles. Successful international managers maintain flexibility and humour in adjusting to local communication patterns.

Organization Characteristics in an International Context

The final aspect of international behaviour relates to organization characteristics. Cross cultural influences are found to exist on environment, technology, organization structure, and organization change.

Environment Across Cultures

Environment across cultures varies. Dissolving borders, growing cross-border trade and investment, the rise of global products and customers, privatization of companies formerly owned by governments, the emergence of new competition in the world market, rise of global standards of quality and production, and the growing sophistication of information technology have not only brought global business to sharp focus but have altered the environment of business everywhere dramatically. China, for example, is an emerging economic power which no international manager can ignore. But the government's desire to balance national, immediate needs with the challenges of a free market economy and globalization contributes to the complexity and risks of the environment over there. Similarly, in France, the 12-year reign of the socialists under Mitterand ended in mid-1995. Mitterand was replaced by Chirac, a more conservative Gaullist, and this heralded a host of political changes impacting on doing business in France. Boris Yeltsin governed Russia throughout the 1990s and when he resigned in 2000 and turned the reins over to Vladmir Putin, the economy was in shambles. One of the major problems before the new administration is corruption.

The *European Bank for Reconstruction and Development* reports that almost a third of firms doing business in Russia indicate that they are required to give bribes to do business and that these monies add more than four per cent to the overall cost of doing business there. As more MNCs invest in Russia, these unethical practices will face increasing scrutiny. To date, many multinationals feel that the risks are too great. But international managers cannot ignore Russia because it is a vast and lucrative market.

Organizations need to be proactive - anticipate changes in the environment and formulate strategies to face the challenges.

Technology and International Business

The technological environment is changing at lightening speed. For example, while semi-conductor firms are now working to develop new memory chips for personal computers, other high-tech firms are creating technologies that will replace the PC with an even better computing architecture. At the same time, computers, telephones, televisions, and wireless forms of communication are being merged to create multimedia products to allow users anywhere in the world to communicate with each other. Today, the number of people who use cellular phones is greater than ever and in countries like Finland, Norway, and Sweden, over half the population are cellular phone subscribers. In addition, a growing number of people have access to the Internet, allowing them to obtain information from literally millions of sources as the number of websites is increasing sharply.

That technology is changing fast is only part of the story. Another dimension of technology is that the attitudes towards it change across cultures. Till recently, Japan was not supporting basic research. For many years, the Japanese government encouraged its companies to take basic research findings from elsewhere (mainly from the US) and figure out how to apply them to consumer products (applied research). Now, however, the government has changed its stance and has started to encourage basic research as well.[31]

Organization Designs

International managers deal with many different types of organizations in international business dealings. Surprisingly, there are similarities between organization designs in different cultures. At the same time there are differences too.

Like Organizations Across Cultures Scholars identify two reasons why organizations from different societies can be similar. These are explained in the **convergence** and **culture-free theories**. Fig.14.8 shows how the convergence and culture-free hypotheses work.[32]

Convergence: Many management practices, specially those related to strategy and structure, are becoming increasingly similar. This growing similarity in management practices is called *convergence*. This trend is more visible in multinational companies. Firms competing in the same industry tend to have similar structures and strategies regardless of the location of the company's headquarters. Since multinational corporations compete in worldwide markets, they not only seek uniform products and strategies but also seek ways of organizing that need not differ because of national boundaries. International managers also lack deep-seated national culture or societal identification. For them, their companies are more important.

Several developments account for convergence.

- Customer's needs across societies are similar. In order to meet identical needs, companies need to produce similar products, for which similarproductive processes are needed.
- Growing industrialization and economic development enable organizations to have the technical and financial capability to use similar technologies.

FIGURE 14-8
ORGANISATIONS ALIKE

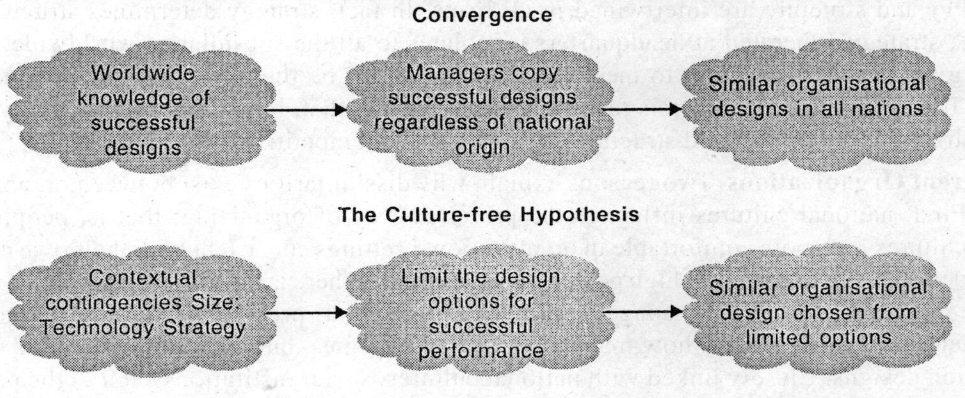

(*Source:* John B.Cullen, *op.cit,* p.339)

- Global competition and global trade contribute to convergence. International competition raises managerial awareness of what people in other societies are doing. Japanese competition with other countries, for example, enabled companies elsewhere to initiate such managerial practices as Just-in-Time (JIT) inventory, Kaizen, open office, and common uniform.
- International strategic alliances contribute to convergence. With international cooperative arrangements among competitors, an increasing number of firms from diverse nationalities combine with one another to form one organization with a unique organizational design. These joint ventures or alliances provide a wealth of information on the organizational practices of other societies. Later, parent organizations use this knowledge to change and improve themselves.
- Business education also serves to harmonize organizational practices. In particular, the large number of international students in US and European MBA programmes helps spread common business techniques. Many students return to their home countries with the intent of adopting management practices that best fit their national cultures.[33] For example, many of the high-tech firms in India, Korea, and Taiwan are staffed with top executives who were educated in the US and stayed on to work for a decade or more. Now they are returning to their homelands armed with technical and managerial expertise.

The Culture-free Theory The second theory on similarities in organization designs relates to organizational contextual factors. Such factors include an organization's size, technology, and strategy.

Large organizations tend to be more formulized, specialized, and less centralized. This implies, that regardless of cultures, large organizations tend to be similar.

Technology affects organization design mostly at the departmental level rather than at the level of organization design. Machines directly influence how people perform their work, regardless of their nationality or constraint of a manager's choice of departmental-level designs. Thus, worldwide proliferation of similar industrial and information technologies means that managers from different countries face similar design options for their departments, irrespective of their national culture. However, not all societies have access to the same technology, nor do people necessarily use technology in exactly the same ways.[34]

Strategy and structure are intertwined in all firms. In fact, strategy determines structures. In any MNC, strategy generated at headquarters percolates to all the subsidiaries worldwide. Since, the strategy is one, the structure to meet the strategy should be the same regardless of national cultures. The culture-free hypothesis rests on the assumption that, regardless of nationality, firms will use strategies and associated structures that give them competitive advantages.

Different Organizations Two reasons explain why dissimilarities exist between organization designs. First, national cultures influence the preferred way of organizing; that is, people from different cultures feel more comfortable in organizational settings consistent with their own cultural values and norms. For example, in high power distance cultures there is a preference for organizations that have a clear hierarchy of management authority. Second, pressures from the institutional environment influence not only how managers choose strategies, but also, how managers choose organization designs. Closely linked with national cultures, social institutions such as the political system, educational system, legal system, and economic system also define what members of a society see as the legitimate or correct ways of organizing and running business.[35]

Thus, one can see that there are pressures for both convergence and divergence in organization designs. Convergence in the similarity of organization design is highest among MNCs that have global strategies, have international products and locations, and hire employees from any country. Inspite of the trend towards convergence, extensive differences still exist among organizations from different societies.

Organization Change Organization change and development were discussed extensively in an earlier chapter. We focus, briefly, on two issues in this context. First is the impact of international environment on change. As we already noted, environment can be a significant factor in bringing about organization change. Given the additional environmental complexities global businesses face, it follows that organization change may be even more critical to them than to purely domestic businesses.

A second factor to be noted is that acceptance of change varies across cultures. In some societies change is normal and an accepted part of organizational life. In other cultures, change causes many problems. The international manager should remember that techniques for managing change that have worked in a domestic environment may not work at all and may even trigger negative responses if used indiscriminately in other cultures.[36]

QUESTIONS

1. What are Hofstede's dimensions of cultural differences that affect work attitudes? Using these dimensions, describe India.
2. How can managers be encouraged towards global thinking? How can managers dispel stereotypes about other cultures?
3. How do cross cultures influence individual behaviour? Discuss.
4. What accounts for some of the motivational differences among employees across cultures?
5. Why are people from high context cultures such as China and Japan likely to be misunderstood by low context Westerners?

Case

GULF STATES

The Gulf States comprise Bahrain, Kuwait, Oman, Qatar, and the United Arab Emirates (U.A.E). These countries lie along the eastern coast of the Arabian Peninsula, with Saudi Arabia bordering on the west and Iran on the east across the Arabian Gulf (called the Persian Gulf by Westerners). Each of the Gulf State countries is very small, but their desert land is strategically located in one of the largest oil-producing regions of the world.

Oil has made these nations some of the richest in the world, with very high per capita income. They generally have free education, free health and social services, and no income tax. Because of the heat, business hours from May to October tend to be from 7 a.m. to 1 p.m. and from 4 p.m. to 7 p.m. During the rest of the year, the hours are from 8 a.m. to 2 p.m. and from 4 p.m. to 6 p.m. The largely government-owned oil industry dominates their economies but does not provide many jobs. The governments are trying to promote economic activities other than oil production to get their people off welfare.

Herman Kerdling's firm has had a very profitable business supplying the Gulf countries with oil production machinery. Last month, Kerdling learned that he would be going to Oman for a one-year assignment servicing the firm's contract. He was delighted, because he knows that all the top managers at headquarters have had similar international assignments. Moreover, Oman is one of the company's most important accounts. Kerdling was determined to be successful in this assignment.

Unfortunately, after several weeks in Oman, things have not worked out quite as he expected. Specifically, Kerdling is finding that doing business with the Arabs is difficult, because their approach is so different from that of the Americans. One of the most disconcerting things is the fact that people stand so close when they talk. He often tries to back away and put some room between them, but the other person usually follows and closes the distance again.

Another problem is the way that meetings are conducted. Last week, Kerdling went to talk to an Arab customer about some new equipment that was to be delivered and installed within the next few weeks. He and the customer talked for about 5 minutes when someone in the next office suddenly barged in and interrupted the conversation. The customer talked to this individual for almost 5 minutes and then turned back to Kerdling and picked the conversation from where he had left off. Within a few minutes, however, someone else came in and another interruption ensued. The meeting, which should have taken approximately 30 minutes, took over 2 hours to complete. As Kerdling left, he turned and saw another person start a conversation with the customer only to be interrupted by a third party. 'How does anyone get anything done around here?' he wondered to himself.

A third problem is the letters and e-mails that Kerdling receives from his customers. These messages are translated by company-paid Arabic interpreters, and the interpreted copy is attached to the original. Herman Kerdling sometimes has trouble with the interpretation, because the interpreters are not very good. Unfortunately, no one on the company's staff is fluent in Arabic, and no better interpreters can be found. There seems to be no way around this problem. Kerdling is convinced that there are many communication breakdowns caused by this lack of language fluency, but he is unsure of how to resolve the matter.[37]

Questions

1. What are some current issues facing the Gulf States? How is the climate for doing business in the Gulf States today?
2. Why is Kerdling upset that his Arab hosts stand so close when they talk to him? What can he do about this?
3. Should Kerdling feel insulted when his conversation is interrupted by outsiders?
4. Is Kerdling right regarding communication break-downs caused by a lack of language fluency? Can anything be done about the problem?[37]

6 Today, many managers work with people from other cultures, both at home and when travelling abroad. What are some of the ways in which your organization could train managers to communicate more effectively with people from other cultures?

7 What are your own assumptions about motivation? Why do you think people work? List your own motivation assumptions and analyse them from a cross-cultural perspective. In which ways are your assumptions similar to those of most of the people from your country? In which ways do they differ?

8 What can Indian managers learn about individual behaviour from other cultures? What can managers in other cultures learn about individual behaviour from Indian managers?

9 What are the advantages and disadvantages of transferring managers across a variety of locations scattered around the world?

10 Add one more column for India in Fig.14.1 and list cultural values peculiar to the country.

REFERENCES

1. John A.Wagner and John R.Hollenbeck, *Organisational Behaviour*, Horcount Callese Publishers, 2002, p.467.
2. Ibid.
3. Richard M.Hodgetts and Fred Luthans, *International Management*, Tata McGraw-Hill, 2003, pp.150-1.
4. Madhukar Shukia, 'Cross Cultural HR', *Human Capital,* November 2002, Pp.52-53.
5. Farid Elashimawi and Philip R.Harris, *Multicultural Managernent,* Synergy Books International, p.62.
6. Darrell Mahancy, *et.al.*, *International Business,* Longman, 1998, p.383.
7. Richard M. Hodgem and Fred Lutham, *op. cit.*, p. 116.
8. Ibid, p.117.
9. Farid Elashmawi and Philip R. Harris, *op. cit.*, Pp 6-7.
10. Ibid, Pp. 144-8.
11. John B.Cullen, *Multinational Management,* South Westem, 1999, p.468.
12. Aswanthappa, K, *HumanResource and Personnel Management,* Tata McGraw-Hill, 2002, p.261.
13. Peter J.Dowling, etal, *International HumanResourcesManagement,* South Westem, 1999, p.199.
14. Ibid, p.133.
15. Nancy J.Adler, *International Dimensions of Organizational Behaviour,* South Western, 2002, p.264.
16. 'Managing Globally Competent People', *Academy of Management Executive,* August 1992.
17. Naucy J.Adler, *Op.cit.*, p.171.
18. Ibid, p.172.
19. John B. Cullen, *Op.cit.*, p. 524.
20. Ibid, p.527.
21. Ibid, p.534.

22. Ibid.
23. Nancy J. Adler, *Op.cit.,* pp. 153-5.
24. Ibid, p. 212.
25. Richard M.Hodgetts and Fred Luthans, *Op.cit.,* p.294.
26. John B. Cullen, *Op.cit.,* p.90.
27. Richard T. Scharfer and Robert P.Lamn, *Sociology,* McGraw-Hill, 1998, p. 73.
28. John B. Cullen, *Op.cit.,* P.91.
29. Ibid, p. 92.
30. Ibid.
31. Gregory Moorhead and Ricky W.Griffin, *Organizational Behaviour,* Jaico.2000, p.718.
32. John B.Cullen, *Op.cit.,* p.338.
33. Ibid, p.339.
34. Ibid, p.340.
35. Ibid, p.341.
36. Gregony Moorhead and Ricky W.Grittin, *Op.cit.,* p.721.
37. Richard M.Hodgetts and Fred Luthans, *Op.cit.,* p.221.

CHAPTER

Fifteen

Foundations of Individual Behaviour

LEARNING OBJECTIVES

After reading this chapter you should understand that –

1. Issues confronting OB specialist in the days to come.
2. The various personal factors which influence individual behaviour.
3. The impact of environmental factors on individual behaviour.
4. How organisational systems and resources are a foundation to individual behaviour.
5. How individual behaviour is influenced by psychological factors.
6. The various behaviouristic models constructed by OB experts.

The behaviour of an individual is determined by several inputs.

In this and the next five chapters we focus on the inputs of individual behaviour in greater detail, followed by other dimensions of OB in the subsequent chapters.

The behaviour of an individual is influenced by many factors, as shown in Fig.15.1. A study of these is useful for a better understanding of OB.

Personal Factors

Personal factors, as shown in Fig.15.1, include age, sex, education, abilities, marital status, and number of dependents.

FIGURE 15-1
FOUNDATIONS OF INDIVIDUAL BEHAVIOUR

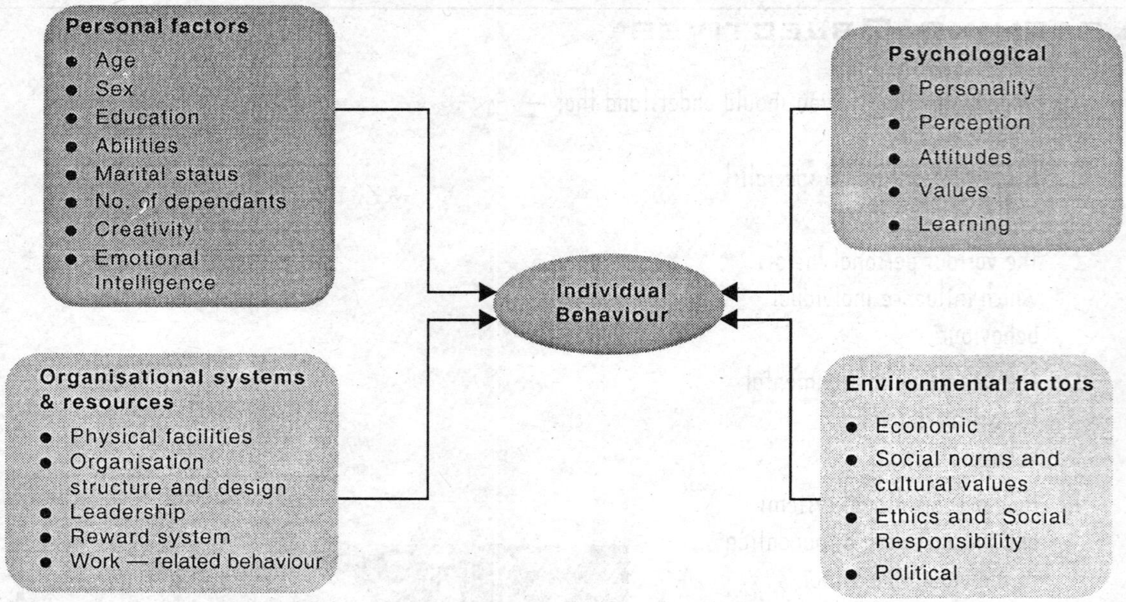

Age The issue of age is multifaceted and individualistic. It has impact on performance, turnover, absenteeism, productivity, and satisfaction.

Performance is dependent on age. As age advances, performance is likely to decline. Similarly, aging also has an impact on *turnover*. The older one grows, the less likely one is to quit the job. Age-absence relationship depends on whether *absenteeism* is avoidable or unavoidable. Generally, older employees have lower rates of avoidable absence than do younger employees. However, they do have high rates of unavoidable absence. This is probably because of poor health associated with oldage. With regard to *productivity*, old age results in reduced productivity. This is because of the decline in an individual's skill as he or she grows older in age. There is a positive association between age and *satisfaction*. However, changes in technology may alter this equation. In jobs where workers are subject to dramatic changes causing their skills to become obsolete, such as those affected by computerization, satisfaction levels of older employees tend to be lower than that of younger ones.

Age can also be a factor in adaptability, although it would be incorrect to stereotype all older people as unadaptable.

The impact of age goes beyond organisational factors. Gender for example, like age, forms the basis for social differentiation. The status of 'older persons' in society frequently influences our perception. Societies often get stratified by age and this stratification varies from culture to culture. One society may treat older people with great reverence, while another sees them as 'unproductive' and 'difficult'. The Sherpas-a Tibetan-speaking, Buddhist people in Nepal-idolize their elders. Almost all elderly members of the Sherpa community own houses and enjoy good health. Similarly, in the Andaman Islands, old people hold dominant positions in the social structure.

Not all societies, however, have a tradition of caring for and valuing the elderly. Among the Fulanis of Africa, older men and women move to the edge of the family homestead. Since this is where people are buried, the elderly actually sleep on their graves, for they are already considered as dead. Some societies are known to have practised *senilicide*-the killing of the aged-because of extreme difficulties in providing basic necessities such as food and shelter.[2]

Sex The issue of male and female employees has received considerable attention from academics, sociologists, and researchers. Research has proved that problem solving ability, analytical skill, competitive drive, motivation, leadership, sociability, or learning ability are not gender-dependent. However, in our male-dominated society, the presence of women employees in organisation is not appreciated or encouraged.

Sex also has an impact on turnover and absenteeism. It has been proved that the tendency to change jobs and to abstain from work is likely to be higher among female than among male employees. The most logical explanation for this phenomenon is that our society has historically placed home and family responsibilities on the female. When a child is ill or someone needs to stay home to await the plumber, it has traditionally been the woman who has taken time off from work to attend to these needs.

Education This has its effect upon individual behaviour, largely through the level and type of education received. Increased levels of education serve to increase an individual's expectations about positive outcomes. These outcomes are generally perceived to be a more satisfying job, higher income level, and greater alternative sources for occupational choice, i.e., the 'good life'. Disillusionment occurs when outcomes do not match expectations.

The type of education received can also affect individual behaviour. Education can be 'general' or 'specialised'. The former includes areas like arts, humanities, and social sciences; whereas the latter covers disciplines such as engineering, medicine, computer science, and the like. Generalist education tends to both attract and develop individuals differently than an education in the specialities. Specialist programmes tend to be relatively narrow and focused, whereas generalist programmes expose individuals to a broad range of subjects designed to enhance an overall understanding of concepts and issues.

Ability It refers to an individual's capacity to perform various tasks in a job. The ability of an individual is made up of two sets of skills-intellectual and physical.

Intellectual abilities are needed to perform mental activities. IQ tests, for example, are designed to ascertain one's intellectual abilities. So, too, are popular college admission tests like GRE, GMAT, and CAT. Some of the more relevant dimensions making up intellectual abilities include number aptitude, verbal comprehension, perceptual speed, and inductive reasoning. Table 15.1 describes these dimensions.

Physical abilities manifest in one's stamina, manual dexterity, leg strength and the like. Management must identify an employee's physical abilities if these are the major inputs required to perform a task.

Nine basic physical abilities (See Table 15.2) have been identified. Individuals differ in the extent to which they have each of these abilities. Not surprisingly, there is also little relationship

TABLE 15-1
DIMENSIONS OF INTELLECTUAL ABILITY

Dimension	*Description*	*Job Example*
Number aptitude	Ability to do speedy and accurate arithmetic	Accountant: Computing the sales tax on a set of items
Verbal Comprehension	Ability to understand what is read or heard and the relationship of words to each other	Plant Manager: Following corporate policies
Perceptual speed	Ability to identify visual similarities and differences quickly and accurately	Fire Investigator: Identifying clues to support a charge of arson
Inductive reasoning	Ability to identify a logical sequence in a problem and then solve the problem	Market Researcher: Fore-casting demand for a product in the subsequent time period
Deductive reasoning	Ability to use logic and assess the implications of an argument	Supervisor: Choosing between two different suggestions offered by employees
Spatial visualisation	Ability to imagine how an object would look, if its position in space were changed	Interior Decorator: Re-decorating an office
Memory	Ability to retain and recall past experiences	Salesperson: Remembering the names of customers

(**Source:** Stephen P. Robbins, *Organisational Behaviour,* p. 41)

TABLE 15-2
NINE BASIC PHYSICAL ABILITIES

Strength Factors	
1. Dynamic strength	Ability to exert muscular force repeatedly or continuously over time
2. Trunk strength	Ability to exert muscular strength using the trunk (particularly abdominal) muscles
3. Static stremgth	Ability to exert force against external objects
4. Explosive strength	Ability to expand a maximum of energy in one or a series of explosive acts
Flexibility Factors	
5. Extent flexibility	Ability to move the trunk and back muscles as far as possible
6. Dynamic flexibility	Ability to make rapid, repeated flexing movements
Other Factors	
7. Body coordination	Ability to coordinate the simultaneous actions of different parts of the body
8. Balance	Ability to maintain equilibrium despite unbalancing forces
9. Stamina	Ability to continue maximum effort requiring prolonged effort overtime

(**Source:** Stephen P. Robbins, *op. cit,* p. 42)

between them. A high score on one is no assurance of a high score on the others. High employee performance is likely to be achieved when management has ascertained the extent to which a job requires each of these nine abilities and then ensures that employees in that job have them.

Ability-Job Fit It is widely known that employees differ in their physical and intellectual abilities and the jobs they perform demand varied abilities. Employee performance is enhanced where there is high ability-job fit.

A perfect ability-job fit is seldom achieved. For one thing, hiring procedures are often imperfect. Managers direct their attention at only the employee's abilities or only the ability requirements of the job and ignore the fact that employee performance depends on a fit between the two. Moreover, people and organisations change. An employee who finds a new job stimulating and exciting to begin with, may find the same job boring and monotonous a few years later. An organisation that adopts new technology needs new skills from its employees. Finally, each person is unique. Measuring skills and performance is quite difficult. Assessing attitudes and personality is far more complex. Each of these makes matching abilities with jobs a difficult and complex process.

What happens when the fit is poor? If the employees are short of the required abilities, they are likely to fail. Performance suffers, even if the employee is highly motivated and has a positive attitude. If the employee's abilities far exceed the job requirements, the consequence will be different. Job performance is likely to be adequate, but there will be organisational inefficiencies and possible decline in job satisfaction.

Marital status This has an influence on absenteeism, turnover, and satisfaction. Married employees have fewer absences, undergo less turnover, and are more satisfied with their jobs than the unmarried ones. Marriage imposes additional responsibility, hence the need for a steady job and steady income.

Number of dependents There is correlation between the number of dependents an employee has and his or her absences and satisfaction. The number of children an employee has is positively related to absence, especially among females. Similarly, there is positive correlation between number of dependents and satisfaction.

Creativity This is yet another personal factor that influences individual behaviour. Creativity refers to the cognitive activity that results in a new or novel way of viewing or solving a problem. Creativity is highly desirable, as it is from creativity that major inventions, scientific breakthroughs, and great works of music, literature, and art emanate.

Creative individuals possess at least three categories of attributes, back-ground experience, personal traits, and cognitive abilities.

Background experience matters much to make an individual creative. It is well understood that creative individuals were raised in environments that nurtured creativity. Pierre and Marie Curie, great scientists in their own right, raised a daughter Irene, who won the Noble Prize in Chemistry. Thomas Edison's creativity was nurtured by his mother.

Personal traits have also been lined to creativity in individuals. The traits shared by most creative people are openness; an attraction to complexity; high levels of energy; independence and autonomy; high level of self-confidence, and a strong belief that one has, in fact, creative. Individuals who possess these traits, tend to be more creative than those do not.

Cognitive abilities are an individual's power to think intelligently and to analyse situations and data effectively. Intelligence is a precondition for creativity. Creativity also depends on one's ability to think divergently and convergently about events. Convergent thinking enables him or her to perceive similarities between situations or events. Creative people are generally skilled both in divergent and convergent thinking.

Organisations seek to promote creativity by making it a part of their culture. Firms that truly want to stress creativity state as goals that some percentage of future revenues are to be generated from new products. This clearly communicates that creativity and innovation are valued.

Firms also seek to enhance creativity by rewarding creative success, but care is taken to avoid punishing creative failures. Punishing an employee for failure of his or her creative idea discourages others from coming out with innovative thinking.

Emotions and Emotional Intelligence Emotions are an affective state of consciousness in which joy, sorrow, fear, hate, love, surprise and anger are expressed. These are part of one's personality and he or she carries them to the work place. And their impact on one's workplace behaviour is considerable. Emotions are a private affair. No individual is willing to share his or her emotions with others. Yet, we are able to recognise the presence of various emotions in others, and we are able to communicate our own fellings to them as well.

Four features are common to all emotions:

- Emotions are highly focused — they have an object towards which emotions are expressed. For example, we love a person, our anger is towards a person, and we hate a specific individual.
- Expression of emotions is universal — people across the globe exhibit similar body language to express same emotions. Facil expression to exhibit joy is same irrespective of the fact that the person is an Indian, Chinese or Japanese.
- Culture determines expression of feelings — notwithstanding the fact that people exhibit identical behaviour to express similar emotion, cuture of each society determines display norms to exhibit feelings. Italian culture, for example, emphasises high expressiveness, but it is a taboo in Thailand.
- Six major categories of emotions have been identified — anger, fear, joy, love, sadness and surprise. These are universal.

Each of these emotions is exhibited (tempered by culture) in a given way. Love, for example, is expressed through smile, excitement, eagerness, anxiety and pleasentness writ large on the face, and anger is seen from the frowning face. How to express emotions while communicating online? Pepole in the recent years have developed ingenious ways to expressing emotions through e-mail messages. Known as *emoticons*, (short for emotional icons), these are created by typing characters such as commas, hyphens, and parentheses, which are viewed by tilting one's head to the left (treating left as top). The most common emotions are as follows:

:–) smile

:–(frown

;–) wink

But the problem with emoticons is their overuse by communicators. Another issue relates to their ineffectiveness in communicating what the sender really wanted to convey. Consequntly, the impact of emoticons has declined over time.

Mood Moods are related to emotions. While emotions are focused and intense, moods are feelings that are diffuse. More specifically, a mood is understood as a feeling that is unfocused, and relatively mild in intensity. For example, one can say tht he or she is in a good mood or bad mood. But this is not as focused and intense as saying that the individual is experiencing anger or sadness. In addition, moods tend to fluctuate rapidly in a given day. A favourable opinion from the boss may make the employee entertain a good mood. A harsh criticism, the next moment or the next day, is likely to put the same person in a bad mood. But emotions tend to endure. Love or sadness is likely to stay longer than a good or a bad mood.

Impact on Performance How do emotions and moods impact job performance? It is being observed that emotions may not have any impact on performance. An individual beset with anger, joy or sadness is likely to focus more on the feeling than on improving performance. The distance between emotions and performance is more where there is negative impact of emotions. An angry employee (because he or she received poor rating from the boss) is unlikely to show any improvement in performance.

With regard to moods, there is correlation between them and performance. This is proved in atleast three ways: (i) mood strongly influences the extent to which people help each other, cooperate with each other, and refrain from exhibiting aggressive behaviour towards others, (ii) moods also influence one's attitude towards work of self as well as of others', and (iii) moods help recall past events and actions. For example, an individual is likely to recollect positive things about the job, the boss and the environment, if he or she starts the day with a good mood. Quite controry happens when he or she starts the day with a bad mood.

Emotional Intelligence Emotional intelligence (EI or EQ) is concerned with an individual's emotional and social skills. EI helps us moitor and shape our emotional responses and those of others. The concept of EI was popularised by Daniel Goleman in 1995. EQ has the following dimensions:

- *Emotional attainment or self-awareness, and people skills.* The person is good at reading his or her own feelings, has the capacity to empathise with others and take into account other people's feelings.
- *Emotional management.* This is reflected in ensuring that the person's emotions (joy, love or anger) do not overwhelm him or her, and that they are appropriate to the situation. It can be seen as an ability to cheer oneself up, or stop a temper tantrum in mid-course by going out for a walk, for example.
- *Using emotions.* A capacity to weight up the emotional aspects of values and attitudes when confronting problems and making decisions.
- *Self-motivation.* This refers to an individual's propensity to delay gratification. It has been observed that an individual who is capable of delaying gratification-i.e., waiting a while to take a reward than taking it immediately-is more socially competent and self-reliant than a person who settles for immediate rewards.

ENVIRONMENTAL FACTORS

Environmental factors include such variables as economic, social, political, and the like. These factors are mainly external and will influence (and are not generally influenced by) individual behaviour considerably. A brief description of the external factors follows.

Economic Factors The economic environment is an important determinant of individual behaviour. All work is performed within economic framework that, both directly and indirectly, impinges on an organisational environment.

Economic environment is a synthesis of several factors, prominent among them being the employment level, wage rates, economic outlook, and technological change.

Employment opportunities will have a strong influence on individual behaviour. Fewer job opportunities (create fear of losing the present job) increase the emphasis on job security and can change the basic motivation pattern of the individual. Where job opportunities are several, tendency of job-hopping will increase. Loyalty to one's organisation becomes irrelevant.

The job that an individual holds has significant influence on his or her behaviour. The behaviour of a professor in a university will be different from an executive in an industrial enterprise. Similarly, the behaviour of a worker in a factory will not be the same as that of cart puller on the street.

Wages satisfy various individual needs. They provide food and shelter, are measures of achievement, and can serve as a status symbol. Money is a complex variable and its effect on behaviour varies tremendously. It is well known that wages attract people to certain organisations and determine their level of job satisfaction. As will be explained in the chapter on motivation (Chapter 8), inequality in wages will have dampening effect on employee performance.

The general *economic outlook* also influences individual expectations, especially of those employed in industries severely affected by economic cycles. In fact, some employees experience layoffs and re-calls in the course of their working life, while others (eg. public sector employees) are insulated from the economy. Individuals who experience frequent layoffs are more likely to be motivated by factors that affect job security, others would consider job security to be relatively unimportant and would be motivated by other factors.[3]

Technological change is considered as an economic factor because of its potential effects upon individual job opportunities. Technological change has the strongest impact on lower level jobs, although increased automation, robotics, computerisation, and more sophisticated production technologies can affect individuals at all levels. In addition to changing employment opportunities, technological change also affects job design. Although the individual may stay employed, the skill required to perform the job may be reduced, thus increasing the downward pressure on wages. Both the reduced skill required and perceived lack of advancement opportunities can have major effect on an individual's level of job satisfaction.

Cultural Environment Cultural environment is made up of institutions and other forces that affect society's basic values, perceptions, work ethics, preferences, and behaviours. People grow up in a particular society that shapes their basic beliefs, values, and behaviours. Culture varies from country to country (even within a country) and these variations result in different behaviours across countries. Work ethics, achievement needs, and effort-reward expectations and values are important cultural factors, having behavioural implications.

Work *ethics* is tinged with morals. In the context of job ethics, it implies hard work and commitment. Strong work ethics ensures motivated employees, and the opposite is true when work ethics is weak.

Achievement need too, influences employee behaviour. A person with a high need to achieve tends to have a high degree of personal responsibility, sets realistic goals, takes moderate risks, and uses personal performance feedback in satisfying his or her need to achieve (Chapter 9 provides more details on achievement needs).

From a cultural perspective, it is important to note that the need to achieve is a learned phenomenon. This suggests that various cultural attributes (eg. educational system, institutional characteristics, media conditioning, etc.) can affect the need to achieve either positively or negatively. Although work ethics and the need to achieve are not the same, they do affect individuals in similar ways. Not surprisingly, individuals with a low need to achieve will be more difficult to motivate using traditional motivation techniques. Similarly, individuals with a high need to achieve would be relatively unhappy in an organisation that does not reward achieving power.

It is well-known that a perfect match between *effect* and *reward* will produce better performance from an individual. When the individual perceives that he or she has been treated unfairly, his or her performance suffers. This phenomenon is observed in most organisation.

Value is tinged with moral favour involving an individual's judgement of what is right, good, or desirable. Values influence one's perception and, attitudes, and through these, his or her behaviour.

Ethics and Social Responsibility Ethics and social responsibility impact individual behaviour considerably.

Ethics refers to a system of moral principles — a sense of right and wrong, and goodness and badness of actions and the motives and the consequences of these actions. As applied to a business firm, ethics is the study of good and evil, right and wrong, and just and unjust actions of business people.

Can personal ethics be different from business ethics? The answer is 'no'. But in reality, circumstances in business may compel an ethically honest person to commit certain immoral acts. What is, therefore, important is that the organisation must have strong ethical conduct. This will make honest people become more strong in their beliefs and actions and often convert morally vulnerable individuals to become ethically strong. Look at the case of a CEO of a car manufacturing company. Chung Mong-Koo, head of Hyundai Motors, the sixth largest car maker in the world, has been sentenced to three years in jail on charges of embezzlement and breach of trust. It is ideal when an honest individual works for an organisation like WIPRO which is known for ethical conduct. The behaviour of such employees will be obviously different from others who work for organisations like Enron.

Social responsibility, also called corporate social responsibility (CSR), is understood as the obligation of decision-makers to take actions that protect and improve the welfare of the society as a whole, along with their own interests. Specifically, CSR refers to the commitment of business to contribute to sustainable economic development, working with employees and their families, the local community and society at large, to improve their quality of life in ways that are good for business. CSR obligations transcend the ethical, legal, commercial and public expectations of business.

An employee working for an organisation (Tatas, for example) known for social consciousness tends to develop similar characteristics—concern in the welfare of others, sharing with others and the like.

Political Factors The political climate in which an individual lives can affect individual behaviour in several ways. The stability of the government can affect employment opportunities, both in quantity and quality. A politically unstable environment has difficulty in attracting industry and therefore experiences problems in maintaining a steady level of employment. The quality of jobs can also be affected by low capital investment. As companies are reluctant to invest large sums of money in a politically unstable country, many available jobs are either agriculture-oriented or in other types of labour intensive industries. Consequently, large segments of the population are either in temporary employment or in jobs that satisfy only their basic needs.

The political ideology of a country affects individual behaviour primarily through the relative freedom available to its citizens. For example, in controlled societies, educational and career opportunities are less available to individuals than in the less controlled ones. Management structures and philosophies in controlled societies have a significant impact on the decision strategies and methods of implementation available to managers. The relative freedom available can affect career choice, job design, motivation methods, and finally, individual performance.[4]

Organisational Systems and Resources

Individual behaviour is also influenced by physical facilities, organisation structure and design, leadership, and reward systems.

Facilities Physical facilities such as lighting, ventilation, air-conditioning, decor, space provided for each employee, equipment, and the like, have an influence on employee performance. In addition, adequate provision of secretarial support and other staff can allow a senior manager to focus his or her attention on issues more critical to the organisation's effectiveness.

Organisation Structure and Design These have to do with the way in which the different groups and departments in an organisation are set up and the way in which, the reporting relationships and lines of communication are established among different positions in the organisation. The behaviour and performance of an individual is influenced by where that person fits into the overall structure and design of the organisation.

Leadership An organisation establishes a system of leadership and supervision to provide direction, assistance, advice, and coaching to individual members. The leader's behaviour is, therefore, a potential source of influence on an individual.

Reward Systems Organisations establish reward systems to compensate their employees for good work done. The behaviour and performance of an individual is influenced by the reward system his or her organisation has established.

Work related Behaviour An individual's behaviour is influenced by what stage he or she occupies in an organisation. The five stages of the individual's stay in the organisation may be distinguished-joining the organisation, remaining with the organisation, maintaining work attendance, performing required tasks, and exhibiting organisational citizenship.[5] (See Fig.15.2).

FIGURE 15-2
STAGES IN ORGANISATIONAL LIFE

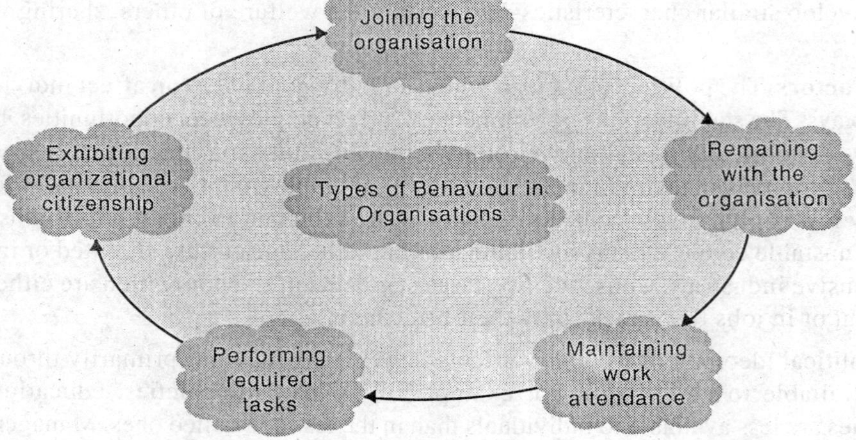

Joining the organisation An individual joins an organisation of his or her choice. He or she needs the job just as the organisation needs the services of the individual. In the induction stage, the new employee experiences excitement because of the new assignment and expectations from it, and anxiety because of the fear that the expectations might not be realised.

Remaining with the organisation The most challenging task before organisations today is to attract talent and retain it for the benefit of the firm. The organisation may succeed in attracting competent employees by offering lucrative remuneration packages and arousing high expectations. Retaining such competent employees is much more difficult. Knowledge workers constitute intellectual capital and the longer they stay, more knowledge they have about work processes, corporate values, and customer needs. Thus, knowledge management involves ensuring that valuable employees stay with the organisation. Towards this end, managers adopt different interventions.

Interventions notwithstanding, employees quit their jobs when they experience dissatisfaction. The behaviour of a dissatisfied employee will be different from that of another who derives satisfaction from his or her job. The dissatisfied employee tends to withdraw and shows less productivity. A satisfied employee, on the other hand, tends to exhibit commitment to work and show better productivity.

Maintaining work attendance Those who stay with the organisation are expected to report to work as scheduled. But some of the employees fail to show up for work and their absences are caused by problems relating to health (of selves or of families), family responsibilities, vehicles breakdown, job dissatisfaction, and lack of motivation in the workplace. These account for absenteeism among the employees.

Performing required tasks People are hired to perform tasks, generally, above minimum standards. Task performance refers to goal-directed activities that are under the individual's control. These include physical behaviours as well as mental processing leading to behaviours. These abilities need to be harnessed and put to use for organisational effectiveness.

Exhibiting organisational citizenship Organisational effectiveness depends on more than just satisfactory job performance. It also relies on organisational citizenship. Organisational citizenship behaviours extend beyond job-related tasks. They include tolerating ambiguities, accepting occasional impositions, sharing resources, and cooperating with fellow employees.

How do employees become good organisational citizens? One way to ensure this is the perceived fairness of the company's treatment of employees. Firms can develop citizenship trait by correcting the inequity felt by an employee. The other is the degree to which employees hold strong ethical values, particularly a sense of social responsibility. An employee with social conscientiousness will reach out to help others and avoid engaging in behaviours that interfere with other's goals. Social responsibility is a trait acquired through life-long socialisation, and it does well for an organisation to hire people with this value.

Psychological Factors Psychological factors are an individual's mental characteristics and attributes that can affect behaviour. Though not always observable, their role in affecting individual behaviour is considerable. There are several psychological factors, but the more prominent among them are personality, perception, attitudes, values and learning. These have been discussed in greater detail in the four chapters.

Models of Individual Behaviour

OB experts have constructed certain models which are useful in understanding individual behaviour. The models are: Theory X and Theory Y model, Economic and Self-actualising model, Behaviouristic and Humanistic model, and Rational and Emotional model.[6]

Theory X and Theory Y Model Theory X assumes the individual to be lazy, non-creative, and in need of constant prodding. Theory Y views the individual as having tremendous potential, which effective management can channelize towards organisational goals. Obviously, depending on the individual manager's philosophy of human behaviour, there may be a divergence of managerial practices in the same organisation.

Economic and Self-Actualizing Model The economic model of the human being conceptualises the individual as totally economic in orientation. The concept has been derived from the scientific management philosophy of the late 1880s. At the heart of scientific management was the concern for standardising jobs, specializing work functions, and providing economic incentives to those whose performance was near or in excess of standard performance.

In contrast to the economic model is the self-actualizing model, which postulates that an individual is motivated by the opportunity to grow, mature, and become all he or she is capable of becoming. The model underlines that the individual cannot be adequately described by economic or physiological consideration alone. People strive for loftier goals, like self-fulfilment and self-actualisation. Adherents of this model see the individual as craving for personal growth, job competence, and self-fulfilment. Although individuals may be temporarily sidetracked in this quest, they will eventually return to it. The challenge of an organisation, therefore, is to provide proper conditions for self-actualization.[7]

Behaviouristic and Humanistic Model Some scholars believe that individuals can be described solely in terms of behaviour. These theorists are interested only in *observable* behaviour as contrasted with thoughts or feelings. In its most radical form, the behaviouristic model holds that all behaviour is environmentally determined.

In the humanistic model, scholars believe that an individual is more philosophical than scientific. Humanists see the individual as capable of surmounting irrational impulses through conscious reasoning. In their view, people control their own destiny to a great degree and their potential cannot be underestimated.

Rational and Emotional Model In the rational model, an individual is perceived to be a highly rational entity, having computer-like characteristics. Whenever faced with a problem, the individual is supposed to collect all relevant information, analyse the data, and then arrive at a solution. Human beings are, thus, deliberative, serious, and computational.

In the emotional model, human beings are understood to be guided by emotions, many of which are unconscious responses. Scholars of the Freudian persuasion rely on this model. Freudians perceive human beings as irrational because of the constant conflicts among the *Id*, and *Ego* and the *Super-ego*. These inner conflicts, according to Freudians, cause individuals to be subject to their emotions. The next chapter contains more details on Freudian theory.

Case

A Worried CEO

Sudarshan, the Managing Director of M.Feeds, a Bangalore-based company, is a worried man. All his efforts to regain the lost market and to wipe out the losses in the company's balance sheet have proved futile. Sitting alone in his chamber, lighting up cigarette after cigarette, and sipping cups of coffee, Sudarshan started recollecting events of 1987, which wrecked the fortunes of a once successful company.

Subbu and his team were defeated in the union election held in the beginning of 1987. Rivals, Gowda and his team, were elected with a comfortable majority. The winning team had a leaning towards CITU, which was known for its militancy. The attitudes and actions of Gowda and his team were not to the liking of the management, particularly Setty, the Factory Manager.

The management was waiting for a way to deal with the new team of unionists. Not reconciled to the loss of power. Subbu and his cronies started a cultural association with the apparent objective of promoting Kannada, the local language. Setty welcomed the formation of the association and, in fact, even encouraged its activities. The management too gave financial support to the cultural outfit.

Emboldened by the encouragement given, Subbu and his team demanded that the management should negotiate with them about all matters relating to employee welfare. This proposal was not acceptable to the management, which turned it down. But Setty began hobnobbing with Subbu, often to the consternation of the leaders of the recognized union.

One day, Gowda and Subbu had a heated exchange of words, which resulted in a physical bout inside the plant. Sridhar, the HRD Manager, placed the duo under suspension on grounds of indiscipline.

An enquiry was conducted and Subbu was acquitted. But Gowda refused to appear before the enquiry officer. Having been acquitted, Subbu demanded reinstatement, which the management readily agreed to. Subbu, with triumph written large on his face, came to the factory but the team led by Gowda protested by calling a strike.

The management assured Gowda that he too would be reinstated provided he was acquitted by the enquiry officer. Gowda was in no mood to listen to the management nor was he prepared to face the enquiry. Subbu demanded reinstatement which Gowda protested against. The stalemate continued and the strike lasted three months.

Work resumed after prolonged talks. But the scars remained. Setty got a sack and Sridhar left and joined an Indo-French company. M.Feeds lost its customers and the efforts (setting up, for the first time, a marketing department) to regain their patronage did not succeed. The company started making losses, which only increased as the years went by.

Questions

1. Using the knowledge you have acquired from this chapter, trace the foundation for the behaviour of each character in the case. Do you think any factor has been left out?
2. Which behaviour model best explains the conduct of each of the characters in the case?
3. Recall Fig.3.2. Where do you place each character in the figure? Why?

Questions

1 State and explain the foundations of individual behaviour.

2 Why do individuals differ in their behaviour?

3 State and explain the different models of individual behaviour.

3 Which biographical factors best predict—

Satisfaction

Absenteeism

Turnover

Stress

Productivity

5 Take a look at yourself. Which of the variables explained in this chapter best explain your actions and performance?

6 What influence do you think an employee's age, experience, and physical abilities have on his or her performance at work?

REFERENCES

1. Shrinivas Pandit, *Thought Leaders*, Tata McGraw-Hill, 2002, pp.222-6.
2. Richard T.Schaefer and Robert P.Lamn, *Sociology*, McGraw-Hill, 1998, p.352.
3. Gray and Starke, *Organisational Behaviour-Concepts and Application*, Merrill, 1998, p.64.
4. Ibid, p.62.
5. Steven L.Mcshane and Mary Ann Von Glinow, *Organisational Behaviour*, TMH, 2000, p.35.
6. Helga Drummond, *Organisational Behaviour-Theory and Practice*, MacMillan, 1991, p.54.
7. Ibid, p.55.

CHAPTER

Sixteen

Personality

LEARNING OBJECTIVES

After reading this chapter you should understand –

1. The nature of Personality.
2. The different theories of personality.
3. The stages that involves in shaping up of personality.
4. The factors that contributed to personality.
5. The "Big five" personality dimensions and Myers-Briggs Indicator seek to explain the structure of personality.
6. The important personality traits relevant to OB.

As stated in the previous chapter, personality is one of the psychological factors that influences individual behaviour. This chapter is devoted to a discussion of nature, theories, shaping, determinants, and attributes of personality which have a bearing on OB.

Nature of Personality

Generally, personality refers to the set of traits and behaviours that characterise an individual. A more comprehensive meaning of personality is that it refers to the relatively stable pattern of behaviour and consistent internal state and explains a person's behavioural tendencies.[1]

The following elements should form the meaning of personality:

1. Personality has both internal and external elements. The external traits are the observable behaviours that we notice in an individual's personality, for example, sociability. The internal states represent the thoughts, values and genetic characteristics that we infer from the observable behaviours.
2. An individual's personality is relatively stable. If it changes at all, it is only after a very long time or as the result of traumatic events.
3. An individual's personality is both inherited as well as shaped by the environment. Our personality is partly inherited genetically from our parents. However, these genetic personality characteristics are altered some-what by life experiences.
4. Each individual is unique in behaviour. There are striking differences among individuals.[2]

Thus, personality refers to the sum total of internal and external traits of an individual, which are relatively stable and which make the individual different from others.

Theories of Personality

More light on the nature of personality has been thrown by theories on personality. There are several theories but the more prominent among them are: (See Fig.16.1).

FIGURE 16-1
THEORIES OF PERSONALITY

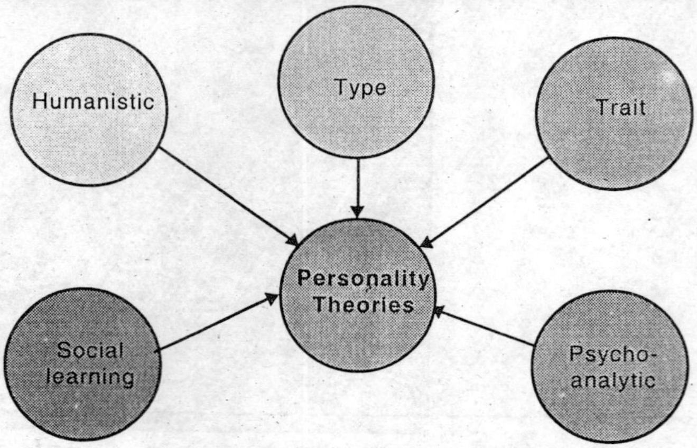

1. type,
2. trait,
3. psychoanalytic,
4. social learning, and
5. humanistic.

A brief description of each follows.

Type Theories

According to type theories, people are grouped into identifiable categories. One basis for classifying personalities is the structure of the body. Kretschmer and Sheldon are credited with this classification. In type theories, a relationship was sought to be established between features of face or body and personality. Thus, a short, plump person (endomorph) was said to be sociable, relaxed, and even-tempered; a tall, thin person (endomorph) was characterized as restrained, self-conscious, and fond of solitude; a heavy-set muscular individual (mesomorph) was described as noisy, callous, and fond of physical activity. Although a person's physique may have some influence on personality, the relationship is much more subtle than this sort of classification implies. Thus, classification of personalities on a physical basis is subjective. Type theories are simple and popular but carry no substance.

Another basis to type personalities is psychological factors. One of Freud's pupils, the Swiss psychologist Carl Jung, divided all personalities into *introverts* and *extroverts*. These terms are normally associated with an individual's sociability and interpersonal orientation. Extroverts are gregarious, sociable individuals, while introverts are shy, quiet, and retiring. In a more technical sense, introverts are characterised by a greater sensitivity and concern for feelings and are more comfortable dealing with abstract things. Extroverts are more oriented towards other people, events, and objects. Typing personalities on psychological factors into introverts and extroverts, though looks simple, serves not much of a purpose, as many people fall between the two extremes. Moreover, as Jung himself pointed out, the introvert and extrovert typology turns out to be more in the nature of continuum than discretely separate types.[3]

Type theories are simple as they are based on physical attributes or psychological factors for categorization of personalities. But the theories fail to reveal all complexities of a personality.

Trait Theory

Another interesting approach to understand personality is the trait. A personality trait is understood as being an enduring attribute of a person that appears consistently in a variety of situations. A trait differentiates one from another in a relatively permanent or consistent way. A trait of an individual is abstracted from his behaviour, and serves an useful 'unit of analysis' to understand personality.

Unlike typologists who tried to stereotype people into distinct types based on physical or psychological characteristics, trait theorists assume that a personality can be described by its position on a number of continuous dimensions or scales, each of which represents a trait. Thus, we could rate an individual on a scale of intelligence, emotional stability, aggressiveness, creativeness, or any of a number of other dimensions. When we informally describe ourselves and others by such adjectives as friendly, cautious, excitable, intelligent, or anxious, we are using trait terms.

It is important to remember that traits are reactions, not something a person 'possesses'. One does not possess shyness, he feels and acts shy under certain circumstances. Actually, he may behave quite forwardly in some other circumstances or at some other time. What is important is what he does typically.

In many ways, the trait theory is a multiple model of the type theory. Rather than classifying a person by just one feature, the trait theory classifies people's personality by a set of features.

Psychologists working in the area of trait theory are concerned with **(a)** determining the basic traits that provide a meaningful description of personality and **(b)** finding some way to measure them. Determining basic traits is rather difficult because thousands of words in the English language refer to characteristics of behaviour. How to reduce them to a small number of meaningful traits? *Factor analysis*, a complex statistical technique, is used for the purpose. Factor analysis helps reduce a large number of measures to a smaller number of independent dimensions.

There are two ways of assessing personality traits: **(i)** the person describes himself by answering questions about this attitudes, feelings, and behaviours; **(ii)** someone else evaluates the person's traits either from what he knows about the individual or from direct observations of behaviour. With the first method, a *personality inventory* is most often used, whereas the second usually involves using a rating scale.

A personality inventory is essentially a questionnaire in which the person reports reactions or feelings in certain situations. A personality inventory asks the same questions of each person, and the answers are usually given in a form that can be easily rated. a personality inventory may be designed to measure a single dimension of personality (such as introversion, extroversion) or it may measure several personality traits simultaneously.

A rating scale is a device for recording judgement about a trait. The rating scale is filled up by someone else by what he or she knows about the individual or by studying his or her behaviour in certain situations.[4]

Trait theory is an improvement over the type theories. The type theories unrealistically attempt to place personality into discrete, discontinuous categories. The trait theory, on the other hand, gives recognition to the continuity of personalities. The theory has also contributed to personality ratings and factor analysis techniques in behavioural science.

However, there are several problems with the trait approach also. Terms are difficult to define, there are contradictions, and the scientific reliability of the results is open to considerable challenge. A major objection to trait theories is that they are very descriptive rather than analytical and are a long way from being comprehensive theories of personality. Further, some theories tend to focus on isolated traits without specifying how these are organised within the personality. Without knowing which traits are most important and how they relate to other traits, we do not have adequate description of an individual's personality. Finally, as mentioned earlier, traits are abstracted from behaviour. But we cannot use the same traits to explain behaviour.

Psychoanalytic Theory

Psychoanalytic theory owes its origin to Sigmund Freud. In his 40 years of writing and clinical practice, Freud, acknowledged as one of the intellectual giants in the history of modern thought, developed **(i)** the first comprehensive personality theory, **(ii)** a method for treating neurotic ills, and **(iii)** an extensive body of clinical observations based on his therapeutic experience and self-analysis.

Freud likened the mind to an iceberg-only a small segment of which protruded above the surface of the water. This small portion of the mind represents conscious experience, while the much larger mass below water level represents the unconscious-a storehouse of impulses, passions, and primitive instincts that affect our thoughts and behaviour. It was this unconscious portion of the mind that Freud sought to explore, and he did so by the method of *free association*. The method requires that the person talks about everything that comes into the conscious mind, no matter how ridiculous or trivial it might seem. By analysing free association, including the recall of dreams and early childhood memories, Freud sought to identify the basic determinants of personality.

Freud saw personality as being composed of three elements-*id, ego, and super ego* (See Fig.16.2). This tripartite division of personality is known as the *structural model* of mental life, although Freud felt the divisions should be understood as hypothetical rather than as specific 'structures' of personality. Freud insisted that these structures be considered as hypothetical constructs, since the field of neuroanatomy was not sufficiently advanced to locate them within the central nervous system.

FIGURE 16-2
LEVEL OF CONSCIOUSNESS OF ID, EGO AND SUPEREGO

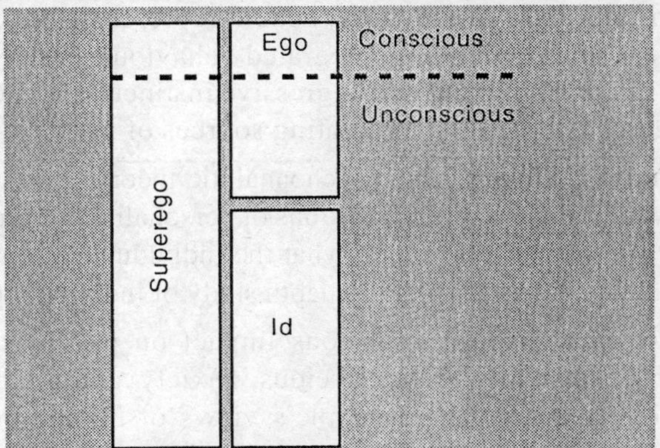

The Id The word 'id' is the Latin word for 'it' and refers exclusively to the innate component of personality. The id is the mental agency containing everything inherited, present at birth, and fixed in the individual's constitution, especially instincts. It is raw, animalistic, unorganised, knows no laws, obeys no rules, and remains basic to the individual throughout life. Operating on a primitive basis, it is free from all inhibitions. The id, as the original personality system, expresses the primary principle of all human life-the immediate discharge of psychic energy (libido) produced by animal drives (especially sex and aggression) which, when pent up, creates tension throughout the personality system. Immediate tension reduction is called the *pleasure principle*, and the id obeys it, manifesting itself in an impulsive and irrational manner, regardless of the consequences of its actions for others or its own self-preservation. Furthermore, since the id does not recognise fear or anxiety, it takes no precautions in expressing its purpose-a fact which Freud felt may result in danger for the individual and/or for society.

The id, according to Freud, employs to rid the personality of tension: *reflex* actions and *primary process*. Primary process refers to attempts of an individual to form a mental image of the object that will remove the tension. A hungry man, for example, experiences partial gratification of his hunger by imagining a delicious meal. In reflex actions, the id responds automatically to sources of irritation, thereby promptly removing the tension which the irritant elicits. Examples of such inborn reflex mechanisms are sneezing, coughing, and blinking.

The Ego Mental images do not satisfy needs. The starving man cannot satisfy his hunger by eating images. Reality must be considered. This is the role of the ego. The ego develops out of the id because of the necessity for dealing with the real world. The hungry man must have food if the tension of hunger is to be reduced.

The Super Ego In order for a person to function constructively in society, he should acquire a system of values, norms, ethics, and attitudes which are reasonably compatible with that society. The super ego, the third part of the personality, represents the internalised representation of the values and morals of society as taught to the child by parents and others. The super ego judges whether an action is right or wrong according to the standards of society. The id seeks pleasure, the ego tests reality, and the super ego strives for perfection. In Freud's view, the human organism is not born with a super ego; rather, children must incorporate it through interactions with parents, teachers, and other 'formative' figures.

Sometimes the three components of personality are at odds with each other: the ego postpones gratification that the id wants right away, and the super ego battles with both the ego and the id because behaviour often falls short of the moral code it represents. But more often, in the normal person, the three work as a team producing integrated behaviour. Freud believed that the conflict between the id impulses-primarily sexual and aggressive instincts-and the restraining influences of the ego and the super ego constituted the motivating sources of personality.

Evaluation of Psychoanalytic Theory The psychoanalytic theory is an improvement over the trait theories. Trait theories try to find the stable dimensions of personality by studying groups of people and much of their data is obtained from self reports-what the individual says about himself or herself. In contrast, psychoanalytic theory is based on the in-depth study of individual personalities.

Psychoanalytic theory has had an enormous impact on psychological and philosophical conceptions of people. The ideas of the unconscious, anxiety, and the childhood causes of adult psychological difficulties have permeated people's views of human behaviour, including their understanding of the cause of their own behaviour.

Freud's emphasis on the unconscious has been partially supported by some of the current research findings of cognitive psychologists. This work has revealed that mental processes about which people are unaware all have an important impact on thoughts and actions. In addition, experimental techniques derived from procedures used to study implicit memory allow the unconscious to be studied in a more scientifically sophisticated manner. The techniques help overcome the reliance of traditional Freudian approaches on single-subject case studies and unverifiable interpretations of dreams and slips of the tongue for support.

The importance of psychoanalytic theory is underscored by the fact that it spawned a significant and enduring method of treating psychological disturbances. For Freud, the basic sources of abnormal behaviour are unresolved past conflicts and anxiety. How to rid oneself of the anxiety produced by the unconscious? The answer, according to Freud is to bring the unconscious to the conscious part. Freud suggested *free association* and *dream interpretation* as techniques to probe the unconscious.

Finally, Freud's emphasis on sexual factors led to an awareness of their role in adjustment problems and paved the way for the scientific study of sexuality.

Freud also contributed to the study of organisational behaviour in at least four areas.

(i) *Creative behaviour* For instance, certain stages of the creative processes are unconscious in nature.

(ii) *Dissatisfaction* Certain behaviours of employees such as day-dreaming, forgetting, apathy, rationalisation, and even some sicknesses, disability, and pain are often analysed in psychoanalytic terms.

(iii) *Group development* Descriptions of the stages which groups must go through to become 'mature' are highly psychoanalytic in nature.

(iv) *Leadership and influence* Freud's great interest in authority and power is reflected in psychoanalytic approaches to the study of the emergence of leadership, the nature of a leader's relationship with his followers, and styles of leadership.

Freud's psychoanalytic theory has been criticised as much as it has been praised. One criticism against the theory is that the approach is not based on empirically verifiable facts. The psychoanalytic elements are largely hypothetical constructs and are not measurable, observable items susceptible to scientific analysis and verification. The id, the ego, and the super ego are primarily a 'black box' explanation of human beings. Hence, the theory fails to reflect clearly human personality and behaviour.

Some critics point out that Freud's theory of personality is based almost entirely upon his observations of emotionally disturbed individuals. It may not represent an appropriate description of the normal, healthy personality. Maslow, the proponent of humanistic psychology, came down heavily on Freud's psychoanalytics. Maslow considered Freudian theory as a one-sided psychology lacking in comprehensiveness since it was grounded on the abnormal or 'sick' part of human behaviour. He felt that psychology had exclusively dwelled on the negative side of human nature (i.e., it frailties and shortcomings), ignoring humanity's strengths and virtues. For example, the nature of graduate students would hardly become evident by exclusively studying high school dropouts. In fact, such a study would be much more likely to discover what graduate students are not like than what they are like. Stated more boldly, Maslow argued that the study of crippled, stunted, immature, and unhealthy persons can yield only a 'crippled' psychology.

About the claim of Freud's theory serving as a basis for scientific study of sexuality, critics point out that Freud overemphasized the role of sex in human motivation. He made his observations during the Victorian period, when sexual standards were very strict, so it was understandable that many of his patients had conflicts centering around sexual desires. In today's permissive society guilt feelings about sex are less frequent, yet the incidence of mental illness remains about the same. Sexual conflicts are not the only causes of personality disturbances-perhaps not even a major cause.

Freud assumed that all human events (actions, thoughts, feelings, aspirations) are lawful and determined by powerful instinctual forces, notably sex and aggression. Thus, human beings are seen as essentially mechanistic, they are governed by the same natural laws that apply to the behaviour of other organisms. In his approach there is no room for concepts such as free will, choice, personal responsibility, volition, spontaneity, and self determination.[5]

SOCIAL LEARNING THEORY

Much of human behaviour is either learnt or modified by learning. Through learning one acquires knowledge, language, attitudes, values, manual skills, fears, personality traits, and self-insight. Therefore, a study of the process of learning throws more light on understanding human's activities.

There are two ways of learning: Learning through reinforcement, direct experience, and learning by observing others, also called vicarious learning. For social learning theorists, reinforcement is not always necessary for learning. They believe that since an individual can make use of complex symbolic processes to code and store his observations in memory, he can learn by observing the actions of others and by noting the consequences of those actions.

The social learning theories of personality regard a situation as an important determinant of behaviour.

A person's action in a given situation depends upon the specific characteristics of a situation, the individual's understanding of the situation, and past behaviour in similar situations (or observations of others in similar situations).

The social learning theory focuses on behaviour patterns and cognitive activities in relation to the specific conditions that evoke, maintain, or modify them. The emphasis is on what an individual does in a given situation. Some of the personal variables that determine what an individual will do in a particular situation include the following:

(i) *Competencies* Intelligence ability, social skills, and other abilities.

(ii) *Cognitive strategies* Habitual ways of selectively attending to information and organising it into meaningful units.

(iii) *Outcome expectations* Expectations about the consequences of different behaviours and the meaning of certain stimuli.

(iv) *Subjective value outcome* Even if individuals have similar expectancies, they may choose to behave differently because of differences in the subjective values of the outcomes they expect. Two students may expect that a certain behaviour will please the professor, but for one this outcome is important, while for the other it is not.

(v) *Self-regulatory systems and plans* Individual differences in self-imposed goals, rules guiding behaviour, self-imposed rewards for success or punishment for failure, and ability to plan and execute steps leading to a goal will lead to differences in behaviour.

All of the above variables interact with the conditions of a particular situation to determine what an individual will do in that situation.

These theorists also believe in reciprocal behaviour patterns. A situation is no doubt capable of evoking, maintaining, or modifying the behaviour patterns of individuals. An individual, in turn, is able to mould the condition of a situation. We are not simply passive reactors to situational conditions. Our behaviour influences the 'situations' of life as well as being influenced by them; the relationship is reciprocal. By selectively attending to what is happening, we can prevent certain conditions from impinging on us. And by our actions we can partly create the condition that do impinge; changes in behaviour towards others are usually followed by reciprocal changes in the behaviour of others.

Evaluation of Social Learning Theory Unlike the trait and psychoanalytic theories on personality, the social learning theory regards situation as an important variable in determining human behaviour. Trait theories assume that personality is consistent so that a person can be characterized according to enduring traits. In other words, behaviour of an individual will be the same irrespective of environmental conditions. However, this assumption may not be correct. After all, actions of the individuals should be in accordance with the demands of the situation.

Psychoanalytic theory assumes that behaviour is influenced by mentalistic (unobservable) concept, namely, the unconscious. B.F.Skinner, one of the social learning theorists, strongly repudiates all explanations of behaviour based on the presumed existence of an inner metaphysical man, the self, the unconscious, or any other hypothetic entity referring to events which 'lie under the skin'. Such mentalists and intrapsychic mechanisms, he notes, originated in primitive animism but persist because there is ignorance of environmental conditions.

Skinner's objection to the use of such hypothetic constructs or inner causes is not that they are inappropriate phenomenon for psychologists to study but rather that they are shrouded in terminology that makes objective definitions and empirical tests impossible. In the history of science, he observes, it has usually been necessary to completely abandon such conceptions rather than modify them to a form which permits empirical study. To explain why a competent student flunks in college we might easily say 'because he lacked motivation', or 'because he cuts classes due to an unconscious fear of success'. Such hypotheses about the student's dismissal from college may sound like explanations, but Skinner warns that they explain nothing unless the motives involved are explicitly defined and unless the antecedents of flunking are established.

Social learning theory has made a major contribution to both clinical psychology and personality theory. It has led us to look more closely at the situation that can modify behaviour. Careful application of learning principles has proved very successful in changing maladaptive behaviour.

Social learning theorists have been criticized for over-emphasizing the importance of situational factors in behaviour to the neglect of individual differences. They show little interest, for example, in innate differences that may predispose one person to be characteristically passive and slow to respond and another to be excitable and quick.

An individual is regarded as a flexible, malleable, and passive victim of external stimuli-the permanent pawn of environmental fate. Environmental conditions are held to be superior to human nature.

As will be studied later in Maslow's humanistic theory of personality, each individual must be studied, as an integrated, unique, organized whole. Maslow felt that for far too long psychologists had concentrated upon minute analysis of separate events, neglecting the basic aspects of the whole person and his human nature. In a common-place metaphor psychologists studied the trees, not the forest. In fact, Maslow's theory was primarily developed as a revolt against those theories (especially learning) which deal in bits and pieces of behaviour while ignoring the person as a unified whole.[6]

THE HUMANISTIC APPROACH

The humanistic approach to the study of personality includes a number of theories which, although different in some respects, share a common emphasis on man's potential for self-direction and freedom of choice. They are concerned with the 'self' and the individual's subjective experiences. The theories stress a man's positive nature-his push towards growth and self-actualization. Their emphasis is also on the 'here and now' rather than on events in early childhood that may have shaped the individual's personality.

Carl Rogers and Abraham Maslow are credited with the humanistic theory of personality. Their views on personality are explained, in brief, in the following paragraphs.[7]

Rogers Self Theory Roger's approach to personality is described as phenomenological. Phenomenology is the study of the individual's subjective experience, feelings, and private concepts as well as his views of the world and self. For Rogers, behaviour is utterly dependent upon how one perceives the world, that is, behaviour is the result of immediate events as they are actually perceived and interpreted by the individual. Such an approach to personality emphasizes the self and its characteristics. Indeed, his theory is often referred to as self theory personality because the best vantage point for understanding behaviour is from the internal frame of reference of the individual himself.

Roger's ideas of human nature, like Freud's, grew out of his experiences in working with emotionally disturbed people. On the basis of his clinical experience, Rogers has concluded that the core of the human nature is essentially purposive, forward-moving, constructive, realistic, and quite trustwörthy. He regards the person as an active force of energy, oriented towards future goals and self-directed purpose rather than a creature pushed and pulled by forces beyond his control.

Freud presented us with a portrait of the person with an id and an self unconscious which, if permitted expression, manifests itself in incest, homicide, thievery, rape, and other horrendous acts. According to this view, humanity is basically irrational, unsocialized, and destructive of self and others. Rogers agrees that people occasionally express all kind of bitter and murderous feelings, abnormal impulses, bizarre and antisocial actions, but he argues that at such times they are not behaving in concert with their inner natures. Thus, the people are functioning as ***fully human beings***, when they are free at experience and satisfying their inner nature, they show themselves to be positive and rational creatures who can be trusted to live in harmony with themselves and others.

Thus, Rogers has a profound (almost religious) sense of respect for human nature. He posits that human organism has a natural tendency to move in the direction of differentiation, self-responsibility, co- operation, and maturity. The expression of this basic nature allows for the continuation and enhancement of the individual and species.

Thus, basic to Rogers' personality theory are two concepts; self and self-actualization. The self consist of all the ideas, perceptions, and values that characterize '1' or 'me'; it includes the awareness 'what 1 am' and 'what 1 can do'. Self-concept denotes the individual's conception of the person he is. The self-concept is one's image of oneself. This perceived self (self-concept) influences both the person's perception of the world and his own behaviour.

Self-actualization, according to Rogers, is the basic motivating force representing the inherent tendency of the organism to develop all its capabilities in ways which serve to maintain or enhance the person. Thus, the primary motive in people's lives is to actualize, maintain, or enhance themselves to become the best that their inherited nature will allow them to be.[8]

Maslow's Self–actualisation Theory

Abraham Maslow is regarded as the spiritual father of humanism in American psychology. The humanistic psychology of Maslow radically differs from the psychoanalytic and learning or behavioristic theories. Psychoanalysis presents man as a creature of instinct and pleasure. Behaviouralism characterizes man as a permanent pawn of environmental fate. The humanist psychology of Maslow, on the other hand, postulates man as a self-actualizer. By self-actualization, Maslow meant the development of full individuality in harmony with all parts of the personality.

Maslow's humanistic psychology is steeped in European existential philosophy and psychology as developed by such thinkers and writers as Kierkegard, Sartre, Camus, Binswanger, and Boss.

Existential philosophy is concerned with man as an individual and each person alone is responsible for his own existence. Contrary to popular belief, he is never static. He is always in the process of becoming something different. He tries to use his potential to become a useful member of society, and to lead a truly authentic and fruitful life. This drive of man which is inherent in him, is called *self-actualisation.*

Existential philosophy also stresses on human consciousness, subjective feelings and modes, and personal experience as they relate to one's existence in the world of other people. This outlook may be called the 'here-and-now' perspective. Existentialists and humanists alike emphasize on subjective experience as the primary phenomenon in the study of human nature. Both theoretical explanations and over-behaviour are secondary to experience itself and its meaning to the experiencing person.

Thus, central to the humanistic approach are the following concepts:

(i) An individual is an integrated whole,
(ii) Animal research is irrelevant to human behaviour,
(iii) Human nature is essentially good,
(iv) Man has creative potential, and
(v) Psychological health of man is most important.[9]

THE SHAPING OF PERSONALITY

How personality develops from its infant to the grown up stage is an interesting and useful study. Psyiologists have come up with different stages in the development of personality. (See Fig.16.3). The most important of them have been explained here.[10]

FIGURE 16-3
SHAPING OF PERSONALITY

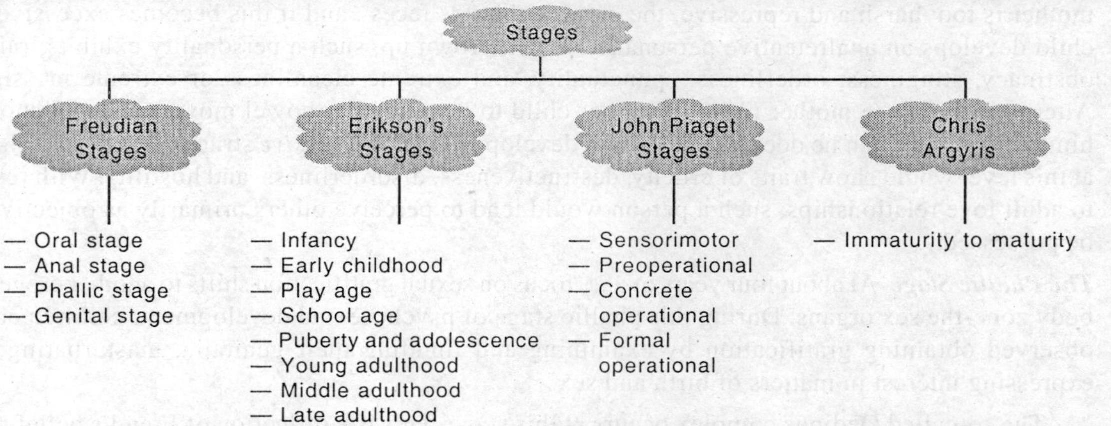

FREUDIAN STAGES

Sigmund Freud was a pioneering stage theorist. Although the analysis of stages of development can be traced as far back as the ancient Greeks, it was Freud who **first** formulated a meaningful stage theory. He was the **first** psychologist to believe that childhood events might have a bearing on adult behaviour and consciousness. Freud theorized that there are four universal stages of psychological development which are decisive for the formation of personality: oral, anal, phallic, and genital-A period of latency, normally occur between the ages of six or seven and the onset of puberty, was included by Freud in the overall scheme of development, but strictly speaking it is not a stage. The first three stages of development extend from birth to **five** years and are called *pregenital* stages, since the genital zones of the body have not attained a dominant role in personality formation.

The fourth stage coincides with the attainment of liberty. The names of these stages are based on the regions of the body whose stimulation allows for the discharge of sexual energy, or libido.

The Oral stage The oral stage extends throughout the first year of life. Infants are totally reliant upon others for survival; dependence is their only way of obtaining instinctual gratification. The mouth is the body zone through which biological drives are sought to be reduced. Thumb-sucking, indulged in by an infant, is one instance of gratifying the sex drive. Later when teeth erupt, pleasure is sought to be achieved through biting. Freud believed that the mouth remains an important erogenous zone throughout life. Even in adulthood there are vestiges of oral behaviour in the forms of gum chewing, nail biting, smoking, kissing, and over-eating, all of which Freudians cite as evidence of the attachment of the libido to the oral zone.

Freud postulated that the infant who is given either excessive or insufficient amounts of stimulation is likely to become an oral-passive personality in adulthood. This is a person who has an optimistic view of the world and who trusts others. He tends to become gullible; passive, and immature. Fixation at the oral stage (particularly towards the end, that is at the teething stage) manifests in adulthood as argumentation, pessimism, and cynicism. People of this personality type also tend to exploit and dominate others as long as their own needs exist.

The Anal Stage During the second and third years of life, the focus of libidal energy shifts from the mouth to the anal region. In other words, the anal becomes the body zone for sexual gratification. Young children derive considerable pleasure from both retention and expulsion of feces and gradually learn to enhance this pleasure by delaying bowel movements.

Toilet-training given to the child by its parents will have its influence on adulthood. If the mother is too harsh and repressive, the child withholds feces , and if this becomes excessive, the child develops an analretentive personality. When grown up, such a personality exhibits traits of obstinacy, stinginess, orderliness, punctuality, and extreme cleanliness or extreme messiness. Alternatively, if the mother pleads with her child to have regular bowel movements and showers him with praise when he does, the child will develop an *anal-aggressive* structure. A person fixated at this level would show traits of cruelty, destructiveness, disorderliness, and hostility. With respect to adult love relationships, such a person would tend to perceive others primarily as objectives to be possessed.

The Phallic Stage At about four years of age, focus on sexual gratification shifts to another erogenous body zone-the sex organs. During this phallic stage of psychosexual development, children can be observed obtaining gratification by examining and fondling their genitalia, masturbating, and expressing interest in matters of birth and sex.

The so-called Oedipus complex occurs at this stage. This is a reflection of Freud's belief that a child both loves and hates his parents, with these feelings being strongest towards the parent of the same sex as the child. If the Oedipus complex is not successfully resolved, severe anxiety and guilt feelings may affect normal personality development. Freud considered unresolved Oedipal problems as the primary source of subsequent neurotic patterns, especially those pertaining to impotency and frigidity.

Adult males fixated at the phallic stage are usually brash, vain, boastful, and ambitious. Phallic types strive to be successful and attempt at all times to assert their masculinity and virility. In the case of women, Freud noted that phallic fixation results in traits of flirtatiousness, seductiveness, and promiscuity, although the individual may appear naive and innocent in sexual relationship.

The Latency Period Between the ages of six or seven and the onset of adolescence, occurs the latency period. During this period, the child loses interest in sexual matters and seeks gratification of the libido from the external world-curiosity, knowledge, and the like.

The latency period (the elementary school age) is very important for the social development of the child, for acquiring the knowledge and skills needed to get along in the workday world.

The Genital Stage The genital stage occurs between adolescence to adulthood. There is a revival of sexual and aggressive impulses coupled with an increased awareness of an interest in the opposjte sex. The individual experiences satisfaction through heterosexual love. Discharge of libido through mature sexual relations with an opposite sex partner paves the way for genuine concern for one's fellow men. The youth begins to love others for altruistic rather than self-gratification reasons.

Freud believed that in order for people to attain the ideal genital character, they must relinquish the passivity of early childhood days when love, security, physical comfort, indeed all, gratification were freely given and nothing was expected in return. They must learn to work, postpone gratification, become responsible, and above all, assume a more active role in dealing with life's problems. Table 16.1 contains a summary of the Freudian stages.

TABLE 16-1
FREUD'S STAGES OF PERSONALITY DEVELOPMENT

Stage	*Age*	***Major** Characteristics*
Oral	0-1 year	Interest in oral gratification from sucking, eating, mouthing, and biting.
Anal	1-3years	Gratification from expelling and withholding faeces; coming to terms with society's controls relating to toilet-training
Phallic	3-4 years	Interest in the genitals, coming to terms with Oedipal conflict, leading to identification with same-sex parent
Latency	4-6 years to adolescence	Sexual concerns large unimportant
Genital	Adolescence to adulthood	Re-emergence of sexual interests and establishment of mature sexual relationships.

Assessment of Freud's Stages

Credit should be given to Freud for he was the pioneering stage theorist. He provided some valuable insights which provoked further study on personality development. Further, Freud's emphasis on sexual factors led to an awareness of their role in adjustment problems and paved the way for the scientific study of sexuality.

There exists hardly a sphere of modem life which has not been influenced to a greater or lesser degree by Freudian thought-sociology, social welfare, politics, law, the family, education, the treatment of delinquency and mental illness, medicine, the arts, propaganda, advertising, entertainment, and even religion. Freud has made our understanding of the human personality both deeper and wider than we chose to dream.

Although the human mind is invisible and intangible, Freud has shown that its study can be carried out with scientific precision. Human behaviour, indeed, seems unpredictable, swayed by unknown motives, but Freud showed that it is possible to discern laws which govern people's words, thoughts, and feelings and that they do not behave irrationally as it might seem, but in tune with their own inner dynamics. His works are considered to be a revolution in our knowledge of the human personality for two reasons: first, because he evolved a new scientific method of studying the human mind, and second, because the application of that method yielded results which compels us to revise our ideas about the human personality.

However, Freud's high reliance on sex to explain stages in personality development has been criticized. The major disagreement centres on Freud's choice of words. As Walter Mischel pointed out, without having at hand a suitable set of learning concepts and terms for personality development, Freud relied on his own preference for a 'body language', he preferred to say 'anal' rather than 'development', 'oral' rather than 'compulsive', 'genital' rather than 'mature'.

A new round of historical research on Sigmund Freud is challenging the reputation of the founder of psychoanalysis.

New revelations depict Freud as one who seems at times a mercenary and manipulative, who sometimes claimed cures where there were none, and who on occasion distorted the facts of his cases to prove his theoretical points. And judged by current knowledge and standards, it is Freud who, at least once, stepped over the line into malpractice.

In one little-known case that barely missed becoming a major scandal, researchers say , Freud induced two patients to divorce their spouses and marry each other. In addition, he hinted that the man should make a generous donation to this psychoanalytic fund.

The most startling discoveries, many not yet published, concern some of Freud's most important cases, including patients he referred to as 'Little Hans' and 'Dora'.

'Each of Freud's published cases plays a role in the psychoanalytic legend', said Frank Sulloway, a historian of science at the Massachusetts Institute of Technology, who is the author of *Freud, Biologist of the Mind,* on the origins of Freud's theories. 'But the more detail you learn about each case, the stronger the image becomes of Freud twisting the facts to **fit** his theory.'

The new historical work is just the kind of inquiry that Freud dreaded. He burned many of his papers at different times in his life and destroyed most of his case notes. Although the Freud Archives at the library of Congress recently opened most papers to scholars, some, like his letters to his future wife, Marthan, remained under lock and key until the year 2000 at the request of the donor, Freud's daughter Anna.

But increasingly over the last few years, that veil of secrecy has been pierced by a determined band of scholars. Some have tracked down people who knew Freud's most famous patients and in one case, a reporter interviewed the patient himself. In the process, the scholars have discovered much that might well have made Freud uncomfortable.

Neo-Freudian Stages

Among the neo-Freudians, Erik Erikson gave a new dimension to the development of personality which, he claimed, was nothing mote than a systematic extension of Freud's psychosexual development. Erikson felt that relatively more attention should be given to the social rather than the sexual adaptation of the individual. He postulated that the social problems encountered in the course of development were more important stages in which the child faces a wider range of human relationships as he grew up. Erikson asserted that a psycho-social crisis occurs within each of the stages and that in order for the person to have a normal, fulfilling personality, each crisis should be optimally resolved. For Erikson, a crisis is not a catastrophe but a turning point in an individual's development. Erikson's eight stages of psychological development are shown in Table 16.2.

TABLE 16-2

ERIKSON'S STAGES OF PERSONALITY DEVELOPMENT

Erikson's Stages	*Age*	*Success in meeting requirements of stage brings*	*Failure to meet requirements of stage brings*
1. Infancy	Birth to one year	*Basic Trust Vs* Pursuit of affection and gratification of needs, recognition.	*Mistrust* Result of consistent abuse, neglect, deprivation of love, too early or hard weaning, artistic isolation.
2. Early childhood	One to three years	*Autonomy Vs* Child views self as a person in his own right apart from parents, still dependent.	*Shame & Doubt* Feels inadequate, doubts self, curtails learning basic skills like walking, talking, wants to 'hide' inadequacies.
3. Play age	Four to five years	*Initiative Vs* Lively imagination, rigorous reality testing, imitates, anticipates rallies.	*Guilt* Lacks spontaneity, infantile jealousy, suspicions, evasive, role inhibition.
4. School age	Six to eleven years	*Industry Vs* Has sense of duty and accomplishment, develops scholastic and social competencies, undertakes real tasks, put-fantasy and play in better perspective, learns world of tools, task identification.	*Inferiority* Poor work habits, avoids strong competition, feels mediocracy, lull before the storms of puberty, may conform as slavish behaviour, sense of futility.
5. Puberty and adolescence	Twelve to twenty years	*Ego Identity Vs* Temporal perspective. Self certain. Role experimenter. Apprenticeship, sexual polarization, leaderelellowship, ideological commitment	*Role Confusion* Time confusion, self-conscious, role fixation, work paralysis, bisexual confusion, authority confusion, value confusion.
6. Young adulthood	Twenty to Twenty four years	*Intimacy Vs* Capacity to commit self to others. Attitude of care, respect and responsibility towards another.	*Isolation* Avoids intimacy, feelings of social emptiness and isolation. Seeks interpersonal encounters which are purely formal (employer-employee). Insulate themselves against any type of real involvement. Attitudes of futility and alienation regarding their vocations.
7. Middle adulthood	Twenty-five to sixty-five years	*Generactivity Vs* Productive and creative for Self and others, parental pride and pleasure, mature, enriches life, estabshshes and guides to next generation.	*Stagnation* Egocentric, unproductive, early invalidism, excessive self-love, personal impoverishment, self-indulgence, feeling of hopelessness and meaninglesness.
8. Late adulthood	Old age (Suns years)	*Integrity Vs* Appreciates continuity of past, present and future, fully satisfied. Death not feared, 'wisdom of old age' comes into being.	*Despair* Time is too short, finds no meaning in life, has lost faith in self and others, wants second, chance at life-cycle with more advantages, fears death. Often senile, depressed spiteful and paranoid.

(***Adapted:*** from L.A.Hjelle's *Personality* and Bischor's *Interpreting Personality Theories*)

ASSESSMENTS OF PSYCHO-SOCIAL STAGES

The eight stages of man, as postulated.by Erikson, offer new perspectives about personality. First, Erikson has formulated a theory in which the roles of society and of persons themselves are accorded equal emphasis with respect to the development and organization of personality. This perspective, in turn, has enabled those in the helping professions to look upon the problems of adults, at least to some extent, as failure to adequately resolve genuine adult personality crises, rather than to see them merely as residual effects of early childhood frustration and conflicts. Second, Erikson has been sensitive to the age of odolescence, a period largely ignored in the formation of the person's psychological and social well-being. Finally, Erikson has stimulated a sense of optimism by demonstrating that each stage of psycho-social growth has the potential for both strength and weakness, so that failure at one stage of development does not necessarily indicate doom at a later stage.

Although Erikson's theory has gained prominence in both clinical and academic settings, research efforts towards testing it have been sparse. Erikson himself admits that his own conceptions of personality may not be directly amenable to experimental verification.

It is useful to dovetail Erikson's stages with those propounded by Freud. This comparison is meaningful because Erikson did a lot to expand and elaborate on Freud's developmental theories. Table 16.3 gives the comparison of the two theories.

TABLE 16-3

COMPARISON OF FREUD'S AND ERIKSON'S STAGE THEORIES

Approximate age	*Freud's Psychosexual Stages*	*Erikson's Psychosocial Stages*
First year	Oral	Basic trust Vs mistrust
2-3 years	Anal	Autonomy Vs shame, doubt
3-5 years	Phallic	Initiative Vs guilt
6 years to puberty	Latency	Industry Vs inferiority
Adolescence	Genital	Identity Vs role confusion
Early adulthood	—	Intimacy Vs isolation
Middle age	—	General activity Vs Self absorption
Late adulthood	—	Integrity Vs despair

(**Source:** Lindal L.Davidoff, *Introduction To Psychology,* New York, MeGraw-Hill, 1987, p. 453).

Cognitive Stages

Jean Piaget, a Swiss psychologist, is credited with the 'cognitive' or 'conscious' stages of personality development. For Piaget, it is the 'conscious' instincts which are important variables in the development of personality. Being a lover of children, Piaget spent most of his life observing children in order to understand when and how they developed their reasoning abilities. He identified four stages of personality development which are shown in Table 16.4. By *sensorymotor* Piaget meant that the infant responds to stimuli quite directly with little in the way of complex information processing. During the *preoperational stage,* the child learns to separate himself from the environmental (all else) and initially classifies objects (the first origin of analytic capacity) through the use of symbols and words. The *concrete operational stage* is characterized by an intellectual understanding of the concept of conservation of a mass, irrespective of its shape. In the final stage, the *formal operational stage,* reasoning can take place on abstract as well as concrete levels.

TABLE 16-4
COGNITIVE STAGES

Stage	*Age*
Sensorimotor	0-2
Preoperational	2-7
Concrete operational	7-11
Formal operational	11 and above

(**Source:** Lindal L.Davidoff, *Introduction To Psychology,* New York, MeGraw-Hill, 1987, p. 453).

Piaget's views on personality are valid in as much as the cognitive stages do have influence on organisational behaviour; particularly the formal operation stage in which most people are active organization members. At this stage, concrete things need not be manipulated to cause behaviour, as employees are capable of analysing, reasoning, imagining and evaluating objects. But the problems with the cognitive theory is that it fails to unravel all dimensions of personality development.

Immaturity to Maturity

Professor Chris Argyris of Harvard had identified specific dimensions of the human personality as it develops. He proposes that the human personality, rather than going through distinct stages, progresses along a continuum from an infancy to maturity as an adult. However, at any stage, people can have their degree of development plotted according to the seven dimensions shown in Table 16.5.

TABLE 16-5
THE IMMATURITY TO MATURITY CONTINUUM

Characteristics of Immaturity	*Characteristics of Maturity*
Passivity	Activity
Dependence	Independence
Limited behaviour	Diverse behaviour
Shallow interests	Deep interest
Short-time perspective	Long-time perspective
Subordinate position	Superordinate position
Lack of self-awareness	Self awareness and control

Argyris argues that healthy individuals tend to move from immaturity to maturity, According to him, such people will display the behaviours of maturity while unhealthy people tend to demonstrate childlike, immature behaviours.

In contrast to the stages theories of Freud and Erikson, Argyris's immaturity-maturity model of personality is specifically directed to the study and analysis of organizational behaviour. Argyris assumes that the personalities of organizational employees can be generally described by the mature end of the continuum. This being the case, in order to obtain full expression of employees' personalities, the formal organization should allow for activity rather than passivity, independence rather than dependence, long-term rather than short-term perspective, occupation of a position higher than that of peers, and expression of deep, important abilities. Argyris argues that too often the exact opposite occurs. The mature organizational participant becomes frustrated and anxious and is in conflict with the modern formal organization. In other words, Argyris sees a basic incongruity between the needs of the mature personality and the nature of the formal organization.

Determinants of Personality

What determinants go into the development of personality? Of all the complexities and unanswered questions in the study of human behaviour, this question may be the most difficult one. The problem lies in the fact that the cognitive and physiological processes, and many other variables, all contribute to personality. However, for convenience of study, the determinants of personality can be grouped into the five broad categories: heredity, environmental, family, social, and situational. (See Fig.16.4).

FIGURE 16-4
DETERMINANTS OF PERSONALITY

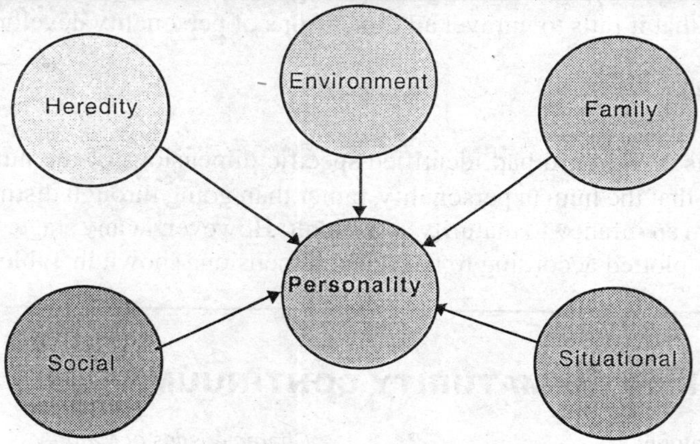

Heredity

The role of heredity in the development of personality is an old argument of personality theory. Heredity refers to those factors that were determined at conception. Physical stature, facial attractiveness, sex, temperament, muscle composition and reflexes, energy level, and biological rhythms are characteristics that are generally considered to be imported either completely or substantially from one's parents.[11] The heredity approach argues that the ultimate explanation of an individual's personality is the molecular structure of genes located in the chromosomes. It is said that at conception, each parent normally contributes 23 chromosomes. These chromosomes contain thousands of genes, which seem to be the transmitters of traits. Even all children of the same parents do not have identical genetic makeups. Only identical twins, who develop from a single fertilized ovum, possess the same pattern of genes[12] but not always as revealed from evidences. The recent tragic deaths of the Bijani twins, Ladan and Lalch is a case in point. The conjoined Iranian twins opted for surgery (which proved to be fatal) because each had a personality distinct and even opposite to that of the other. This is not the only exception. Meera and Meena, Mamata Srinivas MoorChurg and her brother, Alwin John Madtha and his twin Elvin Gabriel, and Tina Garg and her twin sister[13] are instances to demonstrate that twins need not inherit identical characteristics.

The role of heredity on personality development is still an unsettled area of understanding. The problem is that geneticists face a major obstacle in gathering information scientifically on the human being. Animal scientists can conduct highly controlled breeding experiments, but geneticists studying human heredity cannot. Through research on animals, it has been clearly shown that both physical and physiological characteristics can be transmitted through heredity. However, in the case of humans, who cannot be subjected to the necessary controls, the evidence is much less conclusive.[14]

Nevertheless, the role of heredity on personality development cannot be totally minimized. Physical attributes, for instance, may be largely attributed to heredity. To the question posed by a girl as to why her height was not normal for her age, a famous gynaecologist attributed the girl's short height, among other factors, to the height of her parents, implying that had the parent's height been normal, the children would have acquired the same trait. The following classification of characteristics is said to be inherited by all humans:

(i) Physical structure (how tall or short one is, whether one has a long or short nose, large or small feet, briefly, how one is).

(ii) Reflexes (response to external stimuli, such as withdrawing from a pin prick, blinking when something falls in the eye).

(iii) Innate drivers (impulses to act based on physiological tensions; but these must be linked through learning with activities which will reduce the tensions).

(iv) Intelligence (the capacity to learn, to modify responses).

(v) Temperament (patterned and recurrent responses associated with basic emotional make up, for example, phlegmatic, excitable, or lethargic).[15]

Environment

If all personality characteristics were completely dictated by heredity, they would be fixed at birth and no amount of experience could alter them. However, personality development owes as much to environment around it as it does to heredity.

Environment is a broad term and includes such factors as culture which influences norms, attitudes, and values that are passed along from one generation to the next and creates consistencies over time. Anthropologists have clearly demonstrated the important role culture plays in the development of the human personality. The methods by which an infant is fed and is toilet-trained, and makes the transition from adolescence to adulthood are all culturally determined.

While growing the child learns to behave in ways expected by the culture of the family into which he or she is born. One of those expectations has to do with sex roles. Most cultures expect different behaviours from males and females. Sex roles may vary from culture to culture, but it is considered natural in any culture for boys and girls to have predictable differences in personality merely because they belong to one or the other sex.[16]

Every culture has its own subcultures, each with it own views about such qualities as moral values and standards, cleanliness, style of dress, and definitions of success. The cultural sub-group exerts its influence on personality. All boys are excepted to show certain personality traits (as compared with girls), but a poor boy raised in an urban slum is expected to behave differently in some respects from a well-to-do raised in a middle-class suburb.

Although culture has significant influence on personality development, a linear relationship cannot be established between personality and the given culture for two reasons:

(i) The cultural impacts upon an individual are not uniform, because they are transmitted by certain people-parents and others-who are not at all alike in their values and practices, and

(ii) The individual has some experiences that are unique.[17] Each individual reacts in his or her own way to social pressures, the differences in behaviour being caused by biological factors.

CONTRIBUTION FROM THE FAMILY

The family has considerable influence on personality development, particularly in the early stages. The parents play an important role in the identification process which is important to an individual's early development. Usually the parents of the same sex as the child will serve as the model for the child's identification. The process can be examined from three different perspectives:

First, identification can be viewed as the similarity of the behaviour (including feelings and attributes) between child and model.

Second, identification can be looked upon as the child's motive or desire to be like the model.

Third, identification can be viewed as the process through which the child actually takes on the attributes of the model.

From all the three perspectives, the identification process is fundamental to the understanding of personality development.[18]

The overall home environment created by the parents, in addition to their direct influence, is critical to personality development. For example, children with a markedly institutionalized upbringing (orphans) or children reared in cold, unstimulating homes are much more likely to be socially and emotionally maladjusted than children raised by parents in a warm, loving, and stimulating environment.[19]

Siblings (brothers and sisters) also contribute to personality development. It has been argued that siblings position is an important psychological variable because it represents a microcosm of significant social experience of adolescences and adulthood. It is argued that those born first are more prone to schizophrenic, more susceptible to social pressures, and more dependent than those born later. The first-born are also more likely to experience the world as more orderly, predictable, and rational than later-bom children.

SOCIALIZATION PROCESS

Beside heredity, environmental, and family influences on personality, there is greater realization that other relevant persons, groups, and organizations exercise their due role in personality development. This is commonly called the socialization process. It is especially relevant to organizational behaviour because the process is not confined to early childhood, but takes place throughtout one's life. In particular, evidence is accumulating that socialization may be one of the best explanations of why employees behave the way they do in today's organizations.

Socialization involves the process by which a person acquires, from the enormously wide range of behavioural potentialities at are open to him or her, starting at birth, those behaviour patterns that are customary and acceptable to the standards of, initially, the family and later the social group and the employing organization. Thus, socialization starts with the initial contact between a mother and her infant. After infancy, other members of the immediate family (father, brothers, sisters and close relatives or friends), followed by the social groups (peers, school, friends, and members of the working group) play influential roles.[20]

Situational Considerations

The determinants of personality discussed till now are more concerned with the historical nature of personality development. Heredity, family, siblings, and environment are no doubt important to personality development, but it must be recognized that it is the immediate situation which may predominate finally. An example is the worker whose developmental history has shaped a personality which incorporates a high need for power and achievement. When placed in a highly bureaucratized work situation, this individual may become frustrated and behave apathetically and/or aggressively. Thus, on the surface, this worker appears to be lazy and/or a troublemaker, yet developmental history would predict that the individual is a very hard worker, striving to get ahead.[21]

While it seems logical to suppose that situations will influence an individual's personality, a neat classification scheme that would tell us the impact of various types of situations has so far eluded us. However, we do know that certain situations are more relevant than others in influencing personality. What is of interest taxonomically, wrote Lee Sechrest, is that situations seem to differ substantially in the constraints they impose on behaviour. Some situations, such as church or an employment interview may constrain many behaviours while other situations, for a example, a picnic in a public park may constrain relatively few.[22]

From the preceding discussion of the development of personality, it is clear that personality is a complex concept that reflects many influences both within and outside the individual. Personality progresses through identifiable stages and never really stops developing. One can, however, examine personality at any point in time within its developmental sequence in order to compare and contrast individual personalities. One can also do this to show more effectively some of the important components of personality.

Personality Structure

Personality is composed of external traits and no two individuals possess identical characteristics. Since the days of Plato, scholars of personality have been trying to isolate personality traits. However, about 100 years ago a few personality experts tried to catalogue and condense the many personality traits that had been described over the years. They found thousands of words in *Roget's Thesaurus and Webster's Dictionary* representing personality characteristics. They arranged these words into 171 clusters, then further reduced them to five abstract personality dimensions using rare sophisticated techniques. A recent investigation identified the same five dimensions, as the 'Big Five' personality dimensions.[23] As Fig.16.5 shows, these five dimensions include extraversion, agreeableness, conscientiousness, emotional stability, and openness to experience.

Extroversion reflects a person's comfort level with relationships. Extroverts are sociable, talkative, assertive, and open to establishing new relationships, Introverts are less sociable, less talkative, less assertive, and more reluctant to begin relationships.

Agreeableness refers to a person's ability to get along with others. Highly agreeable people value harmony more than they value having their say or their way. The are cooperative and trusting of others.

People who score low on agreeableness focus more on their own needs then the needs of others.

FIGURE 16-5
THE 'BIG FIVE' PERSONALITY TRAITS

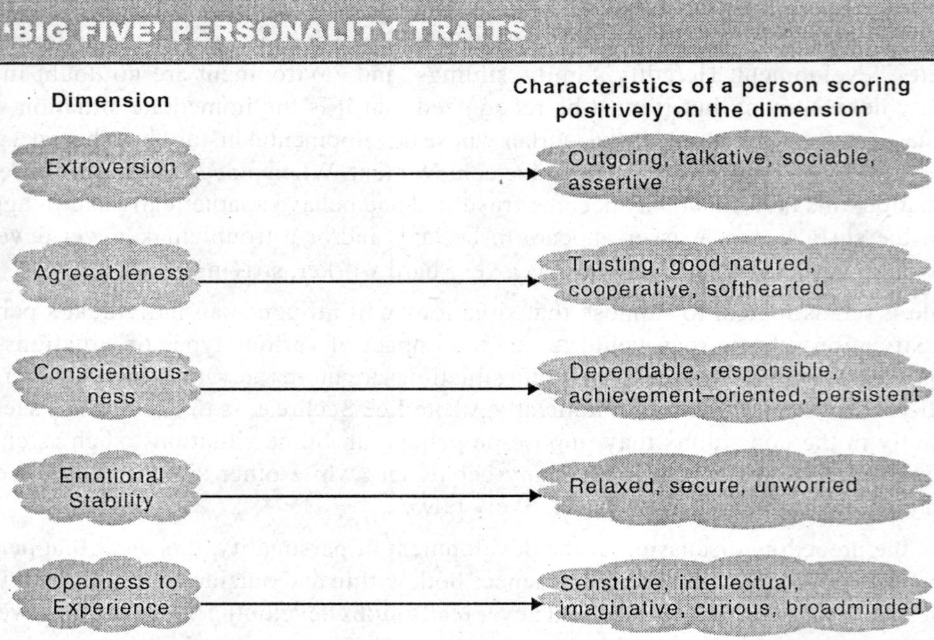

Conscientiousness refers to the number of goals that a person focuses on. A highly conscientious person focuses on relatively few goals at one time. He or she is likely to be organized, systematic, careful, thorough, responsible, self-disciplined, and achievement-oriented. A person with a low conscientious nature tends to focus on a higher number of goals at one time. Consequently, the individual is more disorganized, careless, and irresponsible, as well as less thorough and self-disciplined.

Emotional stability focuses on an individual's ability to cope with stress. The individual with positive emotional stability tends to be calm, enthusiastic, and secure. A person with low emotional stability tends to be nervous, depressed, and insecure.

Openness addresses one's range of interests. Extremely open people are fascinated by novelty and innovation. They are willing to listen to new ideas and to change their own ideas, beliefs, and attitudes in response to new information. On the other hand, people with low levels of openness tend to be less receptive to new ideas and less willing to change their minds. They also tend to have fewer and narrow interests and be less curious and creative.

The 'Big Five' framework continues to attract the attention of both researchers and managers. The potential value of this framework lies in the fact that it encompasses and integrates a set of traits that appear to be valid predictors of certain behaviours in certain situations. However, the 'Big Five' model: primarily based on research conducted in the US. Its generalization to other cultures, therefore, presents unanswered questions.

Myers–Briggs Indicator

During the 1920s, the Swiss psychologist Carl Jung proposed a personality theory that, as stated earlier, identifies the way people prefer to perceive their environment. Twenty years later, the mother and daughter team of Katherine Briggs and Isable Briggs-Myers developed the Myers-Briggs Type Indicator (MBTI), a personality test that measures each of the traits of Jung's model.

Mainly used in the employee hiring process, MBTI measures how people prefer to focus their attention (extroversion versus introversion), collect information (sensing versus intuition), process and evaluate information (thinking versus feeling), and orient themselves to the other world (judging versus perceiving). Extroversion and introversion have been discussed in the earlier section. The other dimensions are examined below.[24]

Sensitivity/intuition Some people like collecting information. Sensing types use an organized structure to acquire factual and, preferably, quantitative details. In contrast, intuitive people collect information non-systematically. They rely more on subjective evidence, as well as on their intuition, and even inspiration. Sensors are capable of synthesizing large volumes of data and draw quick conclusions. Needless it is to say, the work of management demands a combination of intuitive and sensing abilities. (Read Exhibit 16.1 for more details).

Thinking/Feeling Thinking types rely on the rational cause-effect logic and scientific method to make decisions. They weigh the evidence objectively and unemotionally. Feeling types, instead, consider how their choices affect others. They weigh the options against their personal values more than on rational logic.

A good manger uses both mind (thinking) and heart (feeling). It is too well-known that how one feels about a decision can determine the success of its implementation just as much as the logic of that decision. The realities of organizational life often evoke emotions that play a dominant role in a manager's behaviour. Fear of failure, fear of the laws, excitement about a product, compassion for an employee, anger at another person, and the like, are but examples of emotional forces that appear in the day-to-day life of a firm.[25]

Judging/Percieving Some people prefer order and structure in their relationship with their outer world. These judging types enjoy the control of decision-making and want to resolve problems quickly. In contrast, perceiving types are more flexible. They like to adapt spontaneously to events as they unfold and want to keep their options open. To be effective as a manager, one needs to operate at times in perceiving mode and at times in a judging mode. The tensions that develop between 'Perceivers' and 'Judges' can be sources of conflict in organizations.

Besides employee-hiring, MBTI is used in team building too. As members of a team learn to understand and even appreciate differences among them, they are better able to build on complementary strengths and ways of dealing with problems. Intuitive types have the ability to make creative leaps on thinking, but often need the more sensing types to make sure all that facts are being considered. Similarly, perceivers will tend to engage in the endless exploration of alternatives and really need to be balanced by judging types, who are more inclined to move quickly to decisions. An effective team learns to build on these differences.

Other Personality Traits

There are many different personality traits, but some of the more important ones for organizational behaviour are authoritarianism, locus of control, Machiavellianism, introversion-extroversion, achievement orientation, self-esteem, risk-taking, self-monitoring and type A and type B Personalities. (See Fig.16.6).

Authoritarianism Authoritarianism is a concept developed by the psychologist Adorno during World War II to measure susceptibility to autocratic, fascist, or anti-democratic appeals. Since that

FIGURE 16-6
PERSONALITY TRAITS

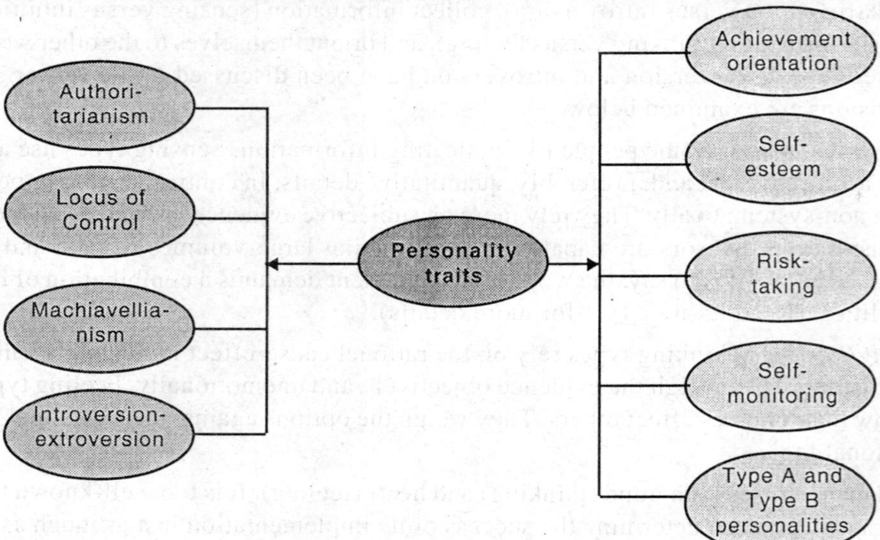

time, the concept has been extended to the authoritarian personality, a generic term used to describe an individual who has a strong belief in the legitimacy of established mechanisms of formal authority, views obedience to authority as necessary, exhibits a negative philosophy of people, adheres to conventional and traditional value systems, is intellectually rigid, and opposes the use of subjective feelings. Authoritarians also tend to be rigid in their positions, place high moral value on their beliefs, and are strongly oriented towards conformity to rules and regulations. They naturally prefer stable and structured work environments which are governed by clean rules and procedures. Similarly, authoritarians are likely to prefer autocratic or directive leadership and would exhibit high respect for individuals in positions of authority.[26]

Locus of Control Locus of control refers to an individual's belief that events are either with in one's control (internal locus of control) or are determined by forces beyond one's control (external locus of control). These personality traits are manifested in different behaviours which are significant to managers.

It has been proved that externals (those who believe that events are determined by external forces) are less satisfied with their jobs, have higher absenteeism rates, are more alienated from work settings, and are less involved on their jobs than internals (those who believe that events are within one's control). Internals typically have more control over their own behaviour, are more active in seeking information to make decisions, and are more active socially than externals.

Table 16.6 reveals the difference between internals and externals more clearly, and Table 16.7 shows the relationships between locus of control and job performance.

Machiavellianism Machiavellianism, a term derived from the writings of Nicolo Machiavelli, refers to individual's propensity to manipulate people. Machiavellians would be prone to participate in organisational politics. They are also adept at interpersonal game-playing, power tactics, and identifying influence systems in organizations.[27]

TABLE 16-6

SOME WAYS IN WHICH INTERNALS DIFFER FROM EXTERNALS

Characteristics of Immaturity	*Characteristics of Maturity*
(i) Information processing:	Internals make more attempts to acquire information, are better at information retention, are less satisfied with the amount of information they possess, are better at utilizing information, and devising and processing rules.
(ii) Job satisfaction	Internals are more satisfied, less alienated, and less rootless.
(iii) Self-control and risk behaviour:	Internals exhibit greater self-control, are more cautious, engaged in less risky behaviour.
(iv) Expectations and results:	Internals are a stronger relationship between what they do and what happens to them, expect working hard leads to good performance, feel more control over how to spend time, perform better.
(v) Preference for skill versus chance:	Internals prefer skill-achievement outcomes, externals prefer chance achievements.
(vi) Use of rewards:	Internals are more likely to use personally persuasive rewards and power bases and less likely to use coercion.
(vii) Response to others:	Internals are more independent, more reliant on own judgement, and less susceptible to influence of others, they resist subtle influence attempts and are more likely to accept information on merit rather than prestige of source.
(viii) Leader behaviour:	Internals prefer participative leadership, externals prefer directive.

(***Source:*** John R.Schermerhom, JR. et.al., *Managing Organisational Behaviour*, John Wiley and Sons, p.109)

TABLE 16-7

LOCUS OF CONTROL AND PERFORMANCE

Conditions	*Performance*
Information processing	
• The work requires complex information processing and complex learning	➢ Internals perform better
• The work is quite simple and easy to learn	➢ Internals perform no better than externals
Initiative	
• The work requires initiative and independent action	➢ Internals perform better
• The work requires compliance and conformity	➢ Externals perform better
Motivation	
• The work requires high motivation and provides valued rewards in return for greater effort, incentive pay for greater productivity	➢ Internals perform better
• The work does not require great effort and contingent rewards are lacking, hourly pay rates determined by collective bargaining	➢ Externals perform atleast as well as internals

(***Source:*** Don Hellrigel, *et al. Organisational Behaviour*, South Western, 2001, p.45)

Do the Machiavellians make good employees? The answer depends on the type of job and whether one considers ethical considerations in evaluating performance. In jobs that require bargaining skills (such as labour negotiation) or where there are substantial rewards for winning (commissioned sales), Machiavllians perform better.[28]

Introversion and Extroversion These are the most common descriptions of personality traits. These terms are normally associated with an individual's sociability and interpersonal orientation. Extroverts are gregarious and sociable individuals while introverts are shy, quiet, and retiring.

It is generally established that introverts and extroverts have significantly different career orientations and require different organizational environments to maximize performance. Extroverts are more suitable for positions that require considerable interaction with others, whereas introverts are more inclined to excel at tasks that require thought and analytical skills. Not surprisingly, managerial positions are dominated by extroverts; thus suggesting that this managerial trait is a significant factor in managerial success.[29]

Achievement Orientation Achievement orientation is yet another personality trait which varies among people and which can be used to predict certain behaviours.

Employees with a high need to achieve, continually strive to do things better. They want to overcome obstacles, but they want to feel that their success or failure is due to their own actions (read internals). This means that they like tasks of moderate difficulty. An easy task shall not evoke challenges and is, therefore, not liked by high achievers. Similarly, a task with high risk is not liked by these people as the failure rates are more. Given the high achievers propensity for tasks where the outcome can be directly attributed to his or her efforts, the high achiever looks for challenges having approximately a 50-50 chance of success.

On the job, high achievers will perform better where there is moderate difficulty, rapid performance feedback, and direct relationship between effort and reward. This means that the high achievers tend to do better in sales, sports, or in management.

Self-Esteem Self-esteem refers to the feeling of like or dislike of one-self. This trait, naturally, varies from person to person. Self-esteem is directly related to the desire for success. People with high self- esteem believe that they have abilities to undertake challenging jobs. They tend to choose unconventional jobs than those with lower self-esteem.

People with low self-esteem are more susceptible to external influence than are those with high esteems. Low esteems are dependent on the receipt of positive evaluations from others. As a result, they are more likely to seek approval from others and more prone to conform to the beliefs and behaviours of those they respect than are high esteems. In managerial positions, low esteems will tend to be concerned with pleasing others and therefore, less likely to take unpopular stands than are high esteems.

Self-esteem is also related to job satisfaction. High esteems are more satisfied with their jobs than the low esteems.

Risk-taking People differ in their willingness to take chances. Their propensity to assume or avoid risk has been shown to have an impact on how long it takes managers to make a decision and how much information they require before making their choice. For instance, 79 managers worked on simulated personnel exercises that required them to make hiring decisions. High-risk-taking managers made more rapid decisions and used less information in making their choices than did low-risk-taking managers. Interestingly, the decision accuracy was the same for both the groups.

While it is generally correct to conclude that managers in organizations are risk aversive, there are still individual differences on this dimension. As a result, it makes sense to recognize these differences and even to consider aligning risk-taking propensity with specific job demands. For instance, a high-risk-taking propensity may lead to more effective performance for a stock trader in a brokerage firm. This type of job demands rapid decision-making. On the other hand, this personality characteristic might prove a major obstacle to accountants performing auditing activities. This type of job might be better filled by someone with a low-risk-taking propensity.

Self-Monitoring Another personality trait that has recently received increased attention is called self- monitoring. It refers to an individual's ability to adjust his or her behaviour to external factors.

Individuals high in self-monitoring can show considerable adaptability in adjusting their behaviour to external, situational factors. They are highly sensitive to external cues and can behave differently in different situations. High self-monitors are capable of presenting striking contradictions between their public, personal, and private selves. Low self-monitors cannot deviate their behaviour. They tend to display their true dispositions and attitude in every situation, hence there is high behavioural consistency between who they are and what they do.

The high self-monitors tend to pay closer attention to the behaviour of others and are more capable of conforming than are low self-monitors. We might also hypothesize that high self-monitors will be more successful in managerial positions where individuals are required to play multiple, and even contradicting roles. The high self-monitor is capable of putting on different 'faces' for different audiences.

Type A personality Finally, there is the Type A personality and Type B personality.

Type A personality typifies a person who is always in a hurry, is extremely competitive, and is often hostile and irritable. Opposite is the Type B personality who is relaxed, incompetent, and easy going. Table 16.8 contracts the two types of behaviours.

TABLE 16-8
TYPE A AND TYPE B BEHAVIOURS

Type A	*Type B*
1. Are always moving, walking, and eating rapidly;	1. Never suffer from a sense of time urgency with its accompanying impatience;
2. Feel impatient with the rate at which most events take place;	2. Feel no need to display or discuss either their achievements or accomplishments unless such exposure is demanded by the situation;
3. Strive to think or do two or more things at once;	3. Play for fun and relaxation, rather than to exhibit their superiority at any cost;
4. Cannot cope with leisure;	4. Can relax without guilt.
5. Are obsessed with numbers, measuring their success in terms of how much of anything they acquire.	

How do the two perform in organizations? Type As are no doubt highly competitive and hardworking. But it is the Type Bs who climb to the top of the organization.

Type As will make most successful sales people and senior executives are usually type Bs. Why this paradox? The answer lies in the tendency of Type As to trade off quality of effort for quantity. Executive positions usually go to those who are wise rather than to those who are merely hasty, to those who are tactful rather than to those who are hostile, and to those who are creative rather than to those who are merely agile in competitive strife.

PERSONALITY AND OB

Understanding personalities is important because personality affects behaviour, as well as perception and attitudes. Personality types also affect human relations and retaliation. People with similar personality types tend to get along well at work, while opposites do not, though there are exceptions.

Personality profiles are used to categorize people as a means of predicting job performance. Some personality characteristics are more productive than others. Conscientiousness is a good indicator of performance, though it is not the only dimension. Many organizations administer personality tests to ensure a proper match between the worker and the job.

The concept of personality is not to be understood in an organizational context only. The need for understanding human characteristics, in general, is more significant than comprehending personality in the context of organizations. Despite serious attempts, experts have not been able to comprehend the real nature of personality. Of all the problems that have confronted human beings since the beginning of recorded history, perhaps the most significant has been the riddle of their own nature. Attempts to answer 'What is man'? are countless and a great many avenues have been explored, with an enormous variety of concepts being employed along the way. Astrology, philosophy, and the life sciences are but a few of the many directions that the quest to understand human nature has taken. At this point in history, some of these avenues have proved to be dead ends, while others are just beginning to flourish. And today, the problem is more pressing than ever, since most of the world's ills, for example, over-population, war pollution, prejudice are brought about by the behaviour of people. So it may not be overstating the case to say that the quality of human life in the future, indeed our own survival, may well depend upon an increased understanding of human nature.

Case: An Over-Confident Employee?

Firms are downsizing. Consumer confidence is plunging. Given the uncertain economic environment, why should anybody give up a secure job?

It may seem odd, but competent people still do it everyday. They job-hop in search of greener pastures. Take Sridhar, a software expert in a Bangalore-based firm, who scribbled the following remarks on his exit interview questionnaire.

'This job is not right for me. I would like to have more input on decisions that affect me, more chance to show what I can do. I do not get enough feedback to tell me if I am doing a good job or not, and the firm keeps people in the dark about where it is headed. Basically, I feel like an interchangeable part most of the time.'

In reply to the question whether the firm could have done anything to retain Sridhar, he replied 'probably not'.

Why do so many promising employees leave their jobs? And why do so many others stay on but perform at minimal levels for lack of better alternatives? One of the main reasons-Sridhar's reasons-can be all but invisible, because it is so common in so many organisations; a systematical failure to keep good people.

Companies should worry about people like Sridhar. By investing in them they may actually help reduce turnover, save on training costs, increase productivity, improve quality, and reap the benefits of innovative thinking and teamwork.

Human resource professionals and managers can contribute to corporate success by encouraging employees' empowerment, security, identity, and competence. How? By recognizing the essential components of keeping their best people and by understanding what enhances and diminishes those components.

Sridhar doubts that his firm will ever change, but other organisations are taking positive steps to focus on and enhance employee retention. As a result, they are reducing turnover, improving quality, increasing productivity, and saving on their training costs.

Questions

1. Do you think that Sridhar's self-esteem had anything to do with his leaving the firm?
2. What do you think were Sridhar's satisfaction with and commitment to the job and firm he is leaving?
3. What lessons can this firm learn from the case of Sridhr? What can and should it now do?
4. Which theory of personality does best describe Sridhar's behaviour?

QUESTIONS

1 Using the personality categories in this chapter, describe the basic sources of personality differences between yourself and a person you know well.

2 Using the 'Big Five' personality factors, describe your perceptions of (a) a close family member, and (b) a person for whom you have worked.

3 Define personality, critically examine the Freudian stages of personality development.

4 What are Erikson's stages of personality development? How do they compare with the Freudian stages?

5 What is personality? What are its determinants? Which of them, you feel, are more important in shaping personality?

6 Describe the concepts, viz., locus of control, authoritarianism, Machiavellianism, and introversion and extroversion. On a scale of 1 to 10, 1 being very low on the scale and 10 being very high, where do you place yourself on each of these personality dimensions?

7 How does the study of personality help in understanding organizational behaviour?

8 Critically examine the psychoanalytic approach to personality.

9 Write notes on (a) type theory and (b) trait theory of personality.

10 Bring out, with comments, the essence of social learning theory of personality.

11 Comment on the humanistic approach to personality.

12 According to you, which theory of personality is more comprehensive? Give reasons.

REFERENCES

1. Steven L.Mcshane and Mary Ann Von Glinow, *Organisational Behaviour*, Tata McGraw-Hill Publishing Company, 2000, p.187.
2. *Ibid*, p.187.
3. *Ibid,* p.188.
4. *Ibid*, p.189.
5. *Ibid,* p.78.
6. *Ibid,* p.81.
7. *Ibid,*
8. *Ibid,* p.82.
9. *Ibid.*
10. *Ibid*, Pp. 83-90.
11. Theodore T. Herbert, *Dimensions of Organisational Behaviour*, Macmillan, 1976, p.136.
12. Fred Luthans, *Organizational Behaviour*, McGraw-Hill, 1989, p.123.
13. The Hindu, 14, July 2003.
14. Theodore T. Herbert, Op.cit, p.136.

15. E.R. Hillgard, et *al, Introduction to Psychilory, Oxford & IBM, 1975, p.364.*
16. *Ibid,* p.366.
17. Fred Luthans, *Op.cit*, P. 129.
18. *Ibid,* p. 130.
19. *Ibid,* p. 131.
20. *Ibid,* p.132.
21. Stephen P. Robbins, *Organisational Behaviour*, Prentice Hall of India, 1989, p.75.
22. Larry A.Hielle and Daniel J.Liegler, *Personality Theories-Basic Assumptions, Research and Applications,* McGraw Hill, 1976, p.4.
23. Steven L. Mcshane and Mary Ann Von Glinow, *Op.cit*, p.188.
24. *Ibid*, p. 190.
25. Allen R. Cohen, *et al, Effective Behaviour in Organisations*, Irwin, 2001, p.188.
26. Gray and Strake, *Organizational Behaviour and Appications,* Macmillan, *1980, p.78.*
27. Joe Kelly, *Organizational Behaviour,* Surjeet Publications, 1987, p.78.
28. Larry A. Hielle and Daniel J. Ziegier, Op.cit, p.1.
29. Stephen P. Robbins, *Op.cit.,* p.65.

CHAPTER

Seventeen

Perception and Attribution

LEARNING OBJECTIVES

After reading this chapter you should understand –

1. The nature of Perception.
2. The steps in perceptual process.
3. The factors that influence stimuli.
4. The meaning of Perceptual organization.
5. The meaning of Attribution.
6. Why Perceptual distortions occur.
7. Perception is an important variable affecting several areas of organizations.
8. The meaning of Social perception.

We propose to discuss, in detail, perception-how it occurs, how it is an important element in OB and other related topics.

PERCEPTION: MEANING AND DEFINITION

In simple terms, perception is understood as the act of seeing what is there to be seen.[1] But what is seen is influenced by the individual, the object, and the situation. Any definition of perception should contain these three elements. Let us consider some popular definitions:

1. *The study of perception is concerned with identifying the processes through which we interpret and organize sensory information to produce our conscious experience of objects and object relationship.*[2]
2. *Perception is the process of receiving information about and making sense of the world around us. It involves deciding which information to notice, how to categorize this information, and how to interpret it within the framework of our existing knowledge.*[3]
3. *Perception includes all those processes by which an individual receives information about the environrnent-seeing, hearing, feeling, tasting, and smelling. The study of these perceptual processes shows that their functioning is affected by three classes of variables:the objects or events being perceived, the environment in which perception occurs, and the individual doing the perceiving.*[4]

The last definition contains all the three elements of perception.

PERCEPTION AND SEMANTICS

There is a great deal of confusion about the terms *perception and sensation.* Often, they are used as synonyms. For the sake of clarity, it may be stated that the study of sensation is concerned with the initial contact between organisms and their physical environment. It focuses on describing the relationship between various forms of sensory stimulation and how these inputs are registered by our sensory organs. The raw sensory inputs are of no consequence-they need to be processed and interpreted. This is the job of perception. Thus, sensation is the first step in the perceptual process. Sensation and other steps constitute the total perceptual process.

Inherited or Learnt? Another question relating to the conceptual clarification of perception is, whether or not it is inherited. It is suggested that normal perception is to some extent learnt. In one experimental study, two kittens were brought in the dark except during the period when the experiment was in progress. One kitten was strapped into a basket and carried around by an active partner on a rotating arm during the experimental periods (See Fig.17.1). The active kitten had the superior view and developed normal perception, where as the passive kitten remained effectively blind.

In another experiment, young animals and human infants were exposed to a visual cliff (see Fig.17.2). This is a patterned area with a steep drop in the middle, which is covered by glass to prevent a fall from the cliff. Both animals and human infants behaved in the same way by avoiding the deep side. The results of this experiment suggest that perception is either innate or learned at a very early stage in the development of the animal or human.[5]

FIGURE 17-1
THE ACTIVE AND PASSIVE KITTENS

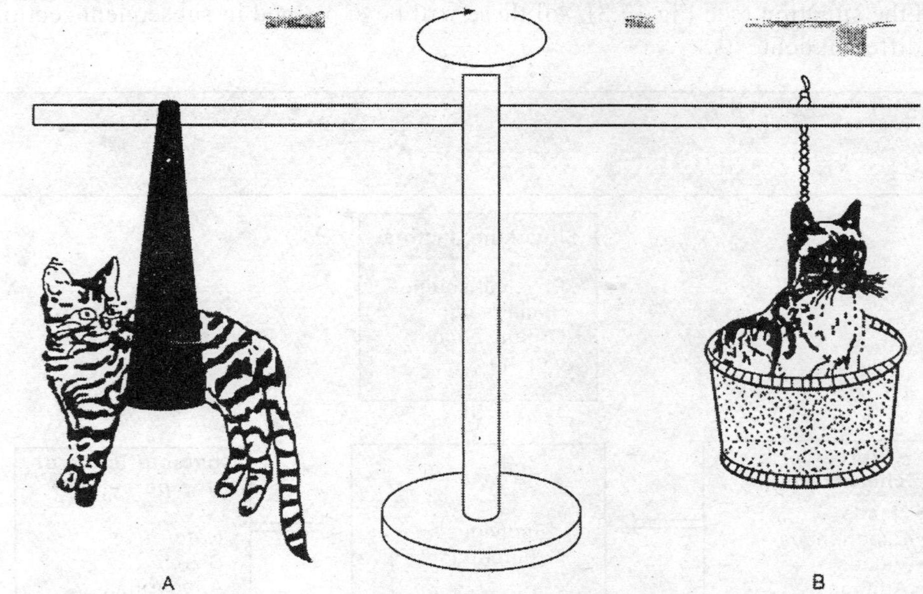

FIGURE 17-2
VISUAL CLIFF

Factors Influencing Perception

As understood from the third definition given above, perception is influenced by the perceiver, the object, and the situation (see Fig.17.3). All these will be explained in subsequent sections in this chapter in different contexts.

FIGURE 17-3
FACTORS INFLUENCING PERCEPTION

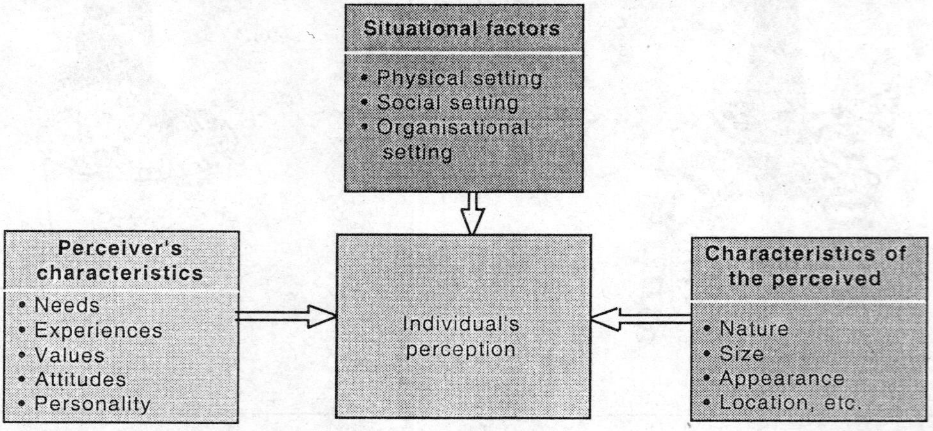

Perceptual Process

Perception is a process of receiving and interpreting stimuli. As shown in Fig.17.4, the process involves a series of steps and the steps are explained in the paragraphs that follow.

Fig. 17.4 shows that the perceptual process begins when stimuli are received through sensory organs. Most stimuli are screened out; the rest are organized and interpreted based on various information-processing activities. The outcomes of the process are covert and overt behaviours.

Receiving Stimuli

Living as we are in the world of objects, we are constantly bombarded with various stimuli. These stimuli enter our organism through the sensory organs-vision, hearing, smell, touch, taste, and kinaesthesis.* Stimuli are received by us through these organs. Sensory organs perceive not only physical objects, they also perceive events or objects that have been repressed. We may not be able to report the existence of certain stimuli, but our behaviour reveals that we are often subject to their influence.[6] Similarly, stimuli need not be external to us. They may be internal also. Examples of external stimuli include light waves, sound waves, mechanical energy or pressure, and chemical energy from objects that one can smell and taste. Internal stimuli include energy generated by

* Kinaesthesis is the sense where one's limbs and body are in space-the way in which you can know where your hand or foot as, even in pitch darkness. The kinaesthesis receptors are loealed throughout the muscles, and joints of the body. These sensors inform us of the relative positions and movements of our limbs and of difficult parts of our body.

FIGURE 17-4
PERCEPTUAL PROCESS

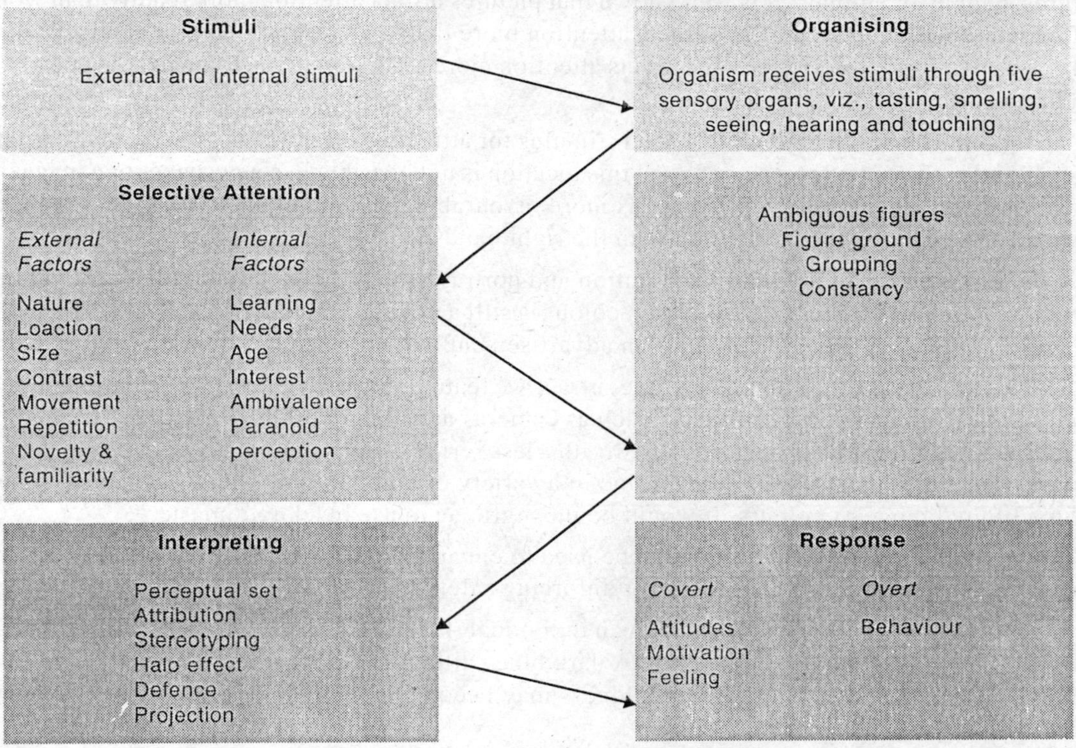

muscles, food passing through the digestive system, and glands secreting behaviour-influencing hormones. External or internal, human beings continue to receive stimuli. When deprived of sensory stimulation, people suffer from disorientation, confusion, and emotional disturbance, and are vulnerable to persuasion and pressure. Under these circumstances, people tend to engage in warding off depression by dwelling on past experiences.

Though stimuli may be external or internal to the organism, we focus on external stimuli in this chapter.

Selecting Stimuli

Not all the stimuli received by the human organism are accepted by it. Some stimuli are noticed and others are screened out. A girl may always need a transistor to be tuned on while she is reading or writing. She happily concentrates on her lessons even as the electronic device beside her blares film songs. A nurse working in a post-operative care might ignore the smell of recently disinfected instruments or the sounds of co-workers talking nearby. Yet a small flashing red light on the nurse station console is immediately noticed because it signals that a patient's vital signs are failing. The process of filtering information received by our senses is called *selecting stimuli* or *selective attention.* Several factors influence selective attention. Some of them are external and others are internal to the body.

External Factors Influencing Selection The external factors influencing selection are nature, location, colour, size, contrast, repetition, motion, and novelty and familiarity.

Nature: By nature we mean whether the object is visual or auditory and whether it involves pictures, people, or animals. It is well known that pictures attract attention more readily than words, that a picture with human beings attracts attention more than a picture of inanimate objects alone, and that a rhyming auditory passage attracts attention more readily than the same passage presented as a narrative.[7]

Location: The best location of a visual stimulus for attracting attention is directly in the front of the eyes and in the centre of a page. When this location is not possible in a newspaper or a magazine, a position in the upper portion of a page is more favourable than one in the lower portion, and the left hand side receives more attention than the right hand side.[8]

Colour Colour is used to attract attention and portray realism. In a mass of black and white, a modicum of colour catches the eye. When colour is still a novelty, as with newspapers till recently, the addition of a cue, a single colour to an advertisement will enhance its attention-getting value.

Colour can be used to emphasize the attractive features of a product or to create a suitable atmosphere. High technology products such as cameras are usually produced in black or methylic finishes although some have been marketed with a less serious, more sporty image, in bright primary colours. Some products, such as cars, come in a variety of colours, but others such as toothpaste, are in a limited range of colours. It would be incongruous to use black toothpaste.[9]

In the work environment, colour can be used to enhance lighting effects, for creating pleasant surroundings, and for putting across and reinforcing safety messages.

Colour has a psychological impact on an individual. It is well known that some colours act as a stimulant and others act as a depressant. A dark blue ceiling may appear to be refreshing to begin with, but after sometime the apparent coldness may become an irritant. Table 17.1 brings out the effects of different of colours.

TABLE 17-1

THE EFFECTS OF DIFFERENT COLOURS

Colour	*Psychological Effect*	*Temperature Effect*	*Distance Effect*
Violet	Aggressive and tiring	Cold	Very close
Blue	Restful	Cold	Further away
Brown	Exciting	Neutral	Claustrophobic
Green	Very restful	Cold/neutral	Further away
Yellow	Exciting	Very warm	Close
Orange	Exciting	Very warm	Very close
Red	Very stimulating	Warm	Close

(***Source:*** Eugene McKenna, *op.cit.*, p.142)

Size Generally, objects of larger size attract more attention than do smaller ones. The maintenance engineering staff may pay more attention to a big machine than to a small one, even though the smaller one costs as much and is as important to the operation.

A 6 foot 4 inch, 260 pound supervisor may receive more attention from his subordinates than a 5 foot 10 inch, 160 pound supervisor. In advertising, a full page spread attracts more attention than a few lines in the classified section.[10]

Contrast The contrast principle states that external stimuli which stand out against the background, or which are not what people are expecting, will receive their attention. Fig. 17.5 illustrates this perceptual principle. The black circle on the right appears larger than the one on the left because of the background circles. In fact both black circles are of the same size. In a similar manner, plant safety signs which have black lettering on a yellow background or white lettering on a red background are attention-drawers. Training managers utilize this factor in organizing training programmes in places far away from work places to create contrast atmosphere.

FIGURE 17-5
THE CONTRAST PRINCIPLE OF PERCEPTION

Movement The principle of motion states that a moving object receives more attention than an object that is stationary. In a work environment the attention of a workman will be focused more on a conveyor belt than on paintings on walls or illumination. Advertisers capitalize on this principle by creating signs which incorporate moving parts.

Repetition The repetition principle states that a repeated external stimulus is more attention-drawing than a non-repetitive one. The same advertisement of a product flashed daily on television is based on the principle of repetition. This principle also explains why supervisors have to give directions to workers over and over again for even simple tasks.

Novelty and Familiarity The novelty and familiarity principle states that either a novel or a familiar external situation can serve as an attention getter. New objects in familiar settings or familiar objects in new settings will draw the attention of the perceiver. Job rotation is an example of this principle. Changing workers' jobs from time to time will tend to increase the attention they give to the task. Anything novel attracts attention fast, for example, humour, animation, and unusual graphics in an advertisement stand out and are noticed.

Internal Factors Influencing Selection Internal factors influencing selection of stimuli include learning, psychological needs, age differences, interests, ambivalence, and paranoid perception. These factors relate to oneself.

Learning Learning, a cognitive factor, has considerable influence on perception. It creates expectancy in people. People tend to perceive what they want to perceive. A number of illustrations have been used by psychologists to demonstrate the impact of learning on perception. Some are shown below.

One tends to read the sentence, because of prior learning, in the triangle as 'Bird in the hand' [see Fig.17.6(a)]. It takes a few seconds for the reader to realize that there is an extra 'the' in the sentence. This illustration shows that learning creates expectancy in an individual and expectancy makes him see what he wants to see. Another illustration is typical.

The individual is likely to read the last word as 'Mac-Hinery' instead of 'machinery' [see Fig. 17.6(b)]. He or she is caught in what is known as 'verbal response set'.

FIGURE 17-6
THE IMPACT OF LEARNING ON PERCEPTION

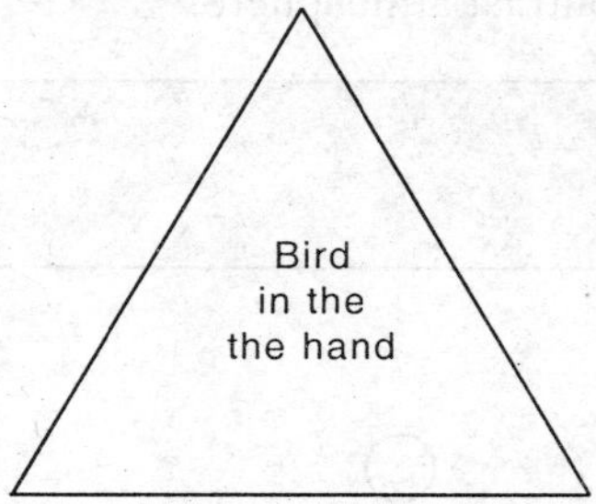

17.6(a)

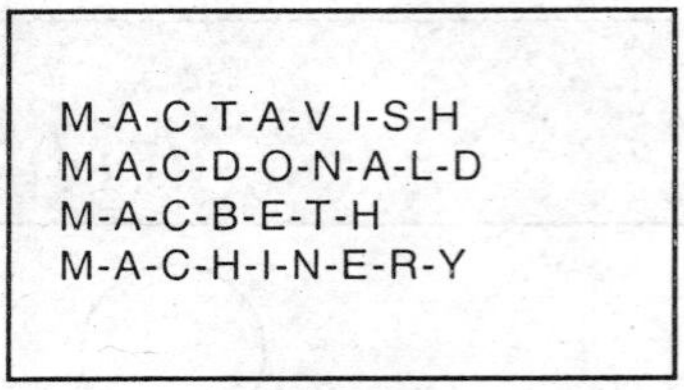

17.6(b)

is some value in conceiving the two as distinct. Once they have been satisfied, most needs no longer influence perception. But if the person has a special interest, his perception is likely to be selective at any time.[13]

Fig. 17.7 is another typical example of learning influencing perception. If one were to see an attractive, elegantly dressed woman, the perception concurs with the majority of the first-time viewers. However, one may agree with a sizable minority and see an ugly old woman.

FIGURE 17-7
ATTRACTIVE OR UGLY WOMAN?

In organizations, managers' and employees' past experiences and learning strongly influence their perceptions. For example, executives are influenced by their functional backgrounds while making decisions. They might perceive their own areas of expertise as being the most important to consider while solving problems. It is also likely that the decision-makers can 'rise above' their own experiences and limitations and solve problems effectively in areas other than those with which they are most familiar.

Psychological Needs Needs play a significant role in perceptual selectivity. Unreal things often look real because of deprived needs. A thirsty person in a desert, for instance, gets the illusion of water when seeing sand from a distance. In one experiment, people who were kept hungry for some time were shown pictures and were asked to describe what they saw in them. Most of them reported more food items in such perceptions.[11]

Maslow wrote (1970) thus: 'For our chronically and extremely hungry man, Utopia can be defined simply as a place where there is plenty of food. He tends to think that if only he is guaranteed for the rest of his life, he will never want anything more. Life itself tends to be defined in terms of eating. Anything else will be defined as unimportant. Freedom, love, community feeling, respect, philosophy, may all be waived aside as fripperies that are useless, since they fail to fill the stomach'.

It may be noted that frequently all of a person's psychic energies are expended in trying to satisfy the basic psychological needs for love, esteem, and adequacy. He may unconsciously interact only with those sectors of another's personality through which he can gratify these needs. Under such conditions he can scarcely perceive the other as a whole person; only when his basic psychological needs are satisfied can he appreciate the full worth of the other.[12]

Age Difference Older, senior executives complain about the inability of the new, young ones to take tough decisions concerning terminating people or paying attention to details and paper work. The young managers, in turn, complain about the 'old guards' resisting change and using paper and rules as ends in themselves. Different perceptions of old and young executives are due to their age differences. The generation gaps witnessed in recent years definitely contribute to different perceptions.

Interest Perception is unconsciously influenced by the interests of the perceiver. An architect will notice many details of buildings though he or she passes by only once. Someone else may pass the same buildings everyday for years without ever observing such details. It has been argued that, in their influence on perception, interests cannot be distinguished from needs. That is, the person with a particular interest has a need to involve himself in activities pertaining to it. Yet there
Ambivalence Another factor of perceptual selection is ambivalence or mixed feelings about a situation. A young man may be ambivalent about his fiancee's virtues and shortcomings. She may be an attractive, charming, and poised woman with whom he likes to be seen, but she may also be insecure and have a poor self-concept. When she tries to compensate for these feelings by taking control of the relationship, he resents it and is anxious about the wisdom of his choice. But because of his physical attraction to her and because he wants to remain a success in his circle by having a beautiful financee, he represses the awareness of her negative qualities and selectively perceives only those that are favourable. Only after several years of marriage, when the selective perception of courtship has given way before the all-inclusive awareness of daily, intimate, and prolonged contact, does he become sharply aware of what he repressed.[14]

Paranoid Perception When a person's perception is so selective that he can find little common ground for communication with others, he is likely to be paranoid. It is the characteristic of the emotionally disturbed person that his perceptual field differs from that of reality and personalized interpretation. His self-concept is poor and he is very insecure, as a result of which he behaves in an inflexible manner.[15]

PERCEPTUAL ORGANIZATION

Perceptual organization is the process by which people group stimuli into recognizable patterns. Selection gives way to organization, and the stimuli selected for attention now appear as a whole. For example, most people have a mental picture of an object made of wood and having four legs, a seat, a back, and armrests: an image of a chair. When people actually see an object having these characteristics, they are able to organize the incoming information into a meaningful whole and recognize the object to be a chair.

There is so much to learn about how the human mind assembles, organizes, and categorizes information. However, certain factors in perceptual organization, such as ambiguous figures, figure background, grouping, and constancy are helpful in understanding perceptual organization.

Ambiguous Figures Perceptual organization becomes a difficult task when there are confusing and disorganized stimuli in the external environment. When we first glance at the lines in Fig.17.8, we tend to conclude that they epitomize disorganization. Then we suddenly begin to realize that it is a drawing and could represent either a duck or a rabbit, and then it fluctuates between the two images. Similarly, in Fig.17.9, we see either kneeling woman or a man's face, or perhaps both. With ambiguous figures, there appears to be a whole image.[16]

FIGURE 17-8
AN AMBIGUOUS FIGURE — A DUCK OR A RABBIT

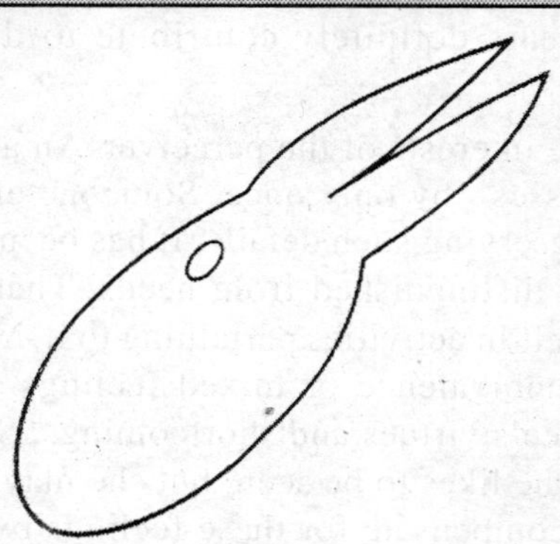

FIGURE 17-9
AN AMBIGUOUS FIGURE — A KNEELING WOMAN OR A MAN'S FACE

Figure Background Figure - ground is considered to be the most basic form of perceptual organization. The figure background principle states that the relationship of a target to its background influences perception. In other words, according to the principle, perceived objects stand out as separable from their general background. For example, in a noisy and crowded restaurant, one is able to hold a meaningful conversation with a colleague. This is possible because the person is capable of distinguishing the sight and sound of the colleague (figure) from the sight and sound of the other people and objects present (background). Although the individual perceives the entire scene, yet he or she responds selectively to the most relevant stimuli.

Managers face similar experiences in organizations. People pay more attention to some stimuli than others and run the danger of overlooking relevant clues.

A quick look at Fig.17.10 and then looking away from the illustration is an experience by itself. Most people focus on the individual figures enclosed with lines and few see any meaning. However, if one were to focus on the space between the figtures, the word WEST appears. Place a piece of paper along the bottom of the figure, the word becomes even more apparent. Fig.17.11 is another illustrator of figure-background principle. At first the figure looks like a white vase. However, if white is taken as the background, we see two grey profiles.

FIGURE 17-10
A FIGURE GROUND EXPERIEMENT

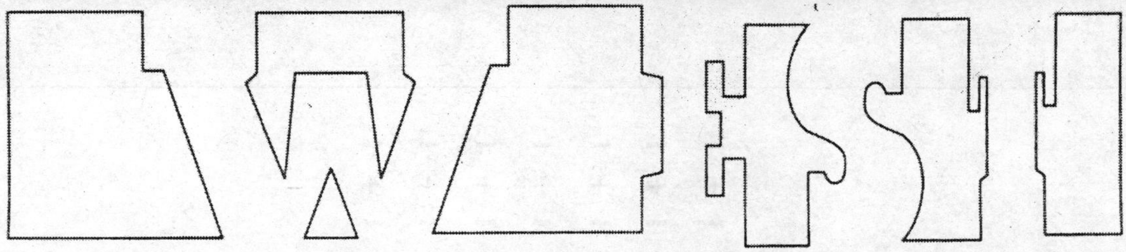

FIGURE 17-11
FIGURE BACKGROUND DEMONSTRATION

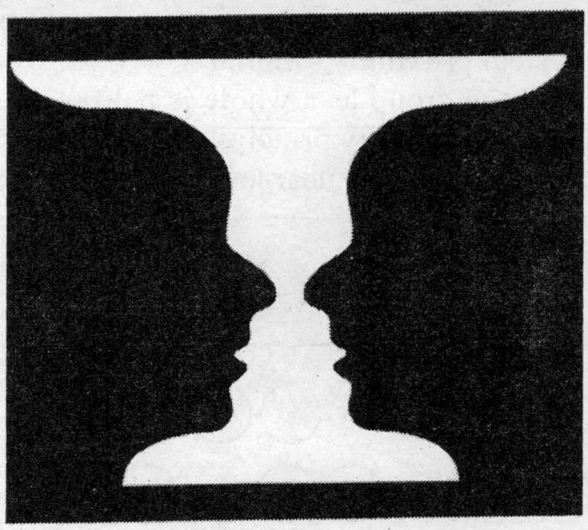

What we see depends on what we see as the figure and what we see as the background. We attend selectively to stimuli by focusing on features that capture our attention. A major purpose of studying OB is to caution the reader about important stimuli. Key theories and concepts (such as motivation and leadership) call attention to variables that affect organizational performance. The trained manager knows what to look for as the dominant figure against a complex background of organizational forces.

Perceptual Grouping The principles of grouping first defined by Gestalt psychologists include similarity, proximity, closure, continuity, and area.

The principle of *similarity* is exemplified when objects of similar shape, size, or colour tend to be grouped together. In an organization, for example, all employees who wear white collars may be perceived as a common group, when, in reality, each worker is a unique individual. A company might require visitors to its plants to wear yellow hard hats and employees to wear white hard hats. Employees can then easily identify people who are unfamiliar with everyday safety precautions and routines when they are in work areas. Although the principle of similarity is useful in helping people make sense of their worlds, a negative aspect of this principle is found in the perceptual stereotyping.

Fig.17.12 illustrates the similarity principle. The signs in the figure are perceived as seven rows rather than the five columns, even though the distances between the rows and columns are equal.

FIGURE 17-12
PRINCIPLE OF SIMILARITY

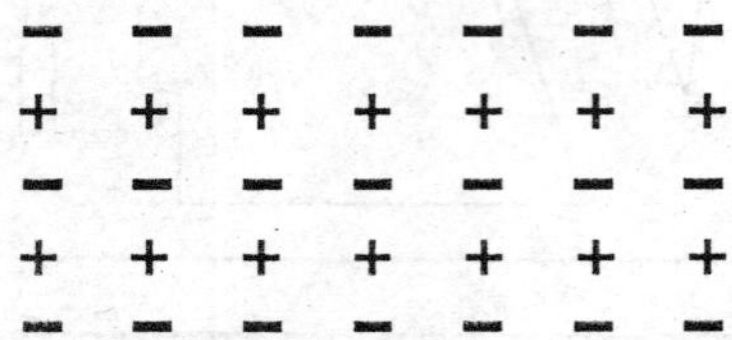

The principle of *proximity* underlines the tendency to perceive stimuli which are near one another as belonging together. For example, several employees in an organization may be identified as a single group because of physical proximity. Similarly, several workers working on a machine are perceived to be one group and the group as a whole is held responsible for any failure in the machine. Fig.17.13 demonstrates the proximity principle. The eight circles in the figure are seen as pairs of two, three, or four, depending on their nearness to one another.

FIGURE 17-13
PRINCIPLE OF PROXIMITY

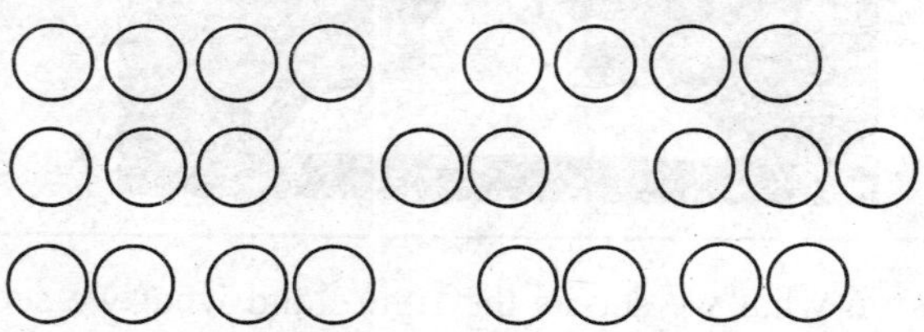

The principle of *closure* states that a person has a tendency to perceive a whole when none exits. The person's perceptual process will close the gaps which are unfilled from sensory inputs. The closure principle demonstrates the perceiver's ability to perceive a whole object even though only part of the object is evident. In an organization, a manager facing a complex decision may be able to develop a fairly accurate understanding of the issues even though some details may be lacking. Based on experience and imagination, the manager can fill in the missing pieces needed to make a decision. Fig.17.14 illustrates the perceptual closure concept.

Continuity is the tendency to perceive objects as continuing patterns. (See Fig.17.15). In the figure, we see curved and straight lines as crossing each other and having dots in common, but it requires some effort on our part to perceive a straight line becoming a curved line at one of these intersecting points or junctions. Continuity is an useful organizing principle, but it may also have negative aspects. For example, the tendency to perceive continuous patterns may result in an inability to perceive uniqueness and detect change. In business forecasting, a common continuity error is to assume that the future will simply reflect current events and trends.

FIGURE 17-14
THE PRINCIPLE OF CLOSURE

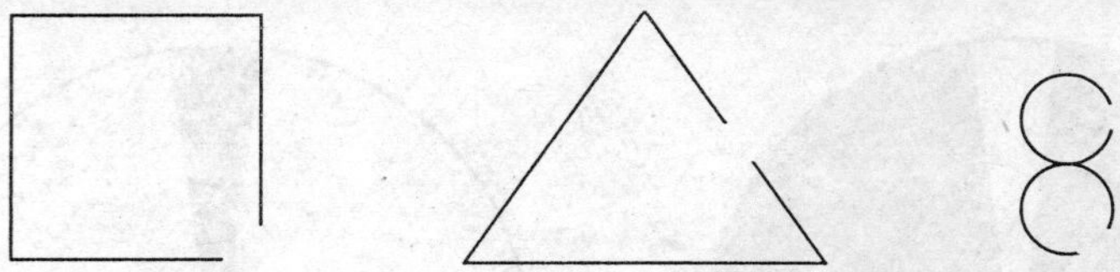

FIGURE 17-15
AN EXAMPLE OF PERCEPTUAL CONTINUITY

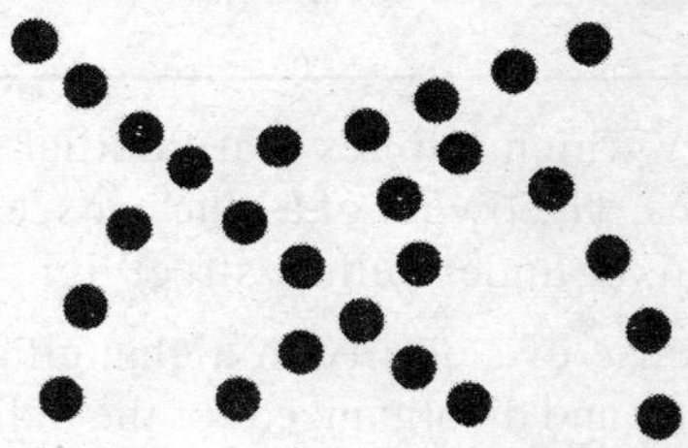

The principle of continuity is closely related to the principle of closure, but there is a difference. Closure supplies missing stimuli, whereas the continuity principle says that a person will tend to perceive continuous lines or patterns.

Area Where one part of an area depicting an ambiguous figure is smaller in size than the remainder, it is more likely that the smaller area will be seen as a figure and the rest of the total area as background. Glancing at Fig.17.16(A), it is usual to see the small areas of white as the figure of a white cross and the large area of black as the background. By contrast, in Fig. 17.16(B), a black cross set in a white background is more likely to be seen.[17]

Perceptual Constancy A more subtle part of perceptual organisation is *constancy,* our ability to perceive certain characteristics of an object as remaining constant, despite variations in the stimuli that provide us with conflicting information. Such constancy amidst changing stimuli is indispensable if we are to adjust to our world. There are several aspects of constancy.

One of these, *shape constancy,* is exemplified whenever an object appears to maintain its shape despite marked changes in the retinal image. For example, we see the top of a glass bottle as 'circular' whether we view it from the side or from the top. Shape constancy works to our advantage by keeping our world of perception orderly. Imagine the confusion you would experience in a crowded car park if your car was seen as a different object according to the different retinal images produced from different viewing positions-front, side, and back.

Another is *size constancy,* which refers to the fact that as an object is moved farther away we tend to see it as more or less invariant in size. For example, football players on the opposite side of the field do not look appreciably smaller than those closer to us on the field even though their images on the retina are much smaller.

FIGURE 17-16
AN EXAMPLE OF PERCEPTUAL CONTINUITY

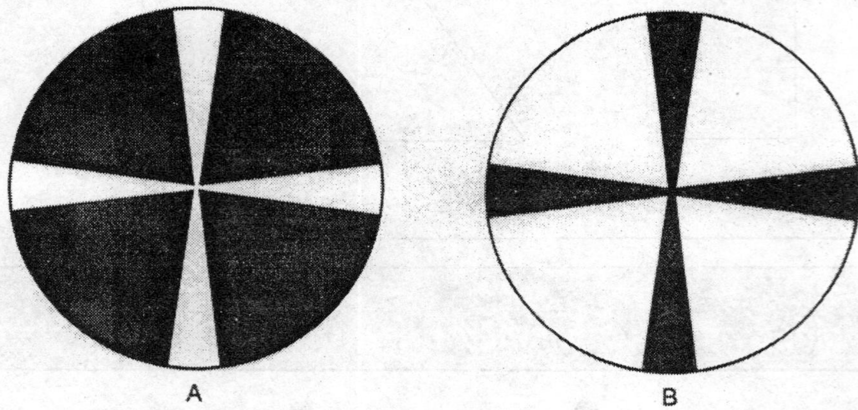

Then there is *colour constancy* which implies that familiar objects are perceived to be of the same colour under varied conditions. The owner of a blue car sees it as blue whether looking at it in bright sunlight, in dim illumination, or under yellow street light.

Constancy gives a person a sense of stability in a changing world. If constancy were not at work the world would be very chaotic and disorganized for the individual. An organizational example would be the worker who must select a piece of material or a tool of the correct size from a wide variety of materials and tools at varying distances from a work station. Without perceptual constancy, the sizes and colour of objects would change as the worker moved about and would make the job almost impossible.

Where Constancy Does Not Hold Good Under certain conditions constancy does not hold good, and what we see appears to be quite different from what we know to be true. These manifestations are called *illusions.* Three such illusions are illustrated in Figures 17.17, 17.18 and 17.19.

FIGURE 17-17

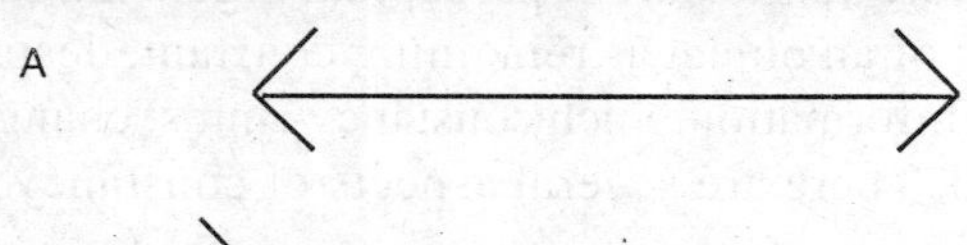

An illusion can be understood as a reliable perceptual error, it is stable and not due to a hasty or careless exploration or processing of stimuli on our part. Though the lines A and B in Fig.17.17 are of the same length, we see A as the shorter one. In Fig.17.18, we see two rectangles, A and B, as different even though they are of the same size. The moon illustration (Fig.17.19) is another typical example of an illusion. The moon seems to be much larger when it appears on the horizon than

FIGURE 17-18

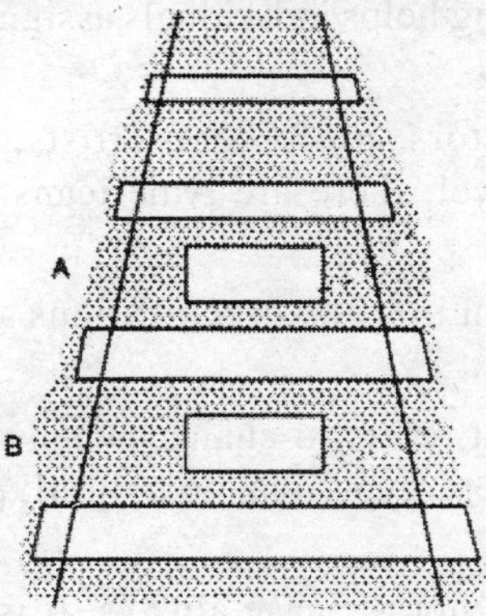

FIGURE 17-19

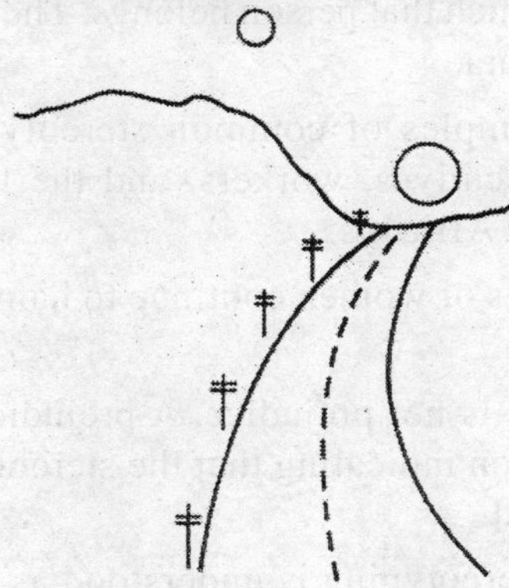

when it is high in the sky. But it is the same distance away from us in both cases and the image projected on to the retina is also the same in both cases. However, we see them as different sizes.[18]

Another instance of illusion is one train that is stationary and the other in motion. It should be the experience of everybody-you are on board a train that is stationary and you look through window at a moving train. You get an illusion that the train you are sitting in is moving though in reality, it is the other train that is moving. This is called the illusion of induced movement. Illusions can also arise for the presentation of stimuli in rapid succession. An example of this phenomenon is the apparent backward movement of wagon wheels in an old Telugu film.

The Process of Interpreting

After the data have been received and organized, the perceiver interprets or assigns meaning to the information. In fact, perception is said to have taken place only after the data have been interpreted. Several, factors contribute towards the interpretation of data. More important amongst them are perceptual set, attribution, stereotyping, halo effect, perceptual context, perceptual defence, implicit personality theory and projection.

Perceptual Set Previously-held beliefs about objects influence an individual's perceptions of similar objects. This is called perceptual set. For example, a manager may have developed general beliefs and attitudes that workers are lazy and shirkers, and that they want to gain whatever is possible from the organization without giving of their best to it. His or her subsequent perceptions will be influenced by this set when he or she meets a group of workers. The manager tends to interpret the behaviour of the workers according to his mental set.[19]

Attribution Attribution refers to the process by which the individual assigns causes to the behaviour he or she conceives. People are interested not only in observing behaviour in organizations, for example, but in determining its causes. Their evaluation of and reactions to others' behaviour may be heavily influenced by their perception that the others are responsible for their behaviour. When plant productivity increases, the manager responsible will be evaluated less favourably if the increase is attributed to new machine installed at the order of the head office than if it is attributed to his or her handling of the employees. A nurse who drops a tray of medicine will be excused if the incident is perceived as caused by a slippery floor, chastised if it is viewed to be caused by her clumsiness, and perhaps fired if it is viewed as a deliberate act.[20] Attribution is discussed in detail in the next section.

Stereotyping It is the tendency to assign attributes to someone solely on the basis of a category of people to which that person belongs. The process of stereotyping helps individuals assign meaning to a mass of data.

Some examples of common stereotypes are women, doctors, professors, artists, software engineers, executives, workers, and the like. At a broader level, there are Americans, Indians, Britishers, and Africans.

Stereotypes of women continue to hamper their advancement in many organizations across the globe.[21]

Stereotype is not prejudice. A prejudice is a stereotype that refers to change when presented with information indicating that the stereotype is inaccurate. Stereotypes can be helpful; prejudice is never helpful.

Though stereotyping is understood as wrong or bad, this is not the case always. It is a useful process that greatly increases one's efficiency in making sense out of his or her environment. Nonetheless, stereo-typing can lead to inaccuracies and negative consequences. To the extent that stereotypes create social injustice, result in poor decision-making, stifle innovation, or cause underutilization of human resources, they contribute to ineffectiveness and inefficiency.

Stereotyping is a four-step process. It begins by categorizing people into groups according to various criteria such as age, sex, race, and occupation. Next, we infer that all people within a particular category possess the same traits. Then we form expectations of others and interpret their behaviour according to our stereotypes. Finally, stereotypes are maintained by (i) overestimating the frequency of stereotypic behaviours exhibited by others, (ii) incorrectly explaining expected and unexpected behaviours, and (iii) differentiating minority individuals from oneself.

Halo Effect The halo effect refers to the tendency of perceiving people in terms of good and bad, and ascribing all good qualities to one who is liked and all bad qualities to another who is disliked. A typical example of the halo effect is a professor awarding more marks to a well-liked student. It is not so much a conscious bias on the professor's part, as that the professor likes the student, he wants him to do well in the examination, and his perception about the student's examination are influenced by what he wants to see. A common phenomenon in communication is the tendency for a receiver to evaluate information on the basis of its source. Information emanating from a VIP tends to be overrated and the same coming from an ordinary individual is likely to be discounted.

Halo effect need not always mean overrating positive characteristics. An individual may be downrated based on the negative evaluation of his or her behaviour. This process is called *rusty halo or horns effect.*

In organizations, the halo effect often occurs when superiors rate subordinates in a formal appraisal. In this context, a manager evaluating one of his employees on certain dimensions may assume that someone who is good in one dimension must also be good at other things and rate the person highly on other aspects (see Fig.17.20). Put another way, the halo effect may be responsible for finding high correlations between the ratings given to people on various dimensions. When this occurs, the resulting evaluations lack accuracy and the quality of the resulting evaluations is compromised.

FIGURE 17-20

THE HALO EFFECT: A DEMONSTRATION

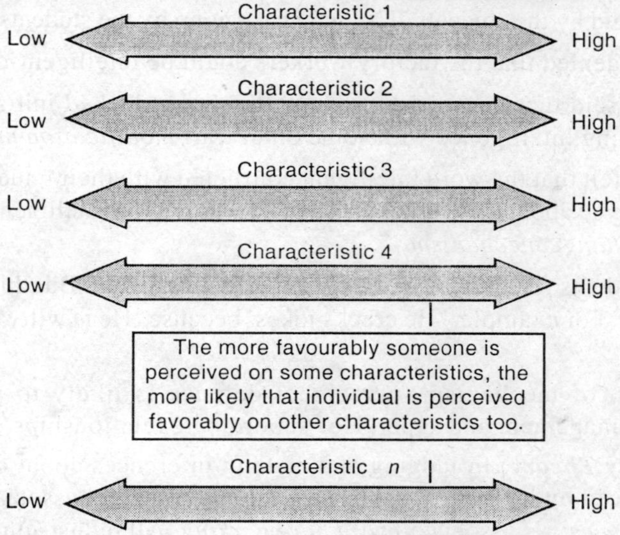

(***Source:*** Greenberg and Baron, *Behaviour in Organisations*)

FIGURE 17-21

GAME OF DODDLES

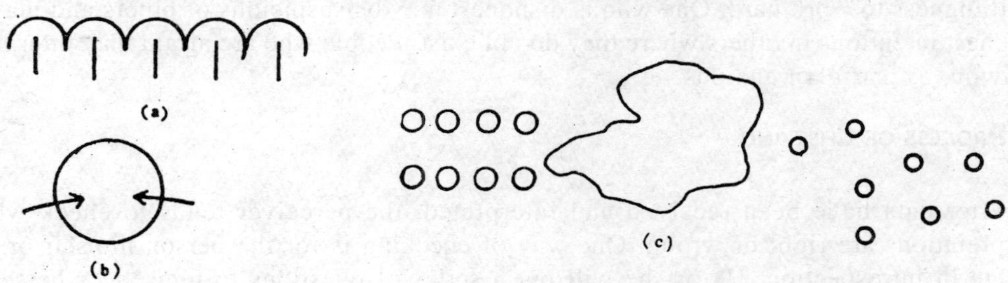

(a) The start of a'rat race' (b) Two mice in a beer can (c) A column of ants marching through spilled whiskey

Perceptual Context The context in which an object is placed influences perception. Fig.17.21 illustrates contextual influence on perception. The visual stimuli by themselves are meaningless. Only when the doodles are placed in a verbal context do they take on meaning and value for the perceiver.

The organizational culture and structure provide the primary context in which workers and managers do their perceiving. Thus, a verbal order, a memo, a new policy, a suggestion, a raised eyebrow, or a pat on the back takes on special meaning and value when placed in the context of a work situation.

Perceptual Defence According to the principle of perceptual defence, an individual is likely to put up a defence when confronted with conflicting, unacceptable, or threatening stimuli. The defence mechanisms put up by the perceiver may assume any of the four forms: outright denial, modification of the data received, change in perception but refusal to change, and change in perception itself. The four defence mechanisms have been culled from a study involving college students. The students were presented with the word 'intelligent' as a characteristic of a factory worker.[22] This was conflicting to the notion about a worker held by the students. The defences put up by the students were:

(a) Some students denied that the factory workers could be intelligent-denial *mechanism.*

(b) Some students said that the worker was intelligent but lacked initiative to rise above his group (associating intelligence with some other trait-*modification mechanism).*

(c) A few students felt that the word intelligent conflicted with their understanding of a worker. What they believed about the worker was that he was not too intelligent-change in perception but *refusal to change mechanism.*

(d) Many of the students felt that the worker was really intelligent. But this change in perception was very subtle. For example, 'He cracks jokes' because 'He is witty'-*change in perception mechanism.*

Whatever the form of mechanism, perceptual defence is likely to play a useful role in understanding union management and supervisor-subordinate relationships.

Implicit Personality Theory In judging and making inferences about others, an individual's perceptions are influenced by his belief that certain human traits are associated with one another. For example, the trait *honesty* is associated with *hardworking,* All industrious people are perceived to be honest.

Projection Under certain conditions, people tend to see in another person traits that they themselves possess. That is, they project their own feelings, tendencies, or motives into their judgement of others. This may be particularly true regarding undesirable traits which the perceiver possesses but fails to recognize in himself. For example, an individual who is himself not very energetic may see others as lazy or may explain their lack of achievement as resulting from their unwillingness to work hard. One who is dishonest may be suspicious of others and may perceive dishonest intentions in others where they do not exist. People who are afraid may interpret others' behaviour as fearful or anxious.

The Process of Checking

After data have been received and interpreted, the perceiver tends to cheek whether his interpretations are right or wrong. One way of checking is for the person himself or herself to indulge in introspection. He or she will put a series of questions to himself or herself and the answers will confirm whether his or her perception about an individual or object is correct or otherwise. Another way is to check the veracity about the interpretation with others.

The Process of Reacting

The last phase in perception is the reaction. The perceiver will indulge in some action in relation to his or her perception. The action depends on whether the perception is favourable or unfavourable: it is positive when the perception is favourable and negative when the perception is unfavourable. A worker responds favourably to the motivational intentions of a manager provided his or her understanding about his or her boss is favourable. The response is negative when his perception of the manager's behaviour is unfavourable.

ATTRIBUTION THEORY

Attribution theory, a relatively new addition to the field of OB, has implications for perception, motivation, and leadership. We shall focus on the impact of attribution theory on perception.

Fritz Heider and H. H. Kelly are well-known contributors to the attribution theory. This theory suggests that we observe behaviour and then attribute causes to it; that is, we attempt to explain why people behave as they do. The process of attribution is based on perceptions of reality and these perceptions may vary widely among individuals.

The theory posits that the behaviour of others can be examined on the basis of its *distinctiveness, consistency, and consensus.* Distinctiveness is the degree to which a person behaves similarly in different situations. Consistency is the degree to which a person engages in the same behaviour at different times. Consensus is the degree to which other people are engaging in the same behaviour. As a result of various combinations of consensus, consistency, and distinctiveness, we form

FIGURE 17-22
THE ATTRIBUTION PROCESS

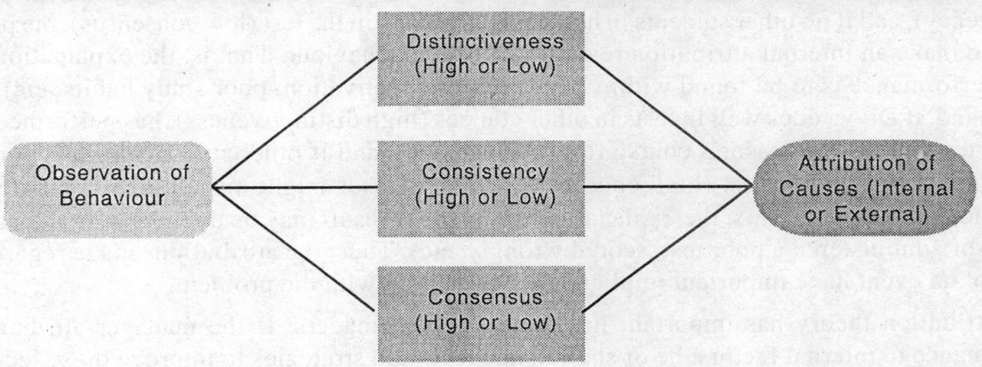

impressions of our attributions to the causes of behaviour. We may believe that behaviour is caused informally (by forces within a person, for example, ability) or externally (by forces in the person's environment, for example, task) (see Fig.17.22).

Under conditions of high consistency, high distinctiveness, and high consensus, the perceiver will tend to attribute the behaviour of the perceived person to external causes. When distinctiveness and consensus are low, the perceiver will tend to attribute the behaviour to internal causes (see Fig.17.23). Of course, other combinations of high and low consistency, distinctiveness and consensus are possible. Some combinations, however, may not provide the perceiver with a clear choice between internal and external causes.

The following example will help clarify the attribution rules. Divya has done poorly in a test in her third semester MBA course and has expressed concern to her professor. Her professor, in trying to understand the possible reasons for her behaviour (doing poorly in the test), tries to determine its degree of distinctiveness, consistency, and consensus. If Divya tends to do poorly in tests in other

FIGURE 17-23
RULES OF ATTRIBUTION

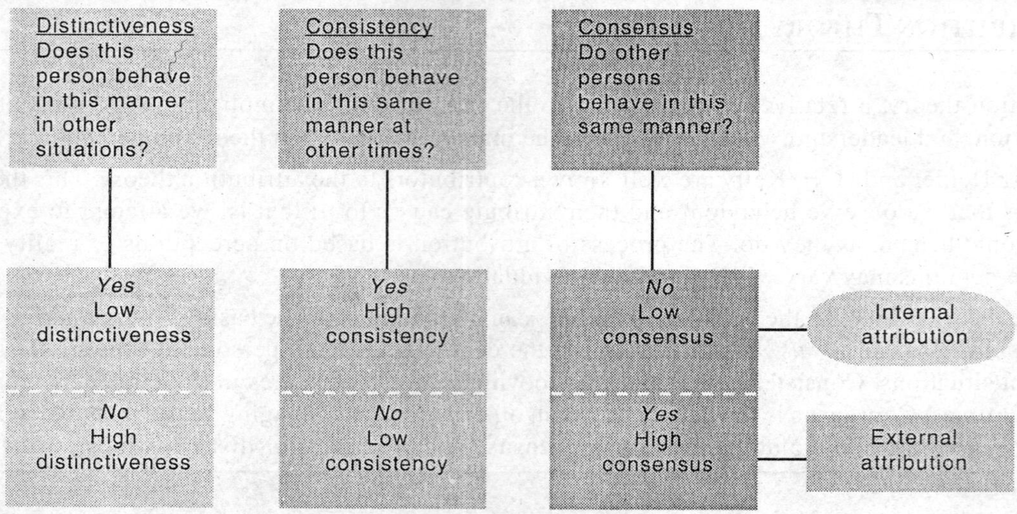

courses (low distinctiveness), has performed poorly on earlier tests in her management class (high consistency), and if no other students in her class did poorly in the test (low consensus), the professor tends to make an internal attribution regarding Divya's behaviour. That is, the explanation for the poor performance is to be found within Divya (lack of motivation, poor study habits, etc). On the other hand, if Divya does well in tests in other courses (high distinctiveness), has performed well in earlier tests in this professor's course (low consistency), and if other students in the course have also done poorly in this test (high consensus), the professor might make an external attribution about her behaviour. That is, the explanation for the poor result may be due to external factors (the professor administered a poor test, scored wrongly, etc). Thus, the attributions made regarding the cause of an event have important implications for dealing with the problem.

Attribution theory has important implications for managers. If the manager attributes poor performance to internal factors, he or she can adopt certain strategies to improve those factors. On the other hand, if the manager attributes poor performance to external factors, he or she can take relevant steps to improve performance.

One can make attribution to oneself. If one attributes a pay raise to hard work, he or she continues to work hard. Instead, if poor performance is attributed to external factors (such as boss's friendliness), he or she may put more effort into cementing that friendship.

When Perception Fails

Perception is the starting point of human behaviour. Through the perception process an individual selects, organizes, and interprets information and this forms the basis for his or her behaviour. Perception often plays spoilsport with our behaviour. For instance, how we perceive others affects how we treat them. If we stereotype people in negative ways, we may not take any interest in them. If we see things only from our frame of reference, we may be in constant conflict with others. If we

FIGURE 17-24
BIASES AFFECTING PERCEPTION

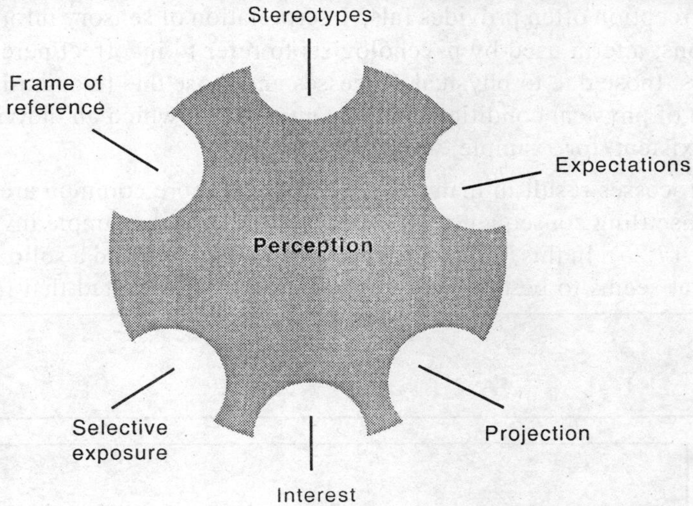

(*Source:* Robert N. Lussier, *Human Relations in Organisations*, P. 58)

see and hear only what we expect, we may turn people off. Selective exposure can cause people to get angry with us for not listening to them. People generally do not like to bear making projective statements about others. Fig.17.24 illustrates the biases affecting perception.

The attribution theory explained earlier is itself an instance of perceptual failure. An important by-product of the theory is the identification of systematic errors or biases that distort attributions. One such error is called the *fundamental attribution error.* This error refers to a tendency to underestimate the importance of external factors and overestimate the importance of internal factors when making attributions about the behaviour of others. An example might be that of a shop floor supervisor who attributes a high injury rate to employee carelessness (a cause internal to the employee), instead of considering the possibility of the equipment being old and in poor condition (a cause external to the employee).[23]

Self-fulfilling Prophecy Self-fulfilling prophecy can be traced back to Greek mythology. According to mythology, Pygmalion was a sculptor who hated women yet fell in love with an ivory statue he carved of a beautiful woman. He became so infatuated with the statue that he prayed to the goddess Aphrodite to bring her to life. The goddess heard his prayer, granted his wish, and the statue came to life. The essence of self-fulfilling prophecy or Pygmalion effect as it is often called, is that people's expectations or beliefs determine their behaviour and performance, thus, serving to make their expectations come true.[24]

Another dimension of self-fulfilling prophecy is that it occurs when our expectations about another person cause that person to act in a way that is consistent with those expectations. In other words, our perceptions can influence reality. If a supervisor believes a new employee will not be able to perform the job, this expectation influences the supervisor's behaviour towards the employee and without realizing it, may cause the new hire to perform the job poorly. Consequently, the supervisor's perception, even if originally incorrect, is confirmed. It is for this reason that employees are more likely to be victims of negative self-fulfilling prophecy than benefactors of positive self-fulfilling prophecy. To block negative self-fulfilling prophecy, firms need to fight negative stereotypes and avoid first impressions.

Illusions Perception often provides false interpretation of sensory information. Such cases are known as illusions, a term used by psychologists to refer to incorrect perceptions. There are two types of illusions: those due to physical processes and those due to cognitive processes. Illusions due to distortion of physical conditions include *mirages,* in which an individual perceives objects which are non-existent, for example, water on a dry road.

Cognitive processes result in many illusions but the more common are *shape* illusions which often result in unsettling consequences. Consider a real-world example involving the *Poggendorf illusion (see* Fig.17.25). In this, a line disappears at an angle behind a solid figure, reappearing the other side at what seems to be the incorrect position. It is reported that in 1965 two aeroplanes

FIGURE 17-25
POGGENDORF ILLUSION

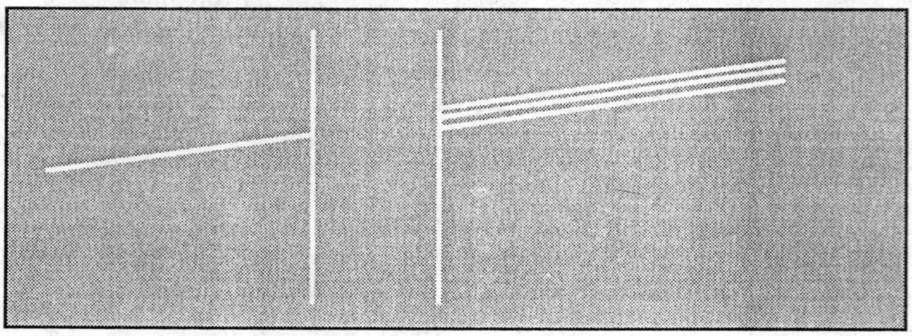

were about to arrive in New York city and because of the Poggendorf illusion, they perceived that they were on a collision course. Both pilots changed their path to correct for what they perceived as an error and thus collided. The result was four deaths and 49 injuries-all because of an illusion.[25]

Incorrect perceptions of the world around them may lead to problems to personnel. Budding managers who flame out do so because they fail to read situations properly and act accordingly. They develop poor working relationships, are too authoritarian, or have conflicts with upper management. As a result, their careers come to a screeching halt. This could have been avoided had they been able to correctly perceive what they should be doing and had the emotional maturity and ability to make the necessary changes.

PERCEPTION AND OB

In the discussion on perception till now, we quoted several organizational contexts demonstrating its relevance. In this section an attempt is made to focus further on the importance of perception.

Perception is a complex cognitive process which, in sum, is a unique interpretation of a situation, not an exact recording of it. It may reveal a picture of the world which is different from reality. Recognition of difference between the perceptual world and the real world is vital to the study of OB. A specific example would be the universal assumption made by managers that subordinates always want promotions when, in fact, many subordinates really feel psychologically forced to accept a promotion. Managers seldom attempt to find out, and sometimes subordinates themselves do not know, whether the promotion should be offered. In other words, the perceptual world of the manager is quite different from the perceptual world of the subordinates, and both may be far-removed from reality. What should be done from the manager's standpoint? The best answer is to understand the perceptual process. The application of what is understood logically follows.

The above being a general statement, specific applications of perception in organisations are analysed in paragraphs that follow.

In an interview for the selection of a candidate, the interviewers' judgement about the suitability or otherwise of a candidate depends on how his behaviour is perceived by them. A rejected applicant might feel that he or she was wronged by the interviewers though he or she deserved selection. But the fact is that interviewers generally form an early impression that becomes quickly entrenched. If the inadequacies of the candidate are exposed early, they weigh against him or her in the final selection.

Another perceptual issue related to hiring new employees is the problem of unrealistic expectations. Every applicant acquires, during the selection proçess, a set of expectations about the organization and about the specific job the applicant is hoping to be offered. It is not unusual for these expectations to be excessively inflated as a result of receiving almost uniformly positive information. There is evidence that now demonstrates that these inaccurate perceptions lead to premature resignations, and that realistic expectations can lead to lower turnover rates.

So what are realistic job expectations? They include both favourable and unfavourable information about the job. If the candidate has been provided with both favourable and unfavourable information about the job, he or she will be better equipped to cope with it and to face boldly the frustrating elements of the job. The result is fewer unexpected resignations by new employees.

Performance appraisal is another area where perception has significant relevance. Assessment of an employee's performance depends on the perception of the person who evaluates. While evaluation can be objective as in a salesman's job where performance is quantifiable, many jobs are evaluated in subjective terms. Subjective measures are easier to implement; they provide managers with greater discretion regarding jobs that do not really lend themselves to objective measures. Subjective measures are, by definition, judgmental. To the extent that the evaluation depends on subjective measures for assessing an employee's performance, perception of who is a 'good' or 'bad' employee greatly influences the outcome of the appraisal.

An individual's future in an organization is usually not dependent on performance alone. In many organisations, the level of an employee's effort is given great importance. Assessment of an individual's effort is a subjective judgment, susceptible to perceptual distortions and bias. If it is true, as some claim, that 'more workers are fired for poor attitudes and lack of discipline than for lack of ability', then approval of an employee's effort may be a primary influence on his or her future in the organization.

Another important judgment that managers make about employees is whether or not they are loyal to the organization. An employee, specially at the managerial level, who disparages the firm or looks for greener pastures outside may be labeled as disloyal, cutting of all future advancement opportunities. The issue is not whether organizations are right in demanding an employee's loyalty, but the fact is that many employers do, and the assessment of loyalty or commitment is highly judgmental. What is perceived as loyalty by one decision-maker may be seen as disloyalty by another, and caring and concerned by yet others. When evaluating a person's attitude, as in loyalty assessment, we must recognize that we are again involved with a person's perception.

Many managerial practices depend on the Theory X or Theory Y assumptions about employees. Theory X assumes that man is (among other things) inherently lazy and irresponsible, creates the unconscious rationale for directing and controlling authoritarian management. Theory Y assumptions, include the responsibility orientation of man and his potential for creativity and contributions, resulting in quite different practices. Both sets of assumptions incorporate many of the perceptual processes that influence managerial behaviour.

Attempts made by individuals to project favourable impressions about themselves in the eyes of their superiors are related to the cognitive process. Popularly called *impression management,* the process refers to the calculated efforts made to get others to think of them in a certain way, preferably in the best possible way. Impression management might involve direct attempts to make oneself look better (such as improving one's appearance, claiming associations with highly regarded people), as well as attempts to make others feel better about themselves (such as by flattering them and showing approval for whatever they say).

Impression management has its impact on the success of getting a job and also on his or her on career. It also has an influence on his or her relationships with others. Superiors feel better disposed towards those subordinates who manage to project better image.

Attempting to look good to others may take its toll on the accuracy of the information communicated. The individual trying to impress management never tells the full story, particularly its negative side.

Impression management is not practised only by individuals. Organizations also seek to create impressions. Called the *corporate image,* organizations gain considerably by the exercise. A good corporate image means better employees, expanded markets, and more responsive investors.

FIGURE 17-26
A MODEL OF THE SELF-FULFILLING PROPHECY

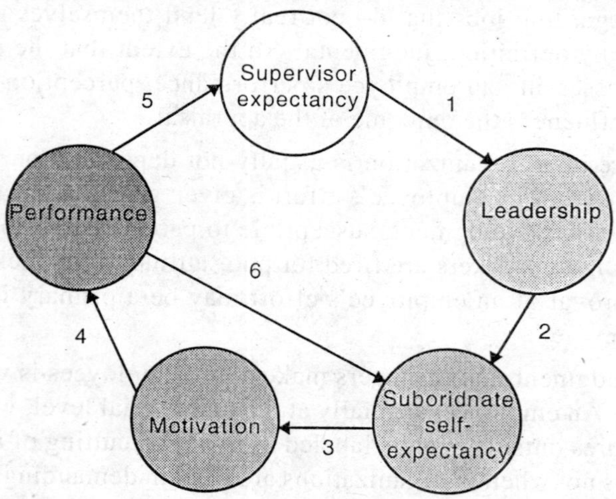

(*Source:* Robert Kreitner and Anglo Kinicki, *Organisational Behaviour,* P. 170)

The Pygmalion effect has important lessons for managers. They need to harness the Pygmalion effect by building a framework (see Fig.17.26) that reinforces positive performance expectations throughout the organization.

Fig.17.26 illustrates how supervisory expectations affect employee performance. As indicated, high supervisory expectancy produces better leadership (arrow 1), which subsequently leads employees to develop higher self-expectations (arrow 2). Higher expectations motivate workers to exert themselves more (arrow 3), finally boosting performance (arrow 4), and supervisory expectancies (arrow 5). Successful performance also improves an employee's self-expectancy for achievement (arrow 6).

Specifically, managers need to do the following:[26]

1. Recognize that everyone has the potential to increase his or her performance.
2. Instill confidence in oneself.
3. Set high performance goals.
4. Positively reinforce employees for a job well done.
5. Provide constructive feedback when necessary.
6. Help employees advance through the organization.
7. Introduce new employees as if they have outstanding potential.
8. Become aware of ones personal prejudices and nonverbal messages that may discourage others.
9. Encourage employees to visualize the successful execution of tasks.
10. Help employees master skills and tasks.

Finally, attributional biases tend to lead to inappropriate managerial actions including promotions, transfers, layoffs, and so forth. This can dampen motivation and performance. Attributional training programmes assume relevance here. Base attributional processes need to be explained and managers need to be taught how to detect and avoid such biases.

Managing the Perception Process

Successful managers understand the importance of perception as an influencing factor on behaviour and they act accordingly. They are aware of perceptual distortions and also know that perceptual differences are likely to exist in any situation. As a result, they try to make decisions and take action with a true understanding of the work situation as it is viewed by all persons concerned. A manager who is skilled in the perception process will:

1. *Have a high level of self-awareness* Individual needs, experience, and expectations can all affect perceptions. The successful manager knows this and is able to identify when he or she is inappropriately distorting a situation because of such perceptual tendencies.
2. *Seek information from various sources to confirm or disconfirm personal impressions of a decision situation* The successful manager minimizes the biases of personal perceptions by seeking out the viewpoints of others. These insights are used to gain additional perspective on situations and the problems or opportunities they represent.
3. *Be empathetic-that is, be able to see a situation as it is perceived by other people* Different people will define the same situation somewhat differently. The successful manager rises

above personal impressions to understand problems as seen by other people.

4. *Influence perceptions of other people when they are drawing incorrect or incomplete impressions of events in the work setting* People act in terms of their perceptions. The successful manager is able to influence the perceptions of others so that work events and situations are interpreted as accurately as possible and to the advantage of all concerned.
5. *Avoid common perceptual distortions that bias our views of people and situations* These distortions include the use of stereotypes and halo effects, as well as selective perception and projection. Successful managers are self-disciplined and sufficiently self-aware so that the adverse impacts of these distortions are minimized.
6. *Avoid inappropriate attributions* Everyone has a tendency to try and explain why events happened the way they did or why people behaved as they did. The successful manager is careful to establish the real reasons why things happen and avoid quick or inappropriate attributions of casualty.[27]
7. *Diversity management programmes* As firms globalize themselves, diversity management assumes greater relevance. The challenge for corporate executives is to leverage the benefits of this diversity while minimizing the perceptual and behavioural problems that tend to accompany heterogeneity.

   OB experts have designed diversity management programmes. Typically, these training programmes serve two purposes. First, they communicate the value of diversity. Second, these programmes help participants become aware of their personal biases and give them more accurate information about people with different backgrounds, thus avoiding perceptual distortions.
8. *Know yourself* Apply the Johari window to know the real self. A powerful way to minimize perceptual biases is to know and become more aware of one's values, beliefs, and prejudice.

Social Perception

Of late, a new concept-*social perception*-is mentioned often in the literature on OB. It is useful to explain what it means.

Social perception is the process of combining, integrating, and interpreting information about others to gain an accurate understanding of them. Viewed from this perspective, social perception is no different from the facets of perception we discussed till now. It may be recalled that we described perception as the process of receiving, organizing, interpreting, and reacting to the sensory stimuli. The idea is to see what is there to be seen. What is there to be seen may be even objects, besides, of course, human beings. But social perception focuses on only people.

Questions

1 Define perception. Explain the perceptual process.
2 What is perception? Why does perception fail?

Case: Prejudices in Work Places: Real or Perceived?

Manjula Srivastav had been head of marketing for the last four years at Blue Chips, a computer products firm. The company's turnover had increased by two-and-a-half times during this period and its market share in a number of products had also moved up marginally. What was creditable was that all this had happened in an environment in which computer prices had been crashing.

Although she had a talent for striking an instant rapport with people-particularly with the company's dealers-Srivastav often found herself battling against odds, as she perceived it, as far as her relationship with her subordinates and peers in the company were concerned. Srivastav had to, all along, fight male prejudice. She found it unfair that she had to prove herself regularly at work and she used to make her displeasure known to everyone.

Six months ago, Blue Chips had been taken over by an industrial group which had a diversity of business interests and was, more importantly, flush with funds. The change of ownership had led to replacement of the managing director, but it had not affected the existing core management team. Anand Prakash, the new managing director, had his priorities clear. 'Blue Chips will go international,' he had declared in the first executive committee meeting, 'and exports will be our first concern.'

Prakash had also brought in Harish Naik as his executive assistant with special responsibility for exports. Naik had been seconded to Srivastav for five weeks as part of a familiarization programme. Much to her surprise, he had been appointed, within two months, as the vice president (exports), with compensation and perks higher than her own. Srivastav had made a formal protest to Prakash who had assured her that he was aware of her good work in the company and that she would have an appropriate role once the restructuring plan he was already working on was put into effect.

One morning, as she entered the office and switched on her workstation, a message flashed on her screen. It was from Prakash. 'Want to see you sometime today regarding restructuring. Will 2.30 be convenient?' it said.

Later, in his office, Prakash had come straight to the point. He wanted to create a new post called general manager (public affairs) in the company. 'With your excellent background in customer relations and connections with the dealer network, you are the ideal person for the job,' he said, 'and I am offering it to you.' Srivastav was quick to react. 'There is very little I can contribute in that kind of job,' she said. 'I was in fact expecting to be promoted as vice president (domestic marketing).' Prakash said that the entire gamut of marketing functions would be looked after by Naik, who would have boardroom responsibility for both domestic and export sales. 'If you continue in marketing, you will have to be reporting to Naik which I thought may not be fair to you. In any case, we need someone who is strong in marketing to handle public affairs. Let me assure you that the new post I am offering will in no way diminish your importance in the company. You will in fact be reporting to me directly.'

'You are being unfair and you are diminishing my importance in the company,' retorted Srivastav. 'You know that I am a hardcore marketing professional and you also know I am the best. Why, then, am I being deprived of a rightful promotion in marketing? Tell me,' she asked pointedly, 'would you have done this to a male colleauge?'

'That is a hypothetical question,' said Prakash. 'But I can't think of any other slot for you in the restructuring plan I want to implement other than what I am offering.'

'If the reason why you are asking me to handle this fancy public affairs business of yours,' said Srivastav, 'is that you can't think of any other slot for me, then I would have second thoughts about continuing to work for this company.'

'May I reiterate,' said Prakash, 'that I value your role and it is precisely because of this that I am delegating to you the work I have been personally handling so far? May I also state that I am upgrading the job not only because it is important but also because it should match your existing stature in the organization?'

'I need to think about this. I will let you know tomorrow,' said Srivastav and left the office.[28]

Questions

1. What role did perception play in Prakash's treatment of Srivastav?
2. Do you think that Srivastav should continue in Blue Chips?

3 What is attribution theory? What is its application in OB?

4 Why is it important for managers to have a working knowledge of perception and attribution?

5 What evidence of self-fulfilling prophecies have you seen lately?

6 From your own experience, provide three examples of perceptual errors. Discuss the outcomes of each instance.

7 Provide an example, from your own experience, of people seeming to interpret the same situation differently. Explain why you think this has happened.

REFERENCES

1. Curtis W. Cook and Philip L. Hunsaker, *Management and Organisational Behaviour,* McGraw-Hill, 2001, Pp. 192-193.
2. Robert A.Baron, *Psychology,* Prentice Hall of India, 1996, p.90.
3. Steven L. McShane and Mary Ann Von Glinow, *Organisational Behaviour,* Tata McGraw-Hill, 2000, p. 166.
4. Joseph Reitz, *Behaviour in Organisations, A Humanistic Approach,* Richard D.Irwin, 1997, p.129.
5. Eugene McKenna, *Psychology and Organisational Behaviour,* Psychology Press, 2002, p.132.
6. Ibid, p. 140.
7. N.I.Munn, *et.al, Introduction to Psychology,* Oxford and IBH, 1972, p.168.
8. Ibid, p. 168.
9. Eugene McKenna, *Op. cit.,* p.142.
10. Fred Luthans, *Organisational Behaviour,* McGraw-Hill, 1989, p.146.
11. Udai Pareck, *et. al., Behavoural Processes in Organisations,* Oxford and IBH Pub. Co., 1981, p.30.
12. Joseph Stein, *Effective Personality, A Humanistic Approach*, Cole Publishing Co., 1972, p.48.
13. Ibid, p. 47.
14. Ibid, p. 50.
15. Ibid, p. 51.
16. Eugne McKenna, *Op. cit.* p. 149.
17. Ibid, p. 150.
18. Ibid, p. 153.
19. Udai Pareck, *Op. cit.,* p.34.
20. Joseph Reitz, *Behaviour in Organisations,* Irwin, 1977, p.129.
21. Don Hellriegel, *et.al., Organisational Behaviour,* South Western - Thomson Learning, 2001, p.81.

22. Mason Haire and William Freeman Grunes, *"Perceptual Defences: Processes Protecting an Organisational Perception of Another Personality"*, as cited in Fred Luthans, *op. cit.*, p.158.
23. Ivancevich and Matteson, *Organisational Behaviour and Management*, Irwin McGraw-Hill, 1999, p.120.
24. Robert Krietner and Angelo Kinicki, *Organisational Behaviour,* Irwin McGraw-Hill, 1998, p.168.
25. Robert A. Baron, Psychology, *Op.cit*, p. 123.
26. Robert Krietner and Angelo Kinicki, *Op.cit,* p. 170.
27. John R. Schermerhon, *et. al., Managing Organisational Behaviour*, John Willy & Sons, 1985, p. 476.
28. R.Chandrasekhar, *The Buck Stops Here,* Macmillan, 1997, Pp. 41-43.

CHAPTER

Eighteen

Attitudes and Values

LEARNING OBJECTIVES

After reading this chapter you should understand —

1. The nature of Attitudes.
2. The three variables of Attitudes .
3. The source of Attitudes.
4. The functions of Attitudes.
5. How difficult to change attitude.
6. The two types of Attitudes.
7. Values distinguish between what is right or wrong, good or bad.
8. Attitudes and values are important concepts in the study of OB.

Nature of Attitudes

Attitudes are understood as the beliefs, feelings and action tendencies of an individual or group of individuals towards objects, ideas and people. This simple meaning has important implications for managers.

- Attitudes are learned. How attitudes are learned will be explained in the next section in this chapter.
- Attitudes refer to feelings and beliefs of an individual or groups of people.
- These feelings and beliefs define one's predispositions towards given aspects of the world.
- Attitudes endure, unless something happens. For example if X is transferred to day shift, his attitude may become positive.
- Attitudes can fall anywhere along a continuum for very favorable to very unfavorable. Such expressions as "This B-School is good", "This leader is corrupt and incompetent" are heard from people.
- Attitudes are organized and are core to an individual.
- All people, irrespective of their status or intelligence, hold attitudes.[1]

A few definitions on the concept of attitude are as follows:

"An attitude is mental state of readiness, learned and organized through experience, exerting a specific influence on person's response to people, object and situations with which it is related."[2]

"Attitudes are learned predispositions towards aspects of our environment. They may be positively or negatively directed towards certain people, service or institutions."[3]

"By attitudes we mean the beliefs, feelings, and action tendencies of an individual or group of individuals towards objects, ideas, and people. Quite often persons and objects or ideas become associated in the minds of individuals and as a result of attitudes become multidimensional and complex."[4]

Are prejudices attitudes? The answer is in the affirmative. An attitude may involve a prejudice, in which we prejudge an issue without giving unbiased considerations to all the evidence. If we are prejudiced against a person, who is accused of a crime, we may regard him as guilty regardless of the evidence. We can also be prejudiced in favour of something.[5]

Components of Attitudes

In general, attitudes comprise three elements. They are: (See Fig 18.1)

- An *affective* component- the feelings, sentiments, moods and emotions about some idea, person, event or object;
- A *cognitive* element – the beliefs, opinion, knowledge, or information held by the individual; and
- A *behavioural* component – the predispositions to get on a favorable or unfavorable evaluation of something.[6]

These three components do not exist or function separately. An attitude represents the interplay of a person's affective, cognitive and behavioural tendencies with regard to a person, group, an

FIGURE 18-1
THREE COMPONENTS OF ATTITUDES

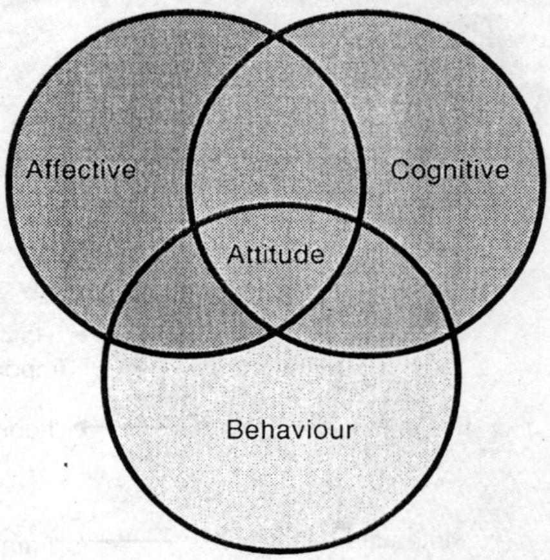

event or an issue. For example, suppose that an individual holds a strong, negative attitude about the use of nuclear power. During an employment interview with the representative of a large firm, he discovers that the company is a major supplier of nuclear power generation equipment. He might feel a sudden intense dislike for the company's interviewer (the affective component). He might form a negative opinion of the interviewer based on beliefs and opinions about the types of person who would work for such a company (the cognitive component). An important element of cognition is the evaluative beliefs held by a person. He might be tempted to make an unkind remark to the interviewer or suddenly terminate the interview (the behavioural component).

The ABC Model

The three components of attitude described above constitute, what is called, the ABC model, the three letters respectively standing for affect, behaviour and cognition. The significance of the model is that to thoroughly understand an attitude, one must assess all the three components. Suppose, for example, one wants to evaluate one's employees attitudes towards flexitime. One would want to determine how they feel about flexitime (affect), whether they would use flexitime (behaviour), and what they think about the policy (cognition). Unfortunately most techniques of measuring attitudes focus only on cognitive component.

Fig 18.2 presents the three components of attitudes in terms of work environment factors. These stimuli trigger cognitive (thoughts), affective (emotional), and behavioural responses.

Formation of Attitude

Individuals acquire attitudes from several sources but the point to be stressed is that the attitudes are acquired but not inherited. The most important sources of acquiring attitudes are direct experience with the object, association, family, neighbourhood, economic and social positions, and mass communication. (See Fig 18.3)

FIGURE 18-2
WORK RELATED COMPONENTS OF ATTITUDES

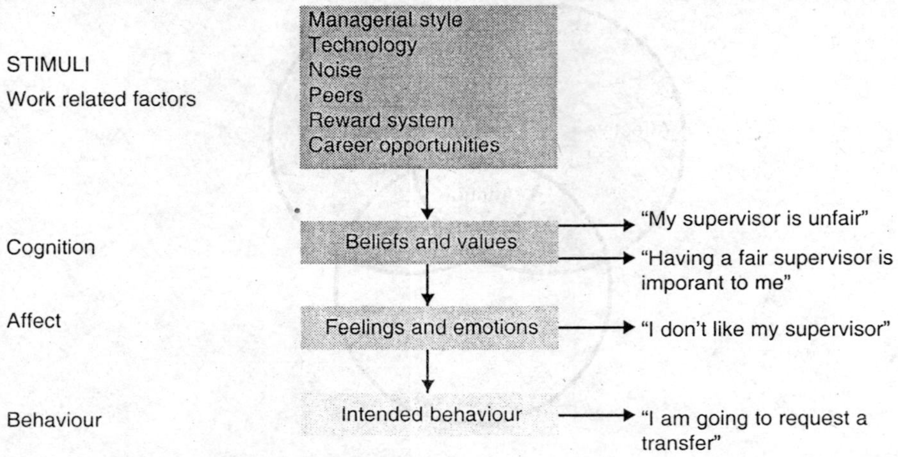

(***Source:*** John M. Ivancevich and Michael T. Matteson, *Organisational Behaviour and Management,* p.120)

FIGURE 18-3
FORMATION OF ATTITUDES

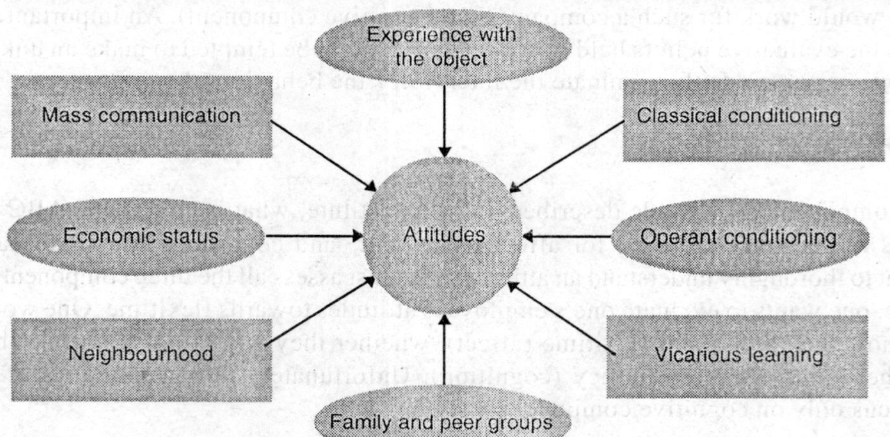

Direct Experience with the Object Attitudes can develop from a personally rewarding or punishing experience with an object. Employees form attitudes about jobs on their previous experiences. For example, if everyone who has held a job has been promoted within six months, current job holders are likely to believe that they will also be promoted within six months. Attitudes formed on experience are difficult to change.[7]

Classical Conditioning and Attitudes One of the basic processes underlying attitude formation can be explained on the basis of learning principles. The same classical conditioning processes that made Pavlov's dogs salivate at the sound of a bell can explain how attitudes are acquired. People develop associations between various objects and the emotional reactions that accompany them. For instance, many soldiers who were stationed in the Persian Gulf during the war with Iraq reported that they never wanted to sit on a sandy beach again. Put another way, the soldiers formed negative attitudes towards sand. Similarly, positive associations can develop through classical conditioning. We may come to hold positive attitude towards a particular perfume because a favourite model wears it.

Advertisers make use of the principles of classical conditioning of attitudes by attempting to link a product they want consumers to buy with a positive feeling or event. For example, many ads feature young, attractive, healthy men and women using a product-even if it is one as uninteresting as toothpaste. The idea behind creating such ads is to create a classically conditioned response to the product, so that just glimpsing a tube of toothpaste evokes a positive feeling.

Operant Conditioning and Attitude Acquisition Another learning process, operant conditioning, also underlies attitude acquisition. Attitudes that are reinforced, either verbally or non-verbally, tend to be maintained. Conversely, a person who states an attitude that elicits ridicule from others may modify or abandon the attitude.

Vicarious learning This referes to formation of attitudes by observing behaviour of others and consequences of that behaviour. It is through vicarious learning processes that children pick up the prejudices of their parents. For example, even if they have never met a blind person, children whose parents say that "blind people are incompetent" may adopt such attitudes themselves.

We also learn attitudes vicariously through television, films, and other media. For instance, movies that glorify violence reinforce positive attitudes regarding aggression, and portrayals of women as subservient to men shape and bolster sexist attitudes.

Family and Peer Groups A person may learn attitudes through imitation of parents. If parents have a positive attitude towards an object and the child admires his parents, he is likely to adopt a similar attitude, even without being told about the object, and even without having direct experience. Attitudes towards the opposite sex, religion, tolerance or prejudice, education, occupations, political parties, and almost all other areas where attitudes are capable of expression are the result of our accepting or rejecting the attitudes held by members of our family.[8] Similarly, attitudes are acquired from peer groups in colleges and organizations.

Neighbourhood The neighbourhood we live in has a certain structure in terms of its having cultural facilities, religious groupings, and possibly ethnic differences. Further, it has people who are neighbours. The neighbours-adults or children-tolerate, condone, or deny certain attitudes and behaviour and as a result we are either northerners or southerners. Further, we accept these moves and conform, or we deny them and possibly rebel. The conformity or rebellion in some respects is the evidence of the attitudes we hold.[9]

Economic Status and Occupations Our economic and occupational positions also contribute to attitudes formation. They determine, in part, our attitudes towards unions and management and our belief that certain laws are "good" or "bad". Our socio-economic background influences our present and future attitudes.

Mass Communications All varieties of mass communications-television, radio, newspapers, and magazines-feed their audiences large quantities of information. The presentation of news or information is constructed so as to cater to the attitude of the audience. In turn, the audience selects the specific form of mass communication that best reflects its attitudes on various subjects. The items of interest include sex and teenagers, crime, divorce, politics, religion, pornographic literature, and the like. The material we select helps us either to substantiate our opinions or to establish new ones.[10]

Once formed, attitudes play an important role in one's life. It applies to every sphere of life, including one's personal and professional life. An executive cannot be good executive without a positive attitude. A student can not be a good student without a positive attitude. A parent, teacher, salesperson, employer, employee cannot be good without positive attitudes.

What an individual needs is positive attitude. When all employees in an organization have positive attitudes, benefits will be many. For example, positive attitude —

- Increases productivity
- Fosters teamwork
- Solves problems
- Improves quality
- Makes for congenial atmosphere
- Breeds loyalty
- Increases profits
- Fosters better relationships with employees, employers and customers
- Reduces stress
- Makes for a pleasing personality.

Functions of Attitudes

People hold attitudes because they serve important functions. In general, attitudes perform four important functions: (i) Adjustment, (ii) Defense, (iii) Value expressive, and (iv) Knowledge. (See Fig 18.4).

FIGURE 18-4
FUNCTIONS OF ATTITUDES

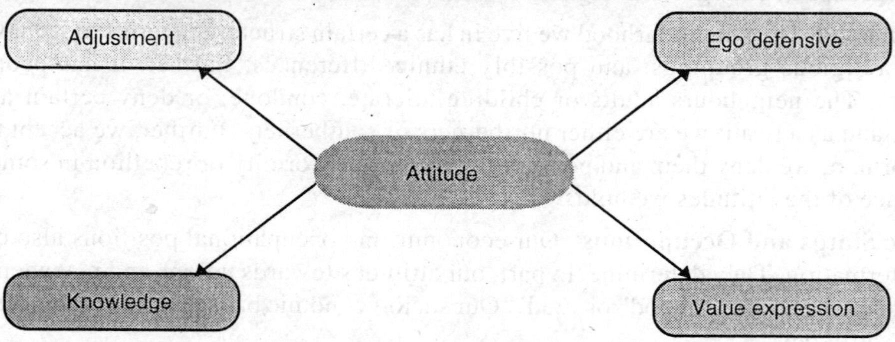

Adjustment Function Attitudes offen help people adjust to their work environment. When employees are well treated, they are likely to develop a positive attitude towards management and the organisation. When employees are berated and paid poorly, they are likely to develop a negative attitude towards the firm and its owners. These attitudes help employees adjust to their environment and are a basis for future behaviour. For example, if employees who are well treated are asked about management or the organisation, they are likely to say good things. Just the reverse may be true for those berated and are poorly paid.[11]

Ego-defence Function People often form and maintain certain attitudes to protect their own self-images. For example, workers may feel threatened by the employment or advancement of minority or female workers in their organization. These threatened workers may develop prejudices against the new workers. They may develop an attitude that such newcomers are less qualified, and they might mistreat these workers. Such an ego defensive attitude is formed and used to cope with a feeling of guilt or threat. Unless this feeling is removed, this kind of attitude will remain unchanged.

Ego defensive attitudes may be aroused by interred and external threats, by frustrating experiences, by the build-up of pressures previously repassed, and by suggestions or directives from an authoritarian source. Ego defensive attitudes are difficult to change bacase of the misdirected nature of the impulses association with them. For example, an employee encounters a frustrating experience at work and feels aggressive as a consequence of the hurt to his or her ego. However, the employee displaces this aggression by directing it at a completely different target such as a member of the family. Though ego defensive attitudes are difficult to change, it is possible to remove the threats to the attitudes through therapeutic means in a supporitive enviroment by giving individuals insight into the dysfunctional parts of their defence mechanism.

Expressive Function This attitudinal function contains three main aspects:[12]

(i) It helps express the individual's central values and self-identity. Consumers express their values in the products they buy, the shops they patronize, and the life style they exhibit.

(ii) The expressive function also helps individuals define their self-concept, and facilitates the adoption of sub-culture values considered important. For example, teenagers may dress and behave in a certain way in order to foster their status in a group.

(iii) The expressive function helps individuals adopt and internalize the values of a group they have recently joined and as a consequence, they are better able to relate to the group. An individual who has joined an ecology group may now express values manifest in the purchase and use of a bicycle and the recycling of bottles.

Knowledge Function People need maintain a stable, organised, and meaningful structure of their world in order to prevent chaos. Attitudes provide the standards or frames of reference by which an individual judges objectives or events, and attitudes that provide consistency in our thinking are particularly relevant. The knowledge function of attitudes is observed more in consumer behaviour.

Attitudes predispose purchasers to prefer a particular brand of car, and they do not have to re-examine their values, habits, and lifestyle prior to the decision to buy. However, if existing attitudes are inadequate in resolving a particular issue, then the acquistion of new knowledge could bring about a changed attitude. Buyers are generally information-seekers; they have a need to know and this drives them to gain information that gives meaning to their social world. But sometimes, individuals take the easy option and rely on stereotypes to simplify reality.

Why do managers need to know about these attitude functions? Such knowledge can serve two purposes. *First,* it helps us understand and predict how a certain person is likely to behave. For example, if a person is "prejudiced" against another, he is less likely to be fair in judging the other person. Moreover, this knowledge helps the manager see why the person has developed such an attitude. *Second*, it can help the manager change the attitude of another person. He can do this by changing the conditions that sustain the attitude. For example, he can change people with low self-images by helping them increase their ability to solve their problems, or by providing them with positive feedback on what they accomplish.

Changing Attitudes

Employee attitudes need to be changed, particularly when they are unfavourable. It is in the best interest of the organization to change attitudes. But changing attitudes is a difficult task as attitudes generally endure. Difficulty is reinforced because of the escalation of commitment, cognitive dissonance, and insufficient information.

Escalation of commitment refers to the prior commitment of people to a particular cause and their unwillingness to change. Escalation of commitment will be explained in detail later in this book.

The second obstacle to change attitude is *cognitive dissonance*. Cognitive dissonance is a term popularized by psychologist Leon Festinger to describe a state of inconsistency between an individual's attitude and behaviour. The discomfort experienced by people feeling cognitive dissonance leads to efforts to reduce the tension by *(i)* changing the attitudes, *(ii)* changing the behaviour, and *(iii)* rationalizing the inconsistency. People rather resort to the third course of the action than changing their attitudes or altering their behaviours.

The third barrier results from *insufficient information*. Some times people see no reason why they would change their attitudes. The boss may not like a subordinate's negative attitudes, but the latter may be quite pleased with his behaviour. Unless the boss can show the individual why a negative attitude is detrimental to career progress or salary increases or some other personal objective, the subordinate may continue to have negative attitude. [13]

Ways of Changing

Attitudes need to be changed at two fronts: Changing one's own attitudes and changing the employee's attitudes (see Fig 18.5).

Changing Attitudes Of Self: The following hints can help the individual change his or her attitude:

(i) Be aware of one's attitudes. People who are optimistic have higher levels of job satisfaction. The individual needs to maintain positive attitudes consciously.

(ii) Think for self. The individual should develop his or her own attitude based on other's input.

(iii) Realize that there are few, if any, benefits from harbouring negative attitudes.

(iv) Keep an open mind. The individuals should listen to other people's input and use it to develop positive attitudes.

(v) Get into continuous education programme

(vi) Build a positive self esteem

(vii) Stay away from negative influences, such as smoking, drugs, alcohol, pornography, negative movies and television programs

Changing Attitudes of Employees The following hints can help a manger change attitudes of his or her employees:

(i) Give feedback Employees to be told about their negative attitudes, if any, and their harmful consequences. The manager needs to offer alternative attitudes.

FIGURE 18-5
CHANGING ATTITUDES

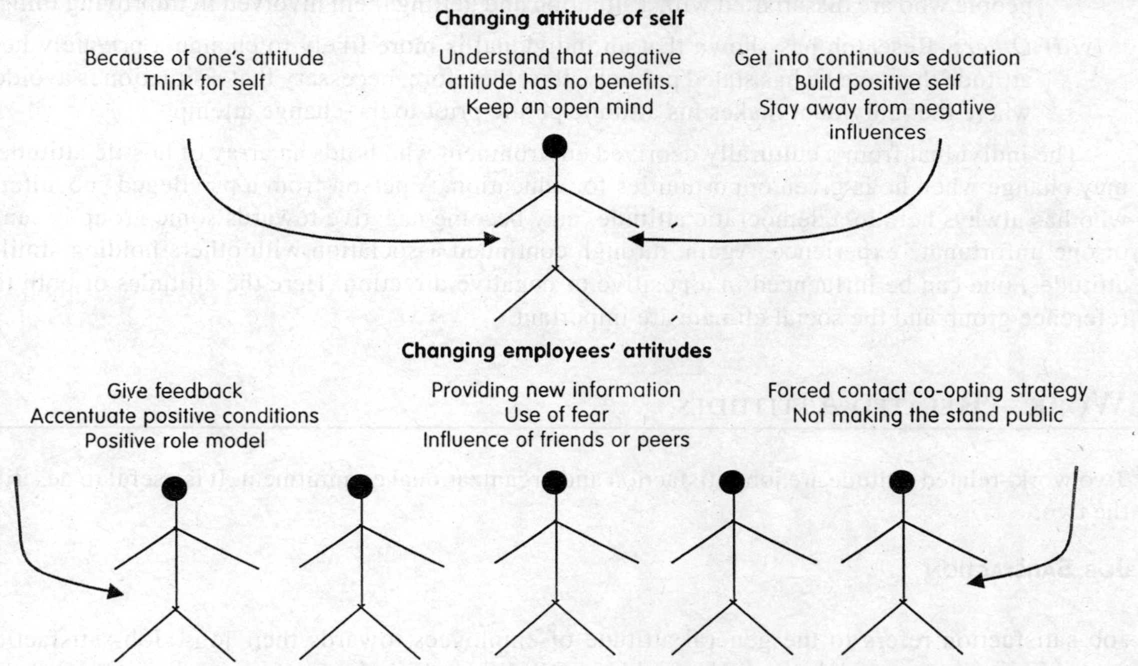

(ii) *Accentuated positive conditions* Employees tend to develop positive attitudes towards the work they do well. Manager should make sure that the working conditions are pleasant and also that the employees have all the resources and training to do a good job.

(iii) *Positive role model* If the manager has a positive attitude, employees may also have similar attitudes.

(iv) *Providing new information* New information will help change attitudes. Negative attitudes are mainly formed owing to lack of or insufficient information. Workers generally become pro-union because of the ignorance about the good intentions of the management. Once they come to know how the management cares for the welfare of the workers, they change their attitude and might turn pro-management.

(v) *Use of fear* Fear can change attitude. However, the change depends on the degree of fear. For example, if low levels of fear arousal are used, people often ignore them. The warnings are not strong enough to warrant attention. If moderate levels of fear arousal are used, people often become aware of the situation and will change their attitudes. However, if high degrees of fear arousal are used, people often reject the message, because it is too threatening and thus not believable. [14] On the contrary, high degree of fear may prove counter productive. On being threatened too far, people tend to become *stubborn* in their attitudes and may refuse to change.

(vi) *Influence of friends or press* Change of attitude can come about through persuasion of friends or peers. Credibility of the others, specially peers, is important to effect change.

Peers with high credibility shall exercise significant influence on change. The same is not true with peers who have low credibility.

(vii) *The coopting approach* Coopting is another way of changing attitude. This means taking people who are dissatisfied with a situation and getting them involved in improving things.

(viii) *Others* Research has shown that an individual is more likely to change a privately held attitude than one he has stated publicly. It is, therefore, necessary that a situation is avoided where the individual makes his attitude public prior to the change attempt.

The individual from a culturally deprived environment who holds an array of hostile attitudes, may change when he is given opportunities for education. A person from a privileged subculture, who has always held to a democratic attitude, may become negative towards some group because of one unfortunate experience. Again, through continued association with others holding similar attitudes, one can be influenced in a positive or negative direction. Here the attitudes of both the reference group and the social climate are important.

WORK – RELATED ATTITUDES

Two work–related attitude are job satisfaction and organizational commitment. It is useful to describe the two.

JOB SATISFACTION

Job satisfaction refers to the general attitude of employees towards their jobs. Job satisfaction probably is the most widely studied variable in OB. When the attitude of an employee towards his or her job is positive, there exists job satisfaction. Dissatisfaction exists when the attitude is negative.

Job satisfaction often is a collection of attitudes about specific factors of the job. Employees can be satisfied with some elements of the job while simultaneously dissatisfied with others.[14] For example, a lecturer may be dissatisfied with the management of the institution but may derive satisfaction while handling a course on OB in the class. Different types of satisfaction will lead do different intentions and behaviour. An employee might complain to the supervisor when dissatisfied with low pay but not with co – worker satisfaction.

Job satisfaction is important for management as it has impact on turnover, productivity, absenteeism and other job related aspects. These will be explained later in this chapter.

THEORIES ON JOB SATISFACTION

What makes some people like their jobs? Others dislike them? An explanation to these is provided by various theories on job satisfaction. Two such theories are Herzberg's two-factor theory and Locke's value theory.

Two-Factor Theory Herzberg and his associates discovered, through their extensive research, (explained in detail later in chapter 8) that the factors that contributed to job satisfaction and job dissatisfaction were different. In particular, dissatisfaction was associated with conditions surrounding the jobs (e.g working conditions, pay, security, quality of supervision, interpersonal relations) rather than the work itself. Because these factors prevent negative reactions, the researchers referred to them as hygiene (or maintenance) factors. By contrast, satisfaction was associated with factors associated with work itself or to outcomes directly derived from it such as the nature of job, achievements, advancement, and recognition. Because such factors were associated with high levels of job satisfaction, Herzberg called them motivators. Herberg's distinction between motivators and hygiene factors is referred to as the two-factor theory of job satisfaction.

The two-factor theory has been carped because of the distinction it seeks to maintain between the hygiene factors and motivators. In practice, it is believed, both the categories of elements exert influence both on satisfaction as well as dissatisfaction. Working conditions for example, can be a maintenance factor for some employees but motivators for others. However, the theory is useful for describing the conditions that people find satisfaction and dissatisfaction on the job. The theory also has been useful in emphasizing the importance of factors such as recognition, advancement, and responsibility.

Locke's Value Theory

This theory posits that job satisfaction is the relationship between job outcomes realized as compared to those desired. In other words, satisfaction is high when an employee receives outcomes which he or she values high. Satisfaction is less when the outcomes received are valued less by the employee. Locke's approach focuses on any outcomes that people value, regardless of what they are and not necessarily lower order needs (lower order needs are explained in chapter on motivation.) The key to satisfaction, according to the theory, is the discrepancy between those aspects of the job one has and those one wants; the greater the discrepancy, lesser the satisfaction.

Locke's theory calls attention to those aspects of the job that need to be attended for job satisfaction to result. Specifically, the theory suggests that these aspects might not be the same for all people, but any valued aspects of the job about which people perceive serious discrepancies. By emphasizing values, Locke's theory suggests that job satisfaction may be derived from many sources, some of which are explained in the next section.

Model of Job Satisfaction

Fig 18.6 shows the causes and consequences of job satisfaction. Causes for job satisfaction comprise organizational factors, group elements and individual needs. All these factors contribute to satisfaction or dissatisfaction. Between the causes and consequences of job satisfaction, there are two variables, namely outcomes valued/expected and outcomes received.

Causes of Job Satisfaction

Organizational Factors There are five major organizational factors which contribute to an employee's attitude towards his or her job: pay, opportunities for promotion, the nature of work, policies of the organization and working conditions.

Wages Wages play a significant role in influencing job-satisfaction. This is because of two reasons. First, money is an important instrument in fulfilling one's needs; and two, employees often see pay as a reflection of management's concern for them.

Employees want a pay system which is simple, fair, and in line with their expectations. When pay is seen as fair, based on job demands, individual skill level, and community pay standards, satisfaction is likely to result. What needs emphasis is that it is not the absolute amount paid that matters, rather it is one's perception of fairness.

FIGURE 18-6
JOB SATISFACTION MODEL

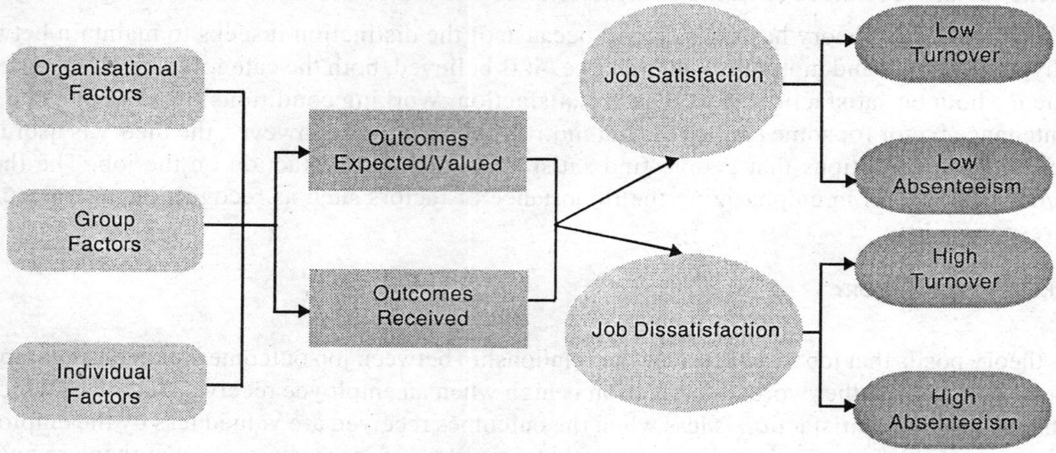

Promotions Promotional opportunities affect job-satisfaction considerably. The desire for promotion is generally strong among employees as it involves change in job content, pay, responsibility, independence, status and the like. An average employee in a typical government organization can hope to get two or three promotions in his entire service, though chances of promotion are better in the private sector. It is no surprise that the employee takes promotion as the ultimate achievement in his career and when it is realised, he feels extremely satisfied.

Nature of Work Most employees crave intellectual challenges on jobs. They tend to prefer being given opportunities to use their skills and abilities and being offered a variety of tasks, freedom, and feedback on how well they are doing. These characteristics make jobs mentally challenging. Jobs that have too little challenge create boredom. But too much challenge creates frustration and a feeling of failure. Under conditions of moderate challenge, employees experience pleasure and satisfaction.

Organizational Policies and Procedures Organizational policies include the basis for effecting promotions (seniority versus merit), transfer of people, foreign assignments, lay-off and retrenchment, appraisal and reward systems, motivational methods, skill based versus job based pay, and the like.

Working Conditions Working conditions that are compatible with an employee's physical comfort and that facilitate doing a good job contribute to job satisfaction. Temperature, humidity, ventilation, lighting and noise, hours of work, cleanliness of the work place, and adequate tools and equipment are the features which affect job-satisfaction.

The assumption that working conditions and satisfaction are interrelated contradicts the two-factor theory of motivation. According to this theory, working conditions are a part of maintenance factors which, when provided, help remove dissatisfaction. And the opposite of dissatisfaction is no-dissatisfaction but not satisfaction.

Thus, while working conditions constitute a source of job-satisfaction, they are a relatively minor source. Generally, unless working conditions are either extremely good or bad, they are taken for granted by most employees. Only when employees themselves change jobs or when working conditions change dramatically over time(e.g., moving into new facilities) do working conditions assume more relevance. In order words, all employees are not satisfied nor dissatisfied by favourable or unfavourable work environment (See Fig 18.7).

FIGURE 18-7
WORK ENVIRONMENT AND JOB SATISFACTION: SOME POSSIBLE RELATIONSHIP

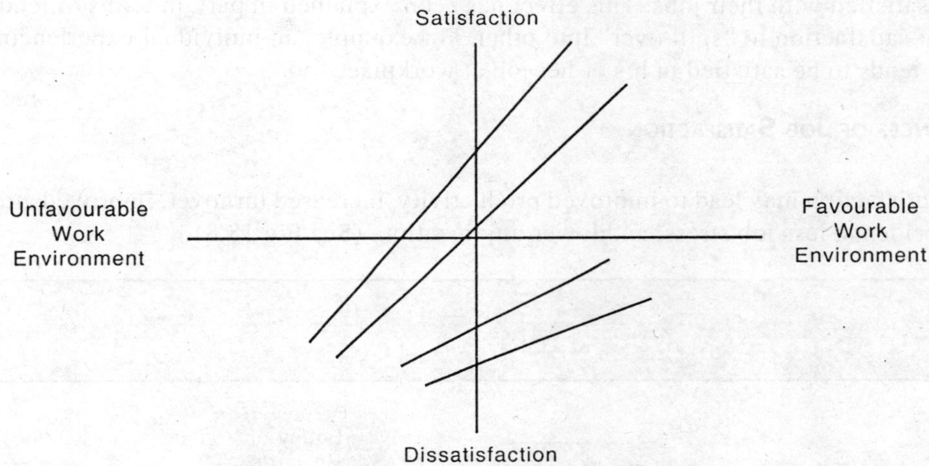

(*Source* : Richard M.Hodgetts, *Organisational Behaviour*, Macmillan, 1991,p.87)

As seen in the Fig 18.7, all the four are dissatisfied when work environment was unfavourable. However, as the favorableness of the environment increased, the job satisfaction of individuals 1 and 2 increased sharply while individuals 3 and 4 had only minor increases in satisfaction.

Group Factors Group factors wielding influence on satisfaction include group size and supervision.

Size: It is truism to say that longer the size of the group, lower the level of satisfaction. As size increases, opportunities for participation and social interaction decrease, so also the ability of members to identify with the group's performance. More members mean dissension, conflict, and groups within groups. All these do not augur well for satisfaction of members.

Supervision Perceived quality of supervision is another determinant of job satisfaction. Satisfaction tends to be high when people believe that their supervisors are more competent, have their best interests in mind, and treat them with dignity and respect. Communication is another aspect of supervision. Satisfaction of members tends to be high when they are able to communicate easily with their supervisor.

Individual Factors In addition to organizational and group factors, there are certain personal variables that have a bearing on job satisfaction.

First, several *personality* variables have been linked to job satisfaction. Among these are self – esteem , **TYPE A** behaviour pattern and the ability to withstand job stress. Stronger an individual is on these traits, more satisfied he or she tends to be on his or her job.

Second, *status* tends to influence one's job satisfaction. Generally speaking, the higher one's position in an organizational hierarchy, the more satisfied the individual tends to be. Put another way, a dissatisfied employee may not stay at one place to reach higher positions in organizational hierarchy.

Third, job satisfaction is related to the extent to which people perform jobs *congruent with their interests.* A recently graduated **MBA** is cut out to join a firm as a management trainee. Instead, if she or he takes up a teaching assignment, because other openings are not coming by, the individual tends to be dissatisfied with teaching.

Finally, job satisfaction has been found to be related to one's *general life satisfaction.* The more the people are satisfied with aspects of their lives unrelated to their jobs, the more they also tend to be satisfied with their jobs. This effect has been explained in part, in terms of tendency for one type of satisfaction to "spill over" into other. For example, an individual experiencing happy family life tends to be satisfied in his or her job at workplace too.

Consequences of Job Satisfaction

High job-satisfaction may lead to improved productivity, increased turnover, improved attendance, reduced accidents, less job stress, and lower unionization. (See Fig 18.8)

FIGURE 18-8
LAWLER-PORTER MODEL OF PERFORMANCE AND SATISFACTION

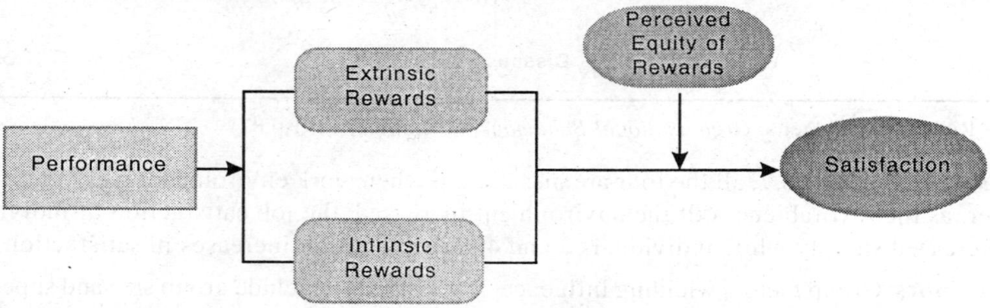

Productivity: The relationship between satisfaction and productivity is not definitely established. However, in the long-run job-satisfaction leads to increased productivity.

On the other hand, job performance leads to job satisfaction and not the other way round. Fig 18.8 illustrates the similarity between performance and satisfaction. An employee who performs well in his or her job gets both intrinsic and extrinsic rewards which will lead to his or her satisfaction. A poor performer will feel worse about his or her incompetence and will receive fewer rewards. He or she will be less satisfied with his or her work experiences.

However, there are some conditions under which high productivity more clearly leads to job-satisfaction. One condition is that the employees perceive that intrinsic and extrinsic rewards are contingent upon their productivity. The second condition is that the extrinsic rewards (pay, for example) be distributed equitably. Inequitable distribution fails to convince the employee about the close correlation between hard work and rewards.

However, the adage " a happy worker is a productive worker" is not always wrong. True, there may not be a relationship between job-satisfaction and productivity, but performance may be affected indirectly by absenteeism or turnover which is related (negatively) to satisfaction.

Job-satisfaction and Employee Turnover High employee turnover is of considerable concern for employers because it disrupt normal operations, causes morale problems for those who stick on, and increases the cost involved in selecting and training replacements. The employer does whatever possible to minimize turnover, making the employees feel satisfied on their jobs, being one such.

Unlike the relationship between satisfaction and productivity, the connection between job-satisfaction to employee turnover is established beyond doubt. It has been demonstrated that workers who have relatively low levels of job-satisfaction are the most likely to quit their jobs and that organizational units with the lowest average satisfaction levels tend to have the highest turnover rates.

However, the withdrawal behaviour of employees is modified by certain factors. Loyalty to the organization is one such. Some employees cannot imagine themselves working elsewhere, however dissatisfied they are in their present jobs. Availability of other places of employment also influences turnover. If greener pastures are available, an employee does not mind going in search of them, notwithstanding the present level of job-satisfaction he or she enjoys.

Satisfaction and Absences Correlation of satisfaction to absenteeism is also proved conclusively. Workers who are dissatisfied are more likely to take "mental health" days, i.e., days off not due to illness or personal business. Simply stated, absenteeism is high when satisfaction is low. As in turnover, absenteeism is subject to modification by certain factors. The degree to which people feel that their jobs are important has a moderating influence on their absences. Employees who feel that their work is important tend to clock in regular attendance. Besides, it is important to remember that while high job-satisfaction will not necessarily result in low absenteeism, low satisfaction is likely to bring about high absenteeism.

Satisfaction and Safety Poor safety practices are a negative consequence of low satisfaction level. When people are discouraged about their jobs, company, and supervisors, they are more liable to experience accidents. An underlying reason for such accidents is that discouragement may take one's attention away from the task at hand. Inattention leads directly to accidents. For example, many hand injuries from power tools can be attributed to the operator not paying careful attention.

Satisfaction and Job Stress Job stress is the body's response to any job-related factor that threatens to disturb the person's equilibrium. In the process of experiencing stress, the employee's inner state changes. Prolonged stress can cause the employee serious ailments such as heart disease, ulcer, blurred vision, lower back pain, dermatitis, and muscle aches.

Chronic job-dissatisfaction is a powerful source of job stress. The employee may see no satisfactory short-term solution to escaping this type of stress. An employee trapped in a dissatisfying job may withdraw by such means as high absenteeism and tardiness; or the employee may quit.

Employeės under prolonged stress stemming from job-dissatisfaction often consume too much alcohol, tobacco and drugs. These employees are costly to the management in terms of time lost due to frequent absences and increased payments towards medical reimbursements.

Unionization It is proved that job-dissatisfaction is a major cause for unionization. Dissatisfaction with wages, job security, fringe benefits, chances for promotion and treatment by supervisors are reasons which make employees join unions. Another dimension is that job-dissatisfaction can have an impact on the tendency to take action within the union, such as filing grievances or striking.

Other Effects of Job-satisfaction In additions to the above, it has been claimed that satisfied employees tend to have better mental and physical health and learn new job-related tasks more quickly.

All things considered, practising managers and organizational behaviour researchers would agree that job-satisfaction is important to an organization. Critics however, point out that this is pure conjecture because there is so much we do not know about the positive effects of satisfaction. On the other hand, when job-satisfaction is low, there tends to be negative effects on the organization. So, if only form the standpoint of viewing job-satisfaction as a minimum requirement or point of departure, it is of value to the organization's overall health and effectiveness and is deserving of study and application in the field of organizational behaviour.

MEASURING JOB-SATISFACTION

Also called survey of morale, opinion, attitude, climate, or quality of work life, job satisfaction survey is conducted by management in order to get information for making sound decisions. A job-satisfaction survey is a procedure by which employees report their feelings towards their job and work environment. The responses are then combined and analyzed. Various ways of measuring job-satisfaction are available. Before discussing the ways, an explanation of the benefits of such survey is in order.

Benefits of Job-satisfaction Study

(i) One benefit of job-satisfaction surveys is that they give management an indication of general levels of satisfaction in a company. Survey also indicates specific areas of satisfaction or dissatisfaction (as with employee service) and particular groups of employees (as in the tool department or among those over the age of forty). In other words, a survey tells how employees feel about their jobs, what parts of their jobs these feelings are focused on, which departments are particularly affected, and whose feelings are involved (for example, supervisors, employees, or staff specialists). The survey is a powerful diagnostic instrument for assessing employee problems.

(ii) Improved communication is another benefit of the surveys. Communication flows in all directions as people plan the survey, talk, and discuss its results. Particularly beneficial to the company is, the upward communication when employees are encouraged to comment about what they really have in their minds.

(iii) An unexpected benefit from a job-satisfaction survey is improved attitudes. For some employees, the survey is a safety valve, an emotional release, a chance to get things off their chest. For others, the survey is a tangible expression of management's interest in employee welfare, which gives employees a reason to feel better towards management.

(iv) The job-satisfaction survey can help discover the causes of indirect productivity problems, such as absenteeism, turnover and poor quality of work. As was discussed earlier, absenteeism and employee turn over are highly correlated with job-satisfaction. It was also noted that these, in turn, affect productivity. If an organization is disturbed by a high rate of absenteeism or turnover, it might appropriately turn to job-satisfaction surveys to diagnose the cause. The causes could be low pay, lack of promotional, opportunities, unchallenging jobs, unjust treatment, and the like. Without proper surveys, there could be random guessing on the part of management. A job-satisfaction survey helps management both to get a better handle on why employees are lagging and to plan better solution to problems.

(v) Another benefit of satisfaction survey's is that they help management assess training needs. Usually, employees are given an opportunity to report how they feel their supervisor performs certain parts of the jobs, such as delegating work and giving adequate job instructions.

Since employees experience these supervisory acts, their perceptions may provide useful data about the training of their supervisors.

(vi) A job-satisfaction survey is an indicator of the effectiveness of organizational reward systems. As was discussed earlier, there is a positive relationship between performance and satisfaction. This relationship will be strong when rewards (intrinsic and extrinsic) are distributed equitably contingent upon performance. Now, job-satisfaction surveys can provide some clues as to the effectiveness of organizational rewards system. They help managers judge whether the best performers are receiving the most reward and the most satisfaction from their jobs. The best performers are likely to quit if they are not suitably rewarded.

(vii) One of the best uses of job-satisfaction surveys is in the evaluation of the impact of organizational changes on employee attitudes. For example, the managements wants to know whether the job redesign programme recently implemented in the organization has resulted in increased satisfaction to the employees. By comparing pre-change data and post-change data, it is easy to determine what impact the redesigned work has on employee attitudes.

(viii) Finally, it is not that satisfaction surveys benefit only management. They are useful to unions too. Often, both management and union argue about what the employees want, but neither really knows. The job-satisfaction surveys is one way to find out. It is for this reason that unions support surveys.

But the benefits discussed above would be realized subject to certain prerequisites. Following are the conditions:

- Top management actively supports the survey.
- Employees are fully involved in planning the survey.
- A clear objective exists for conducting the survey.
- The study is designed and administered consistent with standards of sound research.
- Management is capable and willing to take follow up action.
- Both the results and action plans are communicated to employees.

Ways of Measuring Job-satisfaction There are a number of ways of measuring job-satisfaction. This is not surprising since hundreds of studies have been conducted over the past three and half decades, employing varied techniques. The most common ways of measurement include rating scales, critical incidents, interviews, and action tendencies.

Rating scales The most common approach for measuring job-satisfaction is the use of rating scales. These scales fall in to two general categories. One is called tailor- made scales, which are constructed for a particular setting or a project. The second set comprises standardized scales which, before their use, have been developed to establish group norms on the scales and to ensure reliability and validity of the measuring instruments. It is the tailor-made scales which are frequently used in practice.

One of the most popular standardized scales is the Job Descriptive Index (JDI) developed by Smith, Kendall, and Hulin. The JDI has separate scales for satisfaction with pay, promotion, supervision, work and co-workers (see Fig.18.9)

It has been used with a large scale variety of employee samples, and norms are provided for employees according to their age, sex, education, income, and type of community. Requiring only

FIGURE 18-9
SAMPLE ITEMS FROM SATISFACTION QUESTIONNAIRE

Job Descriptive Index

Think of the work you do at present. How well does each of the following words or phrases describe your work? In the blank beside each word given below, write

__Y__ for "yes" if it describes your work

__N__ for "No" if it does Not describe it

__?__ if you cannot decide

WORK ON YOUR PRESENT JOB:

______ Routine

______ Satisfying

______ Good

Think of the majority of the people that you work with now or the people you meet in connection with your work. How well does each of the following words or phrases describe these people? In the blank beside each word, write

__Y__ for "Yes" if it describes the people you work with

__N__ for "No" if it does NoT describe them

__?__ if you cannot decide

CO-WORKERS (PEOPLE)

______ Boring

______ Responsible

______ Intelligent

Minnesota Satisfaction Questionnaire

1 = Very dissatisfied

2 = Dissatisfied

3 = I can't decide whether I am satisfied or not

4 = Satisfied

5 = Very satisfied

On my present job, this is how I feel about:

______ The chance to work alone on the job (Independence)

______ My chances for advancement on this job (Advancement)

______ The chance to tell people what to do (Authority)

______ The praise I get for a good job (Recognition)

______ My pay and the amount of work I do (Compensation)

10-15 minutes to administer, JDI has been widely used by behaviour researches over the years and provides a broad picture of employee attitudes towards the major component of jobs.

Critical Incidents The critical incidents approach to the measurement of job satisfaction was developed by Herzberg and his associates in their research on the two factor theory of motivation. Employees were asked to describe incidents on their job when they were particularly satisfied or dissatisfied. These incidents were then content analysed in determining which aspects were closely related to positive and negative attitudes.

Interviews Personal interviews are yet another method of measurement of satisfaction. Employees are interviewed individually and the responses reveal their satisfaction or dissatisfaction.

Action Tendencies These represent the inclinations people have to avoid or approach certain things. By gathering information about how they feel like acting with respect to their jobs, the job-satisfaction can be measured. Fig 18.10 provides some examples of action tendencies.

FIGURE 18-10
SAMPLE OF ACTION TENDENCIES

1. When you wake up in the morning, do you feel reluctant to go to work?
2. Do you ever feel reluctant to go home from work at night because of the enjoyment you are getting from the job?
3. Do you often feel like going to lunch at work sooner than you do?
4. Do you feel like taking coffee break more often than you should?
5. Do you ever wish you could work at your job on evenings or weekends?
6. Are you sometimes reluctant to leave your job to go on a vacation?
7. When you are on vacation, do you ever look forward to getting back to work?
8. Do you ever wake up at night with the urge to go to work right then and there?
9. Do you ever wish holidays or weekends would get over soon that you could go back to work?
10. If you were starting over in your working career, would you lean towards taking the same type of job you have now?
11. Would you be tempted to recommended your present job to a friend with the same interests and education as yours?

Likert Scale This method of standardized survey was developed by Likert in 1932 and is widely used even today. In this, an individual is asked to indicate agreement or disagreement with job factors. The individual is also required to state how strongly he or she agrees or disagrees with a statement. This is normally done on a 5-point scale, though it is possible to use a 7-point scale also (See Fig. 18.11). The normal practice is to incorporate the various statements in a questionnaire. The subject is asked to repond to these statements, indicating the extent of his or her agreement or disagreement.

FIGURE 18-11
AN EXAMPLE OF LIKERT-SCALE

1. Strongly Disagree
2. Disagree
3. Tend to Disagree
4. Neither Agree nor Disagree
5. Tend to Agree
6. Agree
7. Strongly Agree

A value may be given to each response category in order to produce a numerical score, and the different scores in each category may be added together to arrive at a total score. A high overall score can be viewed as positive, whereas a low score indicates negative.

Use of Existing Information Before conducting any formal satisfaction survey, managers do well to examine two other methods of assessing employee feelings-daily contacts and existing data.

Managers are in contact with their employees through constant interaction and communication. This is a practical and timely method of determining job satisfaction. Besides, there are a number of indicators already available in the organization, and their collection in the form of reports will throw much light on the degree of employee satisfaction or dissatisfaction. Some of the available data relate to turnover, absenteeism, performance, suggestions, accidents, grievances, and the like.

Satisfaction and Managerial Implications Job-satisfaction has behavioural implications, particularly on such aspects as absenteeism, turnover, and unionization. A clear understanding of the causes and consequence of job-satisfaction can help managers better diagnose and solve employee problems. In particular, manager must be clear that:

(i) Employee dissatisfaction is lost frequently caused by what is perceived to be low pay and boring work;

(ii) Employees dissatisfaction is largely influenced by their feelings of inequity;

(iii) Individual satisfaction or dissatisfaction is more important, than overall satisfaction or dissatisfaction of employees;

(iv) Job-satisfaction has an impact on employee turnover, absenteeism, and unionization; and

(v) If designed and administered effectively, satisfaction surveys can prove to be invaluable help to assess the degree of satisfaction or dissatisfaction of employees.

Responses to Job Dissatisfaction The last thing about job satisfaction is the ways through which employees express their job dissatisfaction. There are several ways of expressing employee dissatisfaction. For example, employees can complain, be insubordinate, steal organisational property or shirk a part of their work responsibilities. Most serious is quitting the organization itself. Fig 18.12 offers four responses that differ from one another along two dimensions: constructiveness/destructiveness and activity/passivity.

FIGURE 18-12
RESPONSES TO JOB DISSATISFACTION

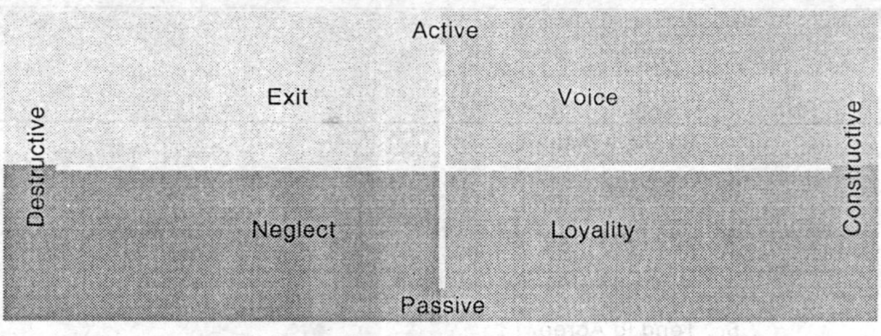

(*Source:* Stephen P. Robbins, P. 79)

Exit Exit represents behaviour directed towards leaving the organization. Also includes looking for a new position as well as resigning.

Voice Actively and constructively attempting to improve conditions. Includes suggesting improvements, discussing problems with superiors, and some forms or union activity.

Loyalty Passively but optimistically waiting for conditions to improve. Includes speaking for the organization in the face of the external criticism and trusting the management and the organization to do the right things.

Neglect Passively allowing conditions to worsen. Includes chronic absenteeism, reduced effort, and increased error rate.

ORGANIZATIONAL COMMITMENT

Organisational commitment is another job related attitude which is of considerable significance to OB. Organisational commitment refers to the strength of an employee's involvement in the organization and identification with it. There are three kinds of organizational commitment: affective, continuance and normative.

Affective commitment is an employee's intention to remain in an organization because of a strong desire to do so. It consists of three factors:

- A beliefs in the goals and values of the organization.
- A willingness to put forth effort on behalf of the organization.
- A desire to remain as a member of the organization.[16]

Affective commitment encompasses loyalty, but it is also a deep concern for the organization's welfare.

Continuous commitment is an employee's tendency to remain in an organization because the person cannot afford to leave. Alternative to leaving the organization is probably securing a less lucrative job or remaining jobless.

Normative commitment is a perceived obligation to remain with the organization. Individuals who experience normative commitment stay with the organization because they feel they should do.

Affective and normative commitments are related to lower rates of absenteeism, higher quality of work, increased productivity and several different types of performance.

Organizational commitment varies across countries. One study of workers in Saudi Arabia found that Asians working there were more committed to the organization than were Westerners and Arab workers. Another study revealed that American workers displayed higher affective commitment than did Korean and Japanese workers.[17]

Building Organizational Commitment As with job satisfaction, sources of organizational commitment are several and tend to vary from person to person. The more important sources of organizational commitment are explained here.

Job characteristics affect organizational commitment considerably. For example, commitment tends to be greater when people have high levels of responsibility over the jobs they perform and ample opportunities for advancement. Similarly enriched jobs tend to command commitment from job incumbents.

The most valuable ingredients for organizational commitment are *positive* and *equitable* work experiences. New hires must believe that the organization is fulfilling its obligations. Organizational commitmént tends to suffer when employee are overworked, not accompanied by commensurate rewards but senior executive enjoy perks disproportionate to their contribution to the success of the organization. This has precisely what happened in most public sector undertakings. The CEO of a Bangalore based Central Government undertaking reportedly spent more than Rs 20 lakhs recently to put up a swimming pool at his residence, the cost being met by the company which has been fighting hard to pay even minimum wages to its workers. Such stories of " fences eating crops" are several and the consequence has been huge losses being piled up in state and central undertakings.

Employees need to feel some *permanence* in the employment relationship. Not that employees should be assured of the type of job security once enjoyed by them, particularly in government undertakings, there should be enough permanence to nurture a relationship in which workers believe their efforts will be rewarded eventually and generally.

The other factors, (which also lead to job satisfaction) that contribute to organizational commitment include pay, relationship with supervisors and co-workers, working conditions, opportunities for advancement and so on. Overtime, organizational commitment tends to become stronger because —

(i) Individuals develop deeper ties to the organization and their co-workers as they spend more time with them;

(ii) Seniority often brings advantages that tend to develop more positive work attitudes; and

(iii) Opportunities in the job market may decrease with age, causing workers to become more strongly attached to their current jobs.

VALUES

Values represent stable, long–lasting beliefs about what is important. They are evaluative standard that help us define what is right or wrong, good or bad, in the world.[18] Some people value money while others consider morals as more important. Some value frugality while others value generosity.

Values differ from attitudes. Values are general beliefs about life, whereas attitudes are directed towards specific objects, events, or people. Of course, values influence our attitudes towards those objects. Further, a value stands in relation to some social or cultural standards or norms. While attitudes are mostly personal experiences.

There are similarities too between values and attitudes. Both are acquired essentially from the same sources. Both values and attitudes endure and are resistant to change.

There are two types of values: terminal and instrumental. *Terminal values* are desired states of existence that we think are worth striving for. A world of beauty, equality, wisdom, and a comfortable life are some of the terminal values that people might hold. *Instrumental values*, on the other hand, are desirable modes of behaviour that help us reach the objectives of terminal values. Some instrumental values include being polite, courageous, logical, self-controlled and ambitious.[19]

Another way of categorizing values is as follows:[20]

1. **Theoretical** Values the discovery of truth and emphasises critical and rational approache to problems.
2. **Economic** Values utility and practicality and emphasizes standard of living.
3. **Aesthetic** Values form grace, and hormony and emphasizes the artistic aspects of life.
4. **Social** Values love of people and altruism and emphasizes concern for others.
5. **Political** Values power, position, and influence and emphasizes competition and winning.
6. **Religious** Values unity and people's relationship to the universe and emphasises high ideals and the search for the purpose of being on earth.

It may be stated that the values people emphasize vary with their occupations. For instance, priests value religious value, scientist and professors are theoretically inclined, business people are strong on economic values, artists have high aesthetic values, psychologists and social workers talk about social values; and politicians have a high political value.

Merging Personal and organizational Values

The discussion on values till now is focused on personal values. An individual enters an organization with a *personal value system* - a relatively permanent framework of beliefs that influences the general nature of his or her behaviour. Individuals enter the organization with their own value systems, which often clash and together may conflict with organizational values.

What values a manager carries to the organization are called *intended values*. These are ideals that are personally important. However, to be successful in an organization, managers need to learn *adopted values*, a set of values that are part of the organization's culture. When personal values (intended) and organizational values (adopted) are congruent, these become highly pragmatic *operative values*. Thus, they provide a frame of reference for consistency in making decisions and relationships with others.[21] Organisations grow and prosper when operative values are strong.

Attitudes, Values and OB

As stated in the beginning of this chapter, attitudes influence behaviour. But this is not always absolute. In other words, a simple direct link between attitudes and behaviour does not exist.

Why direct link does not exist between attitudes and behaviour is explained by *behavioural intentions model*. The model suggests that focusing on a person's intention to behave in a certain way makes the relationship between the attitude and behaviour more definite than if intention is not considered. Fig 18.13 illustrates the model and shows that intensions depend on both norms and attitudes regarding the behaviour. Norms are rules of behaviour, or proper ways of acting, that members of a group or a society have accepted as appropriate. Norms thus impose social pressure to behave or not to behave in certain ways. If both attitudes and norms are positive with regard to a behaviour, an individual's intention to behave in a certain way will be strong. If attitudes and norms conflict, their relative strength may determine an individual's intentions and actual behaviour.[22]

FIGURE 18-13
BEHAVIOURAL INTENTIONS MODEL

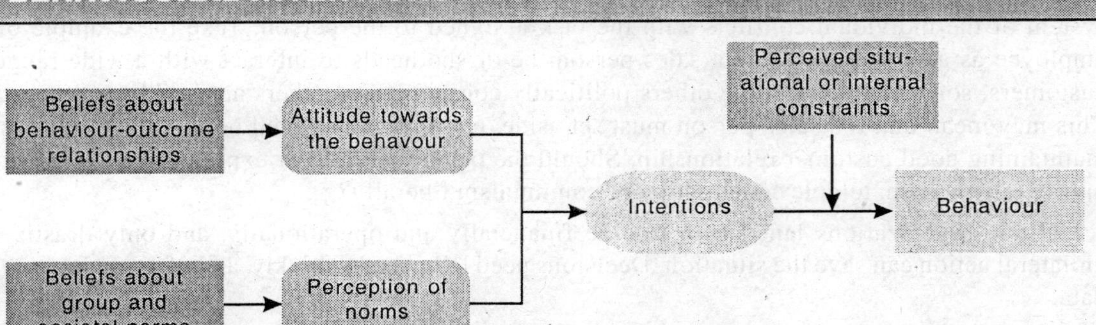

(*Source:* Don Hellriegel, *et.al. op. cit*, P. 51)

The behavioural intentions model indicates that an individual's beliefs regarding behaviours affect both attitudes and norms. In the case of attitudes, beliefs concern the relationship between the behaviour and its consequences (outcomes). Beliefs regarding norms reflect and individuals perceptions of how others expect that person to act. This model helps explain why the relationship between attitudes and behaviour sometimes is strong and at other times it is weak.

The behavioural intentions model also explains another possible explanation of behaviour. Real or perceived situational or internal obstacles may prevent a person from behaving in an intended manner. For example, someone might fully intend to perform a task quickly and effectively but lack competency to do so. Moreover, the perception or beliefs that the individual lacks the necessary competencies might prevent him or her from performing the task. [23]

Attitudinal Influence on Perception Perceptual outcomes are derived from past experiences and perceptions, but they also influence the way we perceive stimuli. Such saying as " Beauty is altogether in the eye of the beholder" and " One person's trash is another person's treasure" emphasize the importance of attitudes in perceiving the world around us. If our attitudes are positive, things will look brighter to us than if they are negative.

Job-satisfaction One of the tasks of managers is to provide satisfaction to employees from their respective jobs. The term job-satisfaction refers to an individual's general attitude towards his job. A person with high job-satisfaction holds a positive attitude towards his job, while a person who is dissatisfied with his job holds a negative attitude about his job. When people speak of employee attitudes more often than not they mean job-satisfaction. In fact, the two terms are used interchangeably.

Job Involvement The term job involvement refers to the degree to which a person identifies psychologically with his job and considers his perceived performance level important to his self worth. A person with a high degree of involvement will identify with his job and will care about the kind of work he does on his job. Besides, such involvement in the job results in reduced turnover and minimized absenteeism. Needless to say that attitude is an important variable in developing job involvement.

Organizational Commitment If job involvement refers to one's identification with a particular job, organizational commitment means one's involvement with his employing organization. Being another name for organizational loyalty, organizational commitment results in a stable workforce. As with job involvement, attitude is an important variable in determining organizational commitment.

As stated earlier, an individual enters an organization with a value system. Often, the value system of the individual conflicts with the task assigned to the person. Take the example of an employee as a sales person. As a sales person, he or she needs to interact with a wide range of customers, some religious, some others politically conscious and others are highly conservative. This may mean that the sales person must set aside, even deny, personal beliefs in the interest of maintaining good customer relationship. Should the person withold or express views on political parties, alcoholism, temple construction or communism liberally?

Often, organizations land up in trouble financially and operationally, and only drastic and unilateral action can save the situation. Decisions need to be made quickly, and often on incomplete data.

Roles of people need to be changed or some even may be fired. The manager needs to be tough and be prepared to even hurt people so that organization can be saved. The manager cannot be rigid on being honest and kind in such situations.

1. Values are important to the study of organizational behaviour because they lay the foundation for the understanding of attitudes and motivation as well as influencing our perceptions. Individuals enter an organization with preconceived notions of what "ought" and what "ought not" to be. Of course, these notions are not value free. On the contrary, they contain interpretations of right and wrong. Further, they imply that certain behaviours or outcomes are preferred over others. As a result, cloud objectivity and rationality.
2. Values generally influence attitude and behaviour. Suppose an individual enters an organization with the view that allocating pay on the basis of performance is right, whereas allocating pay on the basis of seniority is wrong or inferior. He or she is likely to get disappointed if the organization rewards seniority and not merit, disappointment is likely to lead to dissatisfaction and decline in performance. His or her attitude and behaviour would be different if his or her values are aligned with the organization's pay policies.
3. The challenge and re-examination of established work values constitute important cornerstones of the current management revolution all over the world. Hence, an understanding of values becomes a necessity.
4. Values differ across cultures. What is permissible in the United States is not appreciated in our country and what we hold as dear to our hearts may be simply laughed off in Germany. Strangely, majority of the principles and concepts of OB have been developed by Americans using American subjects within domestic contexts. A study of more than 11,000 articles published in 24 management and organizational behaviour journals over a ten-year period reveals that approximately 80 percent of studies have been done in U.S and have been conducted by Americans. This implies that OB specialist should remember that no theories and principles are universally applicable to managing people around the world. They should take into consideration cultural values when trying to understand the behaviours of people in different countries.[24]

However, values are important as they lay the foundation for the understanding of attitudes and motivation as well as influencing our perceptions.

QUESTIONS

1. What do you understand by attitudes? What are their functions?
2. Discuss how attitudes are formed?
3. Do you think it is possible to change attitudes? If yes, what are the ways?
4. What actions might the management take if it wanted to change a specific employee attitude? For example, a negative view towards the introduction of a new information system that requires many of the office personnel to make significant changes in the forms they have and the reports they fill out?
5. Discuss how an understanding of attitudes is useful for the study of organisational behaviour.
6. What is job-satisfaction? What is its relationship with productivity, absenteeism, turnover, and accidents?

Case

CRISIS BLOWN OVER

November 30 1997 goes down in the history of a Bangalore-based electric company as the day nobody wanting it to recur but every one recollecting it with a sense of pride.

It was a festive day for all the 700 - plus employees. Festoons were strung all over, banners were put up, banana trunks and leaves adored the factory gate, instead of the usual red flags; and loud speakers were blaring Kannada film songs. It was the day the employees chose to celebrate *Kannada Rajyothsava,* annual feature of all Karnataka based organizations. The function was to start at 4 p.m. and everybody was eagerly waiting for the big event to take place.

But the event, budgeted at Rs1,00,000, did not take place. At around 2 p.m., there was a ghastly accident in the machine shop. Murthy was caught in the vertical turret lathe and was wounded fatally. His end came in the ambulance on the way to hospital.

The management sought union help, and the union leaders did respond with a positive attitude. They did not want to fish in troubled waters.

Series of meetings were held between the union leaders and the management. The discussions centered around two major issues- (i) restoring normalcy, and (ii) determining the amount of compensation to be paid to the dependants of Murthy.

Luckily for the management, the accident took place on Saturday. The next day was a weekly holiday and this helped the tension to diffuse to a large extent. The funeral of the deceased took place on Sunday without any hitch. The management hoped that things would be normal on Monday morning.

But the hope was belied. The workers refused to resume work. Again the management approached the union for help. Union leaders advised the workers to resume work in all departments except in the machine shop, and the suggestion was accepted by all.

Two weeks went by, nobody entered the machine shop, though work in other places resumed. Union leaders came with a new idea to the management - to perform a *pooja* to ward off any evil that had befallen on the lathe. The management accepted the idea and *homa* was performed in the machine shop for about five hours commencing early in the morning. This helped to some extent. The workers started operations on all other machines in the machine shop expect on the fateful lathe. It took two full months and a lot of persuasion from the union leaders for the workers to switch on the lathe.

The crisis was blown over, thanks to the responsible role played by the union leaders and their fellow workers. Neither the management nor the workers wish that such an incident should recur.

As the wages of the deceased grossed Rs 6,500 per month, Murthy was not covered under the ESI Act. Management had to pay compensation. Age and experience of the victim were taken in account to arrive at Rs 1,87,000 which was the amount payable to the wife of the deceased. To this was added Rs 2,50,000 at the intervention of the union leaders. In addition, the widow was paid a gratuity and the monthly pension of Rs 4,300. And nobody's wages were cut for the days not worked.

Murthy's death witnessed an unusual behaviour on the part of the workers and their leaders, and magnanimous gesture from the management. It is a pride moment in the life of the factory.

Questions

1. What made employee union respond positively towards solving the crisis?

2. Apply the following concepts to the case and write a note on each:

(a) Attitudes, (b) Values, (c) Job satisfaction, (d) Organizational commitment.

7. Describe each of the following measures of job-satisfaction: rating scales, critical incidents, interviews, and action tendencies.

8. In general, how satisfied are young people with their jobs? Blue-collar workers? Middle managers? Women?

9. What are values? How do they differ from attitudes?

10. Why are values important to the study of organisational behaviour?

11. Described the ABC model of attitude. How should each component be measured?

12. Suppose you have an employee whose lack of commitment is affecting others in the work group. How would you go about persuading the person to change this attitude?

REFERENCE

1. John M.Ivancevich and Michale T. Matteson, *Organizational Behaviour and Management*, Irwin McGraw Hill,1999, p.120.
2. *Ibid.*
3. N.L. Munn, *et.al., Introduction to Psychology*, Oxford and IBH Publishing Co., 3rd Edn, p.606.
4. M.L. Blum and J.C. Naylor, *Industrial Psychology,* Harper and Row, 1968, p.275.
5. N.L. Munn, *et.al., Op.cit.,* p.606
6. Don Hellriegel, *et.al., Organizational Behaviour,* South Western, 2001, p.49.
7. Fred Luthans, *Organizational Behaviour*, McGraw Hill, 1998, p.141.
8. K.H. Chung and L.C. Hegginson, *Organizational Behaviour,* Harper and Row, 1981, p.124.
9. Steven L Mc Shane and Mary Ann Von Glinow, *Organizational Behaviour,* TMH, 2000, p.204.
10. Jerald Greenberg and Robert A. Baron, *Behaviour in Organizations*, PHI, 1999, p.174.
11. Fred Luthans, *Op.cit.,* p.141.
12. Eugene McKenna, *Business Psychology and Organisational Behaviour,* Psychology Press, 2002, p. 254.
13. K.H. Chung and Megginson, *Op. cit.,* p.124.
14. Steven L McShane and Von Glinow, *Op. cit.,* p. 204.
15. D.C. Feldman and H.J. Arnold, *Op. cit*, p.204.
16. Don Hellriegel, *et.al., Op. cit.,* p. 54.
17. Debra L. Nelson, *et.al, Organizational Behaviour*, Thomson, 2003, p.125.
18. Miner, J.B., *Industrial and Organizational Psychology*, McGraw-Hill, 1992, p.124
19. A Sagie and D.Elizur, "Work Values: A Theoretical Overview and a Model of Their Effects", *Journal of Organizational Behaviour*, 1996, p.503
20. M. Rokeash, *Understanding Human Values*, Free Press, 1979.

21. John R. Schermerhorn, *et.al., Managing Organizational Behaviour*, John Wiley & Sons, 1985. p.101.

22. Curtis W. Cook and Phillip L Hunsaker, *Management and Organizational Behaviour,* McGraw-Hill, Irwin, 2001, p.179.

23. Don Hellriegel, *et.al., Op.cit,* p.50.

24. K.H. Chung and L.C. Megginson, *Op. cit,* p.125.

CHAPTER Nineteen

Learning

LEARNING OBJECTIVES

After reading this chapter you should understand –

1. The nature of Learning.
2. The Four theories of learning.
3. The Learning principles need to be observed in any training programme.
4. How Learning is an important component of OB.
5. The organizational learning too.

Learning is powerful incentive for many employees to stick to certain organizations. It is not uncommon to listen employees speaking: "We stay here not very much for pay cheques, but we keep learning." Learning has significant impact on individual behaviour as it influences abilities, role perceptions, and motivation. Along with its role in individual behaviour, learning is essential for knowledge management. Knowledge management enhances an organization's capacity to acquire, share, and utilize knowledge in ways that improve its survival and success.

In today's fast-changing world, employee who works is periodically required to learn new knowledge and skills. This is dramatically apparent from the mushrooming uses of the Internet, as it changes the ways people perform routine functions and discover new ways of obtaining and acting on information.

MEANING AND DEFINITION

Simply told, learning is understood as the modification of behaviour through practice, training, or experience. This simple meaning needs to be supplemented with five important components of learning so as to make its import clear.[1]

First, learning involves change, although the change may be for good or bad from an organization's point of view. The change may not be evident until a situation arises in which the new behaviour can occur. Learning is not always reflected in performance.

Second, not all changes reflect learning. To constitute learning, change should be relatively permanent. Temporary changes may be only reflective and fail to represent any learning. This requirement, therefore, rules out behavioural changes caused by fatigue or drugs.

Third, learning is reflected in behaviour. A change in an individual's thought process or attitudes, not accompanied by behaviour, is no learning. It should be further clarified that learning needs to result in behaviour potentiality and not necessarily in the behaviour itself. The reason for this distinction lies in the fact that an individual may learn but owing to lack of motivation, may not exhibit any changed behaviour.

Fourth, the change in behaviour should occurs as a result of experience, practice, or training. This implies that behaviour caused from maturaity, disease, or physical damages does not constitute learning.

Fifth, the practice or experience must be reinforced in order for learning to occur. If reinforcement does not accompany the practice or experience, the behaviour will eventually disappear.

The last, through not implied in any standard definition of learning that, contrary to popular belief, learning is not confined to one's schooling. Learning occurs throughout one's life.

Three definitions which contain the above five important components of learning are-

- *"Learning may be defined as a relatively permanent change in behaviour that occurs as a result of prior experience."*[2]
- *"Generally, it (learning) is described as the process of having one's behaviour modified, more or less permanently, by what he does and the consequences of his action, or by what he observes."*[3]
- *"Learning can be defined as relatively permanent change in behaviour potentiality that results from reinforced practice or experience."*[4]

Learning – Explicit and Tacit Knowledge

When employees learn, they acquire both explicit and tacit knowledge. Explicit knowledge is organized and can be communicated from one person to another. The information a student receives in a class room is mainly an explicit knowledge because the professor packages and consciously transfers it to the students. Explicit knowledge can be written down and given to others. However, explicit knowledge is only a small portion of the total knowledge.

Majority of the people have tacit or implied knowledge. Tacit knowledge is the idea that one knows more than what he or she can tell. Implied knowledge is embedded in our actions and ways of thinking, but is not clearly understood and therefore cannot be communicated explicitly. The knowledge and skills one wants to give others are not sufficiently articulated, so they cannot be communicated through verbal messages. Further, since implicit knowledge is not documented, it is quickly lost when employees leave the organization.

Tacit knowledge is acquired through observation and direct experience. For instance, a truck driver does not learn how to operate the vehicle through lectures. He masters the necessary skills by watching the subtle details as others perform the tasks, and by directly experiencing this complex interaction of behaviour with machine's response. Similarly, organizations acquire tacit knowledge when employees experiment with new technologies or work on unique problems for clients. Most knowledge in organizations is tacit and one of the challenges in knowledge management is to make implicit knowledge explicit so that it may be stored and shared more easily.[5]

How Learning Occurs?

There are four theories which explain how learning occurs. They are **(i)** Classical conditioning, **(ii)** Operant conditioning, **(iii)** Cognitive theory, and **(iv)** Social Learning theory. (see Fig 19.1)

FIGURE 19-1
THEORIES OF LEARNING

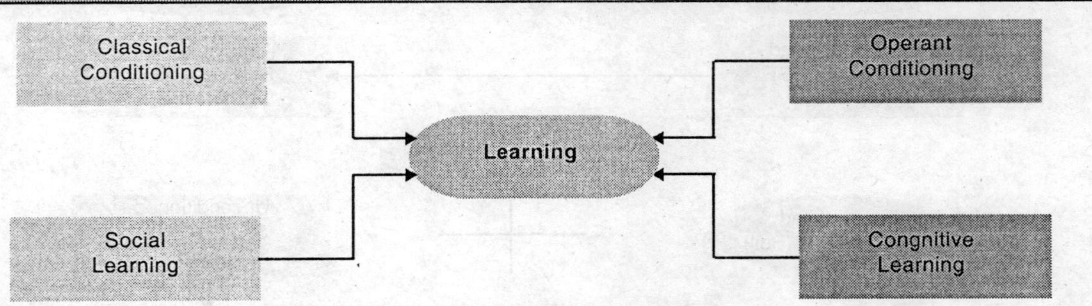

Classical Conditioning

Classical conditioning is based on the premise that a physical event-termed a stimulus-that initially does not elicit a particular response gradually acquires the capacity to elicit that response as a result of repeated pairing with a stimulus that can elicit a reaction. Learning of this type is quite common and seems to play an importamt role in such reactions as strong fears, taste aversions, some aspects of sexual behaviour, and even racial or ethnic prejudice.[6] Classical conditioning became the subject of careful study in the early 20th century, when Ivan Pavlov, a Nobel prize-winning psychologist from Russia, identified it as an important behavioural process.

Pavlov conducted an experiment on a dog and tried to relate the dog's salivation and the ringing of a bell. A simple surgical procedure allowed him to measure accurately the amount of saliva secreted by the dog. When Pavlov presented the dog with a piece of meat, the dog exhibited a noticeable increase in salivation. When he withheld the presentation of meat and merely rang a bell, the dog has no salivation. Then Pavlov proceeded to link the meat and the ringing of the bell. After repeatedly hearing the bell before getting the food, the dog began to salivate as soon as the bell rang. After a while, the dog would salivate merely at the sound of the bell, even if no food was offered. In effect, the dog has learnt to respond (salivate) to the bell.

From the brief description given above, certain key concepts of classical conditioning can now be introduced. Salivation in response to food is a natural, unlearned response-in short, a reflex. This response was called the *unconditioned reflex.* The food, because it elicited the unconditioned reflex automatically, was called the *unconditioned stimulus.* When Pavlov's repeated presentation of the bell followed by food led the dog to salivate in response to the bell alone, this salivation was designed as *conditioned reflex*, which emphasized that arousal of the reflex was dependent upon a stimulus, as the *conditional stimulus.* Thus, the concepts central to classical conditioning are unconditioned stimulus (US), unconditioned response (UR), conditioned stimulus (CS), and conditioned response (CR).

The relationship among these components of classical conditioning is shown in Figure 19.2. The essential feature of this process is that a previously neutral stimulus acquires the capacity to elicit a certain response, which is then called a conditioned response.

FIGURE 19-2

CLASSICAL CONDITIONING

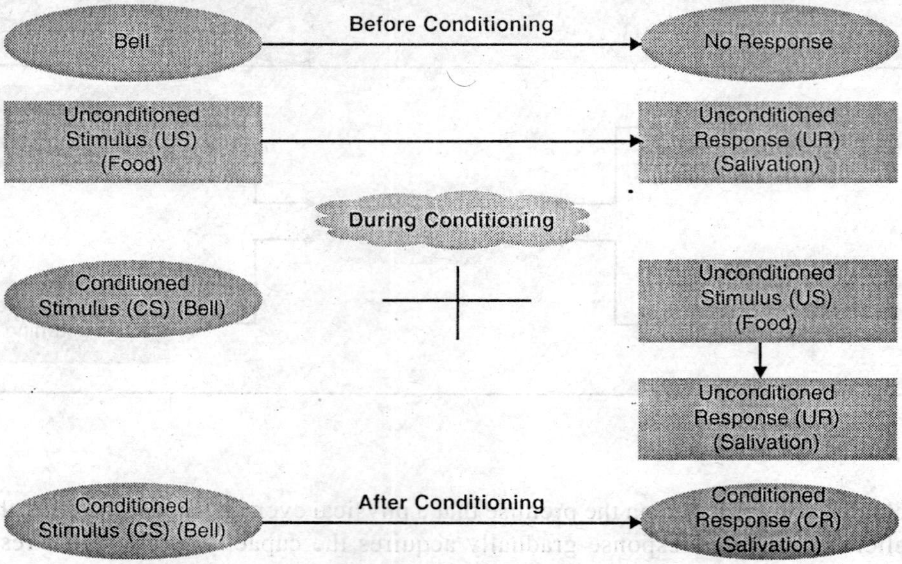

In an organizational setting, we can see classical conditioning operating. For example, at one manufacturing plant, every time the top executives from the head office would make a visit, the plant management would clean up the administrative offices and wash the windows. This went on for years. Eventually, employees would turn on their best behaviour and look prim and proper whenever the windows were cleaned even in those occasions when the cleaning was not paired with the visit from the top brass. People had learnt to associate the cleaning of the windows with the visit from the head office.

Classical conditioning is best observed in the police department, particularly in police personnel regulating traffic in a city. Every circle will be manned with inspectors, sub-inspectors or constables to control movement of vehicles and pedestrians. During peak hours, an Asst. Commissioner of Police (ACP), who is in overall control of traffic, goes round the city and monitors the way the traffic is being regulated. It is the practice of the personnel under the ACP, to salute whenever he passes by in his vehicle. The police at the circles are so used to saluting their boss, that they do so even when only the vehicle passes without the ACP being seated inside.

Despite the theoretical possibility of the widespread applicability of classical conditioning, most modern theorists agree that it represents only a very small part of total human learning. Skinner, in particular, felt that classical conditioning explains only respondent (reflexing) behaviours. These are the involuntary responses that are elicited by a stimulus. Skinner felt that the more complex human behaviours cannot be explained by classical conditioning alone. He felt that most human behaviour affects, or operates on, the environment. The latter type of behaviour is learnt through operant conditioning.

Operant Conditioning

Operant conditioning, also called instrumental conditioning, refers to the process that our behaviour produces certain consequences and how we behave in the future will depend on what those consequences are. If our actions have pleasant effects, then we will be more likely to repeat them in the future. If, however, our actions have unpleasant effects, we are less likely to repeat them in the future. Thus, according to this theory, behaviour is the function of its consequences.

Operant conditioning emphasises voluntary behaviours. Researchers call them "operant behaviour" because they operate on the environment (hence the term operant)- they make the environment respond in ways that we want. For example, you insert a coin in a coffee vending machine and press a certain button so that the machine will offer a cup of coffee. You learnt from past experience how to cause the environment (the machine) to deliver a cup of coffee.(see also Table 19.1 for more such rewards). Examples of application of operant conditioning in organisational settings are many.

Operant conditioning has a much greater impact on human learning. It also explains much of OB. For example, it might be said employees work eight hours a day, six days a week, in order to feed, clothe and shelter themselves and their families. Working is instrumental only in obtaining food, clothing, and shelter. Some significant insights can be gained directly from this kind of analysis. The consequences of OB can change the environmental situation and greatly affect subsequently employee behaviours. Managers can analyse the consequences of OB to help accomplish the goals of prediction and control.

TABLE 19-1

OPERANT BEHAVIOURS AND THEIR CONSEQUENCES

	Behaviours	*Consequences*
	Works	Is paid
	Talks to others	Meets more people
The Individual	Enters a restaurant	Obtains food
	Enters a library	Finds a book
	Increases productivity	Receives merit pay
	Completes a difficult assignments	Receives praise and promotion.

Difference between Classical Conditioning and Operating Conditioning

There are two vital differences between classical conditioning and operant conditioning. The *first* point of difference relates to the type of response. In classical conditioning, a specific stimulus, such as food, is used to elicit a specific response. The response is *elicited*. In operant conditioning, the response is not elicited by controlled stimulation but rather is spontaneously emitted by the subject. The precise stimuli producing the response at the beginning of the learning period cannot be identified. Hence, it might be said that the emphasis in classical conditioning is upon involuntary responses, while the emphasis in operant conditioning is upon voluntary responses.

The *second* difference relates to the consequences of response. In the operant procedure, as its name implies, the subject's response operates on the environment to achieve some result, such as access to food or water, recognition by others, escape from pain or discomfort, or some other desirable circumstances. In classical conditioning, the organism's behaviour is not instrumental in achieving any such result, the organism is unable to change the events of the experiment by its behaviour. Thus, food is presented or not presented in accordance with the design of the experiment-the subject's behaviour does not influence the occurrence of these events. Then there are other less important differences also.

Table 19.2 brings out the differences between classical conditioning and operant conditioning more clearly.

TABLE 19-2

DIFFERENCES BETWEEN CLASSICAL CONDITIONING AND OPERANT CONDITIONING

Classical Conditioning	*Operant Conditioning*
1. Responses are elicited from a person (reactive)	1. Responses are emitted by a person. (proactive)
2. Responses are fixed to stimulus (no choice)	2. Responses are variable in types and degrees (choice)
3. CS is stimulus such as sound, an object, a person.	3. CS is a situation such as office, a social setting, a specific set of circumstances
4. Reinforcement is not received by choice	4. Person of instrumental in securing reinforcement by "operating" on the environment.

COGNITIVE THEORY OF LEARNING

Contemporary perspective about learning is that it is a cognitive process. Cognitive process assumes that people are conscious, active participants in how they learn. Cognitive theory of learning assumes that the organism learns the meaning of various objects and events and learned responses depending on the meaning assigned to stimuli. Fig 19.3 illustrates some underpinnings of the cognitive view of learning.[7]

FIGURE 19-3
COGNITIVE PROCESS OF LEARNING

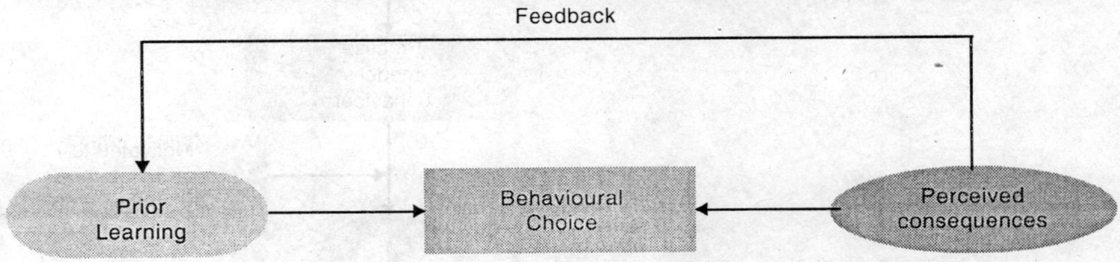

First, in the cognitive view, people draw on their experiences and use past learning as a basis for present behaviour. These experiences represent presumed knowledge or cognitions. For examples, an employee faced with a choice of job assignment will use previous experiences in deciding which one to accept. Second people make choices about their behaviour. The employee recognizes his or her two alternatives and chooses one. Third, people recognize the consequences of their choices. Thus, when the employee finds the job assignments rewarding and fulfilling, he or she will recognise that the choice was a good one and will understand why. Finally, people evaluate those consequences and add them to prior learning, which affects future choices. Faced with the same job choices next year, the employee very likely will choose the same one.

The cognitive theory of learning is relevant in the contemporary managerial practices. Many motivation theories center around the concept of cognition. Expectations, attributions, and locus of control (which are in the forefront of work motivation) are all cognitive concepts requiring attention while motivating employees.

SOCIAL LEARNING THEORY

Also called observational learning, social learning theory, emphasizes the ability of an individual to learn by observing others. The important models may include parents (see opening case), teachers, peers, motion pictures, TV artists, bosses and others.

An individual acquires new knowledge by observing what happens to his or her model. This is popularly known as *vicarious* learning. A learner acquires tacit knowledge and skills through vicarious learning.

Observational learning involves several processes as shown in Fig 19.4

To start with, the learner must pay *attention* to the model-the greater the attention, the more effective the learning will be. Second, the observer must have good *retention* of the model's

FIGURE 19-4
PROCESS OF OBSERVATIONAL LEARNING

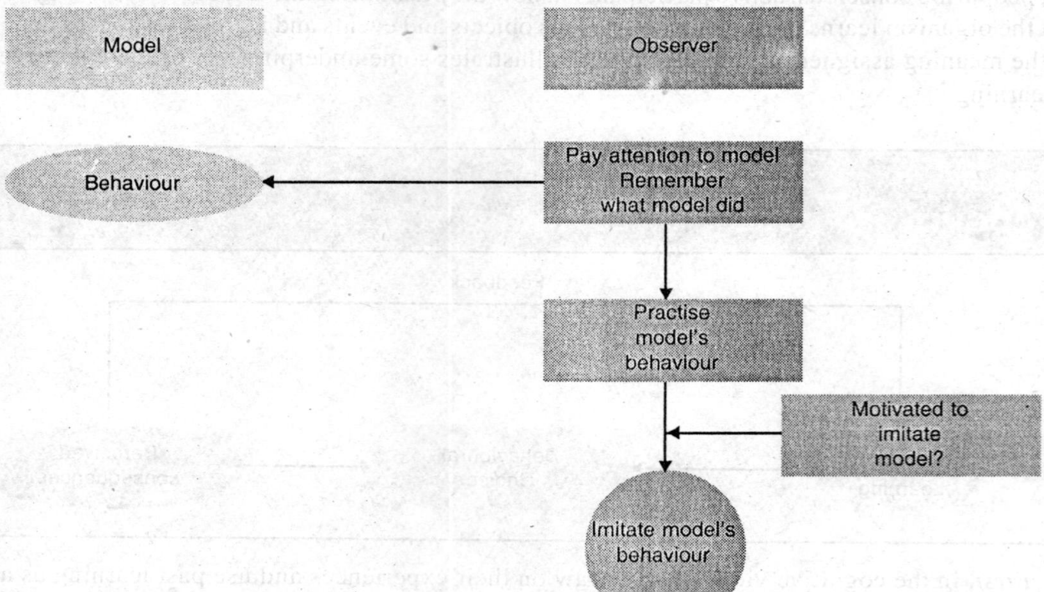

(*Source:* Greenberg and Baron, *op. cit*, p.67)

behaviour. Remembering helps develop a verbal description or mental image of someone's actions in order to remember them. Third, observers must *practice* model's behaviour. Unless, the learner is capable of doing exactly what the model does, he or she will not be able to learn from observing peer, teacher or parent. Finally, the observer must have some *motivation* to learn from the model. One does not emulate every behaviour he or she sees, but focuses on that he or she has reason or incentive to match-such as, an action for which the model is rewarded.[8]

Social learning has considerable relevance in OB. A great deal of what is learned about how to behave in organizations can be explained as the result of the process of observational learning. A new hire acquires job skills by observing what an experienced employee does. Observational learning also occurs in a very informal, unarticulated manner. For instance, people who experience the norms and traditions of their organizations and who subsequently incorporate these into their own behaviour may be recognized as having learnt through observation.

Social learning is also valuable because it enhances the *self-efficacy* of the learner. Self-efficiency refers to a person's belief that he or she has the ability, motivation, and situational contingencies to complete a task successfully. People strong in self-efficiency have a 'can do' attitude towards a specific task and, more generally, with other challenges in life.[9]

Social learning increases self-efficiency because people gain self-confidence after observing some one else do it than if they are simply told what to do. This is particularly true when observers identify with the model, such as someone who is similar in age, experience, gender, and related features.

Yet another benefits from observational learning is that it enables employees to *shape* behaviours that benefit the organization. Shaping is based on the principle that a little can eventually go a long way. Subjects receive a reward for each small step towards a final goal- the target response-rather than only for final response. Initially, actions even remotely resembling the target behaviour-termed *successive approximations* are followed by a reward. Gradually, closer and closer approximations of the final target behaviour are required before the reward is given. An example substantiates the shaping principle more clearly. When a baby suddenly blurts out the sound "Mmmmuuh" the parents are ecstatic: They immediately lavish attention and affection on the child and do so each time the baby repeats the sound. Although initially the parents respond enthusiastically to any sound the child makes, gradually they respond only to sound approximate actual words. Shaping, therefore helps organisms acquire or construct new and more complex forms of behaviour from simple behaviour.[10]

Managers can shape employee behaviour by systematically reinforcing each successive steps that moves the individual closer to the desired response. If an employee, for example, who has been chronically a half-hour late for work comes in only twenty minutes late, the boss can reinforce that improvement. Reinforcement would increase as responses more closely approximate the desire behaviour.

PRINCIPLES OF LEARNING

Principles of learning are highly useful for trainer in order to impart maximum knowledge and skills to the trainees. However, blind adherence to these principles can cause more harm than good. Each principle should, therefore, be interpreted and applied carefully in full consideration of the particular task being learned and the context in which the learning takes place. [11] Principles of learning are many but the most important of them are: motivation, reinforcement, whole versus part learning, learning curves, meaningfulness of material and learning styles.

MOTIVATION

The concept of motivation is basic because, without motivation learning does not take place or, at least, is not discernible. Motivation may be seen at different levels of complexity of a situation. A thirsty rat will learn the path through a maze to a dish of water; it is not likely to do so well, or even more purposefully at all, if it is satiated. On a broader level, a college student must have the need and drive to accomplish a task and reach a specific goal. [12]

REINFORCEMENT, PUNISHMENT AND EXTINCTION

Reinforcement, punishment and extinction play a key role in learning process. Reinforcement is used to enhance desirable behaviour, punishment and extinction are employed to minimize undesirable behaviour.

Reinforcement Reinforcement is the attempt to develop or strengthen desirable behaviour. There are two types of reinforcement: positive reinforcement and negative reinforcement.

Positive reinforcement strengthens and enhances behaviour by the presentation of positive reinforcers. There are primary reinforcers and secondary reinforcers. **Primary reinforcers** satisfy basic biological needs and include food, water, and sexual pleasure. However, primary reinforcers do not always reinforce. For example, food may not be a reinforcer to someone who has just completed a five course meal. Most behaviours in organizations are influenced by **secondary reinforcers.** These include such benefits as money, status, grades, trophies, and praise from others. These become positive reinforcers because of their association with the primary reinforcers and hence are often called **conditioned reinforcers.**

It should be noted that an event that functions as a positive reinforce at one time or in one context may have a different effect at another time or in another place. For example, food may serve as a positive reinforcer for a person who is hungry, but not when the person, as stated above, has already a large meal. Clearly, a stimulus that functions as a positive reinforcer for one person may fail to operate in a similar manner for another person. [(13)]

Within itself, positive reinforcement has several principles.

- *The principle of contingent reinforcement* states that the reinforcer must be administered only if the desired behaviour has occurred. A reinforcer administered when the desired behaviour has not been performed becomes ineffective.
- *The principle of immediate reinforcement* states that the reinforcer will be most effective if administered immediately after the desired behaviour has occurred. The more time that elapses after the behaviour occurs, the less effective the reinforcer will be.
- *The principle of reinforcement size* states that the larger the amount of reinforcement delivered after the desired behaviour, the more effect the reinforcer will have on the frequency of the desired behaviour. The amount, or size, of reinforcer is relative. A reinforcer that may be insignificant to one person may be significant to another person. Thus, the size of the reinforcer must be determined in relation both to the behaviour and the individual.
- *The principles of reinforcement deprivation* states that the more a person is deprived of the reinforcer, the greater effect it will have on the future occurrence of the desired behaviour. However, if an individual recently has had enough of a reinforcer and is satisfied the reinforcer will have less effect.[14]

Negative Reinforcement In negative reinforcement an unpleasant event that precedes a behaviour is removed when the desired behaviour occurs. This procedure increases the likelihood that the desired behaviour will occur.

Just as there are positive reinforcers, there are negative reinforcers as well. Negative reinforcers are the stimuli that strengthen responses that permit an organism to avoid or escape from their presence. Thus, when we perform an action that allows us to escape from a negative reinforcer that is already present or to avoid the threatened application of one, our tendency to perform this action in the future increases. Some negative reinforcers such as intense heat, extreme cold, or electric shock, exert their effects the first time they are encountered, whereas others acquire their impact through repeated association.[15]

We see negative reinforcement in organizations and in personal life. Supervisors apply negative reinforcement when they stop criticizing employees whose poor performance has improved. By withholding the criticism, employees are more likely to repeat behaviours that enhance their performance. Negative reinforcement also occurs when parents give in to their children's tantrums-especially in public places, such as restaurants and shopping malls. Over time, the parent's tendency to give in may increase, because doing so stops screaming.

Thus, both positive and negative reinforcement are procedures that strengthen or increase behaviour. Positive reinforcement strengthens and increases behaviour by the presentation of desirable consequences. Negative reinforcement strengthens and increases behaviour by the threat of and the use of an undesirable consequence or the termination or withdrawal of an undesirable consequence.

Negative reinforcement is sometimes confused with punishment, because both use unpleasant stimuli to influence behaviour. However, negative reinforcement is used to increase the frequency of a desired behaviour, where as punishment is used to decrease the frequency of an undesired behaviour.

Schedules of Reinforcement Reinforcement, positive or negative, needs to be properly scheduled. Schedules of reinforcement determine when reinforcers are applied. Psychologists have identified several different schedules of reinforcement. For example, where reinforcement is administered uninterruptedly, it is called **continuous reinforcement.** Unlike animals performing tricks in a circus, people on the job are rarely reinforced continuously. Instead, in organizations, reinforces are administered following *partial* (or intermittent) *reinforcement* schedules, This means, that rewards are administered intermittently. Four varieties of partial reinforcement schedules have great relevance to organizations: fixed interval schedule, variable interval schedule, fixed ratio schedule, variable ratio schedule.

Fixed interval schedule Fixed interval schedule means providing reinforcement on a predetermined, constant schedule. The first desired behaviour to occur after the interval has elapsed is reinforced. For example, in a fixed interval, 1 – hour schedule, the first desired behaviour that occurs after an hour has elapsed is reinforced. Monthly pay cheque is one example of fixed interval reinforcement.

A fixed interval schedule tends to lead to average and irregular performance. It may result in fast extinction of behaviour too. For example, employees who know that their boss will pass by their desks everyday at 1 p.m. will make sure they are working hard at that time. However, without the boss around to praise them, they may take an early break for lunch, or otherwise work less hard because they know that they will not be positively reinforced for their efforts or punished for not working.

Variable Interval Schedule Variable interval schedule also uses time as the basis for applying reinforcement, but it varies the intervals between reinforcements. Reverting to the example of the boss passing by employees desks. Suppose that instead of coming by at exactly 1 P.M. every day, the boss visits at a different time each day: 9:30 A.M.on Monday, 2 P.M on Tuesday, 11 A.M on Wednesday, and so on. The following week, the times change. Because the employees do not know just when to expect the boss, they tend to work fairly hard until his or her visit. After the visit, the employees may drop back to lower levels because they know the boss will not visit till the next day. As in the fixed interval schedule, there is extinction of behaviour but the process is slow.

Fixed Ratio Schedule In fixed ratio schedule, reinforcement is administered after the desired behaviours occur a specified number of times. Piece rating of wages is an example to be stated in this context.

A worker gets paid wages equal to the number of units produced multiplied by rate per unit. Similarly, a salesgirl knows she will earn a bonus for each Rs 25,000 worth of goods she sells. Immediately after receiving the first reward, performance may slack off. But as her sales begin to approach Rs.50,000, the next level at which reward is expected, performance will once again improve. There is moderately fast extinction of behaviour too.

Variable Ratio Schedule In this, a certain number of desired behaviours must occur before the reinforcer is delivered, but the number of behaviours varies around some average, as for example, reinforcement after 19, then 15, then 12, then 24, and then 17. This type of reinforcement schedule provokes most interest and is preferred by employees for some tasks. It tends to be the most powerful of all the reinforcement schedules.

An interesting fact is that slot machines and a number of other gambling devices operate on a variable ratio schedule. Most of the time when people put a coin into a slot they lose. But, after some unknown number of plays, the machine will payoff. Because gamblers can never tell which pull of the handle will win the jackpot, they are likely to keep on playing for a long time. Obviously, this reinforcement leads to a very high performance. Extinction of behaviour is also very slow.

Comparison of Schedules Table 19.3 summarises the four types of intermittent reinforcement schedules. Which is superior? The answer is ratio schedules-fixed or variable. The reason is that ratio schedules are more closely related to the occurrences of desired behaviours than are internal schedules, which are based on the passage of time.

TABLE 19-3
COMPARISON OF SCHEDULES OF REINFORCEMENT

Schedules	*Description*	*Example*	*Influence on performance*	*Effect on behaviour*
Fixed interval	Reinforcers administered after a constant amount of time has elapsed	Pay cheque at the end of each month	Average and irregular performance	Fast extinction of behaviour
Variable interval	Reinforcers administered after a variable amount of time has elapsed	Boss passes by employees desks at different times on different days	Leads to moderately high and stable performance	Slow extinction of behaviour
Fixed ratio schedule	Reinforcers administered after a constant number of actions performed	Piece rating of wages or bonus for every given amount of sales.	Leads quickly to very high and stable performance	Moderately fast extinction of behaviour
Variable ratio schedule	Reinforcers administered after a variable number of actions performed	A slot machine pays a jackpot, on average, one time per million plays	Leads to very high performance	Very slow extinction of behaviour

Punishment Punishment is the attempt to eliminate or weaken an undesirable behaviour. It is used in two ways. One way to punish a person is to apply a negative consequences called punishers - following an undesirable behaviour. For example, a professional athlete who is excessively offensive to an official (undesirable behaviour) may be ejected from a game (punished). The other way to punish a person is to withold a positive consequence following an undesirable behaviour. For example, a sales representative who makes few visits to companies (undesirable behaviour) is likely to receive less commission (positive reinforcer) at the end of the month.

Fig 19.5 shows how positive and negative reinforcers may be applied or withheld in reinforcement and punishment.

Reverting to the principles of punishment, it may be stated that punishment may end up in unintended results - mainly negative outcomes. Even though punishment may stop an undesirable behaviour of an employee, the potential negative outcomes may be greater than the cost of withdrawn

FIGURE 19-5
REINFORCEMENT AND PUNISHMENT

	Reinforcement (desirable behaviour)	Punishment (undesirable behaviour)
Positive reinforcers	Apply	Withhold
Negative reinforcers	Withhold	Apply

undesirable behaviour. Fig 19.6 illustrates some potential negative effects of punishment. As shown in the figure, punishment tends to minimize undesirable behaviour. But if repeated, punishment many result in undesirable emotions, hostility towards boss, low performance, and even high turnover and absenteeism.

FIGURE 19-6
NEGATIVE EFFECTS OF PUNISHMENT

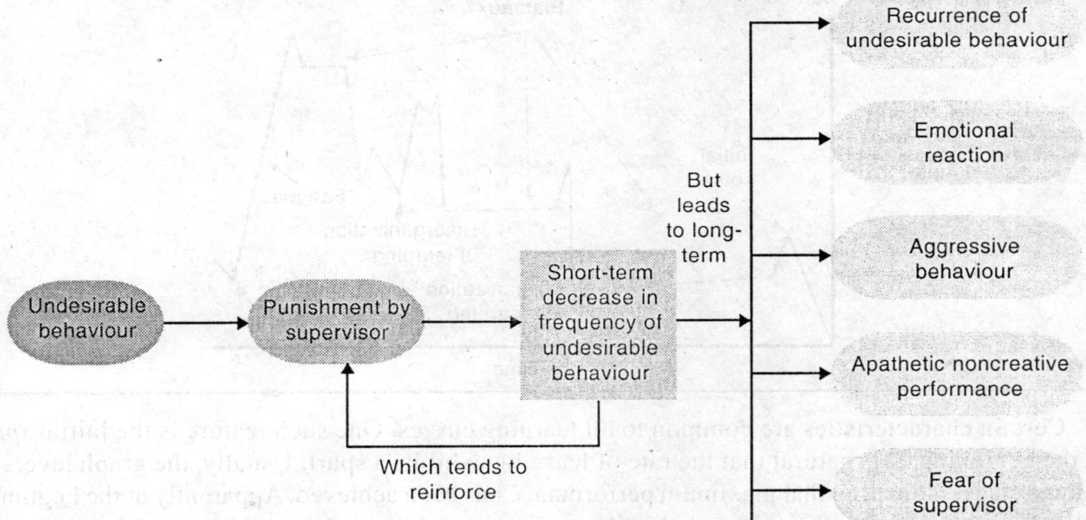

(***Source:*** Adapted from *Organizational Behaviour* by Don Hellriegel, *et al*, p.113)

Extinction An alternate to punishing undesirable behaviour is *extinction.* Extinction is the weakening of a behaviour by ignoring it or making sure it is not reinforced. The rationale for using extinction is that a behaviour not followed by any reinforcer is weakened. In other words, if rewards are for behaviour that were previously reinforced, the behaviours probably will become less frequent and die out. But extinction needs time and patience to be effective.

Whole Versus Part Learning

A great deal of work has been done in psychology of learning to decide whether learning a whole job is superior to breaking the job into parts and learning the parts. In parts learning, the individual is not only required to learn each individual part but must be able to combine the separate parts so that the whole performance can be accomplished. No overall conclusion, however, has been reached in this field.

Learning Curves

A highly useful learning concept, which is valid for a wide range of situations, is the learning curve, a diagrammatic presentation of the amount learned in relation to time. A typical learning curve will show on the Y-axis the amount learnt and on the X-axis the passage of time. Fig 19.7 represents a generalized learning curve, which shows the extent to which the rate of learning increases or decreases with practice.

FIGURE 19-7
GENERALIZED LEARNING CURVE

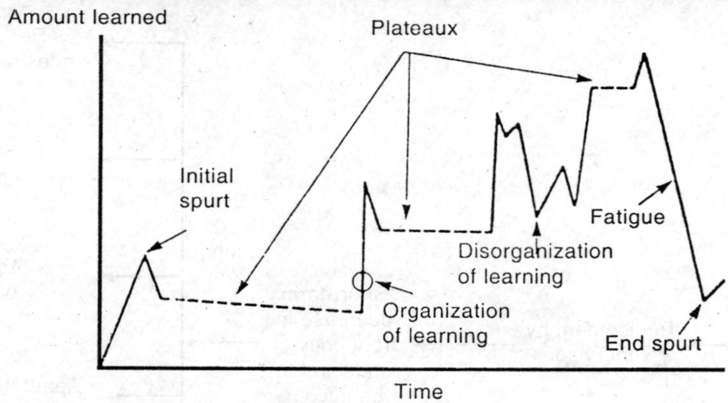

Certain characteristics are common to all learning curves. One such feature is the initial *spurt.* At the beginning, it is natural that the rate of learning exhibits a spurt. Usually, the graph levels off at some stage, indicating that maximum performance has been achieved. Apparently at the beginning of the learning process, the subject is highly motivated and seems to exhibit a significant surge of effort. Many experienced trainers exploit this initial spurt by selecting the most important items to be communicated and presenting them as a package to the students at the beginning of the training unit. In many ways, it is possible to exemplify the initial spurt with the aphorism "the first step is the best step".[16]

Another feature of the curve is the *learning plateau.* At some point in the learning process there is a flattening off in terms of the improvement, a plateau. Frequently, the process of learning is marked by discontinuities and involves escalating from one plateau to another. Most learners are only too aware of the experience of finding themselves on a plateau, which manifests itself in the feeling that they are never going to get anywhere.

Jumping from one plateau to another is called *organization of learning*. Organization of learning is achieved when the learner discovers a new and more effective method of performing particular tasks. For example, when he learns to apply the calculus to solve problems of business.

Disorganization of learning is an actual fall off in performance. This arises when the subject has to choose between alternative methods of tackling a task.

The last characteristic of the learning curve is the *end spurt*. The end spurt is preceded by fatigue which is likely to set in with the passage of time. When the training session draws nearer to an end, and the subject realizes this, there occurs resurgence of interest and effort to learn more. This revival is called the end spurt.

Meaningfulness of Material

A definite relationship has been established between learning and meaningfulness of the subject learnt. The more meaningful the material, the better does learning proceed. Learning of nonsense syllables proceeds more slowly than that of prose or poetry. On a broader scale, a programme of learning, where, each task makes for meaningfulness, trainers do have certain techniques that increase meaning for the trainees. Organizing meaningfulness units, creating association with already familiar terms, and providing a conceptual basis of logical reason for the material are some of the practical possibilities.

Learning Styles

The final principle of learning is the learning styles. Learning style refers to the ability of an individual to learn. A manager's long-term success depends more on the ability to learn than on the mastery of the specific skills or technical knowledge. There are four styles people use when learning: accommodation, divergence, assimilation, and convergence. Fig 19.8 depicts the four styles. The four styles are based on two dimensions: feeling versus thinking and doing versus observing.

FIGURE 19-8
LEARNING STYLES

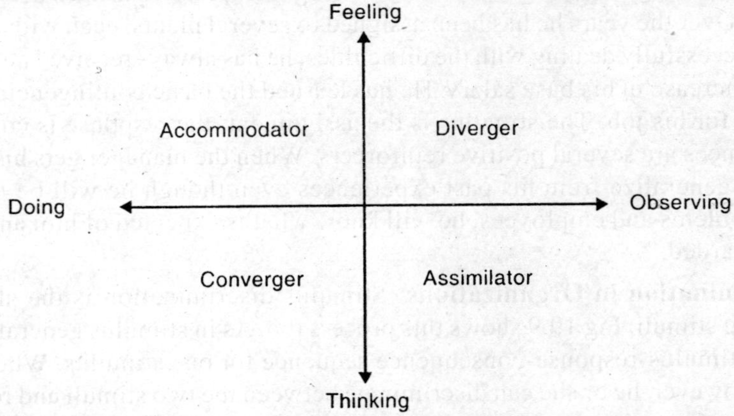

Accommodator An accommodator learns by doing and feeling. He/she tends to learn primarily from hands-on experience. He or she tends to act on gut feeling rather than on logical analysis. An accommodator tends to rely more heavily on people for information while making decisions. He or she seeks action-oriented careers such as marketing, politics, public relations and management.

Diverger A diverger learns by observing and feeling. The diverger has the ability to view concrete situations from different angles. When solving problems, diverger enjoys brainstorming. He or she takes time and analyses many alternatives. Diverger is imaginative and sensitive to the needs of the other people. He or she seeks careers in entertainment, arts and services sector.

Converger A converger learns by doing and thinking. The converger seeks practical use for information. When presented with problems and making decisions, the converger tends to focus on solutions. Converger tends to prefer dealing with technical tasks and problems rather than social and interpersonal issues. Converger seeks technical careers in various scientific fields and work at engineering, production supervision, IT and managerial jobs.

Assimilator An assimilator learns by observing and thinking. The assimilator is effective at understanding a wide range of information and putting in to concise and logical form. It is more important for the assimilator that an idea or theory is logical than practical. Assimilator tends to be more concerned with abstract ideas and concept than with people. He or she tends to seek careers in education, information, and science.

LEARNING AND OB

In addition to the application of learning in OB, as explained earlier, there are several other dimensions (of learning) which have a bearing on individual behaviour in organizations. A few important aspects are explained below.

Stimulus Generalization in Organizations: Stimulus generalization refers to how people recognize the same or similar stimuli in different settings. In other words, it is the process by which they can generalize a contingent reinforcement from one setting to another. Fig 19.9 illustrates a simple example of the process. Following an initial stimulus-response-consequence sequence, a person learns the behaviours likely to produce some kind of reinforcement. Later, when presented with a similar stimulus in different surroundings, he or she knows that the same response is likely to elicit a similar consequence.[17]

Consider the plant manager of a manufacturing company who has a history of effective troubleshooting. Over the years he has been assigned to several plants, each with a serious operating problem. After successfully dealing with the difficulties, he has always received an extended vacation, a bonus, and an increase in his base salary. He has learned the basic contingencies, or requirements of reinforcement for his job. The stimulus is the assignment, the response is correcting problems, and the consequences are several positive reinforcers. When the manager gets his next assignment, he will probably generalize from his past experiences even though he will be in a different plant with different problems and employees, he will know what is expected of him and understand what it takes to be rewarded.[18]

Stimulus Discrimination in Organizations Stimulus discrimination is the ability to recognise differences among stimuli. Fig 19.9 shows this process too. As in stimulus generalization, the person learns the basic stimulus-response-consequence sequence for one stimulus. When confronted with a new stimulus, however, he or she can discriminate between the two stimuli and respond differently.

FIGURE 19-9
STIMULUS GENERALISATION AND DISCRIMINATION

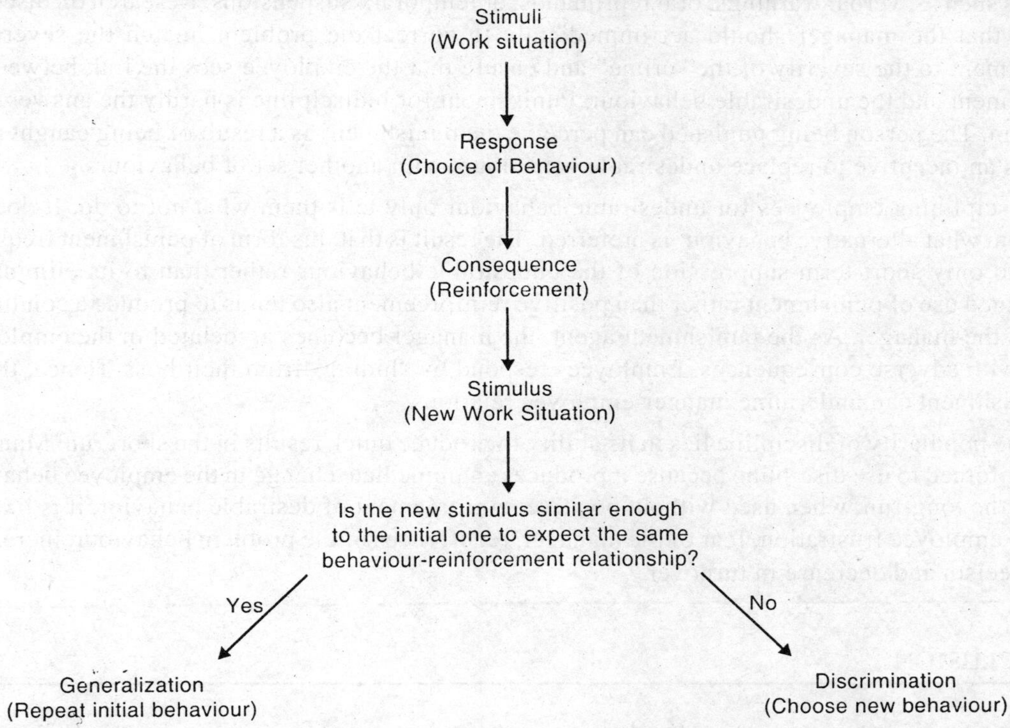

(*Source:* Moorhead & Griffin, *op. cit*, p.73)

Assuming that the troubleshooting plant manager is assigned to the plant that is running smoothly. His routine response to new situations has always been to identify and solve problems, but he must now discriminate between his new situation and his earlier ones. He will also recognise that he will need a different set of behaviours, or responses, to meet performance expectations and receive positive reinforcement.[19]

Learning and Training Learning is the major objective of training. If conducted keeping learning principles (described earlier) in mind, training becomes effective. Many organizations devote vast resources to training and development to expand the skills and abilities of their employees.

Learning Through Feedback Feedback is any information that people receive about the consequences of their behaviour. Feedback has a powerful effect on behaviour and job performance by improving role perceptions, ability and motivation. With regard to role perceptions, feedback lets people know what behaviours are appropriate or necessary in a particular situation. Feedback improves employee ability by frequently providing information to correct performance problems. Employees develop better skills and acquire job-related information by watching instrument dials or non verbal cues from customers. This is known as *corrective feedback*, because it makes people aware of their performance errors and helps them correct those errors quickly.[20] Feedback is a source of motivation. Positive feedback fulfills personal needs and makes people feal more confident that they are able to accomplish certain tasks.

Employee Indiscipline Employee indiscipline exhibited in such acts as drunkenness on the job, late arrivals to work, insubordination, stealing company property and the like is common. Every manager is frequently confronted by such indiscipline. The manager will respond with disciplinary actions such as, verbal warnings, oral reprimands, or temporary suspensions. Research on discipline shows that the manager should act immediately to correct the problem, match the severity of punishment to the severity of the "crime" and ensure that the employee sees the link between the punishment and the undesirable behaviour. Punishment for indiscipline is hardly the answer to the problem. The person being punished can perceive the punishment as a result of being caught rather than as an incentive to replace undesirable behaviours with another set of behaviours.

Disciplining employees for undesirable behaviour only tells them what not to do. It does not tell them what alternative behaviour is preferred. The result is that this form of punishment frequently leads to only short-term suppression of the undesirable behaviour rather than to its elimination. Continued use of punishment rather than positive reinforcement also tends to produce a conditional fear of the manager. As the punishment agent, the manager becomes associated in the employee's mind with adverse consequences. Employees respond by "hiding" from their boss. Hence, the use of punishment can undermine manger-employee relations.

The popularity of discipline lies in its ability to produce quick results in the short run. Managers are reinforced to use discipline because it produces an immediate change in the employee behaviour. But in the long-run, when used without positive reinforcement of desirable behavior, it is likely to lead to employee frustration, fear of the manager, recurrences of the problem behaviour, increase in absenteeism and decrease in turnover.

Conclusion

This chapter focused on individual learning. Just as there is intra – personal learning, there is organizational learning too. *Organizational learning* is the process through which managers seek to improve organization members' desire and ability to understand and manage the organization and its environment so that they can enhance organizational effectiveness.[21]

Questions

1. Give an example of how the manager of an e-commerce unit might apply each of four learning theories: (1) classical conditioning, (2) operant conditioning, (3) social learning theory and (4) cognitive theory of learning.
2. Define the term learning. What is its impact on an employee behaviour?
3. How might a teacher use reinforcement theory to get students to come to classes in time, turn in assignments on time, and take proper notes?
4. In the context of your role as a student, identity examples of each schedules of reinforcement that influence your behaviour. Which works best? Why?
5. What is your opinion about the merits of punishment?
6. Name four different schedules of reinforcement. Describe how each may be used in organizations.
7. Describe how various principles of learning might be used in a training programme.

Case

He Always Did the Best

Sudheer Tilloo (53), group chief executive, DGP Hinoday Industries Ltd and DGP Windsor Ltd. Hinoday now has a turnover of Rs 123 Crore and 1200 employees compared to Rs 1.6 crore and 140 employees in 1980, when Sudheer joined the company, then known as Morris Electronics Ltd. This confidence-inspiring wizard is a picture of innocence and pleasantness in a slight frame.

It was Tilloo's struggle with himself to excel as a manager that led him to spot opportunities. His father's exhortation: "Polish shoes, but ensure that they shine well", in other words, "Do whatever, but do your best" sowed the seeds of his search for growth and excellence. His father, a self-made man, had established himself as the best lawyer in Mandleshwar district, Madhya Pradesh. Sudheer's father passed on to his son his respect for value-based learning and his drive to be the best; while his mother's loving care and fortitude in looking after Sudheer's mentally retarded brother taught him to handle adversity with calm and patience.

Having decided to do something different instead of following in his father's footsteps, Sudheer took his first step in that direction by graduating from BITS, Pilani in 1963. He went on to do his masters from the University of Wisconsin and then worked in a couple of American companies for a year. He came home and joined Siemens India as a project engineer, moving on to become an export sales engineer two years later. Sudheer kept learning. He subscribed to the *Harvard Business Review*, which provided him with major inputs in general management approaches and strategies. After spending six years in exports, he felt the need for some managerial exposure; so he joined Automatic Electric in Mumbai, a small company making industrial panel instruments, as a manager. His one-year stint there bought him in close contact with the mercurial engineer proprietor M G Bhat, from whom he "learnt to learn" and get results.

Sudheer's big break came in 1980 when he joined the Piramal Group as project manager for diversifications. That year group chairman Dilip Piramal bought over the then Morris Electronics Ltd, Pune, from the pioneering American scientist who had started it in 1963. Sudheer moved to Pune and assumed office as executive assistant to the chairman.

The impact of a world-class organization and the opportunity to practice general management on the Morris Electronics turf opened up a challenging career path for Sudheer. He instinctively knew that technology induction had to be his first anchor for building Morris Electronics. The learning and practising voyage had begun.

In his search for appropriate technology, Sudheer turned to big corporations in specific domains of expertise. He activated earlier contacts that had been forged when he was with Siemens, which led him to the offices of Hitachi Metals in Tokyo. During his first visit to Japan he met general manger Mr. Kanayama. The first task was to gain his confidence. Sudheer informed him: "India has enormous iron oxide stocks. If you were to convert it into quality oxide for ferrites". There was silence. Sudheer sensed that the Japanese had a problem: How to trust an Indian whom he was meeting for the first time? Conceptually Sudheer knew what was in it for them. He said: "The Indian market will grow. With your support we will become number one". Sudheer invited Hitachi Metals to visit India to do a feasibility study, and offered to pick up the tab. The proposition was a confidence-building measure. It laid the foundation of a commercially viable relationship that turned out to be durable.

JAPANESE GURUS AND INDIAN SHISHYA

Sudheer won the trust and friendship of Mr Kanayama. He treated the Hitachi Metals chairman, Mr Matsumo, with appropriate reverence. In his first meeting, he took on the role of a *shishya* in front of a *guru* learning the secrets of becoming a manager. He reports the conversation verbatim:

Sudheer : What is your working schedule?

Matsumo : I get up at 6 o'clock in the morning and sleep at 11 at night. History and music are my hobbies.

Sudheer: What is the best way to develop managers?

Matsumo: On the job.

Sudheer: What are India's strengths and weakness?

Matsumo: Population size and people are its strength as well as weakness.

Sudheer: What is your goal for Hitachi Metals?

Matsumo: To make it a global organization.

Sudheer: How would you do it?

Matsumo: By catching growth where it happens. Let local people manage.

Such encounters are culturally welcomed and traditionally respected by the Japanese. The process helped Sudheer sell himself first, rather than sell his company or make appeals for selling the technology. In fact, as he puts it, "*I developed the craze to become the product of what I was doing.* You can become as good as your *guru.* If you take a second-rate teacher, you become second-rate; whereas if you take an excellent one, you are bound to become superb. I created few such *guru-shishya* relationships between me and a few of Hitachi's executives over the years. In other words, I created my own *gurukul* and thereby learnt a lot." In the process, Sudheer developed a formidable reputation in the course of the 50 visits he made to Japan from 1982 onwards.

DGP Hinoday Industries Ltd is a joint venture between Hitachi Metals and Dilip Piramal's Rs 800 crore DGP group, of which the VIP brand of luggage is the flagship. Sudheer explains: "Since Hitachi was not allowed to lend its name to joint ventures, we chose 'Hinoday' from the Japanese word 'Hinode', which means sunrise. With the connotation of 'suryoday', it also sounds suitably Indian." Morris Electronics was thus rechristened Hinoday in 1996.[22]

Questions

1. Which theory of learning, you have studied in this chapter, better explains Tilloo's learning?
2. "Tilloo's struggle with himself to excel as a manager that led him to spot opportunities". Substantiate this statement with the help of reinforcement schedules described in this chapter.

References

1. E.R. Hilgard, *et.al., Introduction to Psychology,* Oxford and IBH Pub. Co., 1975, p.196.
2. *Ibid.*
3. N.L.Munn, *et.al., Introduction to Psychology,* Oxford and IBH Pub. co., 1972, p.201.
4. Richard M. Steers and Lyman W. Porter, *Motivation and Work Behaviour,* McGraw-Hill, 1975, p.478
5. Steven L. Mcshane and Mary Ann Von L Glinow, *Organizational Behaviour,* Tata McGraw-Hill, 2000, p.41.
6. Robert A. Baron, *Psychology*, Prentice Hall of India, 1996, p.177
7. Moorhead and Griffin, *Organizational Behaviour,* Jaico, 2000, p.66
8. Jerald Greenberg and Robert A Baron, *Behaviour In Organizations,* Prenitice Hall of India, 1999, p.67
9. Steven L. Mcshane and Mary Ann VonGlinow, *Op.cit,* p.52
10. Robert A Baron, *Op.cit,* p.194
11. Blum and Naylor, *Industrial Psychology,* Harper and Row , 1968, p.241
12. Blair J. Kolasa, *Introduction to Behavioural Sciences for Business,* Wily Eastern, 1968, p.180
13. Robert A Baron, *Op.cit* p.190
14. Don Hellreiegel, *et.al., Organizational Behaviour,* South Western, 2002, p.109
15. Robert A. Baron, *Op.cit* p.190
16. Joe Kelly, *Organizational Behaviour,* Surject Publications, 1987, p.236
17. Moorhead and Griffin, *Op.cit,* p.72

18. Ibid
19. Ibid, p. 73
20. Steven L. McShane and Mary Ann Von Glinow, *op. cit,* p.47
21. P.M. Senge, *The Fifth Discipline - The Art and Practice of the Learning Organization,* 1990, p.20
22. Shrinivas pandit, *Op.cit* Pp 347-351.

CHAPTER

Twenty

Group Dynamics

LEARNING OBJECTIVES

After reading this chapter you should understand —

1. The nature of Small groups — formal, or informal.
2. The various types of Groups.
3. Why people join groups.
4. The stage of a group formation.
5. The purpose of forming groups.
6. The need for effective structuring groups.

"God created the world in 6 days – but had the advantage of working alone" so goes a statement. It was God who could do it but for lesser mortals like us, the position is different. We need to work in groups to accomplish tasks. A group is an important subsystem in any organisation. Although many students and managers think of organisations as comprising individuals, each doing a separate and distinct job, a large and increasing portion of the world's work is actually done in some kind of group. Even when an employee is not formally assigned to a group, much of his or her work is likely to be carried out in conjunction with a particular set of other people and feelings of "being part of a group" will emerge. Even executives, who often think that they walk in isolation, seldom do so. They are members of committees, task forces, study groups and the like.[1]

But working in groups is not always a pleasant job. Anyone who ever had to coordinate activities and come to decisions in conjunction with other people will remember having felt something like, "If only I could get rid of the others, I could do this job much better myself and save a lot of time, too!" Working together, at least in Indian society is not easy as the people are known for leg-pulling-intolerant of other people's success.

This chapter covers such topics as nature of groups, usefulness of groups, determinants of group behaviour, group norms, group cohesiveness and other related issues. The next chapter will focus on teams-special forms of groups.

NATURE OF GROUPS

In the broad sense, a group is any collection of individuals who have mutually dependent relationships. A formal definition of group is that it refers to "a collection of two or more interacting individuals with a stable pattern of relationships between them, who share common goals and who perceive themselves as being a group."[2] Thus, groups possess four common characteristics: (1) interaction among members, (2) common interests or goals, (3) people see themselves as members, and (4) two or more people are needed to form groups. (See Fig. 20.1)

FIGURE 20-1
GROUP CHARACTERISTICS

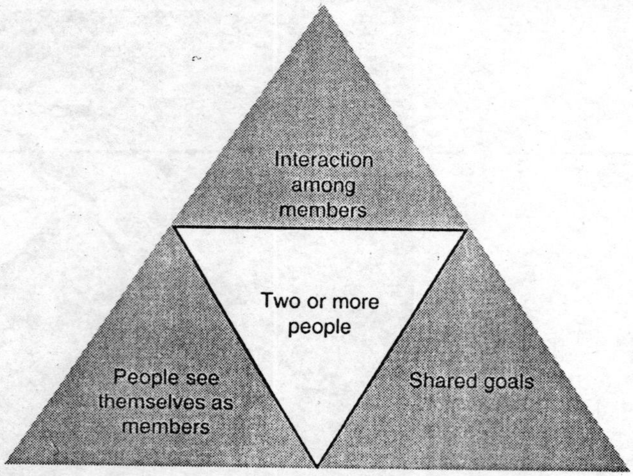

Though according to the last characteristic the membership of a group may be two or more, the size will be generally small. The size is limited by the possibilities of mutual interaction, shared interest and mutual awareness. Mere aggregates of people, a crowd in a street-corner watching some event, for example, do not constitute a group because they do not interact, do not perceive themselves to be a group even if they are aware of each other and do not share a common interest. A total department, a union, or a whole organisation would not be a group in spite of thinking of themselves as "we", because they generally do not interact and are not aware of each other. Though they share a common interest, the interest generally is diffused. Hence, committees, subparts of departments, cliques and various other informal associations among organisational members constitute groups for our purpose here.

Types of Groups

Sociologists and psychologists who study the social behaviour of people in organisations identify several different types of group. Examples of each of these types can be found in most large organisations. (See Fig. 20.2)

FIGURE 20-2
TYPES OF GROUPS

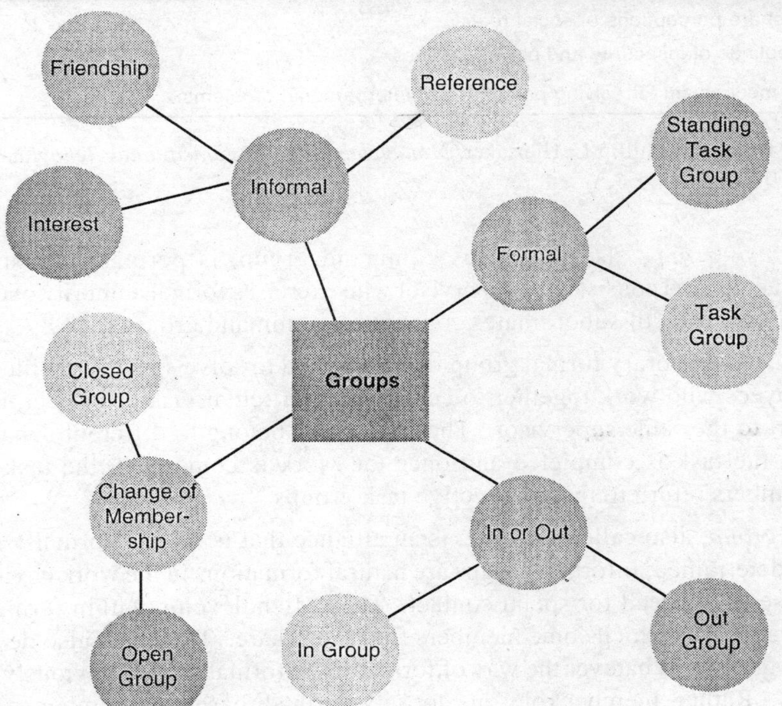

Formal and Informal Groups A *formal group* is one that is deliberately created to perform a specific task. Members are usually appointed by the organisation, but it may not always be the case. A number of people assigned to a specific task form a formal group. One example of such a group is a committee and other examples are work units, such as a small department, a research and development laboratory, a management team or a small assembly line. A distinctive feature of formal groups is that a hierarchy of authority exists, with specified member rules and regulations. Rules, regulations, incentives and sanctions guide the behaviour of small groups. Table 20.1 brings out the contributions of formal groups. Standing task group and task group are two variations of formal groups.

TABLE 20-1
CONTRIBUTIONS OF FORMAL GROUPS

Contributions to Organisations

1. Accomplish complex, independent tasks that are beyond the capabilities of individuals.
2. Create new ideas
3. Coordinate interdepartmental efforts.
4. Solve complex problems requiring varied information and perspectives.
5. Implement action plans.
6. Socialise and train newcomers.

Contributions to Individuals

1. Satisfy needs for affiliation.
2. Confirm identity and enhance self-esteem.
3. Test and share perceptions of social reality.
4. Reduce feelings of insecurity and powerlessness.
5. Provide a mechanism for solving personal and interpersonal problems.

(***Source:*** Curtis W. Cook and Phillip L. Hunsaker, *Management and Organisational Behaviour*, McGraw – Hill Irwin, 2001, p. 340)

A *standing task group*, also known as command group, is permanently specified in the organisational structure and consists of a supervisor who exercises formal authority over subordinates. The foreman and his group of subordinates constitute a command group.

A *task group* is a temporary formal group that is created to solve specific problems. The group comprises employees who work together to complete a particular task or project, but who do not necessarily report to the same supervisor. The employees belong to different departments. They stay together till the task is completed and once the work is completed, the task group usually disbands and members return to their respective task groups.[3]

An *informal group*, also called a clique, is an alliance that is neither formally structured, nor organizationally determined. Informal groups are natural formations in the work environment which appear in response to the need for social contact. They often develop within formal group out of certain values or concerns which some members find they share. They may also develop across or outside of formal groups. Whatever the way of formation, informal groups obviously do not possess formal structures. Rather, member roles are loosely defined, based on member expectations and the needs of a group at any particular moment. A member's behaviour is guided by his own internalised perception of what is appropriate and sanctioned by the bestowing or withholding of social approval.[4]

Interest group, friendship group and reference group are part of informal groups.

An **interest group** is made up of individuals who affiliate to achieve an objective of mutual interest that may have nothing to do with their formal task group memberships. Working mothers who lobby together to get their organisation to facilitate their multiple roles by providing day care facilities on the premises, flexi time and shared job assignments is an example.[5]

A **friendship group** also develops on common characteristics such as marital status, political views, college affiliations and sports. Friendship groups are important because they satisfy affiliation needs of their members. Enlightened managers maintain good relations with friendship groups because these groups have tremendous influence on their members that managers would prefer to have directed towards organisational goals.[6]

A **reference group** is any group with which an individual identifies for the purpose of forming opinions or making decisions. Reference groups are the bases for many interest and friendship groups, but they may also exist outside of the organisation and still influence a person's behaviour at work. Reference groups are based on such factors as race, gender, politics, religion, social class, education level, profession and the like. Reference groups provide values for individuals on which to base personal decisions and norms that justify social behaviour, both of which may or may not be congruent with organisational preferences.

Although informal groups exist to satisfy individual needs, they also provide contributions to the formal organisation. Table 20.2 contains some of the primary contributions of informal groups.

TABLE 20-2

CONTRIBUTIONS OF INFORMAL GROUPS

Contributions to Individuals

1. Satisfaction of social and affiliation needs.
2. Satisfaction of needs for security and support.
3. Enhanced status for members if the group is perceived by others as prestigious.
4. Enhanced feelings of self-esteem if a member is valued by other group members.
5. Feeling more competent by sharing the power of the group to influence and achieve.

Contributions to Organisations

1. Solidify common social values and expectations congruent with organisational culture.
2. Provide and enforce guidelines for appropriate behaviour.
3. Provide social satisfaction unlikely for anonymous individual workers to experience.
4. Provide a sense of identity that often includes a certain degree of status.
5. Enhance members' access to information.
6. Help integrate new employees into the formal expectations of the organization.

(***Source:*** Curtis W. Cook and Hunsaker, *op. cit.*, p. 343)

Open and Closed Groups Another basis for classifying groups is whether they are open or closed. At the one extreme is the completely *open* group, which is in a constant state of change; at the other extreme is the completely *closed* group, which is quite stable. Open groups differ from closed groups in four respects – changing membership, frame of reference, time perspective and equilibrium.[7]

With regard to *changing group membership*, in open groups, true to their nature, members keep changing – new members joining and existing ones leaving.

A good deal of time is devoted to socializing new members. A closed group maintains a relatively stable membership, with few additions and losses in members overtime. Power and status relationships are usually well established and fixed.

With regard to *frame of reference*, it may be mentioned that a high rate of turnover in an open group helps it to expand its frame of reference. New members bring new perspectives to the group's activities and problems. The expanded frame of reference in an open group can enhance creativity. The stability of membership in closed groups, on the other hand, usually results in a relatively narrow frame of reference. Bereft of the challenge from new members who bring in fresh ideas, a closed group can become very unlikely to change its established perspectives.

An open group has a relatively short *time perspective*. The instability and constant change of an open group make it difficult for the group to have long time horizons. Since membership may be brief, members' perspectives for group activities are oriented towards the present or very near future. In contrast, the stable membership of a closed group enables it to maintain a much longer time horizon. Members, because of their long association with closed groups, are able to recollect the history of the group and their expectations for continued long association enable them to use long-term planning.

Equilibrium refers to the process of restoring to the state of balance and stability from imbalance and instability. Because of changing membership, an open group is easily susceptible to imbalance and instability, though closed groups are relatively free from such problems. An open group must develop method for counteracting the disequilibrium, for any disruption is detrimental to the interests of the group. One way to make an open group stable is to make members committed to group ideals. This makes changes in members less frequent. Another way is to enhance group membership. The larger the number of members, the more stable does a group emerge.

An organisation may have both open and closed groups. Many groups whose function is evaluation or review may be relatively open. For example, membership on a promotion committee is often limited to one or two years and terms are staggered so that half the members are replaced every year. Boards of directors exemplify closed groups; they have been described by critics as "self perpetuating cliques" whose members hold sufficient votes or proxies to re-elect themselves each year. The closed nature of such groups enables them to develop historical perspective and to engage in long-term planning, often at the cost of developing new perspectives.

In-groups and Out-groups A distinction is also made between in-groups and out-groups. The groups to which we belong are in-groups and groups to which we do not belong are out-groups, especially if we look upon them with a certain amount of antagonism. The in-group versus out-group concept is applicable to friendly rivalries between schools, clubs and associations, but is also applicable to much more hostile groups. On a small-scale it is descriptive of violent neighbourhood gangs; on a larger scale it is descriptive of wars between nations.

The in-group versus out-group concept is intimately linked to *ethnocentricism*, which means that one's own group is the best and the other is to be judged on its terms. Ethnocentric attitudes are mentioned most frequently in relation to national rivalries, but ethnocentricism has many applications. One can be ethnocentric about one's community, state, social class, or even race.[8]

WHY DO PEOPLE JOIN GROUPS?

There is no single reason why individuals join groups. Since most people belong to a number of groups, it is obvious that different groups offer different attractions and benefits to their members.

The most popular reasons for joining a group is related to our needs for security, esteem, affiliation, power, identity, huddling and task functions.

Proximity, Interaction and Influence One of the most common reasons why people join groups is because they work near each other. Informal groups seem to form among those who are in close proximity. Additionally, when people have frequent interaction or contact with one another there is likelihood that they will form a group. Finally, if the behaviour of one individual influences that of others, they are likely to form a group.

Security: Probably the strongest reason for group formation is the people's need for security. By joining a group we can reduce our insecurity – we feel stronger, have fewer self-doubts and are more resistant to threats. New employees are particularly vulnerable to a sense of isolation and turn to the group for guidance and support. New or experienced, no employee likes to stay alone. We derive reassurance from interacting with others and being part of a group. This often explains the appeal of unions – if management creates an environment in which employees feel insecure, they are likely to turn to unionization in order to reduce their feelings of insecurity.

Esteem An individual can increase his self esteem through group membership. First, one may gain esteem by becoming a member of a high status group. Associating with high status people is reinforcing and one who belongs to such a group is usually accorded a high status by outsiders.

Second, the close relationship an individual can develop as a group member provides opportunities for recognition and praise that are not available outside the group.

Affiliation Another reason why people join groups is that they enjoy the regular company of other people, particularly those who possess common interests. Individuals may seek out others at work who share common hobbies or common backgrounds. Especially when people are new to an organisation, they are eager to find friends with whom they can check their perceptions of new, or uncertain environment.

Power Membership of groups offer power to members in at least two ways. First, there are sayings such as "united we stand, divided we fall" and "there is strength in numbers." These are driving forces behind unionisation in organisations. Workers enjoy much greater power collectively than they do as individuals. Even belonging to an informal group gives the individual a sense that his group will not let him or her be overcome by the impersonal bureaucracy of the organisation.

Second, leadership of an informal group enables an individual to exercise power over group members, even if he or she does not enjoy a formal position of authority in the organisation.

Identity Group membership contributes to the individual's external quest for an answer to the question. "Who am I." It is common knowledge that we try to understand ourselves through the behaviour of others towards us. If others praise us, we feel we are great, if others enjoy our jokes, we see ourselves as funny persons, and so on. Groups provide several "others" who will laugh, praise or admire us.

Huddling One more reason why individuals want to join groups is for huddling. Because of the way bureaucracies work, individuals, particularly executives, make use of informal get-togethers called huddles. These are intimate task-oriented encounters of executives trying to get something done.

Huddling enables executives to deal with emerging matters and minimise the amount of surprise. It also serves to reduce red tape by cutting through hierarchical channels of communication and minimizing misunderstandings. Because organisation charts represent real duties, huddling can compensate for a lack of leadership by taking collective and unofficial responsibility for getting things done.

Functions of Groups The last reason why groups are so common is that they fulfill a wide range of functions both for their members and for the larger organisation. While the former have been explained above, the task functions are listed here.

The organisational functions of groups help realise an organisation's goals. Such functions include the following :

(i) Working on a complex and independent task that is too complex for an individual to perform and that cannot be easily broken down into independent tasks.

(ii) Generating new ideas or creative solutions to solve problems that require inputs from a number of people.

(iii) Serving liaison or coordinating functions among several work groups whose work is to some extent independent.

(iv) Facilitating the implementation of complex decisions. A group composed of representatives from various working groups can coordinate activities of these interrelated groups.

(v) Serving as a vehicle for training new employees, groups teach new members methods of operations and group norms.[9]

The list is not comprehensive. The importance of groups in organisations cannot be overemphasised because most organisational activities are carried out by groups. Since jobs in organisations are becoming more complex and interdependent, the use of groups in performing task functions will become increasingly important.

Group Development

Groups have life cycles similar to people. They are born, grow, develop and often die. A group's effectiveness is influenced by its stage of development and how well its members have learnt to work together. A group passes through five stages in its life cycle. The stages are : forming, storming, norming, performing and adjourning (See Fig. 20.3).[10] It may be stated that different groups will remain at various stages of development for different lengths of time and some may remain at a given stage permanently, either by design or because the group is stalled. By being aware of a group's process, its leader can facilitate members' functioning at each stage and the transition to the next stage of development.

Forming In the forming stage there is a great deal of uncertainty about group's purpose, structure and leadership. Members are concerned about exploring friendship and task potentials. They do not have a strategy for addressing the group's task. Nor are they sure of what behaviours are acceptable as they try to determine how to satisfy needs for acceptance and personal goal satisfaction. As awareness increases, this stage of group development is completed when members accept themselves as a group and commit the group goals.

Storming At this stage of group development conflict arises because of the need to clarify roles and behavioural expectations. Disagreement is inevitable as members attempt to decide on task procedures, role assignments, ways of relating and power allocations. One objective at this stage is to resolve the conflict about power and task structure. Another is to work through the accompanying hostility and replace it with a sense of acceptance and belongingness that is necessary to reach to the next stage. Failure to realise these objectives results in splitting the group itself.

FIGURE 20-3
STAGES OF GROUP DEVELOPMENT

(***Source:*** Curtis W. Cook and Phillip Hunsaker, *op.cit.*, p.344)

Norming At this stage a single leader emerges and this may bring about group cohesion. There is now a strong sense of group identity and comraderie. New group standard roles and behaviour expectations are formed for members. Desired outcomes for this stage of group development are increased member involvement and mental support as group harmony emerges. If groups become too contended, they can get stalled at this stage because they do not want to create conflict or challenge established ways of doing things.

Performing This stage is marked by teamwork, role clarity and task accomplishment. Group energy moves from conflict to task accomplishment. Productivity is at its peak. Desired outcomes are achievement and pride and major concerns include preventing loss of enthusiasm and sustaining momentum. Performing happens to be the last stage in permanent work groups.

Adjourning But for temporary task forces and similar other groups, which have specific tasks to perform, adjourning happens to be the last stage. The groups disbandon after the task has been accomplished. Feelings about disbanding range from sadness and depression at the loss of friendship to happiness and fulfillment at task performance. The leader can facilitate positive closure at this stage by recognising and rewarding group performance. Ceremonial events bring closure to the desired emotional outcome of a sense of satisfaction and accomplishment.

There is an alternative theory of group development. According to this, group development proceeds on four stages: (1) Mutual acceptance, (2) Communication and decision making, (3) Motivation and productivity, and (4) Control and organisation.[11] (See Fig. 20.4).

FIGURE 20-4
STAGES OF GROUP DEVELOPMENT

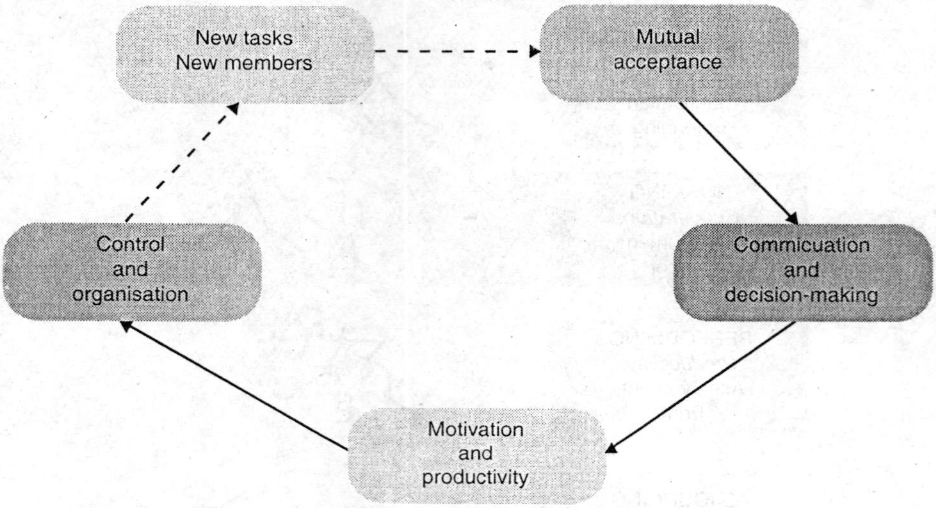

In the *mutual acceptance* stage of group development, members get to know about each other by sharing information about themselves. They discuss subject, often not connected with the group, such as politics, weather, price rise, deteriorating morals, sports or recent events within the organisation. Some aspects of the group's task, such as its formal objectives, may also be discussed at this stage.

As the members get to know one another, discussion may turn to more sensitive issues, such as the organisation's politics or recent controversial decisions. In this way, the participants explore one another's reactions, knowledge and expertise. From the discussion, members may learn one another's views on a variety of issues, how similar their beliefs and values are and the extent to which they can trust one another. Eventually, the conversation will turn to the business of the group. When this discussion becomes serious, the group is moving to the next stage – communication and decision making.

Once group members have begun to accept one another, the group progresses to the *communication and decision making stage*. Here, the group members discuss their feelings and opinions more openly. They may show more tolerance for opposing view points and explore different ideas to bring them about a reasonable solution or decision. Members discuss and eventually agree on the group's goals. Then they are assigned roles and tasks to accomplish the goals.

In the *motivation and productivity stage*, emphasis shifts away from personal concerns and viewpoints to activities that will benefit the group. Members co-operate and actively help others accomplish their goals. The members are highly motivated and may carry out their activities creatively. In this stage, the group is accomplishing its work and is moving towards the final stage of development.

In the final stage, *control and organisation*, the group works effectively towards accomplishing its goals. Tasks are assigned by mutual agreement and according to ability. In a mature group, the members' activities are relatively spontaneous and flexible, rather than subject to rigid structural restraints. Mature groups evaluate their activities and potential outcomes and take corrective actions if necessary. The characteristics of flexibility, spontaneity and self-correction are essential if the group is to become productive and last long.

Not all groups go through all four stages of development. Some groups disband before reaching the final stage. Others may skip certain stage because of pressure from leaders or deadlines. Group productivity, however depends on successful development at each stage. A group that evolves fully through the four stages of development will become a mature and effective group. Its members will be interdependent, coordinated, cooperative, competent, motivated and in active communication with one another.

Usefulness of Groups in Organisations

It is advisable to understand the usefulness of groups in the first place. Groups are highly useful or organisations and members. They can make important contributions to organisational task accomplishment and can also exert considerable influence on individual work attitudes and behaviours.

Organisational Task Accomplishment Many things in life are beyond the capabilities of one person. It takes group efforts, for example, to build a jet airplane or a multistory office building. It also takes a group to play cricket and to perform a television soap opera. The element common to each of the above examples is the benefit of group synergy. Synergy may be understood as the creation of a whole that is greater than the sum of its parts. It is in this context that the famous 2+2=5 becomes relevant. When synergy occurs, groups accomplish more than the total of individual capabilities. Research shows that :[12]

- When the presence of an "expert" is uncertain, groups make better judgements than would the average individual.
- When problem solving can be handled by a division of labour and the sharing of information, groups are typically more successful than individuals.
- Because of their tendencies to make more risky decisions than individuals, groups can be more creative and innovative in their task accomplishments.

However, *social loafing* may adversely affect task accomplishment by a group. Social loafing is also known as "Ringlemann effect", this description being named after Ringlemann, a German psychologist. Ringlemann pinpointed the social loafing effect by asking people to pull as hard as they could on a rope, first alone then in a group. He found that average productivity dropped as more people joined the rope pulling task. Thus, the Ringlemann effect acknowledges that people may tend not to work as hard in groups as they would individually. This is because their contribution is less noticeable and because they like to see others carry the work load.[(13)]

There is also the problem of *groupthink* which is common to a group. Groupthink refers to a condition in which all members of a group tend to think alike. This condition is especially likely to occur when the group has a high *esprit de corps*. The members desire for accuracy. Under such conditions, critical thinking and the independent and objective analysis of ideas are sacrificed to ensure a smoothly running group. The likelihood of group think increases if the group becomes insulated from outside influences and the fresh flow of information.

Group and Individual Behaviours Formal work groups and informal networks are important aspects of any work setting. Groups are social settings that offer a variety of information, expectations and opportunities that relate to individual need satisfaction. As a result, these groups wield major influences on individual work attitudes and behaviours. Figuratively speaking -

Group involvements	→ offer →	Information Expectations Opportunities	→ that influence →	individual attitudes and behaviour

Groups are mechanisms through which people learn relevant job skills and knowledge. Group members can model correct behaviours, offer feedback on performance and provide direct instruction and assistance to one another. Often, these relationships among group members assist individuals in building abilities and acquiring competencies required to do well at their jobs. These group benefits often make up for deficiencies in the formal training practices of the organisations.

Individual motivation to extend effort on work tasks can also be affected by group involvements. Group members communicate expectations to one another regarding work performance. They may encourage or discourage high levels of effort. Members also influence one another's beliefs and predispositions about various aspects of the work setting. A new employee soon learns, for example, who the "bad" supervisors are of whom you cannot "trust" as co-workers. These influences may even extend to the point of communicating how the individual should feel about his or her job and the organisation. For example, a co-worker may indicate that "this is a good job to have and a great place to work."

Perhaps the most apparent function of groups is their ability to satisfy the needs of their members. Groups provide for obvious social interactions and interpersonal fulfillments. A group can provide individual security in the form of direct work assistance and technical advice or emotional support in times of special crises or pressure. Groups also give their members a sense of identification and offer opportunities for ego involvement by assisting in-group activities.

Pitfalls of Groups

The principal pitfalls identified with groups are[13]:

- status differentials,
- group norms,
- risky and cautious shifts,
- polarization, and
- groupthink

Status differentials As stated earlier, groups are formed for task fulfillment. The fulfillment of purpose requires group members to interact with one another. Interaction implies exchange of emotions and stimuli. Through such exchange people become conscious of other members of the group. But status differentials hinder integration of members. High status individuals receive prominence and their views are accepted and respected, even if they are wrong. Group effectiveness is jeopardized by status differentials.

Group norms Norms, as will be explained later, play an important role in enabling groups to function. The existence of groups can prevent embarrassment or conflict by supporting mention of undesirable subjects. Norms can be economically efficient in that they may enable the group to expedite business by rendering some decisions automatic, such as excluding certain categories of people from membership. However, norms dictate the behaviour of group members. Group norms may force members to support decisions which privately they disagree with and which are detrimental to the organisation.

Risky and cautious shifts Risky shifts occur where a group makes a decision which is more risky than an individual operating alone would make. Cautious shifts occur where group makes a decision which is less risky than an individual alone would make. Both phenomena may not be in the interest of the organisation. Risky shifts can lead groups to accept probabilities which are rationally indefensible and excessive caution can lead to missed opportunities.

Polarisation This means magnifying a dominant view point. For example, if group members are doubtful about a particular issue to begin with, group discussion will focus more on doubts and vice versa. One reason for polarisation to occur is that group members are swayed by one another's advocacy. Another possibility is that the security of group membership induces members to support a decision which is more drastic or more cautious than they would accept as individuals. Whatever the reason, polarisation may render groups ineffective.

Groupthink Groupthink, like norms and status differentials, leads to conformity. But groupthink is more dangerous than norms or status differentials. Where as the latter result in deliberate suppression of judgement, groupthink occurs subconsciously. It involves the involuntary suppression of members' critical faculties.

Determinants of Group Behaviour

Several variables influence group performance and satisfaction. External conditions, resources of group members, group structure are the important inputs in group behaviour.

External Conditions

It should be kept in mind that a group is a subsystem of a formal organisation. All elements of the organisation will have their influence on a group. Such elements include organisation strategy, authority structures, formal regulations, organisational resources, procurement of personnel, performance, evaluation and reward system, organisational culture and physical work setting.

Organisation Strategy An organisation has a strategy that defines what business it is in or wants to be in and the kind of organisation it is or wants to be. It is set by top management, often in collaboration with lower level managers. Strategy outlines the organisation's goals and the means for attaining these goals. It might for example, direct the organisation towards reducing costs, improving quality, expanding market share, or shrinking the size of its overall operations. The strategy that an organisation is pursuing, at any given time, will influence the power of various work groups which in turn, will determine the resources that the organisation's top management is willing to allocate to it for performing its tasks. To illustrate, an organisation that is retrenching through selling off or closing down major parts of its business is going to have work groups with a shrinking resource base, increased member anxiety and the potential for heightened intragroup conflict.

Authority Structures Organisations have authority structures that define who reports to whom, who makes decisions and what decisions individuals or groups are empowered to make. This structure typically determines where a given work group is placed in the organisation's hierarchy, the formal leader of the group, and formal relations between groups. So while a group might be led by some one who emerges informally from within the group, the formally designated leader appointed by management has authority that others in the group do not have.

Formal Regulations Organisations create rules, procedures, policies and other forms of regulations to standardise employee behaviour. The more formal regulations that the organisation imposes on its employees, the more the behaviour of work group members will be consistent and predictable.

Organisational Resources Organisational resources important to the work group include such things as tools, equipment, facilities and work methods and procedures. Just as with individuals, groups need proper resources support if they are to achieve their true potential in task performance. Further more, the relative scarcity or abundance of resources in the organisation can affect what happens within and between groups. When resources are scarce, group members are more likely to compete with one another to access them. Similarly, resource scarcity is often an antecedent to intergroup conflict.

Procurement of Personnel Members of any group are first members of an organisation to which it belongs. The method adopted by the organisation to hire employees will determine the type of people who constitute the group. The procurement factor becomes even more critical if a large segment of the organisation's employees are unionised. In such cases, the terms of the union's collective bargaining contract will play a key part in specifying who is hired as well as acceptable and unacceptable behaviours of group members.

Performance Appraisal and Reward System Groups are influenced by the reward system. Well designed reward systems help establish and maintain proper levels and direction for group efforts. Groups can suffer from reward systems that stress individual level as opposed to group level contributions and outcomes.

Closely related to the reward systems is the performance evaluation method followed by the organisation. Does the organisation provide employees with challenging and specific performance objectives ? Answers to this and other related questions will have bearing on work group behaviour.

Organisational Culture Every organisation has an unwritten culture that defines standards of acceptable and unacceptable behaviour for employees. After a few months, most employees understand their organisation's culture. They know things like how to dress for work, whether rules are rigidly enforced, what kinds of questionable behaviours are sure to get them into trouble and which are likely to be overlooked, the importance of honesty, integrity and the like. While many organisations have subcultures – often created around the work groups – with an additional or modified set of standards, they still have dominant culture that conveys to all employees those values the organisation holds dearest. Members of work groups have to accept the standards implied in the organisation's dominant culture if they are to remain in good standing.

Physical Work Setting Physical or spatial arrangements of the work setting can also influence what goes in a group. Architects, industrial engineers and office designers make decisions regarding the size and physical layout of an employee's work space, the arrangement of equipment, illumination levels and the need for acoustics to minimise noise distractions. These create both barriers and opportunities for work group interaction. It is a lot more easier for employees to loaf if their work stations are close to each other, there are no physical barriers between them, and their supervisor is in an enclosed chamber a couple of yards away.

Physical setting, is to a large extent, decided by technology. Technology either facilitates or impedes interaction among group members. It is one thing, for example, for a group to work intensively on custom crafted products, tailor made to customer specifications, it is quite another to be part of a machine paced automobile assembly line. The former allows for more interaction among group members whereas the latter may not.

Group Members' Resources

Group performance depends, to a considerable extent, on the member resources. Members' resources comprise abilities of members and personality characteristics.

Abilities Part of group's performance can be predicted by assessing the task relevant and intellectual abilities of its individual members. How is this possible? First, evidence indicates that individuals who hold crucial abilities for attaining the group's task tend to be more involved in group activity, generally contribute more, are more likely to emerge as the group leaders and are more satisfied if their talents are effectively utilized by the group. Second, intellectual ability and task relevant ability have both been found to be related to overall group performance. However, the correlation between abilities of members and group performance is subject to the impact of such variables as size of the group, the nature of the task, the actions of the leader and the level of intragroup conflict.

Personality Characteristics There has been a great deal of debate on the relationship between personality traits and group attitudes and behaviour. The general conclusion is that attributes that tend to have a positive connotation tend to be positively related to group productivity, morale and cohesiveness. These include traits such as sociability, self-reliance and independence. In contrast, negatively evaluated characteristics such as authoritarianism, dominance and unconventionality tend to have adverse effect on group performance.

Group Structure As group structure has significant impact on group behaviour, we propose to discuss structure in greater detail.

Group Structuring

Work groups are organised systems. They have a structure that shapes the behaviour of members and makes it possible to explain and predict a large portion of individual behaviour within the group as well as the performance of the group itself. Group structure variables, for our purpose, include formal leadership, roles, group size, group norms, group task, status congruence and group cohesiveness.

Leadership

The leadership role in groups is one of the most important of all group structural characteristics, so important that we will devote an entire chapter to its discussion. At this point, let us simply state that the formal leader of the group is its principal representative and is the one individual who can legitimately exert formal influence on the activities of the group. The leader is responsible for the direction and goal accomplishment of the group and can reward or punish individual members when they do not comply with the directions, orders or rules of the group. Because the organisation supports the leader's influence, he or she has the power to make the group members comply with the directives.

In formal group, the leadership role is equally important. Informal group leaders generally are individuals who are respected by other group members and who have acquired special status. The informal group leader generally :

1. aids the group in directing its activities towards goal accomplishment.
2. embodies the values of the group.
3. acts for the group in presenting their viewpoint when interacting with management or other groups.
4. facilitates the activities of the group by initiating group actions and assisting in resolving group conflict.

The informal group leadership role can and often does change from person to person, depending on the particular conditions that exist. An individual who is not able to maintain the respect, status and prestige of the group can be replaced by others who embody the needed characteristics. To remain an informal leader, a person must have the necessary qualifications, knowledge and skills needed to aid and guide the group towards the goal accomplishment.

ROLE

By "role" – a word borrowed from theatre – is meant the part that an individual plays as a result of occupying some position or status in life. Thus, by virtue of the fact a male is born into a family, he plays the role of a son. Similarly, human beings, as the result of occupying other statuses, play such roles as father, mother, worker, manager, nurse, friend and soldier. All these are separate and well defined roles. Of course, no one individual can play all the roles in a society. There are far too many of them, and some are incompatible with each other, for instance, the roles of father and mother. But every human being plays many roles. Thus an individual may be a worker, a father, a son and so on.

In organisations, individuals play either task-oriented, relations-oriented or self-oriented roles.

An individual who helps the group to reach its goal is playing the task-oriented role. Another employee who is supportive, nurturant and who seeks to make other feel happy is said to play relations-oriented or socio-emotional role. Still others do things for themselves, often at the expense of the group. They obviously play self-oriented role. Many specific role behaviours of group members fall into one or another of these categories. Then there are sub-roles in each of the three categories. Main and sub-roles are shown in Table 20.3.

Clearly, the above are expected roles. Besides the expected roles there are also perceived and enacted roles. The *perceived* role concerns the set of activities or behaviours in the group that an individual believes he or she should do. The perceived role generally corresponds to the expected role. However, many factors make the present in a situation that can distort the individual's perception and thus make the perceived role inaccurate. The enacted role is the way that the individual group member actually behaves. The *enacted* role is generally dependent on the perceived role and hence the *expected* role.

To the extent that there are differences among the expected, perceived and enacted roles, the probability of role ambiguity, role stress, conflict and negative effects on group performance increases (See Fig. 20.5) (These terms are explained in detail in the chapter on conflict).

All of us are required to play a number of roles and our behaviour varies with the role we are playing. Different groups impose different role requirements on individuals.

TABLE 20-3
SOME ROLES COMMONLY PLAYED BY GROUP MEMBERS

Task-Oriented Roles	*Relations-Oriented Roles*	*Self-Oriented Roles*
Initiator-Contributors	**Harmonisers**	**Blockers**
Recommend new-solutions to group members	Mediate group conflicts	Act stubborn and resistant to the group
Information Seekers	**Compromisers**	**Recognition Seekers**
Attempt to obtain the necessary facts	Shift opinions to create group harmony	Call attention to their own achievements
Opinion givers	**Encouragers**	**Dominators**
Share own opinion with others	Praise and encourage others	Assert authority by manipulating the group
Energisers	**Expediters**	**Avoiders**
Stimulate the group into action whenever interest drops	Suggest ways the groups can operate more smoothly	Maintain distance, isolate themselves from fellow group members

(***Source:*** J.Greenberg and B.A. Baron, *Behaviour in Organisation*, PHI, 1995, p. 292)

FIGURE 20-5
ROLE RELATIONSHIPS

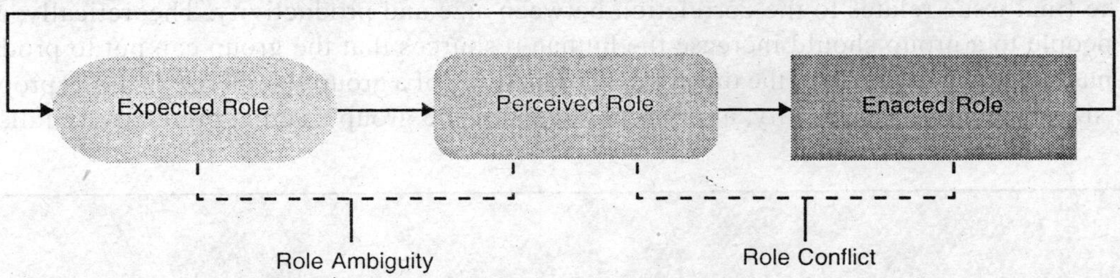

GROUP SIZE

Group size has implications on problem solving, resource and communication trade off, member satisfaction and character of group membership.

Although it is difficult to pinpoint an ideal size group, it has been shown that for problem-solving group -

A. Less than five members result in :
- Fewer people to share task responsibilities.
- More personal discussions.
- More complete participation

B. More than seven members result in :
- Fewer opportunities to participate.
- More members inhibitions.

- Domination by aggressive members.
- Tendency to split into sub-groups.

From the above it is clear that the ideal group size is between five and seven members. It should also be remembered that reducing the group size results in the loss of resources, which might otherwise be available for organisational accomplishment. At the same time increase in-group size will make communication and coordination difficult. Thus, special efforts are needed to minimise the disadvantages associated with the increasing size.

About member satisfaction, it has been proved that, satisfaction increases as group size approaches five and decreases thereafter. Turnover and absenteeism also increase with group size. In general, it appears that the larger groups suffer some disadvantages in terms of the maintainance criterion of group effectiveness. Smaller groups enable members to interact more frequently and to know one another better. This increases member satisfaction.

Another important group size issue is the odd/even character of group membership. Groups with an even number of members (e.g., four, six, eight) as compared with an odd number of members (e.g., three, five) tend to show more disagreement and contest when performing tasks. They also tend to have lower rates of members seeking suggestions from one another. These differences appear to occur because it is easier for members in odd numbered groups to form coalitions and take majority votes to resolve disagreements. Where speed is required, this behaviour is useful. Where careful deliberations are required, as for example, in jury duty or very complex problem-solving, even numbered groups can be more effective if they do not dead lock.

The final issue relates to the correlation between size and productivity. Theoretically, adding more people to a group should increase the human resources that the group can put to productive use. Thus, as shown in Fig 20.6, the theoretical productivity of a group should rise in direct proportion to the size of the group. In reality, after an initial spurt, the group's actual productivity falls as its

FIGURE 20-6
GROUP SIZE AND PROCESS LOSS

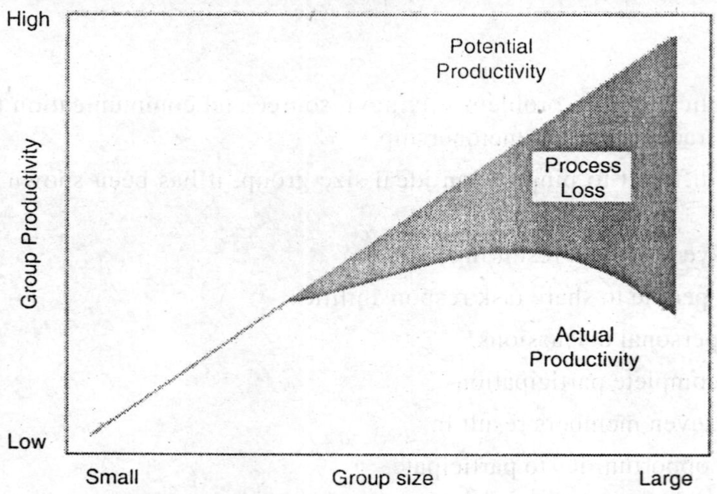

(***Source:*** John A. Wagnor, *et. al., op. cit.*, p. 247)

size continuous to increase. The difference between what a group actually produces and what it might theoretically produce constitutes process loss. It results from the existence of obstacles to group productivity, the most influential of which are production blocking, group maintenance activities, and social loafing.[14]

Production blocking occurs when people get in each other's way as they try to perform a group task – for example, when one member of a moving van crew carries a chair through a doorway and another member waits to carry a box of clothing through the same doorway.

For a group to function smoothly overtime, its members must perform contain *maintenance roles*. These roles help build strong interpersonal relations among members which in turn would ensure longevity of the group. The roles include the following-

- *Encouragers* Who enhance feelings of warmth and solidarity within the group by praising, agreeing and accepting the ideas of others.
- *Harmonizers* Who seek to minimize the negative effects of conflicts among the group members.
- *Standard setters:* Who raise questions about group goals and goal attainment and who set achievement standards against which group members can evaluate their performance.

The above maintenance roles, nodoubt ensure group's continued functioning, but they may also interfere with group's performance. For instance, members of a management group who disagree about a proposal must spend time not only on improving the proposal, but also on harmonizing among themselves. By focusing more on maintenance roles, group members tend to ignore productivity.

Process loss can also result from *social loafing*, the choice by some members of a group to take advantage of others by doing less work, working more slowly, or in other ways decreasing their own contributions to group productivity. Unless someone else in the group takes up the slack, even one person's loafing may lower the entire group's productivity.

Group Norms

These are a set of beliefs, feelings and attitudes commonly shared by group members. These are also referred to as rules or standards of behaviour that apply to group members.

Norms serve three functions in groups : predictive, control and relational.

First, norms provide a basis for understanding the behaviour of others and for deciding one's own behaviour. Second, norms regulate the behaviour of members.

When someone violates a norm, other members are likely to exercise sanctions ranging from a casual remark to physical abuse. Finally, some norms define relationships among roles. For example, while high status members are expected to play leadership roles, low-status members are prohibited from doing so.

Group norms have certain characteristics. They are ;

- the majority of group members generally find them acceptable
- only the significant aspects of group life are covered by them
- group behaviour, rather than the thoughts and feelings of members, is the focal point of attention
- members of the group accept them in varying degrees

- there is variation with regard to the degree of toleration members will accept when it comes to deviations from the norm
- the process of managing the group is facilitated by them
- conformity to norms can be a function of person's status within the gorup — this is conspicuous, e.g., when some members, normally of high status, are given latitude to deviate from the norm
- there is usually an accepted set of rewards and punishment associated with compliance or non-compliance with certain norms.

Many work and non-work norms exist in small groups, but the one most often referred to is the production norm (the group's perception of "acceptable" production behaviour), which is often different from management expectations. The reasons for production norms are :

- fear of rate cutting if production gets too high.
- fear of reprisal against workers if production gets too low.
- fear of production changes if there is too great deviation among individuals.

It was the Hawthorne experiments which gave birth to the concept of work behaviour. Although earlier writers on management such as Taylor had recognised the existence of production norms, their impact was not really assessed until Elton Mayo and his associates conducted their detailed studies. Figure 20.7 indicates the type of production behaviour observed in those studies and the terms workers used to identify those who deviated from the group's production norms.

FIGURE 20-7
PRODUCTION NORMS AND ITS ZONE OF ACCEPTANCE

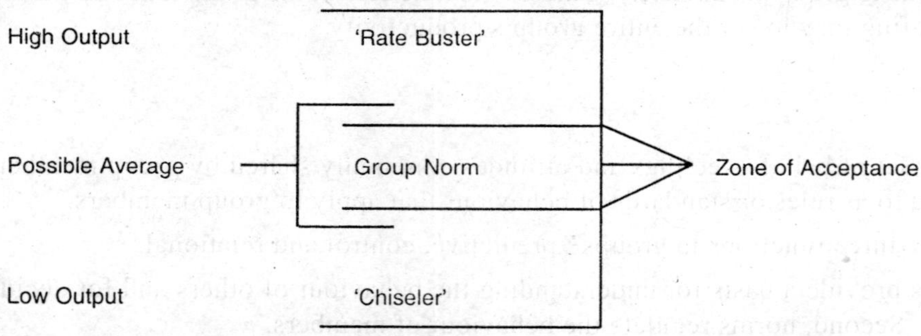

(*Source:* Gray, *et al. Organisational Behaviour, Concepts and Applications*, Merrill Publishing Co., 1988, p. 464)

Fig 20.7 also indicates that the group norm need not be the average of the group's production. The norm indicates which level of production from each individual is considered acceptable by the group, whereas the average may be higher or lower, depending upon the number of workers who deviate from the norm. It is possible to have more than one production norm operating in a group although this tends to divide the group according to different norms.

How do Norms Develop? Norms usually develop gradually and informally as members learn what behaviours are necessary for the group to function. Most norms develop in one of the following four ways.[15]

- Many norms develop because members bring their past experiences from other groups in other organisations.
- Primacy is another way of forming group norms. Primacy refers to the first behaviour pattern that emerges in a group. This behaviour pattern sets group expectations. For example, if the group meeting is marked by very formal interaction between supervisors and subordinates, then the group often expects future meetings to be conducted in the same way.
- A critical incident in the life of an organisation often sets a precedent. For example, in one organisation some employees availed themselves of the "option" of not signing performance appraisal assessments they strongly disagreed with. They were fired the next day. The norm of "sign now, disown later' was established.
- Explicit statements made by supervisors or co-workers themselves may become norms. Norms develop this way to prevent any threats to the status quo. (See also Fig. 20.8).

FIGURE 20-8
FOUR SOURCES OF GROUP NORMS

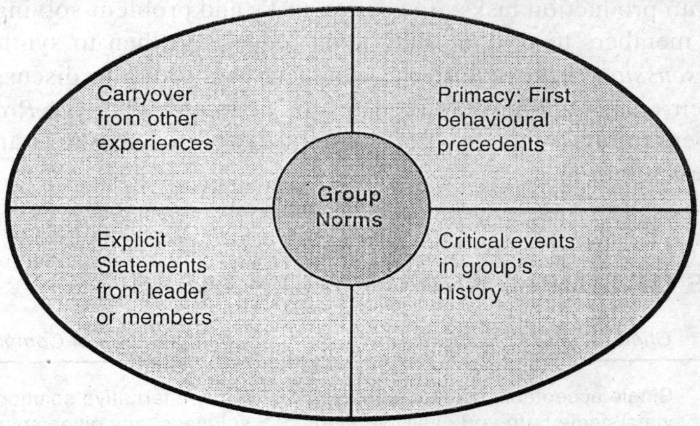

Why are Norms Strongly Enforced? Once norms are established, they are enforced on members particularly when norms help groups meet their twin aims of performing successfully and keeping morale high. To be specific, the reasons why norms are enforced are the following.[16]

(i) Norms are likely to be strongly enforced if they ensure group success or survival.

(ii) They are likely to be strongly enforced if the norms reflect the preferences of supervisor or other powerful group members.

(iii) They are likely to be strongly enforced if the norms predict what behaviour is expected of them. This is particularly true when group members are uncertain about the behaviours they have to exhibit in certain types of situations.

(iv) Norms are likely to be strongly enforced if they help the group avoid embarrassing interpersonal problems.

GROUP TASKS

We had already pointed out, in the beginning of this chapter, that groups facilitate organisational task accomplishment. In this section, our focus will be on what the group actually does, namely, the group task. Group performance, it may be stated, depends on the type of task.

Types of Tasks Tasks can be classified on the basis of time frame, task requirements and task objectives.

Time frame refers to the time required by the group for task completion. On this basis tasks may be sorted into short-term tasks and long-term tasks.

Task requirements include the amount of information to be generated, processed and transmitted; level of interaction between group members required and skills required by the group members. Based on the requirements criteria, tasks may be classified into *routine* and *complex* types. Routine ones are simple and standardized. Complex ones tend to be novel and non-routine (Table 20.4 brings out the attributes of simple and complex tasks clearly). It may be stated that the more complex the task, the more the group will benefit from discussion among members on alternative work methods. If the task is simple, group members do not need to discuss such alternatives. The final means of classifying tasks concerns the objective or purpose of the task. On this basis, tasks can be categorised into production tasks; discussion tasks and problem-solving tasks. *Production tasks* require group members to provide individual inputs and then to synthesise them into an integrative unit. *Discussion tasks* require the members of a group to discuss and resolve some issue, summarise their results and present their results to some authority. *Problem-solving* tasks require group members to review the problem, generate potential solutions and select one of the alternatives as the best solution.

TABLE 20-4
ATTRIBUTES OF SIMPLE AND COMPLEX TASKS

Task Attributes	*Characteristics of Simple Tasks*	*Characteristics of Complex Tasks*
Programmability	Single acceptable solution achieved via a single path and easily verified as correct. People who must perform task have experience with the task. Task requirements remain constant.	Many alternative solutions and means to solutions, any given solution not easily verified. People who must perform the task do not have experience with the task. Task requirements vary.
Difficulty	Little effort is required. Few operations are required. Involves low – level skills.	Great deal of effort required. Many operations are required. Involves complex skills.
Information diffusion	Required knowledge is centralised. Involves few skills.	Knowledge and skills are widely distributed. Several skills or areas of knowledge are necessary.
Member orientation	Agreement on means and ends.	Ego involved. Disagreement over means and ends.

(***Source:*** Schermerhorn, *op.cit.*, p.263)

Each of the three classification schemes for types of task should be evaluated by the manager as a total unit, not as three mutually exclusive classifications. That is, the manager of any group should be able to classify the group in terms of (i) objectives, (ii) requirements, and (iii) time-frame. In this way, a clearer knowledge of group behaviour and performance influences can be identified and evaluated.

Of the three classification bases, tasks requirement scheme is the easiest and widely accepted. As was pointed above, tasks are either simple or complex depending on the task requirements. It may be stated that group performance and satisfaction tend to be high on complex tasks than when the tasks are simple. To elaborate further, a group can be expected to work especially hard on its tasks and members of that group are likely to be satisfied with their work when:[17]

(a) The group task requires members to use a variety of relatively high level skills;

(b) The group task is a whole and meaningful piece of work, with a visual outcome;

(c) The outcomes of the group's work on the task have significant consequences for other people either inside or outside the organisation;

(d) The task provides group members with substantial autonomy for deciding about how they do the work; and

(e) Work on the task generates regular, trustworthy feedback about how well the group is performing.

STATUS CONGRUENCE

Status may be defined as a social ranking within a group and is assigned to an individual on the basis of position in the group of individual characteristics. Status can be a function of the title of individual, level of pay, work schedule, seniority – by far the most important determinant is the job title. The professor in a university has a better status than a lecturer. In some cases, particularly in groups of individuals who have same or similar titles, a person is given status because of some personal characteristics such as age, sex, skill or education.

The existence of status systems in organisations can have both positive and negative consequences for the manager. Status systems, for example, can clarify the relationships between group members by providing for clear definition of authority and responsibility. However, an overemphasis on statuses tends to reduce both the interactions between group members and the frequency of communication.

Statuses can have a direct influence on group performance through status congruence, which is understood as the agreement between group members on the level of status of individual members. When there is full agreement on member status levels (status congruence) the major activity of the group is directed towards goal accomplishment. However, when there is disagreement on status levels within the group (status incongruence) some group activity is diverted from goal accomplishment and directed towards resolving this conflict.

GROUP COHESIVENESS

A characteristic feature of groups which is particularly important for the behaviour of their members is cohesiveness, or the extent to which the members are attracted to each other and to the group. The term *cohesiveness* is understood as the extent of liking each member has towards others and how far everyone wants to remain as a member of the group. It is the degree to which members are attached to and motivated to remain part of a group. Persons in a highly cohesive group value their membership and strive to maintain positive relationships with other group members. Members also experience satisfaction from group affiliation.

Cohesion is an important group property. Managers must offer answers to such questions as (1) "What creates group cohesiveness?" and (2) "What results are expected out of cohesiveness?"

Sources of Cohesiveness Group cohesiveness can be affected by such factors as interaction, threat, severity of initiation, cooperation, shared goals, similarity of attitudes and values, and size.[18]

Interaction Group cohesiveness depends on possibilities of frequent interaction. They become more cohesive when individual members spend more time with each other.

Threat Threat is a powerful unifier particularly when : (a) it comes from outside the group, (b) cooperation can help overcome the threat, and (c) there is little or no chance for escape.

Severity of Initiation Difficulty in getting admission into a group also affects cohesion. More the difficulty, greater the cohesiveness.

Co-operation Sometimes the general atmosphere of group enhances cohesiveness. The overall atmosphere depends, among others on leadership.

Shared Goals Groups that share common goals are likely to be more cohesive than those that do not share such goals. If the group agrees on the purpose and direction of its activities, this serves to bind the group together.

Attitudes and Values One of the strongest sources of group cohesiveness is shared attitudes and values among group members. Two reasons explain why we are attracted to people like ourselves. First, the person who shares the same opinions as we do, provides us with a kind of social validation for four beliefs – he provides us with a feeling that we are right. If someone disagrees with us, this might evoke fear in us that we are wrong. Second, we are likely to make certain negative inferences about the character of a person who disagrees with us on important issues. If we disagree with this person on this issue, we feel much more likely that we shall disagree with him on other issues.

Size It is well-known that as group size increases, cohesiveness tends to decrease. This effect comes about in at least three ways. First, in large size group possibilities of interactions among members are less. Second, as group size increases, it becomes more difficult to get the group to agree on common goals and activities and expression of disagreement and dissatisfaction increases. Third, as group size increases, the need for division of labour also increases, and this places certain restrictions on intergroup communication and leads to a decrease in common activities.

Table 20.5 contains several tips for managers to increase and decrease group cohesion.

Consequences of Group Cohesiveness Group cohesiveness has positive consequences. First, there is increased morale in cohesive groups. Each member of a cohesive group likes the other members, there is increased bonhomie, reduced conflict and better communication among members.

Second, and the most important benefit of cohesiveness is its effect on productivity. Cohesiveness may contribute to increased productivity because of at least three reasons : (i) people in cohesive groups experience fewer work related anxieties, (ii) highly cohesive groups tend to have lower absenteeism and turnover, and (iii) cohesiveness decreases productivity differences among groups.

Third, members of cohesive groups communicate with each other more than members of non-cohesive groups do. Sharing common ideologies, goals, backgrounds, or attitudes gives cohesive groups a lot to talk about, and such discussion is usually reinforcing.

Fourth, conformity and influences are the other benefits of cohesive groups. Cohesive groups, by nature are highly attractive to their members. Members tend to like each other and perceive themselves as similar. These characteristics lead members to be relatively dependent on the group for satisfaction and thus they are susceptible to being influenced.

The four points mentioned above speak about the benefits of groups to members generally. But the critical remaining question is whether or not cohesive work groups are good for their host

TABLE 20-5

TIPS TO INCREASE OR DECREASE COHESIVENESS

Actions to increase cohesion:
Induce agreement on group goals
Increase membership homogeneity
Increase interactions among members
Decrease group size
Introduce competition with other groups
Allocate rewards to the group rather than individuals
Provide physical isolation from other groups.
Actions to decrease cohesion:
Induce disagreement on group goals
Increase membership heterogeneity
Restrict interactions among members
Increase group size
Allocate rewards to individuals rather than to the group as a whole
Remove physical isolation
Introduce a dominating member
Disband the group

(***Source:*** Schermerhorn *et al*, *Managing Organisational Behaviour*, John Wiley, p. 334)

organisations. Effect of cohesiveness depends on performance norms. A basic rule of group dynamics is that, the more cohesive the group, the greater the conformity of members to group norms. When the performance norm is positive, high conformity has a very beneficial effect, however, substantial undesirable result can occur when conformity is high.

Fig. 20.9 illustrates the performance levels predicted for various combinations of group cohesion and performance norms. Performance is likely to be highest in a highly cohesive group with positive performance norms.

In this situation, members with proper competencies can work hard and achieve both performance success and satisfaction with their group affiliation. The worst situation for a manager is a highly cohesive group with low or negative performance norms. Here also members are highly motivated to support one another and experience personal satisfactions. But, the organisation will probably suffer as the group restricts its performance to levels consistent with the low / negative performance norms.

Negative aspects of group cohesiveness should not be lost sight of. One problem with cohesiveness is the groupthink. Groupthink occurs when a group is so cohesive that its members lose sight of its ultimate goals for fear of disrupting the group itself. The second problem of cohesiveness relates to productivity. As stated above, productivity suffers when performance norms are low. (See Fig. 20.10)

The problem for the manager is finding how to direct the activities of highly cohesive groups towards the successful attainment of organisational goals. Following guidelines may be useful :

Emphasis on task accomplishment One approach involves redirecting the activities of the group from interpersonal issues to the emphasis on task accomplishment. If management could

FIGURE 20-9

HOW COHESIVENESS AND PRODUCTIVITY NORMS AFFECT GROUP PRODUCTIVITY

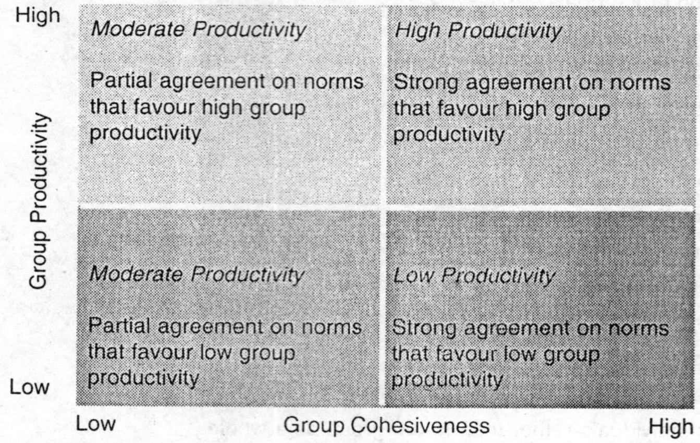

FIGURE 20-10

GROUP COHESIVENESS – CAUSES AND CONSEQUENCES

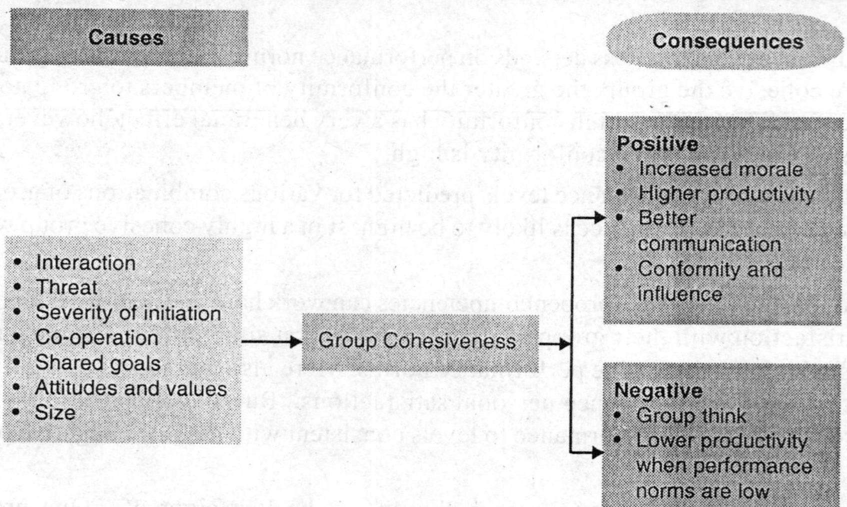

increase the groups commitment towards goals that are more compatible with organisational goals, the level of group performance could be positively influenced. This could be done in some cases by instituting group incentive pay plans or by expanding or changing jobs to be more challenging to the individual.

Participative management Another approach is to incorporate participative management in the group. Participation in establishing goals and norms creates a commitment from those participating. If the established goals and norms are challenging, the group may concentrate more on task accomplishment than on interpersonal issues.

Intergroup competition If managers can get their group members to engage in competition with other groups in the organisation, a team spirit can develop that results not only in higher but also greater group commitment to the accomplishment of the task.

Disband the group Finally, management must disband cohesive groups partially or totally by transferring members to other departments. This can provide the manager the opportunity to begin working with a relatively new group and exerting influence on the entire group formation and development process. This strategy, however, should be considered as a last resort as the unionisation of group members may resist such managerial action.

GROUPS AND OB

As stated earlier, small groups are inevitable in organisations. The prevalence of groups can alter a person's motivation or needs and can influence the behaviour of people in an organisational setting.

Complex task accomplishment requires group effort. Thus, the sayings "two heads are better than one" and "2 + 2 = 5", become relevant and meaningful. Task completion becomes easy when there is group cohesiveness. Managers need to orient organisational systems and resources towards ensuring group cohesiveness.

It is not that groups are confined to organisational settings alone. They are there everywhere. Infact an individual cannot live alone. Man is a social animal. Living alone often is hazardous to one's health. Heart attack patients living alone are nearly twice as likely to suffer another heart attack – and more likely to die of an attack – within six months. Additionally, accidents, suicides, psychiatric disorders, alcoholism and even tuberculosis are more common among socially isolated individuals. When an individual confronts difficulties, the social support and feedback of others can be of immense help. For instance, cancer patients who enjoy the strong emotional support of family, friends or spouses typically survive substantially longer than those who lack such support.(19)

Groups, because of their own pitfalls, tend to outlive their utility in course of time. Where groups fail, teams will emerge.

QUESTIONS

1. Think of a formal group of which you are a member. Describe the group in terms of the characteristics of groups discussed in this chapter.
2. Why is it important for managers to be familiar with the concepts of group behaviour ?
3. Why is groupthink something to be avoided ? How might a manager attempt to ensure that groupthink does not occur in his or her group ?
4. What is the relationship between group norms and group cohesiveness ? What roles do both cohesiveness and norms play in shaping group performance ?
5. Explain what happens in each of the five stages of group's development. When does group address interpersonal issues ? Task issues? Authority issues.?
6. Define the term "group". What are the types of group ? What purposes do groups serve?
7. Explain why people join groups.

Case I

Ben and Jerry's Thrives on Company Spirit

Known for its rich ice cream generously laced with tasty tidbits and for its black-and-white cow logo, Ben & Jerry's Homemade, Inc., began simply enough as an ice cream parlor in a renovated gas station. When it opened in 1978 in Burlington, Vermont, it was a social experiment. Cofounders Ben Cohen and Jerry Greenfield wanted to demonstrate that their business could operate differently from many others. They believed that it could be unconventional, shares its prosperity with employees, interact responsibly with the community and still do well from a business standpoint. In fact, they intended to sell the business as soon as it was established and they had proved their point.

But things didn't turn out quite as they planned. Happily, the ice cream was an instant success. Ben and Jerry considered selling the company, but finally decided instead to keep it and use the profits for social change.

As the company continued to grow, Ben and Jerry worked hard to foster fun, charity, goodwill toward coworkers, and the feeling of a small, close-knit group that had helped make the company successful from the start. The company set up various programs to benefit employees. Such programs included hiring the handicapped; providing for free therapy sessions with drug and alcohol counseling for any worker and taking employees on all company trips to see baseball and hockey games. Ben & Jerry's also had a 5-to-1 salary ratio, whereby the highest salaries paid could not equal more than five times the lowest.

Not surprisingly, dedication to the company ran high among the workers. Such dedication was important because the rapid growth of the company and the somewhat informal ways of operating frequently led to crises that required everyone to pitch in. For example, on one such occasion, a new machine to automatically fill pints did not work and production fell behind. Everyone – including Ben and Jerry – worked the production line to fill orders. Some workers made dinner for the rest of the staff and pizzas were ordered. As always, the group spirit came through.

This spirit that has characterised the company was nurtured by the heavy involvement of the employees in the firm's business affairs. One means was through monthly staff meetings, which all employees were invited to attend. Employees would break into small groups and provide input on solutions to problems.

Gradually, as the company grew bigger, it became more difficult to obtain input from everyone and the meetings became characterised by one-way communication from Ben and other managers. Recognising the problem, Ben attempted to institute the old format by posing the question : "What are the most pressing problems confronting us ?" The approach generated a huge amount of data that were difficult to assimilate. One manager who spent a night helping Ben categorise the responses said, "It was like having this 8-ton dump truck back up and dump its load over you." The overall message to Ben was that the employees were beginning to feel left out.

Growth began to level off at the $ 150 million range. Consumers were becoming more concerned about eating food high in saturated fat. In reaction, the company developed low-fat and nonfat frozen yogurt products. Heavy competition from Grand Metropolitan's Haagen Dazs brand and cheaper premium ice cream emerged. The company began to experience losses.

Ben was forced to conclude that the company had outgrown his management skills and he began to search for a CEO who could recharge the organisation. The company had to abandon the 5-to-1 salary ratio idea because it was difficult to recruit a new CEO of the necessary caliber given the salary arrangement. After a highly publicized search, Ben & Jerry's hired a new CEO, Robert Holland, Jr., a former McKinsey & Co. consultant. He began by instituting tighter controls. Earnings improved. The company began to expand markets in Europe and launched a very successful fat-free sorbet line to compete with the Haagen Dazs brand. After 19 months on the job, Holland resigned amidst rumors of clashes with the founders over meshing their social agenda with shareholder interests. Publicly, Holland said the company needed a CEO strong in marketing and sales. The company then hired Perry Odak as CEO. Odak has 25 years of experience in consumer products and retailing businesses.

Each year, Ben & Jerry's conducts a self-critical "social performance" audit that is included in its annual report. Part of the audit is based on input from employees, who now number over 700. The employee section of one recent annual report noted that focus groups conducted among employees revealed "a continuing sense of confusion, frustration and low morale on the part of many staff members."[20]

Questions

1. What group norms are evident at Ben & Jerry's?
2. What factors have contributed to the development of high cohesiveness among Ben & Jerry's employees ?
3. What could Ben and Jerry do to preserve some of the positive aspects of group dynamics ?

Case-II

THE MANAGER'S MEMO

Following is the letter authored by the Vice President, Consumer Electronics Division and addressed to the Production Manager. The issue raised in the letter relates to Quality First Programme.

"I think it's time to look at a new approach to our Quality First Programme. We've had the suggestion box out for a year and so far we've received only two suggestions for quality improvements, of which only one made any sense.

"Let's try a group approach. We can divide the employees into groups that can meet to come up with ideas for improving the quality of our products and production process.

"I'd like you to prepare a plan for these groups. How should they operate ? How often should they meet ? What should be the size of each group ? Should we divide the groups into engineers, production workers, maintainance personnel and so on, or should we put a variety of workers into each group ? What problems can we anticipate with the group format, and how can we resolve them ? "These questions are meant as a starting point. If you have other ideas or concerns, please include them in your plan."

Questions

Assume you are the production manager and respond to the Vice President's letter with a memo outlining the plan requested. Be sure to respond to the specific questions. Use as many of the concepts in the chapter as you can to develop a complete plan that minimises the pitfalls of group dynamics.[21]

REFERENCES

1. Kathryn M. Bartol, et.al, *Management*, Irwin McGraw-Hill, 1998, p. 485.
2. Robert A. Baron, *Behaviour in Organisations*, Allyn and Bacon, 1986, p. 240.
3. Curtis W. Cook and Phillip L. Hunsaker, *Management and Organisational Behaviour,* McGraw-Hill Irwin, 2001, p. 340.
4. Theodre T. Herbert, *Dimensions of Organisational Behaviour*, Macmillan, 1976, p. 282.
5. M. Dalton, *Men Who Manage*, John Wiley and Sons, 1979, p. 76.
6. Curtis W. Cook and Phillip L. Hunsaker, *Op. cit*, p. 341.
7. Joseph R. Reitz, *Behaviour in Organisations*, Irwin, 1977, p. 293.
8. Blair J. Kolasa, *Introduction to Behavioural Sciences for Business*, Wiley Eastern, 1978, p. 451.
9. Joe Kelly, *Organisational Behaviour – Its Data, First Principles and Applications*, Surjeet Publications, 1987, p. 284.
10. Edgar H. Schein, *Organisational Psychology*, PHI, 1983, p. 152.

11. Gregory Moorhead and Ricky W. Griffin, *Organisational Behaviour*, Jaico, 1997, p. 197.
12. Marvin E. Shaw, "Group Dynamics", *The Psychology of Small Group Behaviour*, McGraw-Hill, 1976, p.6.
13. Schermerhorn et.al, *Managing Organisational Behaviour*, John Wiley & Sons, 1985, p. 252.
14. John a. Wagner and John r. Hollenback , *Organizational Behaviour*, Harcourt College publishes, 2002, p.247
15. Helga Drummond, *Organisational Behaviour*, Oxford, 2000, p. 185.
16. D.C. Feldman and H.J. Arnold, *Managing Individual and Group Behaviour in Organisations*, McGraw-Hill, 1983, p. 445
17. Ibid, p. 438.
18. Richard M. Hodgetts, *Organisational Behaviour – Theory and Practice*, Macmillan, 1991, p. 172.
19. James W. Vander Zanden, *Sociology*, McGraw-Hill, 1996, p. 100.
20. Kathryn M. Bartol, *et al, Op. cit,* p. 504.
21. Adapted from *Organisational Behaviour* by Gregory B. Northeraft and Margaret A. Neole, The Dryden Press, 1990, p. 321.

CHAPTER

Twenty One

Team Dynamics

LEARNING OBJECTIVES

After reading this chapter you should understand —

1. The nature of Teams.
2. The nature of groups.
3. The several benefits of teams to organizations.
4. The different types of groups.
5. The process of team formation.
6. How Teams can be made more effective.
7. Quality circles and self-managed teams.

Teams are common in organizations. Teams and team work have emerged popular terms in management circles these days. Cynics tend to dismiss team work as just another management fad or quick-fix gimmick. But a close look reveals a more profound and durable trend.

The team approach to managing organizations is having a diverse and substantial impact on organizations and individuals. Teams promise to be a cornerstone of progressive management for the foreseeable future. According to the management expert Peter Drucker, tomorrow's organizations will be flatter, information based, and organized around teams.[1] This has been proved in Infosys, no solitary example to be stated in this context. In the Bangalore based software giant, teams are clients or project based. At any given time there are as many as 1800 teams and the strength of each team varies from 5 to 100 depending on size of the project.

In this chapter we focus on the nature, types, model, effectiveness and other related issues on teams and team work.

NATURE OF TEAMS

A team is a small number of people with complementary skills who are committed to a common purpose, common performance goals, and an approach for which they hold themselves mutually accountable.[2]

The above definition needs further elaboration. A team includes few people, same as a small group described in the previous chapter, because the interaction and influence processes, vital for a team to function, can only occur when the number of members is small. When more people are involved, there will be difficulty in interacting and influencing each other.

Teams include people with mix of skills appropriate to the task to be done. Team members need technical, problem solving and decision making, and inter-personal skills. Not all members will have all the required skills, different members will have different skills. However, as the team grows, develops and matures, team members will come to have more of the necessary skills.

Having a common purpose and common performance goals, sets the tone and direction of the team. A team comes together to take action to pursue a goal, unlike a group, in which members report to the same supervisor or work in the same department. The purpose becomes the focus of the team.

Agreeing on a common approach is particularly important for teams, because it is often the approach that differentiates one team from others. The team's approach usually covers how work will be done, social norms regarding dress, attendance at meetings, tardiness, norms of fairness an ethical behaviour, and what will and not be included in the team activities.

Finally, the definition states that team hold themselves mutually accountable for results, rather than merely meeting a manager's demands for results, as in the traditional approach. If the members translate accountability to an external manager into internal, or mutual accountability, the group moves towards acting like a team. Mutual accountability is essentially a promise that members make to each others to do everything possible to achieve their goals, and it requires commitment and trust of all members.[3]

The following distinct features of teams make their meaning more clear[4]:

- They are empowered to share various management and leadership functions.
- They plan, control and improve their own work processes.

- They set their own goals and inspect their own work.
- They often create their own schedules and review their performance as a group.
- They may prepare their own budgets and coordinate their work with other departments.
- They usually order materials, keep inventories and deal with suppliers.
- They are frequently responsible for acquiring any new training they might need.
- They may hire their own replacement or assume responsibility for disciplining their own members.
- They, and not others outside the team, take responsibility for the quality of their products or services.

Teams are also known by other terms such as empowered teams, self directed teams and self management teams.

TEAMS VS GROUPS

Looking at the meaning of a team, there appears hardly any difference between a group and a team. But the two are not same. The following points differentiate between the two.(See also Fig 21.1)

FIGURE 21-1
DIFFERENCES BETWEEN GROUPS AND TEAMS

Groups	Criteria	Teams
Formal-established	Leadership	Shared roles
Individual	Accountability	Shared and Individual
Sum of Individual outputs	Performance	Collective and synergistic
Diverse	Skills	Complementary
Common goal	Orientation	Common commitment

First, in groups work performance typically depends on the work of individual members. The performance of a team, however, depends on both individual contributions and collective efforts of team members working in concert.

Second, groups and teams differ in their accountability for jobs. Typically, members of groups pool their resources to attain a goal, although it is individual performance that is considered while rewarding. Members of groups usually do not take responsibility for any results other than their own. In contrast, teams focus on both individual and mutual accountability. Team members work together to produce an outcome that represents their joint contributions, and each team member shares responsibility for that outcome. Thus, in groups the supervisors hold individual members accountable for their work, whereas in teams, members hold themselves accountable.[5]

Third, group members may share a common goal, but team members share a common commitment to purpose. The commitment to goal attainment is what separates teams from groups. For example, a work team in a financially troubled company may be highly committed to making the plant the top one in its industry. Such commitment may be lacking in a group, though members too share a common interest.

Fourth, both groups as well as teams differ in their respective connections with management. Groups are required to be responsive to demands regularly placed on them by management. In contrast, once management established the mission for a team, and sets goals for it to achieve, it gives the team enough freedom and flexibility to do its job without any further interference. In other words, teams are free to set their own goals, timing, and the approach they wish to adopt without interference from management. The teams are self managing and are autonomous.

Finally, members in a group posses skills diverse but the skills of team members are complementary.

Benefits from Teams

Several benefits accrue to organization from teams. More prominent of these are: enhanced performance, employee benefits, reduced costs, and organizational enhancements.

Enhanced performance can come in many forms, including increased productivity, improved quality and improved customer service. Working in teams enables workers to avoid wasted effort, reduced errors, and respond better to customers, resulting in more output for each unit of employee input.

Employee benefits from teams include, better quality of work life, and reduced stress. Rather than relying on the traditional, hierarchical, manager-based system, teams give employees freedom to grow and gain respect and dignity by managing themselves, making decisions about their work, and really making a difference in the world around them. Consequently employees benefit immensely from teams.

Teams result in reduced scrap, fewer errors, fewer remuneration claims, and reduced *turnover* and absenteeism resulting in significant *cost reduction*. Members are committed to their team's performance. They do not want to let down their teams. Commitment to performance makes team members cost conscious.

Teams result in better *quality decisions*. Teamwork involves the collective effort of a group of people who represent diverse backgrounds, exposure and experiences. As more ideas are produced and alternatives are considered, the team is able to make optimal decisions – decisions that are stronger because they have been made with various perspectives and interest in mind.

Teamwork results in *improved processes*. Because of the coordination between and transfer of learning among team members, teamwork results in organized approach to the situation at hand. For example, a team is more likely than an individual to set up project checkpoints and planning systems to enable all team members to contribute to the project as it unfolds. Team work also permits for distribution of work loads for faster and more efficient handling of large tasks or problems.[6]

Team work contributes to *global competitiveness* to the firms. Firms in the US are relying increasingly on diverse teams to compete in the global economy. Diverse teams have skill sets and perspectives that are superior to what a single individual can marshal. Diverse skills add to the competitive edge to the firms.

Finally, teams benefit management through *organizational enhancements*, which include increased innovation, creativity and flexibility. Teams can eliminate redundant layers of bureaucracy and flatten the hierarchy in large organizations. Employees will have better access to top management. In addition, the team environment constantly challenges teams to innovate and solve problems creatively. Organizational improvements are certain to result.

Empowered teams are catching on among Indian mangers. Companies as diverse as Titan, Reliance, ABB, Tata Information System, Ltd; (TISL), GE Plastics India and Philips are empowering employees both front line as well as production staff. WIPRO Corporation has 29 such teams and their number is expected to go upto 130. WIPRO Infotech, on the other hand, has 10 such teams and the plan is to hike them to around 45 to 50. At Reliance, divisional heads run their divisions like managing directors run their companies.

TYPES OF TEAMS

In view of their wide spread popularity, various types of teams have come to stay. One easy way to classify teams is by what functions do they discharge; for example, some teams make or do things, some teams recommend things, and some teams run things. The most common type of teams are work teams, problem-solving teams, management teams, and virtual teams (See Fig.21.2).

FIGURE 21-2
TYPES OF TEAMS

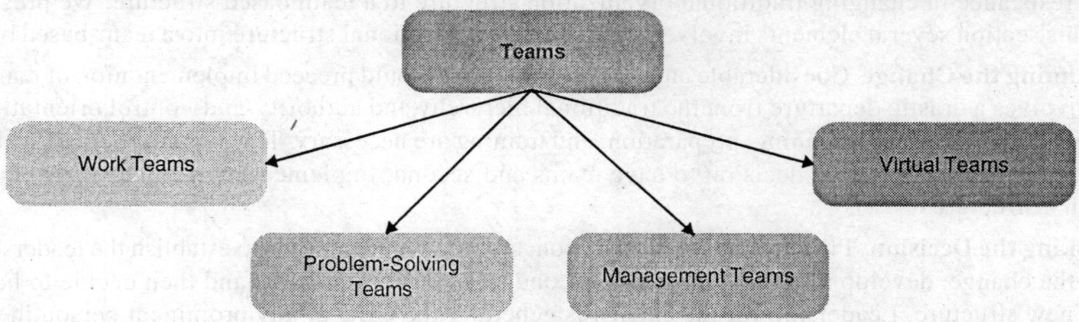

Work Teams These are primarily concerned with the work done by the organization, such as developing and manufacturing new products, providing services for customers, and so on. Their principal focus is on using the organization's resources effectively. Towards this end, work teams are highly empowered.

Problem-Solving Teams These are temporary teams established to attack specific problems in the work place as illustrated in the opening case to this chapter. After solving the problems, the team is usually disbanded, allowing members to return to their normal work. Problem solving teams are often cross-functional, meaning that team members come from different functional areas. These teams generally offer recommendations for others to implement.

Management Teams These consist of managers from various areas and coordinate work teams. They are relatively permanent because their work does not end with the completion of a particular project or the resolution of a problem. Management teams must concentrate on the teams that have the most impact on overall corporate performance. The primary job of management teams is to coach and counsel other teams to be self managing by making decisions within the teams. The second most important task of management teams is to coordinate work between work teams that are interdependent in some manner.

Virtual Teams These are the teams that may never actually meet together in the same room-their activities take place on the computer via teleconferring and other electronic information systems. Engineers in the U.S., for example, can contact audibly and visually with counterparts all around the globe, sharing files via Internet, electronic mail, and other communication networks; all participants can look at the same drawing print, or specifications. Decisions are made much faster. With electronic communication systems, team members can move in or out of a team or a team discussion as the issues demand.

The core features of virtual teams are goals, people, and links. Goals are important to any team, but especially so to a virtual team. Clear, precise, and mutually agreed upon goals are the glue that holds a virtual team together. The roles of hierarchy, including the ability to hire and fire by a superior, and bureaucracy, including the use of rules and regulations to guide outcomes, are minimized in virtual teams.

IMPLEMENTING TEAMS IN ORGANIZATIONS

Creating teams is no easy task. Forming a team requires the right combination of skilled people and individuals who are willing to work together with others as a team. Another difficulty stems from the resistance in changing traditional organization structure to a team based structure. We present in this section several elements involved in converting a traditional structure into a team-based one.

Planning the Change Considerable analysis and planning should preceed implementation of teams. It involves a drastic departure from the traditional hierarchy and authority-and-control orientation. Obviously, significant planning, preparation, and training are necessary. The planning actually takes place in two phases: first, decision to have teams and second, implementing the decision to have such a structure.

Making the Decision Prior to making the decision, top management needs to establish the leadership for the change, develop a steering committee, conduct a feasibility study, and then decide to have the new structure. Leadership for the change is generally the CEO or any prominent person in the organization. The leader shall constitute a steering committee to help explore the organization's readiness to have team based structure. The committee shall comprise plant or division managers, union representatives, human resources representatives and operational level employees.

The steering committee shall conduct a feasibility study. After establishing the leadership, setting up the steering committee, and conducting a feasibility study, the decision to have team based structure is made.

Implementing the Decision Once the decision is made to change to a team based organization, much preparatory work needs to be done before implantation can begin. Preparation involves clarifying the objective, selecting the site for the first work teams, preparing the deign team, planning the delegation of authority, and drafting the preliminary plans.

Preparatory work being done, decision to have team based structure shall be implemented. Implemented is a long and difficult process, often taking two to five years. During this period, the teams go through atleast three phases.

In Phase 1, management must *create performance conditions* for the teams. This means providing to the teams all the needed materials and equipment to do the job. This step also implies that the teams consist of all personnel necessary to perform these tasks.

Phase 2, (form and build the team) involves atleast three things: (i) establish boundaries that is who is and who is not in the team; (ii) arrive at an agreement regarding the tasks to be performed; (iii) clarify the behaviours expected of each team member.

In providing *ongoing assistance stage (Phase -3),* attempts are made to eliminate team problems, if any; replenish or upgrade material resources; and replace members who leave the team.

TEAM ISSUES

Now that teams have been set up, managers face certain issues which need to be tackled if teams were to perform well and last long. The issues are : (i) team performance, (ii) teams and TQM, (iii) workforce diversity and teams, and (iv) reinvigorating mature teams (See Fig.21.3).

FIGURE 21-3
TEAM ISSUES

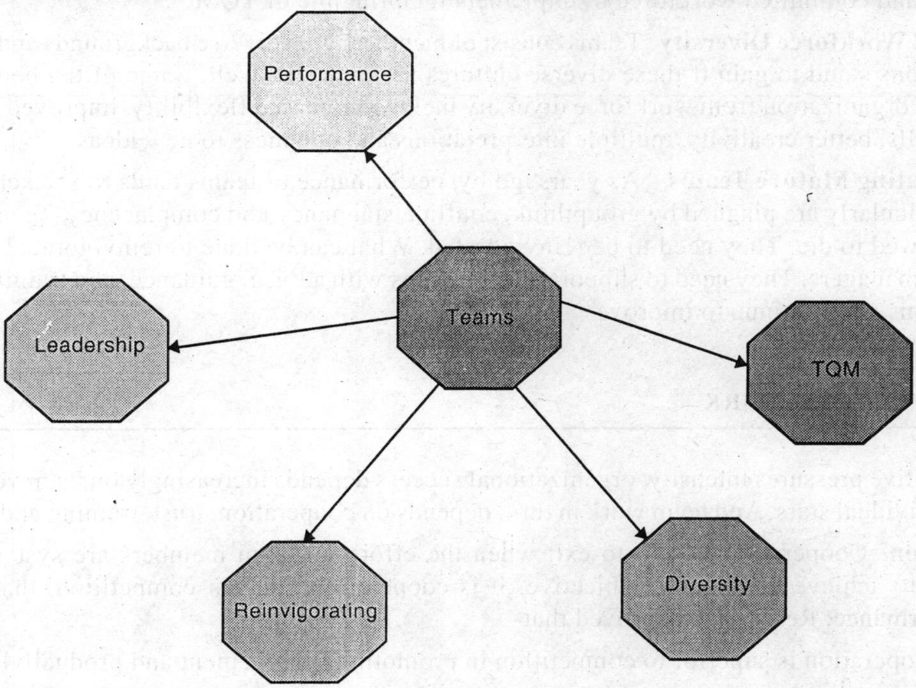

Team Performance Managers expect performance to improve suddenly once teams are constituted. This expectation is not realistic. It takes often a year for more teams to show results. In the meantime, management must take steps on the lines suggested in Table 21.1

TABLE 21-1
GUIDELINES TO ENHANCE TEAM PERFORMANCE

- Have a small team – membership not to exceed 12.
- Take care to ensure that teams comprise members with atleast three types of skill : technical skills, problem – solving and decision – making skills, and interpersonal skills.
- Let the teams have specific goals and develop commitment to realize the goals.
- Have proper leadership and structure for teams. Leadership and structure provide focus and direction.
- Don't allow members to hide inside a group and indulge in social loafing.
- Establish appropriate performance evaluation and suitable rewards system.
- Ensure the team members develop high mutual trust. High performance teams are characterized by high mutual trust.
- Establish demanding performance standards and provide direction.
- Create a sense of urgency in the first meeting.
- Set clear rules of behaviour.
- Regularly challenge the team with new projects or problems to solve.

Teams and TQM Management seeks to implement TQM through teams. The essence of TQM is process improvement. Employee involvement is basic for process improvement. Team offers highly motivated and committed workforce to implement the principle of TQM.

Teams and Workforce Diversity Teams consist of members with diverse backgrounds and cultures. Organizations stand to gain if these diverse cultures are managed well. Some of the benefits that result to an organization from workforce diversity include increased flexibility, improved problem-solving skills, better creativity, multiple interpretations and openness to new ideas.

Reinvigorating Mature Teams As years go by, performance of teams tends to slacken. Mature teams, particularly are plagued by groupthink, conflict, stagnancy and complacency. Teams should not be allowed to die. They need to be reinvigorated. What can be done to reinvigorate? Here lies the role of managers. They need to support mature teams with advice, guidance, and training so that mature teams can continue to improve.

Effective Teamwork

As competitive pressures intensity, organizational success depends increasingly on teamwork rather than on individual stars. And team work in turn, depends on cooperation, trust, training and rewards.

Cooperation Cooperation is said to exit when the efforts of team members are systematically integrated to achieve a collective objective. It is cooperation, but not competition, that ensures team performance. Research has proved that-

(i) Cooperation is superior to competition in promoting achievement and productivity.

(ii) Cooperation is superior to individualistic efforts in promoting achievement and productivity.

(iii) Cooperation without intergroup competition promotes higher achievement and productivity than cooperation with intergroup competition.[7]

Trust Trust has become a causality in recent years because of restructuring, downsizing, mergers and layoffs. Workers have lost trust in managements. Absence of trust affects team performance adversely.

How to build trust? For a start, either management or employees need to take initiative. Let one party trust to other – trust begets trust. Other measures for building trust are-

(i) Communication: Keep team members and employees informed by explaining policies and decisions and providing accurate feedback.

(ii) Support: Be available and approachable. Provide help, advice, coaching, and support for team member's ideas.

(iii) Respect: Delegation, in the form of real decision making authority, is the most important expression of managerial respect.

(iv) Fairness: Be quick to give credit and recognition to those who deserve it. Make sure all performance appraisals and evaluations are objective and impartial.

(v) Predictability: Be predictable and consistent in daily affairs. Keep both expressed and implied promises.

(vi) Competence: Enhance your creditability by demonstrating good business sense, technical ability, and professionalism.[8]

(vii) Leadership in Teams: A leader's role in teams is two fold. One is facilitating the functioning of the team, and the other is managing the external boundary of the teams.

The facilitating function of team leader comprises trouble shooting and resource molsilization. As a trouble shooter, he or she resolves conflict in the team. As resource mobilizer, the leader provides promised inputs to the team and coaches team members to improve their work performance. With regard to managing the boundary the leader maintains contacts with higher ups in the organisation, other teams within the organisation, customers and suppliers, so as to enable teams to function smoothly and effetively.

Training Training is necessary because team members must know how to function effectively as a team, in addition to possessing individual task related skills and abilities. Depending on the type and purpose of the team, training may be needed in problem solving skills, creative thinking, or interpersonal skills. At the very least, team members must be well versed in the company philosophy regarding teams, the team mission, and new roles and responsibilities individuals will have as a consequence of being part of the team.

Rewards The reward system in most organizations is individually based. That is, organizational members are rewarded based on evaluation of their individual performance. While the individual's contribution to team success is a legitimate part of the reward system, team success also should be considered. To the extent that teams perform well, they should be rewarded. There are a number of ways in which rewards may be allocated to teams. With problem solving teams for example, an incentive system is frequently used, wherein the team receives a percentage of the saving realized by the firm. How the rewards are distributed to individual team members is a separate issue.

Table 21.2 contains some more tips to make teams more effective.

TYPICAL TEAMS IN ORGANIZATIONS

Typical teams found in organizations are quality circles and self-managed teams. We purpose to describe these in detail.

Quality Circles Quality circles (QCs)are small teams of employees (usually 7 to 10) who meet for a few hours each week to identify quality and productive problems, propose solutions to management

TABLE 21-2

TIPS FOR EFFECTIVE TEAMS

(a) Make the team highly focused.
(b) Handle conflict directly and be willing to compromise.
(c) Actively participate, and encourage others to do the same.
(d) Keep sensitive issues private.
(e) Communicate openly and positively
(f) Take time to establish operating guidelines and clarify expectations.
(g) Monitor what is going on with in the team.
(h) Work with underperformers to keep them in the flow of the project and prevent them from getting isolated.
(i) Energize the team when motivation is low by suggesting new ideas, humour or enthusiasm.
(j) Be supportive of your team members.

and monitor the implementation and consequences of these solutions in their work area. Usually, the employees are members of a work unit from the same department. Often, their supervisor serves as the circle leader, while a staff member is a facilitator who helps guide the circle through the problem solving process. The primary topics of discussion of most circles is issues related to quality, but they do consider other topics such as cost, safety and efficiency.

Managements facilitate QC programme through skills training and listening to periodic presentations and recommendations. Monetary rewards for suggestions are often awarded but not always. Infact, intrinsic motivation, derived from learning new skills and meaningful participation are the primary payoffs for QC volunteers.

Quality circles are credited with producing quick, concrete and impressive results when correctly implemented. Their advantages include the following: [9]

(i) Employees are involved in decision making. This privilege makes them acquire communication and analytical skills and improve efficiency at work place.

(ii) Saving cost ratios are generally higher than those achieved with other productivity-improvement programmes.

(iii) Because the programme is voluntary, employees and unions generally do not view them as another cost-saving effort.

(iv) Circle members enhance their chances of promotion to supervisory positions.

Started in Japan in the early 1960s, QCs have spread all over the world. In India too, they are being introduced in several firms, BHEL and BEL are only two names that come to one's memory. SKF, Mahindra and Mahindra, Alfa Laval and are other firms which have tired QCs.

Experience in Indian industries has been a mixed one. With Mahindra Jeeps Division (it has, 76 QCs), the experience has been favourable. Technical problems that had plagued the process since its inception were solved eight months after the first circle was formed. To several workers, accustomed to thinking of work as a mindless routine, what happens on the shop floor (through QCs) is a welcome relief. They feel confident of themselves and gain satisfaction that they are being recognised.

On the flip side it may be stated that employee representatives have viewed QCs as attempts to wean employees away from the unions. QCs give added power to the individual worker, not the union.

Yet another criticism, particularly early in the beginning, is that the QC programme stretches the volunteerism concept. When circles are just being formed, they require much time and effort, something employees might not be prepared for. Most QCs begin with a great deal of training in identifying work problems, applying statistics to track and evaluate quality, and work together in a group. This phase can be frustrating for employees who want to get to work on a particular problem straight away. For circles to succeed in the long run the management needs to show its commitment by implementing some of the suggestions of the circles and providing feedback on the disposition of all suggestions.

Table 21.3 shows the phase in the life of a QC and the problems encountered at each stage. Most QCs have a definite life cycle lasting from one to there years. Few circles operate beyond this time, either because they run out of steam or face problems. However, QCs can be an excellent bridge between participative and non-participative management approaches.

TABLE 21-3

PHASES IN THE LIFE OF A QC PROGRAMME

Phase	Activity	Destructive Force
1. Start-up	Publicise, obtain funds and volunteers, train problem solving skills.	Low volunteer rate, inadequate funding, inability to learn group process and
2. Initial problem solving	Identify and solve problems.	Disagreement on problems
3. Presentation and approval of initial suggestions	Present and have initial suggestions accepted	Resistance by staff groups and middle management, poor presentation and suggestions because of limited knowledge.
4. Implementation of solutions	Relevant groups act on suggestions	Prohibitive, resistance by group that must implement.
5. Expansion and continued problem solving	Form new groups, old groups continue	Raised aspirations, lack of problems, expense of parallel organization, savings not realized, rewards wanted.
6. Decline	Fewer groups meet	Cynicism about programme. Burnout.

The QC programme failed in SKF and the company switched to continuous improvement approach. At Alfa Laval, the experience was similar. An earlier attempt at QC had failed. Under a changed management, workers who were sent off on a paid holiday prior to retrenchment, were brought back and redeployed. The fear that it could happen again made the union receptive to the management's new programs. This time, Alfa's QC movement became the best example of shop-floor participation in the Pimpri-Chinchwad industrial belt.[(10)]

Self-Managed Teams Also called empowered teams, autonomous work groups, self-managed teams are catching on everywhere, India being no exception. Companies as diverse as Titan, Reliance, ABB, Tata Information Systems (TISL), GE Plastics India and Phillips are empowering employees-both frontline as well as production staff. Wipro had 29 such teams and their number was expected to go upto 130. Wipro Infotech had 10 such teams and the plan was to hike them to around 40 to 50.[11]

What are these self-managed teams? These are employee groups given a high degree of decision making responsibility and behaviour control for completing their work. Usually, the team is empowered or given the responsibility for producing the entire product or service. A team essentially replaces the boss by taking over responsibilities for scheduling, hiring, ordering, and firing.[12]

Empowered teams have some similarities to QCs because they are based on employee participation, but they also have differences. For example, autonomous work groups usually elect an internal leader who also serves as full time member. Management may appoint an external leader or coordinator. The external leader serves primarily as a facilitator rather than as a supervisor. He or she may assist the team members in receiving feedback on the quality and quantity of their performance as well as make any structural changes in the work design. The coordinator is also responsible for helping the team acquire the needed resources and technical assistance.

Self directed teams will have the following characteristics:[13]

- They are empowered to share the management and leadership functions.
- They plan, control and improve their own work processes.
- They set their own goals and inspect their own work.
- They often create their own schedules and review their performance as a group.
- They may prepare their own budgets and coordinate their work with other departments.
- They usually order materials, keep inventories and deal with suppliers.
- They are frequently responsible for acquiring any new training they might need.
- They may hire their own replacement or assume responsibility for disciplining their own members.
- They, and not others outside the team, take responsibility for the quality of their products or services.

Empowered teams are facilitated by several factors as shown in Fig 21.4. As shown in the Figure, organizational values, human resource systems, and organizational structure and job design lead to employee empowerment which in turn result in continuous improvement actions.

FIGURE 21-4
FACILITATORS OF EMPOWERED TEAMS

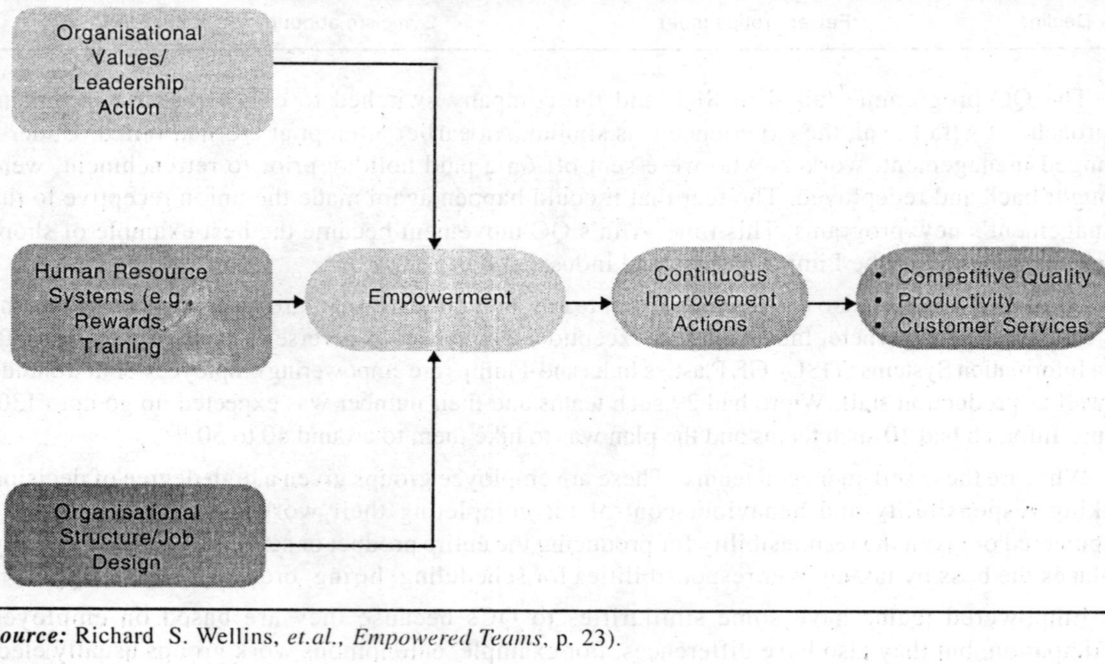

(***Source:*** Richard S. Wellins, *et.al.*, *Empowered Teams*, p. 23).

CAN GROUPS BECOME TEAMS ?

We stated in the previous chapter that groups are inevitable in organizations because they perform several useful functions. But it is not groups that are important, now-a-days the trend is to have teams. Can groups be converted into teams? The answer is 'yes'.

The positive assertion to the above question stems from the fact that groups fail and fail often. One of the attributes of groups is their potential synergism. Synergism is the cooperative action of discrete entities so that the total effect is greater than the sum of the effects taken independently. In the case of groups, discrete entities are individual members of the group. Synergistic groups can create something that is more than the sum total of that produced by individuals. Thus[14]

Potential group performance = Individual performance + Synergy.

But actual performance will be often different. Actual performance is the one shown below:

Actual group performance = Potential performance - Faulty group process.

What this suggests is that synergistic gains from groups may be offset by operating failures within the group. If there is inter-group conflict, communication breakdowns, insufficient interaction, political maneuvering, lack of role clarity, inept leadership, or any number of other counter productive conditions, group performance tends to be negatively affected. No groups operate smoothly and effectively all the time.[15]

When groups fail, teams tend to take over. This does not mean that teams become relevant for wrong reason.

Teams result in increased productivity, reduced errors, cost savings, increased customer satisfaction and reduced turnover. Japanese economic prosperity is, in part, attributed to teams in her organizations. The phenomenal success of Microsoft is attributed to its extensive use of research and development teams.

It is not only organizations that benefit from work teams. Employees report that team membership provides them with more autonomy, flexibility, skill variety, training opportunities, satisfaction, morale, and financial benefits (e.g., group based bonuses). But the benefits do not accrue overnight. It often takes up to two years for some of the positive effects of teams to materialize. Managers need to be patient in expecting results and should guarantee job security to enable employees to feel comfortable taking risks and being creative and innovative.

QUESTIONS

1. What is a team? What are its types?
2. Can groups become teams ?
3. How to make teams more effective ?
4. Think of a successful sport or project team of which you are or have been a member. What key characteristics made it so effective ?
5. Would you like to work in a self – managed team ? Explain.

Case

Teams Enhance Quality at DaimlerChrysler Assembly Plant

On November 17, 1998, Daimler Benz and Chrysler finalized a $35 billion transatlantic merger. The merger made sense economically and provided a number of advantages for both of the previous companies. Chrysler wanted to improve its image as a maker of luxury automobiles; Daimler wanted to improve the marketability of its cars and expand into the light truck segment. Although Daimler Benz has always been known for its German craftsmanship and meticulous attention to detail, Chrysler added its expertise in using the platform team as a method of putting cars together. The platform team is one thing that did not change with the merger and continues to add considerable value to the production process as its application is expanded.

Actually, the platform team, long the standard way of putting cars together among Japanese automakers, was officially embraced by Chrysler executives several years ago as superior to the compartmentalized functional system still prevalent throughout the U.S. auto industry. Simplification is the goal of the platform team. When designers, product engineers, manufacturing engineers, purchasing agents, suppliers, and line workers make decisions together from the beginning, it save time, money, and untold hassles when the car finally goes into production.

A typical example of how teams can contribute to productivity occurred at Chrysler's assembly plant at Brampton, Ontario. Don Callahan and Brian Large huddled around a half-built Dodge intrepid, trying to figure out why the warning light on the instrument panel was on even through the air conditioner was working fine. Both men were members of the LH car's "platform team": Callahan, an hourly assembly-line worker, and Large, a product engineer, have worked together since the intrepid prototype was first built. In a few hours, they managed to fix the electrical glitch and send their car down the line.

If Chrysler had developed the LH like most U.S vehicles have been developed, Callahan wouldn't have contacted Large about the problem because the two would never have met. And the early production cars would likely have reached customers' hands with the electrical system still on the fritz. But the workers, designers, and engineers who collaborated in developing the first test batch of cars thrashed out the final stages of vehicle development process that sought to blur the traditional lines between people in different functional work units – all in the name of building a better car.

The team approach paid off in a number of ways for former Chrysler. The LH team, for example, shaved a full year off Chrysler's average vehicle-development cycle, historically 4 ¼ years. This was an attractive lure for executives at Daimler who sensed that they could learn a lot from Chrysler about how to get a wider variety of cars to market more quickly. And team members did it with 40 percent fewer engineers than a typical product program would use. At a price tag of just over $1 billion, the LH budget came in well under those of two other well-known team efforts, Ford's $3 billion Taurus/Sable and GM's $3.5 billion Saturn.

Questions

1. How did teams benefit Chrysler ?
2. Relate the principles you have learn about teams in this chapter to this case.[16]

References

1. P.F. Drucker, "The Coming of the New Organization", *Harvard Business Review*, Jan-Feb, 1988, Pp. 45-53.
2. Katzenbach and Smith, *The Wisdom of Teams*, p. 45.
3. Moorhead and Griffin, *Organizational Behaviour*, Jaico, 1999, p. 325.

4. Richard S. Wellins, *et.al., Empowered Teams*, Jossey Bass Publishers, 1991, P.3.
5. Greenberg and Baron, *Behaviour in Organizations*, PHI, 1999, P. 298.
6. Suzanne C. de Janasz, *et.al.*, *Interpersonal Skills in Organizations*, McGraw-Hill, 2002, p. 312.
7. Eugene Mckenna, *Business Psychology and Organisational Behaviour,* Psychology Press, 2000, p. 348.
8. Robert Krietner and Angelo Kinicki, *Organizational Behaviour*, Irwin Mc Graw-Hill, 1998, p. 400.
9. Ibid, p. 402.
10. Aswathappa K., *Human Resource And Personnel Management*, TMH, 1999, p. 400.
11. *Business India*, April 26 - May, 9, 1993.
12. *Business World*, July 13-26, 1994.
13. H. John Bernardin and Joyce E.A. Russell, *Human Resource Management*, Irwin Mcgraw-Hill, 1998, p. 349.
14. Richard S.Wellins, *et.al., op.cit,* p.4.
15. John M. Ivancevich and Michael T. Matteson, *Organizational Behaviour and Management*, Irwin McGraw-Hill, 1999, p. 316.
16. Curtis W.Cook and Philip L.Hunsaker, *Managing Organisational Behaviour,* McGraw-Hill, p.337.

CHAPTER

Twenty Two

Conflict and Negotiation

Learning Objectives

After reading this chapter you should understand –

1. The nature of Conflict.
2. The changing views of conflict.
3. The functional and dysfunctional conflict.
4. The process of conflict.
5. The different levels of conflict.
6. The sources of conflict.
7. The nature of Negotiation.

The very mention of the term 'Conflict' envisions fights, riots, or war. In fact, on virtually every day of every year one can find dozens of armed combat situations somewhere in the world. But these extreme situations represent only the most overt and violent expressions of conflict. During the typical workday, managers encounter more subtle and nonviolent types of opposition such as arguments, criticism, and disagreement. Conflict, like power and organizational politics, is an inevitable and often positive force in today's organizations. A study of conflict is, therefore, apt in OB. Hence this chapter.

Nature of Conflict

In simple words, conflict may be understood as collision or disagreement. The conflict may be within an individual when there is incompatibility between his or her own goals or events; may be between two individuals, when one does not see eye to eye with another, and in the process tries to block or frustrate the attempts of another; or between two groups in an organization.[1] Chung and Megginson define conflict as "the struggle between incompatible or opposing needs, wishes, ideas, interests, or people. Conflict arises when individuals or groups encounter goals that both parties cannot obtain satisfactorily."[2] Though intra-personal conflict is not made explicit in the definition, the first sentence implies intra-individuals conflict as well.

Conflict may be *cognitive* or *affective.* Cognitive conflict refers to differences in perspectives or judgements about issues. Affective conflict is emotional and directed at other people. Affective conflict is likely to be destructive because it can lead to anger, bitterness, goal displacement, and poor decisions. Cognitive conflict, on the other hand, can air legitimate differences of opinion and develop better ideas and solutions to problems. Conflict needs to be cognitive and not affective.

Semantics

In a discussion on the nature of conflict, it is customary to draw a distinction between conflict and competition, which are often mistakenly used interchangeably. Competition takes place when individuals or groups have incompatible goals but do not interfere with each other as they try to attain their respective goals. Conflict, on the other hand, occurs when individuals or groups have incompatible goals and they try to interfere with each other as they try to attain their respective goals.[3] Thus, in competition one will not try to frustrate the attempt of another, but in conflict, attempts of one are sought to be thwarted by the other. This difference is clearly illustrated in sports. Track events are examples of competition rather than conflict since each runner attempts to run faster than the others, but no one is allowed to trip or interfere with the other. On the other hand, the games of football, hockey and cricket involve both competition and conflict because each team acts directly to interface with the activities of the other.[4]

Changing Views of Conflict

Attitudes towards conflict in organizations have changed considerably in the last seventy years. Table 22.1 brings out the contrast between the traditional and current views of conflicts.

The traditional view, relevant during the 1930s and 1940s, was that conflict in organizations was unnecessary and harmful. Early managers and management writers generally believed that the appearance of conflict was a clear signal that there was something wrong with the organizations.

TABLE 22-1
TRADITIONAL AND CURRENT VIEWS OF CONFLICT

Traditional View	*Current View*
1. Conflict is avoidable.	1. Conflict is inevitable.
2. Conflict is caused by management error in designing organizations or by trouble makers.	2. Conflict arises from many causes, including organizational structure, unavoidable differences in goals, differences in perceptions and values of specialized personnel and so on.
3. Conflict disrupts the organization and prevents optimal performance.	3. Conflict contributes and detracts from organizational performance in varying degrees.
4. The task of the management is to eliminate conflict.	4. The task of the management is to manage the level of conflict and its resolution for optimal organizational performance.
5. Optimal organizational performance requires the removal of conflict.	5. Optimal organizational performance requires a moderate level of conflict.

They thought that conflict would develop only if managers failed to apply sound management principles in directing the organizations or if managers failed to communicate to employees the common interests that bind management and employees together. If these failures were corrected, according to the traditional view, organizations should operate smoothly. For example, Taylor believed that if the principles of Scientific Management were applied, the age-old conflict between the management and labour would disappear.

The traditional view of conflict started to change as organizational behaviour researchers and management writers began to identify causes of organizational conflict independent of management errors and as the advantages of effectively managed conflict started to be recognised. The current view, also called the interactionist view, is that conflict in organizations is inevitable and even necessary, no matter how organizations are designed and operated. This view still suggests that much conflict is, in fact, dysfunctional; it can harm individuals and impede the attainment of organizational goals. But some conflicts can also be functional – because it may make organizations more effective. Conflict can lead to search for solutions. Thus, it is an instrument of organizational innovation and change.[5]

Functional and Dysfunctional Conflict

Functional conflict refers to confrontation between two ideas, goals and parties that improve employees and the organization's performance. Well managed conflict helps workers anticipate and solve problems, feel confident, strengthen their relationships, and be committed to the organization. Constructive conflict is crucial for effictive functioning of organizations. Specifically, potential benefits of conflict are the following:[6]

1. Conflict increases awareness of what problems exist, who is involved, and how to solve the problem.
2. Conflict motivates organizational members to consider problems. They are energized and psychologically focused on the problems and motivated to put plans into action.
3. Conflict promotes change. Persons are more aware of injustices, inefficiencies, and frustrations, and see the need to correct them.

4. Conflict enhances morale and cohesion. Organizational members deal with and clear up their frustrations and resentments. They conclude that their relationships are strong enough to withstand stress and to handle difficulties. They also learn about each other's needs, styles and values through conflict.
5. High quality decisions result when persons express their opposing views and perspectives. They share their information and check each other's reasoning to develop new decisions.
6. Conflict stimulates interest and creativity. Being in conflict often sparks curiosity and stimulates viewing problems from several perspectives and combining the best of these positions to form a creative solution. Conflict is exciting as peoples learn about what makes them and others angry, frustrated and willing to fight.
7. Conflict adds to the forum of working with others when not taken seriously. Many people find conflict enjoyable to competitive sports, games, movies, plays, books, and eve teasing.
8. Conflict provides a forum for all members of the organization to be self - critical, and to be critical of the organization as a whole.

There is a close relationship between conflict and organizational performance (See Fig 22.1). Organizational performance is low when conflict is extremely high or extremely low, while moderate or optimum level of conflict contributes to high organizational performance. When the level of conflict is low, such as at point A on the curve, performance suffers because of a lack of arousal and stimulation. Employees find the environment too comfortable and they become complacent. When they are not challenged and confronted, they fail to search for environmental changes. On the other hand, when the level of conflict is extremely high (point C), performance suffers because of inadequate coordination and cooperation. The organization is in a state of chaos because of disruption and interference in critical activities. Individuals spend more time defending themselves or attacking others than accomplishing productive work.

FIGURE 22-1
RELATION BETWEEN ORGANISATIONAL PERFORMANCE AND CONFLICT

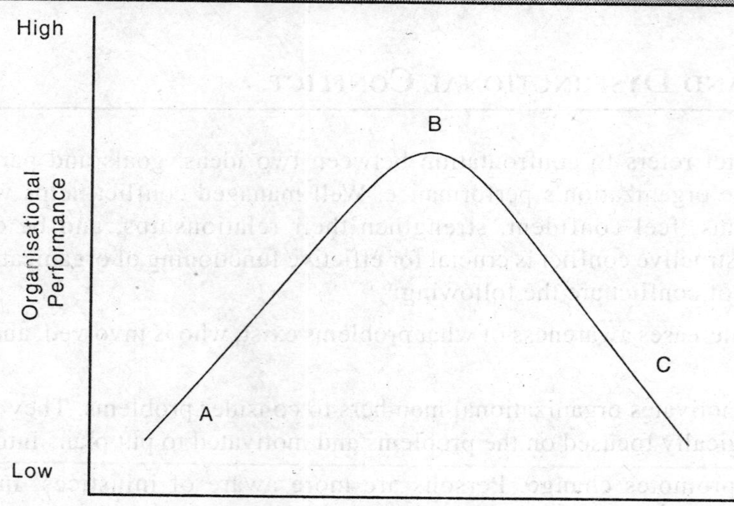

Maximum organizational performance occurs somewhere between these two extremes, where there is an optimal level of conflict. In this situation, at point B on the curve, there is sufficient conflict to stimulate new ideas and a creative search for solutions to problems.[7]

It is true that conflict is inevitable in organizations and also desirable. But without and effective means for handling it, conflict can tear relationships apart and interfere with the exchange of ideas, information and resources in groups and between departments. Dysfunctional conflict hinders and prevents organizational goals from being achieved. (Also see Table 22.2)

TABLE 22-2

POSITIVE AND NEGATIVE CONFLICT

Positive	*Negative*
• Increased involvement	• Unresolved anger
• Increased cohesion	• Personality clashes
• Increased innovation and creativity	• Less self-esteem
• Personal growth and change	• Inefficiency
• Clarification of key issues	• Diversion of energy from work
• Organizational vibrancy	• Psychological well being threatened
• Individual and group identities	• Wastage of resources
	• Negative climate
	• Group cohesion disrupted.

FIGURE 22-2

STAGES OF CONFLICT

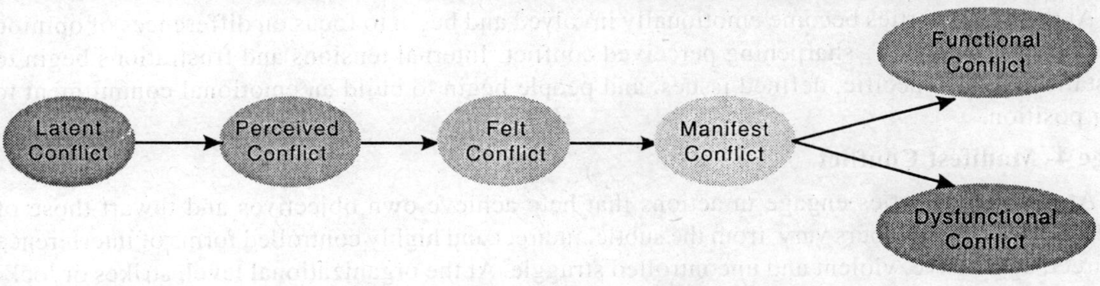

THE PROCESS OF CONFLICT

The final aspect of the nature of conflict is its process. The process generally comprises five stages as shown in Fig 22.2.

Stage 1- Latent Conflict

When two or more parties need each other to achieve desired objectives, there is potential for conflict. Other antecedents (see Table 22.3) of conflict, are interdependence, different goals, and ambiguity of responsibility. They do not automatically create conflict, when they exist - they make it possible. Latent conflict often arises when a change occurs. Conflict is likely to be caused by a budget cutback, a change in organizational direction, a change in personal goals or the assignment of a new project to an already overloaded team.

TABLE 22-3

ANTECEDENTS OF CONFLICT

- Incompatible personalities or value systems
- Overlapping or unclear job boundaries
- Competition for limited resources
- Inadequate communication
- Interdependent tasks
- Organisational complexity (conflict tends to incrase as the number of hierarchical layers and specialised tasks increase)
- Unreasonable or unclear policies, standards, or rules
- Unreasonable deadline or extreme time pressure
- Collective decision making (the greater the number of people participating in a decision, the greater the potential for conflict)
- Decision making by consensus
- Unmet expectations (employees who have unrealistic expectations about job assisgnments, pay, or promotions are more prone to conflict)
- Unresolved or suppressed conflict

(***Source:*** Robert Krietner and Angelo Kinick, *Organisational Behaviour*, McGraw-Hill, 1998, p.337)

Stage2- Perceived Conflict

This is the stage at which members become aware of a problem. Incompatibility of needs is perceived and tension begins as the parties begin to worry about what will happen. But no party feels that it is being overtly threatened.

Stage 3- Felt Conflict

At this stage parties become emotionally involved and begin to focus on differences of opinion and opposing interests - sharpening perceived conflict. Internal tensions and frustrations begin to crystalise around specific, defined issues, and people begin to build an emotional commitment to their position.

Stage 4- Manifest Conflict

At this stage parties engage in actions that help achieve own objectives and thwart those of others. Conflict behaviours vary from the subtle, indirect and highly controlled forms of interference to direct, aggressive, violent and uncontrolled struggle. At the organizational level, strikes or lock-outs are the result.

Stage 5- Conflict Outcome

The conflict finally results in an outcome which may be functional or dysfunctional. If handled well, the result is functional conflict. If mishandled, the consequences is dysfunctional conflict (See also Table 22.2). As conflict proceeds through the stages, resolution becomes more difficult. The parties become more locked into their positions and more convinced that the conflict is win-lose situation. It is usually easier to achieve win-win outcomes when the conflict is recognised early before frustration and negative feelings set in.[8]

Levels of Conflict

There are four levels of conflict in organizational life: (See Fig 22.3)

FIGURE 22-3
LEVELS AND SOURCES OF CONFLICT

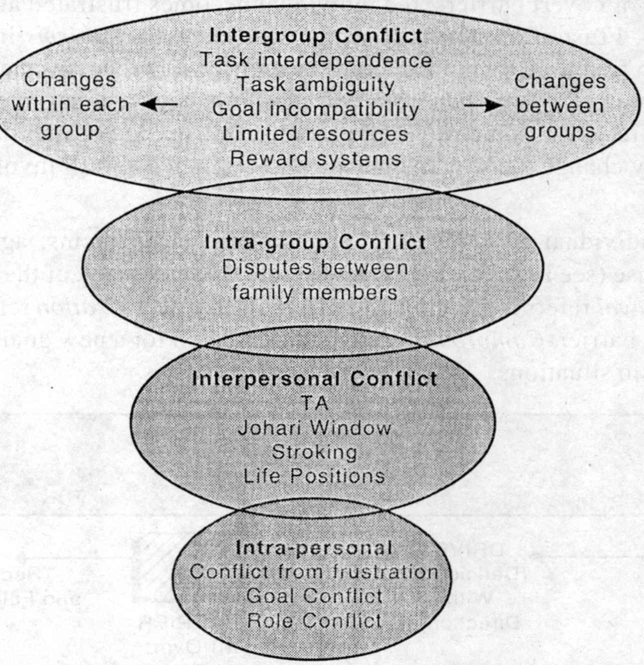

1. Intra-individual conflict
2. Inter-individual conflict
3. Intra-group conflict
4. Inter-group conflict

The causes for each level of conflict are analysed in the paragraphs that follow. The strategies to resolve these conflicts are covered in the later part of this chapter.

INTRA-INDIVIDUAL CONFLICT

This refers to conflict with in an individual. Intra-individual conflict arises from frustration, numerous roles which demand equal attention but is not always possible to devote, goals having both negative an positive aspects, cognitive dissonances, and neurotic tendencies.

Conflict from frustration Frustration occurs when a motivated drive is blocked before a person reaches a desired goal. Fig 22.4 illustrates the way frustration occurs.

An individual driven by an inner state of deficiency engages himself or herself in some action to fulfil the deficiency. But his or her attempts to reach the goal are checked by barriers which may be overt (external) or covert (internal). External barriers include floods, power failures and break-down of transportation. These are non-social in nature. There are external barriers which are social - they are placed by others in the way of reaching one's goals. Examples of social barriers are: parents forcing a child to sit on the toilet, making him refrain from sex play, making him stay in the room, or denying him the pleasure of watching television.[9]

Internal barriers are: personal limitations and disabilities which thwart one's aspirations. Weakness, physical deformities, lack of skill, or low intelligence may stand in the way of achievement. Internal barriers are more lasting than external ones.

Blocked by overt or covert barriers, the individual becomes frustrated as he or she is unable to reach his or her goal. Frustration normally triggers *defence mechanisms* in the person. Defence mechanisms (the term first used by Freud) refer to unconscious processes that protect an individual from anxiety. They protect him or her from external threats or against internal anxiety arousing impulses by distoring reality in some way. Defence mechanisms do not alter the objective conditions of danger, they simply change the way the person perceives it. They all involve an element of self-deception.[10]

The frustrated individual adopts any of four defence mechanisms: aggression, withdrawal, fixation, or compromise (see Fig. 22.4). *Aggression* refers to the attack of the barriers, physically or symbolically. *Withdrawal* refers to backing away from the barrier. *Fixation* refers to the continuation of efforts to break the barrier. *Compromise* refers to the search for a new goal. Conflict occurs in all the defence mechanism situations.

FIGURE 22-4
FRUSTRATION MODEL

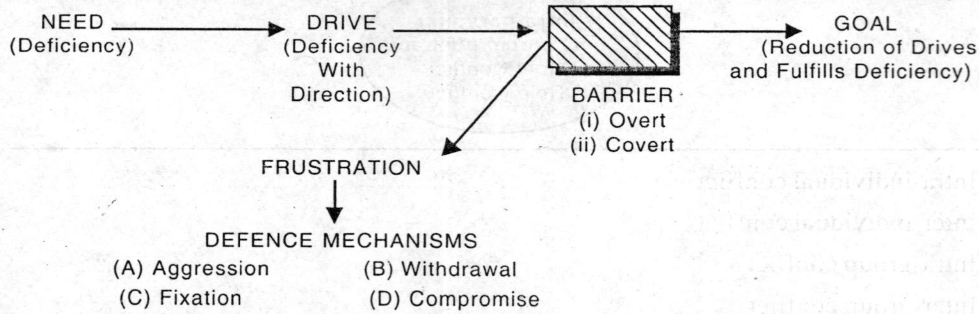

(***Source:*** Fred Luthans, *op. cit.*, p.398)

Goal conflict is more complex than conflict from frustration. Goal conflict occurs when the attainment of one goal excludes the possibility of attaining another. Four major forms of goal conflict may be distinguished:

1. Approach-approach conflict.
2. Approach-avoidance conflict,
3. Avoidance-avoidance conflict, and
4. Multiple approach-avoidance conflict.

Approach-Approach Conflict This conflict arises when the individual is caught between two or more positive but mutually exclusive goals. Approach-approach conflict is hardly a conflict at all, because whichever choice the individual makes, he or she will attain a positively valued outcome. But the problem arises when desirabilities of the choices are more or less equal. For instance, a psychological conflict occurs when a person is hungry and sleepy at the same time. In the social context, a conflict may arise when one wants to go to a political rally or a swimming party which are scheduled for the same night. The proverbial donkey is said to have starved to death because he stood half way between two piles of hay and could not decide which to choose. Actually, neither people nor donkeys starve to death merely because they are in conflict between two positive goals. Such a conflict is easily resolved by satisfying first one goal, then the other, for instance, eating first, then sleeping. Alternatively, this conflict is resolved by giving up one of the goals. Obviously, approach-approach conflict does not generate much anxiety.[11]

If we model the approach – approach situation in terms of the strength of each motive to reach a desired goal, as in Fig 22.5, we can see that a person should initially be caught between the two alternatives (position X in the graph). However, even a slight movement in the direction of one of the choices is enough to break the stalemate and lead to the selection of that particular option.

FIGURE 22-5
APPROACH-APPROACH CONFLICT

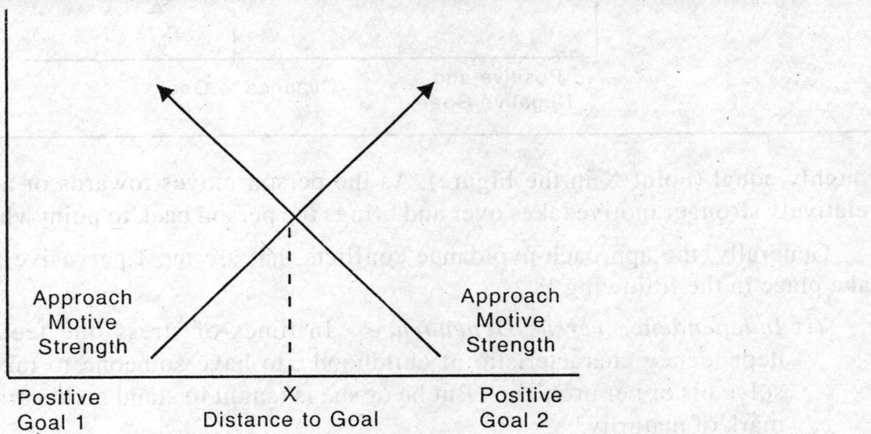

Unfortunately approach-approach conflict does not always end as stated above. Often, when the choice is made, "decision regret" may occur. The option not chosen now becomes more attractive, simply because it was not chosen. Decision regret may lead decision makers to reconsider the positive aspects of the chosen option and give them more weight to justify and validate the decisions made.

Approach-Avoidance Conflict This conflict occurs when an individual is simultaneously attracted to and repelled by a single goal object. For example, a person picks up the telephone receiver and begins to dial the number of someone from whom he or she wants to ask a favour, but fearing he or she may insult the other person or be turned down, he or she quickly puts the receiver back on the hook.[12]

Similarly, a young bride may have been brought up in an atmosphere where sexual activities were treated as ugly and sinful things. As a consequence, sexual matters have a negative valance for her. At the same time, her normal sexual drive, as well as other social values involved in marriage, provide marital situation with a positive valence. Now as she enters marriage, she experiences anxiety because she is caught between her sexual motives and the attitudes learned in her early environment.

Fig 22.6 diagrams the approach-avoidance conflict. If the motive to avoid the goal is stronger than the motive to approach it, the person will be caught where the strengths of the motives are

FIGURE - 22-6
APPROACH-AVOIDANCE CONFLICT

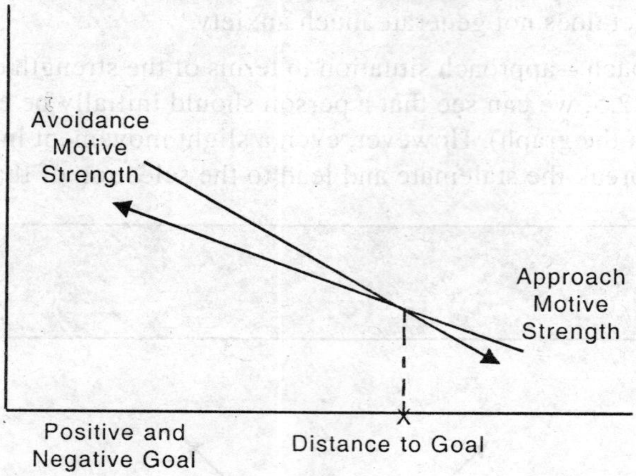

roughly equal (point X in the Figure). As the person moves towards or away from the goal, the relatively stronger motive takes over and brings the person back to point where he or she vacillates.

Generally, the approach-avoidance conflicts that are most pervasive and difficult to resolve take place in the following:[13]

(i) Independence versus Dependence In times of stress one feels like resorting to the dependency characteristic of childhood , to have someone to take care of a person and solve his or her problems. But he or she is taught to stand on his or her own feet which is a mark of maturity.

(ii) Co-operation versus Competition One is taught to compete with others and make a success of one's efforts. At the same time one is taught to cooperate and be helpful to others.

(iii) Impulsive Expression versus Moral Standards All societies place some degree of regulation upon impulse control. Sex and aggression are two areas in which one's impulses most frequently conflict with normal standards, and violation of these standards may generate strong feelings of guilt.

The approach-avoidance conflict is most relevant to the study of OB. Generally, organizational goals have both positive and negative aspects for organizational participants. For example, superior performance on the job and consequent accolades from management, contrasted with sacrifice of family and outside pursuits. Naturally, the organizational goal will arouse a great deal of conflict within a person and can actually cause the person to vacillate anxiously at the point where approach equals avoidance.

Avoidance-Avoidance Conflict This occurs when an individual is forced to choose between two mutually exclusive goals, each of which possesses unattractive qualities. One common instance of avoidance-avoidance conflict involves a choice between bearing the pain from a chronic disease such as ulcers and the fear of going to the hospital for surgery. The net result is that the person is caught between two options. Faced with an avoidance-avoidance conflict, most people will vacillate between the two options, without resolving the conflict (point X in Fig 22.7). In the context of an organization, avoidance–avoidance conflict may be exemplified by a worker who is caught in the

FIGURE 22-7
AVOIDANCE-AVOIDANCE CONFLICT

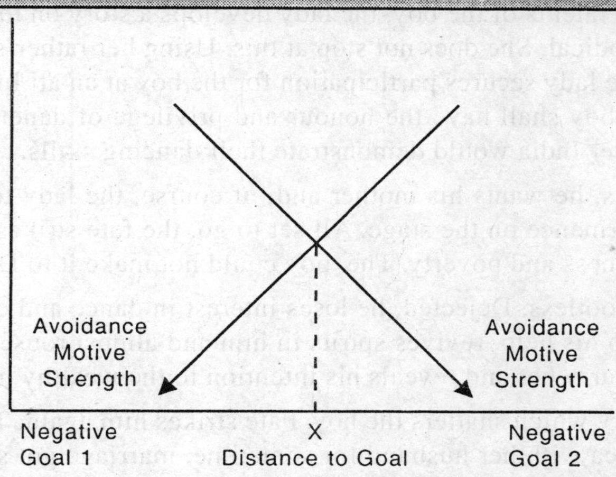

(***Source:*** Figs 22.6 – 22.7 are based on *Organizational Behaviour* by Robert P.Vecchio, P.475).

dilemma of bearing with the supervisor whom he (worker) detests most and quitting the organization and remaining jobless.

Similarly, a child must do his arithmetic or get a spanking. Or, a student must spend the next couple of days studying for an examination or face the possibility of failure. A man must work at a job he dislikes most , or be prepared to lose his income. Such conflicts typify the saying "between the devil and the deep sea".

Two kinds of behaviour are likely to be conspicuous in avoidance-avoidance conflicts. The first is *vacillation*. As is well known, the growth of a goal increases, the closer a person is to the goal. As the person approaches the negative goal, he or she finds it increasingly repelling. Consequently, the person tends to withdraw, but when the person does this, he or she comes closer to the other negative goal and finds it in turn increasing the negative valence.

A second feature of this kind of conflict is an *attempt to leave the conflict situation*. Theoretically, a person might escape avoidance-avoidance conflict by running away from it altogether. In practice, however, there are additional negative goals in the periphery of the situation and these prevent us form leaving. A child who does not want either to do his arithmetic or to get a spanking may think of running away from home. This has more negative consequences, so he does not do it. The person in avoidance-avoidance conflict may resort to other means to get relief from anxiety aroused by the conflict. The person may resort to daydreaming instead of facing upto the problem. A student may at times day dream instead of studying for the examination. A person may even conjure up an imaginary world, or recreate in his or her mind the carefree world of childhood in which no unpleasant tasks have to be performed.

Multiple approach-avoidance Conflict Often we are confronted with several possibilities for action, each having several desirable and undesirable features. Consider the following story.

Here is an young but highly talented boy who is keen on pursuing his career in the art of dance. The boy lost his father early and his mother, who is a daily wage earner, is maintaining not only the boy but is also spending on his professional pursuits. The poor woman too dreams of her son becoming a famous dancer one day.

The boy goes in a search a *guru* and finds one in a nearby town who agrees to teach the budding artiste without fee. While learning under the teacher, the boy happens to meet an young lady who is a photographer cum journalist. The lady is working on a story on South Indian dance for a reputed magazine. Impressed by the talents of the boy, the lady develops a story on the upcoming star and gets it published in the periodical. She does not stop at this. Using her father's clout (who is a rich and influential landlord), the lady secures participation for the boy at an all India dance festival to be organized at Delhi. The boy shall have the honour and privilege of dancing on a stage where eminent dancers from all over India would demonstrate their dancing skills.

Overwhelmed the boy is, he wants his mother and, of course, the lady to accompany him to Delhi and witness his performance on the stage. All set to go, the fate strikes the boy very badly. The boy's mother dies of illness and poverty. The boy could not make it to Delhi.

The boy finds himself rootless. Dejected, he loses interest in dance and everything in life. At this time, the lady comes to his help, revives spirits in him and almost rouses amoral instincts in him. The boy proposes to marry her and reveals his intention to the wealthy man.

The rich man tells a story which shatters the boy. Fate strikes him again. The lady was already married, she lived in America with her husband for sometime, marriage got soured and divorced, she returned to India. She is now active as a journalist. Will the boy marry a divorcee? Yes, says he. All set for the marriage- the former husband comes, regrets his past behaviour and entreats her to accompany him. All (including the boy) are pleased with this development. The lady flies to America. The boy missed yet another opportunity. Disheartened and frustrated, the boy takes to alcohol which kills him eventually.

This poignant story was recently filmed in a vernacular language and the movie became a box-office hit.

A conflict of this type, in which two alternatives - both involving positive and negative features– is referred to as a double approach-avoidance conflict. Dancing at Delhi would have been a breakthrough in the life of the boy, but his mother's death snatched the opportunity from him. Marriage with the damsel would have turned the boy's life for better, but it did not.

Role Conflict The final reason for intra-personal conflict is the need of an individual to play several roles simultaneously but finding time and resources inadequate to do so. For example, it is not uncommon for an adult middle class male to be simultaneously playing the roles of husband, father, son to elderly parents, worker or manager, student (executive MBA programme), member of a social club and the like. Although all the roles which individuals bring into the organization are relevant to their behaviour in the study of OB, the organizational role is the most important. Roles such as assembly line worker, clerk, supervisor, sales person, engineer, systems analyst, department head, and chairman of the board often carry conflicting demands and expectations.[14] The classic example of an organizational role in constant conflict is that of the foreman. The foreman is generally a promotee from among workers. Till yesterday, the foreman was a part of workers. Today he finds himself in management cadre. The dilemma of the foreman becomes acute when there is a dispute between labour and management.

Cognitive Dissonance Cognitive dissonance can lead to intrapersonal conflict. Cognitive dissonance occurs when individuals recognise inconsistencies in their own thoughts and/or behaviours. Such inconsistencies are stressful and uncomfortable, leading to intrapersonal conflict. Employees seek to remove inconsistencies by changing thoughts and/or behaviours, or obtaining more information about the issue that is causing the dissonance. But cognitive dissonance, till it is removed, remains a source of conflict.

Neurotic Tendencies These are irrational personality mechanisms that an individual uses that create inner conflict. In turn, inner conflict often results in behaviours that lead to conflict with other people. One example of neurotic action is the excessive use of tight organizational controls (e.g., budgeting, monitoring systems) by neurotic managers, because they distrust people. Their excessive distrust and need to control triggers conflict with others, especially subordinates who come to feel micromanaged and distrusted. A common reaction to leaders with neurotic tendencies is either overt (open) or covert (hidden) aggression and hostility. Subordinates often try to settle the score and protect themselves from further abuse. These actions give the manager an even stronger sense of employee worthlessness. The manager's hostility and attempts to control and punish become even more vigorous.

INTER–PERSONAL CONFLICT

Inter-individual conflict occurs between two individuals in an organization. It arises mainly because of differences in perception, temperaments, personalities, values systems, socio-cultural factors, and role ambiguities. Transactional Analysis (TA), Johari Window, Stroking, and Life Positions seek to explain the phenomenon of inter-personal conflict.

Transactional Analysis When two people interact with each other there results a social transaction. Analysis of the social transactions is called Transactional Analysis(TA). A formal definition of TA is that it is "The study of moves people make in their dealings with each other and is based on the idea that people's interactions resemble moves in games." (15)

TA was introduced by Eric Berne and popularized by Thomas Harris in the 1960s. TA has found its acceptance everywhere because of several advantages associated with it. The advantages are:

(i) The bases of TA are simple to learn.

(ii) The validity of TA is demonstrable.

(iii) It provides a means for reducing the amount of bad feelings experienced by an individual.

(iv) It increases efficient use of time.

(v) Helps promote effective communication.

(vi) It is applicable at home as it is at work.

(vii) It reinforces and implements other management development activities, including communication, leadership, brainstorming, management by objective, job enrichment, conflict resolution, and the like.[16]

TA has certain limitations which are not to be ignored. They are:

(i) Few scientific studies of its outcome are available.

(ii) Ego states, basic to understand and utilize TA, are difficult to define (although easy to teach and demonstrate operationally).

(iii) If inappropriately applied, TA tends to encourage "amateur psychologising."

(iv) TA jargon may lead to more "cuteness" than insight into human encounter.

(v) It can be used as a put down, or a discount, in inter-personal relations.(17)

Ego States Basic to TA is the assumption that a person has three ego states, viz., parent, adult, and child.

The parent ego state represents the part of a person's personality that is authoritative, dogmatic, overprotective, controlling, nurturing, critical, and righteous. These characteristics are usually learnt from one's parents or other adults who guided one's early life experiences. The parent is, therefore, the "taught" ego state.

The adult ego state represents the mature, rational, and objective part of a person's personality. These characteristics are acquired as one matures into adolescence and adulthood.

The individual gathers relevant information, analyses it carefully, generates alternatives, and makes logical choices. The adult is the "thinking" ego state. In the adult state people do no act impulsively or in a domineering way. In dealing with other people the adult state is characterized by fairness and objectivity.

The child ego state represents the childish, dependent, and immature part of a person's personality. These characteristics grow out of one child hood experiences. Behaviours that are influenced by the ego state are laden with emotion, insubordination, joy or rebellion. Child is the "felt" ego state.

Social Transactions According to Berne, people interact with each other from the child, adult or parent ego state. Depending on the kinds of ego states involved, the interaction can be either complimentary, crossed to ulterior (See Fig 22.8)

FIGURE 22-8
COMPLIMENTARY, CROSSED AND ULTERIOR TRANSACTIONS

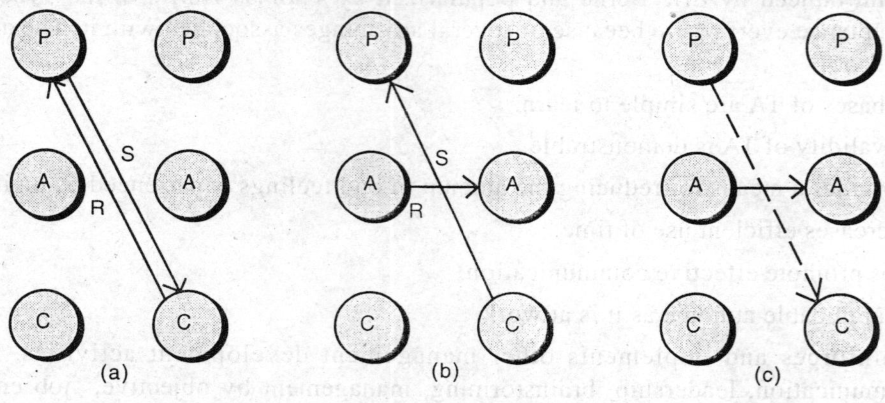

Key : P = Parent, A = Adult, C = Child, S = Stimulus, R = Response.

Complimentary transactions These occur when the message sent or the behaviour exhibited by one person's ego state receives the appropriate or expected response from the other person's ego state. As shown in Fig 22.8 (a) stimulus from the first person is under the influence of the parent ego state and the response from the other person is under the child ego state. There can be more complementary transactions than shown in Fig 22.8(a). For example, parent-parent, adult-adult, parent-adult, and child-child transactions are complimentary in nature. Since these transactions meet the needs and expectations of the initiators, communications flow freely, interactions will continue as inter-personal relations will improve. There is, therefore, no scope for conflict in complimentary transactions.

In *crossed transactions* the stimulus and response lines are not parallel [See Fig 22.8(b). Stimulus comes from the first person under the adult ego stage, but the response from the other person is under the child ego state. There are many more possible crossed transactions than there are complementary transactions. Since the receiver's response is not what was expected by the sender and does not satisfy the sender's needs, the sender sooner or later withdraws from the interaction with the receiver.

Crossed transactions are the source of much inter-personal conflict in an organization. The result can be hurt feelings and frustrations on the part of the parties involved and possible dysfunctional consequences for the organization.[18]

The most complex and subtle are the *ulterior transactions*. Like crossed transactions, ulterior transactions cause much damage to inter-personal relations. As shown in Fig 22.8(c), the ulterior transactions involve at least two ego states on the part of the first person. The individual may say one thing (as in adult) but mean something quite different(as a parent). Although there are many other possibilities besides the one shown in Fig 22.8(c), an example can be, where the boss says, " My door is always open, come in and we shall discuss the problem together and arrive at a solution" (adult state), when what he really means is, "Don't come to me with problems. You solve them yourself, that is what you are getting paid for." (parent state). Obviously, these ulterior transactions are the most difficult to identity and deal with.[19]

Johari Window Developed by Joseph Luft and Harry Ingham (thus the name Johari Window), this model is highly useful in analysing the causes for inter-personal conflict. The model is based on two assumptions:

1. Degree to which the person knows about himself or herself.
2. Degree to which the person is known to others.

The basic premise of the Jahari Window is that our personal and professional relationships can be greatly improved (conflict eliminated) through understanding ourselves in depth and choosing those aspects of self that can be shared with others. The authors believe that more we share of ourselves with others, the more we can develop inter-personal relationships.

The Johari Window is diagrammed in a grid that is divided into four regions, each representing one aspect of personality (See Fig.22.9).

FIGURE 22-9
JOHARI WINDOW

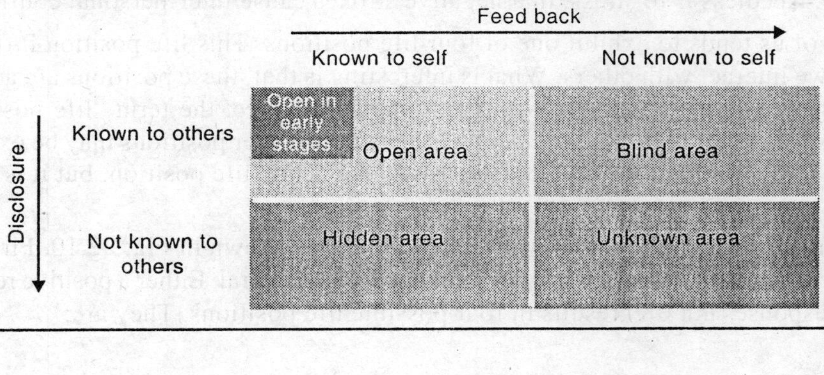

Open area This area consists of details known to self and to others. The information relates to the person's name, job, marital status, region from where the person has come and the like. In the early stages, the open area will be quite narrow. Generally, no individual shares all the details about self with others. As relationship grows, more information is shared. There is openness and compatability. Mutual understanding and friendship between people are the highest in this area. Obviously, there is little or no scope for conflict.

Hidden self This area comprises the knowledge about self but is hidden from others. The person does not share details about self with others lest others would think less of the person or use the information to their advantage. Not sharing hidden information can save the person in the short-run. Overtime, this lack of sharing can lead to distrust and miscommunication. As the person shares more information with others, the hidden area shrinks. It remains large if the person is more reserved. This area has potential for inter-personal conflict.

Blind area This area encompasses certain things about the person that are known to others but not to self. This happens because no one has told the person or he or she has blocked others from telling. For example, the person might have an unknown nervous habit of holding the table fast or wiggling a foot during meetings when he or she is feeling stressed or bored. When others point out such behaviours to the person, the blind area shrinks. The more the person understands strengths and weaknesses of self, and is open to others' views, the better manager he or she will become. As long as the blind area persists, there is scope for inter-personal conflict.

Undisclosed self This is potentially the most explosive situation. This area contains information unknown to self and unknown to others. The person does not know himself or herself because he or she lacks experience and exposure or is unable to recollect past events in life and articulate them effectively. Others are unaware of the details because they have not seen the person behaving in different situations or the person has never shared any details. The unknown window can also contain information that is forgotten or deliberately suppressed. This window can become smaller overtime as people grow, develop and learn. Till then, unknown area carries high potential for conflict.

Stroking Stroking refers to recognition of one's presence by others. When we interact with others, we expect others to say "Good morning" or some such gesture to indicate that we are being recognized. Strokes may be positive or negative. The stroke that makes one feel cheerful is a positive stroke. Words of recognition, affection, cuddling, pat on the back, and pleasant smile are some of the examples of positive strokes. Negative stroke on the other hand, makes one feel sad. Criticism, hatred and scold are examples of negative strokes. People need strokes, mainly positive ones, but not always. In the absence of positive strokes, people seek negative strokes, mainly because of guilt or lack of self-image. Needless is to stress, that negative strokes cause inter-personal conflict.

Life positions Each of us tends to exhibit one of four life positions. This life position influences our behaviour when we interact with others. What is interesting is that, these positions are acquired by us very early in our childhood and stay with us throughout, hence, the term "life positions." Although one life position tends to dominate a person's behaviour, other positions may be exhibited from time to time in specific situations. In others words, there is one life position, but it is not the only one ever taken.

Life position stems from a combination of two viewpoints, as shown in Fig. 22.10. First, how people view themselves? Second, how do they view other people in general. Either a positive response (OK) or a negative response (not 0K) results in four possible life positions. They are:

FIGURE 22-10
LIFE POSITIONS

Positive	I am OK You are not OK	I am OK You are OK
Negative	I am not OK You are not OK	I am not OK You are OK
	Negative	Positive

I am not OK - You are OK

I am not OK - You are not OK

I am OK - You are not OK

I am OK - You are OK

Of the four life positions, the ideal one is I am OK, You are OK. It shows healthy acceptance of self and others. This life position, surprisingly can be learnt. Here is good news and hope for society's well being. The other life positions are less psychologically mature and less effective. What is more, they have potential for interpersonal conflict.

Intra-group Conflict

Intragroup conflict refers to disputes among some or all of a group's members, which often affect the group's performance as happened in the opening case. Family run business can be especially prone to severe intragroup and other types of conflicts. These conflicts typically become more intense when an owner-founder approaches retirement, actually retires or dies. The way the two sons of the late Dhirubai Ambani are fighting on ownership and control of Reliance Industries is a typical example.

Rarely do family businesses make it to the second and third generations. The biggest obstacles to succession are the relationships among the family members who own the business and bear responsibility for keeping it alive for another generation. What determines whatever a family business soars or nosedives?. It depends, in large part, on the respect that family members give each other in the workplace, their willingness to take on roles at work different from those that they have at home, and their ability to manage conflict.

Inter-group Conflict

Inter-group conflict, also called organizational conflict, refers to the conflict between groups, departments, or-sections in an organization. Conflict between groups is frequent and highly visible. The reasons for inter-group conflict are many. The most important of them are explained below.

(i) Task Inter-dependence Task inter-dependence refers to the extent to which two departments depend on each other for assistance, information, compliance, or other coordinative acts in the performance of their respective tasks.[20] Task dependence may be pooled dependence, sequential dependence, or reciprocal dependence .

Pooled inter-dependence exists when two teams function with relative independence but their combined output contributes to the overall performance. *Sequential inter–dependence* occurs when one team's performance depends on another team's prior performance. In *reciprocal inter–dependence* teams exchange outputs, and hence are mutually inter-dependent in accomplishing their tasks. Fig 22.11 diagrams the three sources of task inter-dependence.

FIGURE 22-11
TYPES OF TASK INTERDEPENDENCE

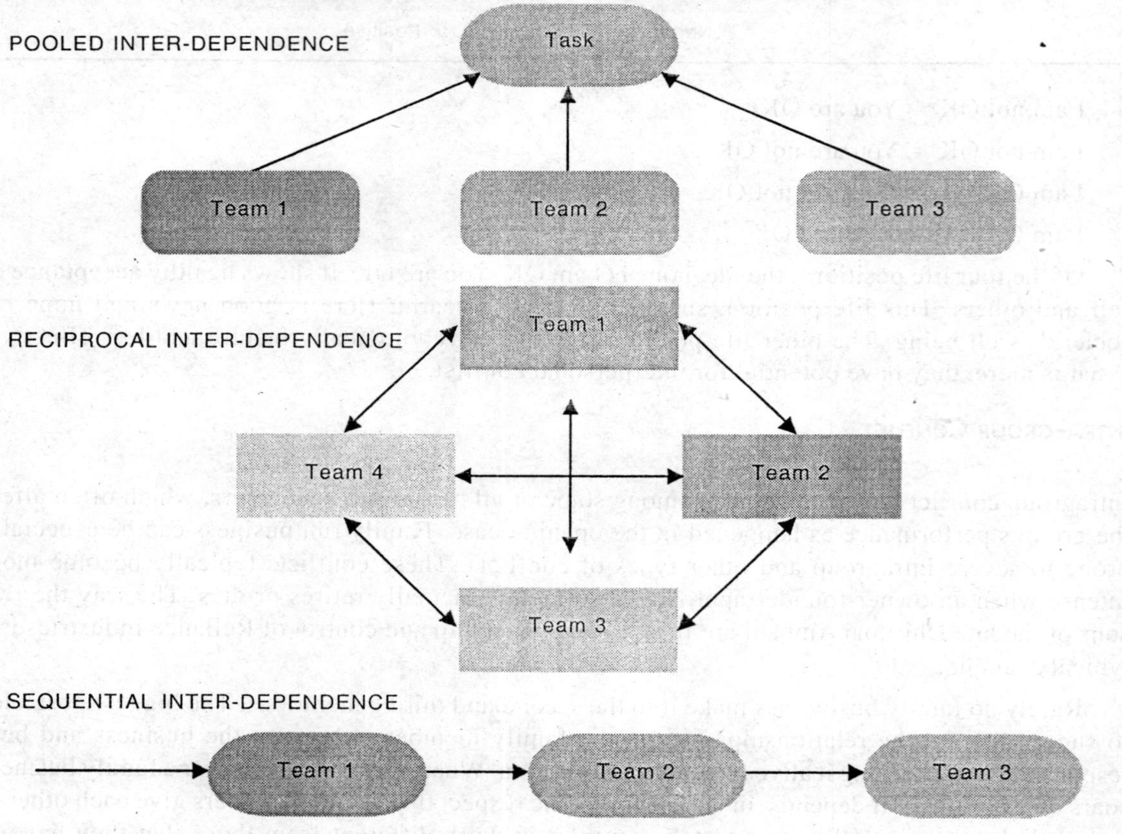

In all the three types of inter-dependence, conflict arises from differences in performance expectations. Conflict as a result of task inter-dependence will be worst when: (a) the more the activities of one group affect the performance of other groups; (b) the wider the range of activities in a group that are affected by another, and (c) the more unstructured the work flow is.[21]

(ii) Task Ambiguity Another important source of inter-group conflict arises when it is not clear which group is responsible for performing certain activities; "things fall between the cracks", and both groups are upset with each other. Task ambiguity arises when the organization is growing or its environment is changing fast. Task ambiguity can also occur from unstructured and non-directive leadership.[22]

(iii) **Goal Incompatibility** Goal incompatibility leads to inter-group conflict. However hard managers try to avoid incompatible goals for different organizational units, they do exist, leading to conflict. The main objective of the quality assurance department, for example, is to ensure uniform quality of all the units of output. This might clash with the production department which desires somehow to push through the units, minor deviations in quality notwithstanding.

(iv) **Competition for Limited Resources** Yet another source of inter-group conflict relates to competition for resources which are limited in their supply. These resources may be tangible such as money, materials, and other physical facilities, or they may be intangible, such as power, status, and prestige. Each department tries to secure a larger share in the resources, and this will result in conflict.

(v) **Competitive Reward Systems** Managers seems to believe that better performance can be achieved through competition, and this belief is reflected in their reward systems. Competition can indeed increase the level of performance in work situations where tasks can be performed independently. However, when tasks require high levels of inter-dependence, competition can hurt cooperation among members and work groups.(23) For example, conflict occurs when the personnel department is rewarded for achieving cost reduction or the production department is given an award for better industrial relations.

(vi) **Line and Staff** The traditional organizational structure which has line officers being assisted by staff officers at different levels has inherent potential for conflict. One reason for conflict lies in the background of line and staff personnel. The line manager, for example, the works manager, may either rise from the lower ranks and reach his position after some years of loyal service, or he may be technically qualified and may enter the industry straight from university. He is not a status keeper or an empire-builder, but is concerned with preserving his present status and authority within his own empire. He is more loyal to his profession than to his employers. He may see his future depending on mobility within the profession as opposed to internal promotion. He is more of an individualist, more sophisticated, and capable of better self-expression. The staff specialist is status conscious.

Their different backgrounds make line and staff officers look at each other with suspicion. A lineman looks upon the staff officer as a theorist, an academic and unrealistic. He resents the easy accessibility of the staff officer to the top management. The staff specialist view the line executives as a mere "Cog in the machine", incapable of thinking and discussing problems. He sees in the lineman a barrier to his pursuit of perfection. He feels that the lineman resists new ides and changes.

(vii) **Intra-personal and Inter-personal Conflict** Intra-personal and inter-personal sources of conflict discussed earlier are reasons for inter group conflict also.

Dynamics of Inter-group conflict Inter-group conflict will have its impact on operations, attitudes and behaviours of participants. There are intra-group and inter-group changes because of conflict.

Changes within each group

The changes that usually occur within a group because of inter-group conflict are:

(i) Group cohesiveness increases.

(ii) Loyalty to the group becomes more important.

(iii) The group becomes more task-oriented.

(iv) Leadership in the group becomes more autocratic and directive.

(v) Organizational structure becomes more rigid.

Changes between groups

Inter-group conflict will result in the following changes between groups:

(i) Groups become more antagonistic towards each other.

(ii) There are distortions of perception, both about one's own group and about the other group.

(iii) Interaction and communication between groups decrease.

(iv) Groups apply double standards, perceiving every act of the other group as bad, while remaining oblivious to one's own misdeeds.

CONFLICT RESOLUTION

Till now we have analysed the various causes for conflict. Strategies for resolving the conflict are considered here. There are separate strategies for resolving intra-personal, inter-personal and inter-group conflicts (See Fig 22.12)

FIGURE 22-12
STRATEGIES FOR RESOLVING CONFLICT

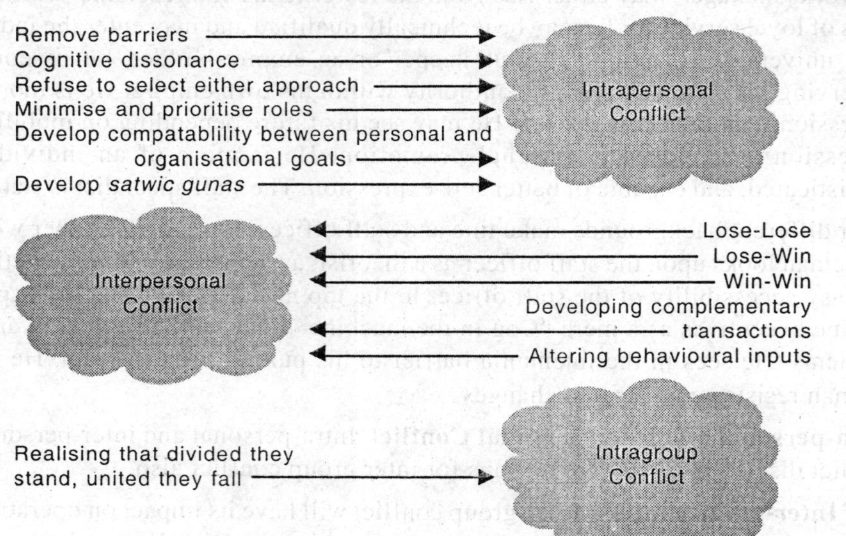

Strategies for Resolving Intra-personal conflict

As was pointed out earlier, intra-personal conflict arises from frustration, competing roles, or goals having positive or negative aspects. To the extent that conflict from frustration results out of blocked goal realization, removal of barriers (covert or overt) will help resolve this conflict. It is the manger's responsibility to clear his employee's path for advancement in his career.

Frustration is not always bad. It may contribute to improved performance. The frustrated individual may divert his attention from barriers towards his job and try to show better results. This is particularly true with an individual who has a self-concept that includes confidence in being able to do a job well. But this is no consolation for a manager to ignore the frustration of an employee. If conflict from frustration is not resolved for long, the manger will be running the risk of losing the services of a competent and sincere employee.

Goal conflict, as was mentioned earlier, has three main dimensions: approach- approach conflict, approach-avoidance conflict, and avoidance-avoidance conflict. Of the three, approach-approach conflict has the least impact on OB. The manager's involvement is not needed to resolve the conflict. It is best resolved by the employee himself or herself. The well-known theory of *cognitive dissonance* helps the individual resolve the approach-approach conflict. In simple terms, dissonance is the state of psychological discomfort or conflict created in people when they are faced with two or more goals or alternatives to a decision. Although these alternatives occur together, they do not belong or fit together. The theory states that the person experiencing dissonance will be highly motivated to reduce or eliminate it and will actively avoid situations and information which would increase it.

Approach-avoidance conflict can be resolved by refusing to select either approach (positive aspect) or avoidance (negative aspect) choice. Referring to the example already quoted, the person may decide not to go near the telephone to dial a number for some favour. This will prevent him or her from being exposed to the conflict situation. But an organizational member cannot avoid the conflict situation. He or she is forced to make a decision, and is, therefore, exposed to conflict. His or her conflict too can be resolved in the same way as cognitive dissonance. Having decided either way (approach or avoidance) the individual may defend the decision. The manager has a responsibility to help the individual defend his or her choice.

Avoidance-avoidance conflict may be resolved by examining and solving the problems causing the conflict. Reverting to the examples quoted earlier, the patient may decide to undergo surgery if that can cure him or her of his or her illness. He or she will be able to make decision upon this course of action if he or she can understand the illness and the causes for it. Similarly, the worker may try to understand the reasons why he or she detests his or her boss. An understanding of the reasons may help him or her overcome any prejudice he or she has developed against his or her superior. Sound counselling from the manager will be highly useful to the affected worker.

Role conflict can be resolved by minimizing the number of roles and fixing priorities for them. Once priorities are determined, there must be no overlapping of roles.

Much of the intra-personal conflict in an organizational member can be resolved by developing compatibility between his or her personal and organizational goals. A realization that he or she is working for the organization and not for the mangers will help him or her regain his or her balance and remain cool, irritants and hassles notwithstanding.

The best solution for intra-personal conflict is to look to Hindu Philosophy and learn a valuable lesson from it. According to the philosophy, an individual is composed of three *gunas* or psychogenic substances. They are: *sattwa, rajas, and tamas*. Roughly translated into English, these three gunas convey the following meanings:

Sattwa Purity, serenity, poise, calmness, discrimination, compassion, clarity, goodness, altruism, dispassion, contentment, etc., or in sum *illumination*.

Rajas Love of fame, passion, lust, strife, impatience, jealousy, pride, display of power, etc., or in sum *movement*.

Tamas Anger, pride, ignorance, stolidity, offering resistance, inertia, forgetfulness, confusion, darkness, brutality, etc., or in sum *obstruction*.

It is essential that one should develop *satwic guna* in oneself, be it the manger or the managed. One can develop *satwic* quality by reading holy scripts, regular prayers, moving with pious people, and leading a disciplined life. Unfortunately, modern organizations are filled with people who are imbedded with *rajasic* or *tamasic* qualities. Hence, the absence of harmonious industrial relations.

Resolving Inter-personal Conflict

The strategies suggested for reducing intra-personal conflict will be useful to resolve inter-personal conflict also. The additional approaches to resolve inter-personal conflict are: the lose-lose, win-lose and win-win strategies. TA, which was discussed earlier, will also be useful in overcoming the inter-personal conflict. Finally, inter-personal conflict can be resolved by changing behavioural inputs.

Lose-lose In a lose-lose approach to conflict resolution, both parties stand to lose. This approach can take several forms. One of the approaches is to take a compromise or middle ground to a dispute. A second approach is to pay-off one of the parties to a dispute. The payment may take the form of bribe. A third approach is to involve a third party as an arbitrator. The final approach is for both parties to resort to existing regulations or bureaucratic rules to resolve the conflict. Lose-lose strategy is sometimes the only one available but is less effective than the win-lose or win-win approach.[24]

Win-Lose In this strategy one party to the conflict tries to marshal all the resources to win, and the other party loses. Examples of win-lose strategies can be fund in superior-subordinate relationships, line-staff confrontations, union management relations, and many other conflict situations found in contemporary organizations. Though win-lose strategy helps defuse conflict, it may not be a permanent solution since the loser will tend to be bitter and vindictive. A most healthier strategy is to have both parties in a conflict situation win.[25]

The following points make win –lose strategy more clear:

(i) The conflicting parties view the issue from their own points of view.

(ii) The emphasis is on solutions rather than on the attainment of goals, values or objectives.

(iii) There is a clear we-they distinction between the parties.

(iv) The parties direct their energies towards each other in an atmosphere of victory and defeat.

(v) Conflicts are personalised and judgmental.

(vi) The parties take a short-run view of the issues.

(vii) There is no differentiation of conflict resolving activities from other group processes, nor is there a planned sequence of those activities.

Win-Win A win-win strategy of conflict resolution is probably the most desirable from the human and organizational standpoint. Energies and creativity are aimed at solving the problems rather than beating the other party. The needs of both parties in the conflict situations are met, and both parties receive rewarding outcomes. Though it is often difficult to accomplish a win-win outcome in an inter-personal conflict, this should be a major goal of the management of conflict.[26]

Transactional Analysis Inter-personal conflict can be resolved by encouraging as many complimentary transactions as possible between parties to the conflict. Of more significance for conflict management is the adult to adult transaction between the parties. Interaction between two adult ego states will improve communication. Improved communication is the sure way of resolving conflict.

Altering the Behavioural Inputs Finally, inter-personal conflict may be resolved by focusing on the behaviour of the individual involved. Conflict arises out of the perceptions and attitudes of people. These can be changed through training programmes. T-group or sensitivity training assumes relevance in this context.

RESOLVING INTRAGROUP CONFLICT

Conflict within a family can be resolved if the members recognize and respect roles of family members. All the members need to realize that divided they stand, united they fall. Probably, a family friend may intervene to resolve the dispute if the members fail to resolve the conflict themselves. This was what happened to the Bajaj family. Sharad Pawar mediated to bring about a truce in the troubled family.

RESOLVING INTER-GROUP CONFLICT

The approaches available for resolving intra-personal and inter-personal conflicts can be used to solve inter-group disputes too. However, certain unique approaches are available for resolving inter-group conflict. They are: problem solving, expansion of resources, avoidance, smoothen, compromise and reorganizing organization structure.

Problem Solving Problem solving is considered to be the most effective approach available as it emphasises the attainment of the common interests of both conflicting parties .In the problem solving strategy, attempts are made to find a solution that reconciles or "integrates" the needs of both the parties. The two parties work together both to define the problem and to identify mutually satisfactory solutions. Moreover, there is open expression of feelings as well as exchange of task-related information.

Organization Redesign Changing organizational structure is another approach for resolving conflict, particularly when the sources of conflict come from the coordination of work among different departments or divisions. One way of redesigning organizations is to reduce task inter-dependence between groups and give each group clear responsibilities. Another way is to transfer or exchange members of conflicting groups. An appeal system may also be developed to eliminate the arbitrary use of power.

Superordinate Goals Appealing to superordinate goals is another way of resolving conflict. The superordinate goal is a common goal of both conflicting parties and the combined efforts of both parties will be needed to realize the goal. It takes precedence over other goals which may separate the conflicting parties. Survival of the organization for example, can be a superordinate goal. Creating an awareness that the organization's survival will be jeopardized if conflicting groups do not work in unison can have a salutary effect on disputing parties.

Expansion of Resources To the extent that scarce resources cause conflict, removing their scarcity will help resolve conflict. If upgradation of one's position has caused ripples elsewhere, some more jobs might be similarly upgraded. If increased budget allocation to one department has caused heart burn to the members of rival department, the rival division's allocation can also be correspondingly increased, and so on.

Avoidance When the issue is trivial, avoidance strategy will be useful. In the avoidance strategy, the party or parties to the conflict may either withdraw from the conflict or conceal the incompatibility. In the first instance, one of the conflicting parties or both will withdraw from the conflicting situation. Where avoidance is not possible, concealing the fact by either or both conflicting parties that there is conflict may help defuse the conflict.

Smoothen The process of playing down the differences between individuals or groups and highlighting their common interests is called smoothening. Finding and emphasising similarities between conflicting parties, while playing down differences, can eventually lead the parties to realize that the two are not as far apart as was first believed. With shared viewpoints on some issue, the ability to work towards a smoothen can help reduce the intensity of the conflict and avoid an escalation of open hostility. However, smoothen is recommended as a stop gap measure to let people cool down and regain perspective.

Resolving Line and Staff Conflict The following remedies have been suggested to resolve line and staff conflict:[27]

(i) The roles, responsibilities, and functions of line and staff officers need to be clearly defined and made known to the people concerned.

(ii) Staff people shall know that their role is advisory. They are to be content with tendering advice on important issues. Line managers need also respect the staff advice and use it for the benefit of the organization.

(iii) Increase possibilities of interaction between the line and staff officers.

(iv) The staff officers are to avoid playing the expert.

(v) The fear complex from which line managers suffer owing to proximity of staff specialists and their intimacy with the top management needs to be removed.

(vi) Both parties are to have the right of appeal to the chief executive.

Conflict Management Styles

There are five conflict management styles, viz., competition, collaboration, compromise, avoidance, and accommodation. The five style are presented in Fig. 22.13.

The figure classifies each style as some combination of a person's-

Co-operativeness: Desire to satisfy the other person's concerns, and

Assertiveness: Desire to satisfy one's own concerns.

As is clear, only the collaboration approach scores high on both dimensions. Hence, this approach is highly effective to resolve conflict.

What needs emphasis is that views and styles of conflict resolution vary across cultures. Important aspects of conflict are viewed and experienced differently in different countries.

FIGURE 22-13
CONFLICT MANAGEMENT STYLES

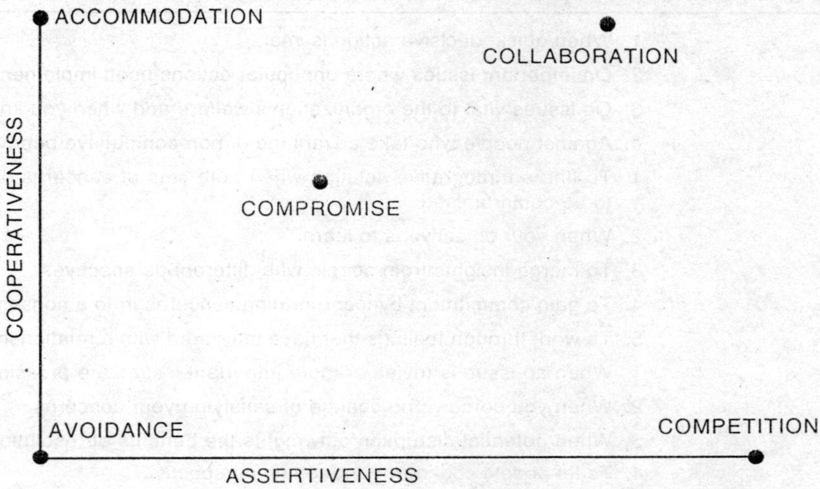

Table 22.4 outlines specific situations where each conflict resolution behaviour is more appropriate and Table 22.5 shows gains and losses from each style.

MANAGERIAL IMPLICATIONS

At the outset a manager must understand that conflict is inevitable, nay desirable, from the point of employee performance and satisfaction. Such activities as hiding information, making misleading statements, postponing meetings, and advising organizational members "not to rock the boat" and "to be a company man", on the part of mangers so that they need not face conflict do no good for furthering the interests of the organization.

Realizing the inevitability of conflict is not enough. Managers must play a positive role to stimulate conflict. Recent developments in conflicts management stress both conflict stimulation and conflict reduction techniques. While the resolution strategies were discussed earlier, the stimulation needs to be mentioned. Following are the indicators:

1. The organization is filled with "yes men."
2. Employees are afraid to admit ignorance.
3. Compromise is stressed in decision-making.
4. Managers put too much emphasis on harmony and peace.
5. People are afraid of hurting the feelings of others.
6. Popularity is considered to be more important than technical competence.
7. People exhibit resistance to change.
8. New ideas are not forthcoming.
9. There is an unusually low rate of employee turnover.

TABLE 22-4

WHEN TO USE THE FIVE CONFLICT-HANDLING ORIENTATIONS?

Conflict-Handling Orientation	*Appropriate Situations*
Competition	1. When quick, decisive action is vital.
	2. On important issues where unpopular actions need implementing
	3. On issues vital to the organization's welfare and when you know you're right.
	4. Against people who take advantage of non-competitive behaviour.
Collaboration	1. To find an integrative solution when both sets of concerns are too important to be compromised
	2. When your objective is to learn.
	3. To merge insights from people with different perspectives
	4. To gain commitment by incorporating concerns in to a consensus.
	5. To work through feelings that have interfered with a relationship.
Avoidance	1. When an issue is trivial, or more important issues are pressing.
	2. When you perceive no change of satisfying your concerns.
	3. When potential disruption outweights the benefits of resolution.
	4. To let people cool down and regain perspective.
	5. When gathering information supersedes immediate decision.
	6. When others can resolve the conflict more effectively.
	7. When issues seem tangential or symptomatic of other issues.
Accommodation	1. When you find you are wrong to allow a better position to be heard to learn and to show your reasonableness.
	2. When issues are more important to others than yourself to satisfy others and maintain cooperation.
	3. To build social credit for later issues.
	4. To minimize loss when you are outmatched and losing.
	5. When harmony and stability are especially important.
	6. To allow subordinates to develop by learning from mistakes.
Compromise	1. When goals are important, but not worth the effort or potential disruption of more assertive modes.
	2. When opponents with equal power are committed to mutually exclusive goals.
	3. To achieve temporary settlements to complex issues.
	4. To arrive at expedient situations under time pressure.
	5. As a back-up when collaboration or competition is unsuccessful.

(***Source:*** K.W. Thomos, "*Towards Multidimensional Values in Teaching: The Example of Conflict Behaviours*", Academy of Management Review, July 1997, p. 487).

Once the need is identified, managers may adapt one or more of the following approaches to stimulate conflict:

1. Encourage individualistic thinking.
2. Increase individual competition.
3. Provide threatening information such as reduction in profits or the loss of a competitive edge in the market.

TABLE 22-5

GAINS AND LOSSES ASSOCIATED WITH CONFLICT STYLES

	Competition	*Avoidance*	*Accommodation*	*Compromise*	*Collaboration*
GAINS	Chance to win everything	No energy or time expenditure	Little muss or fuss, no feathers ruffled	No one returns home empty-handed	Both sides win
	Exciting games-manship	Conserve for fights that are "more important"	Others may view you as supportive	"Keep the peace"	Better chance for long-term solutions
	Exercise own sense of power		Energy free for other pursuits	May or may not encourage creativity	Creativity in problem solving
					Maintains relationship
					New level of understanding of solution
					Improves quality of solution and commitment
LOSSES	Chance to lose everything	Less stimulation	Lowered self assertion and possibly self-esteem	Since neither side is totally satisfied, conflicts are likely to recur later	Time, in the short run
	Alienates others	Less creative problem solving	Loss of power		Loss of sense of autonomy
	Discourage others from working with you	Little under-standing of the needs of others	Absence of your unique contribution to the situation	Neither side realizes self determination fully	
	Potentially larger scale conflicts in the future (or more avoidance of conflict)	Incomplete comprehension of work environment	Others dependent on you may not feel you "go to bat" for them		

(***Source:*** Suzanne C. de Janasz, *et.al, Interpersonal Skills in Organizations*, p.249).

4. Create role conflict
5. Change the organizational structure.

Negotiation and Conflict Resolution

Often , negotiations occur in the process of conflict resolution. Negotiations are viewed as a process in which two or more parties attempt to reach acceptable agreement in a situation characterized by some level of disagreement.[28] Negotiations include a combination of compromise, collaboration, and possibly some coercion on vital issues. A negotiation situation is one in which

- some disagreement or conflict exists. This may be perceived, felt or manifest.
- there is some degree of interdependence between the parties,
- the parties are committed to peaceful means for resolving their dispute, and there exists a possibility of agreement, and
- the situation is conducive to opportunistic interaction.

Situational Factors Favouring Negotiation

Success of negotiation depends atleast on four situational factors, viz; location, physical setting, time, and audience.

Location Negotiating parties feel comfortable when they operate in locations familiar to them. Considering the strategic benefits of familiar locations, many negotiators agree to meet on neutral territory. Increasingly, computer technology is making it possible for two distant groups to negotiate without a location. However, electronic messages are subject to misinterpretation, and conflict can easily escalate if the parties engage in flaming. *Flaming* is the act of sending an emotionally charged message (called flame mail) to others. This occurs because people can post e-mail messages before their emotions subside, whereas the sender of a traditional memo or letter would have time for second thoughts.

Physical Setting Physical setting includes distance between parties and seating arrangements for negotiations. The physical distance between the parties can influence the parties' orientation towards each other and the disputed issues. People who sit face to face are more likely to develop a win-lose orientation towards the conflict situation.

Time Passage and Deadliness Time passage and deadlines are two important factors in negotiations. The more time people invest in negotiations, the stronger is their commitment to reaching an agreement. This increases the motivation to resolve conflict, but it also fuels commitment to a stated position.

Time deadlines may be useful to the extent that they motivate the parties to complete negotiations. However, time deadlines may become a liability when exceeding deadlines is costly. Negotiators make concessions and soften their demands more rapidly as the deadlines approach.

Audience Characteristics Negotiators generally have audiences - any one who has a stake in the negotiation process and its outcome, such as senior management, other team members or the general public. Negotiators tend to act differently when their audience observes the negotiation or has detailed information about the process, compared to situations in which the audience sees only the end results. When the audience has direct surveillance over the proceeding, negotiators tend to be more competitive, less willing to make concessions, and more likely to engage in political tactics against the other party. This hard line behaviour shows the audience that the negotiator is working for their interests. With their audience watching, negotiators also have more interest in saving face. Sometimes, audiences are drawn into the negotiations by acting as a source of indirect appeals. The general public often takes on this role when groups negotiate with governments.[29]

Guidelines for Effective Negotiation

The negotiators need to take care of the situational factors outlined above. In addition, the behaviours of the parties involved need special emphasis because it is they who influence outcome of any negotiation. The most essential behaviours for effective negotiation are summarized in Table 22.6.

Adopting to cultural differences The guidelines for successful negotiation outlined in Table 22.6 are indeed self explanatory but the last point needs elaboration.

Negotiation gets complicated when the negotiating parties hail from different cultural backgrounds. Negotiations approaches vary across countries. Majority of negotiators from India,

TABLE 22-6

EFFECTIVE NEGOTIATION – GUIDELINES

- Consider the other party's situation and viewpoint
- Have a plan and concrete strategy
- Begin with a positive overture
- Address problems, not personalities
- Pay little attention to initial offers
- Emphasise win-win solutions
- Create a climate of trust
- Have open mind
- Insist on using objective criteria
- Adapt to cultural differences.

Japan, China, Argentina, France and the USA tend to adopt win-win approach while sitting for negotiations. While Britishers, Mexicans, Germans, Nigerians and Spaniards generally use win-lose approach for negotiating. Obviously, it is difficult to expect give-and-take approach while negotiating with a Spaniard or a German while it is possible with an Indian or a Mexican. It is important to adopt to the cultural expectations of negotiators from different countries in order to maintain the rapport and credibility for potential outcomes. It is also important to keep in touch with one's own cultural biases and nuances so that they are not exploited by savvy negotiators from other countries.

Beyond Conflict Resolution

The effectiveness of negotiation as a technique of conflict resolution is well recognised and appreciated. But what is not recognised is the fact that negotiation lends itself as a managerial skill for personal and organizational success. A manager for example, can successfully negotiate a salary raise or a good price for supplies. Similarly, a supervisor can negotiate and convince his or her boss to change the shift of his or her subordinates.

Questions

1. Explain approach-avoidance conflict. Give a realistic organizational example of where it may occur.
2. What are some of the major sources of interpersonal conflict? Which do you think is most relevant in today's organizations?
3. What examples of functional and dysfunctional conflict have you encountered?
4. Identify and discuss five styles of conflict management.
5. Identify and discuss guidelines for effective negotiation.
6. Define conflict. What are the sources of conflict?
7. How do traditional assumptions about conflict differ from modern perceptions about it?

Case

HE SAID, SHE SAID

Shirley and Abdul both work for a software development company. The manager of the new product division was originally the leader of a project team for which she interviewed and hired Abdul. Shirley, another project team member, also interviewed Abdul but strongly opposed hiring him for the project because she thought he was not competent to do the job.

Seven months after Abdul was hired, the manager left the project to start her own company and recommended that Abdul and Shirley serve as joint project leaders. Shirley agreed reluctantly- with the stipulation that it be made clear she was not working for Abdul. The general manager consented; Shirley and Abdul were to share the project leadership.

Within a month Shirley was angry because Abdul was representing himself to others as the leader of the entire project and giving the impression that Shirley was working for him. Now Shirley and Abdul are meeting with you to see if you can help them resolve the conflict between them.

Shirley says. " Right after the joint leadership arrangement was reached with the general manager, Abdul called a meeting a the project team without even consulting me about the time or content. He just told me when it was being held and said I should be there. At the meeting, Abdul reviewed everyone's duties, line by line, including mine, treating me as just another team member working for him. He sends out letters and signs himself as project director, which obviously implies to others that I am working for him."

Abdul says: "Shirley is all hung up with feelings of power and titles. Just because I sign myself as project director doesn't mean that she is working for me. I don't see anything to get excited about. What differences does it make? She is too sensitive about everything. I call a meeting and right away she thinks I'm, trying to run everything. Shirley has other things to do - other project to run - so she doesn't pay too much attention to this one. She mostly lets things slide. But when I take the initiative to set up a meeting, she starts jumping up and down about how I am trying to make her work for me."

Discussion Questions A variety of strategies can be used to help resolve the conflict between Abdul and Shirley. Explore the concepts on conflict management presented in this chapter. Put yourself in the position of mediator between Abdul and Shirley and consider the following questions:

Questions

1. Abdul and Shirley seem to have several conflicts occurring simultaneously. Identify as many of these individual conflicts as possible.
2. Are there any general statements you can make about the overall nature of the conflict between Abdul and Shirley?
3. What are the possible ways to deal with the conflict between Abdul and Shirley (not just the ones that you would recommend, but all the options)?
4. Given the choices identified in item three, what is the *best way* for Abdul and Shirley to deal with the conflict between them?
5. Given all the benefits of retrospection, what could or should have been done to avoid this conflict in the first place?[30]

REFERENCES

1. Kae H. Chung and Leon C. Megginson, *Organizaitonal Behaviour*, New York: Harper and Row, 1981, p. 252.
2. *Ibid.*
3. Jerry L. Gray and Frederick A. Strake, *Organizational Behaviour – Concepts and Applications*, Columbus, Merill Publishers Co., 1988, p. 534.

4. David J. Cherrington, *Organizational Behaviour*, Boston, Allyn and Bacon, 1989, p. 441.
5. James A.F. Stoner, *Management*, New Delhi: Prentice Hall of India, 1984, p. 408.
6. Donald D. White and David A. Bednar, *Organizational Behaviour*, Boston, Allyn, and Bacon, 1986, p. 472.
7. David J. Cherrington, *Op. cit.*, p. 444.
8. Curtis W. Cook, *et.al.*, *Management and Organizational Behaviour,* McGraw-Hill, 2001, p. 375.
9. N.L. Munn, *et.al.*, *Introduction to Psychology,* Oxford and IBH, 1992, p. 498.
10. E.R. Hilgard, *et.al.*, *Introduction to Psychology,* Oxford and IBH, 1975, p. 442.
11. Moorgan and King, *Introduction to Psychology,* Tata McGraw-Hill, 1971, p. 247.
12. N.L. Munn, *et.al, Op. cit,* p. 500.
13. E.R. Hillgard, *et.al, Op. cit,* p. 434.
14. Fred Luthans, *Organizational Behaviour,* McGraw-Hill, 1989, p. 404.
15. Morrison and O' Hearne, *Practical Transactional Analysis in Management,* Wiley Publishing co., 1977, p. 7.
16. *Ibid,* p. 1
17. *Ibid,* p.2.
18. Fred Luthans, *Op. cit,* p. 409.
19. *Ibid.*
20. Horlow and Henke, *Behaviour in Organizations,* Little Brown and Co., 1975, p. 359.
21. Feldman and Arnold, *Managing Individual and Group Behaviour in Organizations,* McGraw-Hill, 1983, pp 513-514.
22. *Ibid,* p. 514.
23. *Ibid,* p. 515
24. Fred Luthans, *Op. cit,* p. 413.
25. *Ibid*
26. *Ibid*
27. Aswathappa K., *Factory Organization and Management*, HPH, 1989, P. 170.
28. Ivancevich and Matteson, *Organizational Behaviour and Management,* McGraw-Hill-Irwin, 2002, p. 366.
29. Steven L. Mcshane and Mary Ann Von Glinow, *Organizational Behaviour*, TMH, 2000, P. 42D.
30. Curtis W. Cook and Philip L. Hunsaker, *Op.cit*, p.408.

CHAPTER

Twenty Three

Work Stress

LEARNING OBJECTIVES

After reading this chapter you should understand —

1. The nature of Stress.
2. The Impact of stress varies from person to person.
3. How Stress originates.
4. The Outcomes of stress.
5. The meaning of Burnout.
6. The strategies available to cope with stress.
7. The Stress is negatively related to performance.

There are hundreds of employees who are suffering silently and with helplessness. Stress is a contagion, a black plague, spreading like wildfire and spewing large number of organizational members across the world.

Meaning and Definition

Stress is an individual's response to a disturbing factor in the environment, and the consequence of such reaction. Stress obviously involves interaction of the person and the environment. To quote a definition : *"Stress is an adaptive response to an external situation that results in physical, psychological and / or behavioural deviations for organisational participants."*[1] The physical or psychological demands from the environment that cause stress are called *stressors.* They create stress or the potential for stress when an individual perceives them as representing a demand that may exceed that person's ability to respond.

Stress can manifest itself in both a positive way and a negative way. Stress is said to be positive when the situation offers an opportunity for one to gain something. *Eustress* is the term used to describe positive stress. Eustress is often viewed as motivator since, in its absence, the individual lacks that 'edge' necessary for peak performance. It is negative when stress is associated with heart-disease, alcoholism, drug abuse, marital breakdowns, absenteeism, child abuse and a host of other social, physical, organisational and emotional problems.

Stress is associated with *constraints* and *demands.* The former prevents an individual from doing what he or she desires. The latter refers to the loss of something desired. Aspiring to own a new Ford Ikon and not be able to mobilise the necessary cash is a *constraint.* Desiring to attend a social function but unable to do so because of pressing official work amounts to a *demand.*

Constraints and demands can lead to potential stress. When they are coupled with uncertainty of the outcome and importance of the outcome, potential stress becomes actual stress. Stress is high when there is uncertainty of outcome and the outcome is significant.

What is Not Stress?

To make the meaning of stress more clear, it is useful to state what does not constitute stress. Each of the following does not amount to stress:

Stress is not simply anxiety or nervous tension : These symptoms do not constitute stress. People exhibiting these behaviours may not be under stress. Similarly, individuals who are under stress may not exhibit anxiety or nervous tension.

Stress need not always be damaging : People frequently experience stress without any strain at all. Daily life activities may be stressful, but not at all harmful.

Stress is not always due to overwork : Stressed out individuals are not those who are overworked. Stress may also result from having too little to do.

Stress cannot be avoided : It is necessary to realise that stress is an inevitable part of life, and that it cannot be avoided. What can, however, be avoided are the negative reactions to the stress.

Body has limited capacity to respond : Stress is body's biological response mechanisms. But the body has only limited capacity to respond to stressors. The work place makes a variety of demands on people and too much stress over too long a period of time will exhaust their ability to cope with the stressors as is evident from the preview case to this chapter.

THE STRESS EXPERIENCE

Not all individuals experience stress with same intensity. Some people overact to stressors and get highly stressed. Some others have the stamina, endurance and composure to cope with any stressors. How an individual experiences stress depends on (i) the person's perception of the situation, (ii) the person's past experience, (iii) the presence or absence of social support, and (iv) individual differences with regard to stress reactions.[2] (See Fig. 23.1)

FIGURE 23-1
RELATIONSHIP BETWEEN STRESSORS AND STRESS

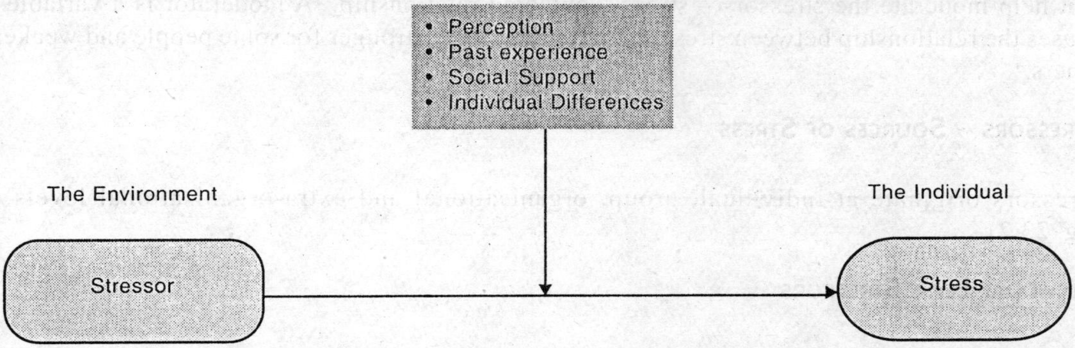

(***Source:*** Don Hellriegal, *et al*, *Organisational Behaviour*, p. 193)

Perception As stated earlier perception refers to a psychological process whereby a person selects and organises stimuli into a concept of reality. Employees' perception of a situation can influence whether or not they experience stress. A simple transfer from one place to another may be perceived by one employee as an opportunity to see new places and learn new things. The same transfer may be understood by another employee as extremely threatening and indicating unhappiness of the management with his or her performance.

Past Experience Whether a person experiences stress depends on his or her past experience with a similar stressor. Writing anonymous letters against the boss or giving leads to the newspaper and getting false stories published in them against the boss are common among disgruntled employees. Over a period of time, the boss will get used to such allegations, though initially he or she underwent stress.

The relationship between experience and stress is also based on reinforcement. Positive reinforcement or previous success in a similar situation can reduce the level of stress that a person experiences under certain circumstances; punishment or past failure under similar conditions can increase stress under the same circumstances.[3]

Social Support The presence or absence of other people influences how individuals in the workplace experience stress and respond to stressors. The presence of co-workers may increase an individual's confidence, allowing that person to cope more effectively with stress. For example, working alongside someone who performs confidently and competently in a stressed situation may help an employee behave in an identical way. Conversely, the presence of fellow workers may irritate some people or make them anxious, reducing their ability to cope with stress.

Individual Differences Individual differences in motivation, attitudes, personality and abilities also influence whether employees experience work stress, and if they do, how they respond to it. What one person considers a major source of stress, another may hardly notice it. Personality characteristics, in particular, may explain some of the differences in the ways that employees experience and respond to stress. Type A individuals, for example (see chapter 16), tend to experience more stress than Type B personalities.

Work Stress Model

Fig. 23.2 contains a typical model of occupational stress. As illustrated in the figure, stressors lead to stress, which in turn, lead to a variety of consequences. The model also contains several variables that help moderate the stressors – stress – outcome relationship. A moderator is a variable that causes the relationship between stress and outcomes to be stronger for some people and weaker for others.[4]

Stressors – Sources of Stress

Stressors originate at individual, group, organisational and extra-organisational levels (see Fig. 23.2).

Individual Level Stressors

These relate directly to a person's personality and job responsibilities. Experts estimate that more than 10 million workers have computer-related vision problems each year that require a trip to an optometrist. Forty percent of these people use special glasses while working with video display terminals.

The most common individual level stressors are type of personality, role overload, role conflict and role ambiguity.

Personality Type In respect of personality, two concepts : Type A personality and Type B personality are relevant in this context.

The **Type A personality** is stress-prone as it is associated with the following behavioural patterns:

- Always moves, walks and eats rapidly.
- Feels impatient with the pace of things, hurries others, dislikes waiting.
- Does several things simultaneously.
- Feels guilty when relaxing.
- Tries to schedule more and more in less and less time.
- Uses nervous gestures such as clenched fist, banging the hand on the table.
- Does not have time to enjoy life.

The achievement orientation, impatience and perfectionism of individuals with Type A personalities may create stress in work circumstances that other persons find relatively stress-free. Type A personalities, in this sense, bring stress on themselves.

The **Type B personality**, on the other hand, is less stress prone. Following are the typical characteristics of Type B personality:

FIGURE 23-2
A MODEL OF OCCUPATIONAL STRESS

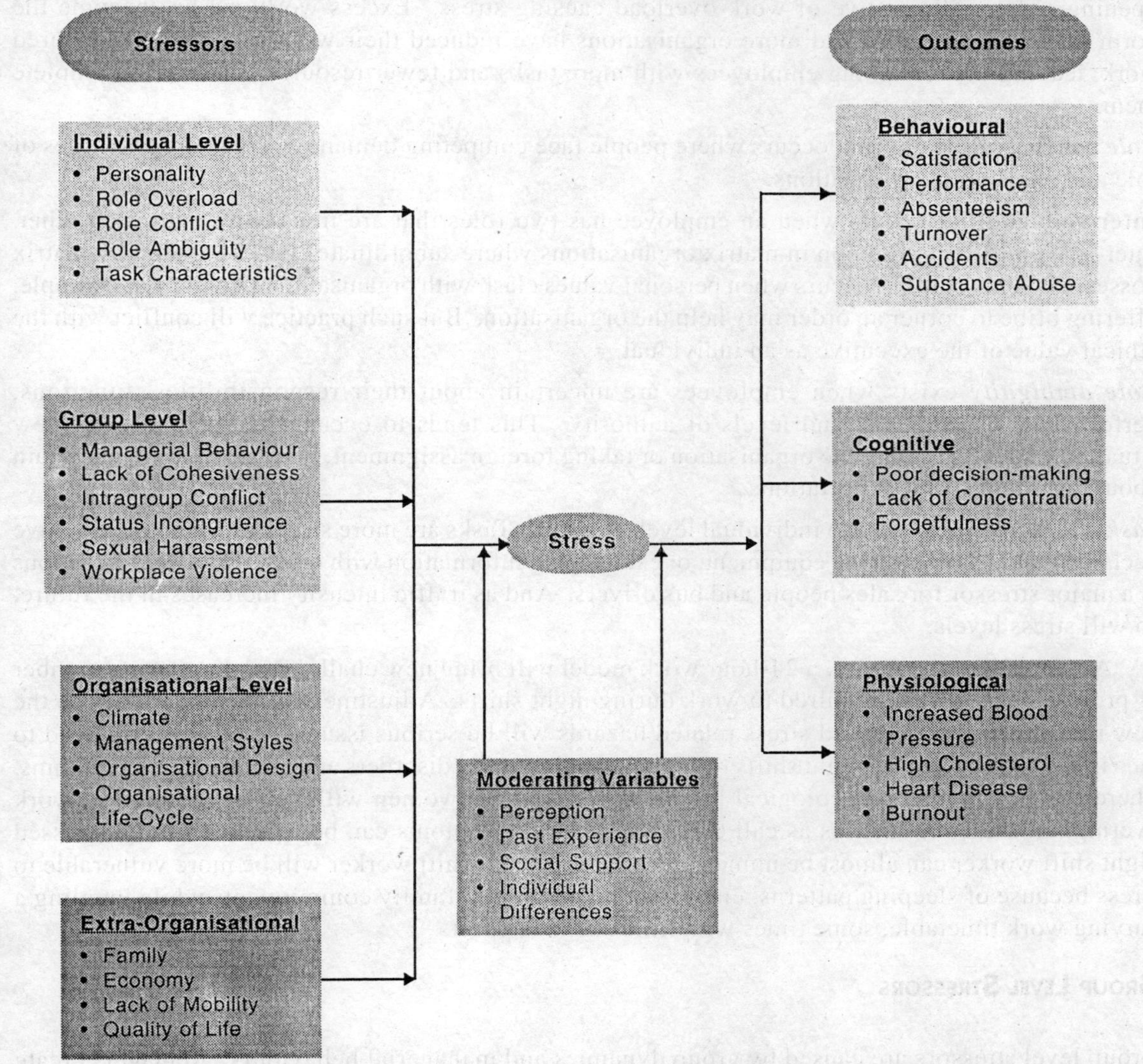

(***Source:*** Adapted from Robert Krietner, et al, *Organisational Behaviour*, p. 530)

- Is not concerned about time.
- Is patient.
- Does not brag
- Play to fun, not to win.
- Relaxes without feeling guilty.
- Has no pressing deadlines.

- Is mild-mannered.
- Is never in a hurry.[5]

Role overload Too much of work causes stress to an employee. The story of Reddy, stated in the opening case, is illustrative of work overload causing stress. Excess workload has become the norm these days as more and more organisations have reduced their workforce and restructured work, leaving the remaining employees with more tasks and fewer resources of time to complete them.

Role conflict Role conflict occurs where people face competing demands. There are two types of role and conflict in organisations.

Inter-role conflict occurs when an employee has two roles that are in conflict with each other. Inter-role conflict is common in matrix organisations where subordinates will be shared by matrix bosses. Personal conflict occurs when personal values clash with organisational goals. For example, offering bribe to corner an order may help the organisation. But such practice will conflict with the ethical value of the executive as an individual.

Role ambiguity exists when employees are uncertain about their responsibilities, functions, performance expectations and levels of authority. This tends to occur when people enter new situations, such as joining the organisation or taking foreign assignment, because they are uncertain about tasks and social expectations.

Task characteristics are also individual level stressors. Tasks are more stressful when they involve decision making, monitoring equipment, or exchanging information with others. Traffic congestions is a major stressor for sales people and bus drivers. And as traffic intensity increases in the future, so will stress levels.

As we go into the future, a 24-hour work model will bring new challenges. Increasing number of professionals will be required to work during night shifts. Adjustment of the body clock to the new routine, health risks and stress related hazards will be serious issues the OB experts need to face in the coming years. Night shifts result in gastrointestinal disorders and abnormal heart rhythms. There can be chronic gynecological problems for women (women will also be required to work overnights in such industries as call centres). Mental symptoms can be so severe that a stressed night shift worker can almost be unmanageable. The night shift worker will be more vulnerable to stress because of sleeping patterns, emotional problems and family commitments while juggling a varying work timetable, some times with little social support.

Group Level Stressors

Group level stressors are caused by group dynamics and managerial behaviours. Managers create stress for employees by (i) exhibiting inconsistent behaviours, (ii) failing to provide support, (iii) showing lack of concern, (iv) providing inadequate direction, (v) creating a high productivity environment, and (vi) focusing on negatives while ignoring good performance.[6]

Sexual harassment is yet another group level stressor. Sexual harassment refers to unwelcome conduct of a sexual nature that affects the job-related performance of an employee adversely. One example of sexual harassment is the male supervisor threatening to fire a female employee if she fails to accept his sexual advances.

Another serious interpersonal stressor is the rising wave of physical violence and aggression in the workplace. It is estimated that more than 1000 employees are murdered at work each year in the US. Workplace violence includes assaults, rape and threats using a weapon.[7]

ORGANISATIONAL STRESSORS

Organisational stressors affect large number of employees. Organisational climate is a prime example. A high pressure environment that places chronic work demands on employees fuels the stress response. In contrast, participative management can reduce organisational-level stressors. Poor lighting, loud noise, improper placement of furniture and a dirty and smelly environment create stress. Managers should monitor these and eliminate them at the earliest.

Organisational structure defines the level of differentiation, the degree of rules and regulations, and where decisions are made. Excessive rules and lack of participation in decision that affect an employee are examples of structural variables that might be potential stressors.

Organisational leadership represents the managerial style of the organisation's senior executives. Some chief executive officers create a culture characterised by tension, fear and anxiety. They establish unrealistic pressures to perform in the short run, impose excessively tight controls and routinely fire employees who fail to measure up.

Organisational life-cycle Organisations like human beings, pass through a life cycle. The life cycle of an organisation comprises eight stages – (i) birth, (ii) growth, (iii) policy, (iv) procedure, (v) theory, (vi) religion, (vii) ritual, and (viii) last rites. In this cycle, the organisation is born and then has its growth. Policies are developed to guide decisions and these are carried out through procedures. These procedures are refined and made more efficient with theories about efficiency. In time, organisation may develop characteristics of a religion, it may worship the way it does things. Performance is by ritual, things are done by habit without questioning. The death and last rites of the organisation will ordinarily follow. Each stage of the life cycle poses its own challenges and problems. While the early stages are exciting, the latter ones create anxiety and tension.

EXTRA-ORGANISATIONAL STRESSORS

Extra-organisational stressors are caused by factors outside the organisation. For instance conflicts associated with one's career and family life are stressful.

Home life certainly impacts one's attitudes and performance at work. Death of a spouse, injury to one's child, war, failure in school or at work, an unplanned pregnancy and similar other life events can be stressful. Socioeconomic status represents a combination of (i) economic status as measured by income, (ii) social status assessed by educational level, and (iii) work status as indexed by occupation. These stressors are likely to become more important in the future.

OUTCOMES

Behavioural scientists are of the opinion that stress has behavioural, cognitive and physiological consequences. Research has proved that stress produces harmful physiological outcomes. Research is now in progress to co-relate stress with work-related behaviours and cognitive outcomes. These studies indicate that stress is negatively related to job satisfaction, organisational commitment and performance and positively related to turnover.[8]

BURNOUT

Burnout is a troublesome outcome of stress. It is desirable to examine burnout in detail.

Burnout is a state of mind resulting from prolonged exposure to intense emotional stress. It manifests through emotional exhaustion and a combination of negative attitudes. Table 23.1 describes 10 attitudinal characteristics of burnout. Table 23.2 draws distinction between stress and burnout.

TABLE 23-1
ATTITUDINAL CHARACTERISTICS OF BURNOUT

Attitude	*Description*
Fatalism	A feeling that you lack control over your work.
Boredom	A lack of interest in doing your job.
Discontent	A sense of being unhappy with your job.
Cynicism	A tendency to undervalue the content of your job and the rewards received.
Inadequacy	A feeling of not being able to meet your objectives.
Failure	A tendency to discredit your performance and conclude that you are ineffective.
Overwork	A feeling of having too much to do and not enough time to complete it.
Nastiness	A tendency to be rude or unpleasant to your co-workers.
Dissatisfaction	A feeling that you are not being justly rewarded for your efforts.
Escape	A desire to give up and get away from it all.

(**Source:** Robert Krietner and Angelo Kinicki, *Organisational Behaviour*, p. 535)

TABLE 23-2
STRESS VS BURNOUT

Stress	*Burnout*
The person feels fatigued	The individual encounters chronic exhaustion.
The person is anxious	The individual is hypertensive.
The person is dissatisfied with his or her job	The individual is bored and cynical about the work.
The person's job commitment has dropped off	The individual's job commitment is virtually nil; he or she is mentally detached from the organisation.
The person feels moody	The individual feels impatient, irritable and unwilling to talk to others.
The person feels guilty	The individual encounters mental depression.
The person is having difficulty concentrating; he or she tends to forget things	The individual does not seem to know where he or she is; forgetfulness is becoming more and more frequent.
The person undergoes physiological changes such as increased blood pressure and heart beat	The individual begins to voice psychosomatic complaints.

(**Source:** Richard M. Hodgetts, *Organisational Behaviour*, p. 345)

Burnout occurs due to prolonged exposure to stress and that too in phases as shown in Fig. 23.3. The three key phases of burnout are emotional exhaustion, depersonalisation and feeling a lack of personal accomplishment. Emotional exhaustion, as shown in Fig. 23.3, is due to a combination of personal, job and organisational stressors. People who expect a lot from themselves and the organisations in which they work tend to create more internal stress, which, in turn, leads to emotional exhaustion. Similarly, emotional exhaustion is fuelled by having too much work to

FIGURE 23-3
A MODEL OF BURNOUT

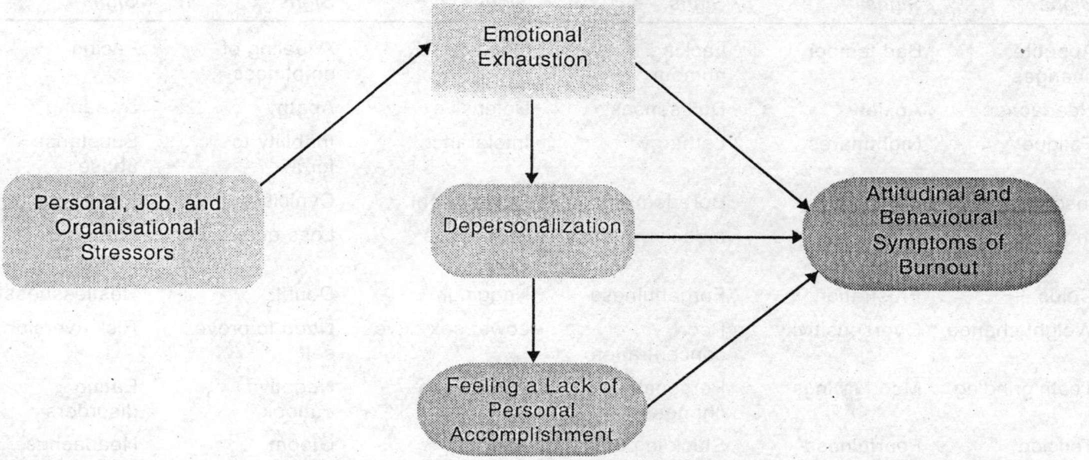

do, by role conflict and by the type of interpersonal interactions encountered at work. Frequent, intense face-to-face interactions that are emotionally charged are associated with higher levels of emotional exhaustion.

Overtime, emotional exhaustion leads to depersonalisation, which is the state of psychologically withdrawing from one's job. This finally results in a feeling of being unappreciated, ineffective or inadequate. The additive effect of these three phases is a host of negative attitudinal and behavioural outcomes.[9]

Stress Management

Stress reduction strategies may be categorized into (a) individual strategies, and (b) organisational strategies.

Individual Strategies

First step in managing stress is to understand that the individual is exposed to stressors. We cannot manage stress unless we know what causes stress and how these causes are affecting us psychologically, physiologically and organizationally. Fig. 23.4 contains series of stressors. If the employee has any of these signs of stress, he or she needs to adopt coping strategies immediately.

Individual strategies to cope with stress include muscle relaxation, biofeedback, meditation, cognitive restructuring and time management.

Muscle Relaxation: This involves slow and deep breathing, a conscious effort to relieve muscle tension and an altered state of consciousness. The technique is inexpensive, may require a trained professional to implement initially.

Biofeedback: A biofeedback machine is used to train people to detect and control stress-related symptoms such as tense muscles and related blood pressure. The machine translates unconscious

FIGURE 23-4
SIGNS OF STRESS

Physical Signs	*Emotional Signs*	*Mental Signs*	*Relational Signs*	*Spiritual Signs*	*Behavioural Signs*
Appetite changes	Bad temper	Lacking humour	Isolation	A feeling of emptiness	Pacing
Headaches	Anxiety	Dull senses	Defensive	Apathy	Swearing
Fatigue	Nightmares	Lethargy	Intolerance	Inability to forgive	Substance abuse
Insomnia	Irritability	Boredom	Resentment	Cynicism	Nail biting
Indigestion	Depression	Indecisiveness	Loneliness	Loss of direction	Slumped posture
Colds	Frustration	Forgetfulness	Nagging	Doubt	Restlessness
Weight change	Oversensitivity	Poor concentration	Lower sex drive	Need to prove self	Risk aversion
Teeth grinding	Mood swings	Personality changes	Aggression	Negative outlook	Eating disorders
Tension	Fearfulness	Stuck in past	Abuse	Gloom	Headaches

(**Source:** Suzanne C. de Junasz, et al, *Interpersonal Skills in Organisations*, p. 72)

bodily signs into a recognisable cue (flashing light or beeper). Muscle relaxation and meditative techniques are then used to alleviate the underlying stress.[(10)]

Meditation: Several meditation techniques are used with results being positive and majority of them are derivatives of Eastern philosophies. Included in this category are Zen Meditation or Sumran. Perhaps the most widely practised technique everywhere is the transcendental meditation (TM) of Maharishi Mahesh Yogi. TM practised 20 minutes twice daily helps reduce stress significantly.

Cognitive Restructuring Cognitive restructuring involves two steps. First, irrational or maladaptive thought processes that create stress are identified. One such thought is entertaining a premonition that something evil is going to befall on you. The second step consists of replacing these irrational thoughts with more rational ones. The fear of evil befalling can be overcome by reasoning and rationalising events and their consequences. Cognitive restructuring would alleviate stress by encouraging a person to adopt a more reasonable belief about the outcomes associated with events.

Time Management Most of us are poor in time management. The result is feeling of work overload, skipped schedules and attendant tension. The truth is, if one can manage time effectively, he or she can accomplish twice as much as the person who is poorly organized. Some basic principles in time management are: (i) preparing daily a list of activities to be attended to; (ii) prioritizing activities by importance and urgency; (iii) scheduling activities according to the priorities set; and (iv) handling the most demanding parts of a job when one is alert and productive.

Organisational Strategies

Besides individuals practising coping strategies, organisations too have been developing and implementing stress – reduction strategies. Some of these programmes focus on a specific issue or a problem, such as alcohol or drug abuse, career counseling, job allocation or burnout. Still other programmes may target a specific group within the organisation, as for example training in relaxation skills.

Organisational coping strategies help reduce the harmful effects of stress in three ways : (i) identify and then modify or eliminate work stressors, (ii) help employees modify their perception and understanding of work stress, and (iii) help employees cope more effectively with the consequences of stress.[11] (See Fig. 23.5)

FIGURE 23-5
TARGETS OF ORGANISATIONAL STRESS MANAGEMENT PROGRAMMES

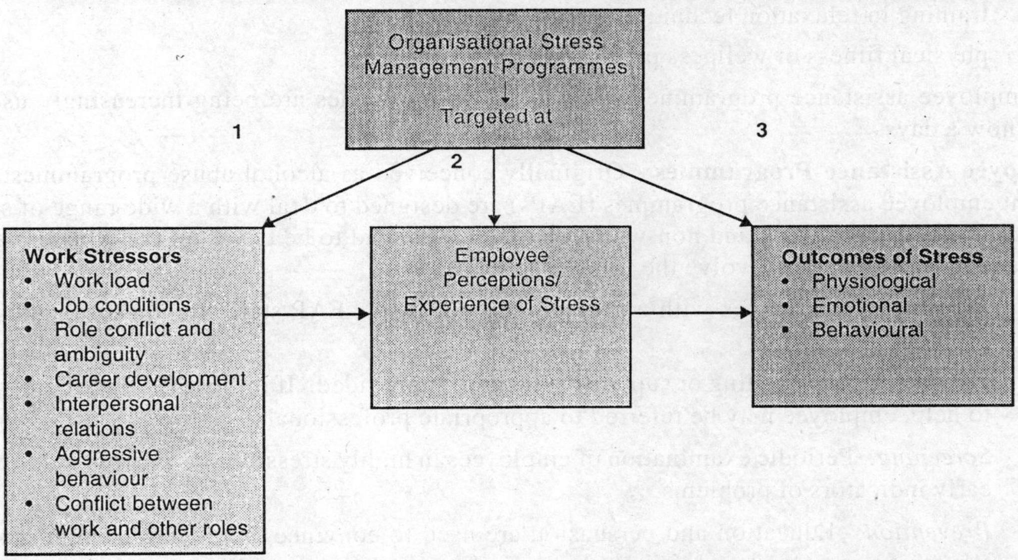

(***Source:*** Don Hellriegel, et al, op. cit., p. 212)

Organisational strategies aimed at eliminating stress often include –

- improvements in the physical work environment;
- job redesign to eliminate stressors;
- changes in workloads and deadlines;
- structural reorganization;
- changes in work schedules, more flexible hours and sabbaticals;
- management by objectives or other goal-setting programmes;
- greater levels of employee participation, particularly in planning changes that affect them; and
- workshops dealing with role clarity and role analysis.[12]

Programmes that promote role clarity and role analysis are of vital importance in removing or reducing role ambiguity and role conflict – the two main sources of stress. While diagnosing stressors in the work place, OB experts should be aware of the fact that uncertainty and perceived lack of control heighten stress. Jobs involving high uncertainty over the outcomes accompanied by low controllability add to the stress. Thus, involvement of employees in organisational change efforts that will affect them, work redesign that reduces uncertainty and increases control over the pace of work, and improved clarity and understanding of roles all should help reduce the work stress.

Programmes of stress management targeted at perceptions and experiences of stress and outcomes of stress (See Fig. 23.5, arrows 2 and 3) include-[13]

- team building;
- behaviour modification;
- career counselling and other employee assistance programmes;
- workshops on time management;
- workshops on burnout to help employee understand its nature and symptoms;
- training in relaxation techniques; and
- physical fitness or wellness programmes.

Employee assistance programmes and wellness programmes are being increasingly used by firms now a days.

Employee Assistance Programmes Originally conceived as alcohol abuse programmes, most current employee assistance programmes (EAPs) are designed to deal with a wide range of stress-related problems both work and non-work related. EAPs tend to be based on the typical medical approach to treatment and involve the following-[14]

- *Diagnosis:* Employees with a problem ask for help. EAP staff attempt to diagnose the problem.
- *Treatment:* Counselling or supportive therapy is provided. If in-hose EAP staff are unable to help, employee may be referred to appropriate professionals.
- *Screening:* Periodic examination of employees in highly stressful jobs is provided to detect early indicators of problems.
- *Prevention:* Education and persuasion are used to convince employees at high risk that something must be done to assist them in effectively coping with stress.

EAPs may be internal company-run programmes or outsourced. Irrespective of the arrangement, crucial to the success of any EAP is trust. Employees must trust that (1) the programme can and will provide real help, (2) confidentiality will be maintained, and (3) use of the programme carries no negative implications for job security or future advancement.[15] If employees do not trust the programme or company management, they will not participate.

Wellness programmes Wellness programmes, often called *Health Promotion Programmes*, focus on employee's overall physical and mental health. Simply stated, any activity an organisation engages in that is designed to identify and assist in preventing or correcting specific health problems, health hazards, or negative health habits falls under wellness programmes. This includes not only disease identification but lifestyle modification too. Among the most prevalent examples of such programmes are those emphasising hypertension identification and control, smoking cessation, physical fitness and exercise, nutrition and diet control and work and personal stress management.

Stress and Performance

As stated earlier, stress is negatively related to performance. In otherwords, higher the stress, lower the performance. Earlier it was believed that moderate levels of stress would energise employees and enhance their performance. But this belief is not held to be true now. The assumption valid now is that performance will be disrupted even by relatively low levels of stress. There are valid reasons in support of this assumption. First, even relatively mild stress distracts an employee. Individuals experiencing stress tend to focus on the unpleasant feelings and emotions rather than on the task at hand and as a result their performance suffers. Second, prolonged or repeated exposure even to mild levels of stress may have harmful effects on health and this may interfere with effective performance. Finally, a large body of research indicates that as arousal increases, task performance may at first rise, but at some point begins to fall. The precise location of this inflection point (the point at which the direction of the function reverses) seems to depend on the complexity of the task being performed. The greater the complexity, the lower the levels of arousal at which a downturn in performance occurs.

There are exceptions to the general rule that stress interferes with performance. Some individuals, for example, are at their best in times of crises. They rise to the occasion and turn in exceptional performance at times of high stress. This may result from the fact that they are truly experts in the tasks being performed, making their inflection points very high. People who are exceptionally skilled at a task may cognitively appraise a potentially stressful situation as a challenge rather than a threat. And, as we noted earlier, by not cognitively appraising a situation as a threat, stress reactions are unlikely to occur. Thus, whether stress can disrupt or enhance performance depends on several different factors (e.g., complexity of the task being performed, personal characteristics of the individuals involved, their previous experience with the task).

QUESTIONS

1. Explain Fig. 23.2 in your own words.
2. What is stress ? What are its effects ?
3. List out the stress coping strategies.
4. What is burnout ? How can burnout be prevented ?
5. "Misfortune loves company". Discuss with reference to workplace stress.
6. It has been suggested that a "stress is in the eyes of the beholder". What does this mean ? Do you agree ?.
7. The issue of who should be responsible for dealing with work stress – the individual or the organisation – is an important one. What do you think ? What are the arguments for and against each position ?
8. What is the relationship between stress and personality ? What aspects of personality might tend to increase stress ? Decrease it ?
9. What are your most common stress symptoms ? How do these symptoms affect your performance, interpersonal relations and happiness ?
10. Several web sites describe problems that people experience at work. Scan through atleast one of these web sites and determine what type of work-related stressor is most commonly described.

Case

Round-the-clock Stress

Many employees feel that on-the-job stress is difficult to control, but at least when they get home they can relax. However, as the nature of work changes, the home is no longer the sanctuary it once was. With advanced information technology and customer demands for 24-hours service, an increasing number of employees are on call at all times or working the "graveyard" shift that used to exist only for factory workers. For example, today there are numerous Wal-Mart stores, Walgreens drugstores and supermarkets that never close. And consider the Heartland Golf Park in Deer Park, Long Island. A golfer who wants a late evening tee-off time can get one up to 3.00 AM. The strategy has proven so popular that within 90 days of the time it was introduced, the wait time at midnight had grown to two and a half hours. Avid golfers do not mind, however, as the course is well lit and they can play as if it were high noon.

All around the country, businesses are realising that there is a great deal of profit that can be added to the bottom line if they remain open outside of "normal" hours. One research firm estimates that this strategy can add 5 percent to overall profits, a hefty sum given that more and more businesses are finding their profit margins being narrowed by the competition.

In some cases, the decision to expand working hours has been a result of customer needs. Kinko's Inc., a privately held chain of photocopy shops, moved to a 24-hour schedule when people literally started banging on their doors after regular business hours and asking them to let them come in for desperately needed photocopies. As a news article recently put it, "The company's ..... stores are magnets for ambassadors of the night : everyone from dreamers pursuing secret schemes and second careers to executives putting the final touches on tomorrow's presentation." In Chicago, Kinko's set up an office in the lobby of the Stouffer Renaissance hotel, a favourite spot of international executives. Customers from different time zones had been coming down at odd hours to ask the hotel to fax materials abroad and to help them with their desktop publishing. The hotel was not equipped to provide these services, so it asked Kinko's to help out. The guests are delighted with the new service, and the hotel is happy to be able to accommodate them thanks to their profitable arrangement with Kinko's.

Banks have also begun to offer 24-hour service. In addition to their ATM machines, which can be found just about everywhere, some banks now offer round-the-clock service : customers can call in and find out within 10 minutes whether they qualify for a new-car loan. A growing number of banks also offer after-hours customer services ranging from safe deposit boxes to $1,000 credit lines to overdraft protection. All the customer has to do is call in at any hour and provide the necessary information.

Some critics are concerned that this development will result in increasing costs to business and added stress to employees. After all, when people work late at night or put in a 15-hour day, they are likely not only to make far more mistakes than if they were on a 9-to-5 schedule but also to become fatigued and burned out. Nevertheless, at the present time approximately two-thirds of all US workers, around 75 million people, do not work traditional 9-to-5 hours – and the number is definitely growing. Additionally, organisations that are engaged in international business, such as brokerage firms, are finding that their operations in Europe and Asia require them to keep odd hours. A US based broker must be up or on call in the wee hours of the morning because Europe's stock exchanges are doing business. By the time the broker wraps up trading on the Pacific Stock Exchange in the early evening (Eastern Standard Time), there are only a few hours before the Asian stock exchanges open. Simply put, in an increasing number of businesses, it is possible to work round-the-clock – and, of course, to pick up the stress that goes along with this lifestyle.

Questions

1. How would a Type A personality feel if his or her organisation suddenly announced that everyone was to be on call 24-hours a day because the company was moving to round-the-clock customer service ?

2. How would psychological hardiness help people deal with these emerging round-the-clock operations ?

3. What are some ways employees and their organisations could cope with the stress caused by these new round-the-clock development ?[16]

REFERENCES

1. Fred Luthans, *Organisational Behaviour*, McGraw-Hill, 1998, p. 330.
2. Don Hellriegel, *et.al., Organisational Behaviour*, South Western, 2001, p. 193.
3. Ibid.
4. Robert Krietner and Angelo Kinicki, *Organisational Behaviour*, Irwin McGraw – Hill, 1998, p. 529.
5. R. Sharpe, "Work Week : Special Report About Life on the Job – And Trends Taking Shape There", *The Wall Street Journal*, April 9, 1996.
6. Robert Knietner and Angelo Kinicki, *Op.cit.*, p. 531.
7. Steven L. McShane and Mary Ann Von Glinow, *Organisational Behaviour*, TMH, 2000, p. 140.
8. Ibid. p. 536.
9. Ibid, p. 547.
10. Ivancevich, Matteson, Freedman and Philips, "Worksite Stress Management Interventions", *American Psychologist*, 1990, 45, p. 252.
11. Don Hellriegel, *et.al., op.cit.*, p. 211.
12. Ibid, p. 212.
13. John M. Ivancevich and Michael T. Matteson, *Organisational Behaviour and Management*, McGraw-Hill, 1999, p. 279.
14. Ibid, p. 280.
15. Jerald Greenberg and Robert A. Baron, *Behaviour in Organizations*, PHI, 1999, p. 258.
16. Fred Luthans, *Organisational Behaviour,* McGraw-Hill, 2002, Pp.425-426.

INDEX

A

B

C

D

E